CONTEMPORARY SUPERVISION

MANAGING PEOPLE AND TECHNOLOGY

McGraw-Hill Series in Management

Fred Luthans and Keith Davis, Consulting Editors

Luthans: Organizational Behavior

Luthans and Thompson: Contemporary Readings in Organizational Behavior

McNichols: Executive Policy and Strategic Planning

McNichols: Policymaking and Executive Actions

Maier: Problem-Solving Discussions and Conferences: Leadership Methods and Skills

Margulies and Raia: Conceptual Foundations of Organizational Development

Mayer: Production and Operations Management

Miles: Theories of Management: Implications for Organizational Behavior and Development

Miles and Snow: Organizational Strategy, Structure, and Process

Mills: Labor-Management Relations

Mitchell and Larson: People in Organizations: An Introduction to Organizational Behavior

Molander: Responsive Capitalism: Case Studies in Corporate Social Conduct

Monks: Operations Management: Theory and Problems

Newstrom and Davis: Organizational Behavior: Readings and Exercises

Newstrom, Reif, and Monczka: A Contingency Approach to Management: Readings

Parker: The Dynamics of Supervision

Pearce and Robinson: Corporate Strategies: Readings from *Business Week*

Porter and McKibbon: Management Education and Development: Drift or Thrust into the 21st Century?

Prasow and Peters: Arbitration and Collective Bargaining: Conflict Resolution in Labor Relations

Quick and Quick: Organizational Stress and Preventive Management

Reddin: Managerial Effectiveness

Rue and Holland: Strategic Management: Concepts and Experiences

Rugman, Lecraw, and Booth: International Business: Firm and Environment

Sartain and Baker: The Supervisor and the Job

Sayles: Leadership: Managing in Real Organizations

Sayles: Leadership: What Effective Managers Really Do . . . . and How They Do It

Schlesinger, Eccles, and Gabarro: Managing Behavior in Organizations: Text, Cases, and Readings

Schroeder: Operations Management: Decision Making in the Operations Function

Sharplin: Strategic Management

Shore: Operations Management

Steers and Porter: Motivation and Work Behavior

Steinhoff and Burgess: Small Business Management Fundamentals

Sutermeister: People and Productivity

Vance: Corporate Leadership: Boards, Directors, and Strategy

Walker: Human Resource Planning

Weihrich: Management Excellence: Productivity through MBO

Werther and Davis: Human Resources and Personnel Management

Wofford, Gerloff, and Cummins: Organizational Communications: The Keystone to Managerial Effectiveness

CONTEMPORARY SUPERVISION

MANAGING PEOPLE AND TECHNOLOGY

Dr. Anne Scott Daughtrey
Old Dominion University

Dr. Betty Roper Ricks
Old Dominion University

McGRAW-HILL BOOK COMPANY

New York St. Louis San Francisco Auckland Bogotá Caracas
Colorado Springs Hamburg Lisbon London Madrid Mexico Milan
Montreal New Delhi Oklahoma City Panama Paris San Juan
São Paulo Singapore Sydney Tokyo Toronto

CONTEMPORARY SUPERVISION

MANAGING PEOPLE AND TECHNOLOGY

234567890 HALHAL 8932109

ISBN 0-07-015586-0

Pages 507–508: Excerpt, p. 218, from *Management* by Arthur G. Bedeian, copyright © 1986 by The Dryden Press, a division of Holt, Rinehart and Winston, Inc., reprinted by permission of the publisher.

This book was set in Times Roman by Waldman Graphics, Inc. (CCU).
The editors were Kathleen L. Loy, Cynthia L. Phelps, and Linda Richmond;
the designer was Scott Chelius;
the production supervisor was Louise Karam.
Arcata Graphics/Halliday was printer and binder.

Library of Congress Cataloging-in-Publication Data

Daughtrey, Anne Scott.
  Contemporary supervision: managing people and technology /
  Anne Scott Daughtrey, Betty Roper Ricks. — 1st ed.
    p. cm. — (McGraw-Hill series in management)
  Includes index.
  ISBN 0-07-015586-0
  1. Supervision of employees.   I. Ricks, Betty R.   II. Title.
III. Series.
HF5549.12.D38   1988   88-13632
658.3'02—dc19

About the Authors

Dr. Anne Scott Daughtrey is a widely recognized author, speaker, and teacher. Among her many publications is a business textbook that has won a gold-book award for sales of over 1 million copies. She is also the recipient of a national award for outstanding teaching in business and economic principles. In addition to many years of teaching, she has served in a supervisory capacity in a variety of settings for over 10 years. She holds masters and doctorate degrees from the University of South Dakota and has been a member of the faculty of the College of Business and Public Administration at Old Dominion University in Norfolk, Virginia, for many years. For the past 9 years, Dr. Daughtrey has held the rank of Eminent Professor of Management at Old Dominion.

   Dr. Betty Roper Ricks served 12 years in a supervisory capacity in public education prior to her appointment to the faculty of Old Dominion University, where she now serves as Associate Professor of Management. Dr. Ricks earned her masters and doctoral degrees from Virginia Polytechnic Institute and State University. She has been a speaker at national and international conferences and is the author of several business textbooks as well as numerous professional articles. Dr. Ricks has been active in professional organizations in the field of business.

Contents

Preface

In these days of increasing pressures for higher productivity on the one hand and greater attention to the desire of the workers for more autonomy over their work lives on the other hand, managers are having a difficult time balancing these diverse interests and keeping the company moving forward. The supervisor, as a part of the management team, plays a critical role in this balancing act. *Contemporary Supervision: Managing People and Technology* is designed not only to help supervisors maintain equilibrium in these changing times but also to prepare them to help as their companies make the transition from a more traditional to a more contemporary management focus.

This text is appropriate for courses such as supervision, introduction to management, and educational supervision taught to freshmen, sophomores, and juniors in departments of business management, educational administration, and continuing education. It is an effective source for the practicing supervisor and for in-house training. This text presents complete and current coverage of research topics involving the transition from the traditional to the participatory approach.

Special features of *Contemporary Supervision: Managing People and Technology* include the following:

1. Focuses on competencies throughout the book. All competencies are presented at the chapter opening, they are presented individually at the appropriate learning point within the chapter, and they form the basis for the competency review at the end of the chapter. There is a competency matrix which relates each end-of-chapter activity to a specific competency.

2. Includes topics of interest to students preparing for transitional management (e.g., participative management) as well as students preparing to deal with current issues (e.g., stress management, drug abuse, ethics, AIDS, employee rights and responsibilities, decision making, and delegation).

3. Provides activities and suggestions to aid the supervisor in translating theory into practice. In addition to realistic examples, these suggestions are featured throughout the text in sections entitled "What Can the Supervisor Do?"

4. Integrates realistic case studies throughout the chapters to illustrate chapter content. These cases are short enough to be easily covered in one class period.

5. Addresses in detail topics often glossed over. There are full chapters on decision making, delegation, and productivity and QWL.

6. Provides a wealth of learning aids, including worked examples and exercises, case studies, applications, illustrations, and more.

7. Is written in an informal, easy-to-read style that makes learning enjoyable.

The supplements include an *Instructor's Manual* and a *Student Activity and Enrichment Guide.*

1. The *Instructor's Manual* includes general and chapter-specific teaching suggestions, lecture outlines, a competency matrix, additional cases, solutions to end-of-chapter activities, a test bank, enrichment activities, and transparency masters.

2. The *Student Activity and Enrichment Guide* provides material to help students review the content of the text as well as to direct their study of each chapter. For example, for each chapter there is a chapter outline and study questions in a variety of formats. In addition, there are applications, cases, and other activities which serve to enrich the students' learning process.

The authors are indebted to many people for their ideas and assistance with this publication. Among those who have made direct contributions are the following:

Chris McAfee, for her invaluable work on the supplements

Patty McClenney, for typing the manuscripts for the supplements

Karen Pinneo, Pascale Tarquis, and Ron Owens, for research assistance

Tom Ricks, for his unwavering support

The authors are also grateful to the following reviewers of the text manuscript: Tommy Gilbreath, University of Texas—Tyler; Dewey Johnson, California State University—Fresno; Dale Scharinger, University of Wisconsin—Whitewater; and Ed White, Danville Community College, Virginia.

Finally, the authors are grateful to the firms, both national and international, which participated in the supervisory management research project, the results of which are included in this text.

No book could find its way to the marketplace without the able assistance of the editorial and production staff of the publisher. The authors gratefully acknowledge the guidance of these professionals at McGraw-Hill.

Anne Scott Daughtrey
Betty Roper Ricks

THE ROLE OF THE SUPERVISOR IN MANAGEMENT

1

A LOOK AT MANAGEMENT— AN OVERVIEW

COMPETENCIES

Studying this chapter will enable you to:

1. Give an example of the universal nature of management.

2. Name the basic approaches in the evolution of management and give a feature of each.

3. Explain the integrative approaches to management.

4. Define *contemporary management.*

5. Identify the levels of management and give an example of each.

6. Explain the functions of management.

7. Explain the methods of entering management.

CHAPTER OUTLINE

As Rhoda Samuels closed her briefcase and prepared to leave for home, she reviewed her busy day in her new job as section supervisor. She had arrived early that morning to meet with three work-team leaders to discuss procedures for the newly formed quality circles. She had had a conference with a worker who had been late to work several times recently, had reviewed vacation requests and made up a tentative schedule to coordinate with other supervisors in the department, had prepared a proposal for a training and development program to present to management, and had started to prepare the budget for the coming year. She had also put the finishing touches on a speech on promotion that she had been asked to give at a regional meeting of a supervisors' professional organization; conducted two performance appraisal interviews; set up a task force to review production standards for her work groups; walked through all the work stations under her supervision, observing for some time two stations that had reported processing problems; and reviewed the draft of a new policy statement on sexual harassment being formulated by management for adoption.

"Yes," she thought as she closed the door to leave, "supervision is different from my job as a worker. It's varied and complex, but it's a challenge I enjoy." She smiled as she realized that she was now going home to "manage" her household. "After all, that's management too, only in a different environment," she thought.

This chapter will introduce you to the nature, functions, and levels of management and will give you a capsulized look at the evolution of management as a profession. The purpose in presenting an overview of management is to establish the appropriate perspective for learning to become an effective supervisor. As Rhoda Samuels noted, as a supervisor she is a part of a management team. Section I of this book will build a framework through which you can examine, in detail, one part of the management structure—first-line management, or supervision. For an in-depth study of management, you will find several sources in the References and Suggested Readings at the end of this chapter.

THE NATURE OF MANAGEMENT

As Samuels noted in reflecting on her job, she manages in two different environments. Most people "manage" in some part of their daily lives. We set goals and try to achieve them. Organizations do that, too. Management affects all of us, and it affects us in many ways. Let's examine what that means.

Management Is Universal

Every person and every organization manages, is managed, or is affected by management. For this reason, we can say that management is universal.

When we try to achieve an objective, several elements are brought into play. We must consider what activities are involved and in what sequence. We must plan the time, the place, and the resources needed to achieve the goal. After the goal is accomplished, we must examine how effective the outcome was. This is, in effect, managing. We manage our education, our homes, our finances, our social activities, and our careers. When we set goals and attempt to achieve them, we are managing.

Organizations must manage also in order to accomplish their goals. When several people get together to accomplish a common goal, they form an *organization*. The organization may be a business, a government, a church, a university, a team, or any other group of people with a common objective. Whatever its type, the organization provides the means for getting done those things that are necessary to reach its goal. The group decides what is to be done, assigns tasks based on its members' interests or expertise, and appoints someone to coordinate its activities and resources so that all tasks will be done and so that members of the group will not duplicate the efforts of others. These and many other management tasks will be performed by the group.

If the organization is a university, the goal is to provide a service—education. Plans must be formulated and implemented for a curriculum, students, faculty, administrators, funding, classroom buildings, housing, libraries, scheduling, maintenance, and all the myriad elements that go into the management of a university.

If the organization is an auto parts wholesaler, the goal is to provide a product— auto parts—to retail firms. Plans would include capital funding, plant and equipment, personnel, sources of supply, marketing, inventory, storage, delivery, and all the other components needed to keep the business operating at a profit.

As you have read, managing, though varied and complex, is common to all organizations. Rhoda Samuels noted the variety and complexity of her new job as section supervisor. It was, indeed, different from her job as worker. She had embarked on a new career path—as a professional manager. She will learn that there are several approaches to the way she handles her tasks.

Competency Check:

Can you give an example of the universal nature of management?

Management Is an Evolving Profession

Modern management is a product of the twentieth century, and it is still evolving. Today, approximately 8 million professional managers make up about 8 percent of employment in the United States.[2] Before the turn of the century, businesses in Europe and America were operated by their owners and their families. Decisions were made from experience and intuition. No principles had yet been developed to guide the decision makers. Owners relied mostly on hunches and true grit to run their firms. As the industrial revolution spread, it spawned the factory system, mass production, and unprecedented growth in the size of business enterprises. Owners began to hire managers for the day-to-day operations. After the turn of the century, applications of research, especially in engineering, began to improve the efficiency of both worker and equipment in the workplace. This was the beginning of the concept of management as a profession. Principles of management that could serve as guidelines in decision making began to evolve.

To review the evolution of management, one might use the first two quarters and the last half of the twentieth century as broad time lines of development. Accumulative knowledge and overlapping of concepts and periods obviously occurred, especially after midcentury, but looking back, we can identify several distinct approaches that were focal points at various times as management evolved. In the next sections, the highlights of these basic approaches will be presented.

The Classical Approach

The classical approach to management grew out of a combination of scientific management and classical organization theory.

Scientific Management.   Beginning in the late nineteenth century, and finding its focus in the first quarter of the twentieth century, scientific management placed its emphasis on improving efficiency in the workplace. Researchers such as Frederick W. Taylor[3] and Frank and Lillian Gilbreth[4] studied jobs and the tools used by workers to perform those jobs. They sought ''the one best way'' to perform each job.

Taylor, an engineer, focused on observing the worker at the job and analyzing the task and the tools. He then redesigned the tools for maximum efficiency. For example, after a study at Bethlehem Steel in which he observed workers shoveling raw materials, such as iron ore and coke, into an open furnace, Taylor tested shovels of various sizes and designed one for maximum efficiency. When his system was installed, it produced impressive results: The number of shovelers needed was reduced from between 400 and 600 to 140; productivity increased from 16 to 59 long tons per worker per day; costs were decreased from 7.1 cents to 3.2 cents per long ton; and worker wages, based on Taylor's piece rate and incentive system, increased from $1.15 to $1.88 per day. The success of Taylor's method prompted the company whose shovels were used in the experiments to let its customers know immediately, as shown in the advertisement on page 7. Taylor's concepts, with some modification, are still used in management.

Two other early scientific-management pioneers, Frank and Lillian Gilbreth, also studied efficiency in the workplace. In their pursuit of ''the one best way'' to perform a task, they analyzed the motions of workers at the job. Frank Gilbreth first studied the motions of bricklayers in construction when he was a bricklayer himself. By analyzing the task, he was able to cut the motions required to lay a brick and managed to move, within a year, from the slowest apprentice to the fastest worker on the job. He cut the motions from 18 to 6; while journeymen were expected to lay 175 bricks an hour, Gilbreth could lay 350. He opened his own construction company and installed his system. His success spread quickly internationally. With his wife Lillian, one of the earliest industrial psychologists, assisting in the analysis, Gilbreth classified 17 basic motions, which he called ''therbligs,'' his name spelled backwards with a slight change. Lillian Gilbreth was so involved in the research that historians have

Give Him a 21-Pound Load Shovel
He'll Double your results

The Wyoming 21-pound Load Shovel is a shovel which is designed to hold an average of 21 pounds a load.

Frederick W. Taylor—the man who first made "scientific management" popular—demonstrates beyond doubt that the shoveler does his best day's work for you when his average is 21 pounds.

Taylor's experiments were conducted with Wyoming Shovels. You can "cash in" on his discovery by adopting

WYOMING
SHOVELS

Source: Arthur G. Bedeian, *Management,* The Dryden Press, Chicago, 1986, p. 36.

been unable to determine much of the authorship of his work. She also continued the work after his death. Their time-and-motion analysis remains, today, a core concept of management.

The scientific approach to designing tools and work flow and to measuring output gave to the period the label ''scientific management'' and to Taylor the title ''father of scientific management.''

Classical Organization Theory.   At the same time, in France, Henri Fayol,[5] an engineer who became a manager, was examining not the work on the shop floor but business activities. He categorized all business activities into six essential groups, as shown in Figure 1-1. Because he felt that ample information was available on the first five of these business activities, he concentrated, in his writing, on the managerial functions. Fayol's management functions, shown under ''managerial'' in Figure 1-1, closely pattern the current functions, which are developed throughout this text: planning, organizing, staffing, leading and motivating, and controlling.

Fayol also felt that several management techniques were applicable to many different circumstances. From this concept, he developed 14 principles of management as guidelines for managing universally. Many of these principles, shown in Figure 1-2, are relevant today. Fayol's work became known as *classical organization theory.*

Other pioneers and their research, such as Henry L. Gantt and his scheduling of work to be accomplished, also contributed to the classical approach to management. Together, the work of these researchers made major contributions to the evolving profession of management by focusing on these two elements of work:

● *the management of work*—by studying the task, the tools, the skills of the worker, and the arrangement of the work station into an efficient work flow
● *the work of management*—by identifying the activities performed by managers and establishing principles of management that could be adapted to different situations

FIGURE 1-1

FAYOL'S 6 ESSENTIAL GROUPS OF BUSINESS ACTIVITIES,
INCLUDING THE 5 FUNCTIONS OF MANAGERS

1. technical (production)
2. commercial (buying, selling, and exchanging)
3. financial (the search for, and optimal use of, capital)
4. security (the protection of property and persons)
5. accounting (including statistics)
6. managerial (planning, organizing, commanding, coordinating, and controlling)

Source: Henri Fayol, *General and Industrial Management,* copyright © 1987 by David S. Lake Publishers, Inc., Belmont, CA 94002.

The emphasis on efficiency and productivity made the classical approach to management mechanistic and authoritarian. The worker was considered a tool of production, to be manipulated in whatever manner would best increase profits. This lack of humanistic concern led eventually to the behavioral science approach.

The Behavioral Science Approach

Concerned by the overemphasis on the technical aspects of the workplace, social scientists began to give attention to the human side of management in an attempt to balance the two. The Hawthorne studies, conducted between 1924 and 1932 by Elton Mayo[6] and others at the Western Electric Company, became an important milestone in the evolution of management thought.

One phase of the research was to determine the relationship of the lighting in a relay assembly room to the productivity of the workers. Lighting was varied for one group and held constant for the other. The researchers were surprised to find that productivity increased during the period of the study whether the lighting was increased or decreased and that no consistent relationship between lighting and productivity existed. This led the researchers to interview the workers in an attempt to find the reason. They formulated these reasons for the higher productivity:

1. The workers enjoyed the experiment, which they considered to be an important and interesting study.
2. A new and more relaxed supervisor-worker relationship developed during the experiments.
3. The workers developed a friendlier group relationship.

In other words, the positive response of the workers resulted not from their changed physical conditions but from their feeling that management was paying attention to them as human beings. This became known as "the Hawthorne effect" in psychology.

FIGURE 1-2

FAYOL'S PRINCIPLES OF MANAGEMENT

1. *Division of work.* This provides for specialization for the efficient use of labor. Fayol applies this to managerial as well as technical work.
2. *Authority.* Authority and responsibility are related and should be equal.
3. *Discipline.* Needed for developing obedience, application, energy, and respect. Fayol recommends that discipline be applied judiciously.
4. *Unity of command.* Workers should receive orders from one superior only.
5. *Unity of direction.* The entire organization should be moving in one direction toward a common objective.
6. *Subordination of individual interest to general interests.* The interests of one individual or group should not have priority over the interests of the organization as a whole.
7. *Remuneration.* Rewards and remuneration should be fair.
8. *Centralization.* The degree of centralization or decentralization should depend on the organization; the rule should be the one that gives the best overall yield.
9. *Scalar chain.* Fayol presents this as a chain of command from the highest to the lowest manager and says that this line of authority should be clearly communicated.
10. *Order.* To promote efficiency and coordination, all materials and people related to a specific kind of work should be located in the same general area. Meaning "a place for everything and everything in its place," this principle is essentially the principle of organization.
11. *Equity.* Workers should be treated with kindness and justice.
12. *Stability of tenure of personnel.* Unnecessary turnover, both the cause and effect of bad management, should be minimized because it is costly.
13. *Initiative.* Workers should be encouraged to exercise initiative in improving their work, thereby improving their job satisfaction.
14. *Esprit de corps.* Managers should encourage harmony and teamwork among workers.

Source: Henri Fayol, *General and Industrial Management,* copyright © 1987 by David S. Lake Publishers, Inc., Belmont, CA 94002.

The findings of this research, highlighting the importance of human relations in the workplace, still influence the study of motivation.

Another significant contributor to this approach, which broadened during this period from human relations to include all the behavioral sciences, was Abraham H. Maslow.[7] Though his work was in the area of psychology, not business, it greatly influenced the field of management. His 1943 "hierarchy of human needs" theory, which relates human behavior to need satisfaction, became one of the most popular and widely known theories of motivation. You will study more about Maslow's theory in Section V.

The contribution of the behavioral science approach is that it adds to scientific management's concern for the work itself a concern for the individual performing the work. This latter concern, as you will read later in this chapter, has intensified in contemporary management.

The Management Science Approach

Concepts formulated in the first half of the twentieth century continued to be applied in the second half, but now new research and technology began to influence management.

The introduction of the computer to the business scene in the 1950s had a profound impact on management theory. This fantastic tool enabled managers to use the science of mathematics to solve business problems at speeds heretofore impossible. But the technology became a hard taskmaster and created some problems of its own, such as information overload, inflexibility, and worker stress. Computer technology and its rapid improvements and growth updated and expanded techniques from earlier scientific management, giving the period the label *management science*.

Competency Check:

Can you name three approaches in the evolution of management and give an example of each?

Growing out of the missile technology of World War II and military operations in which teams of experts were used to develop strategy, management science contributed both the use of statistics and technology and the team approach to problem solving. Management science is also known as *operations research*.

Along with computer technology, behavioral research continued and produced some significant findings during the 1950s and 1960s. The leadership style of the manager and the behavior of the organization were studied by researchers such as McGregor,[8] Argyris,[9] Likert,[10] Drucker,[11] and Herzberg.[12] The complexity of management and theories to explain and cope with it were increasing rapidly.

Integrative Approaches

The proliferation of theories prompted Harold D. Koontz to note that a ''management theory jungle'' had been created, with each movement going its own way without regard for the others.[13] Modern management tries to cut through this jungle by integrating the findings of earlier movements. Two integrative approaches—the systems approach and the contingency approach—emerged.

The Systems Approach.　This approach involves viewing the organization as a set of interrelated parts interacting with each other to accomplish a common goal. That is the meaning of *system*. A heating unit is a system that uses fuel (input) and transforms it through some action such as burning (process) into energy (output). The goal of the system is to provide heat. When one part is affected, the whole system is affected. Inferior fuel, for example, will reduce output and may even cause the entire system to break down.

An enterprise, viewed as a system, will be more productive when its managers treat each part of the organization as important and interrelated. The interactions of the parts are more critical than are the separate actions of the parts. For example, a top-drawer sales force may be setting records taking orders, but if the production department is turning out only 60 percent of its production goals, the system is headed for trouble when deliveries are due. The systems approach emphasizes management interrelationships.

The Contingency Approach.   This approach refutes the ''one best way'' theme from scientific management, yet it was included in the writings of Follett[14] in the 1920s. The contingency, or situational, approach takes into consideration various elements of the situation being managed and chooses the approach most appropriate for that situation. The cartoon below shows how important this concept can be.

One of the situational leadership theorists of the era, Fred E. Fiedler,[15] developed a contingency model in the late 1960s that became highly regarded. Fiedler's model, which will be discussed further in Chapter 11, states that leadership styles have varying degrees of effectiveness in relationship to other variables. These variables include whether leader-member relations are good or poor, whether task structure is high or low, and whether the position power of the leader is strong or weak. Based on the combination of these variables in the situation, Fiedler suggests that different kinds of leadership are appropriate.

The contingency, or situational, approach enables managers to use knowledge from the classical, the behavioral science, or the manageent science approaches as appropriate to the situation. Today's management thinking continues to broaden the integrative process.

Competency Check:

Can you explain the integrative approaches to management?

Contemporary Management

Today's management is marked by its complexity. Managers must guide the internal mechanism of the organization, produce a competitive product or service, and market that product or service at a profit. They must also cope with a variety of external forces unknown to their counterparts in earlier periods. These new external forces may be economic, social, political, environmental, national, or global. The forces

Source: Reprinted with special permission of King Features Syndicate, Inc., 1976, world rights reserved.

have also had an impact on workers, creating a new relationship between employer and employee. Some of these new forces are:

1. the demand for greater productivity, resulting from national and international competition.
2. the wide publicity given to other styles of management, especially those existing in Japan, whose success in international trade has had such an impact on the United States.
3. the emergence of information as a major resource; it has been called a fourth sector of the economy, taking its place along with business, government, and the consumer.
4. the expanding knowledge of behavioral and management science.
5. the changing attitudes and values of today's workers.
6. the changing legal environment, which has increased employer responsibility for the protection of employees' rights.
7. the increasing recognition that the most important resource an organization has is its people.

Among the writers who have addressed these forces during the 1980s are:

- William Ouchi,[16] who examined U.S. and Japanese management and suggested a style (Theory Z) which would allow U.S. firms to adopt features of both into a management style amenable to western culture and conditions
- John Naisbitt,[17] who identified information as the fourth sector of the U.S. economy to which business must adjust and suggested changes which U.S. firms would need to undergo to achieve success
- Thomas Peters and Robert Waterman,[18] who identified "excellent" U.S. companies; cited the source of their success; and, noting the constant changes in the environment affecting business, pointed out ways through which companies may not only survive, but also thrive

All these management writers stressed one of the forces cited above as critical: the importance of management's recognition of the worker as its most important resource.

There is greater emphasis on research into human behavior today, especially as it affects and is affected by the workplace. How can the manager motivate workers to be more productive? Many believe the answer lies in the degree to which workers meet their own needs in the performance of their jobs. Participation in decision making, in control of their work lives, and in gains the employer makes through their efforts are increasingly documented as elements of job satisfaction. One author refers to worker participation in management as "an ethical imperative."[19] Worker participation is looked upon as an essential element of contemporary management.

Management has been defined as the process of accomplishing objectives by, with, and through people. Contemporary management may be defined in more comprehensive terms. *Contemporary management* is management that:

● accomplishes the goals of the organization through the efforts of its people, recognizing that people perform best when meeting their own needs.
● provides equal opportunity for employment, training, and promotion.
● creates and maintains an environment physiologically and psychologically healthful.
● promotes worker participation in decision making and problem solving and encourages innovation.
● tries to balance the demands of technology with the needs of the workers.
● rewards workers on the basis of their performance and shares productivity gains with those responsible for achieving the gains.

Competency Check:

Can you define contemporary management?

For contemporary management to be successful, it must be embraced by all levels of management.

THE LEVELS OF MANAGEMENT

While all managers perform the same functions, there are differences among their jobs. Recall the kinds of tasks that Samuels in the beginning of the chapter performed during one day in her job as supervisor. The manager who is Samuels' boss has different things to accomplish. And the chief executive officer of the company has yet another set of tasks. The vertical relationship among these managers is called *management levels*. While the relationship is portrayed in an exaggerated way in the cartoon on page 14, it suggests that there is a clear hierarchy of managers in most organizations.

The hierarchy of most organizations is composed of three levels: first-line, middle, and top management. Figure 1-3 shows position titles of managers in each level. It also shows the relationship of management to workers; this nonmanagerial group is called *operations*.

The levels of management are also commonly called by other terms. Top and middle management are sometimes grouped under the terms *upper management* or *upper-level management,* with the first line called *lower-level management.* The terms *first-line manager* and *supervisor* are also used synonymously, as they will be in this text.

First-Line Management

First-line managers comprise the largest group of managers in most firms. First-line managers—supervisors—work with the operating personnel who actually produce the product or service that the firm provides. As the term implies, first-line managers form the first line of contact with workers in operations. They direct the workers in carrying out the objectives of the firm and serve as the conduit through which workers communicate with management. They must also work with their peers and with superiors. Unlike middle- and top-level managers, they do not supervise other managers.

Management
hierarchy made
obvious

"This is Wilson T. Morrow, upper-management executive, Harold Bosworth Oakes, middle-management executive, Thomas H. Huxlor, lower-management executive and Billy Wielder, worker bee."

Source: Joseph Farris, © 1978. Reprinted by permission of Joseph Farris.

FIGURE 1-3

Levels of
management and
operations

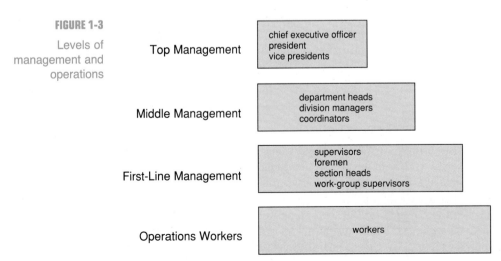

Their managerial tasks are marked by variety, as you noted in the recap of Samuels' day. The supervisor's job is expected to undergo changes in the future; it stands to become more important as the people-productivity link in the firm.[20]

Middle Management

This level of management forms a link between top management, where policies are set, and first-line management, where operations are performed. Middle managers are the administrators who interpret and carry out plans and directives from top management. They integrate the work of the various departments so that the activities of all groups can be directed toward accomplishing company goals. In coordinating the activities of first-line management, they also serve as supervisors of these managers.

Middle management has been the focus of much upheaval in recent years. Japanese firms have few middle managers; American firms have traditionally had many managers at this level. Middle managers have served as information specialists for the firm in the past, but computers are taking over this function. Managers who have been simply a link in the communication chain are finding that this is no longer enough. Organizational redesign and cost-cutting measures in the 1980s have pared the middle level down significantly. Some firms are using value-added analysis, a process that determines whether each step in a work process or a decision sequence actually adds to the previous step. If it does not, the job at that step is viewed as a place for possible cost cutting. Traditional middle managers, whose jobs have consisted mainly of passing on other people's work, will need to accept change or find their jobs in jeopardy.[21]

Top Management

The view from the top may be exhilarating, but responsibility sets heavily on the manager's shoulders in that rarified atmosphere. The ''buck'' stops here. There are many peers for the first-line and middle manager, but only a few at the top. The chief executive officer (CEO), the president, and the vice presidents comprise an executive corps. They establish the character, the mission, and the goals of the firm. They also plan broad strategies to implement the goals and secure the future of the firm. They use a broad brush to create the ''big picture'' and communicate the results downward to middle managers, who fill in the details of implementation by establishing objectives to meet each goal. In this way, top management also direct managers in the middle-management group.

As you have seen, all levels of management perform the same functions, but the emphasis differs. The following section will give you an overview of these functions.

Competency Check:

Can you identify the levels of management and give an example of each?

THE FUNCTIONS OF MANAGEMENT

The management process involves a set of activities called *functions*. As you have read, Fayol cited five functions of management early in this century. Only slightly modified, modern management theory identifies those functions as planning, organizing, staffing, leading and motivating, and controlling. These are shown in Figure 1-4. The time and effort devoted to each function will vary with the manager's position in the hierarchy. The supervisor's role in each of these functions will comprise separate sections of this book. A brief discussion here will introduce you to these functions.

Planning

Planning includes determining the mission, direction, and goals and objectives of the firm and the strategies for achieving them. It includes analyzing economic events and trends and forecasting their implications for the firm. Planning also includes examining alternative uses of resources and choosing among them. It involves thinking, gathering and analyzing data, discussing concepts and ideas, creating innovative and entrepreneurial opportunities, and evaluating decisions. Note from Figure 1-4 that top management devotes the largest portion of time to the planning function.

Organizing

Organizing means creating a structure for the organization. It involves identifying the tasks to be done and grouping those tasks into jobs. It also includes establishing relationships among jobs and people and assigning managerial authority. The organizing function usually results in a graphic organization hierarchy, showing how the efforts of the firm are interrelated and integrated. As shown in Figure 1-4, the organizing function does not vary greatly from one level to another.

Staffing

The process of selecting, training and developing, appraising, and rewarding employees is called *staffing*. Staffing is an integral part of the supervisor's responsibility. It

FIGURE 1-4

Functions of management by levels

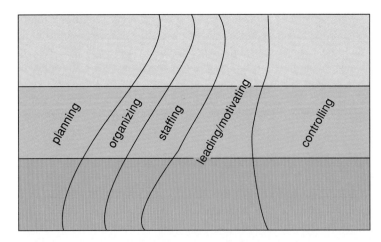

was once considered a part of the organizing function, but with the increasing importance being assigned to human resources management, staffing itself is now commonly considered a major function. In companies with a human resources/personnel department, the supervisor will work in conjunction with that department in carrying out the staffing function. Section IV will address the supervisor's role in staffing.

Leading and Motivating

Influencing workers to act according to company plans is a difficult task. By *leading and motivating,* managers try to create a climate in which workers will willingly perform their jobs and accept their share of responsibility for accomplishing the firm's goals. Leading and motivating means directing the work of people so that their tasks will be performed correctly and on time. This function requires the manager to understand human behavior and motivation and to be an excellent communicator. The supervisor spends a large proportion of time leading and motivating. Section VI will address this function in depth.

Controlling

Controlling is the process through which management determines whether and how well it is accomplishing what it set out to accomplish. In controlling, managers compare actual performance with planned performance. The results determine what action should be taken. Regular monitoring is part of controlling. Monitoring reduces the potential for discovering deviations from plans only at the end of a fiscal period. If a firm has planned a 5 percent sales increase for a quarter, for example, managers will compare sales each week or month to a week or month in a previous quarter. If sales are lower than expected, management may have a special sale to generate more revenue. If sales are higher than expected, sales personnel might be encouraged to push slow-moving or higher-profit products. Note that comparing and taking corrective action go hand in hand in controlling.

The controlling function, like the leading and motivating function, takes a large share of the supervisor's time. You will study the supervisor's role in controlling in Section VI.

Overlapping Nature of Managerial Functions

Managerial functions should not be considered as discrete and independent activities. Planning, for example, goes on most of the time. During the planning stage, managers set standards, which are then used in controlling. For example, the 5 percent increase in sales discussed above was set during planning as a standard for growth. In comparing current sales with the previous quarter in controlling, the manager plans what corrective action, if any, needs to be taken.

In orienting a new worker to a computer terminal work station, the supervisor will observe whether the worker's skills are adequate to the task. These observations will guide the supervisor in planning for additional training, if needed to upgrade the skills. If the skills are better than expected, the manager will plan an adjustment to the orientation period.

In motivating a worker who rarely seems to complete assigned tasks, a manager might observe that the worker seems consistently to have more tasks to perform than other workers. This will call into play the organizing function of examining the job description and possibly redesigning the job.

Competency Check:

Can you explain the five functions of management?

Overlapping of functions is inherent in the managerial process. Samuels in the beginning of the chapter found that to be evident in several of her activities as supervisor. As she conferred with the worker who had a lateness problem, she may have been thinking of ways to motivate the worker. No wonder Samuels remarked that her job was different and varied! No doubt she would include this in the speech she was preparing on promotion, her path to becoming a supervisor.

TOWARD A MANAGEMENT CAREER—BECOMING A SUPERVISOR

We can assume that Samuels wanted to be a supervisor. The desire to influence the performance of others and to gain satisfaction from doing so is a characteristic of most successful managers. Because management is the accomplishment of goals through the efforts of others, an aspiring manager should enjoy working with people. He or she must be willing to continue studying human behavior and motivation. Ability to direct the work of others involves more than just getting along with people and praising good work. It also involves being able to point out incorrect actions or poor performance. Samuels' superiors evidently consider her to have management potential. Let's look at the method through which Samuels became a supervisor.

Promotion

Businesses can hire supervisors directly from outside the firm, but most find it in their interests to provide career development programs for their employees. For this reason, most supervisors move up from the ranks; they have proved themselves on the job. Through career planning, workers' career aspirations can be matched with opportunities available in the firm. When a vacancy occurs, the firm is able to identify workers whose aspirations, skills, and experience qualify them for the job. In this way, the firm retains a good worker and minimizes the cost of staffing.

When vacancy notices are posted in the firm, qualified workers should apply immediately. Success in performing the technical aspects of the job should have been documented in performance appraisals. There should be some evidence that the worker is ready to transfer from the dependency stage of working under a supervisor's direction to working independently and directing the work of others. A U.S. Labor Department publication gives this helpful hint to job seekers:[22]

> In evaluating candidates, superiors look for determination, confidence, innovativeness, high motivation, and managerial attributes, such as the ability to make sound decisions, to organize and coordinate work efficiently, and to establish good personal relations with other workers.

Samuels had evidently proved herself in her former job. She "held the tickets" to win the supervisor's job through promotion.

Management-Trainee Programs

Another common avenue into a management career is through a management-trainee program. A worker may use this entry method to move from operations into management, but the management-trainee method is more common as the entry route for recent college graduates. The financial industry routinely hires recent college graduates as trainees. Figure 1-5 shows that the 309,000 managers in banking represent 18 percent of all banking employees in the United States. Many of these managers began

FIGURE 1-5

10 TOP INDUSTRIES EMPLOYING MANAGERS BY % OF INDUSTRY EMPLOYMENT

INDUSTRY	MANAGERS (thousands)	% OF INDUSTRY EMPLOYMENT
total (all industries)	7851	8
banking	309	18
real estate	185	17
apparel and accessories stores	169	17
general contractors and construction	162	14
miscellaneous retail stores	269	13
membership organizations	195	13
communications	161	12
insurance	151	12
food stores	256	10
special trade contractors (construction)	232	10

Source: U.S. Bureau of Labor Statistics, 1986.

as trainees. In banking, management trainees move through several departments, spending 2 to 6 weeks in each. This rotation gives them an orientation to the entire firm. It also helps to identify the special interests and aptitudes of the individual worker, which may assist in assigning the worker to a department that matches his or her talents.

The management-trainee method also gives the worker an opportunity to work with several managers and to observe different management styles. This is a valuable experience, especially if the worker is preparing for his or her first managerial job. The recent college graduate can flesh out the theoretical skeleton of knowledge learned in the classroom.

Preparing to Become a Manager

Many people who become managers start their careers in operations. Office managers often begin as secretaries, treasurers as accountants, sales managers as salespersons, and school superintendents as teachers.

The first function of management is planning. The aspiring manager should consider planning as an essential step to entering management as a profession. Here are some ways you might prepare to become a manager:

1. Develop a career plan based on your own realistic appraisal of your interests, aptitudes, and abilities.
2. If you are in a firm with a career-development program, take advantage of it.
3. Seek the advice of a career counselor to help you determine your career potential.
4. Some firms offer operations workers or junior managers occasional supervisory assignments, short-term rotation to other departments, or short-term assistant assignments to upper management. If your company provides this opportunity, let your supervisor know you are interested.
5. Participate in management training courses and seminars. These are offered by industry, by management, by universities, and by professional consultants.
6. Pursue a college education. Having a college degree is more important for managers than it is for most other occupations. U.S. Department of Labor statistics show that in a recent year, over 40 percent of all managers had completed 4 or more years of college, about twice the proportion for all occupations.[23]

Competency Check:

Can you cite two methods of entering the management profession?

Preparing well for entering first-level management will make it easier for you to plan your moves upward after you have succeeded as a supervisor.

Maintaining Upward Mobility

It would be a rare manager who planned to stay on that first rung of the professional management ladder. Most want to continue the climb. Competition gets keener as you progress toward the top because there are fewer positions and more aspirants. But obviously some do make it.

Upward mobility is an integral part of career planning. You have already learned to take advantage of training opportunities as you prepared to become a supervisor. Continue to do that. Remember that advancement in business depends on successful performance. Demonstrating loyalty to the firm and promoting its image and interests are also noted by personnel decision makers. Additional college preparation is also an asset. A graduate degree in business administration can enhance your opportunities for promotion and may be essential in technical activities.

In moving upward, it is important to continue training. The U.S. Department of Labor recently noted that 1 out of 3 public administrators took formal company training to improve their skills. Industry sources indicate that top-level managers complete formal academic refresher programs of about a year's duration at least two or three times during their management careers.[24]

In Chapter 2, you will conclude the overview of management and begin to look at what duties you will be performing when you take that first step up the management ladder to a supervisory position.

COMPETENCY REVIEW

1. Give an example of the universal nature of management.
2. Cite the three basic approaches in the evolution of management as a profession.
3. Explain two integrative approaches to management.
4. Define *contemporary management*.
5. Identify the three levels of management, and give an example of a position in each.
6. Explain the functions of management.
7. Explain two methods of entering management.

APPLICATIONS

1. If you have not yet had the opportunity to demonstrate your leadership, you may have much more potential than you think. The following scale is designed to help you evaluate just how much potential you possess. Circle the number that indicates where you fall, from 1 to 10, on the scale. After you have finished, record your score in the space provided. Your instructor will help you interpret your score.

a. I can develop the talent and confidence to be an excellent speaker in front of groups.　　10 9 8 7 6 5 4 3 2 1　　I could never develop the confidence to speak in front of groups.

b. I have the capacity to build and maintain productive relationships with workers under my supervision.　　10 9 8 7 6 5 4 3 2 1　　I'm a loner. I do not want the responsibility of building relationships with others.

c. I intend to take full advantage of all opportunities to develop my leadership qualities.　　10 9 8 7 6 5 4 3 2 1　　I do not intend to seek a leadership role or to develop my leadership skills.

d. I can develop the skill of motivating others. I would provide an outstanding example.　　10 9 8 7 6 5 4 3 2 1　　I could never develop the skill of motivating others. I would be a poor example to follow.

e. I can be patient and understanding with others.　　10 9 8 7 6 5 4 3 2 1　　I have no patience with others and could not develop it.

f. I could learn to be good at disciplining those under me—even to the point of terminating a worker after repeated violations.　　10 9 8 7 6 5 4 3 2 1　　It would tear me up to discipline a worker under my supervision; I'm much too kind and sensitive.

g. I can make tough decisions.　　10 9 8 7 6 5 4 3 2 1　　I do not want decision-making responsibilities.

h. It would not bother me to isolate myself and maintain a strong discipline line between workers and myself.　　10 9 8 7 6 5 4 3 2 1　　I have a great need to be liked; I want to be one of the gang.

i. I would make an outstanding member of a "management team."　　10 9 8 7 6 5 4 3 2 1　　I hate staff meetings and would be a weak or hostile team member.

j. In time, I would be a superior leader—better than anyone I have known.　　10 9 8 7 6 5 4 3 2 1　　My leadership potential is so low it is not worth developing.

TOTAL SCORE _____

Source: Adapted from "A Self-Paced Exercise Guide," *Supervisor's Survival Kit,* 2d ed., Science Research Associates, Inc., 1980.

2. Following are the activities that Samuels performed in her new job as supervisor. By checking the appropriate column, classify each according to the predominant function. If you think that an activity falls within more than one function, check two or more columns as appropriate.

SAMUELS' ACTIVITIES	PLAN	ORGANIZE	STAFF	LEAD/ MOTIVATE	CONTROL
Met with team leaders.					
Conferred with tardy worker.					
Reviewed vacation requests; made tentative schedule.					
Made T & D proposal.					
Prepared budget.					
Prepared speech.					
Conducted 2 performance appraisal interviews.					
Set up task force to review work standards.					
Visited work stations; observed 2 with problems.					
Reviewed draft of new policy statement.					

CASES

Case I: Up! Up! and Away!

Carl Brant has been employed for 4 years in the West Coast plant of Acme Electronics. He has been the top electronics technician at the plant; his performance ratings have always been outstanding. He is admired by his peers in his work group; they call him "Speedy" because he consistently outperforms them on the assembly line. He trained two members of the group when they were hired.

On two occasions, he has been invited to participate in discussions on product design with electronics engineers. When Acme opened its new plant in Reston, Virginia, Brant was offered a transfer and promoted to supervisor of one of the eight assembly work groups, each of which had 10 members. Brant accepted the transfer, pleased that he was now moving into management. The move was right on target with his career plan.

At his farewell party, his group decorated the shop with printed balloons. Some of the messages were: ''Mr. Brant—Boss Man,'' ''Watch out for other Speedys,'' ''The grass is greener,'' ''No overtime pay now,'' ''Can Speedy dish it out?'' and ''Into the hot seat.''

1. Identify Brant's major qualifications for the new job.
2. List several adjustments that Brant will have to make in his new job.
3. Which of these adjustments do you think will be the biggest problem?
4. You will study the concepts referred to in the balloon messages later in this course. Your experience may already have given you some clue, however, to their meaning. See how many you can interpret.

Case II: The Grass May Not Be Greener

Sibyl Garth and Hans Kohl were talking over coffee about their new jobs as supervisors in the stockroom of a large mail-order house. Garth's group filled incoming orders and sent them to shipping. Kohl's group checked in from receiving piers and labeled incoming stock. Business was brisk, and stock groups were kept busy.

GARTH   I'm not sure I like this job. I work harder than my group.

KOHL   I know what you mean, and no more overtime pay, even though I spend hours on the job filling in all these work reports. Last week, two of my group made more than I did.

GARTH   Yeah, and all the problems I have to listen to from my group! You'd think I was a shrink or something.

KOHL   And that's not as bad as the guff we take from the section head when orders get behind. But then, I don't want to go back, do you?

1. Cite two disadvantages of moving from operations to management in addition to those cited in the dialogue.
2. If you could add to Kohl's remark about not wanting to go back to operations, what advantages of the supervisory job would you cite?

REFERENCES

1. John Naisbitt and Patricia Aburdene, *Reinventing the Corporation,* Warner Books, New York, 1985, pp. 52–53.
2. U.S. Bureau of Labor Statistics, *Occupational Outlook Handbook,* April 1986, p. 25.
3. Frederick W. Taylor, *The Principles of Scientific Management,* Harper & Row Publishers, Incorporated, New York, 1911.

4. Frank B. Gilbreth, *Motion Study,* D. Van Nostrand Company, Inc., New York, 1911. Also Frank B. Gilbreth and Lillian M. Gilbreth, ''Motion Study and Time Study Instruments of Precision,'' *Transactions of the International Engineering Congress,* vol. II, 1916; and Lillian M. Gilbreth, *The Quest of the One Best Way,* Society of Industrial Engineers, New York, 1924.

5. Henri Fayol, *General and Industrial Management,* Constance Storrs (trans.), Sir Isaac Pitman & Sons, Ltd., London, 1949.

6. Elton Mayo, *The Social Problem of Industrial Civilization,* Harvard Graduate School of Business Administration, Boston, 1945. See also Fritz Roethlisberger and William J. Dickson, *Management of the Worker: An Account of a Research Program Conducted by the Western Electric Company, Hawthorne Works, Chicago,* Harvard University Press, Cambridge, Mass., 1939.

7. Abraham H. Maslow, ''A Theory of Human Motivation,'' *Psychological Review 50,* July 1943, pp. 370–396. See also *Motivation and Personality,* Harper & Row Publishers, Incorporated, New York, 1954.

8. Douglas McGregor, *The Human Side of Enterprise,* McGraw-Hill Book Company, New York, 1960.

9. Chris Argyris, *Personality and Organization,* Harper & Row Publishers, Incorporated, New York, 1957.

10. Rensis Likert, *New Patterns of Management,* McGraw-Hill Book Company, New York, 1961.

11. Peter F. Drucker, *The Practice of Management,* Harper & Row Publishers, Incorporated, New York, 1954.

12. Frederick Herzberg, *Work and the Nature of Man,* Mentor Books, New American Library, Inc., New York, 1966.

13. Harold D. Koontz, ''The Theory Jungle Revisited,'' *Academy of Management Review,* April 1980, pp. 175–187.

14. Henry C. Metcalf and Lyndall F. Urwich (eds.), *Dynamic Administration: The Collected Papers of Mary Parker Follett,* Harper & Row Publishers, Incorporated, New York, 1942.

15. Fred E. Fiedler, *A Theory of Leadership Effectiveness,* McGraw-Hill Book Company, New York, 1967.

16. William Ouchi, *Theory Z: How American Business Can Meet the Japanese Challenge,* Addison-Wesley Publishing Company, Inc., Reading, Mass., 1981.

17. John Naisbitt, *Megatrends,* Warner Books, New York, 1982.

18. Thomas J. Peters and Robert H. Waterman, Jr., *In Search of Excellence,* Warner Books, New York, 1982.

19. Marshall Sashkin, ''Participative Management Is an Ethical Imperative,'' *Organizational Dynamics,* Spring 1984, p. 5.

20. For three observers' views, see Peter Drucker, ''Twilight of the First-Line Supervisor?'' *Wall Street Journal,* June 7, 1983, p. 34; and Leonard A. Schlesinger and Janice A. Klein, ''The First-Line Supervisor: Past, Present, and Future,'' *Handbook of Organizational Behavior,* Jay W. Lorsch (ed.), Prentice-Hall, Inc., Englewood Cliffs, N.J., 1986.

21. Rosabeth Moss Kanter, ''The Reshaping of Middle Management,'' *Management Review,* January 1986, pp. 19–20.

22. *Occupational Outlook Handbook,* loc. cit.

23. Loc. cit.

24. Loc. cit.

SUGGESTED READINGS

Bedeian, Arthur G.: *Management,* The Dryden Press, Inc., Chicago, 1986.

Carroll, Stephen J., and Dennis Gillen: ''Are the Classical Management Functions Useful in Describing Managerial Work,'' *Academy of Management Review,* vol. 12, no. 1, 1987, pp. 38–51.

Certo, Samuel: *Principles of Modern Management,* 3d ed., Wm C. Brown Company Publishers, Dubuque, Iowa, 1985.

Donnelly, James H., Jr., James L. Gibson, and John M. Ivancevich: *Fundamentals of Management,* 6th ed., Business Publications, Inc., Plano, Texas, 1987.

Hampton, David R.: *Management,* 3d ed., McGraw-Hill Book Company, New York, 1986.

Koontz, Harold, Cyril O'Donnell, and Heinz Weihrich: *Management,* 8th ed., McGraw-Hill Book Company, New York, 1984.

2

THE SUPERVISOR'S ROLE IN THE MANAGEMENT ENVIRONMENT

2

THE SUPERVISOR'S ROLE IN THE MANAGEMENT ENVIRONMENT

COMPETENCIES

Studying this chapter will enable you to:

1. Show the relationship between organizational goals and the environment.

2. Distinguish between the external environments of upper-level and lower-level management.

3. Give an example of goal or objective setting by different levels of management.

4. Define *interface* and cite the interface requirements of management.

5. Define *participative management* and give the premise on which it is based.

6. Give an example of the supervisor's duties in each of the managerial functions.

7. Cite the skills needed by managers and show the importance of each to the levels of management.

CHAPTER OUTLINE

"OK, we all know we can't wish our competition away or solve our problems with some kind of magic," the speaker said after reviewing some of the company's major problems. "But we have had an imposing history of success with quality products, market share, and customer satisfaction. I think we have enough brainpower, skill, and, yes, guts to climb back on top.

"What we need here, it seems to me," he continued, "is a new climate—a new attitude from managers and workers alike—to get this company moving again. After all, we're all in the same boat. Unless we have all our oars in the water and all pull in the same direction, not only are we not going anyplace, we may damn well sink as well."

Hank Enders, president of Mercury Footwear, Inc., was giving more than his usual annual pep talk to company managers. They all sensed the seriousness of his remarks. Competition in recent years from Italy, France, Brazil, and Taiwan had caused market share to plummet from 21 percent to 9 percent in just over a decade. This meeting followed, by 2 months, the closing of the second of the 50-year-old company's five shoe manufacturing plants, displacing a total of 800 employees. Moreover, quality had slipped in the effort to meet competition, and customer complaints had more than doubled. Productivity was on a downslide. Morale was at an all-time low; many good workers were leaving the company. Everyone wondered what—and who—would be next.

"It's up to you," Enders said in closing. "I, for one, think we can turn this thing around. It will take teamwork. And it will take some rethinking of old rules and old routines. Innovation is the name of the new game. I have complete confidence in you to get our ship moving again. You're good managers—that's why you were hired. I've asked the top line managers to spearhead an all-out brainstorming marathon. I expect them to be in touch with you—and with me—30 days from today with a preliminary report."

"Well, at least he acknowledged that someone outside the founding Enders family has some brains," Barney Bailey, a production manager, remarked as they left the room. "But I wonder if this new grass-roots effort will fly in this traditional, lockstep, bureaucratic company."

"Yeah, but it's a mandate, it seems. Enders has some pretty strong goals in mind. No point standing around griping about it," countered Jill Tyson, a sales manager. "It's about time something got moving around here. So let's get on with it."

In recent years, many executives like Enders, finding their firms threatened by environmental forces, have called on their managers and other employees to look for different approaches to their problems. As a supervisor, you too may find yourself involved with the management team and with workers in an effort to guide your company toward its goals. Hopefully, you will respond more like Jill Tyson, who wants to ''get on with it,'' than like Barney Bailey, who reacted negatively.

This chapter will help you understand the environment in which management operates and will help prepare you to assume your role in that environment. In addition, you will review the relationship between organizational goals and the environment and learn how you can participate with the management team in setting goals and objectives. You will examine some of the differences between traditional and participative environments, especially as they affect the supervisor. You will also learn what your duties are and the skills you need to perform them.

As you study the chapter, remember that as a supervisor, you are also a manager. The term *supervisor* refers only to the level at which you carry out your managerial responsibilities. That perspective will help you understand the total management environment, which we shall examine first.

UNDERSTANDING THE MANAGEMENT ENVIRONMENT

The environment in which a business operates has both internal and external components. Internally, the *management environment* encompasses all the human and nonhuman resources in the organization and the interaction among these resources. The *human resources* are the people in the organization: their behaviors, attitudes, skills, motivations, and performance in getting the job done. The *nonhuman resources* are the firm's technology—its equipment, facilities, materials, information, money, and the processes involved in getting the work done. Integrating these resources into an effective operational system is what management is all about. *Managing People and Technology* is the subtitle of this text. As a supervisor, you will interact with your company's human and nonhuman resources as you manage its people and the technology within your assigned unit or department.

An important aspect of the management environment is its relationship to organizational goals. The impact of that relationship will be examined next.

Organizational Goals and the Environment

Goals are the ''end'' to which Geneen referred in the opening quote. He suggested that a business set the goal it wishes to reach and then do everything it must to reach it.

Enders, in the beginning of the chapter, stated his goals for Mercury Footwear. He wanted to regain his company's leadership in the footwear industry by providing a quality product, capturing a large market share, and restoring customer satisfaction. He challenged his managers to be innovative in finding ways to reach these broad goals. Their task was to set definitive objectives to show how the goals could be reached.

Goals are the rationale for an organization's existence. The environment plays a large role in shaping the organization.

The relationship of goals and the environment is evident in several ways. One way is through constraints in the environment. Forces in the environment determine, to a great extent, what a firm may and may not do. A company may sell almost anything that has not been cited by law as harmful to individuals or to society. Laws also govern the way a chemical plant may dispose of its waste materials. A firm must dispose of chemical waste in such a way as to protect humans and the environment, and it must add the cost of doing this to the costs of doing business. Thus, the legal environment imposes many constraints on an organization.

Governments also impose constraints. Our federal government, for example, may not allow a firm to trade with certain countries whose actions it considers unacceptable. This is a constraint from the political environment.

Social disapproval may also affect company goals. Besides outright constraints, the environment sometimes dictates that certain objectives, while not illegal, may not be desirable. Companies that sell alcoholic products, for example, have certainly been affected by the recent actions from many sources to decrease highway fatalities.

Another factor in the environment that can affect organizational goals is the state of the economy. Enders found, for example, that foreign competition had greatly depressed the domestic footwear industry and caused his market share to plummet. In addition to competition, changing prices, the increased cost of capital, or a dwindling supply of resources are among many forces in the economic environment that can influence organizational goals.

Competency Check:

Can you show the relationship between organizational goals and the environment?

Internal forces can also affect management goals. A firm that wishes to expand, for example, may find that it does not have the economic or human resources to do so. Enders suggested a team approach to the company's economic problems, but Bailey doubts if the bureaucratic climate in the firm will permit that approach. Goals sometimes must be modified or discarded because of internal environmental forces.

There are environmental/goal relationships other than the five cited above. Even the weather can influence the goals a firm chooses. For example, a retail store in northern Alaska would be foolhardy to specialize in swimwear and beach clothes. You will detect other relationships as we view the setting of goals by the management team.

The Management Team, the Environment, and Organizational Goals

All levels of management are influenced by environmental forces. The influence at the different levels, however, may stem from different forces and extend in varying degrees.

In setting goals, managers do not work in isolation but function as a team. When a goal is established, each manager must set objectives for his or her department that will feed into and help achieve the goal. Jill Tyson, the sales manager for Mercury

Footwear, might set the objective of increasing sales by 10 percent within a year; this will be her sales unit's part of the broad goal of increasing Mercury's market share. Whether the manager focuses on goals or objectives depends largely on his or her level of management, as we shall see in the discussion which follows.

Focus of the Management Levels on Goal Setting

The major external environmental forces that affect company goals are shown in the outer frames of Figure 2-1, the environment of upper-level management relating to goals, and Figure 2-2, the environment of lower-level management relating to objectives. Note the differences between the forces that influence upper-level management and the forces that influence lower-level management.

The forces that influence goal setting for upper-level management are largely *outside* the firm: customers, creditors, suppliers, stockholders, competitors, the economy,

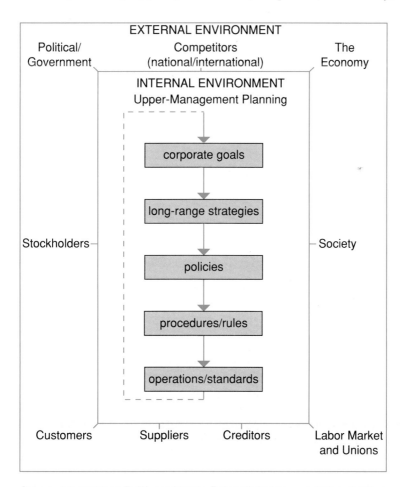

FIGURE 2-1

Organizational goals and the environment—upper-level management

Source: Adapted from R. Wayne Mondy, Robert E. Holmes, and Edwin B. Flippo, *Management: Concepts and Practices,* Allyn and Bacon, Inc., Boston, 1980, p. 61

FIGURE 2-2

Organizational
objectives and the
environment—lower-
level management

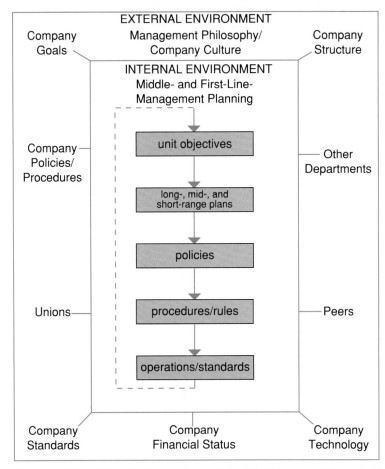

Source: Adapted from R. Wayne Mondy, Robert E. Holmes, and Edwin B. Flippo,
Management: Concepts and Practices, Allyn and Bacon, Inc., Boston, 1980, p. 60

government, unions and the labor market, and society. As noted earlier, these all have an impact on what goals a company chooses to pursue. Upper-level management must be aware of changing conditions in any of these external forces. Enders, judging from the situation in which he now finds himself, either did not keep in touch with Mercury's changing external environment or was slow in responding to it.

The forces in the external environment that affect lower-level management are largely *inside* the firm; that is, they are outside the manager's specific unit or department but within the organization. These include the company's culture, structure, policies and procedures, standards, financial status, and technology as well as management philosophy, other departments, unions, and peers.

Forces external to the firm affect all management to some degree. For example, as a supervisor, you may interface with suppliers and equipment vendors. But upper-level management will typically serve as a buffer between you and most external forces, such as creditors and stockholders.

Competency Check:

Can you distinguish between the external environment of upper-level management and the external environment of lower-level management?

The differences in the external environment are derived from the roles that managers at the different levels play. Let us look at these roles as reflected in the setting of organizational goals and objectives.

Top Management.   The board of directors, the chief executive officer (CEO), the president, and other executive officers look at the "big picture." They formulate goals that answer such questions as:

What is our company all about?

What product or service will we provide?

What level of profit shall we strive for?

What image do we wish to portray?

Where do we wish to be 5 or 10 years from today?

How will we get there?

When Chrysler said "We want to be your car company," it meant that its goal was to develop customer loyalty that would keep its customers coming back for more cars and service. Top management sets the broad goals that will enable the firm to operate in a highly competitive national and international environment.

Before divestiture, AT&T operated in a protected political environment as a limited monopoly. As such, it reminded the public that "all we have to sell is service." Today, without this protected status, it has changed its goals. It now aims to be a competitive manufacturer and retailer of communications products, telecommunications systems, and computer technology. Environmental forces caused AT&T's top management to reshape the company and its goals.

Numerous goals are established by top management to guide the company. Peter Drucker pointed out that objectives should be set in these eight key areas:[2]

1. market standing
2. innovations
3. worker performance and attitude
4. physical and financial resources
5. managerial performance and development
6. social responsibility
7. productivity
8. profitability

Top managers are ultimately responsible for every goal and objective throughout the firm. They direct most of their efforts toward setting broad, long-term goals, as Enders did in his address to the managers. Top managers also formulate strategies for achieving those goals. The setting and implementing of secondary and supporting objectives is delegated to the lower levels of management.

Middle Management.   Enders challenged his managers to find ways to get the foundering firm moving again. He did not suggest that the company's broad goals of manufacturing and marketing shoes be changed. His midlevel managers would have to reexamine their objectives to see how they could help Enders and the company fulfill its mission.

Regional officers, division directors, plant managers, and other middle managers set supportive objectives based on the broad goals established by top management. Bailey and the other production managers at Mercury Footwear might set objectives to support Enders' goal of reviving the company. To do so, Bailey might set objectives to (1) increase units produced by 10 percent, (2) hold increased costs to 6 percent, (3) increase productivity by 3 percent, and (4) realize a 1 percent cost reduction through improved inventory and quality control systems.

At the midlevel, objectives are greater in number and more focused than the broad company goals. Middle managers coordinate objectives with their peers and delegate to first-line managers the setting of additional supportive goals.

First-Line Management.   You have noted that a hierarchy of objectives is created as each level sets objectives to carry out the goals set at the top. The number increases from the few broad company goals at the top to more objectives with greater focus at the middle to more detailed and more narrowly aimed objectives at the supervisor's level.

As you learned in Chapter 1, the supervisor, as a first-line manager, directs operations. This is the level at which the products are made or the services performed. Here the dreams and plans of top management are given physical form. Objectives get more specific. At Mercury Footwear, first-line objectives might include the following:

Increase sales by 10 percent within a year.

Reduce employee turnover by 10 percent this year.

Reduce rejects to 1 percent by the end of the second quarter.

Cross-train four junior line workers by year's end.

Implement an incentive program to reduce absenteeism by 10 percent by midyear.

Reduce customer complaints by 10 percent within 6 months.

Competency Check:

Can you give an example of goal or objective setting by each of the levels of management?

Note that these objectives focus on quality, quantity, and productivity, with special emphasis on worker behavior and motivation. You will learn more about the supervisor and setting objectives in Chapter 3, about motivation in Chapter 11, and about productivity in Chapter 16.

The Interface

Interaction between and among managers and other members of the organization is referred to as *interface*. Regardless of management style, managers must work with each other, with subordinates, with superiors, with work groups, and, often, with unions. These five interface requirements vary with hierarchical levels.

Supervisors spend a large portion of their time interfacing. According to one estimate involving managers of an electrical appliance manufacturer, 15 percent of supervisors' time is spent interfacing with other supervisors and upper-level managers and 55 percent is spent interfacing with subordinates. This means that 70 percent of the supervisor's time is spent relating to other humans.[3]

While top and midlevel managers interface with unions to some extent, their contacts are confined primarily to contract negotiations and working agreements. Supervisors, on the other hand, are in daily contact with union representatives and workers whose performance is based on union standards. Sometimes the standards, schedules, and working conditions have been bitterly negotiated. One author states that ''with few exceptions, American unions have resisted seats on supervisory boards and involvement in the direct management of the business. . . . When they do enter cooperative initiatives, they do so within the collective bargaining framework, within which labor and management see themselves as two separate and distinct institutions.''[4] The author suggests participative management as an effective approach to labor-management relations in this age of change.[5] We shall address participative management later in this chapter.

Another author refers to the supervisor's job as the ''thin line between management and union employees.'' He suggests that the supervisor improve his or her leadership, develop a rapport with the workers in a climate of mutual trust, and practice a management style that fits the supervisor and the situation.[6]

It has been pointed out that many supervisors are weak in their ability to use interpersonal skills effectively and comfortably with their employees.[7] There is a growing consensus that most supervisors could substantially benefit from training in the interactional dimensions of management.[8] A knowledge of group psychology would also be helpful in interfacing with unions, work teams, and other groups. This knowledge would also be helpful in working in a participatory environment, which we shall look at next.

Competency Check:

Can you define *interface* and cite five interface requirements of management?

THE PARTICIPATIVE MANAGEMENT ENVIRONMENT

Participative management is management in which employees are involved, often in teams, in making decisions on such matters as setting goals, production processes, schedules, assignment distribution, and problem solving. The premise is that when workers help to make a decision about their work, they are more willing to accept that decision and to perform in such a way as to bring about its success. The concept is not new. In 1954, Drucker's ''management by objectives'' cited the cooperative setting of objectives by employer and employee as a major element of the model.[9]

Participative management also reflects the motivation and management theories of Maslow,[10] Scanlon,[11] Likert,[12] and Herzberg.[13] Today, participative management is a response to an environmental force—marketplace competition.

Management's Response to Competition

Many firms that have changed to participative management in recent years have done so in response to the conditions described by Enders at the beginning of this chapter: fierce competition and the resultant falling market share, lower quality of output, and decreased customer satisfaction. Many firms have found that participative management works to cure those ills. LTV, Inc., for one example, has experienced many benefits. One team working on a quality-related problem effected an 85 percent improvement in product quality and significant reductions in costs. Another team devised a microfiche records system that not only improved paper-flow efficiency but also resulted in a savings of $72,000.[14] Do you think, in view of Enders' goals, that he would be impressed by these results?

Participative management as a growing trend is a basic premise of this book. There is substantial evidence that participative management does improve the work environment and result in higher productivity. Participative management will be presented throughout the text as a more effective approach to managing. An overwhelming number of upper-level managers from large and small companies (83 percent) responding to a New York Stock Exchange study agreed that participative management is effective in today's environment.[15] While a variety of management styles may be appropriate under certain conditions, participative management offers an alternative that merits consideration in all firms seeking improvement. You will study different management styles in Chapter 11.

In the United States, emphasis on participative management has evolved largely from the Japanese style of management. Ouchi's Theory Z[16] attributes much of the success of Japanese businesses in world markets to their participative-management style. (See Chapters 11 and 16.) Peters and Waterman,[17] in citing over 40 highly successful American companies, point out that employee involvement in management is a typical characteristic. In other evidence that it works, a study of 101 industrial companies found that the participatively managed among them outscored the others on 13 of 14 financial measures.[18]

Focus on Team Problem Solving

As you have read, participative management, by definition, involves workers in problem solving; LTV teams have been cited as a successful example.

Using teams to solve work-related problems is an approach that is being used by a growing number of firms. Among them are Ford, Donnelly Corporation, Honeywell, and 3M.[19] You will read about others in Chapter 16, which presents this approach as a means for increasing productivity.

Team problem solving is not new, but it has been tried by more firms since the wide publicity given to the Japanese use of teams they call "quality circles." (See Chapter 16.) *Problem-solving teams* and *quality circles* are terms used for groups of employees with responsibility for solving problems or addressing specific issues in their work units.

An American Management Association study revealed that 36 percent of 1618 responding member firms were using quality circles. A study by the New York Stock Exchange showed that quality circles were used by 44 percent of 1158 responding firms.[20] The innovative organization plan for General Motors' Saturn plant, scheduled for construction in Tennessee by the 1990s, incorporates a team approach throughout. This is a leading-edge organizational and operational plan whose implementation is anticipated with great interest by management and union leaders.[21]

In spite of its growing use, the team approach may be resisted. When it is attempted, it is sometimes abandoned because it was improperly initiated or administered.[22] Effective team building requires that management align personal and corporate goals, find and build on employee strengths, reduce conflicts and politicking, and help everyone on the team recognize his or her importance to the team. In using a team problem-solving approach, the supervisor's role sometimes changes from director to facilitator and coordinator. The success or failure of the team approach often hinges on the supervisor.

THE SUPERVISOR ON THE LINE

You have seen in the discussion of interfacing that the supervisor's job on the line is not an easy one. It involves working with operations employees, motivating them, and organizing and integrating their activities to achieve company goals. ''On the firing line'' may be a better description of the supervisor's position. A problem which must be dealt with is that people above and below the position have different views of the job, as implied in the cartoon below.

How Others Perceive the Supervisor

In early factory days, the supervisor was viewed by management as an uncompromising drill sergeant whose task was to browbeat the ''troops'' into line with inviolate rules of production and behavior. The plant was aptly called a *sweatshop*. Worker hours were long, and pay was low. Attitudes were slow to change, but improvements

Supervisors may feel this way, too, when first promoted.

Source: Reprinted by special permission of Johnny Hart and NAS, Inc.

rooted in the behavioral movement (Chapter 1) have made significant changes in employer-employee relationships and in the perception of the supervisor's position.

Management today perceives the supervisor as a member of its team, but the distance between top and first level is still formidable and relationships are scant. Two researchers found, in 1981, that supervisors rarely enjoy the privilege of helping establish the goals of the organization they serve.[23] Yet innovative companies, such as those termed "excellent" by Peters and Waterman[24] and many others adapting to participative management, perceive supervision as management's key to increased productivity.[25]

The way that workers perceive the supervisor depends, to a large extent, on the supervisor's management "style." An open, skilled, communicative, and supportive supervisor will be viewed as an excellent manager by subordinates. Conversely, the supervisor who is distant, who barks orders, who chews out the worker for mistakes, or who snoops around looking for rule infractions will be perceived by his or her workers as a Simon Legree and described in unprintable expletives.

Public perception of the supervisor is often better than the perceptions of members of the firm. If the supervisor has been promoted from operations, one often hears that he or she is "on the way up" or, in complimentary tones, that he or she "is management now."

The Supervisor and
the Management Hierarchy

Are supervisors part of management? In 1947, the Taft-Hartley Act placed supervisors unequivocally in the hierarchy of management. The act specifically prohibited supervisors from joining unions of production or clerical workers. Hierarchical status does not always accrue from legal definition, however. "They remain today the bottommost figure on what is essentially a totem pole," according to two researchers.[26]

A study of 225 plants employing over 9000 supervisors disclosed that 97 percent of top management surveyed considered supervisors an integral part of management.[27] They are not always successful in conveying this feeling to supervisors, however. Another study asked 250 supervisors if they truly felt a part of management. In response, 74 percent said yes, 24 percent said "sometimes," and 2 percent said no.[28] Clearly there is room for improvement on both sides to achieve a psychological as well as a hierarchical integration of the supervisor into management.

Career-planning programs are one way to effect this change. A well-defined and communicated system of career opportunities and a clear succession plan will effectively convey management's attitude about the supervisor's role in management. Supervisors would be wise to look for such signs in choosing a company to work for.

Caught in the Middle—
Traditional Management

The first rung on the management ladder is not a comfortable place to be. The supervisor often feels caught between upper management and the workers. He or she is often hanging on tenuously, fingers figuratively bruised by orders pouring down from the top and feet in danger of being dislodged by subordinates who fight for favors or whose failure to produce is cutting the rung from under him or her.

Traditionally, the supervisor was supposed to be fully aligned with management, but his or her association was supposed to be largely with operations workers. Much was expected of the supervisor in the traditional setting. Too much, say two research-ers. They point out that the dizzying range of contradictory subroles and skills required of the traditional supervisor can be overwhelming.[29] In carrying out their varied tasks, supervisors sometimes receive more criticism than support from their managers and are the objects of varying degrees of apathy, distrust, and resentment from their subordinates.

In spite of all these drawbacks, however, there has been much progress under traditional management. The historical record of high productivity in American busi-ness attests to that. The supervisor has played a major role in that productivity. An examination of the supervisory function will help you understand how important that role is.

WHAT DOES A SUPERVISOR DO?

The supervisor plays many roles. Some are well defined; some are not. One study found that supervisors spend more than two-thirds of their time relating with other people. What they do in these relationships covers a broad range of tasks and numerous roles. One of the roles is to link management with workers.

Bridging the Organizational Structure

One of the supervisor's roles is to serve as a connecting bridge between management and operations. Likert described supervisors as linking pins between the upper and lower planes of the organizational structure. This characteristic has been described as ''a series of flexible couplings, transmitting orders and instructions from above while absorbing shocks and disturbances from below.''[30] As you can see, a linking pin serves a very critical function.

More recently, Keith Davis referred to supervision as ''the keystone in the or-ganizational arch,''[31] the supporting structural member which ties together manage-ment and workers. Davis' view and the bridging characterization connote less friction between the elements being joined. That is in keeping with what effective supervision should be. A bridge connecting two productive groups can be a facilitating element. While the bridge is subject to some stress, it can support a lot of traffic when properly planned. The supervisor, when properly trained and supported on both sides, can carry out his or her functions with minimal frustration.

Among the bridging tasks that the supervisor performs are those of communicating and interpreting company objectives and policies to workers, appraising employee performance and making recommendations to upper management, identifying and communicating the needs of workers to management, and serving as a role model in interpreting and carrying out management's philosophy. As shown in Figure 2-3, supervisors spend much less of their time (15 percent) working with people in the same or higher levels than they do working with subordinates (55 percent); but this bidirectional interface will involve all the management functions.

Performing the Management Functions

The bridging characterization should not be interpreted as limiting the supervisor's role to that of facilitator, as important as that role is. The supervisor, as you learned in Chapter 1, performs all five managerial functions: planning, organizing, staffing, leading and motivating, and controlling.

Look at Figure 2-3 again. Note that 15 percent of supervisors' time is spent "thinking ahead." That is part of planning. So is part of the 15 percent of their time that is spent "doing work that cannot be delegated." The supervisor must plan for the

FIGURE 2-3

How managers spend their time

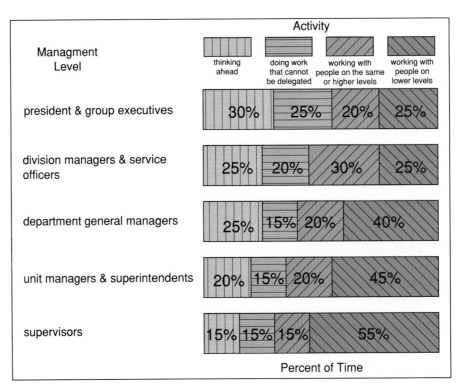

Source: Based on a study of an electrical appliance manufacturer in Donald C. Mosely, Leon C. Megginson, and Paul Pietri, *Supervisory Management* South-Western Company, Inc., Cincinnati, 1985.

long term (How will my department contribute to the company's 5-year plan?); for the intermediate term (Conduct a personnel-needs analysis for the biennium); and for the short term (Plan a meeting with work-team leaders for next week).

The supervisor also organizes. Work must be analyzed and scheduled, and production goals must be set. Vacation requests must be coordinated with workers and with job demands. Conferences must be scheduled for a variety of purposes. Equipment-maintenance schedules must be designed and maintained. Job design and job descriptions must be analyzed and kept up to date. Some of this organizing falls into the 15 percent of time spent ''doing work that can't be delegated.''

The staffing responsibility may be shared with the human resources department, but some personnel tasks must be handled at the source—the unit supervisor. These tasks include determining labor needs, appraising performance, and making compensation and rewards recommendations.

The leading function is a subtle and difficult one. It involves the supervisor's personality and style as well as his or her background in management principles and human behavior. Creating conditions in which workers will be motivated to perform well and willingly is a critical component of leading. Conferring and counseling are also included in this function.

A study by the authors revealed that of the 52 percent of their time devoted to management functions by supervisors, over one-third is spent in leading and motivating. Figure 2-4 shows the allocation of the supervisor's time as disclosed in the study.[32]

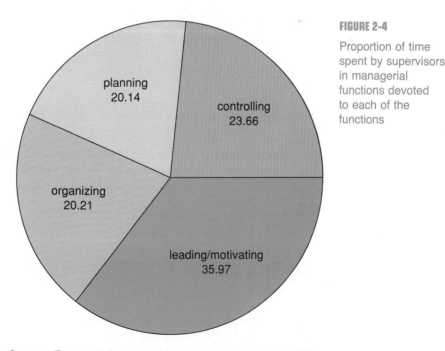

FIGURE 2-4

Proportion of time spent by supervisors in managerial functions devoted to each of the functions

Source: From a study on supervisory management by the authors.

Controlling involves continual follow up on activities initiated in the course of performing the other four functions. Evaluation of a meeting held with work teams; checking to see that equipment is being maintained; determining whether production goals have been met; finding out whether the new self-appraisal system is really motivating workers; finding out whether quality standards are being met—all of these are controlling functions that the supervisor must perform.

Duties of the Supervisor

Another way to look at what the supervisor does is to examine the activities performed on a daily basis without classifying them by function. From the numerous research studies being conducted today on supervision, many sets of supervisory tasks have been compiled. Firms that have supervisory job descriptions have custom-made lists of duties for every supervisor classification.

Competency Check:

Can you give an example of a supervisory duty in each of the five management functions?

Figure 2-5 shows a comprehensive list of duties of supervisors developed by a large corporation. The list resulted from a study of supervisory job content conducted by the firm over several years to aid in the selection of supervisors and to help prepare them for their new jobs. The result is a generic list of duties that could be applied to almost any supervisory position.

Figure 2-6 focuses on supervisory duties in a participative environment. It was prepared by a firm using a form of participative management, including semiautonomous work teams. Note the shared responsibility in decision making with the team approach.

The duties of the supervisor are varied and demanding. Carrying out these duties requires a variety of skills, as we shall see in the next section.

WHAT SKILLS DOES A SUPERVISOR NEED?

How about the wisdom of Solomon and the patience of Job? Even such a formidable combination may not be enough if one is supervising in a technological environment. Certainly today's manager must be more skillful than his or her counterpart in the past. Let us examine the skills needed today.

The Skills of a Manager

Regardless of level in the hierarchy, today's manager must possess certain skills and be able to use them effectively. These can be classified as technical, conceptual, and human skills. Though all managers need all three skills, the importance of each skill varies with the level on which the manager operates, as shown in Figure 2-7.

FIGURE 2-5

PRINCIPAL DUTIES OF SUPERVISORS

RANKED BY PROPORTION OF TIME DEVOTED TO ACTIVITY	DUTIES	FREQUENCY OF OCCURRENCE
1	controlling the work	every day
2	problem solving and decision making	every day
3	planning the work	every day
4	informal oral communications	every day
5	communications, general	every day
6	providing performance feedback to employees	every day
7	training, coaching, developing subordinates	every day
8	providing written communications and documentation	every day
9	creating and maintaining a motivating atmosphere	every day
10	personal time management	every day
11	meetings and conferences	twice monthly
12	self-development activities	weekly
13	career counseling of subordinates	bimonthly
14	representing the company to the community	monthly

Source: Adapted from Charles R. MacDonald, *Performance Based Supervisory Development, adapted from a major AT&T study,* Human Resources Development Press, Amherst, Mass., 1982, p. 20.

Technical Skill

This is the ability to use specific knowledge, methods, procedures, or techniques in performing a job. This ability is crucial to first-level managers. They must work in direct contact with operations workers and must be able to provide technical assistance when needed. Though there are exceptions, supervisors typically should be able to perform the jobs in their work units and to train others to do them. Much respect from workers is derived from supervisors' technical competence. Without this respect, a supervisor's ability to lead and motivate workers is seriously hampered.

As managers move up in the hierarchy, technical skill becomes less critical. The

FIGURE 2-6

DUTIES OF FIRST-LINE SUPERVISORS IN A PLANT WITH SEMIAUTONOMOUS WORK TEAMS

commitment	Supervisors must promote teamwork and convey a genuine interest in and support for the concept. They should encourage cooperation and work with employees in developing team competence and cooperation.
communication	Supervisors are the major link in the communications channel between management and hourly employees. Supervisors must learn to relay daily instructions through the team to reach team members.
training	Supervisors are in a good position to assess the training needs of their employees. They are responsible for identifying, coordinating, and, where possible, conducting the necessary training.
human relations	Since supervision is the key to maintaining positive employee attitudes and high morale, supervisors must develop good human relations skills. This means becoming "employee-centered" by showing an interest in employees' problems, emphasizing communications and team spirit, and demonstrating a sincere concern for workers' welfare.
motivation	Supervisors must learn to be motivators, not just disciplinarians. They can motivate employees by giving them responsibility (with accountability) and a sense of contribution. Supervisors should learn to use such phrases as "What's your opinion?"; "What can I do to help?"; and "Thank you."
delegation	This allows supervisors to take on additional duties by passing on to employees many of the routine details that they can handle efficiently. Delegation helps to bolster both individual and team morale by giving everyone an opportunity to share responsibilities and rewards.
decision making	Supervisors' performance ultimately hinges on the outcomes of decisions. Teams can be allowed to make routine decisions, but supervisors must set priorities and explain why some decisions take precedence over others.
discipline	Supervisors must always remember that employees are individuals as well as members of a group. Most employees will respond to techniques aimed at motivating them, but a few may not. In those cases, the supervisor may have to administer discipline.
feedback	There are times when every team needs guidance, support, and reinforcement. Both oral and written feedback are necessary to make individuals and teams aware of their strengths and weaknesses.

Source: Janice A. Klein, "Why Supervisors Resist Employee Involvement," *Harvard Business Review,* September–October 1984, p. 93.

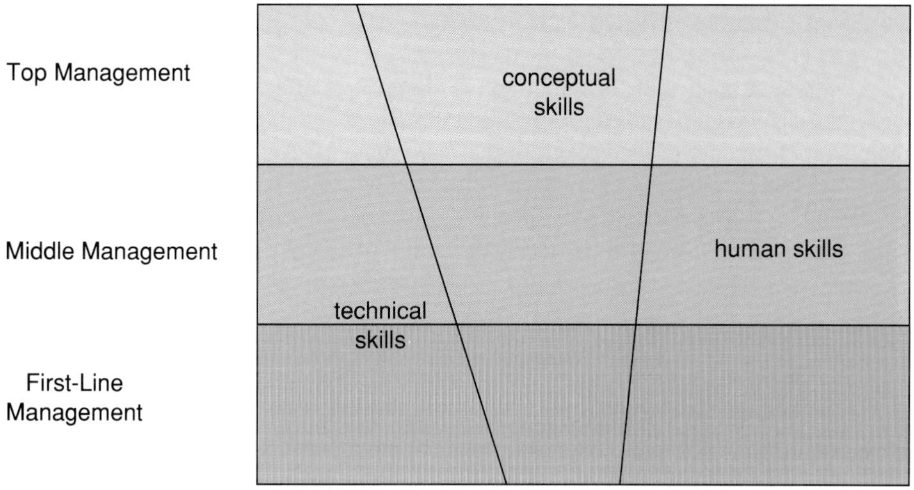

FIGURE 2-7

Skills needed by
levels of
management

CEO need not know how to operate a jackhammer in order to manage a road construction company, but he or she should know what kind of equipment is needed for various construction jobs.

Conceptual Skill

This is the ability to see the big picture, to understand or to create abstract concepts, and to apply these concepts to specific situations. Conceptual skill is more important to top managers than it is to lower-level managers. Top executives must be able to relate events and trends in the environment to their firms. They must be able to visualize the organization as a whole composed of interdependent parts, with the actions of any part having an impact on the whole. Consider Enders in the beginning of the chapter. Has he been using his conceptual skills effectively? The evidence indicates he has not.

Supervisors also need conceptual skills in order to visualize how their units fit into the whole organization. While they are usually given specific guidelines for their units, their plans must mesh with all other units to work toward organizational goals.

Human Skill

This is the ability to understand, communicate with, work with, and interact harmoniously with people. It is the most important skill a manager can possess and it is almost equally important at all levels of management. Human skills enable managers to understand themselves as well as others. Managers also need to understand and be tolerant of different views and values. Most important, they must understand the communications process and be skillful in using it in all their work relationships. It has been said that communication skill is the most important characteristic of a supervisor.[33]

*Competency
Check:*

Can you cite three
skills needed by
managers and show
their importance at
the different levels?

Why Some Supervisors Fail

Lack of good human skills or failure to use these skills effectively will almost surely doom the supervisor to failure. As Figure 2-8 indicates, the transition from the top of the operations ladder to the bottom of the management ladder is precarious. Because the roles of worker and manager are entirely different, some supervisors have difficulty in moving into management from operations. One survey of 225 plant managers with 9000 supervisors under them revealed that the most common weaknesses displayed by supervisors in the performance of their jobs were poor attitude, poor management of their jobs, poor disciplining, and poor communications. Further, the respondents said the most difficult problems faced by new supervisors involved the management functions: adopting a management attitude, human relations, and discipline.[34]

One difficulty faced by the new supervisor is that of breaking away from the "work gang" and forming new "management" relationships. Closely related problems are those of learning to use authority and learning to delegate. Of course, improper selection and training may be the primary reason so many new supervisors face these problems.

These are a few of the common reasons for failure in supervision. There are many others. Knowledge of the pitfalls is a first step in avoiding them. In the next section, you will learn about the stages that managers move through in adjusting to their new jobs.

FIGURE 2-8   The transition from operations to management is difficult

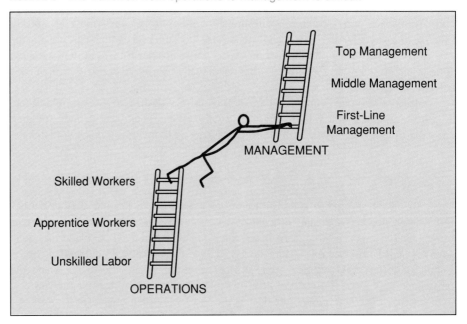

Top Management

Middle Management

First-Line Management

MANAGEMENT

Skilled Workers

Apprentice Workers

Unskilled Labor

OPERATIONS

FIGURE 2-9

STAGES OF DEVELOPMENT FROM BEGINNING TO
PEAK-PERFORMING MANAGER

STAGE	SYMPTOMS
1. initiation stage	Frequent visits with past coworkers. A new manager must, first and foremost, learn to identify with the role of manager after a nonmanagerial history. Until he or she does, the individual may resort to brainstorming excessively, displaying anxiety around subordinates, and procrastinating.
2. fear-of-success stage	May begin to perform so well that he or she actually becomes afraid of prospering on the job, apprehensive of what the consequences of this success may be. May unconsciously fear both increased recognition and expanded responsibilities, which may lead to failure to capitalize on proven, tangible results.
3. team-building stage	Having successfully conquered the earlier obstacles, is now fully committed to the management position. However, may suddenly have difficulty generating new leaders from among key subordinates and forming a tightly knit team among personnel. Unable to relinquish excessive control, inhibits the development of the group into a peak-performing team.
4. affiliation stage	Realizes that while his or her productivity is dependent upon the work of others, the responsibility for managerial performance remains his or hers alone. The task then becomes developing higher-level leadership capabilities. He or she has to relate effectively to both upper and lower levels of the organization and needs to acknowledge the increased importance of people-oriented leadership skills, particularly delegation.
5. elevation-seniority stage	Now operating effectively in the job, the manager is tapped for an upper-management post. If the promotion is to senior management, focus of job may change greatly; for example, from individuals to organization and from products and projects to money issues. The manager must learn to handle the increased responsibility and separation from subordinates that accompany the promotion. In many ways, the development process begins again.

Source: Charles A. Garfield, "The Right Stuff," *Management World,* July 1984, p. 26.

WHAT CAN THE SUPERVISOR DO?

What kinds of fears do you have when you experience a change in your life? If you ever relocated to another city, you probably worried about making new friends and leaving old ones. Or about learning your way around a new city. Or about whether you would like your new environment or be successful in it. If you had any of these anxieties, you are not alone. You were following a natural pattern of adjustment that most people have in moving from one place to another.

There is a natural pattern of development experienced by new managers also. One authority identified five distinct stages in the development of new managers to high-achieving ones. These are shown in Figure 2-9 on the preceding page. Businesses are beginning to use this knowledge in their career development programs in helping managers make adjustments to job changes.

Knowing these stages can help you recognize and move past the blocks that could abort your career development. Becoming acquainted with the stages will alleviate some of the fears of the unknown when you become a supervisor and allow you to concentrate your energies on performing your duties effectively.

In the chapters ahead, look for other sections called What Can the Supervisor Do? These and the remainder of this text are dedicated to helping you avoid these pitfalls on the way to becoming an effective supervisor.

COMPETENCY REVIEW

1. Show the relationship between organizational goals and the environment.
2. Distinguish between the external environments of upper-level and lower-level management.
3. Give an example of goal or objective setting by the different levels of management.
4. Define *interface,* and cite five interface requirements of management.
5. Define *participative management,* and give the premise upon which it is based.
6. Give an example of the supervisor's duties in each of the five managerial functions.
7. Cite three skills needed by managers, and show the importance of each skill to the different levels of management.

APPLICATIONS

1. By the time you are in a course in which this book is used, you may have had several work experiences. If so, you have been able to experience firsthand the management styles and abilities of one or more bosses. Think about the best and the worst of these bosses. If you have never worked, select a leader from another association you have had, such as a teacher or a club president. Then record your

responses in the spaces below to characterize the most effective and the least effective of these managers.

	MOST EFFECTIVE	LEAST EFFECTIVE
a. the level on which this manager operated	_____	_____
b. the characteristic that impressed me most	_____	_____
c. an example of the use of human skills	_____	_____
d. an example of the use of conceptual skills	_____	_____
e. an example of the use of technical skills	_____	_____
f. the characteristic that impressed me most was a _____ skill (human, conceptual, technical)	_____	_____

2. Using a contingency approach, one would examine the situation and determine whether to use a traditional or a participative management style. Below are behaviors typical of a traditional, or directive, approach and of a participative approach, as viewed by a productivity manager in a large corporation. Examine the behaviors; then describe three situations in which you would use the directive approach and three in which you would use the participative approach.

The behaviors typical of a directive management approach include:

1. deciding what needs to be done.
2. planning how to communicate the decision.
3. making arrangements to communicate the decision.
4. telling people the decision and the next steps.
5. answering questions.
6. monitoring subsequent actions.
7. making corrections as necessary.
8. giving feedback to keep the decision on course.
9. documenting the decision or new procedures.
10. deciding when the problem has been resolved.

The management behaviors that characterize a healthy participative approach include:

1. identifying appropriate opportunities for participation.
2. asking interested employees to participate.
3. clearly communicating the task at hand.
4. openly sharing known facts, constraints, and expectations.
5. developing teamwork and a sense of purpose.
6. soliciting and valuing different points of view.
7. acquiring appropriate resources for the team effort.
8. communicating the status of action plans.
9. teaching the process skills needed to participate effectively.
10. providing individual coaching and encouragement to team members.
11. facilitating the process of getting group consensus.

12. demonstrating the behaviors of successful teamwork.
13. actively listening to individuals and responding appropriately.
14. giving both positive and negative feedback (direct, specific, timely, and descriptive feedback) with the intention of helping the person develop.
15. providing recognition for participation and task completion.

Source: Richard Hamlin and Janet Garrison, "Choosing Between Directive and Participative Management," *Supervisory Management,* January 1986, p. 15.

3. From sources such as local newspapers or television, *The Wall Street Journal, Business Week, U.S. News and World Report,* or *Fortune,* identify a firm that has changed its objectives because of some environmental event. Write a brief summary of the event, its impact on the firm, and the changes made by the firm. Classify the environmental factor based on those shown in Figure 2-1.

4. Examine the classified employment section in a metropolitan newspaper or *The Wall Street Journal.* From the ads for managers:
   a. List, by title, the types of managers being sought.
   b. Classify the titles, as far as you are able, by level of management.
   c. List the qualifications specified in each ad.
   d. What conclusion, if any, can you draw about the opportunities for management jobs and the qualifications required for a management job?
   e. If you were in a position to seek one of the jobs, which would you choose? Why?

CASES

Case I: Climbing Back to the Top

Enders, in the beginning of the chapter, asked the top line managers to spearhead an all-out "brainstorming marathon" to get Mercury Footware, Inc., moving again. As a first step, each unit has been asked to call a meeting of its members to get some initial thinking about actions that might be taken. Below are managers representing all three levels. List several ideas that you think might appropriately come from each manager. Your teacher may ask you to form groups to complete this case.

1. Margo Smith, vice president, marketing
2. Barney Bailey, production manager, manufacturing
3. George Cooper, supervisor, shipping
4. Jill Tyson, sales manager, sports footwear
5. Guido Rivera, quality control supervisor, men's footwear

Case II: Who Is Ready to Join Management?

Your department manager has asked the three supervisors to recommend one person from each of their departments to be considered for a promotion to a new position—assistant supervisor. The new assistant will be responsible for helping with the transition to work teams in the plant.

You have given the matter considerable thought and have reviewed the performance appraisals of several good workers. You have also observed the workers closely as they performed their jobs and related to other workers. You have narrowed your selection to these three candidates: Jason Beanstock, Megan Moynihan, and Carlo Valero.

Beanstock has been with the company for 4 years. He is highly skilled, rarely has a reject, keeps a clean work station, and is seldom absent or late. His high productivity rate is the envy of some of his coworkers. He is somewhat of a loner; he never goes to lunch or takes his break with his coworkers, choosing, instead, to stay in and read the latest sci-fi best-seller.

Moynihan joined the firm 18 months ago and has adjusted well to the mostly male environment. She holds her own in production and usually gets good performance ratings. Her reject rate was higher than average at first, but she has improved that to a bit less than average now. She is accepted by her coworkers but lunches in the cafeteria with women from other departments. Her only relationship with her coworkers is at the work station. She is taking a management course at night at the university and hopes to move up in the company.

Valero has been with the firm 3 years. His productivity rate is among the highest in the company and he rarely has a reject. When he does, he takes a lot of good-natured kidding from his coworkers. He is often asked for advice by members of his work group as well as by others in the plant. The supervisor occasionally has to remind him to clean up his work station, and he does so without complaining. He appears to be a role model for his coworkers. Recently he attended a career development seminar sponsored by the firm. "I went just to see what it was all about," he joked. "If I like it, I may go out and get a Ph.D. so I can become the prez."

1. Which one would you recommend for the job? Why?
2. Give your reasons for not choosing the others.

REFERENCES

1. Harold Geneen, with Alvin Moscow, *Managing,* Doubleday & Company, Inc., Garden City, N.Y., 1984, p. 33.

2. Peter F. Drucker, *The Practice of Management,* Harper & Row, Publishers, Incorporated, New York, 1954.

3. As shown in Donald C. Mosley, Leon C. Megginson, and Paul Pietri, *Supervisory Management,* South-Western Publishing Company, Incorporated, Cincinnati, 1985, p. 10.

4. Robert C. Miljus, "Labor Relations Update: Key Ingredients in Cooperative Initiatives," *Personnel,* April 1986, p. 70.

5. Ibid.

6. Charles J. Modzinski, "You're It!" *Supervisory Management,* July 1985, pp. 41–43.

7. Henry B. Clark et al., "Preliminary Validation and Training of Supervisory Interactional Skills," *Journal of Organizational Behavior Management,* Spring–Summer 1985, p. 97.

8. Ibid.

9. Drucker, op. cit.

10. Abraham Maslow, *Motivation and Personality,* Harper & Row, Publishers, Incorporated, New York, 1954.

11. Frederick G. Lesieur (ed.), *The Scanlon Plan: A Frontier in Labor-Management Cooperation,* The M.I.T. Press, Cambridge, Mass. 1958.

12. Rensis Likert, *New Patterns of Management,* McGraw-Hill Book Company, New York, 1961.

13. Frederick Herzberg, *Work and the Nature of Man,* Mentor Books, New American Library, Inc., New York, 1966.

14. William H. Wagel, "Opening the Door to Employee Participation," *Personnel,* April 1986, p. 6.

15. *People and Productivity—A Challenge to Corporate America,* a study by the New York Stock Exchange, Office of Economic Research, 1982, p. 27.

16. William Ouchi, *Theory Z: How American Business Can Meet the Japanese Challenge,* Addison-Wesley Publishing Company, Inc., Reading, Mass., 1981.

17. Thomas J. Peters and Robert H. Waterman, Jr., *In Search of Excellence: Lessons from America's Best-Run Companies,* Harper & Row, Publishers, Incorporated, New York, 1982.

18. William Saporita, "The Revolt Against Working Smarter," *Fortune,* July 21, 1986, pp. 58–65.

19. Robert H. Rosen, *Healthy Companies—A Human Resources Approach,* American Management Association, New York, 1986, pp. 53–56.

20. *People and Productivity—A Challenge to Corporate America,* loc. cit.

21. For one account, see "GMs $4 Billion Bet on a Car to Conquer Imports," *U.S. News and World Report,* Aug. 5, 1985, pp. 23–24.

22. Janice A. Klein, "Why Supervisors Resist Employee Involvement," *The Harvard Business Review,* September–October 1984, p. 88.

23. Jackson Ramsey and Lester R. Bittel, "Men and Women Who Turn the Key of American Productivity," *Journal of Organizational Behavior Management,* Spring–Summer 1985, p. 43.

24. Peters and Waterman, loc. cit.

25. Janice A. Klein and Pamela A. Posey, "Good Supervisors Are Good Supervisors—Anywhere," *The Harvard Business Review,* November-December 1986, p. 128.

26. Ramsey and Bittel, loc. cit.

27. Bradford Boyd, *Management-Minded Supervision,* 2d ed., McGraw-Hill Book Company, New York, 1976, p. 13.

28. Ibid., p. 14.

29. Ramsey and Bittel, loc. cit.

30. Likert, loc. cit.

31. Keith Davis, "The Supervisory Role," *Supervisory Management: Tools and Techniques,* M. Gene Newport (ed.), West Publishing Company, St. Paul, Minn., 1976, p. 5.

32. Anne S. Daughtrey and Betty R. Ricks, supervisory management survey, unpublished, 1986.

33. Thomas DeLong, ''What Do Middle Managers Really Want from First-Line Supervisors?'' *Supervisory Management,* September 1977, p. 8.

34. Boyd, loc. cit.

SUGGESTED READINGS

Hamlin, Richard: ''Choosing Between Directive and Participative Management,'' *Supervisory Management,* January 1986, pp. 14–16.

Hampton, David R.: *Management,* 3d ed., McGraw-Hill Book Company, New York 1986, chaps 2 and 3.

Management Review, February 1988, a special issue featuring views on ''Can Unions Transform Themselves?''

Rubenstein, Sidney P.: *Participative Systems at Work,* Human Science Press, Inc., New York, 1987.

Sashkind, Marshall: *A Manager's Guide to Participative Management,* American Management Association, New York, 1982.

THE SUPERVISOR AND THE PLANNING FUNCTION

3

THE SUPERVISOR'S ROLE IN PLANNING

COMPETENCIES

Studying this chapter will enable you to:

1. Describe the benefits and problems associated with planning.

2. Define the types of plans.

3. Explain the planning focus of the supervisor.

4. Write objectives appropriate for the supervisory level.

5. Describe forecasting as it applies to supervisors.

6. Write an action plan for defined objectives.

7. Describe activities for which supervisors should plan.

8. Describe the tools and aids supervisors can use to help them plan.

CHAPTER OUTLINE

I. WHY PLAN?

   A. Benefits

   B. Problems

II. TYPES OF PLANS

   A. Definition of Types of Plans

   B. Supervisory Focus

III. HOW TO PLAN

   A. Establish Goals and Objectives

   B. Forecast

   C. Develop Action Plan

IV. WHAT TO PLAN

   A. Human Resources

      1. Personnel Needs

      2. Productivity Improvement

      3. Improvement in Quality of Work Life

      4. Self-Improvement

   B. Material Resources

      1. Facilities and Equipment

      2. Materials and Supplies

      3. Quality

   C. Financial Resources

   D. Time Resources

      1. Worker Time

      2. Supervisor Time

V. PLANNING TOOLS AND AIDS

   A. Calendars

   B. Activity Lists

   C. Charts and Boards

   D. Computers

   E. Tickler Files

Juan Gomez felt good about the meeting he had attended this morning. His manager, Mary Gott, had complimented him on the increase in the productivity of data entry operators and the decrease in entry errors since the last work measurement. Further, Gott had discussed in some detail the planning process that would be implemented on July 1. The new system would include supervisory input and require some planning and accountability by first-level managers. Under the present system, supervisors were either told what their goals should be or were simply not given any information at all.

Gomez's good feeling slowly diminished as reality began to intrude. He began to realize that he had no idea how to plan beyond the day-to-day work scheduling for which he was currently responsible.

Planning is the process of determining what you wish to accomplish (*goals and objectives*) and how you are going to accomplish them (*action plan*). Because Juan Gomez is going to become a part of the planning process, he needs to understand why planning is important and how he fits into the total planning function.

WHY PLAN?

Planning provides direction. It helps you to know where you are going and requires that you develop a way to get there. As the quote from Peter and Hull says, ''If you don't know where you are going, you will end up somewhere else.'' Even if you do know where you are going, if you don't have a plan to get there, you will probably also end up somewhere else.

Benefits

The benefits of planning are many, and the following list is not all-inclusive. However, the list provides some insight into the benefits to be gained from the planning process. Planning:

- provides direction.
- encourages managers to think ahead.
- formally allocates resources.
- requires a formal statement of what is to be accomplished.
- provides, in writing, information for successors.
- seeks to prevent problems.

- allows managers at all levels to see how their departments or divisions fit into the total organizational plan.
- lets each supervisor know what is expected of his or her group.
- motivates by providing challenging and realistic goals for employees.
- allows employees to provide input, thus making them a part of the organization.
- leads to better coordination of organizational efforts.
- leads to development of performance standards.
- leads to more profitable organizational performance.

Problems

Although the benefits far outweigh the problems, supervisors must be aware that the planning process cannot be successful if any of the following problems exist:

- untrained planners
- lack of follow-through
- lack of top-management support
- lack of communication of expectations to employees

People at the supervisory level are often asked to plan when they don't know how to do it, they don't know what to plan, or they have little or no knowledge of why planning is important. Planning should answer these questions:

1. What do we want to achieve? (goals and objectives)
2. What must we do to achieve our goals and objectives? (action plan)
3. When should each of the activities identified in the action plan be completed? (checkpoints and deadlines)
4. Who will work on each activity? (task and responsibility assignment)
5. Where should each activity take place? (location)
6. When should all activities be completed? (time frame)

Competency Check:

Can you identify the benefits and problems of planning?

TYPES OF PLANS

There are six basic types of plans. Although first-level managers are concerned primarily with operational and daily plans, they should be knowledgeable about how each of the six types of plans fits into the planning process.

Definition of Types of Plans

The six basic types of plans are:

Strategic, or Long-term, Plans.   These plans are formulated by top management and reflect the vision of the organization for its future. Strategic plans are typically made for a period of 5 to 10 years. Several decades ago, when the business environment was not so volatile, strategic plans were often made for 15 to 20 years. Even today, companies that experience relatively little change in their products or services from year to year (such as manufacturers of matches or boxes) may still make strategic plans for longer periods.

Standing Plans.   Standing plans are plans that seldom change and are used year after year. Standing plans include policies, procedures, rules, and other repetitive-use plans.

Single-Use Plans.   These plans are made for one activity or project and are "used up" once that project or activity is completed. An example of a single-use plan is one that is used to introduce a new product to the market or to add a wing to a building.

Short-Term Plans.   Short-term plans are typically made for 1 to 5 years, depending on the industry. These plans must "fit" the strategic plans and become one of the vehicles for accomplishing the long-term plan of the organization.

Operational Plans.   Operational plans are plans that facilitate the accomplishment of the everyday activities of first-level managers. These and daily plans are the focus of this chapter. Work scheduling, preventive-maintenance scheduling, and the design of new work methods are examples of operational plans.

Competency Check:

Can you describe the six types of plans?

Daily Plans.   Daily plans are plans that show a supervisor's actions for a particular day. Daily plans, of course, flow from operational plans, allowing the supervisor to work toward the accomplishment of the "bigger picture."

Supervisory Focus

Managers at all levels of an organization plan. However, the focus of their planning efforts, as well as the time frames and activities for which they plan, differ. Figure 3-1 shows the planning focus by hierarchical level for one activity.

As noted in Chapter 2, 20.2 percent of the time that supervisors spend on management functions is devoted to planning. The survey respondents, employed by both national and international firms, indicated that their five top planning priorities were as follows:[2]

making decisions	26.5%
setting departmental activities	17.6
planning own work	14.7
planning work schedules	11.8
planning training and development	11.8

As you can see, the planning activities these supervisors are primarily involved in are the operational and daily types.

FIGURE 3-1

HIERARCHICAL PLANNING PROCESS

DECISION LEVEL	DECISION PROCESS	FORECASTS NEEDED
corporate	allocates production among plants	annual demand by item and by region
plant manager	determines seasonal plan by product type	monthly demand for 15 months by product type
shop superintendent	determines monthly item production schedules	monthly demand for 5 months by item

Source: Harvard Business Review, March–April 1984, p. 104.

WHAT CAN THE SUPERVISOR DO?

The focus of the supervisor is at the operational and daily levels of planning. Top-level managers are concerned with strategic and long-term planning; middle managers are concerned with short-term and operational planning. As noted in Chapter 1, as one rises in a hierarchy, the time one devotes to planning increases. Conversely, as one goes down in the hierarchy, the time one devotes to the leading/motivating function increases and the time available for planning decreases.

It has been said that *strategic planning* is "doing the right things" and that *operational planning* is "doing things right." In this way, strategic and operational planning are interrelated and interdependent; the supervisor's role in "doing things right" is particularly important to the success of the strategic plan—"doing the right things."

Competency Check:

Can you explain the planning focus of the supervisor?

HOW TO PLAN

The "how" of planning includes the establishing of goals and objectives, the forecasting of needs, and the writing of an action plan.

Establish Goals and Objectives

The terms *goals* and *objectives* are often used interchangeably. But goals are broader and less definitive than objectives: They may be stated with words such as *understand* and *know* and with other words that are not definite or quantitative. Objectives are more specific and focus on a particular ability, knowledge, or accomplishment. Objectives should be stated with words or phrases that allow the end result to be easily ascertained.

Gomez, as pointed out in the beginning of this chapter, is about to become a part of the planning process. He must, first, know and understand the goals of the organization and then determine how his department can contribute to accomplishing those goals. Gomez will then begin to develop his own departmental objectives and an action plan. He may decide that his department's productivity can be increased and that data entry errors may be reduced still further. Once he has determined the general direction of his department, he must state his objectives in writing.

In general, objectives should:

- be related to the needs of the organization.
- be measurable and quantifiable, whenever possible.
- be designed to prevent rather than solve problems.
- be challenging, but achievable.
- consider internal and external constraints.
- be innovative.
- be written.
- be consistent with each other and with organizational goals.

Techniques for writing meaningful objectives include (1) using specific terms, including what is to be achieved and within what time frame; (2) stating objectives in measurable terms; (3) using language that workers understand; and (4) stating objectives in terms of end results. Let's look at the three objectives that Juan has identified and write these objectives in terms that meet the specific requirements for a "good" objective.

GOMEZ'S THOUGHT	OBJECTIVE
increase productivity	increase average output for data entry operators by 5% over 1/1/88 measurement by 1/1/89
reduce errors	reduce average errors for data entry operators by 3% over 1/1/88 measurement by 1/1/89
reduce turnaround time	reduce average turnaround time for documents from the current 14 hours to 12 hours by 1/1/89

Gomez may also wish to add other objectives that are not so easily quantifiable. Writing qualitative objectives is much more difficult than writing quantitative ones. For example, Gomez may want to include, as an objective, to "increase the quality of work life of the data entry operators." What is "quality of work life"? How do you know if you have it at all, and how do you know if it has increased? To write an objective relating to quality of work life, you must first decide what you want to accomplish (for example, to reduce the fatigue of data entry operators), and then you must write the objective. The "how" will be included in the action plan.

GOMEZ'S THOUGHT	OBJECTIVE
increase quality of work life	reduce the fatigue of data entry operators as measured by decreased absenteeism

Stating the objective in this way clearly shows what you expect to accomplish as well as how it can be measured. If Gomez wanted to be even more precise, he might list as an objective "reduce absenteeism by 10% within a 6-month period."

Competency Check:

Given general information, can you write an appropriate objective?

Forecast

Forecasting is attempting to look into the future and predict future needs. The supervisor's role in forecasting involves projecting the future needs of her or his department. Given Gomez's lack of experience in forecasting, if he were asked to "forecast the needs of your department for the short term (this year) and for the long term (the next 5 years)," he might have a typical reaction: "What do I look like, a crystal ball? I'm no swami, and I don't own a Ouija board, so what do you expect from me?" However, if Gomez were asked specific questions such as the ones in Figure 3-2, his responses would be his forecast. He would probably feel more secure in his answers than if he were just asked to "forecast."

Gomez's responses to these questions will be based on his knowledge in his area of expertise and his experience within the field. In addition, he might want to consult with the staff specialists and with experienced employees to gain the benefit of their knowledge.

Forecasting is predicting the future. It is not an exact science, and of course there is no absolute way to predict what will happen. Too many outside influences over which supervisors have no control affect the accuracy of predictions. For example, if there is an unpredicted downturn in the economy and the demand for a product decreases, projected increases in personnel and equipment will be negatively affected. Forecasting, at best, is an educated guess, but an educated guess is better than no guess at all!

Competency Check:

Can you describe forecasting as it applies to supervisors?

Develop Action Plan

An *action plan* describes how objectives are to be accomplished. What specific actions must be taken, and by whom? What specific activities and tasks must be performed, and by whom? The action plan converts objectives into activities and tasks and assigns responsibility for achieving the objectives.

Let's look once more at Gomez's objectives and see how these objectives can be translated into an action plan.

FIGURE 3-2

Planning questions

For fiscal year 1988–89

Equipment

1. What types of equipment, other than that in current use, will you need to perform the work in your department?
2. What pieces of equipment should be replaced?
3. What additional equipment will be required?
4. Will maintenance contracts expire? Should they be renewed?

Personnel

1. Will additional employees be needed? If so, how many and in what capacity?
2. Will different skills be required by employees? If so, what skills? Do current employees have these skills?
3. Will it be necessary to reduce the work force? If so, by how many and in what area?
4. Are any of the workers' skills obsolete? Identify.
5. Do workers need additional training? If so, in what areas? Identify the employees.
6. Which employees are ready for development and growth within their areas of expertise? What training and development should be provided?

Facilities

1. Are current space allocations adequate for current needs?
2. Will more or less space be required for future needs?
3. Is the current work-space layout efficient?
4. Is the current work-space layout safe?
5. Are the heating/cooling/lighting systems adequate?
6. Is the furniture ergonomically designed to reduce fatigue?

Work Methods and Processes

1. Are current work methods efficient?
2. Are materials required to complete the work available when needed?
3. Are materials of the quality required to produce a quality product?
4. Is the flow of work efficient?
5. Should new or different work methods be analyzed in order to increase efficiency?

OBJECTIVE	ACTION PLAN
increase average output for data entry operators by 5% over 1/1/88 measurement by 1/1/89	provide additional training in keyboarding for 5 operators
	enroll WP supervisor in course for improving interpersonal skills
	institute preventive-maintenance program
reduce average errors for data entry operators by 3% over 1/1/88 measurement by 1/1/89	provide additional training in proofreading skills for four operators
	use additional skill level obtained by providing keyboarding training to operators
reduce average turnaround time for documents from the current 14 hours to 12 hours by 1/1/89	reschedule work assignments so that operators become proficient in each type of document processing
	improve keyboarding and proofreading skills through training, as described above
reduce the fatigue of data entry operators as measured by decreased absenteeism	provide screens to reduce glare from lights and cathode-ray tube (CRT)
	replace existing chairs with ergonomically designed chairs

When the objectives have been determined, the forecast made, and an action plan developed, all of this information should be combined on a form such as the one shown in Figure 3-3. Note that there is space on the form to indicate the date action is to begin and the target date for completion, as well as space to identify the persons involved and the actual outcomes.

WHAT CAN THE SUPERVISOR DO?

"Why should I plan? I spend all of my time 'putting out fires' and trying very hard to 'keep my head above water.' How can you expect me to find time to plan, too?"

Lack of planning often causes supervisors to spend all their time "putting out fires" and trying to "keep their heads above water." It's a vicious cycle, allowing no time to do the planning that would minimize the daily crisis management engaged in by so many supervisors. If supervisors understood that time invested in planning would ultimately pay dividends in daily efficiency, they might be convinced that it was worthwhile to learn how to plan and to follow through on the planning process.

Competency Check:

Can you write an action plan to reach objectives previously written?

FIGURE 3-3

Departmental plans

	Supervisor Juan Perry		Department Information Processing		
Objective	Action	Persons Involved	Date Begun	Target Date	Outcome
Increase average output for data entry operators by 5 percent over 1/1/87 measurement	Provide additional training in key-boarding for five operators	Cox, McMills, Kennedy, Thu, DeMair	1-15-88	1-1-89	
	Enroll WP supervisor in course for improving interpersonal skills	Knight			
	Institute preventative maintenance program				
Reduce average errors for data entry operators by 3 percent over 1/1/87 measurement	Provide additional training in proofreading skills for four operators	Johnson, Szuka, Mathis, Bell	1-15-88	1-1-89	
	Use additional skill level obtained by providing keyboarding training to operators				
Reduce average turnaround time for documents by 2 hours from the current 14 hours to 12 hours	Reschedule work assignments so that operators become proficient in each type of document processing	All data entry operators (see above)	1-15-88	1-1-89	
	Improve keyboarding and proofreading skills through training, as described above				
Reduce fatigue of data entry operators as measured by decreased absenteeism	Provide screens to reduce glare from lights and CRT	All data entry operators (see above)	1-15-88	1-1-89	
	Replace existing chairs with ergonomically designed chairs				

WHAT TO PLAN

Supervisors are charged with the responsibility for using the resources available to them in the most efficient way. They must plan for the efficient use of their human, material, financial, and time resources.

Human Resources

To allocate human resources most efficiently, supervisors should plan for personnel needs, improvement in productivity and quality of work life, and self-improvement.

Personnel Needs

Supervisors must plan for personnel needs in terms of the number of people needed and the skills required now and in the future. For example, Gomez may determine that there are enough workers to run an efficient department at the present time but, if managers continue to increase their use of the information processing department, two additional word processing operators and one additional clerk will be required next year. While the current skill level is adequate for current needs, new graphics equipment may require the hiring of more skilled operators or providing additional training for those already on the job.

Productivity Improvement

Planning for productivity improvement may involve plans for work simplification or methods improvement or both. You will learn more about productivity in Chapter 16, "Improving Productivity and Quality of Work Life."

Improvement in Quality of Work Life

Part of a supervisor's planning responsibility for human resources is to plan for improving the quality of their work life. Quality of work life is also covered in Chapter 16.

Self-Improvement

Supervisors should not neglect planning for their own development and improvement. These objectives should be included in the action plan. For example, a supervisor may wish to improve her interpersonal skills and plan to do so by taking a course at a local community college. This should not be left to chance because it is as important for supervisors to plan for their own development as it is for them to plan for the growth and development of their subordinates.

Material Resources

Planning for material resources includes plans for facilities and equipment, materials and supplies, and quality.

Facilities and Equipment

Efficient use of facilities and equipment requires planning. Space must be properly allocated for most efficient work flow. To evaluate space use, the supervisor should examine the current floor layout. A scale drawing of the floor plan, with each piece of furniture and equipment placed in its current position, provides a basis for tracing work flow and evaluating efficiency. The supervisor can then analyze the allocation and use of space in relation to the tasks performed.

The allocation and use of equipment should also be evaluated. Equipment use should be maximized, with as little idle time as possible. (See the section on Gantt charts for information on scheduling.)

In addition to proper allocation and use, the supervisor must plan for the most efficient equipment to do the job. This will require staying up to date regarding new equipment. Reviewing trade journals and vendor literature, attending professional meetings, and having discussions with colleagues help supervisors stay current. While the resources to replace equipment will not always be available, supervisors should be prepared to make equipment recommendations when the opportunity arises. Records of equipment downtime and maintenance costs provide backup when requesting new or replacement equipment.

The supervisor also needs to plan for a safe place to work and for safe use of equipment. Providing a safe work environment is covered in Chapter 7, ''Managing the Physical Environment.''

Materials and Supplies

Supervisors also plan for the proper allocation, availability, use, and conservation of materials and supplies. For many companies, materials and supplies represent a major expenditure.

When materials and supplies are improperly allocated, not available when needed, improperly used, or when waste is prevalent, costs increase. Additional costs are incurred when workers must wait for materials or supplies required for their work activities. Many companies experience increased costs due to careless use of materials and supplies. Use of materials and supplies must be planned to minimize costs and to increase worker efficiency.

Quality

Planning for higher-quality output and fewer rejects is an important part of the supervisor's activities. Gomez, for example, who is involved with a product (information), plans for the improving of the quality of the output by planning to reduce average errors for data entry operators by 3 percent. A first-level manager who supervises service workers is also concerned with quality. A department store supervisor, for example, may receive too many customer complaints about the sales associates, and so she plans to decrease the number of customer complaints.

Financial Resources

Supervisors may have to plan and submit budgets for their departments. These budgets typically include projected salaries of workers, costs of proposed equipment purchases, allocations for materials and supplies, and training and development costs.

Time Resources

Peter Drucker wrote: "The output limits on any process are set by the scarcest resource . . . time is the scarcest resource, and unless it can be managed, nothing else can be managed."[3]

Most people complain that there is "just not enough time in a day," but time is a valuable resource over which supervisors have some control. To make maximum use of both workers' and supervisors' time, planning is a *must*. No good supervisor would dream of starting a new work method or ordering materials without careful planning, yet many supervisors (and others) think that proper time use does not have to be planned—that it will just happen. Nor do they consider that time is money and that they should be as accountable for its use as they are for the use of all other resources.

Supervisors may use either of two methods of scheduling. *Forward scheduling,* where the schedule results in a projected completion date, is preferred. This type of scheduling allows the supervisor to analyze the job to be completed, schedule tasks leading to project completion, and estimate when the project can be completed. More difficult to implement is *backward scheduling*. Here, the supervisor is given a completion date and must figure out how to get the work completed by that time.

Worker Time

Planning worker time is a large part of many supervisors' duties. A plan must be developed for scheduling normal worker time; overtime, when necessary and appropriate; worker absences; and holidays and vacations. In cases where temporary layoffs are an annual occurrence, this time must be anticipated and plans made to minimize work interruption.

In the 1985 survey of supervisors conducted by the authors,[4] 44.2 percent of the respondents reported that "planning work schedules" was one of their top five planning priorities; 11.8 percent indicated that "planning work schedules" was their *most* important planning activity.

Normal Worker Time.   *Scheduling* is deciding when activities will take place as well as their order, or when specific processes or procedures will begin and end. Different jobs require different levels of scheduling. If the work of one individual or group of individuals affects the ability of others to complete their jobs, the supervisor must plan for coordination of activities. For example, on an assembly line, the task of the worker who places the windshield wipers on the truck is dependent upon the person who installs the windshields. Until that portion of the truck is assembled, the windshield-wiper installer is idle.

Other jobs require a different type of scheduling. Each of the jobs that comes into a word processing center is assigned to an operator who is responsible for completing the job. If an extremely long or complicated job comes in to be processed, several operators may be assigned to complete selected portions and work together to complete the entire project.

Many companies provide breaks or rest periods during the day to help relieve worker fatigue. Breaks are taken by workers according to a predetermined schedule so that they will not all be away from their work stations at the same time.

During the past decade, flextime has become a popular type of work scheduling. *Flextime* allows employees some flexibility in the way they schedule their workday. There is usually a *core time,* a time during which all employees must be on the job, but beginning and ending work hours are flexible. For example, a company may set 10 A.M. to 2 P.M. as the core time—the busy time when it is important that all employees be available to work. The other 4 hours of an 8-hour day may then be set according to the personal needs of the workers, as long as the work can be accomplished and the job covered within the working hours of the company. Suzanne is a ''day person,'' someone who is wide-awake and full of energy early in the day. She may choose to come to work as soon as the doors open at 6:30 A.M. and work until 3:30 P.M. Julian is a single parent whose child must catch the school bus at 8:30 A.M. He may choose to report to work at 9:30 A.M. and work until 6:30 P.M.

Flextime requires very careful scheduling. Everyone cannot work from 6:30 A.M. to 3:30 P.M., leaving the business unattended from 3:30 P.M. until closing. Nor can everyone work from 9:30 A.M. until 6:30 P.M. The supervisor must work with individuals to make a schedule that will maximize worker productivity and worker satisfaction.

Overtime.   Planning for work beyond the normal workday is sometimes necessary. Planning for overtime should not be left to chance nor to the last minute. While supervisors may be unable to anticipate overtime weeks or even days in advance, they can have a plan ready when the need occurs. Knowing who is willing to work overtime hours, on what days, and for how many hours will simplify the task of scheduling overtime work. However, if overtime becomes a normal activity, an investigation of the work methods and employee work loads should be made. Perhaps alternative work methods may be instituted, work loads adjusted, or more workers hired.

Worker Absences, Holidays, Vacations, and Temporary Layoffs.   Just as overtime should be planned for, so should time when employees will not be at work. Workers who are able to do more than one job can often cover for absent workers by performing essential tasks. This, of course, will require an adjustment in the normal work load, but it will allow the department to continue to function without interruption. Unanticipated absences cannot be scheduled, but they can be planned for. If the supervisor knows who is capable of doing other tasks, planning for absences is easier.

Planning for vacations is especially important. Employees get angry if they believe their vacation time has been unfairly scheduled. If the company has a vacation policy, the supervisor should adhere to both the letter and the intent of the policy. As with any other absence, the supervisor must be sure that there are enough people available to handle the work so that productivity will not suffer.

Supervisor Time

In the survey of supervisors cited previously[5] 70.5 percent responded that "planning own work" ranked as one of the five top planning priorities; in fact, 14.7 percent indicated that "planning own work" was their *first* planning priority. Because of the importance of planning one's own work time efficiently, this section will be devoted to identifying time wasters and time leaks. Suggestions for improved use of time will also be provided. Planning tools and techniques for better use of both supervisors' and workers' time will be discussed in the next section.

Numerous studies identifying time wasters have been conducted. Most of the study results show common time wasters among people in different positions and different careers. For example, common time wasters were identified by different groups of workers (including office managers, administrative assistants, engineers, school administrators, city managers, executive secretaries, university administrators, data processing managers, and funeral directors.[6] Figure 3-4 shows a cross-sectional profile of the common time wasters identified by this heterogeneous work group.

Are you having a problem managing your time? Do you recognize any of the problems shown in Figure 3-5? Do you recognize any of these symptoms? If so,

FIGURE 3-4

COMMON TIME WASTERS FOR GENERAL WORK GROUP

TIME WASTER	RANKED IMPORTANCE
telephone	1
drop-in-visitors	2
meetings	3
socializing	4
failure to delegate	5
lack of daily plan	6
inability to say "no"	7
incomplete information	8
crisis management	9
personal disorganization	10

Source: Dennis L. Mott, "Time Management," *NBEA Yearbook,* chap. 14, no. 18, National Business Education Association, Reston, Va., p. 145.

FIGURE 3-5

Self-appraisal

Problem	Yes	No
I never seem to get my work finished.	_____	_____
I spend too much time in meetings.	_____	_____
I have to work overtime.	_____	_____
I take work home on weekends.	_____	_____
I am busy but not as productive as I should be.	_____	_____
I have a cluttered desk all the time.	_____	_____
I feel controlled by the telephone.	_____	_____
I have a steady flow of interruptions.	_____	_____
I am always fatigued.	_____	_____
I am not developing to my potential.	_____	_____

Source: Adapted from *Effective Time Management,* HR&DS Seminars, Human Research and Development Services, Inc., St. Petersburg, Fla.

perhaps you should conduct a time audit. A time audit will help you identify the work time you have available and how you spend it. You may conduct a continuous time audit by dividing each workday over a 2-week period into 15- or 20-minute segments and recording how you spend each segment. Or you may conduct a periodic audit by appointing someone to randomly select (10 to 20 times weekly) a period of time in which to record your activity. Either way, the time audit will provide information about how you use your time and allow you to analyze the results for time wasters and time leaks—inefficient time use. A simple form for analyzing the time audit is shown in Figure 3-6.

FIGURE 3-6

Time-audit analysis

EVALUATE YOUR TIME

How am I presently spending my time? Note every major category on this time audit (meetings, telephone calls, planning daily work, etc.).

	How Much Time Do I Spend?		
Activity	Too little	Just right	Too much
_____			
_____			
_____			

Here are some general guidelines for improving the use of your time.

● Rank tasks in order of importance. Then work through the tasks, beginning with the most important ones.
● Divide tasks into two groups—those for which you can control the timing and those over which you have no control.
● Determine which tasks can be delegated. *Do it!*
● Determine where time can be saved by taking the right steps.
● Make a list or a chart to help you keep track of your progress on each item.
● Follow up. At the end of each week, take a look at your time log and see how you actually spent your time. Was your time used effectively? Why, or why not?

WHAT CAN THE SUPERVISOR DO?

Do you regularly practice timesaving techniques? Are the following techniques a part of your normal routine? Do you

1. arrive at your workplace ½ hour early in order to take advantage of the quiet time before other employees arrive?
2. write a daily "to-do list" of your top priorities?
3. plan your week's activities on Mondays?
4. sort out all important mail items and telephone messages?
5. delegate routine duties?
6. set deadlines for your subordinates when you delegate work?
7. set deadlines for yourself?
8. use waiting time to plan activities?
9. carry blank 3 × 5 cards to jot down spontaneous ideas and notes?
10. know why you procrastinate? (what you are avoiding?)
11. break down unpleasant tasks into smaller ones?
12. cut down on nonproductive activities—phone calls, rambling conversations, water-cooler breaks?
13. handle every piece of paper once by handling it, answering it, or throwing it away?
14. answer letters by writing on the bottom of the letter, when appropriate?
15. keep your work area cleared and ready for action? (Items waiting for attention should be placed in the center of the work area.)
16. schedule a meeting only when you can explain its purpose?
17. listen carefully? (Ask direct questions to obtain needed information quickly or for clarification.)
18. say no to additional tasks if you know you do not have the time to do a good job on them?
19. set aside your most productive time period every day to do creative work?
20. save all trivial matters for a 3-hour session once a month?

21. make an appointment with yourself for 15 minutes late in the afternoon? (Spend 5 minutes of that time assessing the day and how well you've used your time. Then identify the projects that are critical to tomorrow's success, and decide what time should be spent on which projects.)

22. on Fridays, make a 30-minute appointment with yourself? (Plan for the coming week. Schedule the most important tasks for Monday, Tuesday, or Wednesday, when you should be refreshed from the weekend. Thursday and Friday are usually spent playing "catch up."

Source: Adapted from Mary C. Lock, "25 Ways to Save Time," *Modern Secretary*, February 1983, p. 14.

Competency Check:

Can you identify four major categories for which a supervisor must plan?

PLANNING TOOLS AND AIDS

Many planning tools and aids are available to supervisors to help them plan better and increase their efficiency. Among these tools and aids are calendars, activity lists, charts and boards, computers, and tickler files. As shown in the cartoon, planning tools and aids are just that—aids—and must be used properly to be helpful.

Calendars

Calendars may range from one monthly sheet with 31 square blocks to separate pages for each day, with time segments marked and space provided for various other types of information. A simple pocket calendar can help you stay organized. By entering two dates for each task, a deadline and a warning date, you can remind yourself to start working on the task in time. Unless you put important dates and activities in writing, you may forget them in the rush of your day-to-day activities. However, even a calendar won't do you any good if you forget to refer to it, as did Bumgardner in the cartoon. Figures 3-7 and 3-8 show two types of planning calendars.

Source: Jim Smith, *Bumgardner, The Virginian Pilot/Ledger Star*, Jan. 29, 1985.

FIGURE 3-7
Planning calendar

Date *January 22, 198—*	Day *Tuesday*	
	ACTIVITY	PRIORITY	EVALUATION

Date: *January 22, 198—*   Day: *Tuesday*

	ACTIVITY	PRIORITY 1-Urgent 2-Important 3-Routine 4-Discretionary 5-Wasted	EVALUATION Could you have used your time more efficiently? (Example: delegate to _____ ; organize, plan, train someone else to handle it; combine, eliminate, etc.)
8:00	*Work on report for J.O.*	*1*	
8:30			
9:00			
9:30			
10:00	*Meeting with dept. heads*	*2*	
10:30			
3:30	*Performance appraisal - Sam*	*3*	
4:00	*Conference with vendors*	*4*	
4:30	*Return phone calls*	*3*	
5:00	*Order materials*	*3*	*Delegate to Max*
5:30			

Activity Lists

Activity lists, like calendars, come in many forms. The purpose of an activity list is to provide a form for recording tasks to be completed, either by you or by those who report to you. The form you choose to record the tasks on should suit your specific needs. Figures 3-9 and 3-10 show portions of two types of activity lists.

FIGURE 3-8

Planning calendar

DAILY PLANNING CALENDAR   *Date* _____

Priority	*Activity*
	Letters to Write

_____ _____

_____ _____

_____ _____

_____ _____

People to See

_____

_____ _____

_____ _____

_____ _____

Things to Be Done

_____ _____

_____ _____

_____ _____

_____ _____

_____ _____

Things to Be Planned

_____ _____

_____ _____

_____ _____

_____ _____

Items to Be Obtained

_____ _____

_____ _____

_____ _____

_____ _____

Priority

Phones Calls to Make

_____ PERSON   TEL. NO.

_____ _____

_____ _____

_____ _____

Appointments

FIGURE 3-8

(Continued)

8:00	_____
8:30	_____
9:00	_____
9:30	_____
10:00	_____
10:30	_____
11:00	_____
11:30	_____
12:00	_____
12:30	_____
1:00	_____
1:30	_____
2:00	_____
2:30	_____
3:00	_____
3:30	_____
4:00	_____
4:30	_____
5:00	_____

Priority:
1. important and urgent (must be done now)
2. important but not urgent (separates effective managers from ineffective ones)
3. urgent but not important (clamor for attention, but on objective examination, have low priority)
4. busy work (marginally worth doing but not urgent or important)
5. wasted time (subjective—use as criterion for judging how you feel when task is completed)

Charts and Boards

Charts provide a *graphic representation*—a visual interpretation—of activities. Charts allow supervisors to see, at a glance, the status of a project or the output of a worker, to track personnel, or to define activities.

Among the most frequently used charts is the Gantt chart, named for its founder, Henry Gantt. Gantt charts track activities in relation to time. Supervisors may use Gantt charts to track how each worker is progressing on assignments or to examine the status of a particular activity. Figure 3-11 shows a Gantt chart for a 1-week period.

Date assigned	Person responsible	Action	Due date	Completed

FIGURE 3-9

Activity list

FIGURE 3-10

Activity list

Things to Do Today

Activity	Notes about activity
_____	_____
_____	_____
_____	_____

In this case, the chart is used to schedule human resources. For week 10, Matthews and Rice were scheduled to produce 10 units per day each for 5 days; Doolittle and Boston were scheduled to produce 12 units. The supervisor, by looking at the Gantt chart, can see immediately that there were days when some of the workers were on target and days when more or less work than scheduled was produced.

Visual control boards simplify many routine and time-consuming planning tasks.

FIGURE 3-11

Gantt chart

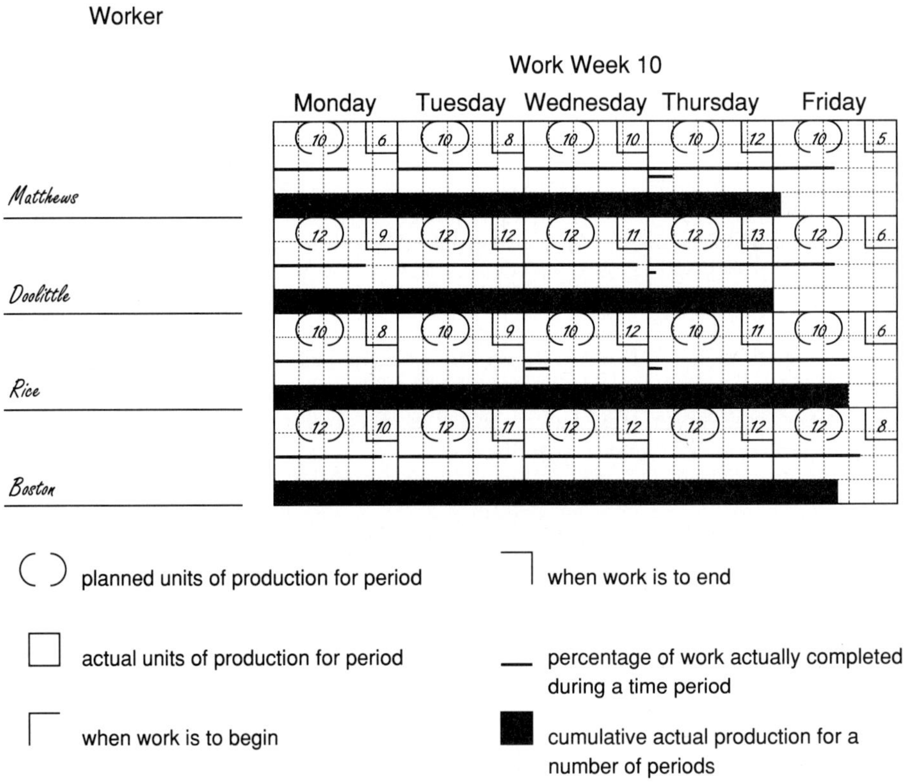

Worker

Source: Adapted from Samuel C. Certo, *Principles of Management,* Wm. C. Brown Company Publishers, Dubuque, Iowa, 1980, p. 137.

They also provide a quick overview of project status, can be used to schedule projects or workers, highlight problem areas, and perform a control function. Two uses of visual control boards are shown in Figure 3-12.

Computers

Computers can be used as planning tools in many different areas. They may be used to schedule space, maintenance, and personnel; to plan for inventory and ordering; to provide information on current levels of production; to provide information on personnel; and to do many other tasks. Periodic printouts (daily, weekly, or monthly)

FIGURE 3-12

Visual control boards

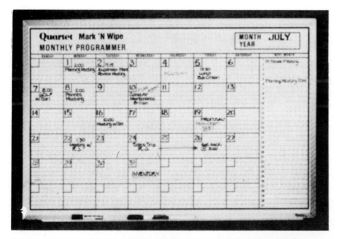

QUARTET MARK 'N WIPE MONTHLY PROGRAMMERS

QUARTET RE-MARK-ABLE GRID BOARD SYSTEM

Source: Quartet Manufacturing Company advertisement in *Office Systems '86,* June 1986, p. 74.

can provide the information needed to make planning decisions. If a computer data base is available to you, use the information as you plan your departmental activities.

Tickler Files

A tickler file "tickles" your memory by reminding you of something you are supposed to do. Set up a tickler file by having divider tabs for each month of the year and tabs for 31 days behind the current month. As you think of things to do later in the month or year, put a note behind the tab for that day or month. At the beginning of each month, move the divider tab for that month in front of the daily tabs and file all of the notes you previously made behind the proper day. Check the file each day for things to put on your daily to-do list.

WHAT CAN THE SUPERVISOR DO?

The supervisor should make use of planning tools and aids that allow for better use of time, more efficient use of materials and equipment, and more effective use of workers.

COMPETENCY REVIEW

1. Describe eight planning benefits.
2. Cite four planning problems, and suggest ways to solve them.
3. Define the six types of plans.
4. Explain the planning focus of the supervisor.
5. Describe the process of writing a meaningful objective.
6. Describe forecasting as it relates to supervisors.
7. Explain the process of writing an action plan.
8. Describe four major activities for which a supervisor should plan.
9. Describe four types of planning tools and aids that a supervisor may use.

APPLICATIONS

1. Juan Gomez completed the following activities on Monday. Analyze the activities, and make suggestions for how he can improve the use of his time. Finally, estimate the amount of time that will be saved if your suggestions are implemented.

ACTIVITY	TIME	SUGGESTION	TIME SAVED
Prepared budget for next year for equipment/personnel/materials/ supplies.	50 min		
Waited 30 minutes to see personnel director about a possible replacement for Sue. Never did get to see her.	40 min (counting time to and from)		
Worked on Jane's project while she was at dentist.	60 min		
Repaired broken piece of equipment. Didn't want to wait for repairman.	30 min		
Interviewed possible addition to staff. Person not qualified.	30 min		
Listened to gripes around water cooler.	20 min		
Helped Jamie reorganize the work area.	30 min		
Returned 6 telephone calls; received 8; all but 4 were business.	45 min		
Was to meet with Nathan from the union. Nathan called to cancel, but I did not receive message and went to Union Hall.	60 min		
Joe, Mike, and Rose dropped by to chat.	45 min		
Discussed the schedule for next week with Mary. Will try to see John later today and Sam tomorrow morning.	20 min		

Source: Adapted from Elwood N. Chapman, *Supervisor's Survival Kit: A Mid-Management Primer,* 2d ed., Science Research Associates, Chicago, 1980, p. 134.

2. Rewrite the following objectives. Explain why you made the changes.
   a. Increase per capita output by 10 percent.
   b. Improve quality of work life (QWL).
   c. Reduce maintenance costs.
   d. Increase productivity.
   e. Reduce absentee costs.

3. For the rewritten objectives, write an action plan. Use the form shown on page 67 and provided in the *Student Activity and Enrichment Guide*.
4. Develop a daily planning calendar for Gomez, using the activities shown in Application 1 and using the form shown on page 78 and provided in the *Student Activity and Enrichment Guide*.
5. Interpret the Gantt chart shown on page 80. What was each worker's output each day? What percentage of the work was actually completed by each worker? What was the cumulative actual production for each worker? For the department? If this is Gomez's department, what actions should he take now?

CASES

Case I: Objectives, Objectives!

As the supervisor of a large office complex, you are asked to submit an annual plan for your department. Your plan, of course, should focus on ways of reaching the objectives of the organization. A portion of the organizational goals are shown below:

to capture 25 percent of the market by 1989

to reduce personnel costs by 10 percent by 1990

to make quality information available to management on a timely basis

to maintain equipment costs and maintenance costs at current levels

1. What specific objectives could you submit for your department to enhance the organization's goals?
2. Write an action plan for your objectives.

Remember that you will be held accountable for accomplishing the targets you set. They should, therefore, be realistic yet future-oriented; challenging, yet achievable.

Case II: Where Is Mr. Gantt When I Need Him?

Connie Barton is the production supervisor for a large manufacturing company. She has recently been promoted to her present job from unit supervisor. Yesterday (March 15) she received orders for five jobs, which she must schedule among four workers. The jobs and the time required are shown below. Prepare two Gantt charts to schedule (1) the jobs and (2) the workers. All work must be completed by June 1.

JOB NAME	TIME REQUIRED	WORKERS
Sampson	4 weeks	Lee
Martin	10 weeks	Berlin
Lockhart	2 weeks	Moscovitz
Reardon	6 weeks	Leon
Johnson	8 weeks	

REFERENCES

1. Laurence P. Peter and Raymond Hull, *The Peter Principle,* William Morrow & Company, Inc., New York, 1969, p. 159.

2. Anne S. Daughtrey and Betty R. Ricks, ''Supervisory Management Survey,'' 1985.

3. Peter Drucker, *The Effective Executive,* Harper & Row Publishers, Incorporated, New York, 1967, p. 25.

4. Daughtrey and Ricks, op. cit.

5. Ibid.

6. Dennis L. Mott, ''Time Management,'' *NBEA Yearbook,* chap. 14, no. 18, National Business Education Association, Reston, Va., p. 145.

SUGGESTED READINGS

Allen, Ken: ''Managing Time Profitably,'' Dartnell Human Resources Development Program, 1981.

Leonard, Joseph W.: ''Why MBO Fails So Often,'' *Training and Development Journal,* September 1985.

McKenzie, R. Alec, and Theodore Engstrom: *Managing Your Time,* Zondervan Publishing House, Grand Rapids, Mich., 1969.

Simmons-Forbes, Maree: ''Facing the Challenge of Space Forecasting,'' *Office Systems '87,* vol. 4, no. 1, January 1987.

Sloma, Richard S.: ''No Nonsense Planning for Administrators,'' *Office Administration and Automation,* April 1985.

Warda, Allan: ''Key Results Planning,'' *CA Magazine,* June 1986.

Wilson, Dorothy: ''Getting Organized: Eight Ways,'' *Modern Secretary,* August 1982.

4

MAKING EFFECTIVE DECISIONS

COMPETENCIES

Studying this chapter will enable you to:

1. Identify and give an example of the types of decisions.

2. Explain the types of decisions made by the three levels of management.

3. Discuss techniques and sources the supervisor can use to develop alternatives in decision making.

4. State, in order, the steps in the decision-making process.

5. Cite factors affecting decision making.

6. Discuss approaches to decision making.

7. Explain follow-through and tell why it is important.

CHAPTER OUTLINE

Woodrow Grant, a supervisor in the assembly plant of Video Systems, Inc., had an agonizing weekend over the decision about Gil Baker, a member of his work group. Baker has been with the firm for 9 years and, until the past year, had been a competent worker. Grant and Baker had been in the same work group for 4 years when Grant was promoted to supervisor a year ago.

Knowing that Baker, who had more seniority, wanted the supervisory job, Grant weighed very carefully this and many other factors about the promotion before he decided to accept it. He accepted because he knew he was better qualified and was confident that he could work out any problems that resulted. But he hadn't counted on Baker's attitude.

Since Grant's promotion, Baker's productivity has fallen, he has been frequently absent or late to work, and he has seemed resentful of Grant's attempts to determine the cause of his behavior and to restore his productivity. The climax came last week when Baker, 30 minutes late 2 days in a row, was called in by Grant for a conference. When Grant asked him what could be done about the problem, Baker responded, ''You're the super; it's your problem.''

Grant was angry with Baker for not seeing that he had been very lenient with him and was trying to salvage his job. He was also angry with himself for having so much difficulty making the decision that now seemed inevitable. At least he was following company policy that the supervisor confer with the worker before suspension or termination recommendations.

''Think about the problem over the weekend, Gil,'' Grant had said. ''See me Monday, 9 A.M.—sharp. We'll make a decision then.''

''Well, Monday is here,'' Grant thinks as he dresses for work after the fretful weekend, ''and I still haven't made a decision.''

Every person faces situations daily in which decisions must be made. Some of the decisions are easy. Some are not. And decisions that are easy for one person may be difficult for another. For some people, deciding how to spend the time on an unexpected day off is troublesome. Making a decision as to whether to sleep late, go shopping, read, catch up on chores, or go swimming may consume half the day for them. Other people can look at an ongoing to-do list and say quickly, ''I'll do this and this and this'' as they choose items deemed appropriate for the day.

The average person rarely thinks about the essentials of decision making, which must be considered by the professional manager in an organization when a decision is to be made.

HAGAR THE HORRIBLE

Source: Reprinted with special permission of King Features Syndicate, Inc.

ESSENTIALS OF DECISION MAKING

Managers must make decisions every day. It is what they are paid to do. As shown in Figure 2-5 on page 45, decision making ranked second of 10 principal daily duties of supervisors. Chapter 3 pointed out that making decisions is a basic part of planning; but managers must also make decisions in all the other functions—organizing, staffing, leading and motivating, and controlling.

There are three essentials of decision making that you must know if you want to make effective management decisions. These essentials answer the questions, What is decision making? What types of decisions are there? Who in the organization is responsible for making decisions?

The Meaning of Decision Making

A *decision* is a choice. *Decision making* is the process of choosing between two or more alternatives. Management is largely a decision-making process. Management decisions are concerned with resources and processes, including people, plant, equipment, strategies, production schedules, work processes, maintenance, compensation, and all other facets of management. Such decisions may have a limited effect on the organization or may be far reaching, depending on the type of decision.

Types of Decisions

Several questions may be asked to determine the classification of a decision. How often does the problem occur? How many members of the organization are affected by the decision? How long does it take to make the decision? On what function of the organization does the decision focus?

Decisions are generally classified into two major types: programmed and nonprogrammed.

Programmed Decisions

Management generally sets up policies or procedures for handling matters involving the daily operation of a business. These routine and repetitive decisions are called *programmed decisions*. All production supervisors in a particular company may follow a standardized procedure for stocking parts inventory for their respective work groups, for example. Personnel supervisors may follow a policy of coordinating with line managers the performance-appraisal schedules for employees. These situations occur regularly and usually affect small groups of people. Since they are routine and recurring, setting policies and procedures for handling them saves the manager time when it comes to making decisions. It also assures that these decisions, while different, will be made in the same way by the different managers. Most of the decisions made in an organization are programmed decisions.

Nonprogrammed Decisions

While most decisions in business are routine and repetitive, many are not. *Nonprogrammed decisions* are usually one-time decisions that can affect the entire organization. They are less structured than programmed decisions. Sometimes called *nonroutine decisions,* they usually involve problems requiring a great deal of analysis before a choice of action is determined.

Some problems may be unique, unexpected, or calamitous; for example, an acquisition that will end the corporate life of the acquired firm; new technology that will make current production processes obsolete; a flood that will bring business to a halt for weeks. But nonprogrammed decisions are made regarding opportunities as well as problems. For example, the nonprogrammed decision of 3M management to market its highly successful Post-it Notes came from an employee's idea for an easily removable bookmark coupled with a product that the company had considered a failure—a glue with a low sticking quality.

Competency Check:

Can you identify and give an example of the types of decisions?

Some decisions may be partly programmed and partly nonprogrammed. For example, a company may have a standard procedure for submitting ideas for new products. The procedure may call for submitting the idea first to the unit head and then, in sequence, to the division director, marketing manager, new product development manager, and research director. Results would then be sent back in reverse order and on to top executives, where a nonprogrammed decision would be made as to whether or not to market the product. Decisions along the way may be programmed, nonprogrammed, or a combination of the two. Note that several managers are responsible for decisions made between the idea and the successful marketing of the product.

Responsibility for Decision Making

All managers make decisions hour after hour and day after day to keep the organization operating smoothly and profitably. Authority for decision making is usually delegated on the basis of the scope of the decision. *Scope* refers to the breadth of the effect of the decision on the company. For example, a decision to move the company to another city would affect all employees. It would, therefore, be broad in scope. A decision to install a conveyer belt on the company's loading pier would affect a limited number of employees, largely those in the shipping and receiving department. Generally, decisions with broad scope will be made at the executive level. As scope decreases, so does the level of management where the decision is made.

Another guideline for determining responsibility for decision making is cost. Generally, decisions should be made at the lowest level consistent with the scope, effectiveness, and cost of the decision. This means simply that a president drawing a six-figure salary shouldn't, as a rule, be making decisions about how many reams of paper to order for the copy machine. You will learn more about this in Chapter 6 in the discussion of delegation of authority.

Top Management

Broad decisions that have an impact on the whole organization are made by top management. These are usually nonprogrammed decisions and may involve several top executives in the process. Top managers generally make fewer decisions than do managers at lower levels, and the cost of making decisions is usually greatest at this level. For example, the recent decision of Lee Iococca, chairman of the Chrysler Corporation, to acquire American Motors, Inc., involved much costly planning. In addition to high-level internal analysis, the Chrysler executive had to confer with government agencies in Washington and corporate executives in the United States and at the French-government-owned Renault division of American Motors in France.[2]

As shown in Figure 4-1, all levels of managers make both programmed and non-programmed decisions. Most of the decisions made by top managers, however, are nonprogrammed.

Middle Management

Middle managers are typically involved with allocating resources within their divisions. They may make decisions regarding the proportion of the budget to assign to each department or the type and number of people to be employed in each department. In Figure 3-1 on page 63, you noted that the plant manager had to decide on a seasonal plan by product type after corporate management had allocated production among plants. This is an example of decisions of decreasing scope being delegated to decreasing levels of management. The decisions of middle managers affect a large

FIGURE 4-1

Responsibilities for decision making by type of decision

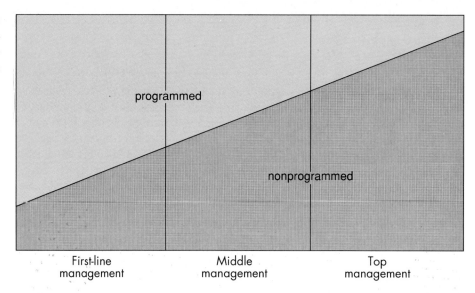

First-line management   Middle management   Top management

segment (the division), while the decision of top management affects all plants in the firm.

Middle managers make both programmed and nonprogrammed decisions. Both top and middle managers make fewer programmed decisions than do first-level managers.

First-Level Managers

First-level managers make more decisions than do managers at higher levels. However, most of their decisions relate to operational concerns and are usually covered by policies and procedures. A few of their decisions will be nonprogrammed or a combination of programmed and nonprogrammed. Decisions at this level are typically less costly than are those at higher levels.

Grant, as pointed out in the beginning of this chapter, followed company policy in conferring with a troublesome employee. That part of his decision was programmed. But the decision that is giving him a headache—the recommendation to discipline— is nonprogrammed.

Supervisors must daily face decisions dealing with individual employee problems. They must also make daily decisions on such operations matters as establishing standards; purchasing supplies and equipment; setting work and vacation schedules; hiring, training, and disciplining workers; making salary and promotion recommendations; planning a budget; measuring productivity; and resolving grievances.

First-level management decisions are usually narrow in scope because they affect only a small segment of the firm. For example, Grant's decision in the Baker case will directly affect only Baker, with perhaps indirect effects on Baker's work group. Regardless of the level at which decisions are made, they are generally more effective when managers follow a sequence of steps to arrive at their decisions.

Competency Check:

Can you explain the types of decisions made by the three levels of management?

THE PROCESS OF DECISION MAKING

Making a decision can be simple or complex. It can be as simple as deciding whether to work overtime or as complex as determining the mission for the organization. The success of the organization is directly related to the effectiveness of the decisions made by its managers. While no one is perfect, every manager strives for a high batting average. Too many strikes and not only will the manager be out but he or she may strike out the company, as well.

Theorists have determined that good decision makers follow a sequence of steps, called the *decision-making process,* in making their decisions. Figure 4-2 shows the six steps in the decision-making process.

Be Aware of Problem

A manager must be aware of a problem in order to solve it. Better still, the manager should be alert to potential problems and make decisions that will prevent the problem from occurring.

While problems are often recognized during planning and controlling, the problem may involve any function of management. Plans must be developed to monitor both the management system and operations to be attuned to potential problems. Some managers may refuse to admit that a problem exists because they are afraid to face it or don't know how to handle it. Do you think that was Grant's problem when he let Baker's problem go on so long without correction? Perhaps, like some managers, he thought the problem would "just go away" if he ignored it. As he learned, it did not.

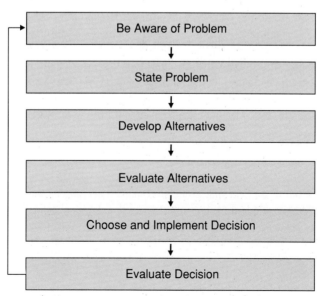

FIGURE 4-2

The decision-making process

Managers must also continually monitor the environment to be aware of potential problems that need attention or opportunities that could improve the workplace. Effective supervisors will be alert to the internal environment. As you learned in Chapter 2, your internal environment includes your unit's objectives, plans, policies, procedures, standards, and operations, including its workers. Any deviation from plans will call for a decision. If workers are regularly failing to meet standards, for example, you will need to examine the cause and decide what action to take. Are workers properly selected, trained, motivated, appraised, rewarded? Is equipment adequate? Are procedures efficient? Are standards realistic? Monitoring your internal environment will keep you in tune with problems and opportunities for improvement.

Your external environment, as shown in Figure 2-2 on page 34, is made up of elements within the firm but outside your unit. These include company objectives and policies, other departments, your peers, and other elements of the firm. Grant, for example, was monitoring his external environment when he made the decision to follow companywide disciplinary policy and confer with Baker before taking action.

The company's external environment, as shown in Figure 2-1 on page 33, also includes forces outside the firm, forces such as customers, suppliers, stockholders, and the economy in general. While supervisors are less concerned with the external environment than is top management, the effective supervisor will, through reading and professional associations, keep aware of changes in the external environment that may have an impact on the company.

State Problem

Before a problem can be solved, it must be identified and stated clearly. Symptoms are sometimes confused with the real problem. A manager must be able to delve behind the symptoms to find the actual cause. For example, Baker has been frequently absent and his work has deteriorated since Grant's promotion. These are symptoms. If Grant wants to improve Baker's behavior, he must find the real cause and not just treat the symptoms. Is it Baker's resentment of Grant's promotion? Is he having personal problems that are affecting his work? Is he ill? If Grant wishes to make the best decision for all concerned, he will try to identify the real problem. Once identified, the problem should be stated clearly. Sometimes putting the statement in writing helps to clarify it. The next step is to try to find some possible solutions.

Develop Alternatives

It has been said that a decision can be no better than the information that shapes it. At this step, information gathering is a primary activity.

This is the time to be creative. Develop as many alternatives as you can in the time you have available. If you leave the best alternative out, you cannot make the best decision. There are several things a supervisor can do to aid in generating alternatives.

WHAT CAN THE SUPERVISOR DO?

Here are several techniques and sources you can use to develop alternatives:

1. Brainstorm. Managers and others can get together, concentrate on a problem, and identify as many solutions as they can. Rules for this technique call for rapid-fire identification of any alternatives that come to mind. "Hitchhiking" onto someone else's idea is encouraged. No analysis or negative reactions are allowed until the evaluation stage, no matter how farfetched an idea might seem. At the end of the session, suggestions are evaluated and several alternatives are selected for in-depth study.
2. Check the files. Has the situation occurred before? Company history may provide alternatives to try again or to avoid. Has a manager previously made a decision in a similar situation? This experience may provide alternatives to repeat or to avoid. A warning is needed here, however: Relying on past experience alone may be detrimental to finding the best solution in the current environment. Examine experiential alternatives carefully.
3. Seek advice from managers, staff specialists, and others in the firm whose expertise enables them to offer suggestions. However, treat a suggestion from this source as just one among many as you develop alternatives. Don't feel that you must blindly follow it solely because it came from a company member. Keep in mind that you are developing as many alternatives as you can.
4. Form a group or task force. A basic tenet of participative management is that workers should be included in problem solving and decision making (see Chapter 2). Who knows more about the problem than the workers who perform the daily tasks? This is certainly something to consider in seeking solutions to operations problems. Groups may consist of work teams, workers and supervisors, special task forces, or committees. Use of the group technique will be covered later in this chapter and developed further in Chapters 12 and 16.
5. Use external sources. To develop awareness, read extensively, and do not restrict your reading to business publications. Branch out to psychology, anthropology, and the social sciences, as well. If your industry has a trade association, read its publications to learn what your competitors are doing. Join a professional association of managers, personnel and human resource specialists, or technical specialists. If you are alert, you might find excellent alternatives in unexpected places.
6. Use your own creativity. Some people are more creative than others. With a little effort, you can improve your ability to examine things from a different viewpoint. Brainstorming will help; so will reading in different fields. Keep your eyes and ears open. Let your mind wander from your typical thought patterns. When considering the problem at hand, ask yourself some What

Competency Check:

Can you cite several techniques and sources the supervisor can use to develop alternatives in decision making?

if? questions. Senator Robert F. Kennedy said "Some men see things as they are and say why. I dream things that never were and say, why not." That's good advice when you're generating alternatives for decision making in today's business environment.

Evaluate Alternatives

At this stage, the manager must compare the costs and benefits of each alternative. The question "What will be the consequences if this action is taken—or not taken?" must be answered as objectively as possible for each alternative.

The evaluation for problems of small scope and significance may be a simple mental analysis before a choice is made. Or the supervisor may make a written comparison of alternatives, listing their costs and benefits in separate columns and choosing the alternative whose benefits outweigh its costs. As problems broaden in scope and significance, the manager might use other analytical tools and procedures, such as risk analysis, payoff tables, cost-benefit analysis, or decision trees. Using statistical tools in which elements of the problem are given numerical values and analyzed mathematically is helpful in many instances. It must be remembered, however, that the tools do not make the decisions; only the manager can do that, after interpreting the numerical data.

Some of these tools, such as the decision tree, can be adapted in a simplified way to aid those who favor a graphical display of material. Figure 4-3 shows a simplified decision tree that might be used by Grant to evaluate his alternatives in handling Baker. Assume that Grant's objective is to improve Baker's performance and productivity and, further, that he has three alternatives: (1) to enforce disciplinary policy, (2) to use positive reenforcement (for example, complimenting him on his progress) and close supervision, or (3) to use a combination of the two. As you can see, the decision tree gives Grant a graphical display of a range of possible outcomes to the three decisions. It shows the probability of success for the three decisions in terms of meeting the objective and based on three possible reactions of Baker to each alternative. For example, if alternative 1 (enforce discipline) is used, improvement will be high only if Baker's reaction is favorable to that decision. It will be low or nil if Baker responds well only to positive reinforcement and close supervision, since that alternative was not chosen. Improvement will be moderate if Baker's reaction is a favorable response to a combination of the two, since only part of the combination (discipline) was used. In choosing alternative 1 or 2, there is a one-in-three (33 percent) risk that little or no improvement will result. Alternative 3, the combination, suggests that at least some improvement will occur, even though the risk is two out of three that the improvement will be moderate. You will learn more about the decision tree later in this chapter.

As a supervisor, you should have at least a basic knowledge of other analysis tools even if you have limited need for their use. Sources presenting these are listed in the Suggested Readings at the end of this chapter.

FIGURE 4-3

Decision tree with alternatives for handling Baker

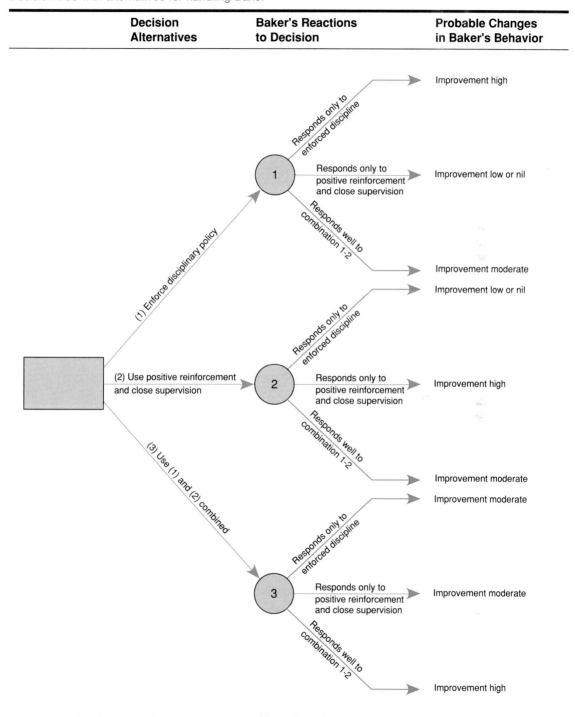

Decision Alternatives	Baker's Reactions to Decision	Probable Changes in Baker's Behavior

Source: Adapted from Lester R. Bittel, *What Every Supervisor Should know,* McGraw-Hill Book Company, New York, 1985, p. 144.

Make and Implement Decision

Making a decision and implementing it are the two sides of the decision-making coin. This is the ''buck-stops-here'' reality of the process. You must choose one of the alternatives. You may have evaluated a long list of alternatives, using broad-based, quality information and statistical tools, but making the choice is the moment of truth that rests on your shoulders. It is not always easy.

Among the pitfalls to decision making are the fear of making the wrong decision, waiting for ''just one more piece of information,'' or delaying the decision for no logical reason. If you have completed the first four steps in the decision-making process correctly, you should not hesitate to choose one of your alternatives. The following checklist may serve as a checkpoint for those who need a final assurance before making the decision.[3]

1. Will the decision actually solve the basic problem, or will it block or divert the solution?
2. Does it form policy, set precedent, or contradict existing policy?
3. Has it been tried by others or tested on a small scale?
4. Has it been thought through all the way to final application, or might unexpected questions arise when the decision is to be implemented?
5. Will it require administrative follow-through; if so, by whom?
6. Is it a permanent solution, or can it be stopped or discontinued? Will it permit switching to other courses of action?
7. What will be the long-term and indirect costs? Will these add to overhead?
8. Has the problem been fairly stated to all persons and interests?
9. Is the solution fair to all concerned, or may it be harmful to someone?
10. Will the solution build goodwill and friendly feelings and provide the basis for good future work relations and business dealings, or might it leave a chain of negative reactions?
11. Will it be profitable?

Most of these questions should have been answered in the evaluate-alternatives step. Of course, you cannot run through the entire checklist every time you have to make a quick decision, and not every question will always be relevant. But in general, among these questions you will find the ones that may help you make your decision.

Making the decision and implementing it go hand in hand. A decision to change a production process needs to be put into action in order to improve the situation that put the decision process in motion. When Grant decides which alternative to use in handling Baker's problem, he must take action immediately. If not, his decision process must begin all over again. The environment is not static. A decision not acted on may not be applicable later because the situation is no longer the same. As a supervisor, you will generally be responsible for implementing decisions involving your unit. If persons other than the decision maker implement the decision, it is the decision maker's responsibility to follow through and see that appropriate action takes place.

Evaluate Decision

How good was the decision? The answer to this question lies in whether or not the objective was met. Was the problem solved without creating serious spin-off problems? Remembering that hindsight is 20/20, the manager should value very highly the results of this last step in the decision-making process. A great deal can be learned from both successes and failures. Both will become a part of your decision-making tool kit when you use experience at the develop-alternatives step. Of course, situations differ, and a past successful decision may not be totally applicable at another time. But knowing what worked and what did not may provide guidelines in similar circumstances. Examine the method by which the decision was made as well as the results. Did productivity increase as a result of the new process? Did the training program improve worker performance? Did the hiring of part-time workers smooth out the seasonal work-load increase at less-than-overtime costs and without damaging worker morale? Grant will want to evaluate the choice he makes regarding Baker by determining whether the choice actually salvaged a formerly productive worker for the company.

Comparing the expected with the actual results of a decision is important to all levels of management, but it is critical to supervisors in operations. Many are learning to make effective decisions not only in order to perform their jobs well but also to help them move up the management ladder. In developing these skills, the supervisor will find that other factors beyond the decision process also have an impact on decision making.

Competency Check:

Can you name, in order, the steps in the decision-making process?

FACTORS AFFECTING DECISION MAKING

Not every decision will be amenable to the full-blown analysis of the decision-making process. A variety of factors may influence the decision. Several of the most common ones are discussed here.

Authority

As you learned earlier in this chapter, responsibility for most decisions is rather clearly delegated to the different levels of management. As a plant work-group supervisor, for example, you would not have the authority to make decisions concerning administrative support staff or sales staff. Nor would heads of these units make decisions concerning your work group. You must know and operate within the limits of your authority for making decisions. Problems you observe outside this boundary should be referred to the appropriate personnel.

Company Policies and Procedures

One of the first things a manager should do when a problem is encountered is to determine whether a policy has been established to cover it. When developing alternatives, such a determination is a must. Policies and procedures set standards for action on recurring problems. They save time and maintain uniformity in handling routine matters.

Policies and procedures may become outdated, however, and may actually prevent a manager from making the best decision. They must be kept up to date and also be flexible enough to take care of situations where they are not clearly appropriate. A company policy requiring automatic disciplining of an employee for three consecutive absences, for example, would not be appropriate in a city where blizzard conditions made driving hazardous for a week.

Generally, policies and procedures keep the firm operating smoothly and uniformly and should guide the decision maker on programmed matters.

Available Time

Many decisions, particularly routine ones, are made in moments. Others require weeks or months. While most managers would prefer plenty of time for information gathering and detailed analysis before making a decision, few can afford this luxury. If a boiler gauge in a small factory registers a critical steam level, the shop supervisor will not have time to do a detailed analysis of alternatives. He or she, hopefully, would make an on-the-spot decision to evacuate the workers and cut off the boiler. Conversely, a decision as to whether to install a robotic production line will require prolonged investigation and analysis. The process for making a decision will necessarily be affected by the time available.

Ethical and Legal Considerations

Decisions are affected by the value system of the organization as well as by legal constraints. The supervisor should be aware of the company's mission and ethical framework and should be guided by them, especially when making nonprogrammed decisions. A supervisor who might decide to conduct a covert antiunion campaign because of problems with the union representative in his or her work group should be aware that there are laws prohibiting such action. A chemical plant manager may be following Environmental Protection Agency guidelines to the letter, but if his or her firm's leaders believe that the firm should go beyond the minimum requirements to protect the health of the community, the supervisor may be violating the firm's code of ethics in deciding to follow only minimum guidelines.

Blanchard and Peale[4] have proposed a set of questions to serve as guidelines for managers who face an ethical dilemma in decision making. Their ''ethics check'' is shown in Figure 4-4.

Suppose you learn that one of your workers has access, through a relative, to information about a competitor's bid for a construction job for which your company is also bidding. The worker offers to get the information for you from the relative's files. Getting the contract will mean jobs for you and your workers, yet your conscience says no. What should you do? Using the ''ethics check,'' you find your answer in the first question: Your worker would be stealing proprietary information, which is clearly illegal.

When an action is legal but still questionable, you move on to the second question. Suppose you are a supervisor on a construction project and have full authority to decide, over the protest of nearby residents, whether to bulldoze a row of handsome old shade trees bordering your site and providing shade to the residents. Getting rid of the trees will give you another quick temporary access for your equipment while construction is in progress. You can legally bulldoze the trees, giving you short-term benefits. But the long-term detriment and displeasure of the community may persuade you to find another solution to your access problem.

When your situation lets you answer yes to the first two questions, your own value system becomes your final guide to making ethical decisions. This may be the most difficult. Suppose you are offered a high-paying job with a company that you know produces a legal but shoddy product and you must decide whether you wish to be a part of what you consider to be a consumer rip-off. Only your own code of ethics will help you answer the third question.

Decision making may be affected by other factors in addition to those presented here. The approach one takes to decision making also affects the process.

Competency Check:

Can you cite the factors affecting decision making?

To guide you in decision making when you face an ethical dilemma, ask yourself these three questions:

Ethics Check	**Consider**
1. Is it legal?	Will I be violating either civil law or company policy?
2. Is it balanced?	Is it fair to all concerned in the short term as well as the long term? Does it promote win-win relationships?
3. How will it make me feel about myself?	Will it make me proud? Would I feel good if my decision was published in the newspaper? Would I feel good if my family knew about my decision?

FIGURE 4-4

Blanchard and Peale's "ethics check"

Source: Kenneth Blanchard and Norman Vincent Peale, *The Power of Ethical Management,* William Morrow and Company, Inc., 1988, p. 27. Text copyright © 1988 by Blanchard Family Partnership and Norman Vincent Peale; illustration copyright © by Norman Vincent Peale. Reprinted by permission of William Morrow and Company, Inc.

CHOOSING AN APPROACH
TO DECISION MAKING

As a supervisor, you will have several approaches to decision making. Will you make decisions systematically or intuitively? Will you make them alone or in participation with groups? Let us examine these pairs of approaches.

Systematic or Intuitive
Approach?

You may follow the decision-making process for all your decisions. A proscribed procedure, based on logic and facts, would be followed in the same way each time you encountered a problem. This is the systematic approach to decision making. Followed strictly, this would not be completely realistic. As has been pointed out, some decisions are so minor that they can be made without going through the entire process. And in some cases, the urgency of the situation may not permit the luxury of following all the steps. On the other hand, nonprogrammed decisions generally require the systematic approach.

Another approach is to arrive at a decision through feelings rather than through facts and logic. This is called an *intuitive approach*. How many times have you heard someone say, "I have a hunch this is the best way"? We have all "played our hunches" in making many kinds of decisions. Successful decision makers use intuition in making some of their decisions. Sometimes it is the only approach available, particularly when the decisions involve future events in a new field. You may have gathered and analyzed the most advanced information using sophisticated technology; but if new and untested concepts are involved, you will probably use your intuition as the final step in making the decision. Astronauts have demonstrated this many times in space exploration. If a decision is a good one, how it was made won't make much difference.

The situational approach to management, presented in Chapter 1, is also relevant to decision making. Using that approach, you would use the systematic approach, the intuitive approach, or a combination of the two as dictated by the situation. The situational approach may also help to determine whether you make the decision alone or in a group mode.

Individual or
Group-Decision Approach?

Making decisions alone is an awesome responsibility for some managers. Others prefer to decide alone. This chapter has dealt largely with individual decision making. "The buck stops here," a frequently used Trumanesque assumption of responsibility, has become a part of American business culture. But, as pointed out in Chapters 1 and 2, a characteristic of companies most often cited as excellent is that they encourage group participation in decision making.

Group decision making follows the "two-heads-are-better-than-one" theory. It brings a variety of skills together to seek a solution to a problem. Also, since the workers are performing the jobs in which many problems occur, it brings to bear a better motivation—and often better knowledge—for solving them. But group decision making is not without problems of its own. The group behaves in ways different from the individuals within it. It sets its own norms for behavior which the supervisor must recognize and deal with. Group behavior as a part of management psychology is beyond the scope of this text. Sources for additional study in this area are given in Suggested Readings at the end of this chapter.

In the traditional firm, decisions are made by management and passed down to workers. Work groups may be allowed—even encouraged—to make suggestions for solving work-related problems, but the supervisor evaluates the suggestions and makes the ultimate decision.

In contemporary participative management, group decision making is often part of the organizational structure. Groups may be given titles such as "work team," "work group," "problem task force," or "quality circle (QC)." These groups usually consist of five to seven people who perform similar jobs. Each group may have some autonomy in setting schedules and procedures. Participation is generally voluntary. The supervisor may serve as team leader, coordinating efforts of the group; in highly participative firms, the team leader is chosen by the group. The group analyzes a problem, develops and evaluates alternatives, and recommends its chosen alternative to management. Implementation often is under the guidance of the group or its team leader, with support from the supervisor.

As part of a recent reorganization at Goodyear aimed at improving its competitive position, an effort was made to harness worker power, in part by encouraging decision making by work teams. Work teams now make personal "business plans" to set production standards, limit absenteeism, and cut product waste. An automatic tire-trimming machine and a tread-gluing machine used in the plant were invented by employees.[5]

The contingency approach to decision making is reflected in the Vroom and Yetton decision model.[6] This approach addresses the question of whether a decision should be made by the manager or by groups. Vroom and Yetton propose that a set of criteria be used to determine what degree of participation by subordinates a manager should allow in decision making. Based on the answers to seven questions, the authors cite five decision-making methods from which a manager might choose, ranging from autocratic to group decision making. The decision tree used to determine the appropriate method and showing the seven questions is shown in Figure 4-5. Note the five decision-making methods listed at the bottom of the figure. The questions at the top of the figure relate to the problem being solved and the subordinates involved. The first three questions relate to the quality of the decision and the last four to the acceptance of the decision by the subordinates. Each path represents a different problem type. Vroom and Yetton identified 12 types, beginning with the top path as type 1.[7]

Suppose you are making a decision as to what office-supply firm to use. To use the tree, begin at the left under question A; the answer is no. The decision is perfunctory, with no extraordinary quality requirements. This answer moves you over to

FIGURE 4-5

Vroom and Yetton's decision tree for determining appropriate decision-making method

A Is there a quality requirement such that one solution is likely to be more rational than another?	B Do I have sufficient information to make a high-quality decision?	C Is the problem structured?	D Is acceptance of the decision by subordinates critical to implementation?	E If you were to make the decision by yourself, is it reasonably certain that it would be accepted by your subordinates?	F Do subordinates share the organizational goals to be obtained in solving this problem?	G Is conflict among subordinates likely in the preferred solution?

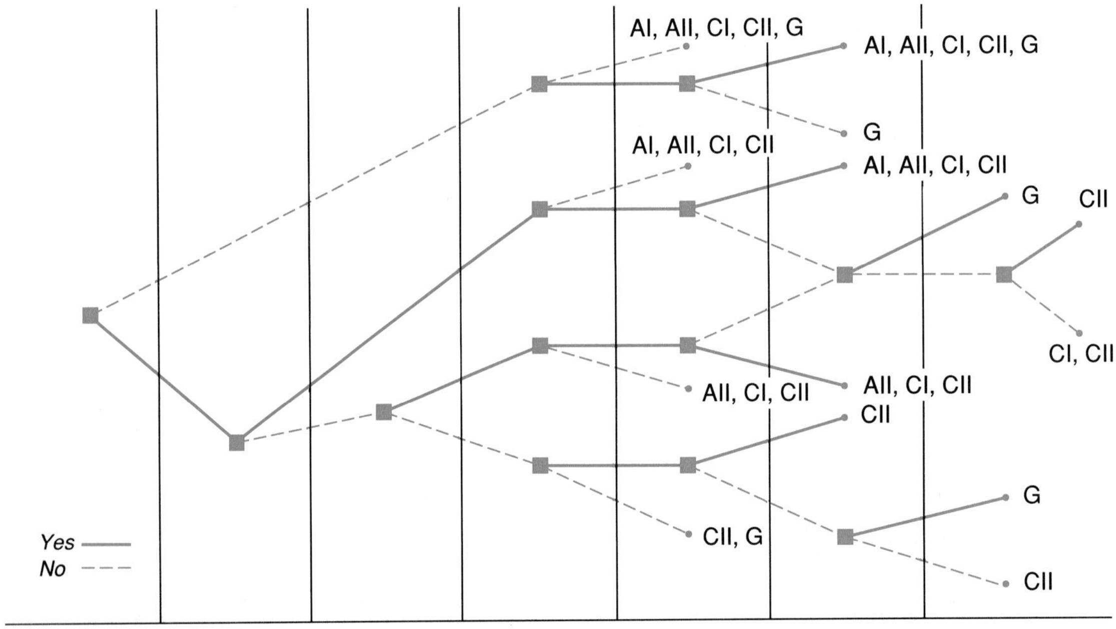

AI, AII, CI, CII, G → AI, AII, CI, CII, G

AI, AII, CI, CII → G

AI, AII, CI, CII → G   CII

CI, CII

AII, CI, CII → AII, CI, CII
CII

G

CII, G

G

CII

Yes ———
No – – –

AI = Authority decision without subordinates' inputs
AII = Authority decision using information gathered from subordinates
CI = Consultative decision with problem discussed individually with each subordinate
CII = Consultative decision with problem discussed with subordinates as a group
G = Group decision

Source: Reprinted from *Leadership and Decision-Making* by Victor H. Vroom and Philip W. Yetton by permission of the University of Pittsburgh Press. © 1973 by University of Pittsburgh Press.

D, the first question relating to subordinate acceptance. Again, the answer is no because, to subordinates, the choice of a supplier is immaterial. According to Vroom and Yetton, the analysis ends here and the decision maker can choose any one of five appropriate methods: AI, AII, CI, CII, or G. The method used may be authoritative, consultative, or group. Vroom and Yetton recommend that the decision among alternative methods then be based on the time available, the development of the subordinates, and the decision maker's choice. You might make the decision without consulting anyone (AI). If you wanted to involve your workers in decision making and plan to change suppliers in the future, you might have a committee research suppliers, establish criteria for judging their products and service, evaluate them, and recommend a list of acceptable suppliers for the department (G).

A decision tree would be useful in helping you decide which problems you could appropriately assign to groups, especially if you are beginning to move from a traditional to a participative management approach.

In addition to operations work groups, management decisions are often made through group efforts. Top managers often work as a group to make decisions on objectives, strategies, and resource allocation. You might participate with other supervisors and your department manager to set objectives for the department. At whatever level, group decision making has some good and some bad features that you will need to consider. The advantages and disadvantages of group decision making are summarized in Figure 4-6.

Competency Check:

Can you discuss the approaches to decision making?

FIGURE 4-6

ADVANTAGES AND DISADVANTAGES OF GROUP DECISION MAKING

ADVANTAGES	DISADVANTAGES
provides broader range of knowledge, ideas, and alternative solutions	takes more time to reach decision
	is more costly process
improves communication within work unit as workers understand better the role of the supervisor	takes workers away from their work stations during group deliberations
improves chances of success since solution is found by workers who then feel part of the process of management	supervisor generally still accountable for decision made by group; may become resentful
improves job dimensions by allowing workers to participate in decision making	may allow strong members to dominate group and exert undue influence on decisions; less strong may become discouraged and stop participating
improves morale of workers	requires high level of supervisory skills to coordinate, communicate, clarify, and implement group's efforts
develops leadership potential of workers within group	

Source: Adapted from *Leadership and Decision-Making* by Victor H. Vroom and Philip W. Yetton by permission of the University of Pittsburgh Press. © 1973 by University of Pittsburgh Press.

As you have learned, the approach selected to make decisions is often determined by the situation. The best approach is the one that will help you make the best decision. Whatever approach is used, implementation of the decision process must be followed through to determine long-term effectiveness.

IMPORTANCE OF THE FOLLOW-THROUGH

In the evaluation step, the supervisor reviews the decision immediately after it is implemented to determine whether it is going as planned. This gives a short-term reading on the effectiveness of the decision. The follow-through is an extension of the evaluation.

Following through over an extended period of time, perhaps several weeks or more, will give you a clearer picture of the quality of your decision. Certain glitches may show up immediately; some will take longer to surface. The reaction of workers, management, and other members of the organization is an example. The effect on subordinates will probably show up immediately because they and their work will undergo change.

To facilitate acceptance of a decision, the supervisor should maintain open communication with the workers and provide proper training of workers for the change. The supervisor should observe the workers more closely and offer assistance during the early steps of the change. These efforts will assist workers in becoming comfortable with the new process or policy. The change process will be treated more fully in Chapter 18.

Invite feedback from workers and give feedback on their progress frequently. A verbal pat on the back will be welcomed by those who adjust quickly and well. Instead of criticizing those having problems, ask ''What can I do to help you with this new process?'' This follow-through with workers will help assure successful implementation of the decision.

Don't forget to communicate the change to other managers in the firm who are affected. Keep the unit manager informed along the way. A memo or short progress report including, if possible, cost savings will alert your superior to the effectiveness of the decision in operations. It will also demonstrate your management skills to upper management.

WHAT CAN THE SUPERVISOR DO?

After you have made your decision, be sure to follow through with the following actions, preferably in the order listed:[8]

1. Inform everyone concerned, precisely and clearly, what your decision is.
2. Be sure they all understand it thoroughly; answer any questions that arise.

3. See to it that the decision is put into effect at the proper time.
4. Supervise carefully how the decision is being carried out, and analyze results as work progresses.
5. Be ready at all times, even immediately after you announce a decision, to listen to any suggestions for, or objections to, your decision. Evaluate these with an eye to improving future decisions.
6. If you find that your decision was not, after all, the best one possible, abandon it at once. Don't fail to let all concerned know about any change. Then make your decision all over again in the light of new facts. And, once more, go through all the steps necessary to make a good decision possible.
7. Document carefully everything connected with your decision as an aid to your evaluation of it. You should learn from each previous decision how to make better and wiser ones.
8. Don't hesitate to discuss the results of your decision with other supervisors and with your immediate supervisor.
9. If you're positive you are right about any decision, stick to it.

Competency Check:

Can you explain follow-through and tell why it is important in decision making?

COMPETENCY REVIEW

1. Identify and give an example of two types of decisions.
2. Explain the types of decisions made by the three levels of management.
3. State, in order, the six steps in the decision-making process.
4. Discuss five techniques and sources the supervisor can use to develop alternatives in decision making.
5. Cite four factors affecting decision making.
6. Discuss two pairs of approaches to decision making.
7. Explain follow-through, and tell why it is important.

APPLICATIONS

1. Blake and Mouton cited three pitfalls in decision making: ''Compromise,'' ''Don't rock the boat,'' and ''Bite your tongue.''[9] Based on your own experience in making decisions at work or in your social life, explain why each of these admonitions might be poor advice to the decision maker.
2. Jenna Reed's company is moving into a new plant in the suburbs. For 5 years, Reed has walked the five blocks from her apartment to work. The company will now be 7 miles away from home, and she faces a transportation problem. She doesn't own a car, mainly because she has been saving to buy a condo. Develop and evaluate a set of alternatives she might consider.
3. One way to distinguish between effective and ineffective managers is by the way in which they cope with decision making. The quiz on page 108 is designed to help you check your decision-making skills. Answer the questions; then, using the point system provided by your instructor, determine your score.

a. Do you often try to avoid or delay making important decisions and even hope that the problem will go away?

Yes ___ *No* ___

b. When required to make a decision fairly promptly, do you become flustered and fail to function at your best?

Yes ___ *No* ___

c. Would you consider it demeaning to consult your subordinates regarding a problem with which they have experience?

Yes ___ *No* ___

d. In deciding a complicated problem where strong arguments exist for either side, would you trust your "gut reaction"?

Yes ___ *No* ___

e. Do you often wish that you did not have to make any decisions?

Yes ___ *No* ___

f. When faced with a serious decision, are your sleep and appetite usually adversely affected?

Yes ___ *No* ___

g. Do you secretly dislike making decisions because you lack self-confidence?

Yes ___ *No* ___

h. Are you uneasy even when required to make unimportant decisions?

Yes ___ *No* ___

i. Would you fire a friend if his continued employment was against the welfare of the organization in which you held a high office?

Yes ___ *No* ___

j. When baffled by a problem within your jurisdiction, would you try to fob it off to others?

Yes ___ *No* ___

k. At home, do you make all or most of the important decisions?

Yes ___ *No* ___

l. Are you usually edgy both before and after making important decisions?

Yes ___ *No* ___

Source: Walter Duckat, "Check Your Decision-Making Skills," *Supervision*, Vol. 41, February 1979, p. 3.

4. This exercise will involve you in a decision-making activity alone and in a group. It will help you consider whether a manager should make decisions alone or with the help of other organization members. Read the incident below, and complete the activity as directed.

Your spaceship has just crash-landed on the dark side of the moon. You were scheduled to rendezvous with a mother ship 200 miles away on the lighted surface of the moon, but the rough landing has ruined your ship and destroyed all the equipment on board except for the following 15 items:

		INDIV. RANKING	ERROR POINTS	GROUP RANKING	ERROR POINTS	NASA RANKING
14	1. box of matches					
6	2. food concentrate					
8	3. 50 feet of nylon rope					
9	4. parachute silk					
3	5. solar-powered portable heating unit					
13	6. two .45 caliber pistols					
11	7. one case of dehydrated milk					
2	8. two 100-pound tanks of oxygen					
4	9. stellar map (of the moon's constellation)					
10	10. self-inflating life raft					
15	11. magnetic compass					
5	12. 5 gallons of water					
7	13. signal flares					
2	14. first-aid kit containing injection needles					
1	15. solar-powered FM receiver-transmitter					
	TIME					

Your crew's survival depends on reaching the mother ship, so the most critical items available for the 200-mile trip must be identified.

Source: Adapted from Jay Hall, "NASA Moon Survival Task" *Telecometrics International,* 1963.

a. Rank the 15 items in terms of their importance for survival. Number 1 should be the most important; 2, the second most important, and so on through number 15, the least important. Record your rankings in the Individual Ranking column on the form. Note the time you begin your ranking and the time you complete it. Record the number of minutes used in the space below the Individual Ranking column.

    b. Form groups of three to five students. Repeat the exercise, using the Group Ranking column. Record the time used.

    c. Determine your score and the group score. Your instructor will tell you how to determine error points.

5. The cartoon below reflects an important point that the decision maker must bear in mind.

Source: Reprinted with special permission of King Features Syndicate, Inc.

    a. What relevant decision-making point is made in the cartoon?

    b. What factors affecting decision making are involved in Dagwood's actions?

6. Form groups of five to seven students to brainstorm one of the following topics:

How can we improve campus parking?

How can registration be improved?

How can participation in campus social activities be increased?

Have one student serve as moderator and one as recorder. The moderator will keep the members actively contributing for a predetermined period of time (about 10 minutes); will prevent negative comments or reactions to suggestions, regardless of how farfetched they seem; and will allow one member to "hitchhike" onto another's idea by amending or embellishing it. The idea is to be as creative as possible. The recorder will write down (on paper or on the chalkboard) all suggestions in as brief a form as possible.

After the predetermined time, all suggestions will cease. The group will then evaluate all suggestions and choose three or four that they would recommend for study as possible solutions to the problem.

CASES

Case I: Monday Morning Headache

Read the Grant-Baker case at the beginning of the chapter; then answer the following questions:

1. Classify the decision Grant must make.
2. What approach to decision making has Grant used up to this point?
3. How would you evaluate Grant's decision making at this point? Give reasons for your answer.
4. If you were Grant, what decision would you make in the Monday session with Baker?
5. How would you implement your decision?

Case II: Get the Lead Out

Ace Marconi is the supervisor of a 10-member work crew at Premier Sports Supply and Manufacturing Company, which specializes in a whole range of fishing tackle and gear. Premier has built its reputation on its handmade fishing lures, a reputation which has sustained the company despite growing foreign competition. Most of its products are sold in the middle 6 months of the year to retailers in the lake area of nearby states, but its lures are distributed internationally. By September, the company begins shifting workers to other products, laying off those who cannot be absorbed into other departments.

On a Friday morning in late August, a large rush order comes in from National Sports Emporium, a good customer that handles the Premier line of lures in all of its stores. It has just bought two competing stores and plans a grand opening next week with a fall fishing promotion. Today's order is conditional: Ship by Monday or forget it.

Premier's marketing vice president hands the order to Marconi at 10:30 A.M. "We need this order, Ace. Inventory tells me that we're short 3 gross of the lead weights on their order of 8 gross. I don't know why we get so low. But 3 gross is such a small amount to trash this big order for—there are sixteen items on the list.

"Are you asking us to turn out 3 gross of lead weights *today?* There's no way we can smelt, mold, anneal, and package those assortments before Monday," Marconi responds. "And you know how the company feels about overtime, particularly now."

"It's important to the company, Ace. You know how tough the competition has been. As I said, see what you can do."

When the vice president leaves, Marconi mutters to himself, "Mary will kill me! She invited guests for this weekend months ago."

He returns to the shop and is met by three of his crew. Greg, one of his best workers, speaks for the group. "We're volunteering to work this weekend to get the order ready for Monday. We're pretty sure we can handle it."

1. What factors affecting the decision will Marconi have to consider?
2. Complete steps 2, 3, and 4 of the decision-making process (state problem, develop alternatives, and evaluate alternatives).
3. What is your decision?
4. How would you implement the decision?
5. How would you follow through?

REFERENCES

1. Jerry Taff, "Tacos and Chopsticks? Do's and Don'ts of Decision Making," *Management World,* July–August 1986, p. 30.
2. *The Wall Street Journal,* Mar. 10, 1987, p. 3.
3. *Dynamic Supervision,* no. 547 (2A), Bureau of Business Practice, 1981, p. 7.
4. Kenneth Blanchard and Norman Vincent Peale, *The Power of Ethical Management,* William Morrow & Company, Inc., New York, 1988.
5. *U.S. News and World Report,* Aug. 24, 1987, p. 44.
6. Victor H. Vroom and Philip W. Yetton, *Leadership and Decision Making,* The University of Pittsburgh Press, 1973.
7. Ibid.
8. *Dynamic Supervision,* op. cit., p. 11.
9. Robert R. Blake and Jane S. Mouton, *Executive Achievement,* McGraw-Hill Book Company, New York, 1986.

SUGGESTED READINGS

Certo, Samuel: *Principles of Modern Management,* Wm. C. Brown Company Publishers, Dubuque, Iowa, 1985, chaps. 5 and 15.

Duncan, W. Jack: *Management,* Random House, Inc., New York, 1983, chaps. 4 and 7.

Edwards, Gary: "Workplace Ethics," *Management Solutions,* December 1986, pp. 12–16.

Einhorn, Hillel J., and Robin M. Hogarth: "Decision Making: Going Forward in Reverse," *Harvard Business Review,* January–February 1987, pp. 66–70.

Herron, Sue, Larry Jacobs, and Brian Kleiner: "Developing the Right Brain's Decision-Making Potential," *Supervisory Management,* March 1985, pp. 16–22.

Hitt, Michael A., R. Dennis Middlemist, and Robert Mathis: *Management Concepts and Effective Practice,* West Publishing Company, New York, 1986, chaps. 3 and 12.

Hodgetts, Richard M.: *Management Theory, Process, and Practice,* Academic Press, Inc., New York, chaps. 6 and 13.

Moore, P. G.: "Techniques vs. Judgment in Decision Making," *Organizational Dynamics,* 2(1973–74), pp. 66–79.

Nutt, Paul C.: "Decision Style and Strategic Decisions of Top Executives," *Technological Forecasting and Social Change,* 1986, pp. 39–62.

Vroom, Victor: "A New Look at Managerial Decision Making," *Organizational Dynamics,* American Management Association, New York, Spring 1973, pp. 66–80.

SECTION III

THE SUPERVISOR AND THE ORGANIZING FUNCTION

THE SUPERVISOR AND THE ORGANIZING FUNCTION

5

THE SUPERVISOR'S ROLE IN ORGANIZING

COMPETENCIES

After studying this chapter you will be able to:

1. Define *organizing* and explain why it is critical to meeting company objectives.

2. Identify the bases for departmentalization.

3. Describe the concepts of centralization and decentralization in delegating authority.

4. Identify and explain the principles of organization.

5. Describe the difference between line and line-and-staff organization.

6. Explain the use of a matrix, or project, organization.

7. State the ways to define a job.

8. Define *job analysis* and tell why it is important.

9. Describe the differences between job description and job specification.

CHAPTER OUTLINE

Tom Sagouris had been thinking for weeks about how he would tell Greg Heinz, his employer and longtime friend, that he was thinking of leaving the young company. He wanted to be sure that Greg would understand there was nothing personal in his decision, even though Mary, Greg's wife, and Sam, Greg's brother, were involved in the problem. Tom was calm but deliberate as he talked over coffee with Greg.

"Look, Greg. It isn't the work. I like repairing foreign wheels. And I think there is a great future here for Foreign Car ServiCenter. The business is growing like crazy. But I can't work in chaos. Let me give you a few examples.

"For one thing, I don't know who the hell is boss. Mary tells me to put the Jag ahead of the Honda, and you tell me the Volks is top priority. Then I find that the parts for two jobs weren't ordered on time, and the owners call me at home to chew me out because we didn't deliver as promised. I turn over the job tickets to Sam, and they get lost. So Mary chews me out because she can't send out the bills. And last week, I even had to cover the front desk and the phone, for Pete's sake, because Sam had to deliver a car and Mary was at the wholesaler's picking up parts. You and I used to do the repairs, but managing takes most of your time now; and since you're back at college part-time, I'm usually left here with the whole can of worms.

"Pete (a part-time worker) can't do but so much in three afternoons a week; he can't take over a whole job. Gino (an apprentice) has promise, but he's pulled from one car to a completely different one right in the middle of a job, so he just throws up his hands and takes a powder. Then I have to chew him out. It's a circus.

"It's not that we don't have the customers—they're coming out of our ears. It's just the opposite—we've grown beyond our ability to handle all the business the way we're set up. I'd like to stay, but I'm losing interest fast. Either we get organized, or I'm going to have to make a change. I'll make a decision by the end of the month."

You may have experienced, either in a job or in your personal life, the same frustration that Tom feels in his auto repair job. Have you ever felt that you had too much to do and everything seemed to fall due at once? You dash frenziedly from one thing to another, never completing anything. As Tom did, you may have reacted by saying, "I've got to get organized." If so, you, also like Tom, will have identified an important management function—organizing.

Overall organizational design is usually handled by top management. It is here that the structure of the firm is created, the number and nature of management personnel are determined, and the lines of authority are established. But as shown in Figure 2-4 on page 43, supervisors also spend over 20 percent of their time organizing. Unfortunately, many supervisors focus only on their narrow functions and do not keep in touch with the total organizational framework—the ''big picture.'' To be effective members of the management team, supervisors must be aware of the overall picture. This chapter will help you develop this awareness by describing the fundamentals of organizing. Chapters 6 and 7 will focus on some specifics of the organizing function, but the first step is to examine its meaning and importance.

WHAT IS ORGANIZING?

As you learned in Chapter 1, organizing is one of the basic functions of managers. *Organizing* is the process of grouping the activities to be performed into manageable components and assigning them in such a way as to achieve the organization's objectives. Organizing follows closely—and sometimes overlaps—the planning function.

Organizing is critical to company objectives for several reasons:

1. It identifies what is to be done and who is to do it.
2. It shows who reports to whom and who is in charge of whom, and it establishes the channels of communication for the process.
3. It focuses resources on the objectives to be achieved.
4. It provides the basis for coordinating the efforts of personnel in the pursuit of company objectives.

Competency Check:

Can you define *organizing* and explain why it is critical to reaching company objectives?

These outcomes of organizing will be grouped into three elements for our discussion. These are (1) dividing the tasks, (2) delegating authority, and (3) assigning resources.

Dividing the Tasks

During the planning stage for Foreign Car ServiCenter, owner-manager Greg Heinz adopted, as his mission, the offering of quality foreign-car repair service to the community at a profit. He also made a list of the tasks to be done. For his small business, these included arranging financing, obtaining licenses, buying equipment, establishing costs and charges, handling inventory, renting a building, ordering parts, hiring workers, repairing cars, handling the payroll, greeting customers, giving estimates, booking jobs, answering the phone, receiving payments, paying bills, preparing and sending statements, advertising, keeping the books, training apprentices, and preparing financial reports.

Heinz's next step was organizing. He had to design the similar tasks into groups, or jobs. Designing jobs will be addressed later in this chapter and further in Chapters 11 and 16. Here we will look at the way each worker specializes in handling certain phases of the business.

Determining Degree of Specialization

An important consideration in dividing tasks is the specialization of labor. As jobs are broken down into smaller and smaller parts, output increases. This is due to the fact that the worker specializing in just one part can become more skillful and thus work faster. Cost per unit, therefore, decreases. But more workers and tools are needed as the number of jobs increases. Sooner or later, the additional labor and capital will outweigh the increased output and the cost per unit will increase. For economic reasons, therefore, the degree of specialization is important.

A second consideration in determining the degree of specialization is the amount of abstraction in the job. A manager does a great deal of thinking, planning, communicating, and other abstract tasks that are difficult to count or measure. A production worker's output, on the other hand, is easily quantifiable—so many silicon chips produced per hour—and is therefore more amenable to specialization.

Let's look at Foreign Car ServiCenter again. Greg noted that some of the tasks to be done were similar in nature; so he made a list, grouping these tasks together. He noted with an asterisk those tasks whose assignment he might want to reconsider. For example, giving estimates, which he listed under ''Job 1,'' might be handled as part of job 2. And booking jobs might be handled as part of job 3. Also, he might want to prepare financial statements himself or have an accountant do them rather than make them part of job 3. Here is his tentative division of tasks into jobs:

Job 1
arranging financing
obtaining licenses
renting a building
buying equipment
hiring workers
establishing costs and charges
giving estimates*
booking jobs*
advertising

Job 2
repairing cars
handling inventory
training apprentices

Job 3
handling the payroll
greeting customers
answering the phone
ordering parts
receiving payments
paying bills
preparing and sending statements
keeping the books
preparing financial reports*

Note that the tasks in job 1 are largely abstract, as are several in job 3. These tasks are varied, and many are not easily measured. Job 2 is far more specialized. It is the production part of the business—repairing cars and keeping the parts inventory to do the job.

A third consideration in determining the degree of specialization is the effect it will have on the motivation of workers. The classical approach to management, as noted in Chapter 1, is to look for the "one best way" to do a job. It emphasizes efficiency through standardization and specialization. Enlightened managers today realize that routine, repetitive tasks in overspecialized jobs decrease motivation and lower productivity. Contemporary management thought stresses designing jobs so as to increase not only the variety of tasks performed by each worker but also worker involvement in decision making about their jobs.[2] This is the purpose of participative programs previously discussed in this text. Figure 5-1 on page 122 summarizes this approach to organizing work. The characteristics of job design will be discussed later in this chapter and in Chapter 16, where the quality of work life is addressed as a means of improving productivity.

Determining the degree of specialization of jobs is not a simple matter. In addition to considering economics, abstraction, and motivation, managers need to use the contingency approach; that is, they need to incorporate the firm's current situation into the organizing function. One thing to consider is the grouping of similar jobs into departments.

Grouping Similar Jobs into Departments

After similar tasks have been grouped into jobs, similar jobs should be grouped into departments. Of course, very small firms, such as Foreign Car ServiCenter, will not need to departmentalize at the beginning. As the firm grows and hires more people for more specialized jobs, Greg Heinz will need to group similar jobs into departments. You can visualize the difference between the degree of specialization and the need for departmentalization between Heinz's business and AT&T.

The overall departmentalization of a firm is determined by top management. Supervisors are usually concerned with functioning within prescribed departments. Even so, there will be times when supervisors will need to use grouping techniques within their own spheres of authority. They may need to form teams, work groups, or quality circles. Supervisors will usually need to seek authority to initiate these grouping techniques. And remember that grouping can be done effectively only in a climate that accommodates participation. For example, establishing quality circles requires not only the approval of top management, but also its support. Because such grouping is becoming more popular in contemporary management, supervisors should become familiar with grouping alternatives. In addition, as members of the management team, supervisors should know the organization of the firm and the basis for its departmentalization because the knowledge will enhance their ability to perform as team members.

There are many bases for grouping jobs that can be used by a business of any size. The most common bases are shown in Figure 5-2 on page 123.

The most widely used form of departmentalization is by function. A functional department groups together people who perform similar or closely related tasks. For

FIGURE 5-1

The changing
approach to
organizing work

THE CHANGING APPROACH TO ORGANIZING WORK

What Management Assumes About Workers

Old Way
Worker wants nothing from the job except pay, avoids responsibility, and must be controlled and coerced.

New Way
Worker desires challenging job and will seek responsibility and autonomy if management permits.

How the Job Is Designed

Old Way
Work is fragmented and deskilled. Worker is confined to narrow job. Doing and thinking are separated.

New Way
Work is multiskilled and performed by teamwork where possible. Worker can upgrade whole system. Doing and thinking are combined.

Management's Organization and Style

Old Way
Top-down military command with worker at bottom of many supervisory layers; worker is expected to obey orders and has no power.

New Way
Relatively flat structure with few layers; worker makes suggestions and has power to implement changes.

Job Training and Security

Old Way
Worker is regarded as a replaceable part and is given little initial training or retraining for new jobs. Layoffs are routine when business declines.

New Way
Worker is considered a valuable resource and is constantly retrained in new skills. Layoffs are avoided if possible in a downturn.

How Wages Are Determined

Old Way
Pay is geared to the job, not the person, and is determined by evaluation and job classification systems.

New Way
Pay is linked to skills acquired. Group incentive and profit-sharing plans are used to enhance commitment.

Labor Relations

Old Way
Labor and management interests are considered incompatible. Conflict arises on the shop floor and in bargaining.

New Way
Mutual interests are emphasized. Management shares information about the business. Labor shares responsibility for making it succeed.

Source: Business Week, Sept. 29, 1986, p. 71.

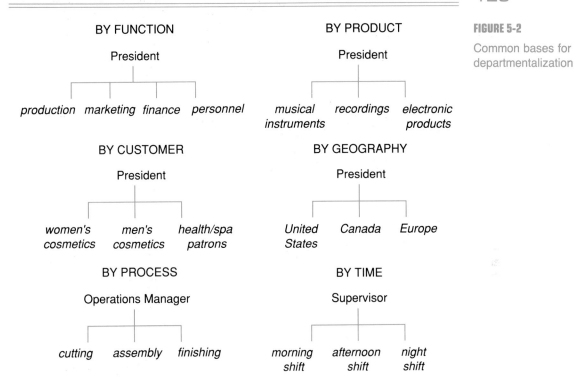

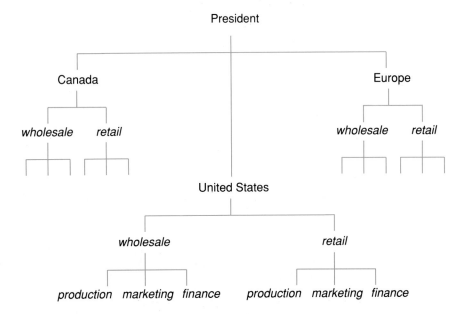

FIGURE 5-2

Common bases for
departmentalization

example, the production vice president is responsible for all production activities and problems; other vice presidents are responsible for the activities related to their particular functions.

Departmentalization by product may be used in firms with several major products. A large wholesale music firm, for example, may have one department or division that supplies retail firms with musical instruments, another that supplies music-related electronic products, and another that supplies recordings. A large department store may set up departments for groups of related products, such as housewares.

Customer departmentalization takes into consideration the differing needs of customers or clients. A cosmetic manufacturing firm may establish separate departments for men's and women's cosmetics. In addition, some large cosmetic firms offer special spa and health services. A special department catering to the needs of both men and women who are health-spa patrons or potential patrons may be established.

Departmentalization based on geography is often used by firms that operate at dispersed locations. Geographical considerations may indicate physical separation as remote as different countries; the division may be by city, state, or region; or the separation may be as close as adjacent buildings or different floors of the same building. Businesses with international components would necessarily consider geographical departmentalization.

Some manufacturing firms find departmentalization by process an appropriate basis for organizing. Examples are manufacturing companies that produce autos, oil products, garments, or furniture. A large furniture manufacturer may have separate departments for cutters of wooden parts for a chair, for workers who assemble the parts, and for finishers of the chair.

A basis for organizing with which supervisors are likely to be directly involved is departmentalization by time. Firms that operate 24 hours a day usually organize by time periods of the workers. The workers may perform the same or different tasks on each shift.

One of the oldest forms of shift work is the 7 A.M. to 3 P.M., 3 P.M. to 11 P.M., and 11 P.M. to 7 A.M. time periods. There are many variations of this today.

Another form is flextime, which was described in Chapter 3. If, for example, core time is set as 10 A.M. to 3 P.M., some workers may choose to arrive at 7 A.M. and leave at 3 P.M. while others choose to arrive at 10 A.M. and leave at 6 P.M. Besides giving workers some freedom to choose their work hours, flextime can help to alleviate rush-hour traffic in highly industrialized areas.

Departmentalization by time is used in a variety of organizations, including the fast food industry, shipbuilding, auto manufacture, hospitals, and large computer service firms.

It is quite common for firms to use overlapping bases for departmentalization. This is called *mixed departmentalization*. A supervisor in a hospital, for example, may supervise only nurses (function) who work on the night shift (time) in the children's ward (customer and geography).

Knowledge of these seven common bases for departmentalization will provide supervisors with a variety of alternatives for organizing work. Other forms of organization are introduced from time to time. Some of these are discussed below.

Competency
Check:

Can you identify
the bases for
departmentalization?

Using Teams and Other Approaches

As you learned in Chapter 2, recent emphasis on productivity and the quality of work life has led to greater use of work teams and other types of work groups.

Work teams. These are commonly subgroups within the departmental organizational structure. A member of a work team may serve as the team leader, or the supervisor may provide the leadership. For example, a supervisor of 12 sewing-machine operators in the swimsuit section of a sports clothing manufacturer may divide the workers into three work groups of four seamsters each. Each group may be assigned a different part of the process, one group seaming all cut front and back pieces, another attaching linings, and the third binding seams and hemming. Or the work teams may include mini production lines within each group, with each worker in the group completing one task and passing the garment on to the next worker until it is completed within the group. These are among a variety of arrangements that can be used in organizing work teams.

Quality circles. These are problem-solving groups of employees with responsibility for addressing specific issues or problems in their work units. These subgroups are composed of workers who perform similar tasks. The number of members varies, but they typically have 10 to 15 members who voluntarily participate to solve problems related to their work. The supervisor may serve as leader, or the leader may be chosen from the group. You will read more about QCs in Chapter 16.

Labor-management participation teams. In the 1980s, labor-management participation teams (LMPTs) made significant gains. After a successful pilot program conducted by the Department of Labor to teach participation techniques to their workers, seven steel companies began a joint effort with the United Steelworkers to institutionalize LMPTs throughout the industry. The initial program involved Inland, LTV, Bethlehem, Wheeling-Pittsburgh, Armco, Acme, and Cleveland-Cliffs steel companies. In 1987, other steel companies joined in the expanded training program.

The function of LMPTs, like the function of QCs, is to tap steelworkers' knowledge of their jobs. Proponents of teams feel that because workers are more intimately acquainted with the shop floor than is management, they should have better ideas about how to improve both safety and efficiency.[3]

Prior to the steel industry's effort, General Motors announced a revolutionary new corporate organization for the Saturn car. Plans for the robotized, restructured plant and the organization to produce the car were announced in 1985, with production to begin in 1989. The Saturn car model of participation organizes workers into small teams of 6 to 15 workers led by a union-member "counselor" elected by the team. The workers perform a wide variety of jobs and decide among themselves how best to do it. The teams also maintain equipment, order supplies, and set relief schedules.[4,5] Figure 5-3 illustrates the changes GM proposed. While the Saturn plan is, at this writing, yet to be implemented, much publicity has been given to its team-oriented approach, and this publicity undoubtedly influenced other organizations to move toward more participatory management.

FIGURE 5-3   The Saturn car model of participation

SATURN'S INNOVATIVE ORGANIZATIONAL STRUCTURE

GM's Heirarchy of Bosses . . .
(Management structure of today's typical assembly plant)

PLANT MANAGER

PRODUCTION MANAGER

GENERAL SUPERINTENDENT

PRODUCTION SUPERINTENDENT
(5 per shift)

GENERAL SUPERVISOR
(15 per shift)

SUPERVISOR/FOREMAN
(90 per shift)

. . . Will Give Way to Management-Union Committees

STRATEGIC ADVISORY COMMITTEE
Does long-term planning. Consists of Saturn president and his staff, plus top
UAW adviser

MANUFACTURING ADVISORY COMMITTEE
Oversees Saturn complex. Includes company and elected union representatives,
plus specialists in engineering, marketing, etc.

BUSINESS UNIT
Coordinates plant-level operations. Made up of company representatives and
elected union adviser, plus specialists

WORK UNIT MODULE
Groups of three to six work units led by a company "work unit adviser"

WORK UNITS
Teams of 6 to 15 workers led by an elected UAW "counselor"

Source: Business Week, Aug. 5, 1985, p. 65.

Work teams, QCs, and LMPTs are also known by other names as companies customize their approaches to alternative organization forms. There are also committees, task forces, and ad hoc groups targeted to specific problems. All of these are aimed at dividing tasks and assigning them to the appropriate personnel. The next step in the organizing function is delegating authority to carry out the tasks.

Delegating Authority

Dividing tasks is one side of the organizing coin; the other is giving to the person assigned the task the authority to do it. *Authority* is the power to make decisions and use resources without getting permission from someone else. As a supervisor, you should have the authority you need to carry out your responsibilities in making decisions, taking action to control costs and quality, and exercising discipline over the workers assigned to you. Whether you have this authority may depend upon your firm's approach to centralization or decentralization.

Centralization and Decentralization

What is the best level at which to delegate authority? Should top management reserve unto itself the authority to make most decisions? Or should authority be assigned throughout the organization by extensive delegation to all levels of management? The first question represents centralization of authority; the second, decentralization.

As you learned in Chapter 2, top management in the traditional organization sets objectives and establishes broad policies; middle management focuses on coordinating, with peers and lower management, the strategies for carrying out objectives; and first-level management focuses on operations. The degree to which a firm delegates authority to the various levels depends upon management philosophy.

A guiding principle is that authority should be delegated to the lowest level of management commensurate with appropriate skill and lowest cost. For example, suppose you are a supervisor for a firm that is considering moving its headquarters from New York to Los Angeles. Your salary would meet the criterion of lowest cost, but you would not normally have the conceptual skill and knowledge of the firm to qualify you to make the decision as to whether to move. Authority for this type of decision should be centralized. Suppose, however, that there is a conflict over the vacation schedule of two members of your work crew. No doubt top management would have the ability to make the decision; but at a six-figure salary compared to first-level management salary, it would be a misuse of resources to centralize authority at the top level for such a decision.

Chapter 6 will address the supervisor's role in delegating authority. Our concern here is the overall concept of authority delegation as a part of organizing. Determining the centralization or decentralization policy is usually a function of the philosophical climate established at the top. What works for one company may not work for others. What works at one time may not be appropriate at another.

Competency Check:

Can you discuss the concepts of centralization and decentralization in delegating authority?

The Contingency Approach

Policy for delegating authority may need to change over the life cycle of the firm to accommodate changing economic conditions, changing technology or resources, or for any number of other reasons. As you learned in Chapter 1, the contingency approach, refuting the ''one best way'' to manage, takes into consideration the various elements of a situation and chooses an approach that best fits that situation. An owner-manager who created and operated a small business, making all the decisions along the way as it grew, may find that centralized authority is no longer efficient when the business has greatly expanded. Have you detected that this is the situation at Foreign Car ServiCenter? The current status calls for an examination of all the elements to determine the most appropriate delegation of authority. The contingency approach requires fluidity. Organizing fluidity has been referred to as *adhocracy,* as opposed to *bureaucracy.*[6] Peters and Waterman, calling adhocracy a hallmark of excellent companies, said:[7]

> In rapidly changing times . . . the bureaucracy is not enough. By "the bureaucracy," [we] mean the formal organization structure that has been established to deal with the routine, day-in, day-out items of business—sales, manufacturing, and so on. By "the adhocracy," [we] mean organizational mechanisms that deal with all the new issues that either fall between bureaucratic cracks or span so many levels in the bureaucracy that it's not clear who should do what; consequently, nobody does anything.
>
> The concept of organizational fluidity . . . is not new. What *is* new is that the excellent companies seem to know how to make good use of it. Whether it is their rich ways of communicating informally or their special ways of using ad hoc devices, such as task forces, the excellent companies get quick action just because their organizations are fluid.

Assigning Resources

A corollary to delegating authority is assigning resources to carry out the responsibility. When Sears Roebuck created a financial services division by acquiring Dean Witter Reynolds, an investment firm, it delegated authority to the Dean Witter Reynolds management to operate the new division. Had Sears not also assigned an operations budget commensurate with the goals set for the acquisition, the new Sears service division would have been doomed.

As supervisor, you will also need the resources to carry out your responsibilities.

Resources assigned must be equal to the responsibility.

FRANCIE

"I HATE IT WHEN THE COMPANY TRIES TO SAVE MONEY!"

FRANCIE GERRARD

Source: Reprinted by permission of UFS., Inc.

Imagine the chaos you would experience as a supervisor of a word processing center in which there were two operators for each keyboard, as indicated in the cartoon. Common sense would dictate to managers that the resources to carry out a job must be allocated at the time that authority is delegated. Basic principles often derive from such logic.

WHAT CAN THE SUPERVISOR DO?

As you now know, organizing is an essential function of all managers at all levels. This suggests that managers should also be well organized in their personal lives. How well organized are you? Before examining the basic principles of organizing, find out by taking the short quiz below.

1. Was everything under control when you last took a vacation—or did you come back to face confused subordinates, dissatisfied superiors, a crisis or two? _____
2. Are you guilty of flagrant time-wasting in the guise of too many unproductive meetings, not enough delegating, getting to work late, knocking off early? _____
3. Do you have the habit of promptly getting things done and out of the way? Or do you tend to let them pile up until their sheer number is discouraging? _____
4. Are you frequently in the office after regular hours in order to catch up on your work? _____
5. Have you developed routine ways to handle routine matters like correspondence, requests for information and so forth; or does every little thing throw you off base? _____
6. Are you intimately familiar with the internal structure of your firm so that you can get specialized information fast? _____
7. When things are going exceptionally well, do you take advantage of the psychological boost by tackling other tough chores, or do you bask in your accomplishment and ease off for the rest of the day? _____
8. Are the meetings you attend always necessary, always productive, always the kind you couldn't afford to miss? _____
9. Do you take maximum advantage of travel time; for instance, to attend to reading chores that get shunted aside on the job, to plan your next day's activities, to just plain think? _____
10. At day's end, do you usually wonder where the time has gone, or do your days seem to drag on endlessly? (If they never seem to end, you are doubtless wasting time.) _____

Now, in view of your answers, *are* you well-organized?

Source: Adapted from Ted Pollock, "A Personal File of Stimulating Ideas and Problem Solvers—How Well-Organized Are You?" *Supervision,* October 1983, pp. 24–25.

PRINCIPLES OF ORGANIZING

Management theorists have presented many principles of organizing over the years. We shall address three significant ones here: unity of command, authority/responsibility parity, and span of control.

Unity of Command

This principle states that each person should have one and only one supervisor. This is the oldest of the classical principles of management. It establishes a two-way relationship for carrying out tasks. It is designed to ensure that directions are clearly transmitted to the worker from the supervisor and that feedback from the worker to the supervisor indicates completion of the task as directed. If you have ever worked in a situation in which two bosses were giving you orders, you know the frustration that Tom Sagouris described in the beginning of this chapter when this principle was violated. Whose work do you perform? In what priority? What happens when you don't have enough time to do the tasks for both? What if one boss countermands the directions of another? While there are some exceptions to this principle, which you will learn later in this chapter, the one worker/one boss principle facilitates the management process best in most situations.

Authority/Responsibility Parity

As you read above, authority is the power to make decisions and use resources without getting permission from someone else. This, too, is a two-sided coin. There must be parity between authority and responsibility. Authority is delegated by a manager to a subordinate; at the same time, the subordinate accepts the responsibility and has the obligation to act. *Responsibility* can be defined as the obligation to carry out assigned tasks.

Suppose, as a word processing supervisor, you are given the authority by your manager to direct workers in your unit to produce a prescribed number of pages of output per day. You are, therefore, responsible to your manager for the output. If you have the authority but don't use it to direct the workers to do the tasks, you are not carrying out your responsibility and will, at some point, be held accountable for your failure to act. Trouble will also arise if you are held accountable for producing the daily output of pages but are not given the authority to direct the workers to do it. You will learn more about this disparity in the discussion of delegation in Chapter 6. Here, the point to be made is that efficient organization requires that authority and responsibility be equal.

Span of Control

The number of subordinates reporting directly to a manager is called the manager's *span of control*. While management theorists have searched for the ideal number, no

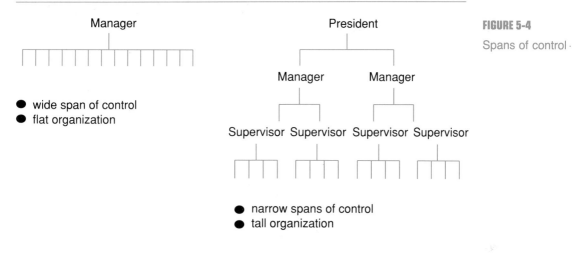

FIGURE 5-4

Spans of control

standard has ever been found. Instead, a principle has evolved which states that there is a limit to the number of workers one manager can supervise and that the span of control should be kept within manageable limits.

A wide span of control (many workers per manager) creates a flat organization because there are few managers. Conversely, a narrow span (few workers per manager) creates a tall organization because more levels of management are needed. These differences are shown in Figure 5-4. American firms typically have taller organizations than do foreign firms, especially those in Japan.

Several factors should be considered in determining the manageable span of control. Examine Figure 5-5 to note how these factors affect the span.

FIGURE 5-5 FACTORS INFLUENCING THE SPAN OF CONTROL

FACTOR	FACTOR USUALLY INCREASES SPAN OF CONTROL WHEN—	FACTOR USUALLY DECREASES SPAN OF CONTROL WHEN—
1. similarity of function	1. subordinates have similar functions.	1. subordinates have different functions.
2. geographic contiguity	2. subordinates are physically close.	2. subordinates are physically distant.
3. complexity of functions	3. subordinates have simple tasks.	3. subordinates have complex tasks.
4. coordination	4. work of subordinates needs little coordination.	4. work of subordinates needs much coordination.
5. planning	5. manager spends little time planning.	5. manager spends much time planning.

Source: Adapted from Samuel Certo, *Principles of Modern Management, Functions and Systems,* William C. Brown Company Publishers, Dubuque, Iowa, 1980, p. 189.

Competency
Check:

Can you identify
and explain the
principles of
organizing?

These principles apply to all areas of the organizing function, whether the consideration is dividing the tasks into jobs, grouping the jobs into departments, or fitting the departments into an overall management structure.

UNDERSTANDING THE OVERALL MANAGEMENT STRUCTURE

After tasks have been assembled into jobs and grouped by jobs into departments, the overall management structure can be formalized to show relationships among all members of the organization. The organization chart, as portrayed in the cartoon, locates each worker in the organization. The overall management structure, usually represented by the organization chart, is commonly determined by top management. The major types of organization structure are line, line-and-staff, and matrix or project.

Line Organization

In most organizations, there is a vertical line of authority which begins at the top—the chief executive level—and goes down through the first level of management—the supervisor's level. Based on the scalar principle first applied to organization in the classical period, this hierarchy is called *line organization*.

The organization
chart tells you where
you are.

Reprinted from *The Wall Street Journal;* permission, Cartoon Features Syndicate.

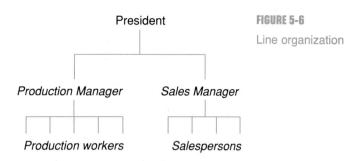

FIGURE 5-6

Line organization

The purpose of line organization is to direct human and capital resources toward the achievement of company objectives. The line is directly concerned with the production and marketing of the goods or services which the company provides. The vertical relationship of the line forms the company's chain of command. As you learned in the section on departmentalization, departments may be formed on several bases; typically, departmentalization is by function, though it may be mixed with other bases, such as product or customer. Small companies often have a pure line structure. Such an organization is shown in Figure 5-6. As the company grows in size and complexity, it may change to another organization structure.

Line-and-Staff Organization

Many factors in the environment today require personnel with specialized technical and professional skills to provide expertise, to advise, and to provide other supportive activities to line managers. These personnel are referred to as *staff*. When these advisers are added, the firm operates as a line-and-staff organization. Figure 5-7 shows

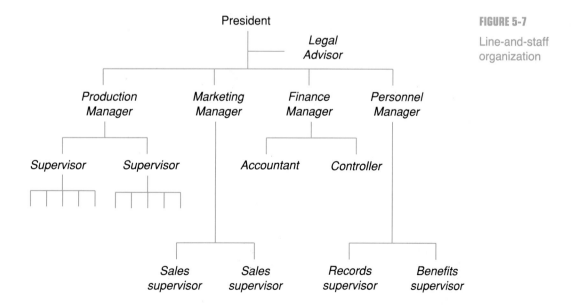

FIGURE 5-7

Line-and-staff organization

such an organization chart. In this chart, the legal adviser and the personnel manager operate as staff. The legal adviser serves as counsel to the president, advising him or her on the legal aspects of proposals, decisions, and actions. If the production manager wants to use a new manufacturing process, for example, the legal adviser may research the environmental implications and advise whether the process would violate Environmental Protection Agency regulations.

Staff personnel usually provide advice or support service to the line and have no direct authority over line personnel. However, if the legal adviser finds that the production manager's proposed new process is illegal, he or she may refuse to approve the line manager's request. As a rule, the refusal would be passed by the attorney to the president, who, in turn, would deny the line manager's request, thereby adhering to the chain of command.

The personnel manager is also considered staff in that he or she serves a support function to all line managers. However, within the human resources department, this manager also has line authority over the subordinates in that department (the records and benefits supervisors, for example).

Competency Check:

Can you describe the difference between line and line-and-staff organizations?

Matrix, or Project, Organization

Organizations today must cope with a complex and changing environment. Traditional organizational structure often is not flexible enough to accommodate this. Indeed, the organizational structure, by definition, is designed to give stability to the firm's internal relationships. The matrix organization provides ''the best of both worlds,'' even though it creates some problems of its own. A *matrix,* or *project, organization* is a structure that combines features of the functional and product departmentalization and is used on an ad hoc basis to manage specific projects.

Such an organization may be used, for example, to research, manufacture, and test a new product before it is added to the firm's existing product line. As shown in Figure 5-8, separate organizations would be established for products A and B. The functional organization would continue undisturbed, with one exception: While product A is being developed, personnel with special needed skills would be ''borrowed'' from their regular departments and assigned temporarily to the product A manager. When the product A project is completed, these workers would return to their functional departments. The product A manager, therefore, would be managing a separate organization that functioned concurrently with the company's permanent organizational structure. He or she would direct the activities of the product A workers. Permanent employment relationships, such as personnel records, would continue to be handled for product A workers by their regular functional managers.

The project, or matrix, structure gives the organization the fluidity that Peters and Waterman cited as a hallmark of ''excellent companies.'' It is adhocracy combined with bureaucracy. But do you see any problems? What about the workers on product A having two bosses? Right! The project, or matrix, structure violates the principle of unity of command.

Firms that use the matrix design feel that its high efficiency and high response to environmental changes outweigh its inherent problems. Careful preparation, clear

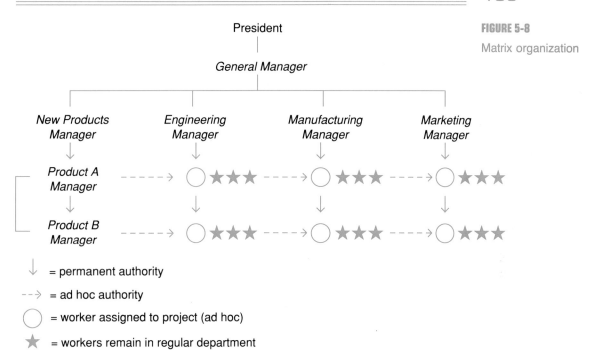

FIGURE 5-8
Matrix organization

assignment of responsibilities, and open communication minimize disruption and help to maintain a smooth operation while the project is in progress.

As a supervisor, you might be involved in a matrix, or project, structure within your own division. For example, a new inventory system or a new computer configuration might necessitate setting up a project team. Technical specialists might be borrowed from all work groups, including yours, to facilitate the implementation. You might need to share your authority over one of your workers while he or she is working on the project. In addition, you might need to reassign the project member's work load while the project is active. You might also need to counteract possible resentment if extra tasks are assigned to the remaining work team and the jealousies which may occur from the temporary assignment of one of your workers to a "special project." Coping with a new organizational structure, particularly one which is superimposed on the existing one, will call for a high level of supervisory skill.

The organizational structure selected by the firm depends on many things, but the main consideration is the function the structure is expected to provide. An architectural axiom says, "form follows function." A look at some of the tools used in organizing will add another dimension to your understanding of the overall structure.

Competency Check:

Can you explain the use of the project, or matrix, organizational structure?

DESIGNING AND ANALYZING JOBS

A fundamental part of the organizing function is designing and analyzing the specific jobs to be accomplished. You may see on an organization chart the job title, "computer programmer,'' but there is nothing on the chart to tell you what the person holding that job title does or what job satisfaction, if any, he or she derives from doing it. Every job must be designed and described so that each person placed at a desk or a work station bearing the job title, including management, will know what is expected of that worker.

This section will introduce you to job design and analysis as parts of the organizing process. It will also discuss two basic tools of organizing, the job description and the job specification. The overview here will be further developed in Chapters 11 and 16, which address motivation and productivity, respectively.

Job Design

Every job must be specifically created and labeled before a worker is selected to fill it. Jobs are the building blocks of an organization. Creating jobs is an organizing task called job design. *Job design* is the process by which job content is identified, work methods to perform the job delineated, and the job's relationship to certain other jobs in the firm specified.

Many factors influence job design. The following questions identify some of the major factors:

- What is the management philosophy?
- Are there government requirements that may affect the job?
- Is technology involved? What type, and at what level?
- Are there union requirements?
- What economic factors may affect the job?
- Are there employee factors that will affect the job?

Giving consideration to these questions early in the job-design process will enable the job designer to avoid costly mistakes that may be disclosed after the job is implemented.

Job design has two elements that are critical to an organization's success:

1. It establishes the work to be done to accomplish the objectives.
2. It has a significant impact on the motivation of the worker and the quality of work life in the firm.

There are distinctive features of each, but there is also some overlap.

In determining the work to be done, the job designer can group together a manageable number of similar tasks. Examples are the movements of a lathe operator, the cleaning and repair tasks of a maintenance worker, the process of writing a computer program, or the supervision of a given number of salespersons. But research findings indicate that the process of selecting and grouping the tasks in job design also affects the motivation of the worker who performs the job.[8] Current methods of job design, therefore, define a job in terms of these characteristics: depth, scope, and core dimensions.

Job depth refers to the degree of freedom a worker has in performing a job. Narrowly specialized jobs, such as operating a drill press, have little depth—the operator performs standardized procedures on a routine basis. A produce manager, on the other hand, may have the freedom to order produce and create displays as he or she chooses, with only budgetary and space limitations.

Job scope refers to the number and combination of tasks a worker is asked to perform. It also includes the *time cycle* of a job; that is, how long it takes to complete a task before it must be repeated. Typically, highly specialized jobs are narrow in scope.

A third way to define a job is through the characteristics called *core dimensions*.[9] This term refers to five characteristics used to evaluate the way in which a job is perceived by the worker. The core dimensions are:

- *skill variety*—the variety of activities and the number of skills required to perform them
- *task identity*—the degree of ''wholeness'' of a task; that is, the completion of a job from beginning to an identifiable final result
- *task significance*—the degree of importance other people see in the job
- *autonomy*—the degree of freedom the worker has in deciding the schedule and process for doing the job
- *feedback*—the degree to which the completed job provides information to the worker on the results of his or her performance

The relationship of job design to motivation makes job design a common approach today to the search for productivity improvement. This will be further discussed in Chapter 16. As a supervisor, you are responsible for meeting production standards. You therefore need to be aware of the impact job design can have on productivity by increasing or decreasing worker motivation. In an established firm, after jobs are initially designed, you may be asked to participate in the analysis of existing jobs, a process which may result in the redesigning of jobs.

Job Analysis

In today's changing environment, it is unrealistic to assume that any job design is permanent. Designs must be kept up to date. In addition, jobs must be described and communicated to the workers so that they will clearly understand their roles in the organization. To do these things, job analysis must be instituted.

Job analysis (JA) is the process of gathering and studying information about jobs and their requirements. In large firms, JA is usually a specialized function of the human resources/personnel department. By nature of the program, involving workers and their jobs, supervisors are usually involved in the data-gathering process. In smaller firms, supervisors may direct the data collection. The data may then be analyzed by internal personnel or by an outside consultant. The job descriptions that result from JA are today so critical to legally mandated nondiscriminatory employment that most businesses—except, perhaps, for mom-and-pop operations—conduct some type of ongoing job analysis.

JA data can be gathered by observing the worker on the job, interviewing the worker, having questionnaires completed by the worker or with the supervisor, or having the worker keep a log of tasks performed over a period of time.

A variety of formats can be used to collect the data. Work sheets and other instruments used must be acceptable under the 1978 Uniform Guidelines on Employee Selection. To be acceptable, the procedure must clearly identify the job duties and behaviors necessary to perform the job. JA work sheets are usually designed to answer questions such as:

- What are the major duties and responsibilities?
- What tools and procedures are used?
- What skills, knowledge, and abilities are required?
- What are the physical requirements of the job?
- What are the environmental conditions of the job?

Competency Check:

Can you define *job analysis* and tell why it is important?

The data gathered in the JA are used to prepare a job description and a job specification, two important tools of management.

Job Description

The *job description (JD)* is a written statement of the duties and responsibilities of any person holding the job. It may be a short statement or a lengthy, formalized one. Whatever the format, JDs are important documents.

The supervisor will use the JD to orient a new worker to the job. The JD will delineate for the worker the tasks to be performed, the tools to be used, and the supervision given or received. It also becomes an important legal document for the firm in case the firm is called upon to show that its personnel decisions and activities are nondiscriminatory.

Job descriptions are sometimes called *position descriptions*. Figure 5-9 shows a position description for a supervisor.

Job Specification

Competency Check:

Can you describe the differences between the JD and the JS?

Another result of the JA is the job specification. A *job specification (JS)* is a statement of the qualifications necessary for performing the job. The major difference between the two documents is that the JD focuses on the job while the JS focuses on the individual who will hold the job. The JS generally shows the job requirements of the worker in terms of education; experience and training; and skills, knowledge, and abilities. Job specifications are commonly used in recruiting and staffing activities.

FIGURE 5-9

Position description

FIDELITY SAVINGS BANK
Position Description

Position Title	Word Processing Supervisor	Position No.	2784-C
Reports to:	Manager of InfoSystems	Effective Date	1/1/89
Approved by:		Status:	Exempt

(Must be signed)

I. General Description of Duties/Position: Manages the Word Processing Department of 6 WP operators. Receives original work from all managers, establishes priorities, sets production schedules. Provides technical expertise for new and nonroutine applications. Establishes and implements turnaround and accuracy standards. Trains new operators and assists incumbent operators with programming and technical problems. Prepares and submits reports to InfoSystems manager and works with that position in executing company and department policies. Cooperates with Human Resources manager on personnel matters relating to WP operators.

II. Responsibilities:

1. Records and logs incoming work from managers. Assigns priorities and establishes method of assigning to operators. Maintains service checks and support communications with originators.

2. Checks progression of jobs to maintain turnaround/accuracy standards. Communicates with originators when deadlines may not be met.

3. Maintains knowledge of equipment capabilities and software updates and problems through vendor contacts and professional publications.

4. Provides or secures expertise on nonroutine applications.

5. Trains new operators and experienced operators on new applications.

6. Prepares and submits monthly reports on productivity and cost/budget analysis.

7. Cooperates with Human Resources manager in performance appraisal schedules and personnel data-gathering activities re WP operators.

Supervision Received: First-level management position. Has limited supervision. Works under the general direction of the InfoSystems manager.

Supervision Given: Supervises 6 WP operators and the WP function for the firm.

COMPETENCY REVIEW

1. Define *organizing,* and explain why it is critical to reaching the company objectives.
2. Identify seven bases for departmentalization.
3. Discuss the concepts of centralization and decentralization in delegating authority.
4. Identify and explain three principles of organization.
5. Describe the difference between line and line-and-staff organization.
6. Explain the use of the project, or matrix, organizational structure.
7. State three ways to define a job.
8. Define *job analysis,* and tell why it is important.
9. Describe the differences between a job description and a job specification.

APPLICATIONS

1. Assume that you have been taking a night course in supervision at a local university. You regularly discuss with your coworkers the new concepts that you learn in class. To help them understand the meaning of the core dimensions of a job, compare the jobs of a sandwich assembler in a fast food restaurant production line and a physician. It might be helpful to use a three-column format, listing the core dimensions in column 1, the sandwich assembler in column 2, and the physician in column 3. Fill in the comparisons for each core dimension in column 2 and column 3.
2. From your own experiences or from the experiences of a firm about which you have some knowledge, describe a situation that violates the principle of authority/responsibility parity. List the problems caused by the disparity. Describe how you might have corrected the situation.
3. Using your present firm, one in which you previously worked, or one for which a relative or friend now works as a basis, describe, on a scale of 1 to 5, the firm's situation in terms of the changing approach to organizing work shown in Figure 5-1. Using a continuum (as illustrated below) for each of the six categories, place your firm on the scale based on its approach to organizing. Example:

What Management Assumes About Workers

1	2	3	4	5
old way				new way

4. You learned in this chapter that the organization chart reflects management organizational philosophy as well as relationships. The following organization charts provide a tongue-in-cheek look at a variety of organizations as they are traditionally viewed or as they were viewed during a publicized event affecting the organization. Describe, in a sentence or two, the organizational philosophy implied in each organization chart.

ORGANIZATIONAL CHARTS

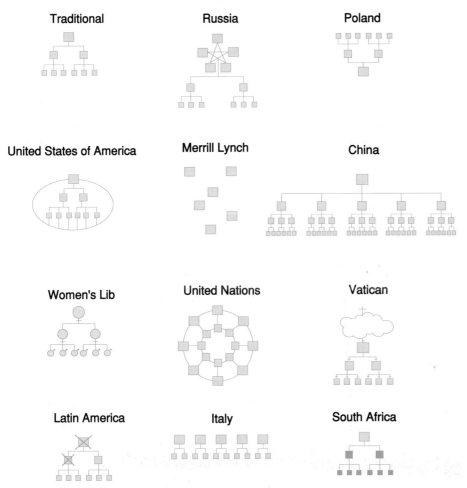

Traditional Russia Poland

United States of America Merrill Lynch China

Women's Lib United Nations Vatican

Latin America Italy South Africa

Source: The Ashwell Division of the Chicago Corporation, Chicago, Ill.

CASES

Case I: Retooling the Car Shop

At the beginning of this chapter, Tom Sagouris is thinking of leaving the company unless some reorganization takes place. He is an excellent worker and runs the repair function of the shop. Owner Greg Heinz doesn't want to lose him. Greg knows business has tripled in 3 years and is still growing. He has been thinking about changes for some time. Based on an analysis of the firm's financial position and its potential, he has decided to expand to larger quarters, hire more personnel, and add a parts department. He will remain as president and make Tom repairs manager. Tom will give cost estimates and manage all repairs. Greg's wife, Mary, will become manager for administration. A new sales manager will handle repair scheduling and counter sales of parts. Greg's brother, Sam, will no longer work for the firm. Other positions to be added include two repair specialists, an apprentice, an accounts clerk to handle bookkeeping and inventory, a secretary to the president, a receptionist, and a counter salesperson.

1. Draw an organization chart to reflect the changes that will take place at Foreign Car ServiCenter.
2. What will the span of control be for each manager? What problems, if any, do you see in the spans of control?
3. Do you see any assignments that may later cause conflict?
4. If Heinz decides to add a full paint shop to the repair service, where would you place the new function in the organization? Explain.

Case II: Rewriting the Book at Metropolitan Community College

Below is the form of JD used at Metropolitan Community College (MCC). The college is not satisfied with its JD and has been reminded by its personnel department that its format needs to be brought into line with current personnel practices. MCC, therefore, is updating and standardizing all its JDs.

CLERK TYPIST B
POSITION NUMBER 661
STUDENT RECORDS

Qualification Standards
Completion of high school or equivalent and at least one year of clerical, typing, or word processing experience. Education may be substituted for experience, or experience involving clerical and/or typing duties may be substituted for education on an equivalent time basis. Typing speed of 60 WPM—95% accuracy is minimum requirement.

Brief Description of Duties
Responsible for maintenance of one-quarter of the student records (4,000 active plus 40,000 inactive estimated), including entering the final grades at the end of each semester and making approved grade changes, entering transfer and advanced placement, updating cumulative totals. Establishes and maintains an active student academic record file each semester; verifies all totals on active records annually. Submits all changes in cumulative academic data to the Computer Center according to established procedures; verifies all totals on active records annually; verifies all transactions upon completion. Processes all name changes, both in office and through the Computer Center; handles all student inquiries, complaints, etc., in his/her file, according to MCC policy with appropriate directions from supervisor; interprets policy to the public as required with direc-

tion. Supervises work-study students who are assigned to student records office, if any. Performs other routine office jobs as directed by Student Records supervisor.

Salary
State Commission scale: $10,800–$13,800

The job holder must be very energetic, capable of assuming responsibility with a minimum of supervision. The job requires hard work, irregular hours at times, last-minute overtime duties. Worker often must work at computer terminal for long periods. The ability to supervise student workers and communicate effectively with a variety of people under stress conditions is more important than the computer skill.

1. Does MCC's present format reflect the text's definition of a JD? Explain.
2. Using Figure 5-10 as a model, write a new JD.
3. Write a JS. (Make assumptions where necessary.)

REFERENCES

1. Thomas J. Peters and Robert H. Waterman, Jr., *In Search of Excellence,* Warner Books, New York, 1982, p. 155. Copyright © 1982 by Thomas J. Peters and Robert H. Waterman, Jr. Reprinted by permission of Harper & Row.
2. "Managers Discover the Human Side of Automation," *Business Week,* Sept. 29, 1986, pp. 70–75.
3. "Steelmakers Want to Make Teamwork an Institution," *Business Week,* May 11, 1987, p. 84.
4. "How Power Will Be Balanced on Saturn's Shop Floor," *Business Week,* Aug. 8, 1985, p. 65.
5. "GM's $5-Billion Bet on a Car to Conquer Imports," *U.S. News & World Report,* Aug. 5, 1985, pp. 23–24. Copyright, *U.S. News & World Report.*
6. Peters and Waterman, Jr., op. cit., p. 121.
7. Loc. cit.
8. See Frederick Herzberg, B. Mausner, and B. Snyderman, *The Motivation to Work,* John Wiley & Sons, Inc., New York, 1959; J. Richard Hackman and Greg Oldham, "Development of the Job Diagnostic Survey," *Journal of Applied Psychology,* April 1975, pp. 159–170; and J. Richard Hackman, Greg Oldham, Robert Janson, and Kenneth Purdy, "A New Strategy for Job Enrichment," *California Management Review,* Summer 1975, pp. 57–71.
9. See Hackman and Oldham, op. cit., and J. Richard Hackman and R. G. Oldham, "Motivation through the Design of Work: Test of a Theory," *Organizational Behavior and Human Performance,* August 1976, p. 256.

SUGGESTED READINGS

Bedeian, Arthur G.: *Management,* The Dryden Press, Inc., New York, 1986.
Bureau of Intergovernmental Personnel Programs, *Job Analysis, Developing and Documenting the Data,* Washington, 1973.

Champion, Michael A., and Paul W. Thayer: ''Job Design: Approaches, Outcomes, and Trade-offs,'' *Organizational Dynamics,* Winter 1987, pp. 66–79.

Dyer, Lee: ''How Does Decentralization Affect Human Resource Departments?'' *Training and Development Journal,* February 1987, pp. 20–23.

Ivancevich, John M., and William F. Glueck: *Foundations of Personnel/Human Resources Management,* 3d ed., Business Publications, Inc., Plano, Tex., 1986.

McCormick, E. J.: *Job Analysis: Uses and Applications,* AMACOM, New York, 1979.

Miner, M. G., and J. B. Miner: *Uniform Guidelines on Employee Selection Procedures,* The Bureau of National Affairs, Washington, 1979.

Roderick, Richard M.: ''Redesigning an Accounting Department for Corporate and Personal Goals,'' *Management Accounting,* February 1984, pp. 56–60.

Schermerhorn, John R., Jr.: *Management for Productivity,* 2d ed., John Wiley & Sons, Inc., New York, 1986.

———: ''Team Development for High Performance Management,'' *Training and Development Journal,* November 1986, pp. 38–41.

U.S. Department of Labor, *Dictionary of Occupational Titles,* 1977.

Vinton, Donna: ''Delegation for Employee Development,'' *Training and Development Journal,* January 1987, pp. 65–66.

6

DELEGATING EFFECTIVELY

6

DELEGATING EFFECTIVELY

COMPETENCIES

After studying this chapter, you will be able to:

1. Define delegation.

2. Cite reasons supervisors should delegate.

3. Identify reasons supervisors fail to delegate.

4. Describe the categories of tasks that should be delegated.

5. Discuss delegation techniques.

6. Describe nontraditional delegation methods.

CHAPTER OUTLINE

66

f I want something done right, I have to do it myself,'' Marty
grumbled. ''This is the second time this week that the job I gave
Jan to do wasn't done the way I told her to do it.''

''You'd think that when a person gives you a job to do and makes you
responsible for getting it done, he'd let you alone to do it your own way,''
Jan thought. ''After all, it's the end result that counts, not the *way* the
job's done.''

Marty and Jan are confused about delegation and its value to supervisors and to
the employees they oversee. Marty apparently believes that he should tell each person
exactly how to do a job; Jan believes that she should be allowed to do the job any
way she wants to so long as it gets done. Who is correct? Marty? Jan? Both? Neither?

WHAT IS DELEGATION?

Supervisors delegate work to varying degrees depending on their definition of *delegation*. First-level managers must know when, to whom, and how to delegate.

Definition

Webster's New International Dictionary defines *delegation* as the ''act of delegating;
or investing with authority to act for another.'' Combine this definition with the
commonly accepted business principle that the delegation of responsibility (obligation)
for performance should never be conferred without the delegation of authority for
directing the performance. In everyday terms, this means that when work is delegated
by one person to another, the authority granted by that person should equal the responsibility given.

Just as a scale must be in balance to provide an accurate measure, so must authority
be in balance with responsibility if a person is to perform effectively. Let's look at
the effects of a situation such as that shown in Figure 6-1. Imagine that Marty has
given Jan responsibility for gathering information from 76 assembly-line workers as
to their perceptions of the quality of work life both in their department and in the
company as a whole. This is in response to a memo from the central office. The
conversation when Marty assigned the task to Jan was as follows:

MARTY   I received a memo today from the central office, and they want to know
how the workers feel about ''the quality of their work life''—whatever
that means.

JAN   Didn't we discuss quality of work life at our group meeting last month?

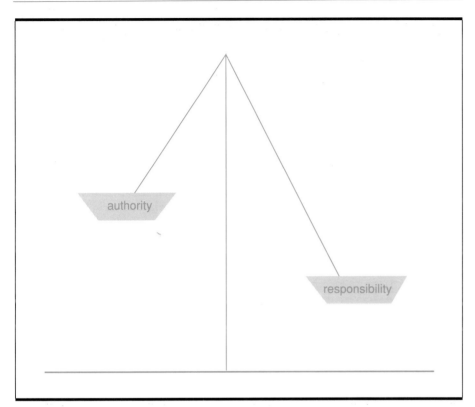

FIGURE 6-1

When authority
does not equal
responsibility,
problems occur.

MARTY   Yeah, I guess we did. I was just being funny. Anyway, they want us to
        find out how the workers feel about the quality of their work life both in
        our department and in the company as a whole. I want you to take care
        of that.

JAN   It sounds like an interesting job, and I'll be glad to take it on. Will you
        give me the authority to call a meeting to explain what we're trying to
        do? Maybe I should ask the central office if they want to do a survey
        throughout the company, using a uniform questionnaire. That way, we'd
        all be gathering the same type of information.

MARTY   You'll just have to do this on your own.

In this case, Marty has given Jan a big job to do and little or no authority to get the
job done.

   Delegation means more than assigning tasks. It means sharing authority with a
subordinate. If you are the type of supervisor who believes that you are the only one
capable of making decisions or completing difficult tasks, delegation will be a difficult
supervisory technique for you to master. But keep trying. Practice makes perfect, and
the more you delegate, the easier it becomes and the better supervisor you become.

   Level of delegation varies among supervisors. The delegation continuum shown in
Figure 6-2 illustrates the degree of authority given to subordinates and the degree of

FIGURE 6-2

Levels of delegation

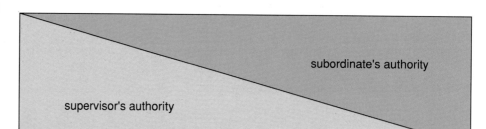

L1	L2	L3	L4
Authority retained by supervisor	Supervisor's approval obtained before subordinate takes action	Subordinate acts and then reports to supervisor	Subordinate has complete authority delegated

Source: Adapted from Tannenbaum and Schmidt's Leadership Model shown in Business Pub- lications, Inc., James H. Donnelly, James L. Gibson, and John M. Ivancevich, *The Fundamentals of Management,* 5th ed., Plano, Tex., 1987, p. 383.

authority retained by the supervisor. This is usually largely determined by the super- visor's philosophy of delegation.

On the first level (L1), the supervisor assigns a job to be completed by the sub- ordinate but is unwilling (or unable) to give more than token authority to the subor- dinate.

On level 2 (L2), the supervisor allows the subordinate to work on an assigned task but requires supervisory approval before the subordinate can take action.

On level 3 (L3), the subordinate is given the authority to act but must then report to the supervisor.

On level 4 (L4), the supervisor delegates full authority to the subordinate. At this level of delegation, the supervisor steps back and allows the subordinate to accomplish the task entirely on his or her own.

Competency Check:

Can you define delegation?

As an organization and its employees move toward participatory management, levels 3 and 4 become more appropriate delegation levels. As worker participation increases, level 4 becomes an ideal toward which to strive. Level 4 is participatory management in action.

Why Supervisors Should Delegate

According to J. C. Penney, founder of J. C. Penney Co., Inc., there are a number of benefits to be derived from delegating tasks to others. The benefits cited by Mr. Penney include:[2]

● Delegation gives you an opportunity to take on additional work yourself. Of course, the additional tasks should be meaningful ones that lead to your develop- ment as a supervisor. Taking on additional work that could be done just as well by others is simply trading tasks.

● Delegation relieves you of petty, routine details that can probably be done just as effectively by others. A note of caution here: Dumping work on others because you find it petty and boring is not the best motivator for subordinates. The added work and responsibility should be meaningful to the subordinate. The way the work is delegated is very important. Never assign someone a task by saying, "I hate this job—it's so boring. Why don't you try it for awhile?"

● Delegation can keep your department from becoming a bottleneck, which is apt to happen if you try to do everything yourself. Delegation spreads the work around, shares the challenges, and helps keep work moving through the department.

● Delegation improves employee morale by giving employees a feeling of shared responsibility. People like to believe that they are important to the organization, and delegation fosters that feeling.

● Delegation keeps you from being harassed. Sharing the work load is one way of reducing the stress that results from unmet deadlines and too much work.

To Mr. Penney's list of the benefits that accrue from delegation, we might add several others. Delegating assignments to subordinates may improve their decision-making skills by requiring them to examine a task critically and make a decision as to how it should be done. In the long run, this develops employees and leads to their growth in the job.

The supervisor may discover some ability in an employee that had not been evident previously, or a problem employee may be tested by offering a challenge. Additional benefits of delegation are training workers in unfamiliar tasks, discovering potential leaders, and demonstrating confidence in subordinates.

Any of the benefits cited above should be enough to encourage supervisors to begin to delegate tasks to their subordinates if they do not already do so. If they *have* been delegating work to their subordinates, they should continue to do so, increasing the authority given until they reach the ideal (L4) or the level at which they and their workers are most efficient and effective.

G. David Adams, manager of employee communications for Puget Sound Power and Light Company, says, "I have only one firm rule. I want to be informed. I let my people do their job in whatever way they want. I just want to be given a brief update, either in a staff meeting or when passing someone in the hall." Mr. Adams is approaching level 4, with some remnant of level 3 (reporting).

Competency Check:

Can you identify seven reasons for delegating tasks to subordinates?

Competency Check:

Can you describe the four levels of delegation?

Why Supervisors Fail to Delegate

In general, supervisors fail to delegate because they are not comfortable with the philosophy or they don't know how to relinquish control. Some of the specific reasons supervisors are reluctant to delegate are presented below.

Lack of Trust

Some supervisors lack trust in their subordinates' ability to do anything beyond routine assignments. The attitude of the supervisor is, as Marty's was in the beginning of this chapter, "If I want something done right, I have to do it myself."

Perceived Threat

"If I give all my work away, who will need me?" is a worry expressed by some supervisors. Others are concerned that someone else may do a good job and thus be a threat to their positions—take their jobs. To supervisors secure in their ability to do their jobs, however, subordinates capable of assuming greater responsibility should not represent a threat.

Lack of Tolerance for Ambiguity

Many managers need to feel "on top of things," to know what is going on at all times; some even believe they must have their "fingers in all of the pies." Supervisors who feel this way need to know what each subordinate is doing at any given time. They have no tolerance for ambiguity, and thus they delegate very few of their responsibilities.

Competency
Check:

Satisfaction That Comes from Work

Can you identify
four reasons
supervisors fail
to delegate?

Many supervisors, and other managers, receive such satisfaction from doing their own work that they are unwilling to relinquish any part of it. Satisfaction from a job well done, from completing work on time, and from knowing that they have the ability to do a task is such a good feeling that it is difficult for them to share it.

WHAT CAN THE SUPERVISOR DO?

The supervisor can learn to let go. Delegation is an important part of supervision. Although delegation can be difficult, if you want your subordinates to grow and develop, delegation is one way to help them in their development.

Do you recognize any of the excuses listed in Figure 6-3? Check the excuses you have used when delegation was an option.

If you have used these excuses to keep from delegating, then perhaps you need to reevaluate your supervisory style. Nobody can do everything. Delegation allows you more time to do other tasks and, at the same time, it contributes to the growth and development of your subordinates. Try it. You'll like it!

WHAT SHOULD BE DELEGATED?

There are some tasks for which delegation is appropriate. Other tasks should *not* be delegated. The effective supervisor knows the difference. One rule of thumb is: If the work does not have a direct bearing on your ability to plan, organize, staff, lead, and control, delegate it; if mistakes would have dire consequences, do it yourself!

Delegate Routine Tasks

Routine tasks can be performed by someone else. Assigning routine tasks to subordinates gives them opportunities to enlarge or enrich their jobs. You should, however,

FIGURE 6-3

Delegation excuses

_____ 1. My employees are too inexperienced to do this. I have to do it myself.

_____ 2. It takes more time to explain the job to someone else than to do it myself. It's not worth the bother.

_____ 3. I can't afford to have a mistake made here.

_____ 4. This job is different. It demands my personal attention.

_____ 5. My staff members are all busy; nobody has time for any additional work.

_____ 6. Nobody else is willing to take on this responsibility.

_____ 7. This is the type of work I'm best at; I'm not going to give it up now to a subordinate.

_____ 8. If I pass it on to a subordinate, I'll lose control of the job. I won't know what's going on.

_____ 9. People will think I'm lazy—that I'm just passing the buck.

_____ 10. No one knows exactly how I want this job done.

_____ 11. If you want the job done right, you have to do it yourself.

_____ 12. This job is too important to trust to someone else.

_____ 13. I've got to approve the final product anyway, so why not do it to begin with?

Source: "Developing Action Plans," _Supervisory Sense,_ vol. 7, no. 7, January 1987, pp. 14–15.

be sure that the tasks assigned have some meaning to the employees; they should not be viewed as meaningless busywork.

Delegate Repetitive Tasks

Repetitive tasks often provide training for more complex jobs. Children crawl before they toddle; they hold your hand before they walk. Subordinates should learn to complete routine and repetitive tasks efficiently with some supervision before they tackle more difficult tasks. Being given that opportunity benefits both the supervisor and the subordinates.

Delegate Tasks That Contribute to Staff Growth

As mentioned earlier in this chapter, tasks that are delegated should be seen as meaningful by the subordinate and provide an opportunity for growth. Learning to do new tasks, becoming involved in departmental operations, experiencing working with others on group projects all lead to employee development. These activities should be encouraged.

Delegate Tasks That Someone Else Is More Qualified to Perform

People like to believe themselves capable of doing any assigned task and doing it well. But it is important to recognize that sometimes others have greater experience, knowledge, or expertise in a particular area. When this is true, recognize that ability and take advantage of having that capability in your department. For example, if someone in your department is more knowledgeable about the capabilities of new equipment, then assign the job of comparing equipment for possible purchase to the person with greater ability to make those comparisons.

WHAT CAN THE SUPERVISOR DO?

Smart supervisors evaluate each delegation. Ask yourself the following questions as you evaluate your delegation decisions:

● Did an emergency or pressure force you to delegate? Or did you plan well in advance?

● What factors prompted you to select this delegate?

● Were other subordinates equally qualified? How do you know? If not, was it due to a failure on your part to provide training and development?

● Did you clearly explain the subordinate's authority? Was it necessary to transmit this information to others? Why?

● Did the subordinate try to avoid acting as your delegate? If so, why? What do you plan to do about it?

● When you communicated with the delegate, did you treat him or her as an equal?

● Did you meet with the delegate to discuss the *completed* delegation? Why? Who took the initiative to arrange the discussion?

● Did you credit the delegate for what was done? How?

● Would you give this subordinate another, perhaps a more difficult, task? If not, why not?

● Do you have a written record of what the delegate achieved? Will you use it during a performance appraisal?

Source: Herbert M. Engel, "Understanding Effective Delegation," *Modern Office Technology,* July 1984, p. 18. Reprinted from the July issue of *Modern Office Technology,* and copyrighted 1984 by Penton/IPC, subsidiary of Pittway Corporation.

HOW TO DELEGATE

There are two sides to the delegation coin—the obligation that workers have to their supervisors and the obligation that supervisors have to their managers. Remember that although you can delegate responsibility and authority to a subordinate, you cannot absolve yourself of your own responsibility for completion of the job. Referring to his office, President Harry Truman once said, "The buck stops here." In this case, it is on the supervisor's desk that the "buck stops."

Dale D. McConkey identified the roles of the supervisor (delegator) and the employee (delegatee) as follows.[3] The role of the delegator in the delegation process, he wrote, is to:

1. communicate clearly.
2. specify authority.
3. encourage subordinate participation.
4. review results, not methods.
5. show trust.
6. seek recommendations.
7. delegate credit, not blame.
8. give support.
9. be consistent.
10. know the delegatees.
11. develop the delegatees.

The role of the delegatee is to:

1. take the initiative.
2. relate to the boss.
3. be sure the delegation is realistic.
4. determine if the task is compatible with the delegatee's goal.
5. determine and give feedback regarding results.
6. report periodically to the boss.
7. carry out delegated assignments effectively.
8. develop himself or herself.

Both roles are important to the success of the delegation process. There are many techniques for successful delegation, among them defining the task, assigning authority, setting clear goals, following up, and giving credit.

Define Task

Tell the person to whom you are delegating a job exactly what you expect. Spell out instructions clearly, including deadlines and any special directions. "Jan, this report is due at the central office on Monday, June 5. Therefore, it must be received by our word processing center by the preceding Wednesday. This is an important report; careful preparation and attractive presentation are critical. I know I can count on you to represent our department in the most positive way." Instructions like these define the task parameters.

Provide Needed Information

The supervisor must provide information regarding the assignment. Initially, all relevant written information should be turned over to the subordinate. In addition, the supervisor will provide any other information that has been received verbally. This is the time for the subordinate to ask any questions or clarify any instructions. For example, the subordinate might want to know if others who will be involved in the assignment have been notified of his or her role; if interaction with other departments is expected, has authority been given to make the contacts and ask for input; how much flexibility there is in time estimates; and so forth.

The supervisor must continue to provide the delegatee with pertinent information as it is received. This routing should be made promptly; information should not be allowed to accumulate on the supervisor's desk. Information received verbally should be transmitted as promptly as that received in written form. However, to minimize misunderstanding, verbal messages should be put in writing before being given to the subordinate.

Assign Authority

Delegation should not take place until authority is assigned. Authority is not the icing on the delegation cake; it is the basic ingredient.

Authority should be given in advance so that it can be exercised when required. After-the-fact authority carries very little weight. And when the authority is granted, everyone who will be involved in the action or affected by the results should be made aware of it.

Be specific. Make it clear from the beginning just how much authority and initiative in decision making you are giving. This definition of parameters will spare you from an ''I didn't expect you to assume so much authority'' future situation.

Set Clear Goals

Let your subordinate know what results you expect, leaving the means for accomplishing those results to the subordinate's discretion. The goals are the results, and that is where your interests are, not in the methods for achieving the results. An effective delegator will say to the subordinate, ''This is what we need to accomplish. What do you think is the most efficient way to achieve these results?'' An ineffective delegator might say, ''We want to achieve these goals. If you follow this procedure, you can reach the goals,'' going on to outline steps 1, 2, and 3 in the procedure. Of course, some employees need more supervision and direction than others; but if you expect your subordinates to develop their decision-making skills and to show initiative, you must give them the opportunity.

Follow Up

Following-up is not ''checking up,'' or constantly looking over the shoulder of the person to whom you have delegated a task. Rather follow-up provides the subordinate with the opportunity to let the supervisor know how the task is progressing and allows the supervisor to stay informed.

When the task (job, project, assignment) is originally delegated, checkpoints should be established. This procedure is particularly helpful when responsibility is being delegated to a subordinate for the first time or when an especially difficult task is being assigned. Follow-up is also necessary when it is obvious that the subordinate is getting into serious trouble. Don't let him drown; throw him a life preserver before it is too late!

Give Credit

Weak supervisors often fail to acknowledge good work done by their subordinates while hastily placing blame when someone fails to meet expectations. Good supervisors, on the other hand, publicly, privately, and promptly recognize and acknowledge good performance and do not advertise blame. Good supervisors also do not leave employees in doubt; nor do they put their workers in the position of the employees in the cartoon below.

So this is the Saunders report.
Who wrote it?

I hate it!

Competency
Check:

Can you discuss six
techniques that
contribute to
successful
delegation?

As presented in Chapter 11, praise is a powerful motivator. When deserved credit is given to a subordinate, it encourages her or him to accept even greater challenges. Blame, on the other hand, should not be broadcast. If a subordinate makes a mistake, try to find out why the mistake was made and give the subordinate support in correcting the error.

NONTRADITIONAL DELEGATION METHODS

Traditionally, delegation is downward—from supervisor to subordinate. Nontraditional methods of delegation include reverse delegation, lateral delegation, and abdication. Sometimes these nontraditional methods are not even recognized as delegation.

Reverse Delegation

Reverse delegation shifts responsibility upward. Responsibility shifts from the delegatee (subordinate) to the delegator (supervisor). William Oncken and Donald L. Wass use the ''monkey on the back'' analogy when referring to reverse delegation.[4] Consider the following examples:

1. You approach the door to your office, and Sue greets you with, ''Good morning. I'm so glad I caught you early this morning. You remember that report you asked me to do last week? Well, we have a problem. You see . . .'' Because you just arrived at work and have a number of activities waiting for you, you respond, ''Thanks for bringing that to my attention. Let me give it some thought, and I'll get back to you in the next day or two.''
2. Joe says to you, ''I have a great idea for a pizza-vending machine to be available at breaks and at lunchtimes.'' Because you are in a hurry, you respond, ''Fine. Send me a memo, and I'll consider your suggestion.''
3. During a meeting with another subordinate, you agree to support a proposal for better lighting in the work area. As you are leaving, you say, ''Let me know how I can help you.''
4. Suppose you have given a subordinate a rather difficult report to write for a VIP. Because you want to be sure the subordinate gets started on the right track, you say, ''I'll do a rough draft so you can get an idea of how the report should be organized. It's just a rough draft, but it should help you get started.''

In all the situations described above, the ''monkey'' has jumped from the backs of the subordinates to you, the supervisor. You have, either wittingly or unwittingly, accepted responsibility for all the delegated tasks. How did this happen? It happened because you and your subordinates did not consider the tasks delegated; rather, you considered the tasks to be joint responsibilities.

How can you avoid reverse delegation? By being aware when a subordinate tries to move the monkey from his or her back to yours and by being prepared for the move, you can prevent the transfer of the monkey from the subordinate's back to yours.

WHAT CAN THE SUPERVISOR DO?

Let's take a closer look at each of the situations described above and see what the supervisor can do to prevent these particular monkeys from landing on the supervisor's back.

1. Your initial response to Sue should have been, "I'm sorry that you have a problem with the report. Why don't you write down some alternative solutions to the problem and meet me in my office at 4 P.M. tomorrow. I think you should be prepared to suggest a solution at that time."
2. You should not ask for a memo on the suggestion. Asking for a memo clearly makes the next move yours—you are going to have to respond to the memo. Instead, ask Joe to come to your office prepared to discuss his suggestion for a vending machine, but make the appointment only after Joe has had time to find out all the information regarding costs and revenues. Chances are you will not see Joe's name on your appointment calendar.
3. If you think a checkpoint is necessary, tell the subordinate that you will be available for a short discussion on Monday from 2 P.M. to 2:30 P.M.
4. Under no circumstances should you have offered to write an initial draft—rough or not. If you have delegated the task to a subordinate, you should have enough faith in your good judgment in selecting the subordinate and in the subordinate's ability to do the job that it should not be necessary for you to write any part of the report.

Lateral Delegation

Lateral delegation involves persuading a colleague on a similar level in the organization to do your work. Passive or compliant peers are primary victims—they just find it very difficult to say no. Employees who are easily intimidated, vulnerable to peer pressure, or who can be manipulated are special targets for lateral delegation. As a supervisor, you should not engage in lateral delegation, nor should you accept it. And you should be aware of your subordinates who try to use a lateral arabesque on one of their peers and promptly act to stop the shift.

Abdication

Supervisors who conveniently "disappear" when a task is to be done or who "forget" when a report is due are delegating by abdication. They simply do not do their jobs, and others must assume the ongoing responsibilities. These supervisors may have reached the first level of management because they were smooth talkers, "con artists" who make people believe they are all they say they are. The chances of their maintaining their supervisory positions for any extended period of time are slim; their superiors will eventually begin to understand that they are all talk and no action, and their subordinates will begin to rebel at having to do their work.

The procrastinator is often an abdicator. Putting off tasks and avoiding meeting deadlines shifts the responsibilities to others. If the procrastination is a result of disorganization rather than intentional abdication, the supervisor may be helped. A disorganized supervisor has difficulty setting priorities and anticipating deadlines; these weaknesses can be addressed through time-management training and an understanding of what is important in the job.

Reverse delegation, lateral delegation, and abdication are negative forms of delegation. Supervisors must learn to identify and deal with them while, at the same time, learning to use positive forms of delegation.

Competency Check:

Can you describe the three nontraditional methods of delegation?

WHAT CAN THE SUPERVISOR DO?

Complete the following checklist and action plan. It will help you identify your delegation strengths and the areas in which you need improvement. You will need to use the following authority codes for questions 16 and 17:

> A = Subordinate may act and need not report.
> B = Subordinate may act but must report
>   to the supervisor as soon as possible.
> C = Prior approval by supervisor is required.

How Much Do I Delegate?

	Yes	No
1. Have I taken all vacations in the last 5 years? Action plan: _____	_____	_____
2. Do I work longer hours than those reporting to me? Action plan: _____	_____	_____
3. Do I usually do work at home? Action plan: _____	_____	_____
4. Do I get more than two business phone calls a week at home? Action plan: _____	_____	_____

5. Do I frequently come into the office when it is closed?   _____   _____
    Action plan: _____
    _____

6. Am I usually behind in my work?   _____   _____
    Action plan: _____
    _____

7. Do I measure my success primarily by time worked or by   _____   _____
    accomplishment?
    Action plan: _____
    _____

8. Do my subordinates request advice once or twice a day?   _____   _____
    Action plan: _____
    _____

9. Do I have limited time for outside interests?   _____   _____
    Action plan: _____
    _____

10. Do my subordinates consistently make recommendations   _____   _____
    to me?
    Action plan: _____
    _____

11. Do my subordinates know specifically the results they   _____   _____
    must achieve?
    Action plan: _____
    _____

12. Are my subordinates consistently qualified for promotion   _____   _____
    when promotions occur?
    Action plan: _____
    _____

13. What tasks have I reserved strictly for myself?   _____   _____
    Action plan: _____
    _____

14. Has authority been clearly defined?   _____   _____
    Action plan: _____
    _____

15. Is the authority in writing?   _____   _____
    Action plan: _____
    _____

16. How much type A or type B authority do my subordinates   _____   _____
    have?
    Action plan: _____
    _____

17. How much type C authority do my subordinates have?   _____   _____
    Action plan: _____
    _____

18. Do my subordinates consistently exercise their authority without checking with me?
Action plan: _____

_____

19. Has authority been tailored to accountability?
Action plan: _____

_____

20. Do my subordinates' questions to me involve details or policy?
Action plan: _____

_____

21. How many times have I overruled my subordinates in the past year?
Action plan: _____

_____

22. How often do I check on my subordinates' work?
Action plan: _____

_____

23. Is all of my checking done overtly?
Action plan: _____

_____

24. Are decisions made at the lowest level at which all information is available?
Action plan: _____

_____

25. Is the development of people a major consideration when I delegate?
   a. Do I really know the strengths and weaknesses of my subordinates?
   b. On what do I base this judgment?
   c. Have I delegated enough to them to justify this judgment?
Action plan: _____

_____

26. Do my subordinates consistently achieve the desired results?
Action plan: _____

_____

27. Do I permit my subordinates to select their own means to agreed-upon ends?
Action plan: _____

_____

28. Do I grant my subordinates the right to be wrong?
Action plan: _____

_____

29. What percentage of my job do I really delegate?   _____ _____
Action plan: _____

_____

30. Would my subordinates agree with the accuracy of this   _____ _____
percentage?
Action plan: _____

_____

31. Could I increase my own productivity and decrease my   _____ _____
supervisory difficulties if I delegated more to my subordinates?
Action plan: _____

_____

Source: Adapted from Dale D. McConkey, *No-Nonsense Delegation,* AMACOM, New York, 1974, pp. 215–220.

Suggestion: Prior to beginning your action plan, ask your subordinates to answer the same questions but from their perception of your supervisory activities.

COMPETENCY REVIEW

1. Define *delegation*.
2. Cite at least six reasons for delegating tasks to subordinates.
3. Identify four reasons supervisors fail to delegate.
4. Describe four categories of tasks that should be delegated.
5. Discuss five techniques leading to effective delegation.
6. Describe the three types of nontraditional delegation.

APPLICATIONS

1. Whose view of delegation do you think was correct in the scenario given at the beginning of this chapter: Marty's or Jan's? Were both of them right? Was neither of them right? Give reasons for your answer as well as reasons for not choosing the other responses.
2. Respond to the following questions regarding delegation. Are you guilty or not guilty of these actions?

	Guilty	*Not* Guilty
I do the job because I fear that my subordinates lack sufficient experience to assume the responsibility.	_____	_____
I believe my subordinates are already overloaded with work.	_____	_____
I perform the tasks out of long-standing habit; it's *my* job, and I simply can't relinquish it.	_____	_____

I believe that no one else is competent to make the required decisions.   _____ _____

I feel it will take so long to explain the work and monitor the performance that it is not worth the effort.   _____ _____

I keep intending to turn the work over "one of these days," but that day never seems to come.   _____ _____

I believe that delegating the task will add to the danger of error or misjudgment, and I am unwilling to take the chance.   _____ _____

The work in question is too important for anyone else to do.   _____ _____

I am unable to pinpoint a subordinate who is willing to take on the added responsibility.   _____ _____

I enjoy the particular task too much to relinquish it.   _____ _____

Delegating the work would require revealing more information about the operation than I care to reveal.   _____ _____

Sometimes I feel that my security is threatened when I delegate too much.   _____ _____

Source: Ken Allen, *What an Executive Should Know About Managing Time Profitably,* A Dartnell Human Resources Development Program, 1981, p. 10.

3. For each of the items above that you checked "guilty," devise an action plan or strategy to overcome the problem. Use a form similar to the following for each "guilty."

Guilty of: _____

Strategy: _____

4. For the job you currently hold or for a job you previously held, use the levels-of-delegation continuum shown on page 150 to identify the level of delegation used by your supervisor. Cite specific incidents to support your decision that your supervisor operated on that level of delegation. Why do you think your supervisor operates or operated at that level?

CASES

Case I: To Delegate or Not to Delegate—That Is the Question!

Joan Brennan was just promoted to a supervisory position. The promotion became effective when her superior was out of town. Due to the illness of one of Joan's subordinates, the work schedule was not being met. She decided to pitch in and help, spending about 4 hours daily in production.

When Joan's superior returns to work, Joan is not available. He is upset and tells Joan that it is the function of the supervisor to accomplish work with and through other people, not to do it herself.

1. What was the initial problem in this case?
2. Of the alternatives given below, which would you select to solve future problems when workers are not available?
    a. Let the scheduled work be late, and catch up when the worker returns.
    b. Lend a hand, as Joan did in this case.
    c. Prepare backup for emergencies.
    d. Work out an acceptable compromise with the superior.
3. Evaluate each of the alternatives in terms of their advantages and disadvantages to the company, to the workers, to Joan.
4. Develop implementation procedures for the alternative you selected.

Case II: Why Should I Do Your Dirty Work?

Supervisors must assign and oversee work done by others. Sometimes the work is routine or tedious, such as cataloging new parts, implementing a new filing system, or ordering supplies.

Marty, our supervisor at the beginning of this chapter, would like to delegate to Jan responsibility for keeping track of supplies and ordering new supplies. The following conversation takes place when Marty tries to make that assignment:

MARTY   Jan, from now on, I want you to inventory supplies and set up a regular time to order new supplies.

JAN   But that's a boring job. Who's been doing it up to now?

MARTY   I have, but it's time somebody else took over. So it's your turn in the bucket.

1. How effectively did Marty handle the delegation?
2. What would you suggest that Marty do differently when he delegates work?
3. Write a role-playing skit in which Marty handles the delegation more effectively.

REFERENCES

1. J. C. Penney, *What an Executive Should Know About Success,* A Dartnell Human Resources Development Program, 1980, p. 14.
2. Ibid. p. 15.

3. Dale D. McConkey, *No-Nonsense Delegation,* AMACOM, New York, 1974, pp. 90–100.

4. William Oncken and Donald L. Wass, "Getting Those Monkeys off Your Back," *Management World,* October 1980, pp. 22–25.

SUGGESTED READINGS

Baldwin, Bruce A: "The Dynamics of Delegation," *Pace Magazine, Piedmont Airlines, Inflight Magazine,* June 1985.

Harrison, James C., Jr: "How to Stay on Top of the Job," *Harvard Business Review,* November–December 1961.

Major, Michael: "Delegating Authority Without Losing Control," *Today's Office,* October 1984.

7

MANAGING THE PHYSICAL ENVIRONMENT

7

MANAGING THE PHYSICAL ENVIRONMENT

COMPETENCIES

After studying this chapter, you will be able to:

1. Discuss the factors that have influenced management's concern about employee safety and health.

2. Discuss top management's role in safety and health programs.

3. Discuss elements of the work environment that may cause accidents.

4. State ways through which the supervisor can develop safety awareness among workers.

5. Explain the importance of observation and inspection in maintaining safety.

6. Discuss the supervisor's role in investigating and reporting accidents.

7. Define methods of measuring worker safety.

8. Discuss current health issues in the physical environment.

CHAPTER OUTLINE

Peg Sutton watched the ambulance carrying Julio Rivera, a stock clerk, pull out and head for the hospital.

"Poor Julio," she said. "His vacation is scheduled to start next week." Then, turning to the five stock clerks who had gathered, she said, "OK, back to the scene of the accident, everybody. We need the facts for the accident report."

On the way back to the produce section, she thought about the accident. She had been a produce supervisor for this giant supermarket chain for 3 years and had recently been chosen over several other candidates for the job in the big new showplace store.

"Two accidents in the first month," she thought. "My safety record is shot. All that training . . . all the pep talks . . . all the work with the union rep to develop safety procedures. And for what? How could Julio slip on a grape and trigger a bone-breaking avalanche of coconuts on his hand? And why in my department?" She mentally ran through the version of the accident she had heard from Sean Bailey, an assistant supervisor, while they waited for the ambulance. Julio had pushed the loaded cart from cold storage to produce at his usual fast clip. To save a trip, he had placed a crate of coconuts on the back of the loaded wagon, partly resting on the handlebars. As he turned the corner at produce, his foot found the grape. As he fell, one of his feet hit the cart, bumping it into the display case. The impact sent the coconuts crashing to the floor onto Julio's hand and foot. That was it, as she recalled it.

On the way back, she picked up her accident report form. Back at produce, she stepped over the rope blocking the area off from customer traffic.

"OK, Sean, you were in charge here when Julio fell. Let's hear again what happened."

Sutton's concern illustrates a major problem facing every manager today. How does a firm provide a safe physical environment for its employees at a reasonable cost? While there are some legislated guidelines, organizations answer the question in a variety of ways.

This chapter will focus on the guidelines and some of the methods of promoting safety and health in the workplace. It will examine the role the supervisor plays in the company's safety program. Finally, it will give an overview of some of the current safety and health issues in the workplace.

EMPLOYEE SAFETY AND HEALTH

A primary goal of an organization's safety and health program is to provide for the well-being of those in the work environment. This responsibility has greatly increased in scope and complexity over the years. Many factors have had an impact on management's concern about worker safety and health.

Factors Influencing Management's Concern

Management concern for employee well-being is still evolving. Many factors have influenced the change from a time when the entire emphasis was on production efficiency, with only a minimal regard for employee safety, to the present time, when some firms provide health programs that are well beyond what is required of them. Let's look at some of the major factors.

Humanitarian and Social Concerns

Sutton's first thought was for Rivera and his vacation. This concern was for Rivera as a person, not as a worker. It is difficult to imagine any manager who would deliberately undermine the safety of the firm's workers. Rational people in a civilized world do not like to see a fellow human injured or killed. Translated to the workplace, this humanitarian concern motivates managers to take reasonable action to provide a safe environment for workers.

Carried further, this humanitarian concern influences the social concern of the business. Though there are differing opinions about the degree of social responsibility, it is recognized today that businesses must do more than simply make a profit. The activities a business performs affect its workers as people and, therefore, affect the whole society. The ethical framework in which management makes its decisions is as applicable to the firm's employee relations as it is to its marketing strategies. (See the ethical checklist in Chapter 4.) Businesses have some responsibility for taking into consideration the effects on society as they plan and operate their organizations. Whatever the degree of social responsibility they assume, effective firms today recognize that the workers are their greatest resource and give employee safety and health a high priority in their planning.

Costs

Even in the unlikely absence of humanitarian and social concern, the costs to the firm of job-related accidents and illnesses would force today's managers to plan a safe workplace. These costs are enormous and rising. While safety statistics differ, research reports invariably show staggering costs. The National Safety Council reported that 75 million days were lost in 1986 due to job-related accidents that occurred in that year and before. The council further projected that another 100 million days would be lost in future years as a result of job-related accidents that occurred in 1986 and that this would cost firms an estimated \$34.8 billion.[2] The costs in related human suffering is incalculable.

Among the many costs for the firm are production stoppage or slowdown; damaged equipment, products, supplies, and materials; medical and insurance costs; and worker replacement costs. Intangible costs, which eventually translate into dollar costs, include worker morale and motivation, public image, and recruitment ability. There are also hidden costs, such as dispensary services, which are sometimes not directly assigned by a firm to a particular accident or illness.

Cost analysis is important. Without cost data, management would be unable even to estimate the savings realized through accident control. As a supervisor, you will be involved in this cost analysis. As you will read later in this chapter, one of your functions in the safety program will be investigating and reporting accidents. To gather cost data, you may be asked to report on a form like that in Figure 7-1. Examine the form; note that the questions include the hidden costs of an accident.

For example, when Rivera had his accident, five clerks stood around with the supervisor as the ambulance took off. Suppose their wages averaged \$8/hour. If they were away from their jobs for 20 minutes, their ''watching time'' cost the company \$13.33; add to this their lost productivity and, possibly, lost sales, and you will see a substantial drain on profit. You will report other financial cost data on other forms, some required by legislation.

Legislation

Perhaps the greatest influence on management's concern for safety and health has been legislation. Federal, state, and local governments have, over the years, passed many laws directed toward improving worker safety and health.

Perhaps the most significant state laws were the worker compensation laws. All 50 states now require organizations to pay workers' compensation insurance premiums. This insurance protects workers from loss of income and from other costs related to occupational injuries.

Various federal labor laws, such as the Walsh-Healy Act of 1936, incorporated safety provisions. That act prohibited companies involved in government contracts from placing workers in unsanitary or unsafe working conditions to perform their contract work.

Among other federal laws concerned with worker health are those affecting a particular industry, such as the Coal Mine Health and Safety Act of 1969, later broadened to the Federal Mine Safety and Health Act of 1977. These laws were aimed at reducing the risks of dust inhalation, said to cause black-lung disease; explosions; structure or ceiling collapse; and improper ventilation. The act established standards for inspections and emergency procedures.

In 1970, Congress passed the Occupational Safety and Health Act which went into effect in April 1971. It supersedes several safety and health acts, such as Walsh-Healy, that are administered by the U.S. Department of Labor.[3] Because this act is the most significant and pervasive legislation on safety and health yet passed, its major

FIGURE 7-1 Department supervisor's accident cost report

DEPARTMENT SUPERVISOR'S ACCIDENT COST INVESTIGATION REPORT

Injury/Accident _____

Date _____ Name of Injured _____ Dept. _____

	Time Lost

1. How much time did other employees lose by talking, watching, or helping at accident? Number of employees _____ x hours =

2. How much productive time was lost because of damaged equipment or loss or reduced output by injured worker?
   Estimate hours =

3. How much time did injured employee lose for which he was paid on the day of the injury?   Estimate hours =

4. Will overtime be necessary?   Estimate hours =

5. How much of the supervisor's or other management's time was lost as a result of this accident?
   Estimate hours =

6. Were additional costs incurred due to hiring and training or replacement?
   Training time estimate hours =

7. Describe the damage to material or equipment. _____
_____

8. If machine and/or operations were idle, can loss of production be made up?
   Yes _____ No _____

9. Will overtime be necessary?   Yes _____ No _____

10. Any demurrage or other cost involved?   Yes _____ No _____

ADDITIONAL ACCIDENT COSTS
To compute the total costs of this accident, it is necessary to complete the following costs. Should the supervisor have access to this information it is advised he complete as much as possible. Safety Department will develop those costs not known by supervisor.

11. Estimate of demurrage or other costs. $

12. Costs associated with giving medical attention, first-aid, ambulance costs, etc. $

13. Workers compensation costs. $

14. Hospital medical costs. $

15. Costs associated with placing injured on other work when unable to perform regular work. $

16. Costs associated with questions 1 through 6.
    16-1 $
    16-2 $
    16-3 $
    16-4 $
    16-5 $
    16-6 $ _____

17. Company dollars lost on accident: TOTAL $

Source: Reprinted with permission from the National Safety Council: *Accident Prevention Manual for Industrial Operations,* 9th ed., National Safety Council, Chicago, 1988, pp. 160–161.

features will be discussed here. Some of your activities as a supervisor that relate to this act will be presented later in this chapter.

Purposes.   Under provisions of this act, the Occupational Safety and Health Administration (OSHA) was created within the U.S. Department of Labor to:[4]

- encourage employers and employees to reduce workplace hazards and to implement new or improve existing safety and health programs.
- provide for research in occupational safety and health.
- establish ''separate but dependent responsibilities and rights'' for employers and employees.
- maintain a reporting and recordkeeping system.
- establish training programs.
- develop and enforce job safety and health standards.
- provide for the development, analysis, evaluation, and approval of state occupational safety and health programs.

While OSHA continually reviews and redefines specific standards and practices, its basic purposes remain constant.

Administration.   OSHA is administered out of the U.S. Department of Labor. There are 10 regional offices. The agency's function is to establish and enforce occupational safety and health standards. This function is carried out through workplace inspections; citations for infractions and resultant penalties, where appropriate; data collection and analysis; consultation services; and training programs.

The act encourages states to develop and operate, under OSHA guidance, state job safety and health plans. Once OSHA certifies a state plan, OSHA funds up to 50 percent of the program's costs and relinquishes authority to the states in areas over which the states have jurisdiction.

Rights and Responsibilities.   Employers and employees have certain rights and responsibilities under the act. These rights and responsibilities are shown in Figure 7-2 on pages 175 and 176. Employer rights and responsibilities in states that have their own programs generally conform to the federal list.[5]

The Occupational Safety and Health Act and other legislation have focused management attention on safety and health in the workplace. Labor unions have played no small part in that focus.

Labor Unions

For most of their history, unions have bargained for better working conditions along with higher wages. The Bureau of National Affairs reported from a recent study that 87 percent of union contracts in manufacturing firms include safety and health features.

In all of the rubber and mining industries' contracts, there are clauses on equipment safety. In addition, 45 percent of union contracts provide for union representation on management safety committees.[6]

Unions have begun to focus on safety and health matters beyond the immediate work station. Some unions have employed industrial health specialists to monitor the work environment and to identify health hazards. For example, the Teamsters Union hired a nationally known health expert to investigate unexplained illnesses at the Robert Shaw Controls Company plant in Ohio.[7] Other unions have bargained for company financial assistance for research to improve worker safety and health. The AFL-CIO has established its own department of occupational safety and health to work with industry in identifying safety problems and reducing industrial accidents and personal injuries.[8] It is no wonder their actions have influenced management's concern for safety and health.

Media Reporting

Safety and health issues and events are much in the news. You've read the headlines: Three Mile Island . . . Hotel Walkover Collapses . . . 17 Die in Mine Explosion . . . Asbestos Removal Demanded . . . Bhopal . . . Nearly Complete Condo Collapses . . . Chernobyl Pollution Continues.

The human suffering and economic costs of these tragedies are vividly related to us by the media almost as they happen. In addition, environmentalists and other advocacy groups exert a great deal of pressure on government to gather data and disseminate information on safety and health. As a result, we are better educated than we have ever been about safety and health, not only in the workplace but in the total environment. This widespread public awareness tends to be translated into pressure on our government and on businesses to provide a safer and more healthful environment in which to live and work. Management concern about safety and health has been heightened by these pressures.

Employee Attitudes

Management concern about health and safety has been influenced by the employees themselves. Employees range from the activist, who may neglect the job in his or her zeal to promote environmental safety, to the apathetic worker, who completely ignores safety rules and procedures. Both types present a challenge. Unless workers can be motivated to cooperate, even the best efforts to promote safety and health or the most careful OSHA inspections or even citations and penalties won't do much to improve worker safety and health.

Economic Conditions

A final factor that has influenced management concern for safety and health is economic conditions. Management typically wants to provide safe working conditions

FIGURE 7-2 Employer and employee rights and responsibilities—OSHA

Employer Rights

- Seek advice and off-site consultation as needed by writing, calling or visiting the nearest OSHA office. (OSHA will not inspect merely because an employer requests assistance.)
- Be active in your industry association's involvement in job safety and health.
- Request and receive proper identification of the OSHA compliance officer prior to inspection.
- Be advised by the compliance officer of the reason for an inspection.
- Have an opening and closing conference with the compliance officer.
- File a Notice of Contest with the OSHA area director within 15 working days of receipt of a notice of citation and proposed penalty.
- Apply to OSHA for a temporary variance from a standard if unable to comply because of the unavailability of materials, equipment or personnel needed to make necessary changes within the required time.
- Apply to OSHA for a permanent variance from a standard if you can furnish proof that your facilities or method of operation provide[s] employee protection at least as effective as that required by the standard.
- Take an active role in developing safety and health standards through participation in OSHA Standards Advisory Committees, through nationally recognized standards-setting organizations and through evidence and views presented in writing or at hearings.
- Be assured of the confidentiality of any trade secrets observed by an OSHA compliance officer during an inspection.
- Submit a written request to NIOSH for information on whether any substance in your workplace has potentially toxic effects in the concentrations being used.

Employer Responsibilities

- Provide medical examinations when required by OSHA standards.
- Report to the nearest OSHA office within 48 hours any fatal accident or one which results in the hospitalization of five or more employees.
- Keep OSHA-required records of work-related injuries and illnesses, and post a copy of the totals from the last page of OSHA No. 200 during the entire month of February each year. (This applies to employers with 11 or more employees.)
- Post, at a prominent location within the workplace, the OSHA poster informing employees of their rights and responsibilities.
- Provide employees, former employees and their representatives access to the Log and Summary of Occupational Injuries and Illnesses at a reasonable time and in a reasonable manner.
- Cooperate with the OSHA compliance officer by furnishing names of authorized employee representatives who may be asked to accompany the compliance officer during an inspection.
- [Do n]ot discriminate against employees who properly exercise their rights under the Act.
- Post OSHA citations at or near the worksite involved. Each citation, or copy thereof, must remain posted until the violation has been abated, or for three working days, whichever is longer.
- Abate cited violations within the prescribed period.
- Meet your general duty responsibility to provide a workplace free from recognized hazards that are causing or are likely to cause death or serious physical harm to employees, and comply with standards, rules and regulations issued under the Act.
- Be familiar with mandatory OSHA standards and make copies available to employees for review upon request.
- Inform all employees about OSHA.
- Examine workplace conditions to make sure they conform to applicable standards.
- Minimize or reduce hazards.
- Make sure employees have and use safe tools and equipment (including appropriate personal protective equipment), and that such equipment is properly maintained.
- Use color codes, posters, labels or signs when needed to warn employees of potential hazards.
- Establish or update operating procedures and communicate them so that employees follow safety and health requirements.

FIGURE 7-2   (Continued)

Employee Rights

Employees have a right to seek safety and health on the job without fear of punishment. That right is spelled out in Section 11(c) of the Act.

The law says employers shall not punish or discriminate against workers for exercising rights such as:

- Complaining to an employer, union, OSHA or any other government agency about job safety and health hazards;
- Filing safety or health grievances;
- Participating on a workplace safety and health committee or in union activities concerning job safety and health;
- Participating in OSHA inspections, conferences, hearings or other OSHA-related activities.

Other Rights

- Review copies of appropriate OSHA standards, rules, regulations and requirements that the employer should have available at the workplace.
- Request information from your employer on safety and health hazards in the area, on precautions that may be taken, and on procedures to be followed if an employee is involved in an accident or is exposed to toxic substances.
- Request the OSHA area director to conduct an inspection if you believe hazardous conditions or violations of standards exist in your workplace.
- Have your name withheld from your employer, upon request to OSHA, if you file a written and signed complaint.

- Be advised of OSHA actions regarding your complaint and have an informal review, if requested, of any decision not to inspect or to issue a citation.
- Have your authorized employee representative accompany the OSHA compliance officer during the inspection tour.
- Respond to questions from the OSHA compliance officer, particularly if there is no authorized employee representative accompanying the compliance officer.
- Observe any monitoring or measuring of hazardous materials and have the right to see these records, as specified under the Act.
- Have your authorized representative, or yourself, review the Log and Summary of Occupational Injuries at a reasonable time and in a reasonable manner.
- Request a closing discussion with the compliance officer following an inspection.
- Submit a written request to NIOSH for information on whether any substance in your workplace has potentially toxic effects in the concentration being used, and have your name withheld from your employer if you so request.

Employee Responsibilities

- Read the OSHA poster at the job site.
- Comply with all applicable OSHA standards.
- Follow all employer safety and health rules and regulations, and wear or use prescribed protective equipment while engaged in work.
- Report hazardous conditions to the supervisor.

- Report any job-related injury or illness to the employer, and seek treatment promptly.
- Cooperate with the OSHA compliance officer conducting an inspection if he or she inquires about safety and health conditions in your workplace.
- Exercise your rights under the Act in a responsible manner.

Source: *All About OSHA,* U.S. Department of Labor.

Competency
Check:

Can you discuss
the factors that
have influenced
management's
concern about
employee safety and
health?

for their employees. But there are products, substances, and working conditions for which the effects are not known or are not completely known. As knowledge becomes available, economic conditions may preclude management from providing the conditions it would choose to provide. Asbestos, for example, was once widely used for insulation and in construction. When it proved to be harmful, the economic costs associated with the change to other materials put some firms out of business. Other substances known to be hazardous have been costly to control in the workplace; x-ray technology, atomic energy, and uranium mining are examples.

Economic conditions play a role in all the functions of management, not only in providing for employee safety and health. As they do in implementing any company-wide policy, top management must take the leadership in setting the climate for acceptance of the safety and health program.

WHAT CAN THE SUPERVISOR DO?

Remember, you are a manager, too. You will also be feeling the pressure from the factors presented above. In some cases, the pressure may be more acute at your level than it is at the top. You might start by upgrading your own understanding of safety and health. You have taken the first step by enrolling in this course. Check out local sources for help. If you have a personnel director and a safety specialist, talk with them. Learn about the training programs offered through the OSHA Training Institute. For information, write to the institute at the U.S. Department of Labor, 1555 Times Drive, Des Plaines, Ill. 60018. Or check with your regional or the federal office of OSHA.

Learn the rights and responsibilities of both the employer and the employee as shown in Figure 7-2. In situations in which more knowledgeable employees try to assert their rights on safety matters, you not only will not be caught by surprise, you probably will have addressed a potential problem before employees call it to your attention.

Get acquainted with the *Federal Register* and other publications that report on safety standards and regulations. OSHA standards and revisions are reported in the *Register*. You can, if you wish to and have the time, read the original standards there, but be prepared to spend some time reading very small print in a voluminous document. Most managers wait for OSHA's interpretation, but knowing where official standards are printed should be a part of your knowledge base. Your human resources/personnel department may receive the *Register* by subscription and thus help you keep in touch with what is happening in OSHA regulations. There are many standards; be prepared to be patient! Some people feel that OSHA goes overboard with standards, as illustrated in the cartoon.

Other organizations publish summaries and updates on safety matters. Two such organizations are the National Safety Council, which publishes *Accident Facts* annually, and the Commerce Clearing House, which publishes a biweekly bulletin called *Human Resources Management Ideas and Trends in Personnel*.

Source: NEA, Inc., © 1978, reprinted by permission of NEA.

Creating the Corporate Climate for Safety and Health

The climate of an organization is reflected in the behavior of its members. The climate is a mirror image of morale. A good climate can produce vigor, enthusiasm, a co-operative spirit, and a supportive "family" feeling. A bad climate can result in a dull, lackadaisical, uncooperative, even apathetic organization. Whatever the climate, it is set by top management.

Top Management's Commitment

"You can't fill a bottle from the bottom" is an adage that can be applied to organizational behavior. Think of filling a glass bottle. You pour liquid into the top. The liquid flows down, through every level of the bottle, to the bottom. Then the bottle begins to fill up solidly, the liquid filling all the space back up to the top. Managers who wish to change the safety behavior of their employees should remember the bottle analogy.

Top managers must have a personal commitment to improve employee safety and health and must include that commitment in the organization's mission and objectives. Moreover, the commitment cannot be just lip service. Top management must show, by its actions as well as its words, that it believes in employee safety and health, that it will implement a program and personally participate in it, and that it will hold every member of the organization responsible for participating in the program.

The commitment must also be sustained. Consider the top manager who approves a program and then responds to a request for funds in the following way: "Of course I believe in safety. But we don't have any money for such things as training and posters. Tell the supervisors to find a way to enforce the safety rules—that's what will improve our shop safety." Workers will take such a short-term commitment as a sign that top management isn't really concerned about safety. Sustained commitment requires allocation of resources to carry out the objectives.

Assigning Responsibility and Resources

The test of top management's commitment to any program is whether it allocates resources adequate to carry out the program. People resources are first. Who will be responsible for carrying out the tasks? The person who is to be held responsible must also have the authority needed to make decisions and take action. A supervisor who is responsible for the safety environment of a team of joggers' headset assemblers shouldn't be required to have four superiors sign off for a fluorescent light to replace one that is flickering over the work stations and causing visual discomfort for the work group. As you learned in Chapter 5, authority and responsibility must be equal.

The level of the resources assigned to safety and health will depend on the size, nature, and complexity of the firm.

In a small retail shoe store, for example, safety would probably be handled by the manager. Larger firms may have personnel departments, which may be responsible for coordinating the safety program with line managers. A safety specialist may be employed. Some firms may have a separate department of safety and health.

A chemical, mining, or energy firm would necessarily have a more complex safety and health program than would an insurance firm. Think of the specialized safety personnel needed by Monsanto Chemical Corporation, Homestake Mining, or the Surry Atomic Energy plant.

OSHA has a significant impact on the level of resources assigned to safety programs. Management must know the standards applicable to its specific firms in order to determine the resources needed for compliance. Firms that go beyond minimal OSHA standards will need to assign resources adequate to conduct their programs effectively. Some firms take an ergonomic approach, encompassing the total environment in planning for the safety and health of their workers.

Taking an Ergonomic Approach

Top management decides the extent of company involvement in safety and health. For some, that means taking an ergonomic approach. *Ergonomics* is a science that tries to design the work, the workplace, and the tools to fit the worker. Ergonomics goes beyond safety in the physical environment, taking into consideration technological, psychological, and aesthetic factors, as well.

Reynolds Metals Company includes selection of workers as part of its ergonomic approach to safety and health. The firm uses "ergonomic testing" as part of its screening process for industrial workers. Administered by the firm's medical department, the objective of the testing is to identify workers who are physically and psychologically able to meet the physical-stress demands of the job.[9] (The psychological environment will be treated in Chapter 13.)

Some firms take an ergonomic approach to improving the work environment because the approach has been shown to improve the quality of work life, thus resulting in improved worker motivation and productivity. Therefore, taking the ergonomic approach to environmental planning in the workplace is not altruistic alone. As G. Gordon Long of Rhone-Poulenc, Inc., points out, "ergonomics can show the way to efficiency and productivity."[10] He describes four factors—utilities, lighting, acoustics, and furnishings—to be considered in the ergonomic planning of an office. Note in the following summary of the four factors the safety and health implications for the workers.

Utilities.   A properly balanced heating and cooling system, providing a properly maintained air environment, promotes higher productivity, better work quality, improved morale, and a lower rate of absenteeism.

Lighting.   Since vision is improved when light is directed toward the actual work surface—such as a desk—the majority of light should be used where it is most needed. This concept of task-ambient lighting should take into consideration problems such as glare, the technical factors involved in fluorescent lighting and computer terminals, and possible eyestrain as workers move from one degree of lighting to another. Color is also related to proper lighting.

Acoustics.   The characteristics of sound—pitch, intensity, quality, and reverberation—must be taken into consideration in designing the work environment. Selecting quieter machines, using sound shields for equipment and sound-absorbing materials for room surfaces, providing proper maintenance, and adding controlled music are techniques for managing the acoustical environment.

Furnishings.   The work-station design, the type and comfort of the furniture, and the relationship between the employee and the equipment should be reviewed in selecting furnishings. *Anthropometrics,* the study of human body dimensions and physical capabilities, such as seating and standing heights and reaching and viewing levels, is fundamental in the selection of furnishings in an ergonomic environment.[11]

An example of an ergonomically designed chair is shown in Figure 7-3 on page 182. It is designed to adjust to the user and to the function the user performs. The computer has been described by many workers who use it all day as "one big pain in the neck." A computer operator's ergonomic chair is designed to alleviate the neck and back stress that often results from long periods of sitting at a terminal. In addition, the chair adapts to workers of different sizes, making it a cost-effective way to provide for individual differences on the job. For example, the same chair might accommodate a 5-ft 2-in woman on the day shift and a 6-ft 3-in man on the night shift.

As a supervisor, you will not be expected to be an ergonomist, but knowledge of the science will make you more alert to stress points in the workplace. You will also be better prepared to suggest improvements in the physical environment to increase worker safety and health. Your more direct responsibilities will be presented in the next section.

Competency Check:

Can you discuss top management's role in safety and health programs?

THE SUPERVISOR'S ROLE IN MANAGING THE PHYSICAL ENVIRONMENT

You are the key person in a safety and health program because you are right there, where most occupational accidents happen. What are your functions? If you learn the six responsibilities presented here, you will be well on your way to becoming an effective safety supervisor.

FIGURE 7-3 What an ergonomic chair does

WHAT AN ERGONOMIC CHAIR DOES

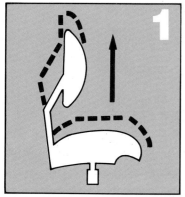

CHAIR HEIGHT
Instant fingertip
pneumatic adjustment

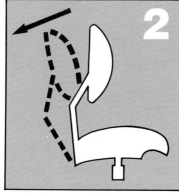

FLOATING BACKREST
Floats pneumatically
as you move

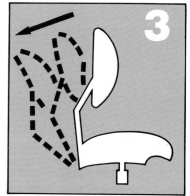

BACKREST POSITION
Lock your backrest
at any position you want

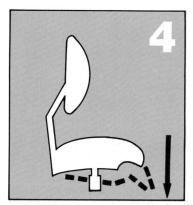

FULL SEAT TILT
Seat pivots 8°
downward at front

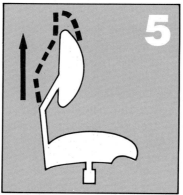

BACKREST HEIGHT
Raise or lower
backrest while seated

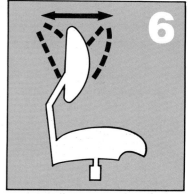

FLEXIBLE BACKREST
Backrest flexes
as you move

Implementing Company Policy

Supervisors carry out company policies at the operational level. That is their main function. Do you know what the company safety and health policies are? The manager to whom you report should provide you with this information and cooperatively develop or approve your plans for administering the policies. You may also need to liaise with the personnel manager or the company's safety specialist.

Company policies should be in writing, but sometimes they are communicated only verbally or in the actions of superiors. If that is the case in your firm, you may have to do a bit of research to find out what is expected of you. Unless you, as the key person, promote safety among the workers, the company might as well forget the safety program.

A safety consultant, Dan Petersen, suggests that supervisors assess where they are now in terms of safety and health by taking the quiz shown in Figure 7-4. It helps to show where the supervisor needs to be headed in safety management. Try it; then check your score with the scoring system at the end of this chapter.

Understanding Causes of Accidents

An old adage tells us, ''An ounce of prevention is better than a pound of cure.'' Prevention should be the primary thrust of safety and health programs. To promote prevention, you must be aware of what causes accidents and whether these causes are present in your workplace.

There are differing approaches to the prevention of accidents. Too often, the approach is far too simple. If a worker receives an electric shock when using a defective drill, for example, we might look simply at (1) the unsafe act, which was using the defective drill, and (2) the unsafe condition (the defective drill). In this case, we would simply repair or discard the defective drill.

If we explored the event further, however, we might begin to ask questions such as:

- Why was the defective drill not found in inspection?
- Why did the supervisor allow its use?
- Did the employee know he or she should not use the drill?
- Was the injured employee properly trained?
- Was the injured employee reminded of the hazard?
- Did the supervisor examine the job before the event?

Looking at the accident from this perspective, we find that there may be a number of root causes, among them poor inspection, procedures, or training; ill-defined responsibilities; poor job planning by supervisors; or poor equipment maintenance.[12] Note that these causes are all related to management.

Another way to look at causes is to look at the three elements in the work environment: people, products, and processes.

People.   Are the workers properly selected, trained, motivated, and supervised? Do some workers seem to be accident-prone? Are they careless? Do they take unnecessary chances? Do they use the prescribed protective garments and equipment? Is the supervisor (people, too!) properly selected, trained, and motivated? Does the supervisor use effective controls?

Products.   Does the product contain hazardous materials such as toxic chemicals or explosives? Does its use involve hazardous procedures (detonation, high-voltage current, testing of cars or planes)?

FIGURE 7-4   Where are you now in safety?

When you begin your job as supervisor, you might want to take stock of where you stand in safety. These 15 questions will direct your thinking. Choose for each question the answer that best describes your situation. (Scoring suggestions appear at the end of this chapter.)

1. Do I have a job description that indicates precisely what I am to do in regard to safety?
   (a) No
   (b) I have a job description, but it doesn't mention safety.
   (c) Yes
2. Do I know exactly how much authority I have in safety?
   (a) No
   (b) Yes
   (c) I've discussed it with my boss, and we've reached some decisions.
3. Do I know exactly how I'm going to be measured in safety?
   (a) No
   (b) Yes
   (c) I've discussed it with my boss, and we've come to some agreements.
4. Do I know exactly what I am expected to do in safety?
   (a) No
   (b) All that counts are results—no accidents.
   (c) Yes
5. Do I know what is considered acceptable performance in safety?
   (a) No
   (b) No accidents, I guess.
   (c) Yes
6. How much time do I spend on safety?
   (a) No time
   (b) It's a constant job.
   (c) A few hours a week
7. Have I read the Federal Register?
   (a) What's a Federal Register?
   (b) Yes
   (c) Those sections that apply to me.

8. Have I made a list of all violations of the law in my area?
   (a) No
   (b) Once
   (c) Regularly
9. Have I set up a system of priorities?
   (a) No
   (b) Yes
   (c) Yes. It's in operation.
10. Have I kept my boss aware of my status in OSHA compliance?
    (a) Heaven forbid.
    (b) Once I did.
    (c) Regularly
11. Have I documented everything I've done in safety and in OSHA preparation?
    (a) No
    (b) In part
    (c) Yes
12. Do I know what turns my people off?
    (a) Who cares?
    (b) Everything, I think.
    (c) Yes, I know.
13. Do I know what turns them on?
    (a) Who cares?
    (b) Nothing
    (c) Yes, I know.
14. Do I know when to use discipline?
    (a) Always
    (b) Never
    (c) Yes, I know.
15. Do I know how to work with problem people?
    (a) The same way as with anyone else.
    (b) No, I don't.
    (c) Yes, I do.

Source: Dan Petersen, *Safety Supervision,* AMACOM, New York, 1976, pp. 2–3.

Processes. Does the manufacturing process include potentially hazardous steps such as mixing minerals or chemicals; sequencing electronic or electrical components; applying extreme heat, as in smelting; construction; or lifting? Does the process involve the use of equipment? (Any equipment is potentially dangerous if improperly maintained or used.) Does the process generate waste that is potentially hazardous (fumes, particles that can be inhaled or absorbed into the skin, water or liquids that can burn or cause slippery floors)?

Accidents happen in all kinds of businesses, but statistics show that the accident potential is greater in some industries than in others. The U.S. Department of Labor shows that in 1984, the accident rate was greatest in construction, with 6.9 injuries or illnesses resulting in lost workdays per 100 full-time employees.[13] Workers need to be made aware of potential dangers and encouraged to take safety precautions.

Competency Check:

Can you discuss the elements in the work environment that might cause accidents?

Developing Safety Awareness

Understanding the causes of accidents will better prepare you to develop safety awareness among your workers. A work force with safety awareness will have fewer accidents because the workers will be more likely to practice safe work habits and avoid potentially dangerous behavior. But how do you develop awareness?

The first step is proper training (see Chapter 10). Each new employee must be thoroughly trained in the company's safety policy and procedures, including, especially, procedures for performing his or her job safely. Experienced employees need refresher courses and information on new products, processes, and equipment. The training should emphasize prevention. Adopting a safety slogan (selected by the workers!) may create interest and keep the training alive. Remember that slogans can become boring, so unless it is a company tradition, you might want to change it periodically.

The second step is making the workers' jobs more interesting. It is generally agreed that workers whose jobs are satisfying, who feel ''in on things,'' and who have some decision-making authority over their jobs are better motivated. Motivated workers are less prone to the negative behavior that leads to accidents. Consider job design that you studied in Chapter 5 as an approach to making jobs more interesting: add task variety, let workers perform the whole job rather than parts of it, make the job significant to others, and give feedback on performance of the job.

The third step is using safety committees. These committees provide worker involvement. This participation will develop the committee members' awareness, which through them will spread to their peers. The following activities have been suggested for safety committees:[14]

- Make regular inspections of the work areas.
- Sponsor accident-prevention contests.
- Help prepare safety rules.
- Promote safety awareness.
- Review safety suggestions from employees.

- Supervise the preparation and distribution of safety materials.
- Make fire-prevention inspections.
- Supervise first-aid equipment maintenance.

Competency Check:

Can you state the ways through which the supervisor can develop worker safety awareness?

Some firms display "accident-free days" signs on the premises. Safety committees often use this as a project. The sign might read: "Koling Steel Works—204 accident-free days." Other signs might be posted on bulletin boards or in the work area. The board might feature awards for safety records, including a photo of the workers who won the awards. Safety committees might maintain the bulletin boards.

Developing and maintaining safety awareness among workers will be a continuing challenge. Figure 7-5 shows activities for developing good safety attitudes through four steps of attitude formation.

Observing and Inspecting

Observing is an informal way to keep informed about safety practices and conditions. As you do your routine "walk-around" supervision, you should be alert to safety and health conditions that may need attention. Unsafe conditions found through observation should be corrected immediately. Quick response may not only prevent an accident, but also confirm for the workers your sincerity about safety. If Sutton in the beginning of this chapter had been observing before Rivera's accident, she could have had someone pick up the grape—or she could have picked it up herself. Of course, no place can be made 100 percent safe. But the supervisor's job is to reduce risk to a minimum consistent with human ability and company resources.

Another point to remember is that you have many other responsibilities and you can't watch workers all the time even if it were desirable. Instead, try to instill in the workers the feeling that each is a "safety specialist." Make observing part of their routine. Do you see any implications here for Rivera? Routine observation by workers will augment observation by the supervisor; together, they will fill in the gaps between inspections.

Safety inspections are usually a more formal way to maintain safe working conditions. Inspections have several objectives:

- to compare results to plans
- to evaluate and improve safety standards
- to note and correct unsafe worker behavior
- to note and correct unsafe equipment or procedures
- to check out new facilities, equipment, processes, and materials
- to spot training needs
- to gather safety data
- to reinforce interest in safety

A newer approach to observation and inspection is monitoring through video terminals called Computerized Supervision Systems (CSS). Taking advantage of the networking of computer terminals, CSS allows supervisors to monitor employees who use computer terminals in their jobs or operate sophisticated machine tools.[15]

FIGURE 7-5

Activities for
developing good
safety attitudes

FOUR STEPS IN ATTITUDE FORMATION	TYPICAL SAFETY ACTIVITIES TO USE
Step I Laying the foundation for the attitude	*Mass Media* Safety slogans, safety posters, safety talks. Motion pictures and sound strip films of general safety nature. Training classes and demonstrations for groups on job methods and theory. Company safety policies. Safety contests and competitions of a group or company nature.
Step II Personalizing the attitude for the individual	*Learned Responses and Habit Formation* On-the-job training in correct safe work methods. Good supervision—immediate correction of violations of safe working practices to build safe habits. Individual participation in safety meetings, safety planning, and safety inspections. Motion pictures and sound strip films dealing with job methods and sequences. Recognition of personal contributions by boss and higher authority figures. Individual safety awards.
Step III Fixation of the attitude	*Emotional Set* Discussion of actual job-related accidents with individual participation. Role playing—permits identification with and projection of self by individual. Motion pictures with high emotional content relating to safety in general and to job performance. Actual demonstration of their personal interest in safety by the boss and higher management—making it the No. 1 item—catching the attitude from authority figures.
Step IV Keeping the attitude alive	*Attention, Memory, and Emotional Set* Checkup on attitude status of individuals and groups using industrial safety attitude scales for employees and supervisors to see where emphasis is needed. Attitude surveys.

NOTE: Plan safety program to offset "safety program fatigue" by using some of the items designed to provide for Steps I, II, and III since employees may be in any one of these steps or may have regressed from III to II, or II to I.

Source: Earle Hannaford, *Supervisor's Guide to Human Relations,* 2d ed., National Safety Council, Chicago, 1976. Reprinted with permission.

These systems have both positive and negative sides. They obviously provide management with more information on how employees are using their time and thus allow for greater control over the workplace. Some workers see it as more objective than a boss's personal and sometimes biased opinion. On the negative side, some employees consider it a ''Big Brother is watching'' technique and an invasion of privacy. Others are concerned about the nature and use of the data collected through CSS.

WHAT CAN THE SUPERVISOR DO?

If CSS is used in your firm, the following guidelines may help you use it effectively:

1. Participate with other managers in deciding what information is needed. Ask "How relevant are these data for supervisory purposes?"
2. Seek workers' involvement. You might say, "We want to know your concerns about CSS. If you feel threatened, we want you not only to tell us how but also to help us find ways to eliminate the threat."
3. Work with other managers to implement a pay-for-performance policy. Give bonuses and pay raises for good performance captured by the monitoring system.
4. Humanize supervision. Don't hide behind the CSS. Keep in daily personal contact with workers. CSS doesn't include the personal and social aspects of the supervisor-employee relationship. You have to take care of that.[16]

Along with internal inspections, you may have OSHA inspections. Every business is subject to inspections by the Compliance Safety and Health Officers (CSHOs) of OSHA. States may also conduct inspections. Almost without exception, inspections are conducted without advance notice to the firm.

With over 5 million workplaces to inspect, OSHA has had to set up inspection priorities. They are, in decreasing order: imminent danger, catastrophies and fatal accidents, employee complaints, programmed high-hazard inspections, and follow-up inspections.[17]

During inspections, CSHOs determine the route of the tour and talk with workers along the way. They examine recordkeeping; check for posting of required OSHA materials; and inspect for unsafe or unhealthy conditions, noting especially any violations of OSHA standards. CSHOs report their findings to an area director, who determines what, if any, citations or penalties will be imposed. Inspections can be costly. In 1986, after a follow-up inspection, Chrysler was cited for violating OSHA recordkeeping standards on injuries at one of its plants and fined $295,332.

WHAT CAN THE SUPERVISOR DO?

Use a checklist derived from your last inspection on your current inspection. The record will provide valuable data on your safety program by giving dated notations of conditions and provide cumulative information on all elements of the workplace under your supervision. Comparing a report to a previous one will alert you to deteriorating conditions, such as loosening floor tiles or corroding pipes, so that the condition can be corrected before it becomes hazardous.

The checklists will also serve as evidence of your ongoing attention to safety in the event that your firm is called on by OSHA or your insurance agency to provide it.

Develop a checklist tailored to your own needs. Figure 7-6 can serve as a pattern. Since OSHA requires you to display the OSHA poster on employee rights and responsibilities, you might want to include ''bulletin board'' on your list.

Competency Check:
Can you explain the importance of regular observation and inspection in maintaining safety?

FIGURE 7-6

Monthly safety check

MONTHLY SAFETY CHECK

Dept. _____ Date _____
Supervisor_____
Indicate discrepancy by ☒

General area		First aid	
floors condition		first-aid kits	
special purpose flooring		stretchers, fire blankets, oxygen	
aisle, clearance/markings		**Fire protection**	
floor openings, require safeguards		fire hoses hung properly	
railings, stairs temp./perm.		extinguisher charged/proper location	
dock board (bridges plates)		access to fire equipment	
piping (water-steam-air)		exit lights/doors/signs	
wall damage		other	
ventilation		**Security**	
other		doors/windows, etc., secured when required	
Illumination—wiring		alarm operation	
unnecessary/improper use		dept. shut down security	
lights on during shutdown		equip. secured	
frayed/defective wiring		unauthorized personnel	
overloading circuits		other	
machinery not grounded		**Machinery**	
hazardous location		unattended machines operating	
wall outlets		emergency stops not operational	
other		platforms/ladders/catwalks	
Housekeeping		instructions to operate/stop posted	
floors		maintenance being performed on machines in operation	
machines		guards in place	
break area/latrines			
waste disposal			

FIGURE 7-6

(Continued)

vending machines/food protection		pinch points	
rodent, insect, vermin control		**Material storage**	
Vehicles		hazardous & flammable material not stored properly	
unauthorized use		improper stacking/loading/ securing	
operating defective vehicle		improper lighting, warning signs, ventilation	
reckless/speeding operation		other	
failure to obey traffic rules			
other			
Tools			
power tool wiring			
condition of hand tools			
safe storage			
other			

Keep on file as evidence of on-going safety program.

Source: Reprinted from *Safety and Security for Supervisors,* published by Business Research Publications, 817 Broadway, New York, N.Y. 10003, 1980, pp. 20–21.

Investigating and Reporting Accidents

In the beginning of this chapter, Sutton's first action after getting Rivera off to the hospital was to get information for a report on the accident. She was right on target. OSHA requires that all accidents be reported. Note in Figure 7-7 that OSHA guidelines for reporting include almost every work-related death, illness, or injury. It is usually the supervisor's job to fill out the accident report of his or her injured worker. The report may then be checked by a safety director or department manager.

Knowing your reporting responsibility will help you in investigating the accident. The accident should be investigated immediately, while observers can recall all the particulars clearly and while the supervisor can examine the accident site. Get the views of more than one observer, if possible, to give you as complete a picture as possible and to verify the accuracy of observers' information.

A copy of the OSHA report should be kept in your files. Your firm may also wish to develop and use its own form, tailored to its own needs for research, safety history, and insurance information. Figure 7-8 on pages 192–193 shows an accident investigation report form developed by the National Safety Council. Note the information on supervision requested in item 24.

When Sutton headed back to the accident site to investigate and fill out the form, she expressed concern about her accident record. Let's look at the way safety is measured.

Competency Check:

Can you discuss the supervisor's role in investigating and reporting accidents?

FIGURE 7-7 Guide for reporting/recording accidents, illnesses, and deaths to OSHA

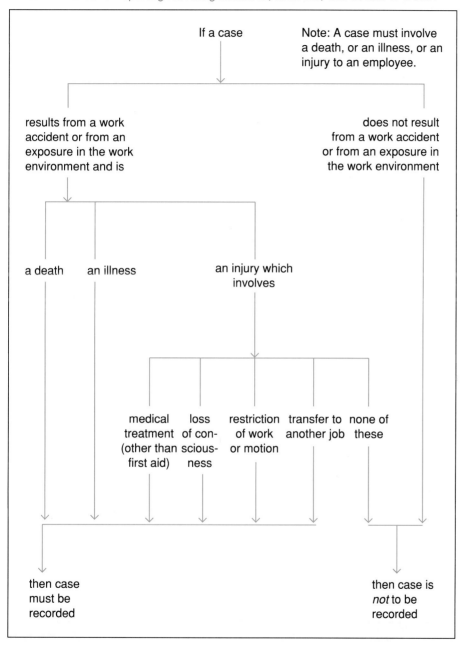

FIGURE 7-8 Accident investigation report form

ACCIDENT INVESTIGATION REPORT

CASE NUMBER

COMPANY _____ ADDRESS _____

DEPARTMENT _____ LOCATION (if different from mailing address) _____

| 1. NAME OF INJURED | 2. SOCIAL SECURITY NUMBER | 3. SEX
□ M
□ F | 4. AGE | 5. DATE of ACCIDENT |

| 6. HOME ADDRESS | 7. EMPLOYEE'S USUAL OCCUPATION | 8. OCCUPATION at TIME of ACCIDENT |

9. LENGTH of EMPLOYMENT
□ Less than 1 mo.   □ 6 mos. to 5 yrs.
□ 1-5 mos.   □ More than 5 yrs.

10. TIME in OCCUP. at TIME of ACCIDENT
□ Less than 1 mo.   □ 6 mos. to 5 yrs.
□ 1-5 mos.   □ More than 5yrs.

11. EMPLOYMENT CATEGORY
□ Regular, full-time
□ Temporary   □ Nonemployee
□ Regular, part-time   □ Seasonal

13. NATURE of INJURY and PART of BODY

12. CASE NUMBERS and NAMES of OTHERS INJURED in SAME ACCIDENT

14. NAME and ADDRESS of PHYSICIAN

15. NAME and ADDRESS of HOSPITAL

16. TIME of INJURY
A.M.
A. _____ P.M.
B. Time within shift
C. Type of shift

17. SEVERITY of INJURY
□ Fatality
□ Lost workdays—days away from work
□ Lost workdays—days of restricted activity
□ Medical treatment
□ First aid
□ Other, specify _____

18. SPECIFIC LOCATION of ACCIDENT

ON EMPLOYER'S PREMISES? □ Yes   □ No

19. PHASE OF EMPLOYEE'S WORKDAY at TIME of INJURY

□ During rest period   □ Entering or leaving plant

□ During meal period   □ Performing work duties

□ Working overtime   □ Other _____

20. DESCRIBE HOW the ACCIDENT OCCURRED

_____
_____
_____
_____

21. ACCIDENT SEQUENCE: Describe in reverse order of occurrence events preceding the injury and accident. Starting with the injury and moving backward in time, reconstruct the sequence of events that led to the injury.

A. Injury Event _____

B. Accident Event _____

C. Preceding Event #1 _____

D. Preceding Event#2, #3, etc. _____
_____

FIGURE 7-8 (Continued)

22. TASK and ACTIVITY at TIME of ACCIDENT	23. POSTURE of EMPLOYEE

22. TASK and ACTIVITY at TIME of ACCIDENT

   A. General type of task _____

   B. Specific activity _____

   C. Employee was working:

      ☐ Alone ☐ With crew or fellow worker ☐ Other, specify _____

23. POSTURE of EMPLOYEE

   _____

24. SUPERVISION at TIME of ACCIDENT

   ☐ Directly supervised   ☐ Not supervised

   ☐ Indirectly supervised   ☐ Supervision not feasible

25. CAUSAL FACTORS. Events and conditions that contributed to the accident. Include those identified by use of the Guide for Identifying Causal Factors and Corrective Actions.

_____

_____

_____

_____

_____

_____

_____

_____

_____

26. CORRECTIVE ACTIONS. Those that have been, or will be, taken to prevent recurrence. Include those identified by use of the Guide for Identifying Causal Factors and Corrective Actions.

_____

_____

_____

_____

_____

_____

_____

_____

_____

_____

PREPARED BY _____   APPROVED _____

TITLE _____   TITLE _____ DATE _____

DEPARTMENT _____ DATE _____   APPROVED _____

    Developed by the National Safety Council   TITLE _____ DATE _____

Measuring Safety

The U.S. Department of Labor periodically issues data on many areas of American life. OSHA safety and health information is one segment. Data from supervisors like you from all over the country are compiled and published. Industries, unions, and private agencies such as the National Safety Council also publish safety and health statistics. Data from the various sources are not always comparable because different methods of collecting and reporting are used. Two common measures of safety and health are the injury and illness incidence rate and the lost workday incidence rate. The OSHA formulas for these rates are shown in Figure 7-9.

Assume that United Energy Company's 150 employees worked fifty 40-hour weeks during a recent year and reported 6 injuries/illnesses for the period. Using formula A in Figure 7-9, the company's injury and illness incidence rate would be 4; i.e., $6 \times 200,000 \div 300,000 = 4$. United would find its safety record a bit better than the national average, which was 4.7 in 1984.

Now, suppose the 6 injured or ill workers lost a total of 12 working days. United's lost workday incidence rate, using formula B, would be 8; i.e., $12 \times 200,000 \div 300,000 = 8$.

Incidence rates can be measured fairly easily; the health part of employee safety and health is much less amenable to measurement, as you will see in the next section.

Competency Check:

Can you discuss the methods of measuring worker safety?

HEALTH ISSUES IN THE PHYSICAL ENVIRONMENT

What is *health?* How can it be measured? And what is the responsibility of business to promote health in the workplace? There are many different answers to these questions.

In the 1980s, health and fitness have become a national pastime. We have become preoccupied with diets, health foods, nutrition clinics, aerobics, and jogging. Health has reached megabusiness proportions. At the same time, the costs of employee in-

FIGURE 7-9

Safety incidence rate formulas.

A. Injury and illness incidence rate $= \dfrac{\text{number of injuries and illnesses} \times 200,000^*}{\text{total hrs worked by all employees for the year}}$

B. Lost workday incidence rate $= \dfrac{\text{number of lost workdays} \times 200,000}{\text{total hrs worked by all employees for the year}}$

*OSHA uses a base of 100 full-time employees working 40 hours a week for 50 weeks ($40 \times 50 \times 100 = 200,000$).

Source: Accident Facts, 1986 Edition, National Safety Council, Chicago. Reprinted with permission.

juries are soaring. In 1985, these costs were over $37 billion.[18] Through insurance programs, employers pay almost half of the health-care costs in the United States; in 1982, that amounted to almost 10 percent of the gross national product. General Motors' employee medical benefits cost the company more than it pays for the steel it buys from its main supplier.[19]

Robert H. Rosen points out that the healthy company takes an integrated view of health and the organization. He cites four critical elements in that concept. These are the impact of:[20]

- the employee's lifestyle on his or her own health.
- the work environment on the employee's health.
- employee health on the organization's profitability.
- the larger environment—family, peers, leisure—on employee health and organizational profits.

The author lists 39 costs to show the impact of employee health on the organization's profitability.[21] This implies that one way to measure employee health is by measuring the health of the company, including worker morale, absenteeism, and productivity that translates into profit.

To improve employee health and to reduce health-care costs, businesses are using a variety of approaches. One that encompasses the broader view of employee health is the wellness program.

Promoting Safety and Health through Wellness Programs

A national health insurance trade association defines *wellness* as a ''freely chosen lifestyle aimed at achieving and maintaining an individual's good health.''[22]

Wellness goes beyond accident prevention and the absence of disease to a state of vitality in the individual. An employee's state of health can affect his or her productivity, motivation, and creativity. Wellness programs offer management an approach to improving these employee contributions and to reducing the costs accruing from absenteeism, fatigue-related accidents, medical claims, and apathy. Hartman and Cozetti report a high degree of participation in wellness programs because employees:[23]

- perceive it to be a quality program because it is sponsored by the company.
- see it as a fringe benefit and feel they should take advantage of it.
- feel it is a convenient way to take care of their health.

Wellness programs take many forms. Among them are physical fitness programs (PFPs); others emphasize drug and alcohol rehabilitation, stress management, counseling, or detection of illnesses such as hypertension or cancer. Among the most popular are the PFPs. The National Industrial Recreation Association estimates that over 50,000 firms have PFPs and that more than 70 percent of these have been formed since 1975.[24] Figure 7-10 shows some of the benefits of physical fitness programs to participants and to the organization.

The supervisor's role in wellness programs, other than personal participation, is mostly supportive. Encouraging employee participation, commenting on individual progress, and communicating to the employees and to other managers any reduced costs or improved productivity by participants will provide positive reinforcement.

The supervisor will play a larger role in addressing some other health issues that have a negative impact on worker environment.

Addressing Health Hazards

It would be great if all the health issues that you will face as a supervisor were as positive as the wellness programs. Unfortunately, they are not. Negative issues that have an impact on the worker and the work environment continue to emerge. They are often emotionally charged, involving the psychological as well as the physical environment. Chapter 13 will address the psychological environment. The focus here will be on two issues that are currently of great concern to managers: substance use and abuse and acquired immune deficiency syndrome (AIDS).

Substance Use and Abuse

While substance abuse is not new, the number of substances, the number of workers involved, and the extent of abuse have increased in recent years. Businesses were

---

FIGURE 7-10   BENEFITS OF PHYSICAL FITNESS PROGRAMS

PHYSIOLOGICAL IMPROVEMENTS	BEHAVIOR CHANGES	BENEFITS TO THE ORGANIZATION
weight and body-fat loss	less absenteeism	lower medical claims and insurance premiums
greater strength and endurance	fewer fatigue-related accidents	fewer disability claims
better nutritional habits	higher productivity	fewer losses due to accidents
less smoking	enhanced mental alertness	lower workers' compensation costs
improved blood pressure and cardiovascular function		higher employee morale and productivity
stress reduction		lower overtime and temporary-worker salaries due to absenteeism reduction

Source: Michael R. Carrell and Frank E. Kuzmits, *Personnel—Human Resources Management,* 2d ed., Merrill Publishing Co., Columbus, 1986, 391. Reprinted by permission of the publisher.

developing alcohol-abuse programs in the 1940s; drug-abuse programs began increasing in the 1960s. During the 1970s and 1980s, the Surgeon General's reports on smoking and its effects on the smoker and the nonsmoker, through secondary-smoke inhalation, made smoking a highly emotional health issue.

A complicating factor is that the *use* of some substances—alcohol, tobacco, and prescribed drugs—is not illegal, while the *use* of other substances—cocaine and heroin—is illegal. The mixed interpretations of substance use and abuse by the federal and state governments, by the courts, by organizations, and by individuals further complicate the matter.

Alcohol abuse has long been a problem in the workplace. The National Council on Alcoholism and other agencies estimate that about 10 percent of workers are alcoholics.[25] While some of these can perform their jobs satisfactorily, at least for a time, many cannot. Alcoholics are typically absent more often and are involved in more job-related accidents than are nonalcoholics.[26] In addition, alcoholics may:[27]

- cause accidents and injury to others through negligence.
- disregard job details, use poor judgment, and make bad decisions.
- perform unevenly in terms of quantity and quality.
- minimize contact with coworkers and supervisors and exhibit antisocial behavior.

Firms may address alcoholism on the job in any of several ways. They may offer in-house counseling, rehabilitation programs, referrals to medical or other specialized agencies, employee assistance programs, or educational programs.

The formation of a company policy toward alcoholism should be a top priority. Figure 7-11 shows one company's policy. Note that the role of the supervisor is part of the policy.

The term *drug use* usually refers to the use of substances such as marijuana, heroin, and cocaine. The cost of drug use to the American economy is estimated to be over $25 billion per year.[28] The impairment of skills, decision-making ability, and reaction time by users makes the potential for danger in certain jobs enormous. Think of the possible disastrous results from drug abuse by pilots, workers in chemical or nuclear power plants, doctors, bus drivers, and the military. Drug testing, required by some organizations to detect employee use of drugs, is a hotly debated issue.

Drug use creates the same kinds of problems in the workplace as alcoholism, plus some of its own. One of these is the increased potential for theft, to which many addicts resort to support their habits. Unlike alcohol, the use of these drugs is illegal. The legal difference has a significant impact on company policy. Commonwealth Edison Corporation has the following policy on drug abuse at work. Note the specific penalties for policy violation.[29]

- The illegal use, sale, or possession of controlled substances while on the job or on company property is a dischargeable offense.
- Off-the-job illegal-drug use that can adversely affect an employee's job performance or that can jeopardize the safety of others is cause for administrative or disciplinary action up to, and including, termination of employment.

FIGURE 7-11   Policy on alcoholism

Policy.

The underlying concept of Kemper's personnel policies is regard for the employee as an individual as well as a worker. Reflecting this concern, the company has devised a policy with six principles.

1. We believe that alcoholism, drug addiction, and emotional disturbances are illnesses and should be treated as such.

2. We believe the majority of employees who develop alcoholism, other drug addiction, or emotional illness can be helped to recover, and the company should offer appropriate assistance.

3. We believe the decision to seek diagnosis and accept treatment for any suspected illness is the responsibility of the employee. However, continued refusal of an employee to seek treatment when it appears that substandard performance may be caused by any illness is not tolerated. We believe that alcoholism, other drug addiction, or emotional illness should not be made an exception to this commonly accepted principle.

4. We believe that it is in the best interest of employees and the company that when alcoholism, other drug addiction, or emotional illness is present, it should be diagnosed and treated at the earliest possible date.

5. We believe that the company's concern for individual alcohol drinking, drug taking, and behavior habits begins only when they result in unsatisfactory job performance, poor attendance, or behavior detrimental to the good reputation of the companies.

6. We believe that confidential handling of the diagnosis and treatment of alcoholism, other drug addiction, or emotional illness is essential.

The objective of this policy is to retain employees who may develop any of these illnesses, by helping them to arrest its further advance before the condition renders them unemployable.

Supervisory Practices.

Supervisors are instructed not to attempt to identify alcoholics or drug abusers among their employees, since diagnosis is the job of trained professionals. The firm's Personal Assistance Program provides training and assistance to supervisors and handles such problems through referrals. Supervisors' responsibility is to closely and accurately monitor employee *performance and work habits.* They should concern themselves only with job performance except when there are observable signs that the employee is drinking or taking illegal drugs on the job, is under the influence of alcohol or drugs, or is behaving in an abnormal manner. Supervisors are told to discuss referral with the Program's staff when an employee has a serious problem in any job area or difficulties in two or more of these job areas: sporadic performance, periods of poor judgment and confusion, increased sick time and tardiness, irritable attitudes toward other employees, quick or unreasonable anger, and strained relations with agents, policyholders, and the general public. Supervisors are warned to beware of three don'ts: don't play the expert, don't feel guilty about referring, and don't get emotionally involved.

The Program staff uses a variety of internal and external sources for consulting, counseling, and treatment for employees with alcohol, drug addiction, or other living problems.

Source: The Kemper Approach to Alcoholism, Drug Addiction, and Other Living Problems, Kemper Group, Long Grove, IL 60049, pp. 13–19.

● Employees who are arrested for off-the-job drug activity may be considered to be in violation of the company policy.

● Employees undergoing prescribed medical treatment with a controlled substance should report this to their supervisor or the company medical department.

As a supervisor, your top priority will be to know company policy and to communicate it to workers. The policy is the company's standard for disciplinary action in cases of drug use.

Smoking has been declared by the Surgeon General to be potentially dangerous to the smoker's health. Recent disclosure of the hazardous effects of secondary smoke to the nonsmoker has caused upheaval in the workplace and elsewhere. An estimated 29 percent of workers in a typical organization smoke cigarettes.[30]

The smoking issue is highly emotional, and remedies are hotly debated by smokers and nonsmokers. Each thinks his or her rights are being violated if the remedy favors the other's view. This creates a dilemma for organizations that wish to treat employees equally. Some states and localities are beginning to legislate where smoking may take place. The division of planes and other public places into smoking and nonsmoking sections, while still typical, is being challenged by nonsmokers. A 1987 law in California forbade smoking in public "restaurants," with the exception of "bars." The exception quickly transformed many former "restaurants" into "bars." As the cartoon suggests, it is hard to go anywhere these days without running into the smoking/nonsmoking problem. Some states now prohibit smoking in public buildings, and airlines do not permit smoking on short flights.

"Smoking or nonsmoking . . . ?"

Source: © 1987 Bill Schorr/Los Angeles Times Syndicate.

In spite of copious research, no evidence on the dangers seems clear enough to sway everyone. Yet with so much emphasis on health and safety, many managers feel that the risks of smoking are great enough to take action. Approaches usually take one of four forms: (1) a total ban—no smoking on the premises, (2) a ban on smoking at the work station, (3) a ban on smoking other than in designated areas such as lounges, and (4) voluntary quit-smoking programs to help workers stop smoking. Only a brave company would have banned smoking in the 1970s; more and more are doing so today.

Approaches to substance use and abuse are still evolving and will continue to do so as societal attitudes change. The supervisor is sometimes perplexed about what he or she can do about it.

WHAT CAN THE SUPERVISOR DO?

1. Know the company policy and the law governing your company. This will give you greater confidence in meeting your responsibility.
2. Recognize that your primary responsibility is to supervise the performance of the workers in meeting company objectives. Every action you take should be in terms of the worker's performance on the job. If you see a worker behaving strangely and you suspect that he is using drugs, don't say, "Hank, are you on drugs? I've suspected it for some time. No wonder your work is lousy." A better approach would be to say quietly, "Hank, we need to talk about your production over the past month. Please come to my office for a conference today at 3 o'clock. Maybe there's something I can do to help you meet your standards this week." At the conference, confine your discussion to job performance. Point out how his performance has changed. Be specific. "Your record shows, Hank, that your productivity over the last 6 months is down 20 percent; from last month alone, your output has slipped 6 percent. What can I do to help you reverse that?" If Hank volunteers information on his use or abuse of substances (he probably won't for fear of losing his job), then you must take action. If it is clearly a violation of policy, tell him it is your responsibility to report it to the appropriate person in the firm. If it is alcohol abuse, follow policy. This often means referring the worker to a person in the firm who is qualified to help.
3. Remember that substance abuse is a medical problem to be handled by a professional. Don't try to play doctor, psychologist, or clinician. Even professionals have had difficulty changing the behavior of some drug users.
4. Don't let your personal judgments about the individual influence your actions, and don't let your biases enter your appraisals. Resist the temptation, if you have it, to say, "Dora, you're a bum. My father was an alcoholic, and he was a bum. You're all bums. So don't give me your sob story." Keep your value judgments out of it.

    At the same time, don't play mother, father, or best friend and continue excusing a known abuser. "Just this one last chance, Tim, but I promise

> you this time is the last'' won't solve your problem or the worker's. Stick to job performance as the basis for your appraisals and your actions.
>
> **5.** If you observe a worker drinking or using drugs on the job, report it. Illegal acts or violation of company policy should not be tolerated. In this case, *not* taking proper action is a violation of company policy, and you will be held responsible.

Substance abuse has been around long enough to give organizations an experiential basis for their actions. But new health problems have arisen, among them AIDS.

Acquired Immune Deficiency Syndrome (AIDS)

No health issue in recent history has so frightened the world as has AIDS. A virulent virus with no known cause or cure, AIDS is not only a death sentence to those who acquire it but is spreading at an alarming rate. While the major methods of transmission have been identified, the Centers for Disease Control has been unable to classify a likely method of transmission in 6 percent of the cases studied.[31] The disease is thus causing generalized fear throughout society.

AIDS is different from the communicable diseases that businesses have had some experience in handling. It thus causes many new problems, and businesses are learning to handle these problems mostly by trial and error. Concerned for the health of their other workers, some firms have fired AIDS victims. Others have refused to do so. Court decisions have tended to be ambivalent, though recent judgments have tended to place the worker under the protection of nondiscrimination laws governing the handicapped. Federal policy now prohibits discrimination in personnel actions involving people with AIDS.

Some insurance companies have threatened to exclude coverage for AIDS patients, while others have extended coverage for them. One recent survey disclosed that ''two-thirds of the companies responding have adopted nondiscrimination policies for workers with AIDS. Only 1 percent required job applicants to take AIDS tests, and almost 100 percent cover AIDS expenses in health plans.''[32]

One of the greatest problems stems from the stigma attached to the disease. Because the majority of victims so far have been homosexual males or intravenous drug users, the patients suffer a social stigma as well as the life-threatening illness. Victims are often shunned by their fellow workers, friends, and even their families out of fear of contagion. One worker refused to work on a computer keyboard that was used by an AIDS patient on another shift. Some will not even shake the hand of an AIDS patient. A recent lawsuit charged an AIDS victim with criminal assault for having contact with a noninfected person without first informing the person of the condition. These fears of the unknown, coupled with a lack of definition and direction by government, the medical and legal professions, or the general public, make policy setting by business both elusive and risky. Added to the fears of its workers is the public relations headache the firm faces from customers who may refuse to buy its products if they believe that AIDS patients have handled them. At this point, case-by-case handling is preferred over a policy. Policy statements are being deferred until more is known about the disease.[33]

One approach that business can take is to make sure that facts are disseminated to all workers, including management, as soon as they become known. Counseling and employee assistance can also be offered to known victims and to workers for whom the issue causes stress. To get the known facts about AIDS to the public, the Surgeon General in 1988 mailed a brochure explaining the disease to every household in the United States. The media, medical and health agencies, schools, and other organizations offer programs to educate the public about the facts, to allay fears, and to promote prevention. But there are no clear answers at this writing.

Where does that leave the supervisor? The answer is, in a very sensitive and often stressful position. If top management isn't sure what to do about the situation, how can the supervisor be expected to handle it? The next section will provide guidelines that may be helpful until research can clarify our responsibilities and shape our policies.

WHAT CAN THE SUPERVISOR DO?

1. Learn as much as you can about the disease. You will be serving as a role model for your workers, whether you intend to or not. Attend company-sponsored educational seminars. Stay as objective as possible in your dealings with your workers. Remember that your job is to supervise the *performance* of your workers; the workers should know that you are doing so.

2. Confer with your peers and your superiors. Discuss with them the handling of each case until a policy is set. A representative of IBM has said his company's policy is to "offer treatment, support, and guidance."[34] Generalized statements like this are typical and will probably remain so until more is learned about AIDS. Under the circumstances, your best action is to confer and refer. If you become aware that someone in your work group has AIDS or is an AIDS carrier, confer with your manager; if a policy exists, refer the worker to the authority it designates. Management awareness about the problem is great enough so that you will probably have much support in handling the situation. Remember that you do not have to handle it alone; so don't be hesitant about asking for advice and help.

Competency Check:

Can you discuss current health issues in the physical environment?

COMPETENCY REVIEW

1. Cite seven factors that have influenced management's concern about employee safety and health.
2. Discuss top management's role in safety and health programs.
3. Discuss three elements of the work environment that may cause accidents.
4. State three ways through which the supervisor can develop safety awareness among workers.
5. Explain the importance of observation and inspection in maintaining safety.

6. Discuss the supervisor's role in investigating and reporting accidents.
7. Describe two methods of measuring worker safety.
8. Discuss two health issues in the physical environment.

APPLICATIONS

1. As a supervisor, your top responsibility is the safety and health of the employees reporting to you. It is not only a managerial responsibility but a moral responsibility. Equally important, it is a responsibility which, if fulfilled conscientiously, will ensure your peace of mind.

   If you are a supervisor, answer the questions on the questionnaire that follows based on your present situation. If you are not a supervisor, assume the role of a former supervisor or manager you have had and answer as you perceived his or her safety and health actions. Your instructor will help you determine and analyze your score.

	Yes	*No*
a. Do you try on a continuing basis to create and sustain employee awareness with regard to the importance of safety?	_____	_____
b. Are you tough and rigid when it comes to the enforcement of safety regulations and rules?	_____	_____
c. Are you constantly on the alert to track down hazardous conditions in your department?	_____	_____
d. If an accident occurs, or if you uncover a safety hazard, do you always make the best effort you can to track down its cause and take steps to prevent its recurrence?	_____	_____
e. Do you make special efforts to indoctrinate new employees in such a way that they will be conscious of the importance of safe performance from the first day they start working?	_____	_____
f. Do you give all your people the training they need to ensure safe job practices and conduct?	_____	_____
g. Do you promptly make a written report of all accidents?	_____	_____
h. Do you encourage first aid for every injury no matter how minor it may be?	_____	_____
i. Do you firmly insist on good housekeeping practices?	_____	_____
j. Do you inspect your operation on a regular basis to make sure drawers are kept closed, flooring is in	_____	_____

good repair, objects do not protrude from shelves, etc., so that the possibility of tripping and falling is kept to a minimum?

k. Do you check all machines to make sure they are properly grounded and that electric cords are in good condition? _____ _____

l. Do you rigidly enforce NO SMOKING regulations in areas where flammable liquids or combustibles are stored? _____ _____

m. Where machine guards or shields are called for, do you always insist on their use? _____ _____

n. Do you also insist that employees wear safety goggles, safety shoes, helmets, and safety gloves as required? _____ _____

o. Do you encourage your people to report hazards as soon as they are spotted and give you suggestions for safer performance? _____ _____

Total no. of Yes answers _____ _____

Source: "Safety: You're Responsible," Dartnell Corporation, April 26, 1983.

2. Morgan Santos, Inc. (MSI), filed OSHA reports for five accidents involving missed workdays during the past year. The injured employees missed a total of 15 days as a result of the accidents. The company's 125 full-time employees worked 40 hours per week for the full year, less 2 weeks of vacation time.

MSI is preparing its annual safety and health report and wishes to know its incidence and severity rates. Using the OSHA formulas, calculate the two measures.

3. To simplify and standardize your reporting of accidents as required by your firm and OSHA, you might want to prepare a checklist that will help you identify and describe the facts of each incident. Reading *All About OSHA* (1985 revised edition), especially pages 13–17, will help you design a form that will meet both your firm's and OSHA's requirements. The form below can serve as a guide which could be adapted to your needs.

Assume that you are preparing to report Rivera's accident as described in the opening scenario of this chapter. Use the form below to identify the facts of the incident. Was there a part of the accident for which you found no appropriate term? If so, explain that part in brief terminology like that on the checklist.

IDENTIFYING ACCIDENT FACTS

What part of the body was injured?

Description: right/left, location, etc.

_____ head _____

_____ eyes _____

_____ ears _____

_____ teeth _____

_____ face _____

_____ neck _____

_____ shoulders _____

_____ arms _____

_____ hands _____

_____ chest _____

_____ abdomen _____

_____ back _____

_____ hips _____

_____ legs _____

_____ knees _____

_____ feet _____

_____ other _____

Identify and describe the nature of the injury.

_____ cut _____

_____ fracture _____

_____ sprain _____

_____ amputation _____

_____ puncture _____

_____ bruise _____

_____ burn _____

_____ foreign body _____

_____ skin eruption(s) _____

_____ hernia _____

_____ other _____

Identify and describe the cause of the injury.

_____ fall _____

_____ collision with or struck by moving object(s) _____

_____ inhalation/absorption of toxic substance(s) _____

_____ electric shock _____

_____ exposure to temperature extremes/burns _____

_____ caught in/by/between objects _____

_____ other _____

Identify and describe the hazardous condition which caused the injury. If none, check here. _____

_____ defective tools/equipment _____

_____ faulty design/construction _____

_____ workplace arrangement _____

_____ inadequate lighting _____

_____ improperly guarded or unguarded area _____
_____ inadequate ventilation _____
_____ improper clothing _____
_____ improper housekeeping _____

Identify the equipment/facilities involved. If none, check here. _____

_____ machines/equipment _____
_____ tools _____
_____ materials/supplies _____
_____ vehicles _____
_____ elevators
_____ doors/windows/walls _____
_____ floors _____
_____ stairs _____
_____ ladders _____
_____ electrical apparatus _____
_____ other

Identify and describe the human act which caused or contributed to the accident. If none, check here. _____

_____ using equipment/tools unsafely _____
_____ failure to follow correct operating procedure(s) _____
_____
_____ failure to report unsafe condition(s) _____
_____
_____ operating without authority _____
_____ using unsafe speed _____
_____ using defective equipment _____
_____ unsafe loading/mixing _____
_____ improper lifting/carrying _____
_____ horseplay _____
_____ poor housekeeping _____
_____ being in unsafe area/position _____
_____ other _____

Identify and describe other factors which contributed to the accident. If none, check here. _____

_____ failure to follow instructions _____
_____
_____ lack of skill/knowledge _____
_____ involvement of other persons _____
_____ lack of training _____
_____ late or no report to medical staff _____
_____
_____ other _____

CASES

Case I: But I Didn't *Say* I Saw the Accident

In the beginning of the chapter, Sutton meets the produce group back at the scene of the accident to continue her investigation. She has reviewed the account of Bailey, one of the assistant supervisors, and thinks she has a clear picture of the mishap. On her way back, within earshot of produce, she stops briefly to let a loaded bread dolly pass and overhears an interesting conversation between Bailey and Quan, a new produce clerk.

QUAN   Why did you give her the impression you were here, Sean? You know you were back at the Coke machine.

BAILEY   Oh, knock it off, Ann. I didn't say I saw Julio fall. She just asked me how it happened. Besides, you know every clerk is responsible for watching the floor. I can't do it all. Why didn't you pick up the grape?

QUAN   Don't put the blame on me! You were on duty, and. . . .

Seeing Sutton approach, Quan stops. Sutton ignores the conversation for the moment—she will handle that problem later.

"Let's hear it, Sean," she says as she dates her report. Bailey gives essentially the same story, and the others corroborate it.

"Was there any horseplay before the accident?" she asks. All agree there was none. She examines the cart and the display case. Except for a few scratches and some mashed fruit, there is no damage. Coconuts are all over the floor, but only a few are cracked.

"Well, Julio seems to have suffered the worst of this," Sutton says as she looks over the accident report she has to fill in. She will complete items 20 and 21 first, while her memory and notes are fresh.

"OK," she says. "Let's get the place cleaned up and get back to work. Sean, get maintenance out here to do the floor." As she turns to leave, she says, "And Sean, see me in the produce office when your shift ends, please."

1. Using the Accident Investigation Report in Figure 7-8 and the information in the case, carry out Sutton's responsibility for items 20 and 21.
   a. Describe how the accident occurred (item 20).
   b. Report the accident sequence in reverse order (item 21).
2. What suggestions can you make for improving the safety of the produce operation? Consider people, processes, and equipment. (You might want to review the checklist for identifying key facts to help here.)
3. If you were Sutton, what would you say to Bailey about item 24 when he came to your office?

Case II: Heavy-Duty KP

At the Crispo Chip Company, business has been growing by leaps and bounds since the company won a government contract to supply potato chips to overseas commissaries. Conveyer belts and automatic peelers and cutters have replaced manual handling of the potatoes. The work force has been doubled to 75, and still the firm has difficulty keeping production equal to orders. New people are being hired regularly, sometimes right off the street.

Milo Osborne is one of these walk-in hires. He is sent to Jake Brandon, supervisor for peeler group 4, to be put to work. Brandon puts him at the start of peeler line 4. He is required to lift 100-pound bags of potatoes onto the peeler that is at the start of the automatic chip process.

"Just keep dumping the bags onto the belt—that's your job," Brandon tells Osborne.

Brandon is not used to this type of sustained physical effort. He is 6 feet tall and weighs 140 pounds. After an hour, he's pooped. He can't keep up with the process. Production is down, and the packers at the end of the line, who are paid by the box, are yelling.

Brandon tells Osborne to "just keep at it. You'll get the hang of it soon."

OSBORNE   But my back is hurting something awful. I don't think it's safe to put a man on a job like this, just cold, with no thought about his back. I ain't used to lifting.

BRANDON   Look, you want the job or not? Just keep trying. And I don't want any beefing about safety. I've got a quota to get out on line 4. If you don't want the job, you can check out now.

Brandon walks away.

Source: Adapted from Dan Peterson, *Safety Supervision*, AMACOM, 1976, p. 183.

1. What safety problems do you see in Osborne's situation?
2. Do you see any problems in the design of the equipment or the job process?
3. Were any OSHA rights violated? Explain.
4. Based on the chapters you have studied so far, can you cite any other management problems in the case?

Scoring System for Quiz, Figure 7-4

Give yourself 3 points for any *c* answer, 2 points for a *b* answer, and 1 point for an *a* answer. If you scored 45, you have no worries and probably no accidents. If you scored between 35 and 44, you need to work at it still. If you scored between 25 and 34, you're not quite there, and if you scored under 24, maybe you ought to see the boss about a transfer.

REFERENCES

1. *Accident Prevention Manual for Industrial Operations,* 7th ed., National Safety Council, 1974, as presented in Dan Petersen, *Safety Supervision,* AMACOM, New York, 1976, p. 66.

2. *Accident Facts, 1987 Edition*, National Safety Council, Chicago, p. 24.

3. *All About OSHA,* U.S. Department of Labor and OSHA, 1985, rev., p. 3.

4. Ibid., p. 2.

5. The discussion of OSHA is based on *All about OSHA,* ibid.; *Occupational Safety and Health Act of 1970,* 91st Cong., Pub. L. 91-596, 5.2193, Dec. 29, 1970; and *OSHA: Safety and Health Is Our Middle Name, Four Ways OSHA Can Help,* OSHA 3076, 1984.

6. *Collective Bargaining Negotiations and Contracts,* 95, Bureau of National Affairs, May 26, 1983, pp. 1–4.

7. John M. Ivancevich and William F. Glueck, *Foundations of Personnel, Human Resources Management,* rev. ed., Business Publications Inc., Plano, Texas, 1983, p. 585.

8. Wendell L. French, *Human Resources Management,* Houghton Mifflin Company, Boston, 1986, p. 589.

9. J. Vernon Glenn, ''Ergonomic Testing,'' *Human Resources Management Ideas and Trends,* May 2, 1986, pp. 70–72.

10. G. Gordon Long, ''Ergonomics Can Show the Way to Efficiency and Productivity,'' *Office Systems,* December 1985, pp. 65–68.

11. Ibid.

12. Based on Dan Petersen, op. cit., pp. 46–47.

13. *Accident Facts, 1986 Edition,* op. cit., p. 30.

14. George Terry, *Self Review in Supervision,* Learning Systems, 1975, p. 73.

15. Discussion based on Ravinder Nath and Barry Gilmore, ''Managing Computer Supervision Systems,'' *Management Solutions,* July 1987, pp. 5–11.

16. Ibid., pp. 7–9.

17. *All About OSHA,* op. cit., pp. 18–23.

18. *Accident Facts, 1986 Edition,* op. cit., p. 6.

19. Michael R. Carrell and Frank E. Kuzmits, *Personnel—Human Resource Management,* 2d ed., Charles E. Merrill Books, Inc., Columbus, Ohio, 1986, p. 399.

20. Robert H. Rosen, *Healthy Companies, A Human Resources Approach,* American Management Association, 1986, p. 17.

21. Ibid., pp. 20–21.

22. *Your Guide to Wellness at the Worksite,* Health Association of America, 1983, p. 3.

23. Stephen W. Hartman and Janet Cozzeto, ''Wellness in the Workplace,'' *Personnel Administrator,* vol. 29, no. 8, August 1984, pp. 108–109. Copyright, 1984, The American Society for Personnel Administration, Alexandria, Virginia.

24. Jack N. Kondrasuk, ''Corporate Physical Fitness Programs: The Role of the Personnel Department,'' *Personnel Administrator,* vol. 29, no. 12, December 1984, pp. 75–80.

25. Christine A. Flipowicz, ''The Troubled Employee: Whose Responsibility?'' *Personnel Administrator,* vol. 24, June 1979, p. 18.

26. Frank E. Kuzmits and Henry E. Hammonds, II, ''Rehabilitating the Troubled Employee,'' *Personnel Journal,* April 1979, p. 239. Reprinted with permission. All rights reserved.

27. Carrell and Kuzmits, op. cit., p. 393.

28. Peter Bensinger, ''Drugs in the Workplace,'' *Harvard Business Review,* November–December 1982, pp. 48–50.

29. Ibid., p. 48.

30. Robert H. Rosen, loc. cit.

31. *AIDS—The Workplace Issues,* American Management Association, 1985, p. 9.

32. "Job Security for Aids Victims," *U.S. News & World Report,* June 1, 1987, p. 44.

33. *AIDS—The Workplace Issues,* op. cit., pp. 21–22.

34. Ibid., p. 22.

SUGGESTED READINGS

AIDS—The New Workplace Issues, American Management Association, 1988.

Blanchard, Kenneth, and Norman Vincent Peale: *The Power of Ethical Management,* William Morrow & Company, Inc., New York, 1988.

Byrne, John A.: "Businesses are Signing Up for Ethics 101," *Business Week,* Feb. 15, 1988, pp. 56–57.

Brennan, Andrew J. J.: "Wellness Comes to Work," *Management World,* February 1985, pp. 12–15.

Dickinson, Daniel: *It's Their Business, Too—A Manager's Guide to Corporate Awareness,* American Management Association, New York, 1985.

Drug Abuse, the Workplace Issues, American Management Association, New York, 1987.

Hayden, Donald F., Tinker D. Murray, and Ted L. Edwards: "Texas Employee Health and Fitness Program," *Journal of Physical Education, Recreation, and Dance (JOPERD),* October 1986, pp. 28–32.

Saad, Henry W.: "Aids and the Law," *Management Solutions,* September 1986, pp. 12–16.

IV

THE SUPERVISOR AND THE STAFFING FUNCTION

THE SUPERVISOR AND THE STAFFING FUNCTION

8

THE SUPERVISOR'S ROLE IN STAFFING

COMPETENCIES

After studying this chapter, you will be able to:

1. Describe the roles of the supervisor and the human resource/personnel (HR/P) department in the hiring process.

2. Explain the importance of a good match between the applicant and the job.

3. Forecast human resource needs, given basic information.

4. Describe the roles of the supervisor and the HR/P staff in recruiting.

5. Cite the methods used by the HR/P staff to screen applicants.

6. Describe the supervisor's activities in planning for the interview.

7. Describe the supervisor's activities in beginning the interview.

8. Describe the supervisor's activities during the interview.

9. Describe the supervisor's activities in closing the interview and after the interview.

10. Explain the role of the supervisor in selection.

11. Cite laws that protect against discrimination in employment, and define the protected groups.

12. Identify types of questions that should be avoided during a pre-employment interview.

CHAPTER OUTLINE

Eagles don't flock, you have to find them one at a time.

H. Ross Perot[1] on the value of finding the best people for the job

Barbara Michaels, sales supervisor for Publishers Promotions, Inc., just received the following note from the human resource/personnel department. Attached to the note is a projection of staffing needs in the sales department for next year and for the following 2 years.

> From the Desk of
> Toni Rosso
>
> Barbara,
>   I realize Ray was sales supervisor when these projections were made. Would you review the report and revise as needed.
>
>   Toni

The projected requirements list six additional sales associates and one additional clerk for next year and three additional sales associates and one additional clerk for each of the following 2 years.

This is Michaels's first experience in projecting staffing needs. She is not sure where to begin. Michaels is unable to find any data in the files; she has no idea where Ray obtained his figures.

THE SUPERVISOR'S STAFFING RESPONSIBILITIES

A decade ago, Michaels would not have faced the challenge she has now. At one time, supervisors were not concerned with planning for future staffing needs; staffing consisted primarily of finding a replacement for someone who had left the job. "I quit," "You're fired," or "I am being transferred" triggered a help-wanted advertisement in the local newspaper. This method of staffing is no longer acceptable.

Interacting with the Human Resource/Personnel Department

Staffing responsibility is shared by the human resource/personnel (HR/P) department and the supervisor, with the common goal of having the right number of people with the right skills, knowledge, and abilities (SKAs) available at the right time to meet the organization's goals. That's a tall order; and it requires mutual trust, communication, and interaction among the HR/P department, top and middle managers, and supervisors.

Supervisors are responsible for forecasting the human resource needs of their departments and for communicating these needs to the HR/P department. This forecast may be for a period of 6 months, 2 years, or more. Forecasting human resource needs is discussed later in this chapter.

Supervisors are also responsible for communicating their immediate needs to the HR/P department. When John quits, Marsha is transferred, Mike is fired, or Sue is promoted, the supervisor must complete a requisition and submit it to the HR/P department before the vacancy can be filled. In a small company, a telephone call to the person responsible for hiring may serve as the ''requisition.'' Larger companies usually rely on a more formal procedure, requiring the completion of a requisition form such as the one shown in Figure 8-1 on page 218. This requisition form is completed in triplicate. One copy is used by the interviewer in the personnel department; one is retained by the personnel manager until the position is filled and the first copy is returned to the requestor; and the originating department retains one copy.

WHAT CAN THE SUPERVISOR DO?

The responsibilities of the supervisor and the HR/P staff in hiring are summarized in Figure 8-2 on page 219. You will note that the responsibilities are interrelated and dependent on each other.

The roles of the HR/P staff and the supervisor in other areas of staffing (appraising, rewarding, training, and developing) are described in Chapters 9 and 10.

Competency Check:

Can you differentiate the roles of the supervisor and the HR/P department in the employment process?

Matching the Employee and the Job

You will recall from Chapter 5 that a job specification and a job description are outcomes of a job analysis. Both the job specification and the job description provide a supervisor with the information necessary to match the applicant and the job.

A *job specification* provides information about the requirements necessary to per-

FIGURE 8-1

Requisition form

SOVRAN
FINANCIAL CORPORATION

SOVRAN JOBS NO. _____

PERSONNEL REQUISITION NO. **22244**   DATES POSTED FROM _____ TO _____

KEEP IN MIND SOVRAN'S POLICY OF HIRING AND PROMOTING FROM WITHIN WITHOUT REGARD TO RACE, COLOR, RELIGION, SEX, AGE, NATIONAL ORIGIN, HANDICAP OR VETERAN STATUS.

1. TO: PERSONNEL DEPARTMENT	From Dept. or Branch Name	Location of (Dept., Br., Etc.)	Cost Center Number	Co. No.	Reg. Code

REQUIREMENTS

OBTAIN INFORMATION FROM POSITION CONTROL REPORT, EPR OR CONTACT YOUR PERSONNEL MANAGER

Salary Grade _____ Job Code _____

Job Title _____

Position Control No. _____

CLASS: ☐ Cleaning & Guarding
☐ Off. ☐ Exempt ☐ Non-Exempt Staff

☐ Full-Time   ☐ Part-Time   ☐ Temporary

Date Needed | If Travel Required Specify Approx. %

If Temporary Specify Period (From – To)

☐ Full-Time   ☐ Part-Time

OUTLINE OF DUTIES:

EXPERIENCE AND SKILL REQUIREMENTS: (Minimum necessary Only)

Office Location _____

Office Phone _____ Phone Extension _____

Specific Work Days _____ Specific Hours _____

Is overtime required? ☐ Yes   ☐ No

Total Number of Scheduled Work Hours Each

Week _____

Who Will Supervise This Employee?

How Many Employees Will This Person Supervise?

Any Special Or Unusual Working Conditions?

Who Will Interview Applicants for this position?
Phone No.

2. IF REPLACEMENT, COMPLETE THE FOLLOWING

Employee Replaced	Job Title	Grade	Date Job Vacant

VACANCY IS DUE TO: ☐ Termination   ☐ Transfer   ☐ Promotion

Signature - Office Mgr./Dept. Head/Reo/Div. Head	Date	Signature - Personnel Manager	Date

DATE RECEIVED BY HIRING OFFICE
_____

3. FOR USE OF PERSONNEL DEPARTMENT

Name _____   Rehire ☐ Yes ☐ No

DATE FILLED
_____

Starting Date _____ Salary _____

INTERVIEWER'S SIGNATURE
_____

Hiring Location Code _____

Filled From: ☐ Outside ☐ Job Posting ☐ In House Transfer ☐ On-Call, Inc.

WHITE   1. FOR USE BY INTERVIEWER IN PERSONNEL DEPARTMENT.
YELLOW   2. PERSONNEL OFFICER: RETAIN THIS COPY UNTIL POSITION IS FILLED AND WHITE COPY RETURNED.
PINK   3. ORIGINATING DEPARTMENT: RETAIN THIS COPY.

Source: Sovran Bank, N.A., Norfolk, Va.

FIGURE 8-2

HIRING RESPONSIBILITIES

SUPERVISOR		P/HR STAFF
forecast HR needs	⟶	develop HR plan
submit requisition	⟶	locate qualified workers
		↓
		conduct preliminary employment
conduct interviews	⟵	procedures (screening, first interview, testing, references)
↓		
make recommendations	⟶	make hiring decision

form the job. For example, a job specification might include some of the following statements:

Must be able to input on a word processor at the rate of 50 words per minute with errors corrected.

Must possess a valid California driver's license.

Must demonstrate an ability to communicate effectively with students.

Must be able to work effectively without supervision in a solitary work environment.

Must have completed high school and 2 years of technical school, or its equivalent.

A *job description* provides information about the tasks required by the job, the working conditions, whom the worker reports to, and any other information necessary to describe the job properly.

Using the information from the job analysis and the information about the applicant obtained from the application and from subsequent employment procedures, the supervisor tries to match the job and the person. The match must consider the skills, knowledge, abilities, and interests of the applicant as well as the requirements of the job. For example, if the job to be filled is one in which there is little opportunity for creativity and independent thinking and the applicant has indicated that he or she works best without supervision and is looking for a job that will allow her or him to try new ideas, then there is obviously not a match—even if the applicant meets all of the other job specifications.

Matching the job and the applicant—finding a good ''fit'' between the requirements of the job and the requirements of the applicant—results in a more productive employee. And more productive employees, satisfied with their jobs, remain with the company longer. When the match is bad, either the company will be dissatisfied with the performance of the employee or the employee will be dissatisfied with the job and with the company. In either case, the company loses an employee and must go through the entire hiring process once more.

Competency Check:

Can you explain why it is important to have a good match between job and applicant in the staffing process?

THE STAFFING PROCESS

The supervisor's role in the employment process is shown in Figure 8-2. It is important, however, to understand the entire process and then focus on the components that more specifically relate to the duties of the supervisor.

Forecasting Work-Force Requirements

Forecasting work-force requirements means projecting future staffing needs in terms not only of quantity of employees but also of skills necessary to perform the jobs of the future.

As Barbara Michaels realized at the beginning of this chapter, you can't forecast without data. And she had no data to either verify or reject Ray's projections for human resource needs. How can Michaels determine the right number of people and the right skills, knowledge, and abilities needed at the right time for her department?

The department Michaels supervises is the telemarketing arm of the sales department. Michaels has asked for and received the company sales plan for the next 5 years. Publishers Promotions, Inc., has set a 20 percent increase in telemarketing sales as one of its sales goals for next year. Telemarketing sales goals for the following 2 years are 20 percent and 15 percent, respectively. Barbara's charge is to determine how many additional sales associates will be necessary to generate the increased sales and how many clerical workers will be necessary to support the sales associates. At the present sales level, the 20 sales associates are currently working about 6 hours out of 8. The five clerks always have a backlog of orders to process—at least a day's work each week. To determine the number of sales associates and clerks required to meet projected sales levels, Michaels should take the following steps:[2]

1. Determine the output necessary to meet the goals. The current sales associates make about 2400 telecalls a day (20 sales associates working about 6 hours a day, each making about 20 calls per hour). On the average, 1 phone call in 6 results in a sale. This means 400 sales a day. A 20 percent increase, therefore, would increase sales to a total of 480 a day.

2. Determine how many sales-associate hours would be required to meet the goal of a 20 percent increase in sales.

   2880 calls per day ÷ 20 calls per hour = 144 work hours

3. Allow for equipment downtime, coffee breaks, unavoidable delays, and normal level of employee interaction. (An hour to an hour and a half per day is a fair estimate.)

8 hours − 1.5 nonproductive hours
   = 6.5 productive hours per day per employee
144 hours ÷ 6.5 productive hours per day
   = 22.15 sales associates required to reach new
      sales goals of 20 percent increase

4. Allow for worker absences, vacations, and holidays. On the average, the sales associates have been absent a combined total of 80 days for each of the past 3 years. Each sales associate earns 10 vacation days and 5 legal holidays a year.

10 vacation days + 5 legal holidays for each
   of 20 employees = 300 days
80 absences + 300 vacation/holidays
   = 380 days away from work
52 weeks × 5 days = 260 days available per year
380 days off work = 1 year, 120 days, or 1.46 year
22.15 employees + 1.46 employees
   = 23.61, or 24 sales associates required to reach goal

5. Determine worker hours for clerks necessary to support the sales associates, keeping in mind that there is a 1-day backlog of work each week. The clerks are now processing 1600 orders a week (four-fifths of the orders generated).

1600 ÷ 5 clerks = 320 orders processed by each clerk each week
320 orders ÷ 5 days = 64 orders per day per clerk

New Target:

2400 sales ÷ 5 days = 480 orders per day to be processed
480 orders ÷ 64 orders per day = 7.5 clerks required to process orders

6. Allow for absences, vacations, and holidays for clerks. On the average, clerks have been absent from their jobs a combined total of 20 days for each of the past 3 years. They earn the same vacation and legal holidays as the sales associates.

10 vacation days + 5 legal holidays × 7.5 clerks = 112.5 days
112.5 days + 20 absences = 132.5 days away from work
132.5 days = 0.51 of a year
7.5 + 0.51 = 8.01, or 8 clerks required to process
   the sales resulting from the new target

Competency Check:

Provided basic information such as that Barbara Michaels was given, could you forecast human resource needs?

The same kind of analysis Michaels has made to forecast the needs of her department (24 sales associates, an increase of 4 over the present level, and 8 clerks, an increase of 3) can be used to forecast the human resource needs of other types of workers. Substitute "widgets" for number of successful telecalls to determine number of workers required to produce "x" number of the product. Substitute number of custodial workers or supply workers for the clerks to obtain the required number of support people for production workers. Or substitute the number of documents flowing through a word processing center.

Recruiting

Recruiting is the process of building up an applicant pool from which to select employees. The primary responsibility for recruiting rests with the HR/P department. They recruit externally and internally to obtain qualified applicants.

External Sources

Walk-ins.　　Walk-ins are applicants who "walk in" and inquire if there are any vacancies. They are not responding to a call for applicants.

Educational Institutions.　　Students are a good source of applicants, and many companies recruit directly at schools.

Employment Agencies.　　Each state has a state employment agency; the agencies do not charge either the applicant or the employer since they are tax-supported programs. In addition, there are private employment agencies, which charge a fee for placing someone on the job. The fee may be paid by either the applicant or the employer. Temporary-help agencies may also add to the applicant pool.

Media.　　Advertising positions through newspapers, periodicals, or radio is another way to obtain applicants. More companies use newspaper advertisements than any other source to generate applicants.

Professional and Trade Associations.　　Advertisements may be placed in professional and trade journals when applicants are needed for positions requiring specialized technical and professional skills.

Competitors.　　Some companies raid their competition to get employees. One advantage of this type of recruiting is that the employee needs less training on the job. A disadvantage, of course, is that your firm is subject to the same raiding technique.

Unions.　　Labor unions have long been a source of employees for certain types of jobs. The union hall is the contact point between organizations and potential employees.

Internal Sources

Many organizations prefer to recruit internally before going to external sources. Internally, applicants may be obtained through:

Job Posting and Job Bidding.   When there is a vacancy, a description of the job and the specifications are posted in an area where employees are most likely to see it. Typical postings are made on bulletin boards, near water coolers, or in the company newsletter, inviting employees to ''bid'' on a job.

Present Employees.   Present employees provide a pool of applicants, particularly for jobs that represent upward mobility. Present employees may also recommend friends or family members for jobs (if that is permitted in the organization).

Former Applicants and Employees.   Although these applicants and employees are not presently with the company, they may represent a potential candidate pool for current jobs.

WHAT CAN THE SUPERVISOR DO?

Supervisors have a role in recruiting, too. They should know the SKA requirements for the job and communicate that information to the HR/P department. Supervisors may be asked to review advertisements, post job openings, and ''sign off'' on job bids.

Supervisors can let current employees know that there is (or will be) a vacancy, describe the skills the applicant needs to fill the job, and encourage employees to make recommendations. The supervisor may also recommend that current employees be promoted when they possess the requisite skills.

Competency Check:

Can you describe the roles of the HR/P department and the supervisor in recruiting?

Screening Applicants

As shown in Figure 8-2, the initial screening process is done by the HR/P department. The supervisor becomes involved after the initial screening has been completed. In a small company, however, the supervisor might have responsibility for the entire process.

Initial Screening

The initial screening process begins when the applicant submits an application or résumé to the employment office. The application or résumé itself is a screening device. A comparison of the job description and job specification with the applicant information will reveal if there is a match and if, therefore, the applicant should go on to the next stage.

In some firms, the applicant has a brief screening interview *before* completing the application form; in others, the brief screening interview follows submission of the application. The purpose of this initial, very brief interview is to determine if the applicant meets the minimum job qualifications.

Tests

Tests are administered, when appropriate, by the HR/P department. Typical tests include *tests of proficiency,* which measure levels of achieved skill or acquired knowledge; *aptitude tests,* which measure an applicant's potential to perform a job; *personality tests,* which evaluate characteristics such as emotional maturity, sociability, and responsibility; *honesty tests,* which are paper-and-pencil tests that purport to measure an applicant's honesty; *intelligence tests,* which measure a person's knowledge; and *vocational-interest inventories,* which evaluate an applicant's likes and dislikes in relation to occupations and hobbies.

If tests are a part of the employment process, they should meet the criteria of validity, reliability, and job relatedness.

Validity.   A valid test measures what it is represented to measure. For example, if a test is to measure an applicant's ability to perform the math functions required on the job but it really measures only the ability to follow instructions, then the test is said to be *invalid.*

Reliability.   A reliable test produces the same results with repeated use. If Scot, for example, is given a test to measure his manual dexterity and scores very low, and then he is given the same test a week later and scores very high, the test is not a reliable measure of his ability.

Job Relatedness.   Any test given for employment purposes must be job-related. For example, if a shorthand test is required for all secretarial applicants when the actual duties of the secretary do not require shorthand, the test is not considered job-related.

References

References may be requested either before or after the supervisor conducts an in-depth interview. Some companies want to have all of the preliminary information available before the supervisor's interview; others wait until after the supervisor has indicated an interest in the applicant before asking for references.

Some employers place little credence in references. Frequently, former employers will provide only limited information. Many firms limit the information they provide on previous employees to dates of employment and job title or simply acknowledge that the person requesting the reference was, indeed, employed by the firm. Because of possible legal ramifications, former employers are reluctant to give a negative reference and, therefore, give a rather neutral evaluation of the former employee's performance. The worst-case scenario is one in which a less-than-honest reference is given because it is a way of getting a current employee ''out of our hair'' and into a new position. While references should continue to be a part of the employment

Competency Check:

Can you cite the methods used to screen applicants?

process, it is not wise to overemphasize references when making a decision to employ or not to employ.

Interviewing

After an applicant has gone through the initial screening and met the qualifications for the job, the next step is an in-depth interview by the supervisor. This is the stage at which the supervisor tries to determine, based on all the preliminary information, if this applicant is the person for the job. This is also the time at which the supervisor will describe the job and provide some information about the company.

Planning for the Interview

The supervisor, as well as the applicant, must prepare for the interview. One of the best ways for the supervisor to prepare is to become familiar with the job description, job specification, and applicant information. Applicant information will come from the application or from a résumé, from references, from the test results, and from any notes made by the HR/P staff following the initial interview. Figure 8-3 on page 226 is a good checklist to follow when becoming familiar with the job requirements.

Set the stage for the interview by creating a comfortable environment. Conduct the interview in a room that is private and in which the atmosphere is pleasant (comfortable temperature, enough light, attractive). If your office doesn't meet these requirements, there may be a conference room available for the interview. Keep in mind that the interview offers you an opportunity to present the company in a positive way to a potential employee who may be an invaluable asset to the company. At the same time, however, be honest about any requirements of the job that may be perceived as negative. For example, if overtime is required, if there is a dress code, or if there is a no-smoking policy, applicants should be made aware of these requirements.

Prepare questions to be asked during the interview. The questions should focus on the applicant's employment history, education, outside activities and interests (if appropriate), strengths and weaknesses. A form that can be used to develop your questions is shown in Figure 8-4 on page 227. A list of possible questions is presented later in this chapter.

Competency Check:

Can you describe the supervisor's activities when planning for an interview?

Many companies use a structured interview format (one that follows a set pattern of questions provided to the interviewer). If this is the case, your preparation for the interview should consist of becoming so familiar with the questions that they will seem to be your own.

Beginning the Interview

When the applicant comes into the room, stand, greet him or her with a firm handshake, and introduce yourself. Indicate where the applicant should sit. Make every effort to put the person at ease. If the applicant appears to be nervous, offer a beverage and spend a moment in small talk. But be careful to avoid questions that might later be considered discriminatory.

Let the applicant know the purpose of the interview. ''You have completed the

FIGURE 8-3

WHAT THE INTERVIEWER SHOULD KNOW ABOUT THE REQUIREMENTS OF THE JOB

SKILL/KNOWLEDGE/EDUCATION

technical knowledge required
job expectation—output, quality, costs
special equipment required
specific experience required
specific skills required
formal education required
job duties involved

RESPONSIBILITIES

potential loss to company—equipment,
    products, $$, good will
supervision of others
safety of others
confidential information
customer contact
vendor contact
public contact

PHYSICAL

activity—energy required
mobility—speed required
strength
visual/auditory requirements
sensitivity of touch/smell
dexterity
general health
appearance (if relevant)
sex (if bona fide requirement)

ENVIRONMENT

working conditions
safety hazards
hours
location
travel

INTELLECTUAL

intelligence required
judgment required
independent action required
amount of supervision

MISCELLANEOUS

pay—benefits
future potential of job

EMOTIONAL

pressures of job
variety or monotony of work
job satisfactions
adaptability required
relationships with others
personality and attitudes of supervisors,
    coworkers, subordinates

Source: Sovran Bank, N.A., Norfolk, Virginia.

*Competency
Check:*

Can you describe
the supervisor's
activities when
beginning the
interview?

initial screening process, and our purpose today is to try to establish if there is a proper fit between you and the job for which you have applied.'' Keep in mind that the interview should provide information about the applicant that may not be completely covered by the application. Therefore, you should talk no more than 20 to 25 percent of the time. Otherwise, you may become the interviewee, and the purpose of the interview will be lost.

Maintain control of the interview. Control means that you establish the direction of the questions and the time spent on the answers. Do not allow the interviewee to wander off in other directions; keep the purpose of the interview in mind. Begin with a leading question such as ''How did you learn about this job opening?'' or ''Why are you interested in this job?''

FIGURE 8-4

Structured
interview form

Fill out questions prior to the interview to ensure you cover all the areas you need to know about in order to predict an applicant's future performance in the position.

Applicant's Name _____

Position Applied For _____

Interviewer _____

WORK HISTORY

Opening Question: _____

Specific Questions: _____

_____

EDUCATION

Opening Question: _____

Specific Questions: _____

_____

NONPAID ACTIVITIES

Opening Question: _____

Specific Questions: _____

_____

PROBLEM-SOLVING SKILLS

Opening Question: _____

Specific Questions: _____

_____

PERSONALITY FACTORS

Opening Question: _____

Specific Questions: _____

_____

OTHER CRITERIA

Opening Question: _____

Specific Questions: _____

_____

Source: Suzanne Reiffers, *How to Hire and Supervise Women Legally,* Executive Enterprises Publications Co., Inc., New York, 1979, p. 19.

During the Interview

Once the lead-in has been done, you can get to the heart of the interview. To gain the type of information that will be helpful, however, there are certain types of questions that should be avoided. Try to avoid:

Questions That Can Be Answered with a Yes or No.   "Were your business courses helpful to you?" "Do you think you have the skills to do this job?" Change these yes or no questions (this can really tax the interviewer's skills) to open-ended questions that allow the applicant to respond in more than monosyllables. Perhaps the first question could be changed to "How were your business courses helpful to you?" The second question could be changed to "Describe the skills that you would bring to this job." Open-ended questions also provide the interviewer with an opportunity to see and hear the applicant use communication skills that may not be apparent in yes or no responses.

Leading Questions.   These questions often telegraph the right response. For example, "Would you say that you have good interpersonal skills?" or "Don't you think that it is important to plan for personal growth?" say to the interviewee "Your response should be a very strong yes."

Obvious Questions.   "So you graduated from John Marshall High School?" is a question that is answered on the application and is a waste of time to ask. "You worked for John Cool for 2 years right after college?" is another example of an obvious question. Use the limited time you have to obtain information not available to you prior to the interview.

Questions That Are Not Job-Related.   Confine your questions to ones that are related to the job. "When overtime is necessary, is that a problem for you?" "What kind of lathe have you operated?" "Is your driver's license current?" are all job-related questions. Questions that are not job-related might include "Are you a Redskins fan?" or "What do you think of (the current 'hot topic')?" or even "What do you do for recreation?"

Questions That May Be Considered Discriminatory.   This issue is addressed later in this chapter.

A major employer has divided the questions to be asked during the interview into these categories: work experience, education and training, leadership, initiative, persistence, motivation, and communication skills.

Work Experience

- Describe your work experience at your previous position.
- What additional responsibilities did you have?

- What was the most fulfilling aspect of that job?
- What was the least fulfilling aspect of that job?
- Why did you leave?
- How do you feel about your progress on that job?
- Which of your previous jobs did you find most fulfilling?
- Which of your previous jobs did you find least fulfilling?
- What recognition for outstanding performance did you receive in your previous job?
- Why did you choose to work for your previous employer?
- What skills did you develop in your previous position?

Education and Training

- What was your major course of study?
- Why did you select that course?
- What was your minor course of study, if any?
- What courses did you prefer? Why?
- What courses did you dislike? Why?
- What courses did you find most valuable? Why?
- What courses did you find least valuable? Why?
- What training have you had that would help you in this position?
- What further training or education do you anticipate obtaining?
- What extracurricular activities were you involved in?

Note: As the applicant's educational experience becomes less recent, it decreases in relevance. Educational experience is also less important than the amount and quality of the applicant's work experience.

Leadership

- How do you feel about making decisions? Why?
- How do you feel about supervising others? Why?
- How would you evaluate your degree of self-confidence? Why?
- How do you feel about authority?

Initiative

- What is your idea of challenging work?
- How do you feel about working in an unstructured environment?
- How do you feel about regularly increasing your job responsibilities?

Persistence

- How do you feel about working in a high-pressure area?
- How do you feel about working in a position in which there are many obstacles to overcome?
- How would you react if given an unpleasant task?

Motivation

- What are your short-term career goals?
- What are your long-term career goals?

Communication Skills (if Job-Related)

- What is important to you in communicating with others?
- What written communication skills have you developed?
- Have you taken any communication courses? Describe them.
- What public speaking experience do you have?

The interviewer should be objective during the interview and wait until the interview is over before making a decision about whether to recommend this applicant for the job.[3]

Avoid snap judgments. It has been said that many interviewers make a decision about an applicant within the first 3 minutes of an interview. It is very difficult to overcome an initial negative impression. For example, if the applicant is late for the appointment, the interviewer may decide, justly or unjustly, that this applicant is not dependable. Rather than jumping to a conclusion, a good interviewer will file that bit of information away and evaluate the applicant based on the total interview.

Avoid personal biases. Objectivity is the key; evaluate the applicant on the basis of all the information you have available. You may believe that pregnant women should not be working or that members of minority groups take longer to learn a job. These are personal biases not based on fact. The first step in avoiding decisions based on biases is to recognize that you have biases and that you must put them aside when you make employment decisions.

Avoid the "halo effect." The halo effect occurs when you let one factor influence your assessment of all other factors of an applicant's employability. For example, Mason scored very high on her aptitude test; therefore, you assume that she is also a good performer and a responsible person. You are guilty of letting the halo effect color your assessment of Mason's entire potential. On the other hand, Jeff is late for his interview and so you assume that he must be irresponsible and lack good thinking skills. Negative halo effect is at work here.

Avoid emphasizing the negative. One negative can outweigh several positives because the focus is often on the negative rather than the positive. As the song says, "Accentuate the positive, eliminate the negative." This does not mean that you should ignore negatives; it simply means that negative factors should not receive greater weight than positive ones. Keep them in perspective.

If possible, wait until after the interview to make notes and complete any required forms. It is very distracting to the applicant if you are writing while he or she is talking. Interviewers can also be distracted if they try to take notes while listening to the applicant.

Competency Check:

Can you describe the supervisor's activities during the interview?

Closing the Interview

When you have all the information you require to make your recommendation, close the interview. You may do that by saying "Is there anything else we should cover?" or "Do you have any additional questions that I can answer at this time?" If there are none, you may close the interview by thanking the applicant for coming in and explaining that he or she will be notified of the employment decision by the HR/P department within 2 weeks (or whatever time frame has been established).

After the Interview

A written record of the interview should be made immediately following the interview. If you wait until later, you may forget some points you wished to make. Or if you interview several people before making your written report, it is possible to confuse some of the applicants and to attribute qualities to the wrong person. Two examples of applicant interview reports are shown in Figures 8-5 and 8-6 on pages 232–234.

Competency Check:

Can you describe the supervisor's activities in closing the interview and after the interview?

Selection

In a large organization, selection will be made by the HR/P department based on all the information received, with special emphasis on the supervisor's recommendation. Frequently, a supervisor will be asked to recommend several candidates for the job, and the final selection will be made by the HR/P staff. In a small company, however, the selection may be made by the supervisor based on the preliminary employment information.

If the responsibilities of the supervisor include telling the applicant of an employment decision, care should be exercised in communicating either acceptance or rejection. Communicating acceptance is easier because giving good news is always more pleasant than giving bad news. Communicating good news can also be a trap, however. This is more fully described in Chapter 17. It is enough here to caution against making promises along with the offer of employment. Remarks such as, "If you do a good job, you'll be here until you retire," or "Welcome aboard. You're probably the most qualified person we've had around here in the past few years" may be construed as a contractual obligation and should be avoided.

FIGURE 8-5   Applicant interview report

SOVRAN FINANCIAL CORPORATION
APPLICANT EVALUATION REPORT
MANAGEMENT ASSOCIATE PROGRAM
INITIAL INTERVIEW

Applicant's Name: _____   Date: _____

Referred by: _____   Interviewer: _____

Rate on scale of 1–5 with   1   2   3   4   5
                            Poor   Good   Excellent

1. **IMPACT** — Ability to create a good first impression, to command attention and respect, to demonstrate confidence, and to achieve personal recognition.   _____

    +/− Business Dress   +/− Poise   +/− Maturity   +/− Grooming
    +/− Confidence   +/− Assertiveness   +/− Enthusiasm

2. **ORAL COMMUNICATIONS SKILLS** — Effectiveness of expression as demonstrated by clarity of speech, vocabulary, and grammar.   _____

    +/− Vocabulary   +/− Syntax   +/− Clarity   +/− Rate   +/− Grammar
    +/− Eye Contact   +/− Animation   +/− Volume

3. **SALESMANSHIP** — Ability to persuade and to sell oneself in the interview.   _____

4. **LEVEL OF ACHIEVEMENT** — Factors which comprise this person's record, quality of life's experience or indicate a commitment to achievement and success.

    College _____

    Major _____

    GPA _____ Date Graduated _____
                                    (or will graduate)

    +/− Business Coursework   +/− Activities   +/− Leadership
    +/− Community Involvement   +/− Work Experience

5. **INTEREST** — Extent to which this individual is knowledgeable about Sovran, has adequately prepared for a career in banking, and matches up to Sovran's current goals.   _____

    +/− Industry Knowledge   +/− Level of Ambition
    +/− Banking Career Interest   +/− Quality of Questions
    +/− Sovran Knowledge   +/− Realistic Expectations
    +/− Management Interest   +/− Business Development Interest

FIGURE 8-5   (Continued)

GEOGRAPHICAL INTERESTS
(Rank for Priority (1,2,3)

    AREA   CITY PREFERENCE

___Central Region   _____
___Eastern Region   _____
___Hampton Roads Region _____
___Maryland   _____
          _____
___Mountain Region _____
___Northern/Potomac Regions _____
___Skyline Region   _____
___Southside Region _____
___Western Region   _____

FUNCTIONAL INTERESTS
(Check appropriate areas)

___Retail   ___Fin. Serv./Invest.
___Commercial ___Real Estate Finance
___Trust   ___Personnel
___Marketing ___Audit
___Accounting ___Systems
___Operations ___Mortgage Lending
___Leasing

OVERALL RATING _____
(Rate on scale of 1-5)

RECOMMENDATION (check one)

☐ Drop from consideration (circle reason for decision)
 a. applicant not qualified
 b. applicant not interested in M.A. position – do not refer to other areas
 c. competition too stiff

☐ Consider for next step in selection process

☐ Definitely move to next step in selection process

☐ Other: Drop from consideration for M.A. position and refer to: (check appropriate area)

   Commercial (CBA) _____ Accounting _____
   Real Estate Finance (REFA) _____ Systems _____
   Other _____ (Specify department below)
   _____
   _____

APPLICANT IS A CANDIDATE FOR (check one) _____ February Program _____ June Program

Interviewer's Signature _____

Source: Sovran Bank, N.A., Norfolk, Va., used in Betty R. Ricks and Kay F. Gow, *Business Communications: Systems and Applications,* John Wiley & Sons, Inc., New York, 1987, p. 438.

FIGURE 8-6 Interviewer report form

Job Title:							Candidate Name:				Date:	
Rating factors Consider all factors in relation to the position for which the interview is being conducted	**Rating** Check the appropriate boxes.											
	Below acceptable level						Accept-able	Good	Superior	Out-standing		
	10	20	30	40	50	60	70	80	90	100	WT* (1-3)	Score
Relevant previous experience												
Possession of critical knowledge, skills, abilities (see job specifications)												
Oral communications skill (ability to communicate ideas)												
Interpersonal style, personality attitudes consistent with job requirements												
Reasoning/ judgment (ability to problem-solve at necessary level of expertise)												
Interest in the position/compatibility with career plans												
Appearance, physical condition (if appropriate)												
Others:												

*WT: Assign weights to criteria and multiply by factor of   TOTAL
        1 = desirable, but not essential
        2 = important
        3 = critical to job success.
Comments: Give justification for extreme ratings (below 50, above 80) on the back of this form.

Interviewer's signature _____

Source: Betty R. Ricks and Kay F. Gow, *Business Communications: Systems and Applications,* John Wiley & Sons, Inc., New York, 1987, p. 439.

It is sometimes necessary to reject one applicant in favor of a more qualified one. When this happens, the turndown should be made objectively and briefly.[4] "We have made our selection for the accounting clerk, but we thank you for your interest in our company." Do not offer the applicant reasons for the rejection unless you are forced to. If you have asked applicants to specify in their applications exactly the type of job they are seeking, and then have them document their own specifications, you have had the applicants select themselves out of the pool for other jobs.

One last caution: Beware of making casual notes on rejected applicants' applications or on the interview forms. Notations such as "mature," "nice girl," or "pregnant" may be used in court to support claims of age or sex discrimination.

Let's review and trace the applicant flow through the employment process, as shown in Figure 8-7 on page 236.

Competency Check:

Can you describe the role of the supervisor in selecting employees?

LEGAL IMPLICATIONS

We live in a litigious society where it is not unusual for courts to award large sums, often in six or more figures, to employees or former employees who charge that they have been treated in a discriminatory manner. To avoid charges of discrimination in employment, supervisors should be aware of laws that protect certain groups from discriminatory practices. In addition to being aware of the laws, supervisors must also know how to follow legal staffing procedures.

Equal Employment Opportunity (EEO)

At the federal level, there are four basic laws governing equal employment opportunity. These laws are outlined in Figure 8-8 on page 237. The laws are designed to protect certain groups from discriminatory practices in all stages of employment— hiring, promotion, transfer, and termination.

1. *Title VII of the 1964 Civil Rights Act, as amended,* is the basic act that protects against discrimination based on race, color, religion, sex, and national origin. This act extends to discrimination in employment. Employers may not discriminate in their employment decisions on the basis of an individual's race, color, religion, sex, or national origin.
2. *The Equal Pay Act of 1963* is a gender-based act that makes it unlawful to pay females less than males who perform similar duties. This law relates to the sex of the employee only and does not extend to race, color, religion, or national origin. For example, a female flight attendant must be paid the same salary as a male flight attendant with equal seniority. However, the act does not protect a black male who is paid less than a white male for the same job.
3. *The Age Discrimination in Employment Act of 1967, as amended,* protects against discrimination in employment decisions on the basis of an individual's

FIGURE 8-7 Applicant flow

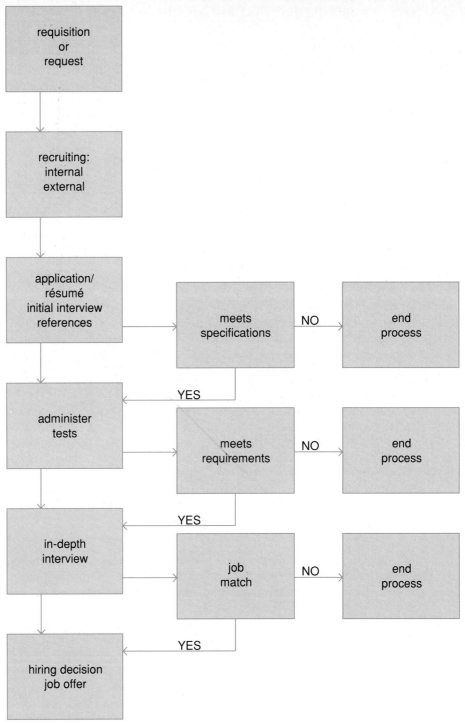

FIGURE 8-8

BASIC LAWS GOVERNING EQUAL EMPLOYMENT OPPORTUNITY

ACT	PROTECTS AGAINST
Title VII of the 1964 Civil Rights Act as amended	discrimination on the basis of race, color, sex, religion, national origin
Equal Pay Act of 1963	discrimination in pay between males and females performing similar duties
Age Discrimination in Employment Act of 1967 as amended	discrimination in employment on the basis of age
Pregnancy Discrimination Act of 1978	discrimination in employment based on sex; pregnancy must be treated as any other temporary disability

age. The law protects all persons over the age of 40 and extends to both the private sector and the federal government. For example, an employer may not refuse to promote qualified persons because they are 60 years old and the employer believes that they do not have enough productive years left until their retirement.

4. *The Pregnancy Discrimination Act of 1978* protects against discrimination in employment because of pregnancy. Pregnancy should be treated as an employer would treat any other temporary disability. For example, an employer who grants special treatment to an employee who is temporarily disabled with a broken leg should extend the same treatment to a pregnant woman or a new mother. An employer may not refuse to hire a qualified female because she is pregnant.

There are several exemptions to the above laws. If there is a seniority clause in a union contract, promotion may be determined by seniority. Another exemption is if the company can show that the qualification is a bona-fide occupational qualification (BFOQ). A BFOQ may specify, for example, that a model for women's clothes must be female; that someone advertising cosmetics for black females must be both black and female; or that a flight attendant must meet minimum height requirements to reach overhead storage areas.

All employment decisions should be based on the qualifications of the worker, not on whether the person is black, white, or oriental; male or female; young, middle-aged, or older; Catholic, Protestant, or Buddhist; or from the United States or France. The basic question should be, "Is this the person most qualified to do the job?"

In addition to the laws discussed, federal contractors or subcontractors may not discriminate against Vietnam veterans or the physically or mentally handicapped.

Competency Check:

Can you identify four major federal acts governing equal employment opportunity and describe the groups they protect?

Larger federal contractors may be required to examine their work force to be sure there is no underutilization of women or minorities. Being aware of the law is the first step toward protecting your company from lawsuits.

Following Legal Staffing Procedures

In order to follow legal staffing procedures, supervisors must know what constitutes discrimination and must conduct themselves in such a way as to avoid even the perception of discriminating practices. Supervisors have little influence on what is included on the employment application or how preliminary screening is done; these decisions are made at higher levels in the organization. Therefore, the primary staffing responsibility of supervisors is to interview all applicants in a nondiscriminatory manner.

Nondiscriminatory interviewing means asking only job-related questions. Figure 8-9 was developed by New York State's Division of Human Rights as a guide to which pre-employment questions to ask and which to avoid. It should be noted, however, that although the figure is labeled ''Legal and illegal pre-employment questions,'' it is not the questions themselves that are legal or illegal. For example, if you ask an applicant, ''Have you ever been arrested?'' you're not going to be charged with a crime, handcuffed, and hauled off to jail. What may be considered illegal is the way the applicant perceives that the information has been used. ''I believe I wasn't hired because the interviewer asked if I had ever been arrested and I said yes. Well, I was arrested 10 years ago for a minor offense of which I was later found innocent. But I didn't get a chance to explain. I believe I was discriminated against.''

Competency Check:

Can you list 10 questions that should not be asked during a pre-employment interview?

Treat all interviewees the same. Don't ask female applicants if they are free to travel unless you ask the same question of male applicants. Don't ask minority applicants about their credit ratings unless you ask nonminority applicants the same question. Be consistent in your treatment of applicants.

WHAT CAN THE SUPERVISOR DO?

Supervisors should take the following precautions when interviewing job applicants. This list, of course, is not inclusive, but it does provide some guidelines.

1. Age should not be an item for discussion.
2. Female applicants should not be questioned about their child-care arrangements.
3. An applicant's religious preferences are his or her private affair and should not be discussed.
4. It is unwise to seek information about the employment of an applicant's spouse unless the applicant indicates that this is a factor to be considered.

FIGURE 8-9 Legal and illegal pre-employment questions

Here is a series of questions which the New York State Division of Human Rights has compiled as being lawful and unlawful pre-employment inquiries. As New York appears to be stricter than most states and the federal government, by following these recommendations, lawyers suggest that a company may be less likely to find itself in difficulty with the authorities because of pre-employment inquiries.
(Verified with N.Y. State Division of Human Rights as of January 1980.)

SUBJECT	LAWFUL*	UNLAWFUL
Race or Color:		Complexion or color of skin. Coloring
Religion or Creed:		Inquiry into applicant's religious denomination, religious affiliations, church, parish, or religious holidays observed. Applicant may not be told "This is a (Catholic, Protestant, or Jewish) organization."
National Origin:		Inquiry into applicant's lineage, ancestry, national origin, descent, parentage or nationality. Nationality of applicant's parents or spouse. What is your mother tongue?
Sex:		Inquiry as to gender.
Marital Status:		Do you wish to be addressed as Mr.? Mrs.? Miss? or Ms.? Are you married? Are you single? Divorced? Separated? Name or other information about spouse.
Birth Control:		Inquiry as to capacity to reproduce, advocacy of any form of birth control or family planning.
Age:	Are you 18 years of age or older? If not, state your age.	How old are you? What is your date of birth? What are the ages of your children, if any?
Disability:	Do you have any impairments, physical, mental, or medical, which would interfere with your ability to perform the job for which you have applied? If there are any positions or types of positions for which you should not be considered, or job duties you cannot perform because of physical, mental or medical disability, please describe.	Do you have a disability? Have you ever been treated for any of the following diseases . . .? Do you now, or have you ever had, a drug or alcohol problem?
Arrest Record:	Have you ever been convicted of a crime? (Give details)	Have you ever been arrested?
Name:	Have you ever worked for this company under a different name? Is additional information relative to change of name, use of an assumed name or nickname necessary to enable a check on your work record? If yes, explain.	Original name of an applicant whose name has been changed by court order or otherwise. Maiden name of a married woman. If you have ever worked under another name, state name and dates.
Address or Duration of Residence:	Applicant's place of residence. How long a resident of this state or city?	
Birthplace:		Birthplace of applicant. Birthplace of applicant's parents, spouse or other close relatives.

Inquiries which would otherwise be deemed lawful may, in certain circumstances, be deemed as evidence of unlawful discrimination when the inquiry seeks to elicit information about a selection criterion which is not job-related and which has a disproportionately burdensome effect upon the members of a minority group and cannot be justified by business necessity.

(continued over)

FIGURE 8-9 (Continued)

SUBJECT	LAWFUL*	UNLAWFUL
Birthdate:		Requirements that applicant submit birth certificate, naturalization or baptismal record. Requirement that applicant produce proof of age in the form of a birth certificate or baptismal record.
Photograph:		Requirement or option that applicant affix a photograph to employment form at any time before hiring.
Citizenship:	Are you a citizen of the United States? If not a citizen of the United States, do you intend to become a citizen of the United States? If you are not a United States citizen, have you the legal right to remain permanently in the United States? Do you intend to remain permanently in the United States?	Of what country are you a citizen? Whether an applicant is naturalized or a native-born citizen; the date when the applicant acquired citizenship. Requirement that applicant produce naturalization papers or first papers. Whether applicant's parents or spouse are naturalized or native-born citizens of the United States; the date when such parents or spouse acquired citizenship.
Language:	Inquiry into languages applicant speaks and writes fluently.	What is your native language? Inquiry into how applicant acquired ability to read, write or speak a foreign language.
Education:	Inquiry into applicant's academic, vocational or professional education and the public and private schools attended.	
Experience:	Inquiry into work experience.	
Relatives:	Name of applicant's relatives already employed by this company	Names, addresses, ages, number of applicant's spouse, children or other relatives not employed by the company.
Notify in Case of Emergency:		Name and address of person to be notified in case of accident or emergency.
Military Experience:	Inquiry into applicant's military experience in the Armed Forces of the United States or in a State Militia. Did you receive a dishonorable discharge? Inquiry into applicant's service in particular branch of United States Army, Navy, etc.	Inquiry into applicant's military experience other than in the Armed Forces of the United States or in a State Militia. Did you receive a discharge from the military in other than honorable circumstance?
Organizations:	Inquiry into applicant's membership in organizations which the applicant considers relevant to his or her ability to perform the job.	List all clubs, societies and lodges to which you belong.

Prima Facie Discriminatory Inquiries

In the absence of business necessity, a selection criterion should not be used if it has a disproportionately burdensome effect upon those of a particular race, creed, color, national origin, sex, age, marital status, or disability group. In Griggs v. Duke Power Company, 401 U.S. 424, 431 (1971) the U.S. Supreme Court said:

> "The touchstone is business necessity. If an employment practice which operates to exclude Negroes cannot be shown to be related to job performance, the practice is prohibited."

It is considered prima facie discriminatory to inquire about a subject which, because of its disproportionately burdensome effect, may not properly be used as a basis for selecting employees. The inquirer may justify the making of such inquiry by the showing of a business necessity such as a bona fide occupational qualification.

*Inquiries which would otherwise be deemed lawful may, in certain circumstances, be deemed as evidence of unlawful discrimination when the inquiry seeks to elicit information about a selection criterion which is not job-related and which has a disproportionately burdensome effect upon the members of a minority group and cannot be justified by business necessity.

Source: Division of Human Rights, New York State, 1980.

5. Matters related to the applicant's race, ancestry, or national origin are not open for discussion.

6. Value judgments about workplace social life which could be expected to discourage unmarried or minority applicants should not be expressed. Provide only factual information, and leave the appraisals to the applicants.

7. Attempts at ''in'' jokes related to race, national origin, religion, or sex should be avoided.

8. Discussion of military discharge or rank at time of discharge should be avoided.

9. Asking a handicapped applicant to describe the severity of his or her handicap is inappropriate.

10. Questions about civil rights litigation with former employers should be avoided.

11. Questions about arrests are unwarranted because the person is not judged guilty by an arrest.

12. Avoid discussion of political affiliation or membership in any political organizations.

Source: AA/EEO Department, Old Dominion University, Norfolk, Va.

COMPETENCY REVIEW

1. Describe the roles of the supervisor and the human resource/personnel department in the hiring process.

2. Explain the importance of a good match between the applicant and the job.

3. Forecast human resource needs, given basic information.

4. Describe the roles of the supervisor and the HR/P staff in recruiting.

5. Cite the methods used by the HR/P staff to screen applicants.

6. Describe the supervisor's activities in planning for the interview.

7. Describe the supervisor's activities in beginning the interview.

8. Describe the supervisor's activities during the interview.

9. Describe the supervisor's activities in closing the interview and after the interview.

10. Explain the role of the supervisor in selection.

11. Cite four laws that protect against discrimination in employment, and define the protected groups.

12. Identify five types of questions that should be avoided during a pre-employment interview.

APPLICATIONS

1. The projections for Barbara Michaels's department for next year are shown on page 220. Using the information provided on pages 220–221, complete the projections for the following 2 years.

2. Test your equal employment opportunity knowledge by answering the following questions. Answer *Yes* if you believe the question is legally defensible. Answer *No* if you believe the question is not legally defensible.

	Yes	*No*
Are you married?	_____	_____
Do you have children?	_____	_____
What is your age?	_____	_____
Where do you live?	_____	_____
How long have you lived there?	_____	_____
Tell me a little about yourself.	_____	_____
Do you believe in God?	_____	_____
Can you speak, read, or write fluently in any language other than English?	_____	_____
How did you acquire this ability?	_____	_____
What educational experience have you had?	_____	_____
Have you ever been arrested?	_____	_____
Are you willing to work an evening shift?	_____	_____
Are you willing to work on Christmas or Easter?	_____	_____
What organizations or clubs do you belong to?	_____	_____
What kind of credit rating do you have?	_____	_____
What is your height and weight?	_____	_____
Do you have friends or relatives employed here?	_____	_____
Are you pregnant?	_____	_____
What kind of military discharge did you receive?	_____	_____
Do you have any handicaps which might affect your ability to perform the duties of the job for which you are applying?	_____	_____
How do you feel about working for a woman?	_____	_____
What happens if you or your husband gets a job transfer?	_____	_____
Do you feel that your race or color will be a problem in your performing the job?	_____	_____
Where were you born?	_____	_____
What is your maiden name?	_____	_____

Source: Adapted from "Interviewing Checklist," AA/EEO Department, Old Dominion University, Norfolk, Va., which was adapted from State of Virginia EEO Office Training Program, 1982.

3. Conduct an interview with a fellow student for a telemarketing position, using the interview questions provided on pages 228 through 230.

4. Develop a set of questions that you think are appropriate for interviewing a candidate for a secretarial position. Use the form shown in Figure 8-4. Compare your questions with those developed by a fellow student. Discuss the similarities and differences.

CASES

Case I: It's a Man's World

Yesterday, two bus drivers retired, one quit, and one was fired. "Mac" McNeil, the supervisor of bus drivers for Independent Transit Company, is in the process of hiring replacements. The first of two interviews scheduled for this afternoon is in progress.

MCNEIL   Hello, Mrs. North. It is Mrs., isn't it? You know this job is a man's job. You may have to deal with some rowdies and even a few drunks. And this is a big piece of equipment for a little gal like you. Why, you probably can't even reach the pedals. How tall are you, anyway?

Why don't you sit down and tell me all about your family. You're mighty young-looking to have three kids. How old are you?

Little lady, don't you think you ought to be home with those kids and not taking a man's job away from him? Well, with all that feminist mumbo jumbo, I guess we'd better go through the formalities. You worked for Union Transit for 5 years?

Ever been arrested?

While you're out driving a bus, what does your husband do? And who are you going to get to take care of the kids? You know, we can't have you missing work because one of the kids is sick. You aren't pregnant again, are you?

What was your maiden name? Kowalsky? Isn't that Polish? I guess if you're Polish you support the Pope? You hear the joke about the Polack who . . .

Well, honey, I'll let you know about the job. I've got several men, WASPs, to interview first, and then I'll make a decision. Don't call me, I'll call you.

1. What did McNeil do wrong? List each interviewing mistake he made.
2. What questions *should* McNeil have asked to determine the applicant's qualifications for the job?

Case II: I Can Spot a Good Employee Right Away

Gerry Mahoney, area supervisor for the Mini Markets at the beach, must hire workers for the summer season that starts 6 weeks from now. She will need stock clerks, cashiers, custodians, and outside maintenance workers. The people she hires will work only through the summer; there are enough regulars for the winter months.

The home office of Mini Markets has advertised in local newspapers in college towns and actively recruited through high school counselors. Mini Markets hopes to attract students who will be willing to work crazy hours at the minimum wage just to be at the beach all summer. In fact, the advertisement reads "young, willing to work irregular hours."

The area supervisor must interview all the applicants, make all the hiring decisions, and inform the applicants. Gerry has received over 50 applications from the home office. Most of the applicants indicated that they would take any job that is available so long as it is at the beach.

Gerry has just told Carson Blankenship, the director of personnel, that she is going to interview at least 25 applicants this afternoon and another 25 on Friday. When Carson asks how that is possible, Gerry says, "Oh, I can spot a good employee right away. I have an eye for good employees. I can tell immediately if I want to hire them by the way they walk in, shake my hand, and look me in the eye."

1. Is Gerry correct? Is that the best way to select an employee? Explain your answer.
2. What would you suggest to Gerry prior to her afternoon interviews?

REFERENCES

1. H. Ross Perot, *Bits and Pieces,* vol. F, no. 4M, The Economics Press, Inc., Fairfield, N.J., 1985, p. 23.
2. Adapted from Lester R. Bittle, *What Every Supervisor Should Know,* 5th ed., McGraw-Hill Book Company, New York, 1985, pp. 189–190.
3. Betty R. Ricks and Kay F. Gow, *Business Communications: Systems and Applications,* John Wiley & Sons, Inc., New York, 1987, pp. 429–430.
4. Peter M. Panken, "The Road to Court Is Paved with Good Intentions," *Nation's Business,* June 1985, p. 46.

SUGGESTED READINGS

Bacas, Harry: "How Companies Avoid Mistakes in Hiring," *Nation's Business,* June 1985.
Barton, William M.: "The Interactive Interview," *Management World,* April–May 1986.
Clipp, Richard: "Avoiding Legal Hassles When Hiring and Firing," *Office Systems '86,* March 1986.
"The Danger of Overstaffing," *Supervisory Sense,* American Management Association, New York, 1986.
Kiechel, Walter: "How to Pick Talent," *Fortune,* Dec. 8, 1986.
"Religious Accommodation," *HRM Ideas and Trends,* Nov. 26, 1986.
Sheppard, I. Thomas: "Seeking Substance," *Management World,* July–August 1985.

9

APPRAISING AND REWARDING PERFORMANCE

9

APPRAISING AND REWARDING PERFORMANCE

COMPETENCIES

After studying this chapter, you will be able to:

1. Define *performance appraisal.*

2. Cite the major purposes of performance appraisals.

3. Diagram and describe the performance appraisal sequence.

4. Identify uses of performance appraisal information.

5. Cite and explain types of rater errors.

6. Describe performance appraisal formats.

7. Cite the importance of performance appraisal feedback.

8. Describe methods of providing feedback to employees.

9. Explain the importance of the supervisor's role in performance appraisals.

10. Describe planning steps a supervisor should take when preparing for a performance appraisal interview.

11. Cite actions a supervisor should take when conducting a performance appraisal interview.

12. List the general types of rewards and give examples of each type.

13. Describe the role of the supervisor in establishing and communicating compensation criteria.

14. Explain criteria for recommending and administering rewards effectively.

15. Tell how a supervisor can conduct nondiscriminatory appraisals.

16. Tell how a supervisor can implement nondiscriminatory reward systems.

17. Define *comparable worth* and tell how it differs from "equal pay for equal worth."

18. Describe how job evaluation is linked to comparable worth.

CHAPTER OUTLINE

I. APPRAISING PERFORMANCE

  A. Purposes of Performance Appraisal

  B. Appraisal Sequence

  C. Using Appraisal Information

  D. Appraisal Errors

  E. Appraisal Formats

II. PROVIDING FEEDBACK

  A. Written Appraisals

  B. Postappraisal Interviews

III. REWARDING PERFORMANCE

  A. Types of Rewards

  B. Establishing and Communicating Compensation Criteria

  C. Recommending and Administering Rewards

IV. LEGAL IMPLICATIONS

  A. Making Nondiscriminatory Appraisals

  B. Implementing Nondiscriminatory Rewards

  C. Monitoring Comparable Worth

Pat Collins looks at the clock. It is 9:10 A.M. He is tired; he got very little sleep last night. Today he is to conduct his first performance appraisal interview since becoming supervisor at Midwest Tool and Dye Works. And frankly, he is worried. Collins has come up through the ranks, and he is concerned about how his former peers, the workers he now supervises, will react to their appraisals and to him.

Collins has established a good working relationship with most of the workers. Still, it is not going to be easy to tell Jo Simmons that she must correct her habit of reporting to work 5 to 10 minutes late every day. She has been warned several times, and now her tardiness is being made a part of her performance appraisal. On the other hand, Collins is looking forward to commending Michael Forbes on his improvement. Forbes has reduced his scrap rate from 10 percent to 3.5 percent since his last evaluation.

Midwest Tool and Dye Works is committed to helping its employees do their jobs well. Last month, all supervisors went through a 1-week training workshop on how to evaluate workers objectively and how to provide feedback to improve worker performance. Collins excelled in the role-play exercise conducted in class. He hopes he can do as well in the "real thing," but he is nervous as time for the first interview approaches.

APPRAISING PERFORMANCE

Everyone wants to know, "How am I doing?" Performance appraisals provide one opportunity to give feedback to workers and to let them know how they are doing. *Performance appraisal* is the process of measuring and reporting employee behavior and accomplishments for a given period for the purpose of improving job performance.

Supervisors play a major role in performance evaluation because their input carries more weight than does any other information source. In an American Management Association study published in 1984, respondents overwhelmingly acknowledged the influence of the immediate supervisor's input. This is shown graphically in Figure 9-1. Note that 96.2 percent of the respondents reported that the immediate supervisor has moderate or extreme influence, with 78.9 percent citing the influence as having extreme weight.

Competency Check:

Can you define performance appraisal?

248

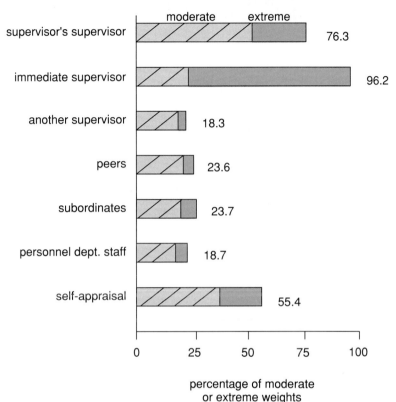

FIGURE 9-1

Supervisors'
influence on ratings

Source: Evelyn Eichel and Henry E. Bender, *Performance Appraisal: A Study of Current Techniques,* American Management Association, New York, 1984, p. 16.

Purposes of Performance Appraisal

Performance appraisals have two purposes: employee evaluation and employee development. For most companies, evaluation is the more important purpose. Appraisals of employees' performance provide the basis for administrative decisions about promotions, demotions, terminations, transfers, and rewards. The development purpose—to improve performance on the job—has generally been secondary, but the AMA study referred to earlier shows that the focus of performance appraisals is shifting to a more balanced approach. Purposes for which responding companies use performance evaluation are shown in Figure 9-2 on page 250.

Appraisal Sequence

Performance appraisal follows a sequence of activities, as shown in Figure 9-3 on page 251. This sequence is (1) to set performance standards, (2) to communicate these

Competency Check:

Can you cite the importance of the immediate supervisor's input into the performance appraisal process?

FIGURE 9-2 PURPOSES FOR WHICH RESPONDING COMPANIES USED PERFORMANCE EVALUATION

PURPOSE	PERCENTAGE OF RESPONDENTS
compensation	85.6
counseling	65.1
training and development	64.3
promotion	45.3
manpower planning	43.1
retention/discharge	30.3
validation of selection technique	17.2

Source: Evelyn Eichel and Henry E. Bender, *Performance Appraisal: A Study of Current Techniques*, American Management Association, New York, 1984, p. 7.

standards, (3) to observe the employees doing their work, (4) to collect data, (5) to have employees do self-appraisals, (6) to do a supervisor's appraisal, (7) to evaluate performance, and (8) to provide feedback.

Set Performance Standards

Performance standards provide a benchmark against which to measure employee performance. In some firms, performance standards based on historical data have already been set. For example, a standard day's work may be defined as ''produces 1800 widgets with no more than 1 percent rejects,'' and employees who produce above that average (standard) receive a higher evaluation than do those who produce the average or below the average. Other firms set individual employee standards through a management by objectives (MBO) process, where managers and subordinates set goals cooperatively. MBO is typically used for management positions and where employees have some flexibility or control over their work. An assembly-line worker, for example, has little control over the quantity of work performed and, therefore, is not a good candidate for MBO.

Communicate Standards

Employees should know from the beginning the basis for their evaluations. Will they be evaluated on the quality of their work? The quantity? Initiative? Dependability? If so, what do these mean, and what is the measure applied to them? What quality is expected? What quantity? What does *initiative* mean, and what behaviors must be exhibited to show initiative? For example, if quality is judged by percent of rejects, what percent is considered high performance, acceptable performance, marginal performance, and unacceptable performance?

Observe Employees Performing Work

During the appraisal period, employees should be observed as they perform their daily tasks, and information regarding their performance should be recorded.

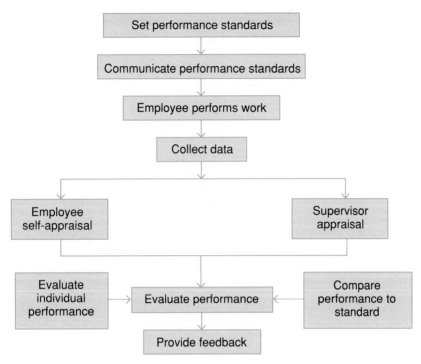

FIGURE 9-3
Performance
appraisal process

Collect Data

Data for the performance appraisal should be gathered throughout the appraisal period, not in the last minutes prior to the formal evaluation. Supervisors should record both positive and negative incidents on the job. These incidents become a part of the workers' files and can be referred to when evaluating worker performance. Examples of supervisor's notes are shown below:

3/31
The report John gave me today was completed on time, well written, requiring no revisions.

4/6
Joanne's scrap rate continues to increase. The measurement this week showed a 10% increase. Talked to her again today.

4/12
Mitchell was on break for an additional 15 minutes today — second time this week.

Have Employees Complete Self-Appraisal

Workers may be asked to complete an appraisal of their own performance. When this is a part of the performance appraisal process, this procedure should be followed:

1. Discuss the purpose of the self-appraisal with the employee.
2. Go over the format, and clarify what the employee should do.
3. Provide the employee with the form at least a week before it is to be completed.
4. Set a specific time for the self-appraisal to be completed.
5. Stress the importance of the self-appraisal to the total performance appraisal system.

Appraise the Employee

The supervisor needs to plan before beginning the employee evaluation. Plan a time when you will not be disturbed, when you can concentrate on the evaluation without being interrupted. Plan to work in a place that is comfortable and where you will be able to work with full concentration on the task. Plan the procedure that you will use, and follow the same procedure with each worker. Gather all the performance data and place it in each employee's folder. Review all the data before beginning to write. Write a draft copy. Put the draft aside for at least an hour, longer if possible. Then go back to the draft copy, and try to read it as if someone else had written the evaluation. Rewrite as necessary for clarity and objectivity.

Evaluate Performance

Evaluation should be based on the worker's performance *on the job* and not on traits or characteristics. This is more fully presented later in this chapter.

*Competency
Check:*

Can you diagram
and describe the
appraisal sequence?

Provide Feedback

Feedback may be provided in written form or in oral form and is discussed later in this chapter.

SALLY FORTH

Source: Reprinted by special permission of NAS, Inc.

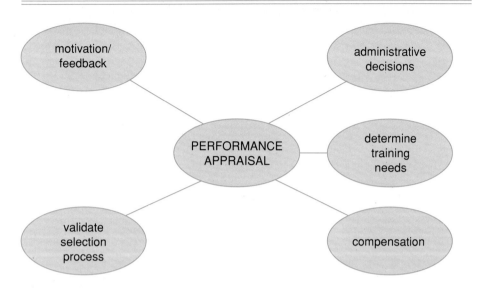

FIGURE 9-4

Uses of
performance
appraisal information

Using Appraisal Information

As shown in Figure 9-4, appraisal information may be used in five primary ways.

1. To make administrative decisions, such as whom to promote, suspend, terminate, demote, or transfer.
2. To identify training and development needs, such as what kind of training and development is needed and who can benefit by it.
3. To motivate and provide feedback by letting workers know how they are performing, what their strengths are, and in what areas they need improvement.
4. To validate the selection process by comparing worker performance with desired outcomes. For example, if 75 percent of new employees are performing below effective levels, the selection criteria should be examined to see whether the job description and job specification accurately define the requirements of the job.
5. To make compensation decisions, such as who should receive merit increases.

Competency Check:

Can you identify five uses of performance appraisal information?

Accurate, current information is required to make objective judgments that affect workers' careers. Unfair, inequitable, subjective decisions are often made because performance data are incomplete and not arrived at objectively.

Appraisal Errors

Sin Yu was a Chinese philosopher of the third century. He discussed the system of using an imperial rater to evaluate the official family of the Wei dynasty. Sin Yu said,

''The Imperial Rater of Nine Grades seldom rates men according to their merits, but always according to his likes and dislikes.''[1] Sin Yu's criticism is still valid today because performance appraisals are subject to rater errors. Some of the more common rater errors to be avoided when evaluating worker performance include:

Personal bias against members of a different race, religion, sex, or national origin.

The *halo effect,* which lets your rating of one factor affect your rating of all other factors. ''John displays an excellent knowledge of nursing techniques; therefore, I judge that he is excellent in all other nursing activities.''

Central tendency, judging most workers as average, thus not making a distinction between high and low performers.

Harshness and leniency. These are opposite sides of the same coin. Supervisors who are harsh raters tend to rate everyone at the low end of the scale; supervisors who are lenient raters evaluate everyone at the high end of the scale.

Similarity, rating people who are like you higher than those who are different from you.

Recency of events, letting what happened yesterday (or last week) affect your judgment of a worker's performance for an entire rating period.

Competency Check:

Can you explain five rating errors?

WHAT CAN THE SUPERVISOR DO?

To avoid rating errors, a supervisor should:

● Put aside personal biases, and evaluate a worker on performance only. (personal bias)

● Realize that workers have both strengths and areas where they need improvement, and rate each job dimension on its own merits, not on the basis of one strength or weakness. (halo effect)

● Understand that some workers are more productive than others; not everyone is average. Be willing to make the distinction among above average, average, or below average workers. (central tendency)

● Recognize that *all* workers are not exceptional, nor are *all* workers less than satisfactory performers. Acknowledge worker differences, and appraise individuals according to their performance. (strictness/leniency)

● Be willing to accept people who are different, and don't expect everyone to be like you. Variety in experiences and backgrounds is desirable. (similarity)

● Keep notes about events that happen throughout the appraisal period, and refer to the entire list of incidents when making an appraisal so that a worker's actions last week will not affect your rating to a greater degree than will all previous actions. (recency of events)

Appraisal Formats

The format of a performance appraisal may be comparative, absolute, or outcome-based.

Comparative Formats

If a comparative format is used, the supervisor evaluates employees in relation to each other. Most frequently used comparative methods include ranking, paired comparisons, and forced choice.

Ranking.   This method requires the evaluator to compare employees on the basis of their overall performance and then to list the employees in either *ascending* (lowest-to-highest) or *descending* (highest-to-lowest) order. This is frequently done by identifying the best performer and the worst performer, the next-best and the next-worst, and so on until all employees have been placed in rank order. Ranking is the simplest way to do a comparative appraisal.

Paired Comparison.   Under this method, each person is compared with every other person being appraised. For example, in a department with six people (Jay, Michelle, Alice, Maureen, Bob, and Ray), Jay would be compared to each of the others in turn and given a ranking of ''1'' or ''2.'' Then Michelle would be compared to the remaining employees, and so on until all have been compared one to the other, as shown below:

Jay	2	Michelle	1
Jay	1	Alice	2
Jay	2	Maureen	1
Jay	1	Bob	2
Jay	2	Ray	1
Michelle	1	Alice	2
Michelle	1	Maureen	2
Michelle	2	Bob	1
Michelle	1	Ray	2
Alice	2	Maureen	1
Alice	1	Bob	2
Alice	2	Ray	1
Maureen	1	Bob	2
Maureen	2	Ray	1
Bob	1	Ray	2

To arrive at a ranking, the number of times each person receives a ''1'' rating is calculated as follows:

Jay	2
Michelle	4
Alice	1
Maureen	3
Bob	2
Ray	3

When there are duplicate numbers (as Maureen and Ray, Jay and Bob), the original comparisons would be reviewed in order to make the decisions. Note that when Maureen and Ray were compared directly, Ray ranked first and Maureen second. Therefore, the ranking for these six people would be:

Michelle
Ray
Maureen
Jay
Bob
Alice

Forced Choice.   When this method is used to make a comparative appraisal, percentages of performers to fit in any one category are established. For example, all employees may be "forced" into the following groups:

excellent	10%
above average	20
satisfactory	40
below average	20
unsatisfactory	10

Although comparative formats are relatively simple, there are problems associated with them. One problem is that they do not provide any measure of the differences between rankings. For example, the employee ranked eighth may be considerably more productive than the one ranked ninth, while there may be very little difference in the performances of the employees ranked ninth and tenth. As you can imagine, as the number of employees increases, ranking becomes much more difficult. Because comparisons are usually made on a *global* (overall) basis, there is very little information available about strengths and weaknesses. For the employee, it is like receiving a grade of *C* on a test without being told which questions were answered correctly and which answers were wrong. It therefore provides no basis for employee development.

Absolute Formats

When absolute formats are used, the supervisor evaluates each employee's performance without comparing it to the performance of others. Frequently used absolute methods include narrative, critical incidents, graphic rating scales, weighted checklists, and behaviorally anchored rating scales (BARS).

Narrative. This method requires the rater to give a written description of a worker's performance. As its name implies, a narrative describes the worker's strengths, weaknesses, and potential, as well as providing suggestions for improving the worker's performance.

The success of the narrative method depends largely on the supervisor's ability to observe performance and translate that observation to written form. Just as important are the supervisor's writing skills and ability to describe the worker's performance clearly. A standardized form may be used to provide some uniformity to the information recorded. One form used for a narrative appraisal is shown in Figure 9-5 on page 258.

Critical Incidents. This method is closely related to the narrative method. Under this method, the supervisor records both the good and the bad things that employees do in performing their jobs. The supervisor's notes shown on page 251 are examples of positive and negative job behaviors recorded as critical incidents.

Graphic Rating Scales. This is the oldest absolute appraisal method. A graphic rating scale is a form containing a number of items relating to job performance. The rater simply checks where the employee scores on a continuum. Graphic rating scales have been criticized for lacking definition; that is, the items being used to appraise employees are frequently vague. Figure 9-6 on page 259 is one example of a graphic rating scale.

All too often, the dimensions included in a graphic rating scale are traits, or characteristics, rather than job behaviors. Traits are difficult to measure unless a job behavior is used to describe the trait. For example, the word *dependability* means different things to different people. What is your definition of the word? If the clue given is the word only and supervisors are expected to rate employees' dependability on a scale of 1 to 5, the responses will differ according to what *dependability* means to the rater. If, however, *dependability* is described as ''completing assigned work on schedule'' or ''arriving at work on time prepared to begin work,'' raters (and employees) know the basis for the rating. To be used effectively, graphic rating scales should also include a description of the behaviors required to earn a 1, 2, 3, 4, or 5 on the scale.

Weighted Checklists. Like graphic rating scales, weighted checklists give traits or job behaviors along with a scale, but weighted checklists assign a value to each of the items. The degrees of performance within a category may also vary according to the value assigned. Figure 9-7 on page 260 shows a weighted checklist that assigns

FIGURE 9-5

Narrative format

Employee's Name _____   Dept. _____

Employee Title _____   Dates of Evaluation _____

Major accomplishments for the period of evaluation.

Major areas in which performance was less than expected.

Evaluation of special skills required for the job.

Description of major areas of strength.

Description of areas needing improvement.

Signature of Supervisor _____   Date _____

Source: Adapted from Evelyn Eichel and Henry E. Bender, *Performance Appraisal: A Study of Current Techniques,* American Management Association, New York, 1985, p. 38.

differing values within each trait rather than weighting the value of each trait. A weighted checklist may also provide a method for valuing each item according to its perceived importance. For example, ''quality of work'' might be more important than ''quantity of work'' and therefore count 20 percent, while 15 percent is assigned to quantity. Either format may be used.

Behaviorally Anchored Rating Scales (BARS).   This method concentrates on job behaviors, not on personal traits or characteristics. BARS gets its name from the ''behavioral anchors,'' or statements that describe each job dimension. The behavioral anchors are usually developed by a committee or task force including managers,

FIGURE 9-6

Graphic rating scale
format

Employee's Name ———————————— Date ——————————

Evaluator's Name —————————— Period of Evaluation ——————————

Directions: Circle the number on each scale that best approximates the
employee's performance.

	Poor	Below average	Average	Above average	Excellent
job knowledge	1	2	3	4	5
quality of work	1	2	3	4	5
quantity of work	1	2	3	4	5
cooperation	1	2	3	4	5
customer courtesy	1	2	3	4	5
company loyalty	1	2	3	4	5
ability to learn	1	2	3	4	5
dependability	1	2	3	4	5
safety habits	1	2	3	4	5
ability to follow directions	1	2	3	4	5

Source: Michael R. Carrell and Frank E. Kuzmits, *Human Resource Management,* 2d ed.,
Charles E. Merrill Books, Inc., Columbus, Ohio, 1986, p. 183.

supervisors, and subordinates. Using job analyses as a basis, the committee identifies
job clusters; that is, jobs that have similar characteristics and requirements. Performance dimensions are then derived by identifying critical aspects of performance
for each of the job clusters. For example, in a BARS developed for a hospital, some
of the critical nursing dimensions were identified as nursing process, patient and family
education, interpersonal relationship skills, and organizational ability.[2] For each of
the dimensions of performance, the task force is asked to provide specific behavioral
examples of highly effective and highly ineffective performance. The committee then
evaluates each of the behavioral descriptors, discarding incidents where unresolved
disagreements exist. An example of a BARS from one nursing dimension, organizational ability, is shown in Figure 9-8 on page 261.

Outcome-Based Formats

When these formats are used, employees are judged on the basis of performance
outcomes. Two of the best-known outcome-based methods are standards of performance and management by objectives (MBO).

FIGURE 9-7   Weighted checklist format

SUPERVISOR'S APPRAISAL OF EMPLOYEE'S JOB PERFORMANCE

Name of Employee _____

Job Title _____

Department _____

Date of Appraisal _____

	0 PTS	1–5 PTS	6–10 PTS	11–15 PTS	16–20 PTS
QUALITY OF WORK	☐ Much of work just gets by. Work requires constant checking to eliminate mistakes he [or she] should recognize. Low standards as to neatness.	☐ Work requires checking due to some lack of care, interest or other reasons. Work not quite as neat as it should be.	☐ Most of work done well. Usually acceptable in both accuracy and neatness.	☐ Very few errors, usually minor in nature. Work seldom has to be done over.	☐ Mistakes extremely rare. Merits complete confidence in ability to do quality work without close supervision. If checking work of others, rarely fails to find existing errors.
QUANTITY OF WORK	☐ Seldom gets work done in required time. Slow.	☐ Output not always up to amount described in performance standard for job.	☐ Turns out the normal amount of work but seldom more.	☐ Output exceeds amount described in the performance standard for this job.	☐ Volume of work is extraordinarily high. Usually does considerably more than expected of average person in job.
JOB KNOWLEDGE	☐ Leans heavily on others for procedures he [or she] should know. Slow learner.	☐ Has acceptable knowledge of most phases of job, but leans on others in some phases of job.	☐ Shows adequate personal knowledge of all parts of job. Can proceed without special instructions on all regular work.	☐ Has very good knowledge of all parts of job. Without special instructions can proceed correctly on many unusual (as well as routine) matters.	☐ Has most exceptional knowledge of job and spends time studying other phases of dept. work. Others in job class look to him [or her] for correct procedures.
APPLICATION TO WORK	☐ Spends much time away from desk. Often interrupts work for idle talk. Usually tardy. Waits for assignments.	☐ Spends more time than necessary in talk or away from desk. Due to own poor planning is idle at some times but unable to handle volume at others. Often tardy.	☐ Spends no more time than necessary in talk or away from desk. Shows fair planning to keep busy. Sometimes tardy.	☐ Usually on the job at all times. Very little idle time. Industrious. Rarely tardy. Does day's work.	☐ Energetic. Loses no time in starting and works right to the last minute. Plans work in advance so as to avoid delays. Never tardy.

Source: Evelyn Eichel and Henry E. Bender, *Performance Appraisal: A Study of Current Techniques*, American Management Association, New York, 1984, p. 40.

FIGURE 9-8 Behaviorally anchored rating scale format

RN DIMENSION 4: ORGANIZATIONAL ABILITY

The ability to organize work effectively; to effectively allocate time; to set priorities in the workplace; to complete one's work within reasonable time limits.

HIGHLY EFFECTIVE PERFORMANCE

9 Frequently has time to assume additional responsibilities because she/he organizes and sets priorities so well; usually remains calm and organized and is able to function effectively when emergencies and unexpected events occur; is a resource to other nurses in prioritizing their daily routine.

8 Consistently begins pre-op teaching prior to surgery; organizes and prioritizes activities in order to effectively handle a heavier-than-usual patient assignment.

EFFECTIVE PERFORMANCE

7 Organizes and prioritizes activities in order to effectively handle a standard patient assignment; completes the initial assessment and initiates the care plan when admitting a new patient.

6 Organizes each work day to effectively complete the necessary patient care and other activities within the time at work; consistently completes the necessary care plan; correctly prioritizes activities to allow completion of the essential activities; is able to adapt the day's activities to unexpected events; allocates time effectively.

MARGINAL PERFORMANCE

5 Completes all essential patient care but leaves some nonessential care for the next shift; occasionally forgets about hospital meetings that were scheduled during the shift; has difficulty adjusting the schedule to meet changing patient needs; can organize a workload under usual circumstances, but becomes disorganized when something unusual happens; occasionally needs help prioritizing the day's activities.

4 Completes essential patient care during the shift but rarely completes nonessential patient care; usually misses meetings; consistently stays overtime to get his/her daily work done; usually relies on charge or head nurse to prioritize and organize work.

3 Sometimes leaves essential patient care to be completed by the next shift; makes several trips to the supply room to get what is needed when only one trip should be necessary; can organize and prioritize for small patient assignments, but is unable to do so for standard patient assignments; nursing care plan is frequently incomplete.

INEFFECTIVE PERFORMANCE

2 Must have the charge or head nurse organize the day's activities to complete the nursing care required; leaves work for the next shift and does not care about the problems it might cause; does not finish all care and resists staying overtime to finish; rarely completes the initial assignment and rarely initiates the care plan when admitting a new patient.

1 Never completes the nursing care plan; fails to organize and prioritize the day's activities and needs frequent reminders throughout the day to complete certain activities on time; generally leaves essential patient care undone because of poor organizing of the work; is flustered during the shift if demands are presented.

NOTE: This is one of several dimensions used to evaluate nurses. A separate summary sheet is used to record the ratings and devise an action plan (called PIP, Personal Improvement Plan).

Source: Glenn L. DeBiasi, "The Development, Implementation, and Evaluation of a Nursing Performance Evaluation System," position paper, August 1982.

Standards of Performance. This method involves comparing actual accomplishments with a list of conditions that will be fulfilled if the job is considered to be done well. Figure 9-9 is an example of a standards-of-performance form for a production foreman. The standards are established through negotiation between the individual subordinate and the manager. At the end of the appraisal period, the individuals meet to compare the actual results with the agreed-on standards, recording those that have been fully met, almost met, partially met, and so on. At this meeting, the subordinate

FIGURE 9-9

STANDARDS OF PERFORMANCE FORMAT

SIGNIFICANT JOB SEGMENTS	THE JOB OF THE PRODUCTION FOREMAN IS WELL DONE WHEN:
1. safety	**A.** monthly safety meetings are conducted in accordance with company schedules.
	B. safe operating procedures are followed by all employees.
	C. regular monthly inspections are held in the department in accordance with the approved checklist.
	D. action is taken within 5 days to correct any unsafe conditions.
	E. monthly safety reports are submitted by the fifth of the month.
2. controlling costs	**A.** waste and scrap are kept below 2% of total production.
	B. one cost-saving improvement per month is developed and put into operation.
	C. overtime costs are held to a maximum of 3% of direct labor costs.
	D. overhead costs are kept within budget limitations.
	E. salary controls are exercised in accordance with the salary administration plan.
	F. at least two team projects a year are undertaken to eliminate causes of significant scrap losses.
	G. the ratio of productivity to costs is improved by 1% every 6 months.
3. developing subordinates	**A.** new employees are inducted and trained in accordance with a definite plan.
	B. performance reviews are held with all subordinates on at least an annual basis.
	C. discussions are held with subordinates at least quarterly to see that performance improvement takes place according to plan.
	D. responsibilities and authority are delegated to subordinates on a planned basis.

Source: Adapted from an exhibit in Donald L. Kirkpatrick, *How to Improve Performance Through Appraisal and Coaching,* New York: AMACOM, 1982, and shown in Eichel and Bender, *Performance Appraisal: A Study of Current Techniques,* American Management Association, New York, 1984, p. 47.

is given an opportunity to explain how any discrepancies occurred, and a revised standard may be agreed on.

Management by Objectives (MBO). This method is similar to the standards-of-performance method in many ways. Goals are established through negotiation between subordinate and supervisor. Results are measured by the level of goal achievement. Follow-up at appraisal time focuses on achievements, and an action plan is developed for discrepancies. The difference between these two outcome-based methods is that MBO focuses on specific *goals* (changes) to be achieved within a specified time frame, while the standards-of-performance method focuses on a level of performance that is considered to be acceptable on a continuing basis. Figure 9-10 is an example of MBO goals for a sales manager.

Competency Check:

Can you identify the three major types of performance appraisal formats?

FIGURE 9-10 Management-by-objectives (MBO) format

Key results as detailed here will be attained during fiscal 198___.

1. Increase penetration (in share of market) in the Southeast Region for the _____ Division from _____% to _____% during 198___.

2. Open _____ branches in the Southeast Region before September 15.

3. Revise field sales reporting procedures during 198___ so consolidated reports can be issued _____ days earlier.

4. Establish by April 15 a procedure for handling and analyzing customer complaints.

5. Send a bulletin on minimum order size and trade discounts to the company's customer list for Product X by February 15.

6. During fiscal 198___, increase direct product profit for Product Family Z by _____% over the fiscal 198___ rate.

7. During August, conduct a series of regional meetings to review past results and introduce the marketing plans for Product M.

8. During fiscal 198___, reduce direct selling expense to _____% of net sales.

9. Issue by January 30 a new bulletin on collecting credit information on new accounts.

10. By July 30, investigate the potential net gain in sales volume and standard profit contribution that could be realized if hardware stores are added to present channels of distribution.

Source: Evelyn Eichel and Henry E. Bender, *Performance Appraisal: A Study of Current Techniques,* American Management Association, New York, 1984, p. 50.

Competency
Check:

Can you describe
several methods
within each of the
major performance
appraisal formats
cited above?

WHAT CAN THE SUPERVISOR DO?

Most supervisors have little control over the types of appraisal formats used in their companies. However, they should be aware of the various formats and their individual strengths and weaknesses, be able to use the current format to its best advantage, and be prepared to suggest alternative methods when appropriate.

PROVIDING FEEDBACK

Performance appraisal feedback may be given to employees by providing a copy of the written appraisal and by conducting a postappraisal interview.

Written Appraisals

Feedback through written appraisals is usually provided by making a copy of the supervisor's appraisal available to the employee. The written appraisal may be accompanied by a transmittal note from the supervisor calling attention to the more salient points made in the performance appraisal. The note may also include an invitation for the employee to make an appointment with the supervisor to discuss the appraisal.

Postappraisal Interviews

Following the performance appraisal, many supervisors conduct postappraisal interviews. The purposes of the interview are to be sure there are no misunderstandings about the performance appraisal ratings, to allow employees to share their attitudes and feelings about their job performance, to provide an opportunity for a straightforward and honest discussion with ample time for questions and answers, and to build a better relationship between supervisors and subordinates.

Preparing for the Interview

The supervisor's objectives for the performance appraisal interview should be to inform, encourage, and give recognition. To accomplish these objectives, the supervisor must plan. The planning checklist in Figure 9-11 provides some general guidelines for preparing for the appraisal interview.

Conducting the Interview

Many supervisors feel the way Collins did at the beginning of this chapter. The first performance appraisal interviews, and sometimes even subsequent interviews, make supervisors nervous and uncertain. The careful planning described in Figure 9-11 is

FIGURE 9-11

Planning checklist

	Yes	No
1. Did you find a setting for the interview in a quiet, comfortable, and relaxed place?	___	___
2. Did you refresh your memory by reviewing the employee's job description, performance standards, job objectives, employee education, training, and experience?	___	___
3. Did you give your employee enough advance warning of the appraisal interview?	___	___
4. Did you ask your employees to come to the interview prepared to appraise their own performance?	___	___
5. In your advance warning did you make it clear that the purpose of the appraisal interview was to improve his or her performance on the job?	___	___
6. Did you list specific good things the employee has done and plan to compliment him or her on them?	___	___
7. Did you list bad things the employee has done and plan to discuss those?	___	___
8. Did you note what reactions you think he or she will have and how you plan to handle them?	___	___
9. Do you keep a detailed list of facts supporting your appraisal?	___	___
10. Have you made a list of corrective actions you plan to take for each employee?	___	___
11. Have you written down any approach you plan to use to help you gain acceptance of your corrective action?	___	___
12. Have you noted what follow-up activities you can use?	___	___

Source: D. Keith Denton, "How to Conduct Effective Appraisal Interviews," *Administrative Management,* June 1986, Issue W '86, p. 15. Republished with permission from Administrative Management, copyright 1986, by Dalton Communications, Inc., New York.

one way to reduce the apprehension usually associated with appraisal interviews. If you are well prepared for an interview, are comfortable with your appraisal of the employee's performance, and have reviewed all the information mentally, much of your apprehension will disappear.

Conducting the interview requires planning also. Review what you wish to say to the employee. Define the order in which you will discuss the evaluation. Be prepared to develop an action plan with the employee. Make the performance appraisal interview a productive experience for both you and the employee. Keys to a productive performance appraisal interview are:[3]

1. *State the purpose, and create a positive attitude.* Explain the purpose of the interview. You might say, "As we discussed when this meeting was arranged,

our purpose today is to discuss your performance since the last appraisal and determine what we can do to help you improve your performance. Let's together review our performance appraisals—your self-appraisal and my evaluation. Then we can work on an action plan for both the areas of strength and the areas in which some improvement may be needed.''

By setting the stage in this manner, the supervisor provides a structure for the session. The subordinate also realizes that the discussion will be a two-way one, with both the subordinate and the supervisor having an opportunity to state their views. In addition, the subordinate is aware that the outcome of the discussion will be an action plan for his or her development—one that the employee has played a major part in developing.

2. *Be specific.* You should provide specific examples of both good and bad job performance. It is not enough to say to a subordinate, ''You're doing just fine. Perhaps there are a few things you could improve on, but they are really minor.'' Or ''You just don't seem to be doing as good a job as you could.'' These appraisals do not give any information that will help the employee improve. More helpful feedback is given when the supervisor specifies performance that is satisfactory as well as performance that could be improved.

3. *Give behavioral feedback.* Behavioral feedback provides information about something the employee does and something over which the employee has control. ''You're too tall'' is feedback about something over which the employee has no control. ''You were 5 minutes late for work yesterday and again today'' describes an employee's behavior and something that can be changed. ''You have a poor attitude'' is too general; that appraisal could mean any number of things. ''You have not been getting along with your fellow workers recently. Can you describe the problem as you see it?'' is more specific and behavioral.

4. *Be flexible.* Sometimes your appraisal on a particular dimension may be incorrect because you have not had access to all the information. If you have rated an employee ''average'' on interpersonal relations and the employee brings to your attention that he has been helping a new employee get acquainted on the job and that he often helps out when another employee is overscheduled, you should be flexible enough to change your rating if the change is justified.

5. *Share responsibility.* Ask ''What can I do to help you in the performance of your job?'' Make the appraisal a joint venture, offering whatever help it is within your authority to offer.

6. *Listen.* Be an active listener. Encourage the subordinate to do most of the talking. If you talk 25 percent of the time and listen 75 percent of the time, the performance appraisal interview will be much more productive and informative. The interview should not be a ''telling'' experience; it should be a ''sharing'' experience.

7. *Agree on an action plan.* After discussing the performance appraisal and commenting on the employee's strengths and weaknesses, you and the subordinate should agree on an action plan. The action plan should include notes on the employee's strengths, identify areas in which improvement is needed, specify actions to be taken and who will take those actions, and note when improvement can be expected.

8. *Follow up*. The action plan should include a time frame for follow-up to see if the improvement has occurred. Follow-up is vital if improvement or correction is expected. If the action plan specifies that improvement should be noted within 6 weeks, then you and the subordinate should meet in 6 weeks to discuss the outcomes.

Competency Check:

Can you cite six keys to a successful performance appraisal interview?

WHAT CAN THE SUPERVISOR DO?

After conducting the performance appraisal interview, the supervisor can compare his or her technique with the following checklist:

	Yes	No
Opening		
Did you put the employee at ease?	_____	_____
Did you state the purpose of the interview?	_____	_____
Find Out Employee's Viewpoint		
Did you ask how they see their job and working conditions?	_____	_____
Did you ask if there are any problems you need to discuss?	_____	_____
Identify Your View of Their Performance		
Did you make a summary statement only?	_____	_____
Did you avoid making comparisons to other workers?	_____	_____
Mention Desirable Behavior You Would Like to Continue		
Did you mention one or two such points?	_____	_____
Did you capitalize on identified strengths?	_____	_____
Identify Opportunities for Self-Improvement		
Did you mention one or two such points?	_____	_____
Did you avoid presenting "shortcomings?"	_____	_____
Did you keep discussed topics work-related?	_____	_____
Prepare Employee Improvement Plans		
Did you try to make it the "employee" plan, not yours?	_____	_____
Did you play the role of helper or counselor?	_____	_____
Review Future Opportunities		
Did you mention any advancement opportunities?	_____	_____
Did you review future possible pay increases?	_____	_____
Did you warn poor performers, if necessary?	_____	_____
See If They Have Any Questions		
Did you answer questions of general concern?	_____	_____
Did you close interview with constructive, encouraging note?	_____	_____

Source: D. Keith Denton, "How to Conduct Effective Appraisal Interviews," *Administrative Management,* February 1987, p. 15. Republished with permission from Administrative Management, copyright 1987, by Dalton Communications, Inc., New York.

REWARDING PERFORMANCE

Supervisors give too little salary information to employees, according to a survey of managers in 330 of the 500 largest industrial and service companies.[4] The Towers, Perrin, Forster, and Crosby survey also found:

76 of the surveyed managers believe supervisors are uncomfortable talking with employees about pay.

60 percent believe the supervisors in their organizations may not have a clear understanding of the mechanics of the pay system.

92 percent said supervisors in their organizations do know where they can get answers to pay questions.

Based on the responses to the survey, Towers, Perrin, Forster, and Crosby recommend that companies deal with the sensitive pay issue in a frank and credible way. According to the authors, the key is a thorough ongoing training program for supervisors that would teach them how to explain the pay program, how to tell employees how their performance affects their pay, and how to respond knowledgeably to questions.

Types of Rewards

As shown in Figure 9-12, rewards may take many forms. The three general types of rewards are those that are given by the company, those that come from the tasks or the job itself (*intrinsic rewards*), and those that the supervisor or manager gives.

Company-Established Rewards

Supervisors have no control over company-established rewards except to see that they are administered according to company policy. Note in Figure 9-12 that both monetary compensation and benefits are included in the company-granted rewards. Benefits may include life insurance, hospitalization, dental plans, pension plans, day care centers, and all the other nonmonetary benefits shown in column 1, and some others not mentioned. Many companies are offering flexible benefits plans, sometimes called "cafeteria-style" benefits programs. These plans may combine a group of benefits into a package, with workers selecting the cluster that suits their needs, or employees may receive an allowance to apply to the benefits they select.

Intrinsic Rewards

Supervisors have some indirect control over rewards that are intrinsic to the task or job (those shown in column 2 of Figure 9-12). Although the feeling of achievement

FIGURE 9-12

TYPICAL EMPLOYEE REWARDS

COMPANY	INTRINSIC TO JOB	SUPERVISOR RELATIONSHIP
awards	achievement	advancement
bonuses	challenge	attention
cafeteria	flexibility	autonomy
clear, consistent	growth	clear goals/rewards
policies	interesting work	development
company car	responsibility	feedback
contests/prizes	variety	friendship
discounts on company		honesty
products		information
expense accounts		involvement/participation
flexible working hours		praise/recognition
free dinners for family		support
free lunches		trust
free tickets to games		
and plays		
gifts		
leisure time		
life insurance		
loyalty/appreciation		
medical insurance		
offices		
office decorations		
office furnishings		
parking space		
pay		
profit sharing		
promotions		
promotions from within/		
advancement		
salary		
security		
social outings		
stocks		
titles		
transfers		
use of company		
equipment		
use of company		
facilities		
wages		

Source: Adapted from J. Kenneth Matejka and Richard J. Dunsing, "Managing Employee Rewards," *Administrative Management,* June 1986, p. 23, with permission from Administrative Management, copyright 1986, by Dalton Communications, Inc., New York.

one gets from performing a job well is internal to the person doing the job, the supervisor can add to this feeling of achievement by assigning additional responsibilities, providing opportunities for growth, or redesigning jobs to make them more interesting or to provide more variety. Refer to Chapter 11 for a discussion of motivation.

Rewards Given by the Supervisor

Competency Check:

Can you list the three general types of rewards and give five examples of each type?

The area of rewards over which supervisors have direct control is shown in column 3 of Figure 9-12. These are tools, techniques, and strategies that supervisors can use to reward their subordinates. All of these rewards are not appropriate for all workers; some workers respond more positively to some rewards than to others. For example, some subordinates have no interest in advancement but crave attention. Within appropriate boundaries, supervisors can provide that attention. Praise and recognition are powerful rewards if used correctly with those who respond to praise. They can also be overused, as is shown in the cartoon below. Praise and other motivators are described in Chapter 11.

Establishing and Communicating Compensation Criteria

Criteria for rewarding employees for their work are usually established by the company and may differ according to the level or position of the employee in the company. Communicating the criteria to employees is a role supervisors need to strengthen. Recall that the Towers, Perrin, Forster, and Crosby survey found that supervisors give too little salary information to employees.

Source: CATHY © 1985 Universal Press Syndicate. Reprinted with permission. All rights reserved.

Bases for Rewarding Employees

Companies may choose to reward their employees on the basis of seniority, or they may give cost-of-living increases or across-the-board increases, or they may adopt merit-pay or pay-for-performance reward systems. The supervisor's role in seniority, cost-of-living, and across-the-board pay increases is minimal. Supervisors, however, play a major role in reward systems based on pay for performance or merit because it is the supervisors who are responsible for evaluating the workers' job performance.

Communicating Bases for Rewards

Employees should know the criteria for compensation decisions. What does an individual employee have to do to receive a pay increase? Changing the criteria for pay adjustments without communicating the changed expectations to the employees is no longer acceptable.

Bases for rewards can be communicated to subordinates in several ways: through conferences in which the supervisor tells the individual worker what level of performance is expected for what level of pay increase; through group meetings in which the criteria for various levels of pay increases are described; or through a company handbook in which expected performance is clearly described. Whatever the method used to communicate the bases for pay adjustments, the supervisor has a responsibility to provide the information to subordinates and to ensure opportunities for questions and answers. This, of course, assumes that the supervisors are aware of and understand company compensation policies and practices.

Open or Closed Pay System

Some companies choose to have an open pay system, one in which information is made available to employees who wish to inquire about salaries. A system is considered to be open if salary information is available about either individual pay or about pay ranges for a specific job. Closed systems provide no salary information, and some companies have a policy prohibiting any discussion among employees about their individual salaries. Employees who violate the policy may be subject to dismissal. Supervisors are obligated to support the company's policy on availability of pay information whether it is an open or a closed policy.

Competency Check:

Can you describe the responsibility of the supervisor in establishing and communicating compensation criteria?

Recommending and Administering Rewards

Supervisors play a major role in recommending rewards based on merit or pay for performance. It is therefore important that recommendations for rewards be based on *objective* performance evaluations.

Although merit pay and pay for performance are both based on results of work, the pay method for the two may differ. In a pay-for-performance system, employees receive their salaries or wages based on how well they do their jobs. Top performers receive greater monetary rewards than do average performers; average performers receive more than below-average performers. In a merit-pay system, additional compensation is usually awarded only to employees whose work is above average; that is, above the expected standard of performance.

To recommend and administer rewards effectively, supervisors should observe the following:

Competency
Check:

Can you cite the
four criteria for
recommending and
administering
rewards?

1. Workers should be able to see a relationship between their work effort and their pay. When employees see a relationship between work effort and pay, they are more likely to perform in a way that will give them the rewards they desire.
2. Workers should perceive pay recommendations as being equitable. When workers believe that pay recommendations have been based strictly on work performed, there is less conflict among workers and more incentive to perform at higher levels.
3. Workers should perceive the salary administration as being consistent and fair. When employees believe the salary administration is fair and consistent among workers, there are better relationships among workers and between workers and supervisors. Supervisors are considered to be more objective in the performance of their duties.
4. Supervisors should be sure that all salary decisions are made within legal guidelines. This is discussed in more detail later in this chapter.

WHAT CAN THE SUPERVISOR DO?

Supervisors can provide salary information to employees in keeping with company policies regarding how much information is to be made available. Supervisors can also, provided the appropriate systems are in place, make sure that better performance leads to better rewards by maintaining an objective appraisal system. Use the following checklist as a self-check noting the interdependence of the appraisal and reward criteria.

	Yes	No
1. Do job descriptions accurately reflect job content and the skills, effort, and responsibility required?	_____	_____
2. Are employees accurately classified into jobs based on the work they perform, their skills, and their actual responsibilities?	_____	_____
3. Is the method and process used to determine job value fair?	_____	_____
Does it provide due process?	_____	_____
4. Are jobs graded accurately, considering skill, effort, responsibility, and working conditions?	_____	_____

5. Are pay ranges competitive with other organizations who employ people in similar jobs?   _____   _____
6. Do employees understand the criteria used to appraise performance and how the measurement is done?   _____   _____
7. Are performance criteria appropriate and weighted correctly given their relative performance?   _____   _____
8. Are employees given an adequate opportunity to review appraisals, and do they have an adequate appeal process?   _____   _____
9. Are current pay scales equitable, given the skills and performance level of individuals?   _____   _____
10. Do employees understand the pay program and how it is supposed to work? If not, what is unclear?   _____   _____

Source: Robert J. Greene, "Effective Compensation: The How and Why," *Personnel Administrator,* February 1987, p. 115.

LEGAL IMPLICATIONS

Much has been written about our litigious society, and, indeed, more and more employers are being sued by their employees and former employees. It is therefore incumbent upon supervisors to protect both their companies and themselves by being knowledgeable about what is legal and permissible in appraising and rewarding employee performance.

Making Nondiscriminatory Appraisals

The key to making nondiscriminatory appraisals is really quite simple—but not always so easy to do. The key is to *evaluate all employees on the basis of job performance only, be consistent in your application, and apply criteria objectively to all employees.*

Evaluating employees on the basis of job performance means judging only the way they do their jobs without regard to their age, race, sex, religion, or national origin and putting aside any personal likes or dislikes. For example, you may have a preconceived notion that older workers are dependable but not open to new ideas and, therefore, resistant to change. As an *individual,* you can believe anything you choose; as a *supervisor,* you must put aside your preconception about age when judging Mary Ardsley, age 51. What is the evidence that she is dependable? Do you have evidence that she is not willing to try new ideas? Or you may simply like Jim Jenkins. He is friendly, enthusiastic—a personable guy who is hard to dislike. But judge his performance on the way he does his job, not on the fact that you like him.

Consistency in evaluating performance means that given the same information, the way you evaluate Susie Perkins today is the way you will evaluate her 2 weeks from now—or 2 months from now.

Applying criteria objectively to all is simply being fair and not letting your personal feelings interefere with your appraisal. If Bob Jones is penalized because his reports are often late, then Connie Grossman must also be penalized if her reports are late. If you consider Maureen O'Hara an exceptional nurse because she has initiative and good interpersonal relations with her peers and patients, then Paul Juniper should also be rated "exceptional" if he exhibits the same qualities. The same criteria should be applied to all.

Implementing Nondiscriminatory Rewards

The key to implementing nondiscriminatory rewards is the same as that for administering nondiscriminatory appraisals—make them job-related, consistent, and objective.

Competency Check:

Can you describe the keys to administering nondiscriminatory performance appraisals and implementing nondiscriminatory rewards?

All decisions regarding what a worker will earn must be related to the job requirements and performance on the job. A supervisor who consistently awards a poor performer satisfactory ratings and average salary increases and then one day says "I can't put up with your poor performance any longer—you're fired!" is placing the company in a vulnerable position if the fired employee chooses to sue the company. Even though the supervisor may have given the poor performer worse appraisals and smaller pay increases than any other worker in the department, the supervisor has still, by giving satisfactory ratings and salary increases, indicated to both the company and the employee that the worker's performance is okay. There is therefore no basis for terminating the employee. To avoid situations such as this, both performance appraisals and recommendations for rewards should be based on job performance, consistently applied criteria to all workers, and objective application of criteria.

Monitoring Comparable Worth

In biblical times, according to Lev. 27:3–4, females of working age were valued at 30 silver shekels while males were valued at 50 shekels.

Comparable worth has been called the "issue of the 1980s," and the controversy associated with it will doubtless extend beyond the 1980s. Comparable worth goes beyond equal pay for equal work, which was addressed in the Equal Pay Act of 1963. That law, a gender-based act, says that people performing essentially the *same* jobs should receive the same pay, except as that pay may be affected by seniority or union contracts. Comparable worth, on the other hand, addresses the issue of pay based on the *value* of the job, whether the jobs are the same or different.

Most working women remain in nursing, secretarial, light-industry, and waitressing jobs that make up a low-paying "pink-collar" ghetto. Supporters of comparable worth say the only way to eliminate the pay bias left from the days of sex-segregated jobs is to revalue all jobs on the basis of the skills and responsibility required. Thus a clerk-typist might seek the same pay as, for example, a warehouse worker, claiming that the jobs are of equal value.[5]

To determine a job's value, a job evaluation must be conducted. A job evaluation defines the various factors required, such as job knowledge, communication, accountability, education, planning and decision making, or whatever other factors the company considers important. Typically, the process of doing a job evaluation involves three steps:[6]

1. Develop composite job descriptions, based on information obtained through questionnaires and interviews for the jobs to be evaluated. The use of this information ensures that all job tasks performed by an employee are explicitly stated.
2. Assign each job a number of points for each of a variety of factors, such as skill, effort, responsibility, and working conditions.
3. Compare jobs with similar numbers of points to see whether the salaries are similar and, if they are not, determine whether the difference is related to the gender of those filling the jobs.

Studies show that patterns of discrepancies in pay still exist in the workplace. Job evaluations have uncovered a consistent pattern of undervaluing jobs held by females. An example of that pattern is shown in Figure 9-13.

FIGURE 9-13

PATTERNS OF DISCREPANCIES IN PAY

JOB TITLE	MONTHLY SALARY	NO. OF POINTS
Minnesota		
registered nurse (F)	$1723	275
vocational ed. teacher (M)	2260	275
typing pool supervisor (F)	1373	199
painter (M)	1707	185
San Jose, Calif.		
senior legal secretary (F)	665	226
senior carpenter (M)	1119	226
senior librarian (F)	898	493
senior chemist (M)	1119	493
Washington State		
licensed practical nurse (F)	1020	173
correctional officer (M)	1436	173
secretary (F)	1122	197
maintenance carpenter (M)	1707	197

Source: Robert L. Farnquist, David R. Armstrong, and Russell P. Strasbough, "Pandora's Worth: The San Jose Experience," *Public Personnel Management Journal*, vol. 12, no. 4, Winter 1983, p. 398.

Competency
Check:

Can you define
comparable worth?
How is it related to
job evaluation?

Advocates of comparable worth believe it is a fair way to value jobs and establish pay. They try to value jobs that are traditionally female more objectively and equitably and to reward workers based on the value of the jobs they hold. Opponents of comparable worth believe it is an artificial way of elevating pay and that the *marketplace* (supply and demand) should determine the pay for a particular job. Opponents also point to the difficulty of valuing jobs except in an artificial way. As expressed by a Washington attorney, ''You tell me how to set up a system outside the marketplace that objectively compares rock musicians and brain surgeons, and I'll tell you whether nurses and plumbers should have comparable pay. But I suspect it can't be done in any but an artificial way.''[7]

WHAT CAN THE SUPERVISOR DO?

A pay equity problem arises when men and women are employed in such a way as to create male-dominated and female-dominated job classifications, and there are pay differentials between them. Usually, a classification or job family is considered to be gender-dominated if 70% or more of the employees are male or female. With that parameter in mind, the following measures to minimize the pay equity liability are recommended.

1. *Job design.* Job responsibilities/tasks should be analyzed to minimize the number of stereotypical ''male'' or ''female'' tasks: typing, manual dexterity, weight lifting, etc. Dispersing these tasks will assist in integrating the job categories.
2. *Recruiting.* Diligently seek to attract males (or females) into gender-dominated jobs. Equal utilization of males and females in a job negates major pay equity problems. Recruiting specifications need to be scrutinized to eliminate gender segregation in the selection process (heavy lifting, typing, excessive experience or education, and any skill or trait favoring one sex).
3. *Job evaluation.* Examine methods and factors for their impact on sex stereotyping. Evaluators need to be schooled to eliminate their intentional and unintentional biases. Evaluate jobs based on content—not title of the incumbent, and be sure that both males and females are active in the process. Provide for an independent review of evaluation results by someone sensitive to, and knowledgeable about, pay equity problems.
4. *Market pricing.* Carefully designed market pricing of jobs is still a strong defense against pay equity claims. The selection of surveys—i.e., quality, industry, geographic area covered, number of surveys used—must be carefully evaluated.
5. *Internal/external reconciliation.* A conflict often arises when trying to reconcile the internal ranking or hierarchical order of jobs with external job worth as measured by market pay levels. Consistency of system application is the key for all levels of jobs. If the external market takes precedence over the internal evaluation of V.P. Marketing (male) it should also be the deciding factor for the typist (female) position.

6. *Upward mobility*. Job-posting programs, career ladders, cross-training and skill training programs can provide mobility for both sexes into and out of gender-dominated positions.

7. *Management training*. Sensitivity to the liabilities of pay equity can eliminate current and future problems.

8. *Salary administration*. Analysis of position in salary range, years of experience in the position, starting salaries, promotional increases, merit increases, performance evaluation by gender assists in identifying historical, current and prospective problems. Sound policy design and definition should include constant audit mechanisms.

Source: Human Resource Management Ideas and Trends in Personnel, Commerce Clearing House, issue 104, Nov. 18, 1985, p. 182.

COMPETENCY REVIEW

1. Define *performance appraisal*.
2. Cite the two major purposes of performance appraisals.
3. Diagram and describe the performance appraisal sequence.
4. Identify five uses of performance appraisal information.
5. Cite and explain five rater errors.
6. Describe three performance appraisal formats.
7. Cite the importance of performance appraisal feedback.
8. Describe two methods of providing feedback to employees.
9. Explain the importance of the supervisor's role in performance appraisals.
10. Describe eight planning steps a supervisor should take when preparing for a performance appraisal interview.
11. Cite six actions a supervisor should take when conducting a performance appraisal interview.
12. List the three general types of rewards and give five examples of each type.
13. Describe the role of the supervisor in establishing and communicating compensation criteria.
14. Explain four criteria for recommending and administering rewards effectively.
15. Tell how a supervisor can conduct nondiscriminatory appraisals.
16. Tell how a supervisor can implement nondiscriminatory reward systems.
17. Define *comparable worth*.
18. Describe how job evaluation is linked to comparable worth.

APPLICATIONS

1. Each of the statements given below is an example of performance appraisal feedback. If you think that the statement gives specific behavioral feedback, state your reason(s) for believing that. If not, rewrite the statement to describe specific behavior. You may make any assumptions about performance standards in your rewrite.

    a. Receptionist: "You get entirely too many personal calls. You should not let personal business interfere so much with your job."

    b. Dental technician: "You seem to be having a problem relating to our patients."

    c. Hotel maid: "The hotel rooms don't look as clean as they should."

    d. Assembly-line worker: "The level of rejects for your part of the line is good. Keep up the good work."

    e. Parts counter person: "You're not as courteous to our phone customers as you are to our over-the-counter sales customers."

    f. Telemarketer: "You are really doing a good job for a person so new to the job. You have already exceeded our goal by 18 percent."

    g. Welder: "Your safety record is below standard."

    h. Salesperson: "The language you use around your peers as well as our customers is unacceptable. You had better clean up your act, 'or else!'"

2. Jack Monroe and several other supervisors are discussing the performance appraisals they conducted last week. An eavesdropper overhears these comments:

    a. "I just don't believe women are capable of handling hard physical labor."

    b. "Personally I like Sue. She's very much like me."

    c. "All of my employees are pretty much the same, so I give them all a satisfactory rating."

    d. "It's really hard to forget all the times Marie was late. Why, only last week she was late twice!"

    e. "Well, from my point of view, people really have to show me something if they want better than a satisfactory rating from me."

    f. "I'd rather rate everybody 'good' than hassle about it."

    g. "Barbara is so knowledgeable about repairs; she just seems to be good in everything she does."

Identify the rater errors present in the comments from Jack Monroe and his colleagues.

3. You are the mailroom supervisor at Midwest Tool and Dye Works. There have been complaints about the performance appraisal format currently in use, and you have been asked to recommend a format to be used in evaluating mailroom employees. Which format would you choose? Why? If you were asked, would you recommend that the same format be used throughout the company in all departments? Why, or why not?

4. Rate a performance appraisal system, using the checklist in Figure 9-14.

CASES

Case I: No More Free Beer!

An old tradition at Anheuser Busch has gone down the drain. When the company negotiated a new 3-year contract with the Teamsters Union, which represents 9000 workers at the company's 11 breweries, the parties agreed that the practice of supplying free beer to workers during lunch and rest breaks would cease on March 1,

FIGURE 9-14 Performance appraisal checklist.

PERFORMANCE APPRAISAL CHECKLIST

	Yes	No
1. Is the performance appraisal system based on the measure of effective employee behavior?		
2. Is the performance appraisal based on an accurate reflection of job performance? (The overall measure of job performance is fundamentally related to critical aspects of the job).		
3. Is the performance appraisal system based on a thorough analysis of the job?		
4. Is the performance appraisal system based on job analysis data pertaining to:		
(a) knowledge and skills?		
(b) specific rates or levels (standards) of performance?		
5. Does the appraisal system meet the criteria of Title VII federal guidelines?		
6. Has empirical data been collected to prove the validity of the method for the purpose for which it is being used?		
7. Does the performance appraisal method differentially discriminate against a specific subgroup of the working population?		
8. Are performance ratings all job related?		
9. Were performance measures developed through job analysis?		
10. Are raters able to observe the performance they are to rate?		
11. Are ratings collected and scored under standardized circumstances?		
12. Have the employees been advised of the critical requirements of their jobs?		
13. Are performance appraisals conducted at least once a year?		

	Yes	No
14. Are the employees evaluated solely on the extent to which they fulfill the critical requirements of the job?		
15. Are rewards tied directly to performance?		
16. Was the job analysis conducted at a time when the job was reasonably stable?		
17. Are criterion measures reliable?		
18. Does the appraisal instrument enable the appraiser to differentiate good from poor performers?		
19. Do appraisers:		
(a) have a thorough knowledge of the job?		
(b) have ample opportunity to see the individual on the job?		
(c) have the expertise in interpretation of what is seen?		
20. Do appraisers have formal training in:		
(a) the appraisal system?		
(b) the appraisal instrument?		
(c) the job of individuals being evaluated?		
21. Are raters trained to reduce rating errors?		
22. Do subordinates have a high degree of participation in the performance appraisal?		
23. Do subordinates participate in the setting of specific goals they are to achieve?		
24. Are subordinates "free" to discuss problems that may be hampering their current job performance?		
25. Do the supervisor and subordinate agree on a plan of action to be taken until the next review?		

Source: Evelyn Eichel and Henry E. Bender, *Performance Appraisal: A Study of Current Techniques*, American Management Association, New York, 1984, pp. 58–59.

1986. In return, the company agreed to different methods of compensation, such as distribution of beer to take home or increased contributions for employee benefits. The "right to drink the product" had been "a tradition since before the days of the American Revolution," said a Teamsters negotiator, who explained that "the mood of the country is such that we thought the time had come" to eliminate the practice.

1. As a worker, how would you feel about this break with tradition?
2. As a supervisor, how would you feel about this break with tradition?
3. Why do you think the "time had come" to eliminate the practice of free beer on the job?

Source: CompFlash (sample copy), May 1985, no. 85-05.

Case II: You Discuss Your Salary, and You're Fired!

Midwest Tool and Dye Works has long had a policy of pay secrecy. The employees have generally ignored the policy and, while not discussing individual pay in front of the supervisors, have discussed their salaries with each other. Company policy includes a statement that "any employee overheard discussing salary with another employee may be subject to immediate dismissal."

Colin Janssen is relatively new to Midwest Tool and Dye Works. He was hired 6 months ago as supervisor of the design department. Janssen came to the company with 10 years' experience with a competitor who had a very liberal open pay policy. Although he read the handbook and is aware of the policy, Janssen chooses to ignore it when he overhears employees discussing their pay. In fact, Janssen believes such a policy is archaic and foolish.

After the performance appraisals last week, when employees were told what their annual pay would be for the next year, there was a lot of grumbling among workers as they openly discussed their salaries. Mark Jacksen, an employee with a great deal of seniority, was particularly upset when he heard that other employees with less seniority had gotten larger pay increases than he had. Mark even discussed this discrepancy with workers in several other departments. When the other supervisors overheard these discussions, they agreed that Janssen should be told and that he should take action.

1. Should Janssen follow company policy?
2. Do you favor a closed or an open pay system?
3. Does your preference depend on whether you are a worker or a supervisor? Why?
4. What are the benefits and what are the potential problems with a closed pay system? An open pay system?

REFERENCES

1. Evelyn Eichel and Henry E. Bender, *Performance Appraisal: A Study of Current Techniques,* American Management Association, New York, 1984, p. 9.

2. Glenn L. DeBiasi, "The Development, Implementation, and Evaluation of a Nursing Performance Evaluation System," position paper, Norfolk, Virginia, August 1982.

3. Ibid.

4. Towers, Perrin, Forster, and Crosby survey, reported in *Human Resource Management Ideas and Trends in Personnel,* Commerce Clearing House, issue 124, Aug. 22, 1986, p. 133.

5. Iamar Lewin, "Comparable Worth," *The Virginian-Pilot and the Ledger-Star,* Jan. 29, 1984.

6. Robert L. Farnquist, David R. Armstrong, and Russell P. Strausbaugh, "Pandora's Worth: The San Jose Experience." *Public Personnel Management Journal,* vol. 12, no. 4, Winter 1983, p. 397.

7. Lewin, loc. cit.

SUGGESTED READINGS

Allen, Ken: "What an Executive Should Know About the Art and Science of Self-Assessment," *A Dartnell Human Resource Development Program,* 1981.

Bianco, Virginia: "In Praise of Performance," *Personnel Journal,* June 1984.

Cumming, Charles M.: "New Directions in Salary Administration," *Personnel,* January 1987.

Deets, Norman R., and D. Timothy Tyler: "How Xerox Improved Its Performance Appraisals," *Personnel Journal,* April 1986.

Fritz, Roger: "There's a World of Difference Between Activities and Results," *Office Systems '85,* May 1985.

Geis, A. Arthur: "Making Merit Pay Work," *Personnel,* January 1987.

Hart, Jerry: "Job Performance Evaluation: Be Sure to Touch All Bases," *Office Systems '86,* March 1986.

"If Your Organization Sent People to China, How Would You Compensate Them?" *Human Resource Management Ideas and Trends in Personnel,* Aug. 23, 1985.

Kanter, Rosabeth Moss: "From Status to Contribution: Some Organizational Implications on the Changing Basis for Pay," *Personnel,* January 1987.

King, Patricia: "How to Prepare for a Performance Appraisal Interview," *Training and Development Journal,* February 1984.

"Making It Through the Difficult Performance Review," *Supervisory Sense,* July 1986.

Phillips, Kenneth R.: "Red Flags in Performance Appraisals," *Training and Development Journal,* March 1987.

Waldrop, Heidi: "Rating with Mirrors," *Computer Decisions,* September 1986.

Wallach, Arthur E., and Lauren Hite Jackson: "Getting an Answer to 'How Am I Doing?'" *Personnel,* June 1985.

10

TRAINING AND DEVELOPMENT

COMPETENCIES

Studying this chapter will enable you to:

1. Identify the elements in the relationship of training and development to the staffing function.

2. Discuss the supervisor's role in training and development.

3. Cite the sources for identifying training and development needs.

4. Discuss the conditions which affect learning.

5. Cite ways to encourage participation in training and development programs.

6. Discuss the importance of making training and development results visible to employees and management.

7. Identify and define the training methods for operations personnel.

8. Give examples of training methods that can be used for operations or developmental training.

9. Cite the factors to consider in choosing a training method.

10. Discuss the methods of trainee evaluation of the program.

11. Give the meaning of the levels of training evaluation.

CHAPTER OUTLINE

t is 8:15 A.M. "A beautiful Monday morning," Rita Columbo says to herself as she runs up the steps of the big government building where she will today begin her career. Rita has just graduated from vocational-technical high school, and she is excited about her new job as clerk-typist in the regional office of a federal supply facility. As she traveled to work on the bus, many questions went through her mind: Can I really handle the work? What will my first assignment be? Will the supervisor like me? What happens if I make mistakes? Will somebody help me get started? Will the other workers like me? Where will I get lunch? Suppose I get sick and miss a day—what do I do? How long will it be before I get a raise? Or get promoted?

The questions seemed endless. She has not had much work experience—a paper route when she was younger and a part-time job for a while at Burger King. But she was an excellent student and is sure she can do the work.

"And all my questions will be answered by the supervisor, I'm sure," she assures herself as she arrives at the receptionist's desk.

The receptionist announces her arrival, and Tony Maxwell, the supervisor to whom she is assigned, rushes out to greet her.

"Glad to see you, Rita. I'm Tony Maxwell, support services supervisor. Come with me, and I'll talk about your job on the way. I know you were hired as a clerk-typist, but we're shorthanded in the document production center today and so we're going to start you out there. Personnel noted that you've worked on a Kaypro at Vo-Tech, and when you've worked on one system, all others are easy. You'll learn our Xerox Network without any trouble.

"Well, here's your work station. Have a seat. Let me show you the ON button. All your instructions will be on the screen; just do what it says. Here's the manual in case you need to look anything up. If you get into a jam, call on Jack Gantos over there. I'll tell him to look out for you. He's doing double duty today, but he'll help if you need him. I'll be in and out all morning. Don't worry about your W-2 and the personnel info. I'll tell personnel I've put you directly to work; they'll get to you shortly. OK, it's all yours."

"Well, so much for answers to my questions," Rita thinks as she sits down at the terminal. She is no longer excited. Instead, she is frustrated and scared.

RELATIONSHIP OF TRAINING AND DEVELOPMENT TO THE STAFFING FUNCTION

If Rita Columbo's day continues as it began, her employer not only may lose her but may also have wasted the cost of recruiting and selecting her for the job.

As you learned in Chapter 8, both the supervisor and the personnel staff devote a great deal of time and effort to recruiting and selecting the best candidate for each job. Staffing is an expensive process. Proper training and development must follow selection; otherwise staffing costs are a direct drain on profits. Since profit is essential to effective organizational continuity, any breakdown in the staffing-training-development chain threatens that goal. Figure 10-1 shows the six elements which graphically portray the relationship of training and development to the staffing function.

Recruitment and selection bring the new employee into the firm. Orientation and training help the new worker become a productive member of the firm's "family" and the experienced worker adapt to changing job demands. Developmental programs give workers the opportunity to grow and progress in their careers within—and sometimes outside of—the firm. Performance appraisal is conducted for both new and experienced workers. The appraisal often triggers additional training or development for the workers. The entire process provides the organization with its own high-quality human resource pool from which to fill its job needs and thus provide for organizational continuity. This chapter will focus on the training and development part of the process.

Training and *development* are related terms, but they can be viewed as having special focuses that differentiate them.

Training refers to company-directed activities and experiences designed to develop the skills, knowledge, and behaviors that will lead to effective job performance. Training usually relates to a specific job or to related jobs. It includes, for example, the training of a newly hired sanitation worker in the technical and mechanical aspects of the waste-collection truck to be driven and on the pick-up schedule and route the

FIGURE 10-1   Relationship of training and development to the staffing function

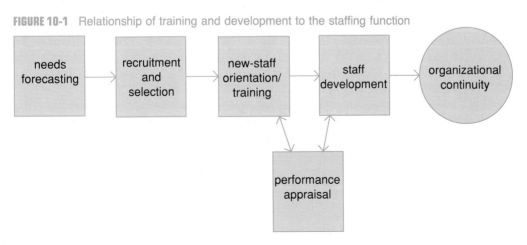

worker will follow. Training also includes preparing a worker to change to newer methods of performing a job; for example, training an accountant to change from a manual recording method to computerized accounting.

Development refers to programs aimed at educating workers beyond the present technical demands of their jobs in order to enhance the firm's ability to achieve its current and future goals. For example, to prepare you to move from supervisor to a higher level of management, your firm may offer management and leadership training as part of its developmental program.

Training and development (T&D) is now a specialized field of management support. It is estimated that there are 50,000 training specialists serving organizations in the United States[1] and that over $100 billion is spent on T&D programs.[2] The estimated ratio of training to development is 80:20, but this varies greatly among organizations.

T&D programs cover a broad range of sophistication and complexity. In small companies, they may be as simple as start-up instruction for new employees by the supervisor. At the other end of the spectrum are company-owned training centers like Hamburger University, operated by McDonald's Corporation in Oak Brook, Illinois, and the customized centers of GE and IBM. Regardless of their size, the objectives of all T&D programs are the development and retention of a productive work force in order to meet company goals. High priority is given to training new workers to become productive as quickly as possible.

Moving Employees to Productive Status

If Rita Columbo in the opening case has been selected on the basis of what you learned in Chapter 8, she is the one person among all the applicants whose qualifications best matched the demands of the job. But even if she is highly qualified, she is still an expense to the firm until her performance meets company standards. Through orientation and training, new employees move from being an expense to the firm to a point where they "earn their keep" by being productive.

Changing the productive status of workers through training is not limited to new employees. Experienced workers, for a variety of reasons, often need training to increase their productivity. Efforts to reduce waste, to cut costs, or to increase productivity often lead to changes in job requirements. New methods, new technology, or new equipment may necessitate the retraining of workers.

Keeping workers productive through training and retraining is an ongoing activity. In addition, developmental programs help to motivate productive workers by providing growth opportunities.

Providing for Employee Growth

Effective human resource planning includes providing opportunities for employees to develop beyond the technical demands of their current jobs. Developmental programs that allow workers to stretch their skills, knowledge, and abilities beyond their daily routine benefit the firm in a number of ways. Participating in these programs not only makes workers more valuable to the firm but improves their motivation by giving them a feeling of self-fulfillment. It also tends to make them more loyal to the firm. Finally, these programs improve management of the firm by helping to identify and develop future managers from within.

As you have read, developmental programs are directed largely, though not exclusively, to management. Objectives of these developmental programs are:

- to identify and develop potential managers from nonmanagerial personnel.
- to improve the skills and abilities of current managers to enable them to manage more effectively.
- to provide for the personal growth of managers.
- to provide for organizational continuity through planned managerial succession.

Because this text is directed to you as a current or future supervisor, it emphasizes the training of nonmanagerial personnel. Preparing you to move from supervisor to a higher level of management is an example of organizational planning for continuity.

Maintaining Organizational Continuity

Through T&D, firms not only prepare employees for promotion but prepare others to fill the vacancies created by the promotions. Through succession planning, organizational continuity can be maintained. Effective T&D programs help to minimize the disruption caused by personnel changes and help to keep the organization operating smoothly.

While succession planning is usually associated with managerial development, it also applies in a lesser degree to operations. For example, if one of your group leaders is promoted to section foreman, you should have a plan for moving someone in the group up to become group leader. In operations, a promotion often leaves a vacancy that can be filled only by hiring a new worker. Your knowledge of planning (Chapter 3) and staffing (Chapter 8) will enable you to use succession planning to help maintain organizational continuity.

Now let us look specifically at your role in T&D.

Competency Check:

Can you identify the elements in the relationship of training and development to the staffing function?

THE SUPERVISOR'S ROLE IN TRAINING AND DEVELOPMENT

As a supervisor, you will play an active role in the overall training and development program. In a small company, you may be the only trainer available. Your program will be limited to the time you can spare from your other responsibilities. In a large company, you will cooperate with the human resources/personnel (HR/P) department, but you will have some specific responsibilities in these three areas of the training of your workers: (1) in identifying the training needs of your workers, (2) in their job-specific training, and (3) in interfacing with the HR/P staff. Let us first look at your function in finding out what training is needed.

Identifying Training Needs

Since you are considered the technical specialist for the requirements of jobs under your supervision, you are the primary source of information about the qualifications of workers who are to be hired. As the workers become experienced, you will, through daily supervision and performance appraisal, be able to identify training that will help them improve their performance. In addition, you will be aware of workers with special skills or abilities who may benefit from development courses to prepare them for promotion.

At all stages of your workers' tenure, your daily contact with them will enable you to identify the training needs that will benefit both the workers and the firm.

Providing Job-Specific Training

In most firms, the supervisor carries the responsibility for training new workers in the specific jobs for which they are hired.

After you have oriented new workers to the work area, introduced them to co-workers, and assigned them to their work stations, you will give instructions on what is to be done and how it is to be done.

In firms where initial training is done by a training specialist, it is usually the supervisor's responsibility to see that the new worker performs the job according to established procedures.

If there is an HR/P department in your firm, your training and development role is shared with that department.

Interfacing with Human Resources/Personnel

Competency Check:

Can you discuss the supervisor's role in training and development?

While line managers look after the needs of their specific units, the function of HR/P is companywide. In the orientation of new workers, for example, HR/P carries the responsibility for acquainting new workers with overall aspects of the company while line managers handle information about the immediate work area. You will learn more about orientation later in this chapter.

As Figure 10-2 shows, you and HR/P have some separate responsibilities and share others. As the figure points out, T&D is a cooperative effort. For example, HR/P's companywide T&D needs analysis is one source of information when identifying the training needs of your workers; other sources will be discussed in the next section.

FIGURE 10-2

THE SUPERVISOR AND HR/P INTERFACE

HR/P DEPARTMENT	SUPERVISOR
conducts companywide training-needs analysis; sets objectives for overall T&D program; designs, implements, and evaluates program	orients workers to specific work environment
may assign specialist to teach job-specific skills to new workers based on supervisor's identification of skills	reviews and approves training program relating to supervisor's department
designs and implements training program for general knowledge and ability needs of workers	identifies skills to be performed in each job
provides feedback to supervisors regarding results of training of their workers	usually trains, or supervises training by a senior worker, new workers in job skills; if training is by a specialist, provides feedback to HR/P department
provides feedback to all managers regarding overall T&D program	identifies training needs of workers in general knowledge and skills, and communicates these needs to HR/P department
	identifies and recommends candidates for developmental programs
	encourages workers to participate in growth and developmental programs available through HR/P department
	provides performance data to HR/P department relating to training and development

SOURCES FOR IDENTIFYING TRAINING NEEDS

There are many sources from which you can identify the need for training and development. Records and reports are the most common.

Records and Reports

You can learn a great deal about training and development needs from records and reports relating to your employees. In a small firm, you may maintain your own file of employee applications, test records, and interview and performance appraisal results. In firms that maintain a human resources information system, you will have the benefit of the extensive records system kept by HR/P. Some of the most common records sources are discussed below.

Employee Applications and Test Records

Applications and test records provide useful clues to the training needs of new employees, particularly where skills are involved. Tony Maxwell in the beginning of the chapter determined from Rita Columbo's initial employment records that she had had some word processing experience. Even though he used the information with more thought to his own predicament than to proper orientation for Columbo, he was aware of the data available to him from her records. He might have noted the information and, after conferring with Columbo, recommended a word processing training program for her. That would not have solved his immediate problem, but it probably would have salvaged a new employee.

You will need to work cooperatively with the HR/P department in obtaining and using information about new employees because much of this information is subject to confidentiality laws.

Performance Appraisals

The appraisal system provides you with information about the degree to which a worker is meeting expected standards of performance. Productivity deviations are one measure. If you see, for example, that a worker is producing only 8 units per hour in an area where the standard is 12 and the average is from 11 to 17, you should try to determine the reason. If the worker's skills are deficient, additional training is in order. Examining a series of appraisals of this worker will show whether the production rate is typical, is increasing or decreasing, or is erratic. Your findings, together with your observations of the worker, will help you determine what type of training would help improve the productivity. The worker may, for example, need additional supervised practice of the job skills taught in orientation or in previous training sessions or the worker may need training in new skills. The summary report of the productivity of all workers will serve as another source of information relating to training possibilities.

The appraisal process keeps you informed about workers' strengths and weaknesses, which will help you identify both their training and their developmental needs.

Human Resource Demand Schedule

As you learned in Chapter 3, your planning responsibility includes forecasting the personnel needs of your unit or department. You must determine how many people are needed, what skills are needed, whether the skills of current workers are up to date, and who among your workers would benefit from developmental programs.

Considering such questions for each position on your human resource demand schedule will enable you to identify training needs.

Employee Skills Inventory

Information on the skills, knowledge, and abilities of all workers in the firm provides an inventory of its human resources. In addition to skills information, the inventory may include information on the worker's experience, education and training, special knowledge, time in current job, performance appraisals, and compensation record. By showing the skills available within the firm, the inventory helps identify the skills that must be acquired through outside sources or through training and development programs within the firm.

Career and Succession Plans

Like the skills inventory, the firm's career and succession plans provide information that can help identify training and development needs. Career planning motivates employees by informing them of growth opportunities within the firm; T&D programs help them prepare for these opportunities.

Training and Development Results

You can use the results of T&D programs to identify new training needs. As the cartoon shows, not all training is 100 percent successful. If a worker's behavior does not change after the training, additional training or a different type of training may

Source: Reprinted by permission: Tribune Media Services.

be called for. If, on the other hand, a worker in a training program masters the new skills easily and quickly and the training report shows that other trainees call upon him or her for help and advice, you would probably want to mark this worker as a candidate for promotion through a leadership training program.

Employee records and reports such as those presented here serve as historical data which you can analyze for planning and development in the quiet of your office. But you will learn much about training needs as you observe workers on the spot in your daily rounds.

Observation of Workers

Peters and Waterman described "management by walking around" (MBWA) as a characteristic of "excellent companies."[3] As a supervisor, you will find that MBWA helps you get to know your workers. The better you know them, the better able you will be to keep in touch with their training and development needs.

Through MBWA, you can see how the worker performs on the job, whether safety rules are being followed, how the equipment is being operated, and the condition of the work station.

One of your MBWA rounds might be for general observation of operations. Or you might have a specific objective. The safety observation described in Chapter 7, using a safety checklist (Figure 7-6), is an example.

Suppose you are a supervisor in a company that manufactures leather handbags and wallets. You have noted an increase in waste and rejects, and you wish to observe the cutting process. Before making your rounds, you might prepare a matrix for observation of cutting skills such as that shown in Figure 10-3. Say that an on-the-spot demonstration helped Julio improve his marking of the skins and setting of the cutters. But Sam did not respond as well to your demonstration because he was having trouble with the entire process. You make a note to follow up on your observation of

FIGURE 10-3

MATRIX FOR OBSERVATION OF CUTTING SKILLS

			Skills		
WORKERS	PRE-EXAMINING SKINS FOR FLAWS	MARKING BEST CUTS	POSITIONING PATTERN; SETTING CUTTERS	OPERATING CUTTING MACHINE	SORTING & STORING CUTTINGS & UNUSED SKINS
Jake	√	√	√	√	√
Sam	X	X	X	X	X
Mary	√	√	√	√	√
Julio	√	X	X	√	√

Julio to make sure that his improvement is maintained. For Sam, you note that additional training in the entire process is needed.

Observation of workers in your daily rounds helps you keep on top of training and development needs. Your MBWA activities will need to be intensified when operational changes are made in your department.

New Systems, Equipment, and Processes

Operational changes necessitate training. Before installing a new system, new equipment, or a different process, you will have worked with vendors, engineers, or systems consultants to determine what skills will be needed in the new work environment.

When an automated factory changes from a traditional assembly-line process to robot assembly, new skills and fewer workers will be required. Workers who are retained will need training in robotic technology. Those who are displaced will need training for other jobs within the firm. Some firms also offer training to displaced workers to help them move into other jobs outside the firm. If you are a supervisor of the new robotic assembly line, you will probably participate with HR/P in identifying training needs disclosed in the change. Typically, you will either train or supervise the training in any new system, equipment, or process for the workers in your department.

In this section, you have learned the major sources from which to identify training and development needs. Other situations may clue you to other training needs. New health or safety information may be released, or problems may be spotted by you or by an OSHA inspector. Workers themselves may identify training needs through suggestion systems or quality circles.

Identifying training needs, however, is only one of your jobs. Establishing a climate in which the training can take place is also necessary if the program is to succeed.

Competency Check:

Can you cite the sources for identifying training and development needs?

WHAT CAN THE SUPERVISOR DO?

Keep alert to the sources for identifying training and development needs. All the sources noted above are either a part of your daily job as supervisor or are part of the human resource information available in your interface with HR/P. Your reading, your participation with your peers in professional associations, and your own growth program will generate ideas that may help you see where employee training is needed. But it is your daily association with workers that will be your best source.

Keep a T&D note pad handy so that as, or immediately after, you observe, talk with, or appraise a worker, you can note training and development needs.

Awareness is the key. Be aware of your company needs, your workers' needs and potential, and your workers' skills, knowledge, and abilities. T&D should serve both the company *and* the workers.

ESTABLISHING THE CLIMATE FOR TRAINING AND DEVELOPMENT

The climate of an organization is established at the top. Both the philosophy and the reward system for implementing that philosophy are set by top management and then passed down through every level and to every member of the organization. For T&D to be successful, top management must "buy" it as a strategy for growth, "sell" it to the entire organization, and reward successful participation in it.

Even in an excellent organizational climate, there is another dimension of T&D that must be considered. The worker-participant is expected to learn in the program. How will that be accomplished?

Conditions for Learning

How do people learn? And why? The psychology of learning is a complex body of knowledge beyond the scope of this text. Our focus here is on an overview that will help you, as supervisor, apply some of the findings of research to your training program.

Research to date has told us more about *why* people learn than about *how* they learn. While we do not yet have complete answers to how people learn, scientists continue to probe the human brain in their search for knowledge about the learning process. Behavioral scientists have already given us considerable insight into *why* people learn.

Learning has been defined as a change in behavior. If we observe behavioral changes, we can assume that learning has taken place. For example, to move from one place to another, an infant first crawls. Then, after coaxing from parents to walk to their outstretched arms, the child learns how to reach the goal in an upright position. From then on, the youngster begins to abandon crawling in favor of walking. The child's behavior has changed through learning. Studying the conditions under which a person learns new behavior provides some insight into "why" a person learns. An understanding of certain conditions of learning will enable you to plan and implement your training program. Here are some conditions which are now considered basic to learning.

Desire to Learn

The worker must *want* to learn. You cannot force workers to learn anything. There must be some internal willingness to make the effort. The desire to learn is called *motivation,* a concept that will be discussed in Chapter 11. Motivation is greatly influenced by a person's perceptions, values, and attitudes, which vary from one person to another. Workers may look at the training program and ask, "What's in it for me?" or "Do I want this job enough to learn this new skill?" How Columbo in the beginning of this chapter answers these questions will determine whether she stays in her new job or leaves. She will need to be well-motivated in order to learn under the frustrating conditions in which she has been placed. As supervisor, your job will be to recognize that you must create conditions that will stimulate the workers' desire to learn.

Purpose of Learning

Trainees must know the purpose of the training. Why is it being given? Is it designed to improve safety? Increase productivity? Cut costs? Improve quality? Make the task easier for workers? If workers know the purpose and feel that the purpose is worthwhile, they will respond better to the training. For example, if workers know that training in cutting procedures for making wooden chairs is designed to control unit cost and increase the company's and their earnings, they will more willingly respond to training for cutting as many chair legs as possible from a given piece of wood, consistent with standards of quality.

Applicability of Learning

Knowing that the learning will be applicable to their lives will facilitate learning for the workers. To be applicable, learning should meet the following conditions:

1. It should be meaningful. Requiring all shop workers to take a sales training course would meet with some protest because it would not be meaningful for most shop workers.
2. It should be realistic. Training workers to use manual typewriters in a firm with a computerized word processing system would not be realistic; nor would training toy salespersons on selling approaches geared to senior citizens. Meeting the "real-world" test is an important condition for most work-related learning.
3. It should be transferable to the workplace. Skills training is generally more transferable than some other kinds of training because it can either be given at the work station or, if given off-the-job, can be on identical or closely simulated equipment. Even so, such elements as physical settings, interpersonal relationships, and supervisory styles may be different on the job from those in the training situation. Research shows that the more similarity between the training and the job, the more transferable the learning. Columbo's experience on a Kaypro in her school environment may be only marginally transferable to her new employer's Xerox Network system.

Involvement of Learner

Learning is an active, not a passive, process. The more a worker is involved in the situation, the easier the learning. This suggests that instruction should involve as many of the senses as possible. Let the learner see, hear, touch, smell, taste. Imagine training people to become chefs by using only their visual and auditory senses! They must touch the tomato to judge its firmness, smell the milk to judge its freshness, and taste the broth to judge its seasoning. By the same token, lecturing is the least effective way to teach television repair. Lectures with visuals and demonstrations are somewhat better, but hands-on experience by the trainee is the most effective way to teach television repair because the worker is involved in the learning.

Organization of Content

The material to be learned should be organized in such a way as to make learning easier. "One thing at a time" is a good rule. Breaking down a skill into small components and arranging these components in the correct sequence is an appropriate way to organize most job-skill training. For example, welding instruction might follow this sequence: (1) an overview of welding technology; (2) the safety rules and the protective garments needed for the task; (3) the preparation of materials to be welded; (4) the parts of the welding torch, its fuel supply, its operation, its ignition and control; and (5) proper close-down and storage of equipment. The training might extend over a period of time in order to provide for an evaluation of each part of the learning before the worker progresses to the next component.

Timing is important so that learning of the different parts can be assimilated by the worker. The parts serve as building blocks to learning the whole process. Organization for learning should consider the components of the content, the sequence in the job process, and the interval between learning segments.

Feedback

Learning takes place more readily when learners are given feedback on how they are progressing. Training specialists know the power of a pat on the back for a job done well. They also know that it is important to point out weak points in the learning as they are spotted and to put the learner back on track immediately by explanation or demonstration.

Both positive and negative feedback serve a purpose. Positive feedback gives the learner encouragement to move ahead. Pointing out errors helps the worker get back into the learning sequence and may prevent the compounding of errors into another step of the process. In some situations it may prevent hazardous events. Telling a worker "Go ahead; I'll tell you when you're wrong" does not provide appropriate feedback. Nor does frequent faultfinding help a worker progress. If frequent errors are occurring, it might be wise to observe the worker move backward in the steps until you and the learner together find out where the problem originated. You might say, "Let's see if together we can find out where the problem is. Let's go back to the previous step and see if that's where my instruction was not adequate." Negative feedback can be given in a positive way.

Expectations and Rewards

Learning is closely related to the expectations of the learner. Research shows that workers are motivated to act based on their expectations of rewards. The questions they ask themselves are: Will I be rewarded for my effort? Is the reward worth the effort involved? Can I be sure that the reward will be forthcoming?[4]

Management can offer rewards such as higher pay or promotion for participating in training programs. In deciding whether to participate, workers might have views such as these:

''Yeah, there's a pay increase, but it's not enough to make me spend 6 weeks in a training program. No way!''

''What do they mean, 'higher pay'? It's the same as I'll get next year when I move up to grade 2—and for doing nothing extra.''

''Promises, promises. I did two of those sessions 2 years ago, and I'm still right where I was before.''

Reward systems must be established and adhered to as part of the training and development program because expectations often influence the motivation of the worker to participate or not.

Competency Check:

Can you discuss the conditions which affect learning?

Encouraging Participation

One of your first tasks in T&D will be to communicate the reward system to the workers. Then you must convince them that personal and near-term benefits will accrue to them as a result of the training. Successful completion of training will further *their* interests, give *them* more salary, prepare *them* for promotion. In addition, you must show them that as they progress, the whole organization progresses. As the company grows, they, in turn, reap further long-term benefits, and so the cycle continues.

Since most workers today want to progress in their careers, encouraging participation in T&D is not too difficult. But there are always some who, for a variety of reasons, avoid training programs. They may fear the learning situation, fear failure, resent having to learn something new, or simply be satisfied with the status quo.

Research shows that tying pay to performance is a good motivating device. Giving raises or bonuses to those whose training results in improved performance sends a message to nonparticipants. Limiting or withholding pay increases from those who do not meet standards may also move some to get the training. In some cases, especially those involving safety or new systems, you may have to present an alternative—train or be terminated. To the holdout, you might finally have to say, ''Alex, you've chosen not to participate in two training programs in the new system. We've discussed this several times, and you've indicated that your only reason for not taking the training is that you don't want to. We can't accept that. We're under OSHA pressure to get all our people certified; we have no choice. So I must notify you that the final program will begin June 1. If you do not take advantage of it, you will be terminated as of that date. As you know, that's company policy. If you want to talk to me about it, I'll be glad to meet with you.'' Then follow through on your proposal. Hopefully, you'll be able to persuade most workers to participate by emphasizing the benefits to themselves and to the company.

Another way to encourage participation is through career pathing. Today's workers want to know what their opportunities are for growing within the company. Career paths will let them see how they can move up.

Career paths may be dual. A quality-control technician in plant operations, for

*Competency
Check:*

Can you cite ways
in which you can
encourage
participation in
T&D programs?

example, may move into engineering management. A dual-career ladder would show how this worker might move up in either department.

There may also be horizontal moves. In a mid-1980s reorganization, IBM provided training programs to prepare many of its systems specialists to move into sales or other areas.

New technology and new market strategies also create new jobs. Employees on one career path may enter training programs in order to move into one of these emerging careers.

Importance of Visible Results

In an organization that supports T&D, every employee is aware that the program is available. Internal communications announce T&D opportunities, report results, and feature successful participants. Visibility becomes the fuel for keeping the program alive.

In addition to encouraging employee participation, making results visible shows management the effect of the program on profits. This means that results should also be measurable. You should follow up on participants after the training to document the benefits to the worker and to the organization.

Let's say that one of your workers produced an average of 20 units per hour before skills training. A month after she completed the training, she was averaging 24 units per hour, a 20 percent increase. She should be commended for her accomplishment, and her performance appraisal should show her improvement. Her work group and the department should be apprised of her and the program's success. Management should be given a report, not only of her personal accomplishment, but also of the increased productivity for the work group and the department.

A graphic presentation often helps to dramatize results because of its visual impact. A before-and-after graph of the results of a program aimed at improving quality control will enhance the report to management. Figure 10-4 shows one form that may be used. Posted on the department bulletin board, it will advertise to all workers how training can improve their performance.

*Competency
Check:*

Can you discuss the
importance of
making T&D results
visible to employees
and management?

Wherever possible, training results should be translated into dollars and cents and communicated to management and the employees. The financial results of some types of T&D programs are not immediately visible, but those that the supervisor deals with often are.

To get good results, you need to know what training and development methods are available and how to select the most appropriate one. Let's look next at the methods you can use for training and development.

TRAINING METHODS

There are many methods of training. The staff of specialists in larger firms may choose from a wide array of methods. In small firms, the supervisor may do all the training in "show-and-tell" sessions at the worker's job station. In most firms, however,

FIGURE 10-4

Effects of training on product rejects

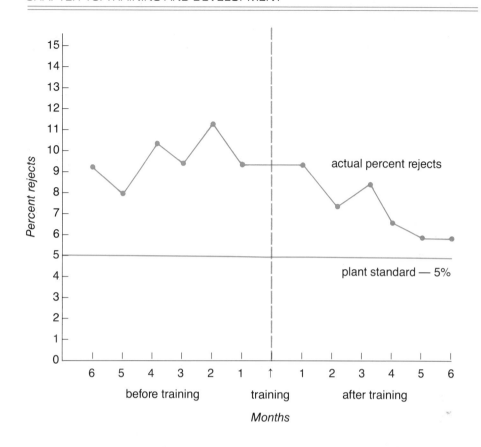

workers are given some type of introduction to their new work environment before they are put on the job.

Orientation

The introduction that workers are given to the firm and their jobs is called *orientation*. Employees form their initial impressions of the company during the first few days. These impressions may be positive or negative. Rita Columbo in the beginning of the chapter was put to work immediately, without any orientation. No wonder her initial thoughts about her new job were negative!

To get the new employee-employer association off on a positive note, most firms provide an orientation to welcome new workers into the "family." This not only helps to create a good interpersonal beginning but also helps employees adjust to their new surroundings.

The orientation may consist of a few hours during which the worker is informed about company benefits, pay, and vacations and is introduced to his or her workplace and coworkers. A handbook describing the company history and its employer-employee relations may be given to workers to review after the orientation session.

Some orientation programs are spread over a longer period of time. One such program might be conducted over 2 or 3 days or partial days and include an in-depth look at the firm. The first day might begin with a welcome to the workers by a member of top management. There might be introductions of functional officers and other managers who then make brief remarks about their roles. A visual presentation of the firm's history, philosophy, and products or services might precede a luncheon to close the first day's general orientation. Subsequent sessions might focus on company policies, employee benefits, relevant legislation, and other topics of concern to all employees. A final session may be conducted by the supervisor in the assigned work area. In this session, the supervisor might give the worker a tour of the department and introduce her or him to coworkers. Then the supervisor might discuss with the new employee the unit policies, the work station, the worker's job description, or other topics relevant to the specific job and unit.

Topics covered in orientation sessions vary with the nature, size, and complexity of the organization. One comprehensive list shows 130 possible topics.[5] Figure 10-5 shows, in checklist form, the topics that might be included in a 2-day orientation. Note the follow-up at the end of 2 weeks.

The HR/P department usually designs the orientation program and conducts the general sessions. The supervisor handles the part that relates to his or her specific unit. A checklist should be used to see that all planned topics are covered. To ensure that coverage is complete, it is recommended that the person handling each topic initial and date the checklist after completion. Many firms also require that the new employee sign the checklist to show that instruction was received.

Orientation is the first step in training the new employee. Following orientation, training focuses on the worker's specific job. As the employee becomes more experienced, training may focus on developing the worker for growth in the firm. Figure 10-6 on pages 302–304 describes common methods of training and development. Your involvement in developmental training will usually be limited to recommending workers for these programs or to participating in them yourself. But you will be actively involved in operations training.

Operations Training

Your major role in T&D will be job-intensive training of the operations workers for whom you are responsible. Immediately after orientation, your workers will begin learning their jobs under your direction, usually at their job stations.

The operations training methods shown in Figure 10-6 are typically one-on-one sessions in which you, or a senior employee under your direction, show the worker how to do the job.

While *on-the-job training (OJT)* is the term applied to a specific method, all the operations training methods shown in Figure 10-6 occur on the job. In OJT, the trainer uses the demonstration method to show the worker how to follow the job procedure, operate equipment, handle supplies, and follow safety rules. Key points or "tricks of the trade" in performing the job are explained by the trainer to help the learner master

FIGURE 10-5 Orientation checklist

Name of Employee _____   Name of Employee _____
Starting Date _____   Starting Date _____
Department _____   Department _____
                                              Position _____

PERSONNEL DEPARTMENT

Prior to Orientation

_____ Complete Form A and give or mail to new
      employee
_____ Complete Form B
_____ Attach Form B to "Orientation Checklist—
      Supervisor" and give to the supervisor

Employee's First Day

Organization and Personnel Policies and Procedures

_____ History of XYZ Inc.
_____ Organization chart
_____ Purpose of the company
_____ Employee classifications

Insurance Benefits
_____ Group health plan
_____ Disability insurance
_____ Life insurance
_____ Workers' compensation

Other Benefits
_____ Holidays
_____ Vacation
_____ Jury and election duty
_____ Death-in-the-family leave
_____ Health services
        _____ Professional discounts
        _____ Appointments

End of Orientation—First Day
_____ Make appointment for second day
_____ Introduce employee to supervisor

Other Items
_____ Job posting
_____ Bulletin board—location and use
_____ Safety
_____ No drinking
_____ Where to get supplies
_____ Employee's records—updating

At the end of the employee's first two weeks, the
supervisor will ask if the employee has any questions
on the above items. After all questions have been
satisfied, the supervisors will sign and date this form
and return it to the Personnel Department.

SUPERVISOR

Employee's First Day

_____ Introduction to coworkers
_____ Tour of department
_____ Tour of company

Location of
_____ Coat closet
_____ Rest room
_____ Telephone for personal use and rules
      concerning it

Working Hours
_____ Starting and leaving
_____ Lunch
_____ Breaks
_____ Overtime
_____ Early departures
_____ Time clock

Pay Policy
_____ Pay period
_____ Deposit system

Other Items
_____ Parking
_____ Dress

Employee's Second Day

_____ Pension retirement plan
_____ Sick leave
_____ Personal leave
_____ Job posting
_____ Confidentiality
_____ Complaints and concerns
_____ Termination
_____ Equal Employment Opportunity

During Employee's First Two Weeks

Emergencies
_____ Medical
_____ Power failure
_____ Fire

_____
SIGNATURE
_____
DATE

_____
ORIENTATION CONDUCTED BY

Source: Robert L. Mathis and John H. Jackson, *Personnel—Human Resource Management,* 4th ed., West Publishing Company, St. Paul, Minn., 1985, p. 280. Reprinted by permission.

FIGURE 10-6

COMMON METHODS OF TRAINING & DEVELOPMENT

OPERATIONS TRAINING
(basically job-intensive)

Apprentice training: Provides on-job experience under guidance of a skilled and certified worker. Requirements may be set for training, length of training, equipment, and skill level. Usually for skill crafts. May be monitored by U.S. Department of Labor.

Demonstration: Trainer performs a process or operates equipment while trainees observe. Usually accompanied by an oral explanation of the procedure. Typical in skills training.

Job-instruction training (JIT): Form of on-the-job training developed during World War II. "Trainer card"-guided instructor. Card lists a 4-step instruction process: preparation, presentation, performance tryout, and follow-up. Still widely used.

Job rotation: Worker rotates through a series of jobs, staying in each a few days or weeks. In operations, worker may rotate through several jobs in a production process. Rotation may also be in different functional areas to enable the worker to learn several phases of the business. Commonly used to develop employee, to expand variety of tasks performed by worker, and to provide organizational flexibility. Sometimes called *cross-training.*

Mentor/buddy system: Worker is assigned to another employee recognized for high ability. Mentor serves as role model for new worker. Worker emulates mentor and may seek advice on job or other problems. Buddy system usually operates within work group, where experienced worker serves as buddy or big sister/ brother to new worker to teach him or her the job and to guide in adjusting to the job environment.

On-the-job training (OJT): Worker is placed in the job situation. Training is done by supervisor or by an experienced worker. Most common of all types of training.

Vestibule: Training conducted away from the job site in a training simulation created to resemble the employee's actual work area and conditions of the job. Commonly used for skills training and for developing trainees' ability to react to variable conditions. Uses include training for pilots, astronauts, drivers, and police officers.

FIGURE 10-6 *(Continued)*

DEVELOPMENTAL TRAINING
(may be current-job related or
preparation for growth within firm)

Assessment center (AC): Management training method used to identify & select management personnel. In the AC process, a potential manager goes through several days of activity, including role playing, discussions, tests, cases, in-basket exercises, simulations, and peer evaluations. Results also help identify areas where participants need further training.

Case study: Written description of a business situation that trainee must analyze and offer solutions. Often used in management development to give trainee practice in citing good and bad features of the situation in the case; spotting violations of management principles, such as poor organization; and developing alternative solutions.

Conference/seminar/discussion: Training that involves verbal interaction between instructor and participants or among participants. Discussion may be used in operations for problem solving by workers in quality circles; in management for problem solving; or for development of employees at all levels.

Counseling and coaching: Ongoing informal training in which supervisor provides information on improving performance or behavior. May be follow-up coaching to refine skills; counseling workers on group interaction; or giving personal assistance or guidance to workers for individual growth.

In-basket: Written situations based on the company's business activities as they would arrive in the manager's "in" basket daily. Trainee responds, usually in writing, by describing what action he or she would take in the situation. Typically management development.

Lecture: Oral presentation by a person knowledgeable in the topic given to a group of employees. Usually given in "classroom" mode. May or may not include visual illustrations. A "telling" method, the lecture, used alone, is not considered effective for producing lasting results.

Off-the-job training: Training performed away from the workplace. May be in-house training conducted in the company's training facility. May also be off-site training conducted in vendors' training facilities, educational institutions, commercial training facilities, or by trade or professional associations in a variety of places.

Programmed instruction/computer-assisted instruction (CAI): Learner is given material in a series of small sequential units. He or she must respond correctly to test of each unit before progressing to the next unit. May be in printed form or on a computer. Commonly used for cognitive learning; also used for developing computer skills.

Role playing: Learners assume roles of other people and interact with other learners in acting out a business situation. In sales training, one learner assumes the role of salesperson, another the potential customer. May follow a prepared script or communicate extemporaneously to act out the wrong way and a better way to close a sale, for example. May be used in attitude training to visualize good and bad job behaviors, such as following

303

FIGURE 10-6 (*Continued*)

DEVELOPMENTAL TRAINING
(may be current-job related or
preparation for growth within firm)

safety rules or in interpersonal relations. Often used in supervisory training.

Gaming: Using a model of a business situation, including many variables, learner must make decisions and take actions by choosing from among several alternatives. Business simulations and games usually answer "what if" questions; e.g., "If we follow strategy *A,* what market share might we capture?" Gives practice in decision making. Usually developmental.

Video/audio self-directed instruction: Instruction given through TV, videotapes, cassettes, or other audiovisual devices. Commonly used in cognitive learning; may also be used for behavioral learning by depicting right and wrong attitudes or interpersonal relations. May be as diverse as a lecture by an authority on management for developing of managers to learning the parts of a new piece of equipment.

---

the tasks as quickly as possible. After demonstrating the tasks, the trainer watches the worker repeat the process.

The advantages of OJT are that (1) it is done at the actual work station, (2) it requires no special equipment, and (3) the worker is producing during the training process. A disadvantage is that when a worker is used as a trainer, the pressures of his or her own job may lead to neglect or shortcuts which can result in a poorly trained and disenchanted worker. Worker-trainers should be carefully chosen and prepared themselves to do the training. They should also be rewarded for their training efforts.

A structured on-the-job method developed during World War II to improve production is called *job instruction training (JIT).*[6] When this method is employed, special trainers first train the supervisors in a four-step instruction process. This process is printed on a "trainer card" for quick reference by the supervisor. The four-step JIT card is shown in Figure 10-7.

Apprenticeship is intensive on-the-job training that extends over a longer period of time ranging from a few months to 2 years or more. The training is usually provided by a skilled worker who may be certified by the firm, the union, or some other agency. Apprentice training is often required in crafts such as electrical work, plumbing, and shipbuilding.

Apprentice programs may include classroom training in the relevant technology as well as on-the-job training. Apprentices are usually required to progress through prescribed skill levels before they can practice the craft on the job.

Vestibule training, as the term implies, is entrance preparation for a job. While vestibule training may be used for a variety of jobs, it is typically used to teach the

FIGURE 10-7   Job instruction training (JIT)

First, here's what you *must do* to *get ready* to teach a job:

1. Decide what the learner must be taught in order to do the job efficiently, safely, economically, and intelligently.
2. Have the right tools, equipment, supplies, and material ready.
3. Have the workplace properly arranged, just as the worker will be expected to keep it.

Then, you should *instruct* the learner by the following *four basic steps:*

Step 1—*Preparation* (of the learner)
1. Put the learner at *ease.*
2. Find out what he or she already knows about the job.
3. Get the learners interested in and desirous of learning the job.

Step II—*Presentation* (of the operations and knowledge)
1. *Tell, show, illustrate,* and *question* in order to put over the new knowledge and operations.
2. Instruct slowly, clearly, completely, and patiently, one point at a time.
3. Check, question, and repeat.
4. Make sure the learner really knows.

Step III—*Performance tryout*
1. Test learner by having him or her perform the job.
2. Ask questions beginning with *why, how, when,* or *where.*
3. Observe performance, correct errors, and repeat instructions if necessary.
4. Continue until *you know learner knows.*

Step IV—*Follow-up*
1. Put the employee "on his own."
2. Check frequently to be sure learner follows instructions.
3. Taper off extra supervision and close follow-up until person is qualified to work with normal supervision.

Remember—if the learner hasn't learned, the teacher hasn't taught.

Source: Training Within Industry Report, War Manpower Commission, Bureau of Training, 1945.

operation of complex equipment. Models called *simulators* are used when operation of the actual equipment could be hazardous to the operator or others or prohibitively costly if the real equipment were damaged. Pilots, for example, are trained in cockpit simulators; astronauts are trained in zero-gravity chambers and spacecraft simulators. This training simulates ''the real thing'' as closely as possible, giving the trainees experience in reacting to variables and unexpected events without jeopardizing their safety, the safety of others, or the expensive equipment.

Vestibule training is also used for workers such as drivers, police and fire personnel, and disaster workers.

The *mentor, or buddy, system* may be used to extend the learning of a new employee after the initial training period. If the mentor, or buddy, is a willing and effective participant, the relationship can be a positive training support system. The mentor-buddy not only serves as a role model but is also a source of help for new workers after they are put on their own in their jobs.

The mentor-buddy system may be used alone for the initial training or in combination with supervisor training followed by assignment to a mentor-buddy for an extended period.

In *job rotation,* workers are trained in several different jobs within a work unit or department. They move from one job to another and work at each for a specified period. Initial training at each rotation is like initial training at any new job. Assignments at each rotation should be long enough for the worker to develop proficiency at the job.

*Competency
Check:*

Can you identify
and define the
methods for training
operations
personnel?

Job rotation has also been used to add variety and interest to routine jobs. After all the stations have been learned, however, monotony tends to return. An advantage is that job rotation helps workers to understand an entire process rather than a small part of it, increasing the core dimensions of the job. Job rotation also increases departmental flexibility; when one worker is absent, another can fill in.

While the seven methods for training operations personnel discussed here are the most common for on-the-job training, off-the-job and developmental methods may also be used.

Developmental Training

Though you will not be actively involved in developmental training programs, you should be familiar with the methods used in these programs so that you can (1) recommend workers for them and (2) participate in them yourself.

Figure 10-6 describes 11 developmental training methods. All of them might also conceivably be used for some type of operations training. For example, as you have read, role playing might be used in sales training. Our purpose here, however, is to point out how four of these methods might be used in operations training. While you may occasionally be involved, most training using these methods will be handled by HR/P or training specialists.

You will certainly be involved in *counseling and coaching* your workers in the course of your ongoing relationship with them. The counseling may be strictly informal. For example, you might stop by a worker's station on your rounds and say, "I noticed, Megan, that you were late twice this week. That's unusual for you. Is there something I can help you with? I'll be in my office at 4 P.M. today if you'd like to stop by and talk." In a few words, you've called attention to a symptom, alerted the worker that you're aware of the tardiness without condemning her, and offered to help. That combines effective supervision with initial counseling.

You may also use the *lecture* and *discussion* methods on occasion when you need to instruct your workers as a group. You may give a brief lecture apprising them of a change in company policy or the installation of a new system. A follow-up discussion by workers may be used to further explain and clarify the points presented.

Computer-assisted instruction (CAI) may be used as a preliminary to on-the-job instruction or in conjunction with it. CAI involves the use of a computer to teach a unit of learning on a *programmed* basis. In programmed instruction, one step or small part of the instruction is presented, in printed form or on a computer terminal; the learner responds, and, if the response is correct, the next part of the unit is presented. This continues until the entire unit is presented.

Video/audio instruction is also used in cognitive learning, such as parts of equipment for machine operators, recognition of dental problems for dental technicians, or warehouse organization for stock clerks. CAI, video/audio instruction, and programmed instruction may reduce on-the-job learning time and therefore reduce the time the supervisor must spend on training; but they do not substitute for the entire on-the-job training process.

In addition to knowing what operations training and developmental training methods are available, you must also be able to select a method appropriate to your workers' needs. We shall address that problem next.

Competency Check:

Can you give examples of methods that may be used for operations or developmental training?

Selecting the Training Method

With so many training methods available, you might ask, "How do I select the best one?" Let's examine several factors that need to be considered in answering that question.

When selecting a method, the first factor you should examine is your *objectives*. If the job is fairly routine and your major objective is to move the worker to productivity as quickly as possible, OJT or JIT at the work station would be infinitely preferable to off-the-job methods such as lecture or discussion. On the other hand, if the objective is to improve customer relations among salesclerks, a conference or seminar using role-play, gaming, and case study might be appropriate.

It is generally agreed that when the objective is to develop the manipulative skill of machine operators, on-the-job training is usually the most effective method. But what method is best when the objective is to improve attitude, better personal relations, or enlarge knowledge of the company's product or service? Figure 10-8 on page 308 shows how training directors in one study rated training methods for specific objectives.

Whether to train individually or in groups would also be influenced by objectives. If the objective is to improve a manipulative skill such as keyboarding, for example, the worker would progress faster working on the actual equipment. Keyboarding could be taught to groups of workers in an off-the-job setting, such as in the company training center or in a community college or technical school. If off-the-job equipment was not available in multiple units so that each trainee could use a keyboard, however, individual on-the-job instruction at the worker's work station might be used to improve skills.

If the objective is to develop interpersonal skills, training in groups would provide an opportunity for trainees to role-play, discuss, and interact with each other in learning sessions.

The second factor to consider in choosing a method is *cost*. While you might wish that your machine operators could be trained to high proficiency in vestibule simulations before you risked placing them on plant equipment, it would be far too costly

FIGURE 10-8

COMPARATIVE EFFECTIVENESS OF NINE TRAINING METHODS FOR SPECIFIC OBJECTIVES

TRAINING METHOD	KNOWLEDGE ACQUISITION MEAN RANK	CHANGING ATTITUDES MEAN RANK	PROBLEM-SOLVING SKILLS MEAN RANK	INTER-PERSONAL SKILLS MEAN RANK	PARTICIPANT ACCEPTANCE MEAN RANK	KNOWLEDGE RETENTION MEAN RANK
case study	2	4	1	4	2	2
conference (discussion) method	3	3	4	3	1	5
lecture (with questions)	9	8	9	8	8	8
business games	6	5	2	5	3	6
movie films	4	6	7	6	5	7
programmed instruction	1	7	6	7	7	1
role playing	7	2	3	2	4	4
sensitivity training (T-group)	8	1	5	1	6	3
TV lecture	5	9	8	9	9	9

Note: 1 = highest rank.
Source: Adapted from Stephen J. Carroll, Frank T. Paine, and John M. Ivancevich, "The Relative Effectiveness of Training Methods—Expert Opinion and Research," *Personnel Psychology* 33, 1972, pp. 495–509.

to use that method. On-the-job training by you or by a senior employee would thus be more appropriate. Cost is also a consideration when determining how training time should be divided between personal teaching and written instruction. Your time is limited, and you will not be able to stay by the trainee's side during the entire learning period. After you go through the JIT process, for example, an operator's manual might be used by the trainee in the intervals between follow-ups while you are performing other supervisory tasks.

A third factor influencing method selection is *resources*. Some firms have large training staffs and sophisticated facilities. Yours may not be one of them. If it is not, you will need to select an on-the-job method that you or one of your workers can handle. It may also be up to you to train the senior employee who will serve as trainer. An alternative might be low-cost, off-the-job sources such as a public community college or a technical school.

Evaluation of each training program will help you become more adept at selecting methods. Evaluation will be the final section of this chapter.

Competency Check:

Can you cite the factors to consider in choosing a training method?

WHAT CAN THE SUPERVISOR DO?

Getting yourself ready for one-on-one teaching at the job station and the actual teaching when you get there will be easier for you and the worker if you follow these tips:

1. **Do your homework.** Learn the conditions under which workers learn best. In addition to the overview presented in this chapter, do some reading in the behavioral sciences, especially in the psychology of learning and motivation. Texts in principles of management and human resources management will also help you put the behavioral principles into the workplace context.

2. **Prepare the worker for learning.** New workers are usually eager to get started on the job, but they also have some apprehension about learning a new task. Put them at ease with a pleasant, unhurried manner. Pick out something from their background and experience that might relate to the job, and get them to talk about it on the way to the work station. You might also walk through the work group to let the new worker observe coworkers at work. Say, for example, ''You've already met your work group in your orientation. We'll do a walk-through to let you see them at work. We're pretty informal, as you can see; and we get the job done. In no time at all, you'll be operating the equipment as easily as they do. Well, here's your station; let's get you started.'' Your attitude at this stage should be supportive.

3. **Give an overview of the job and the work station.** Keep it brief—too much will overwhelm the worker. ''Your job will be to fix the picture tube to the frame in the TV cabinet. The tubes will come on the belt from *C* group over there. The cabinets are on the rack in front of you. When you assemble the two, they move on the belt to the spot welders. There's more, but we'll handle that later.''

4. **Break the job into manageable components, and demonstrate one part at a time.** ''First, let me show you how to seat the tube onto the frame.'' This is the show-and-tell part. Point out reasons for each step in the process as you demonstrate. Be alert to questions, whether voiced or simply registered on the worker's face. Explain again, if necessary.

   Caution: Remember, workers learn at a different pace, so don't bore a fast learner by moving too slowly or laboring over a point. Experience will help you judge pretty closely the learning pace of each worker.

5. **Let the worker perform as you observe.** ''Now, let me watch as you seat the tube, Joe.'' Stay with the worker. Don't run off to the phone or to your office. Let the worker explain to you each part of the process as she or he performs it. Refrain from interrupting to add new data at this point. Correct only if the worker varies widely from the accepted method. Reinforce the learner's effort. ''Very good, Joe. You might want to use a bit more caution moving the tube into the cabinet to avoid scarring. You'll get the hang of it.''

   Go through steps 4 and 5 for each part of the process. Then let the worker put the parts together by going through the whole process. If a process has many steps, you might want to put them together in groups so the learner won't have to recall them all at once on the first attempt.

6. **Gradually put the worker on his or her own.** As the worker gains confidence and you feel that he or she can do the job without close supervision, let the worker ''go it alone.'' But continue to be supportive. Return occasionally during the first day or so to answer questions or see if there are problems.

> As far as possible, allow the worker some leeway for making decisions in performing the job, such as sequencing the tasks or scheduling. Don't forget the importance of a verbal pat on the back. "You're coming along fine, Joe; give me a call if you need help before I drop by in a couple of hours."

EVALUATING THE TRAINING PROGRAM

How effective was your training and development program? Did it accomplish the objectives you established for it? Improvement in worker performance is the critical measure of its success. But you will also need feedback from workers to determine the effectiveness of the program. Did you select the method most appropriate for the type of participants and for your objectives? Answers to these questions should come from an evaluation of the program by trainees and the training staff.

Evaluation by the Trainees

Competency Check:

Can you cite the methods of trainee evaluation of the training program?

The degree of participation by workers is another measure of the success of a program. Word gets around. Successful programs are often the best advertising you can use. Conversely, it doesn't take many boring courses to kill the whole T&D program. Trainees tend to evaluate a program both by the behavior they exhibit after the training and by the judgment they share with their peers.

Even before you attempt to measure after-training performance, therefore, you should ask trainees to evaluate their own training sessions. Questionnaires distributed at the close of the session, to be filled in before the trainees leave, are one device used for this purpose. As shown in Figure 10-9, Chick-fil-A Corporation asks its training participants to fill out a questionnaire rating (1) their overall reaction to the session, (2) how well it related to their jobs, (3) the effectiveness of the instructor, and (4) any visual aids used. They are also asked to make suggestions for improving the training.

Combined with your own evaluation, the trainee evaluation will assist you in planning future training sessions.

Evaluation by the Trainer

When planning a training session, you establish the criteria by which you will judge the effectiveness of the session. After a session, you might ask yourself the following questions:[7]

TRAINING SESSION QUESTIONNAIRE

Title or Course Number _____ Date _____

Instructor _____ Location _____

1. Please circle your overall reaction to the training session just completed.

          Very Good   Good   Fair   Poor

Comments: _____

_____

_____

_____

2. How well do you expect the material presented will relate to your job as a Chick-fil-A unit Operator?

          Very Much   Quite a Bit   Some   Very Little

Comments: _____

_____

_____

_____

3. Will you be able to use and apply the material presented in your daily duties as a unit Operator?

          Very Much   Quite a Bit   Some   Very Little

Comments: _____

_____

_____

_____

4. Would you please give your overall reaction to the way the instructor presented the session.

          Very Good   Good   Fair   Poor

Comments: _____

_____

_____

_____

5. What is your reaction to the visual aides used if any?

          Very Good   Good   Fair   Poor

Comments: _____

_____

_____

_____

6. What suggestions do you have for improving this particular training session?

_____

_____

_____

_____

_____

_____

Source: Chick-fil-A, Inc.

FIGURE 10-10

COSTS AND BENEFITS OF TRAINING

COSTS	BENEFITS
trainer's salary	increase in production
materials for training	reduction in errors
living expenses for trainer and trainees	reduction in turnover
cost of facilities	less supervision necessary
equipment	ability to advance
transportation	new skills lead to ability to do more jobs
trainee's salary	attitude changes
lost production (opportunity cost)	
preparation time	

Source: Robert L. Mathis and John H. Jackson, *Personnel—Human Resource Management,* 4th ed., West Publishing Company, St. Paul, Minn. 1985, p. 299. Reprinted by permission. Copyright © 1985 by West Publishing Company. All rights reserved.

Reaction: How well did the trainees like the training?

Learning: To what extent did the trainees learn the facts, principles, and approaches that were included in the training?

Behavior: To what extent did their job behavior change because of the program?

Results: What final results were achieved (reduction in cost, reduction in turnover, improvement in production, and so on)?

Questionnaires can be used to evaluate trainee reaction. Tests are commonly used to evaluate cognitive learning. Before-and-after training tests can be used to compare growth.

On the behavioral level, evaluation is designed to measure the degree to which training has affected job performance. Behavior is much less amenable to measurement than are the other levels. A decrease in tardiness and absence can be counted; but other behaviors, such as attitude and teamwork, may be more difficult to measure. Interviews with trainees and their coworkers may reveal behavioral changes. Also, fewer grievances and a better work atmosphere are often observable as a result of improved behaviors.

At the results level, evaluation measures the contribution of the training to the achievement of company objectives. Improved productivity and reduced costs can be measured fairly easily. A cost-to-benefit comparison will show to management the degree of effectiveness of T&D to the organization. Figure 10-10 lists the costs and benefits of training.

Some costs and benefits are not easily quantifiable. For example, if a worker who successfully completes a training program leaves a few months later for a better job in another firm, the cost to your firm may be difficult to measure. Some benefits, such

Competency Check:

Can you give the meaning of the levels of T&D evaluation?

as attitudinal changes, are also difficult to translate into monetary terms. Even so, a cost-to-benefit comparison is a good way to show whether training is cost-effective, and the firm needs to determine the contribution each of its activities is making to the accomplishment of its objectives.

COMPETENCY REVIEW

1. Identify the elements in the relationship of training and development to the staffing function.
2. Discuss the supervisor's role in training and development.
3. Cite three sources for identifying training and development needs.
4. Discuss six conditions which affect learning.
5. Cite two ways in which to encourage participation in training and development programs.
6. Discuss the importance of making training and development results visible to employees and management.
7. Identify and define seven training methods for operations personnel.
8. Give three examples of methods that may be used for either operations training or developmental training.
9. Cite three factors to consider in choosing a training method.
10. Discuss two methods of trainee evaluation of the program.
11. Give the meaning of the four levels of training evaluation.

APPLICATIONS

1. For your current job or one you have held in the past, respond to the questions below. If you have not worked, interview someone who now works.
   a. Describe the orientation program the company conducted when you began your job.
   b. List the training methods used by your firm.
   c. Using a format similar to that shown in Figure 10-9 on page 311, evaluate your initial training.
2. In groups of four or five, outline an orientation program for incoming freshmen at your college. Compare your group's plan to other groups' plans, and discuss the differences.
3. "It is necessary for new employees to be trained by the company to perform the jobs for which we hire them; but the company shouldn't spend money on employee development." Do you agree or disagree with this statement by an executive? Defend your position.

4. For each training situation listed in the left column below, select a method from those in the right column that you consider most appropriate. Give your rationale for each selection.

Training Situation	**Method**
a. Train 10 new pari-mutuel betting window cashiers.	programmed instruction
	OJT
b. Train 20 new bricklayers for a large unionized construction firm.	case study
	lecture
c. Train 16 employees to teach basic reading and writing skills.	conference or seminar by a local university
d. Train 1 registration clerk in a college to retrieve records on a new display terminal.	CAI
	vestibule training
e. Train 2 senior workers for possible promotion to group-leadership positions.	

CASES

Case I: One Day Is Enough

Rita Columbo in the beginning of the chapter was unceremoniously placed at a work station and told to learn a job for which she was not hired and on which she was given no help.

The day was a disaster. She had had only 2 days on a Kaypro at her school just to get acquainted with a computerized keyboard and terminal, a fact she had noted on her application. She had been hired as a clerk-typist but was told that as she became experienced with government work, there would probably be opportunities for her in the document-production center. She was pleased but had no idea that she would be put into that higher-rated job on her first day.

She struggled through the menus on the screen, but everything seemed to go wrong. She found that the Xerox was nothing like the machine in her classroom. And the manual, she discovered, might as well have been written in a foreign language. Every instruction, she thought, assumed she already knew a lot of things about the machine, which she surely didn't.

She tried to get Jack Gantos' help, but he kept saying he'd be over as soon as he finished the rush job he was on. The next thing she knew, he had gone to lunch.

Tony Maxwell came by once and told her to "use the manual and hang in there."

By 2 P.M., without a break of any kind and hopelessly bogged down with a machine that kept displaying "systems error" and a string of numbers, she gave up. Fighting back tears of disappointment, she picked up her purse and walked out.

1. Cite several T&D errors that are evident in this case.
2. Evaluate the on-the-job method used to train Columbo.
3. What would you advise Maxwell to do about Columbo?
4. If you were Maxwell's manager, what would you do about the situation?

Case II: You're Grazing in My Pasture

Judd Bovine is known as a hard-nosed, hardworking, no-nonsense shop supervisor in the equipment maintenance division of National Mills, Inc., a large firm with 3000 workers in five plants in the Midwest. He is respected as a skilled worker who has found his niche as a shop supervisor after 10 years with the company. He claims to have no desire to move up. He likes his workers, and they like him. His success, he proudly states, is due to the fact that ''I train 'em right because I'm good at every job in my section.'' No one argues with him about that. The workers kid around about ''Bovine's guarding his pasture.''

Recently, the firm centralized its HR/P division at Chicago headquarters. As part of the reorganization, T&D was expanded and moved into a separate center under HR/P at headquarters. Sable Whitney, a new MBA with impeccable academic credentials, was hired as T&D director.

After 2 months as director, Whitney sends a memo to all plant managers stating that in the future, all training will be under her direction and conducted at the center. This will include all orientation, job training, and developmental training. Whitney's memo says that it is felt that new employees can be better oriented at company headquarters and that job training can be standardized to save money.

A copy of the memo is sent by plant managers to all their managers. When Bovine reads his copy, he storms into the plant manager's office and hits the ceiling.

''Who does this upstart MBA think she is? Let her come here and see what these guys on the shop floor do. Where does she get off thinking she can train my grease monkeys at a tea party on the tenth floor at headquarters? She's out of her cotton-pickin' mind! Well, if you want me to keep our good record going, just tell her to stay out of Bovine's pasture.''

1. Evaluate the new T&D director's proposal.
2. Evaluate Bovine as a trainer.
3. What changes, if any, would you make in the training program?

REFERENCES

1. Irwin I. Goldstein, *Training: Program Development and Evaluation,* Brooks/Cole Publishing Company, Belmont, Calif. 1974. See also ''Employment Training: Current Trends, Future Challenges,'' *Training and Development Journal,* August 1983.

2. S. Norman Feingold, ''Tracking New Career Categories Will Become a Preoccupation for Job Seekers and Managers,'' *Personnel Administrator,* December 1983, pp. 86–91.

3. Thomas J. Peters and Robert H. Waterman, Jr., *In Search of Excellence,* Warner Books, New York, 1982, pp. 2–3.

4. Victor Vroom, *Work and Motivation,* John Wiley & Sons, Inc., New York, 1964.

5. Walter D. St. John, ''The Complete Employee Orientation Program,'' *Personnel Journal,* May 1980, p. 377.

6. Fred Wickert, "The Famous JIT Card: A Basic Way to Improve It," *Training and Development Journal,* February 1974, pp. 6–9.

7. Ralph F. Catainello and Donald L. Kilpatrick, "Evaluating Training Programs—the State of the Art," *Training and Development Journal,* May 1968, pp. 2–3.

SUGGESTED READINGS

Beardsley, Carolyn: "Improving Employee Awareness of Opportunity at IBM," *Personnel,* April 1987, pp. 58–63.

Carrell, Michael R., and Frank E. Kuzmits: *Personnel—Human Resource Management,* 2d ed., Charles E. Merrill Books, Inc., Columbus, Ohio, 1986.

Gordon, Jack: "What They Don't Teach You About Being a Training Manager," *Training,* June 1986, pp. 22–34.

Ivancevich, John M., and William F. Glueck: *Foundations of Personnel/Human Resource Management,* 3d ed., Business Publications, Inc., Plano, Tex., 1986.

Magnus, Margaret: "Training Futures," *Personnel Journal,* May 1986, pp. 61–71.

Mathis, Robert L., and John H. Jackson: *Personnel—Human Resource Management,* 4th ed., West Publishing Company, St. Paul, Minn., 1985.

Schermerhorn, John R., Jr.: *Management for Productivity,* 2d ed., John Wiley & Sons, Inc., New York, 1986.

SECTION V

THE SUPERVISOR AND THE MOTIVATING AND LEADING FUNCTION

THE SUPERVISOR AND THE MOTIVATING AND LEADING FUNCTION

11

THE SUPERVISOR'S ROLE IN LEADING AND MOTIVATING

COMPETENCIES

Studying this chapter will enable you to:

1. Discuss the dimensions of leadership.

2. Contrast the terms *leader* and *manager.*

3. Briefly describe several leadership theories.

4. Identify the forces the supervisor should learn about to help in choosing a leadership style.

5. Describe the basic concepts of several motivational models.

6. Tell what is meant by a "motivational climate."

7. Cite several demotivators, and suggest what action the supervisor can take to eliminate them.

CHAPTER OUTLINE

The supervisors left the meeting in which a pervasive systems change had been introduced. Most of them stopped by the desk of Meg Standing, a competent and charming supervisor, to continue discussing the change. They were more relaxed and talkative than they had been in the meeting. The general manager, observing the gathering from his office, remarked to the consultant, "That happens all the time. It's not only with her peers. Her work group is tops in morale and productivity. She's a born leader."

"He's always ramming orders down our throats and then standing over us to see that it's done his way. We do what he assigns—and no more," a worker remarked to a new employee. The two workers had just watched supervisor Jason Polik, after reading his list of things to be done that day, return to his office, which overlooks the work area.

"I know it's hot in the shop today," Al Matson, the repair supervisor bellowed, "but this job has to be done by 5 P.M.—period. Besides, we've worked in hotter weather than this. Get a Pepsi when you want, but get out there and get the job done!"

"We're going to handle this job differently," Bayne Smith, the supervisor, explained. "We have four new workers and two trainees on the line, so the situation calls for a standardized procedure and closer supervision for a while. At the end of 2 weeks, we'll all look at the situation again and decide from there."

"OK, we realize there's a problem in shipping," supervisor Jean Ballou said in summarizing a discussion with three work-group leaders. "Let's shut down half an hour early today so your groups can get together and see what they can work out. I'll have coffee ready, and we'll put our heads together to solve this thing."

Each of the situations above represents a different approach to leading. Some are good. Some are not so good. Each leader represented has the same goal: getting the job done. Each job must be done by people. The workers in each case will follow their leader or not depending on their feelings about themselves, their jobs, and the leader. Considering all the variables in both the leader and the follower, is there one best way to lead? If there is, no one has yet discovered it, although a great deal of research has been devoted to the subject. We know that many managers are not as effective in leading as they should be, often because they lack the skills or because they do not know how to adapt their leadership style to the situation.

This chapter will focus on some of the research findings in the areas of leadership and motivation. While both topics are highly complex, our purpose here will be confined to introducing some basic leadership styles and motivation models and to illustrating the use of different styles in different situations. First, let us look at what *leadership* is.

WHAT IS LEADERSHIP?

There are many answers to this question. As already noted, the incidents at the beginning of this chapter reflected five managers' approaches to leadership. Each, at least in the short run, will probably accomplish the task at hand. Is *leadership* synonymous with "getting the job done"? Current thinking about leadership would answer no. Let's see why.

Dimensions of Leadership

Is *leadership* the same as *authority?* In Chapter 5, *authority* was defined as the "power to make decisions and use resources without getting permission from someone else." In each incident in the beginning of the chapter, authority had been delegated and was used. Why did Standing's manager call her a "born leader" when he observed other supervisors asking her views on the change rather than asking the manager's? She had no authority over her peers. Some other factor was at work here, as we shall see later. The authority used by all the other managers illustrates that authority is a *dimension* of leadership; it is not *synonymous* with it.

Another dimension of leadership is power. *Power* can be defined as "the ability to influence the behavior of other people." Consider the concepts of authority and power in the following:

> An agent of the Textile Workers Union likes to tell the story of the occasion when a new manager appeared in the mill where he was working. The manager came into the weave room the day he arrived. He walked directly over to the agent and said, "Are you Belloc?" The agent acknowledged that he was. The manager said, "I am the new manager here. When I manage a mill, I run it. Do you understand?" The agent nodded, and then waved his hand. The workers, intently watching this encounter, shut down every loom in the room immediately. The agent turned to the manager and said, "All right, go ahead and run it."[1]

Power comes from a variety of sources. Think of the influence of these people: Albert Einstein, O. J. Simpson, Sylvester Stallone, Lee Iacocca, Ayatollah Khomeini, Margaret Thatcher. Each is from a different walk of life, and though all have or have had power, each has had it for a different reason.

How does one get power? In some cases, it can come simply from overwhelming physical size, as shown in the cartoon on the next page.

In the view of J. R. P. French and B. Raven,[2] there are five kinds of power.

Source: Reprinted by permission of Mal Enterprises, Inc., 1984

1. *Reward power*: You have reward power when your workers see that you have the ability to provide them with something they want, such as pay increases or promotions or feelings of pride, belonging, or sense of worth.

2. *Coercive power*: As a supervisor, you have coercive power if your workers see you as a source of punishment, such as assigning difficult jobs, isolating a worker from the group, blocking promotions, or giving low performance appraisals.

3. *Legitimate power*: When you are given the job of supervisor and the authority that accompanies it, legitimate power is part of the package. This is sometimes called "position power." Workers tend to view their bosses as having a certain inherent level of power and the authority to carry out the job.

4. *Referent power*: If workers see in you qualities such as competence, fairness, and consideration, they are likely to accept you as a role model and may even try to emulate you. This gives you referent power. This personal power may derive from an attractive personality and charm, sometimes called *charisma*. Standing, in the beginning of the chapter, may be viewed as having referent power.

5. *Expert power*: If your workers see you as highly skilled and knowledgeable in your field, you may lead through expert power. Their respect for your expertise will make them more willing to follow your direction on the job. Standing may also be viewed as having expert power.

Competency
Check:

Can you discuss
two dimensions of
leadership?

As you can see, power, like authority, is a dimension of leadership, but *power* and *leadership* do not mean the same thing. Yet some people equate managing with leading. Do you think a manager is also a leader? Let's examine that concept next.

Are Managers and Leaders the Same?

Is a manager also a leader? In Chapter 1, *management* was defined as "the process of accomplishing objectives by, with, and through people." That also applies to leadership, but a part of the definition is missing.

Management involves people and other resources, while leadership focuses on people, individually and in groups. Look at the "people" situations in the opening cases. If you were a worker and had your choice, which supervisor would you prefer? Both subordinates and peers thought highly of Standing. How about the team approach of Ballou? In that situation, you would be given an opportunity to help make the decisions. Would Smith's adaptation to changing conditions provide an easier environment for you than, say, the inflexible styles of Polik or Matson?

If your choices are typical, you have injected concepts such as willingness, respect, and inspiration into the definition. This means, then, that a person can manage without being a leader. Polik will accomplish the company's objectives by getting his workers to produce a certain number of widgets per day, but the workers will not produce for him beyond a certain minimal standard. As you study leadership styles and motivation, keep these supervisors in mind. We will return to them at the end of the chapter.

A management consultant recently told a group of executives that the title of *manager* or even *owner* did not make them leaders. "Leadership is not something you take," he explained. "Leadership is something that is given to you—you have to earn it."[3]

Competency Check:

Can you contrast the terms *leader* and *manager*?

A Definition

The view of leadership dimensions and the difference between a manager and a leader leads us to a definition: *Leadership* can be defined as "the ability to influence people to set and accomplish goals willingly while, at the same time, engendering their respect, loyalty, and cooperation." As you can see, several operative words in this definition—*influence, willingly, respect*—make leadership something more than authority, power, or management. Of course, when you find leadership and managerial ability in the same "package," you have a winning combination. Being a leader of your workers as well as their supervisor will make your job easier and help to accomplish your objectives. To work toward this goal, you must develop and improve your leadership skills. To help you better your understanding of leadership styles, the next section presents some of the most common leadership styles.

BASIC LEADERSHIP STYLES

All the supervisors in the beginning of the chapter thought they were leading. Each approached the job differently. What styles were they using? There have been many attempts to identify and describe leadership styles. We shall examine the essence of several of these styles.

The Trait Theory

Do you agree that Standing was "born" a leader? Or was her seemingly innate ability only in the eyes of the beholder? Perception is important because leadership style is not what the leader thinks it is but what the followers think it is.

Early leadership theories focused on what the leaders were like rather than on the actions they took. Researchers tried to identify the personality traits of known leaders that could be used in predicting leadership success in others. Ghiselli and other researchers found certain traits to be common among successful leaders.[4] Among these traits were supervisory ability, occupational achievement, intelligence, self-actualization, self-assurance, and decisiveness.[5]

Personality and social traits, as well as physical characteristics, were examined, and findings seemed to suggest that leaders tended to be more intelligent, more extroverted, more dominant, and more decisive than followers, as well as bigger and taller. Closer examination, however, revealed some contradictions. It was noted that the traits were not applicable to all situations, leading one researcher to conclude that "the chances of finding a set of universally effective leadership traits is nil."[6]

While it is acknowledged today that certain traits may influence a person's ability to lead, the same traits have not been shown to be reliable predictors of leadership success for all managers or in all situations. Some researchers have viewed the traits in broader contexts, as we shall see in the next section.

Leadership Influenced by Management Philosophy

Some management theories center around the way in which the manager views people in the work environment. A classic among these is Douglas McGregor's theory on the assumptions we make about people in the workplace. This theory is often viewed in both a leadership and a motivation context.

McGregor felt that a manager's views about people and their behavior largely determined his or her style of operating. He cited two sets of assumptions and labeled them *theory X* and *theory Y*.[7] These assumptions are shown in Figure 11-1.

If you are a theory-X supervisor, you assume your workers are not responsible people and you therefore do not assign them responsibilities. This can become a self-fulfilling prophesy—your workers have no responsibilities and so, in your view, they are not responsible workers. We should not conclude that McGregor's theory X and theory Y are "polar opposites and that X is bad and Y is good."[8] Where workers *do* behave irresponsibly, are lazy, and respond only to coercion, the supervisor should examine all the elements of the situation to find the reason for the behavior and to find the best leadership "fit" among people, tasks, and the organization.[9] This thesis suggests a situational approach to leadership, which will be addressed later.

Another leadership theory, conceived in 1947, was based on the Ohio State Leadership Studies. The purpose of these studies was to determine the relationship between effective leader behavior and subordinates' satisfaction and performance. The studies disclosed two principal dimensions of effective leader behavior:

FIGURE 11-1 MCGREGOR'S THEORY X AND THEORY Y:
ASSUMPTIONS ABOUT PEOPLE

THEORY X	THEORY Y
1. People inherently dislike work and will avoid it if they can.	1. The expenditure of physical and mental effort in work is as natural as play or rest.
2. People must be coerced, controlled, directed, and threatened, in order to make them work.	2. People can exercise self-direction and self-control in the service of objectives to which they are committed.
3. The average human being prefers to be directed, wishes to avoid responsibility, and has relatively little ambition.	3. The average human being learns, under proper conditions, not only to accept but to seek responsibility.

Source: Douglas McGregor, *The Human Side of Enterprise,* McGraw-Hill Book Company, New York, 1960.

> **1.** *Consideration*: a close psychological relationship between leader and followers
> **2.** *Initiating structure*: concern for close direction of subordinates to get the job done

According to this theory, four combinations of the two dimensions were common. A leader might be high in consideration and low in initiating structure, or the reverse; or, the leader might be high in both or low in both. Moreover, the leader could use a different combination of the two dimensions, based on the situation.

The Ohio State Leadership Studies served as a springboard for much of the leadership research that followed.[10] One such study introduced another two-dimensional approach, which we shall look at next.

A classic leadership model that treats the influence of managerial philosophy on leadership is the Managerial Grid® theory of Blake and Mouton.[11] As shown in Figure 11-2 on page 328, the Managerial Grid is a two-dimensional display of five leadership styles. Through an interactive process with feedback, managers are assisted to locate their own managerial assumptions regarding their concern for people and concern for production in relation to these five styles and paternalism, which is not shown. Although there are 81 points on the Grid, Blake and Mouton used the corners to show the extremes and the center for a balanced position. For example, a 9,1 leader (authority-obedience) corresponds to the classical school of management thought (Chapter 1), in which efficiency of operations is the paramount concern. A 1,1 position (impoverished management) indicates leaders who do only enough to keep their jobs. The ''country club'' manager (1,9) assumes that attention to human needs in the workplace is primary and will lead to a friendly workplace. The 5,5 leader (''organization man'') tries to balance the concerns for people and production, though this leader provides only an adequate level of concern for the two dimensions. Most leaders tend to be in this center position on the Grid. The 9,9 position (team management)

FIGURE 11-2

The Managerial Grid

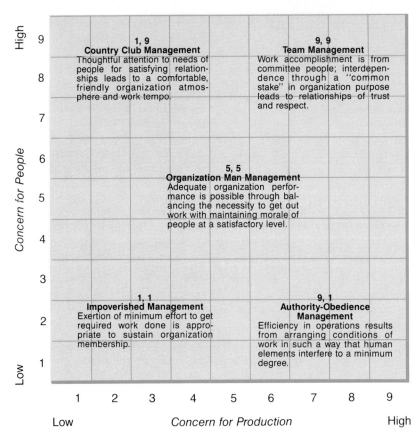

Source: Robert R. Blake and Jane Srygley Mouton, *The Managerial Grid III: The Key to Leadership Excellence*, Gulf Publishing Company, Houston, © 1985, p. 12. Reproduced by permission.

is, according to Blake and Mouton, the ideal toward which managers should strive. This position reflects a high level of concern for both people and production; it has a participative focus. When people are committed to the organization and feel a part of it, the resultant atmosphere of mutual trust and respect will lead to high productivity.

Through the Managerial Grid, you can determine what your managerial style is and develop a plan to work toward a 9,9 style, if that style is appropriate to your situation. Let's now consider what impact the situation has on leadership style.

Situational Leadership

Leadership has also been portrayed in terms of the degree of decision-making input the manager allows from the followers. According to Robert Tannenbaum and Warren H. Schmidt, there is a continuum of leader behavior, with two extremes. One extreme is the authoritarian or autocratic leader, who makes all the decisions. The other is the democratic leader, who not only encourages participation in decision making but also

FIGURE 11-3   The continuum of leadership behavior

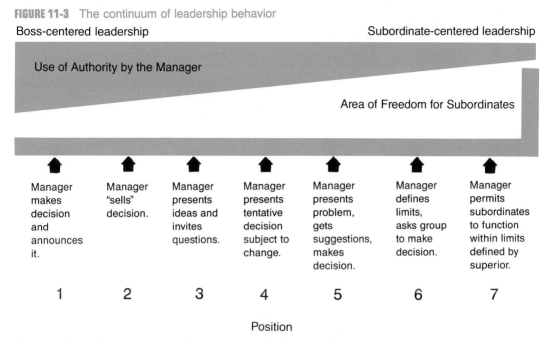

Boss-centered leadership   Subordinate-centered leadership

Use of Authority by the Manager

Area of Freedom for Subordinates

Manager makes decision and announces it.	Manager "sells" decision.	Manager presents ideas and invites questions.	Manager presents tentative decision subject to change.	Manager presents problem, gets suggestions, makes decision.	Manager defines limits, asks group to make decision.	Manager permits subordinates to function within limits defined by superior.
1	2	3	4	5	6	7

Position

Source: Robert Tannenbaum and Warren H. Schmidt, "How to Choose a Leadership Pattern," *Harvard Business Review,* May–June 1973, p. 164.

allows workers to function on their own within prescribed limits. Tannenbaum and Schmidt presented these concepts on a continuum of leadership behavior, as shown in Figure 11-3.[12]

The leadership continuum theory holds that different situations require different leadership styles. Tannenbaum and Schmidt stress that style should be determined by examining three forces—the manager, the subordinates, and the situation—and the way in which these forces are combined in each situation. The forces are shown in Figure 11-4 on page 330.

Using the continuum and these forces, for an authoritarian supervisor who is accustomed to directing dependent workers under boss-centered leadership in a centralized organization, a leadership style near the left end of the continuum, such as position 1 or 2, may be the most appropriate. But if you are a new supervisor with a participative orientation and come to a workplace with the other conditions described, you will have some adjusting to do to prevent confusion among the workers who are accustomed to receiving orders. Before your participative style can be effective, the workers and the work climate will have to be changed; this will take planning and must occur over time. (Chapter 18 will address the problems of change.)

Among other situational theories is that proposed by Fred E. Fiedler, who defined two basic styles of leadership: task-oriented leadership and relationship-oriented leadership.[13] Through a questionnaire technique, Fiedler identified leaders who gained satisfaction from task performance and those who gained satisfaction from interpersonal relationships.

FIGURE 11-4

FORCES IN THE LEADERSHIP SITUATION

FORCES IN THE MANAGER	FORCES IN THE SUBORDINATES	FORCES IN THE SITUATION
value system: how the manager personally feels about delegating, degree of confidence in subordinates personal leadership inclinations: authoritarian vs. participative feelings of security in uncertain situations	need for independence: some people need and want direction, while others do not readiness to assume responsibility: different people need different degrees of responsibility tolerance for ambiguity: specific vs. general directions interest and perceived importance of the problem: people generally have more interest in, and work harder on, important problems degree of understanding and identification with organizational goals: a manager is more likely to delegate authority to an individual who seems to have a positive attitude about the organization degree of expectation in sharing in decision making: people who have worked under subordinate-centered leadership tend to resent boss-centered leadership	type of organization: centralized vs. decentralized work-group effectiveness: how effectively the group works together the problem itself: the work group's knowledge and experience relevant to the problem time pressure: it is difficult to delegate to subordinates in crisis situations demands from upper levels of management demands from government, unions, and society in general

Source: Leslie W. Rue and Lloyd L. Byars, *Management Theory and Application,* 4th ed., Irwin Publishing Co., Homewood, Ill., 1986, p. 391.

Fiedler also examined leadership styles in relation to the situation within which the leader was operating. He identified three situation dimensions:

1. *Leader-member relations*: friendliness of the leader and the degree of trust and respect for the leader by the workers
2. *Task structure*: the degree to which the job is structured or routine
3. *Position power*: the power inherent in the leader's position, which increases with the power to hire, fire, or discipline as opposed to the power only to supervise performance

FIGURE 11-5 Matching leadership styles to situations according to Fiedler

Forces in the Situation	Situations 1–8							
	1	2	3	4	5	6	7	8
Leader-member relations	good	good	good	good	poor	poor	poor	poor
Task Structure	structured	structured	unstructured	unstructured	structured	structured	unstructured	unstructured
Leader position power	strong	weak	strong	weak	strong	weak	strong	weak
	Favorable for leader						Unfavorable for leader	
Most productive leadership style	task	task	task	relation	relation	no data	task or relation	task

Source: Adapted from Leslie W. Rue and Lloyd L. Byars, *Management Theory and Application,* 4th ed., Irwin Publishing Company, Homewood, Ill., 1986, p. 393.

Using these three dimensions, Fiedler developed an eight-cell classification continuum of leadership. He also identified the most effective style of leadership for each of the eight cells. His work emphasized finding a match between the leader and the situation. Figure 11-5 shows the classification of leadership and identifies the styles Fiedler suggests as most productive for different situations.

In general, the Fiedler approach proposes that the success of either task-oriented or people-oriented leadership depends on its being applied to the right situation. In searching for a style that would achieve better group performance in favorable, intermediate, and unfavorable situations, the Fiedler findings can be summarized as follows:[14]

- Task-oriented leadership is associated with effective group performance in situations that are either very favorable or very unfavorable to the leader.
- People-oriented leadership is associated with effective group performance in situations of intermediate favorableness.

Let us look at an example. A first-line supervisor with good leader-member relations and strong position power, working at an auto manufacturing plant where the tasks are highly structured, would find task-oriented leadership most effective (situation 1 in Figure 11-5). In this situation, the employees respect the technical expertise of the supervisor, recognize his or her power, and follow his or her leadership.

Among other approaches to situational leadership is the Hersey-Blanchard model, which, like Fiedler's model, examines the subordinate in the situation.[15] Paul Hersey and Kenneth Blanchard term the leadership characteristics *task behavior* and *relation-*

ship behavior. These generally correspond to the autocratic and participative dimensions of Tannenbaum and Schmidt's continuum and the task- and people-centered leadership styles of Fiedler's situational model.

A more recent presentation of this model is presented by Hersey in his book, *The Situational Leader*.[16] Distinctive features of the model are the readiness of the followers and the mix of task and relationship in the leadership style. Figure 11-6 shows the four styles (S) of leadership correlated with a continuum of follower readiness (R).

Hersey defines *readiness* as how a person performs a particular task.[17] A low readiness level (R1) means that a worker is both unable and unwilling to perform a

FIGURE 11-6

Hersey leadership model

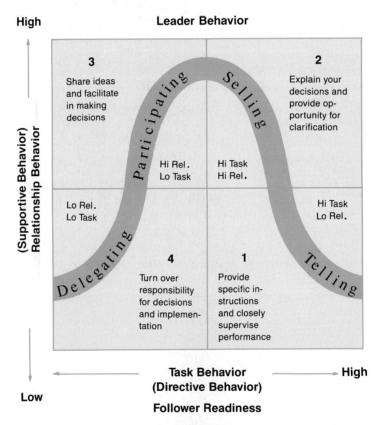

	HIGH	MODERATE		LOW
	R4	**R3**	**R2**	**R1**
	able & willing or motivated	able but unwilling or insecure	unable but willing or motivated	unable & unwilling or insecure

Source: Paul Hersey, *The Situational Leader,* Warner Books, New York, 1984, p. 63.

FIGURE 11-7

MATCHING STYLE AND READINESS IN THE HERSEY MODEL

READINESS	STYLE	DESCRIPTOR
R1 unable and unwilling or insecure	S1 HT/LR	Provide specific instructions and closely supervise performance.
R2 unable but willing or confident	S2 HT/HR	Explain decisions and provide opportunity for clarification.
R3 able but unwilling or insecure	S3 HR/LT	Share ideas and facilitate followers in decision making.
R4 able and willing or confident	S4 LR/LT	Turn over responsibility for decisions and implementation.

Source: Paul Hersey, *The Situational Leader,* Warner Books, New York, 1984, p. 71.

particular task. This would call for a high-task and low-relationship style (S1), which the author labels the "telling" style. Here, workers who do not have the skills and have no desire to learn the task need closer supervision with firmer controls. Hersey says that matching leadership and worker readiness to each situation is "just organized common sense."[18] Moving up the scale of readiness to R2, workers who may be willing but unable to take responsibility for the task need direction and supportive supervision (S2).

Highly competent workers who are also willing to take responsibility for their tasks (R4) might prefer the freedom to work on their own. This combination of skill and willingness greatly reduces their need for direction and support (S4). The matching of readiness and style in the Hersey model is summarized in Figure 11-7.

It is likely that in view of all the leadership theories available, you are now asking yourself, "How can I choose the right style?" The next section will help you address that question.

Competency Check:

Can you briefly describe six leadership theories?

CHOOSING A LEADERSHIP STYLE

As you have learned, leadership styles vary. You must choose the one that is most appropriate for you. According to Tannenbaum and Schmidt, to choose the right style, you must examine three forces: (1) forces in the manager, (2) forces in the subordinate, and (3) forces in the situation.[19]

Forces in the Manager

What are the forces within you—your values, your personality, your abilities—that influence your leadership style? What type of leader are you now? Is your style effective? Can it be improved? Can you change your style? Are you willing to do so? These questions suggest that you do a self-appraisal to learn more about yourself.

WHAT CAN THE SUPERVISOR DO?

You can start learning about yourself by examining your assumptions about people at work. Respond to the quiz shown in Figure 11-8. Your instructor will help you determine and interpret your score.

Do you lean toward theory X or toward theory Y? Over a few days, jot down your supervisory actions on the job, and classify them as X or Y characteristics. For example, do you watch as workers arrive each morning and punch in on the time clock? Do you have an attitude that says, "I have to let them know I'm checking. We've got a job to do. That lazy Joe Burton would never get here on time except for payday." This clearly reflects theory-X leadership. While there must be attendance controls, a more objective method would be to examine time cards periodically in your office and individually counsel those whose tardiness is reflected in their productivity. For early offenses, an approach might be, "Joe, your productivity was down on 5 days last month; on 4 of those days, you were more than 30 minutes late. As you know, we're expected to meet standards. Some unusual circumstances must be causing your tardiness. What can we do to help you pull your rate back up?" This approach reflects assumptions closer to theory Y: that Joe is not necessarily lazy; that some unexplained and correctable circumstances are causing his tardiness; that Joe does not necessarily work only for pay; and that Joe's job may not be designed in such a way as to motivate him to report to work promptly.

This approach, based on the Managerial Grid, would move you from a 9,1 toward a 5,5 position, one in which you show concern for people (Joe's problem) as well as concern for production (meeting standards) at least at an adequate level. When you are comfortable at this level and you feel that your situation would accommodate more worker participation, you might move toward a 9,9 position.

Continue to examine your supervisory actions. Where you feel that a different style of leadership may be more appropriate, don't be afraid to try it. Whether a different style is appropriate will also be influenced by the workers themselves.

Forces in the Subordinate

It is relatively easy for you to assess the technical skill of your workers because you supervise their work daily. Knowing what makes them tick, however, is another dimension you should consider when determining how to lead them. Remember that workers are influenced, just as you are, by their values, their personalities, their goals, and many other variables.

How the workers feel about you is another important factor to consider when choosing a leadership style. Do they respect your technical ability? What kind of responses do they expect from you in work situations? What level of direction do they

FIGURE 11-8 Your assumptions about people at work

	Strongly agree	Agree	Disagree	Strongly disagree
1. Almost everyone could probably improve his or her job performance quite a bit if he or she really wanted to.	—	—	—	—
2. It's unrealistic to expect people to show the same enthusiasm for their work as for their favorite leisure-time activities.	—	—	—	—
3. Even when given encouragement by the boss, very few people show the desire to improve themselves on the job.	—	—	—	—
4. If you give people enough money, they are less likely to worry about such intangibles as status or individual recognition.	—	—	—	—
5. Usually when people talk about wanting more responsible jobs, they really mean they want more money and status.	—	—	—	—
6. Being tough with people will usually get them to do what you want.	—	—	—	—
7. Because most people don't like to make decisions on their own, it's hard to get them to assume responsibility.	—	—	—	—
8. A good way to get people to do more work is to crack down on them once in a while.	—	—	—	—
9. It weakens a person's prestige whenever he or she has to admit that a subordinate has been right and he has been wrong.	—	—	—	—
10. The most effective supervisor is one who gets the result management expects, regardless of the methods used in handling people.	—	—	—	—
11. It's too much to expect that people will try to do a good job without being prodded by their boss.	—	—	—	—
12. The boss who expects his or her people to set their own standards for superior performance will probably find they don't set them very high.	—	—	—	—
13. If people don't use much imagination and ingenuity on the job, it's probably because relatively few people have much of either.	—	—	—	—
14. One problem in asking for the ideas of subordinates is that their perspective is too limited for their suggestions to be of much practical value.	—	—	—	—
15. It's only human nature for people to try to do as little work as they can get away with.	—	—	—	—
Total Checks	—	—	—	—

expect? Some workers need or expect more direction than others, as you noted in the Hersey and Blanchard and the Fiedler models. If a supervisor with an authoritarian orientation is asked to supervise a work group that has been operating under participatory management, some adjustment in the supervisor's leadership style will be necessary in order to prevent a complete breakdown of morale.

The level of direction is another important consideration in choosing a leadership pattern. According to Robert Tannenbaum and Warren H. Schmidt, greater subordinate freedom can be allowed when certain essential conditions exist. These essential conditions are shown in Figure 11-9. Tannenbaum and Schmidt point out that managers will tend to use their own authority if the conditions shown in Figure 11-9 do not exist and that "at times there may be no realistic alternative to running a one-man show."[20] At this point, it might be worthwhile to reexamine, in Chapter 2, Application 2, the list of behaviors that help in choosing between a directive and a participatory approach.

Generally, if the level of confidence the workers have in you is high, it will be easier for you to adapt your leadership style to the situation. If your workers respect your technical and managerial skills, they won't feel threatened if, in a normally participative climate, you occasionally find it necessary to make a decision on your own.

The climate of the firm leads us to the third factor to consider in choosing a leadership style—the organization and the situation.

FIGURE 11-9 Essential conditions for greater subordinate freedom

Generally speaking, the manager can permit his or her subordinates greater freedom if the following essential conditions exist:

- If the subordinates have relatively high needs for independence. (As we all know, people differ greatly in the amount of direction that they desire.)

- If the subordinates have a readiness to assume responsibility for decision making. (Some see additional responsibility as a tribute to their ability; others see it as "passing the buck.")

- If they have a relatively high tolerance for ambiguity. (Some employees prefer to have clear-cut directives given to them; others prefer a wider area of freedom.)

- If they are interested in the problem and feel that it is important.

- If they understand and identify with the goals of the organization.

- If they have the necessary knowledge and experience to deal with the problem.

- If they have learned to expect to share in decision making. (Persons who have come to expect strong leadership and are then suddenly confronted with the request to share more fully in decision making are often upset by this new experience. On the other hand, persons who have enjoyed a considerable amount of freedom resent the boss who begins to make all the decisions himself or herself.)

Source: Robert Tannenbaum and Warren H. Schmidt, "How to Choose a Leadership Pattern," *Harvard Business Review,* May–June 1973, pp. 175, 178.

Forces in the Situation

The third factor that influences the choice of leadership style is the organization itself. What kind of leadership is at the top? It is unlikely that an authoritative chief executive with a centralized structure will tolerate participative, subordinate-centered supervisors on the production line.

Organizations have cultures that reflect values, traditions, and accepted mores. These cultures develop over a long period. There is evidence that firms with strong cultures are the most successful over the long term. Terrence E. Deal and Allen A. Kennedy report that less than one-fourth of the 80 companies they studied had strong cultures; but these 18 firms were uniformly outstanding performers, a correlation they did not find in the other firms studied.

Deal and Kennedy stress the importance of corporate culture to all members of the organization. They feel that a return to high productivity in U.S. companies will not come from mimicking Japan or other countries nor from the scientific tools of management now available. Instead, they feel that

American business needs to return to the original concepts and ideas that made institutions like NCR, Procter and Gamble, 3M, General Electric, IBM, and others great. We need to remember that people make businesses work. And we need to relearn old lessons about how culture ties people together and gives meaning and purpose to their lives.[21]

Further, the authors say that early leaders of long-term successful firms

. . . believed that the lives and productivity of their employees were shaped by where they worked. These builders saw their role as creating an environment—in effect, a culture—in their companies in which employees could be secure and thereby do the work necessary to make the business a success. They had no magic formulas. In fact they discovered how to shape their company's culture by trial and error. But all along the way, they paid almost fanatical attention to the culture of their companies. The lessons of these early leaders have been passed down in their own companies from generation to generation of managers; the cultures they were so careful to build and nourish have sustained their organizations through both fat and lean times. Today these corporations still have strong cultures and still are leaders in the marketplace.[22]

If you are employed by a company with a strong culture, one like those described by Deal and Kennedy, you are fortunate. While not all companies have cultures that promote a familylike atmosphere, they all have cultures of one type or another. New employees learn to adjust to whatever culture exists in their firms. Failing to do so may have unpleasant consequences. One's own value system must be considered when making such an adjustment. If your values conflict with the corporate culture, you will probably either have to adjust or leave the firm.

Ideally, you should learn something about the corporate culture before you accept a position with any firm. Firms usually select their employees on the basis of their potential for fitting in with the organization, but this doesn't always happen.

You also have to consider the organization's culture when deciding how to lead your workers. You will need to examine several elements of this culture, including whether the company is centralized or decentralized. As you learned in Chapter 5, a decentralized organization pushes decision making downward. This permits a more participative approach to decision making than in the centralized organization, where the chief executive makes all or most of the decisions. For example, you would have difficulty developing the right climate for problem solving by your workers through quality circles in a company where the top manager, as owner and founder of the company, insists that he or she sign off on every decision.

The nature of the problem will also be a factor in the organizational environment. If the problem involves technical skill beyond the ability of your workers, you probably need to have a more task-oriented approach, one in which you or a specialist provide more direction than usual. If the task is less complex, such as scheduling routine work, you may wish to allow workers the freedom to perform the task in their work groups.

Another organizational element you must consider is the time limitation. Most working people feel the pressure of time. The supervisor is no exception. Where you are under stress to get the job done, it is likely that you will tend to make the decision alone rather than take the time to have workers participate. In such a situation, your leadership will lean toward the authoritarian. This does not mean that when time is short, boss-centered leadership is necessarily the best; it is simply the most expedient leadership.

Competency Check:

Can you cite three forces the supervisor should consider in choosing a leadership style?

As you can see, the organizational factors considered here largely reflect short-term, "do-it-now" influences on the choice of leadership style. The reality is that the style you select may not be the one you prefer but, considering the three factors (you, the workers, and the organization), the style that best fits the situation at hand. Changing these factors takes time, a process that will be discussed in Chapter 18. For now, let us turn our attention to the other side of the leadership coin—motivation of the workers.

MOTIVATION OF THE WORKERS

Leadership was defined as "the ability to influence workers to set and accomplish goals willingly." *Motivation* is defined as "the desire or drive within a person to achieve some goal." *Within* is the operative word here, for motivation is an internal condition based on a person's values, perceptions, and needs. What can you do as a leader to ignite this internal flame? Creating a climate in which your workers will be motivated on a continuing basis will probably be your greatest challenge as a supervisor.

This part of the chapter will focus on helping you develop an understanding of human behavior so that you can create a workplace climate in which workers will willingly strive to achieve company goals as well as their own. First, let us look at a few popular motivation models, selected from the large volume of research in the field.

Some Theories of Motivation

A great deal of research has been conducted to try to find out why people behave as they do. An interesting disclosure from these efforts is that human beings are all alike and yet they are all different. From this contradictory assumption, we know what, in general, "makes us tick." For example, all human beings need food, clothing, and shelter; and most find some way to get it. But to use this knowledge of similarity, we must recognize that people have their individual views of those basic needs. The amounts and types of food, clothing, and shelter needed differ from person to person, depending on their individual perceptions, values, goals, and even other needs. Psychologist A. H. Maslow put these concepts into a model of human motivation.

Maslow's Hierarchy of Needs

The behavior of human beings is based on their needs, according to Maslow.[23] The first of two principles of Maslow's theory is that needs can be classified into five groups and arranged in a hierarachy; when one need is satisfied, another need emerges to be satisfied. His hierarchy of needs became a widely accepted model of human behavior. Maslow's hierarchy of needs is shown in the left section of Figure 11-10.

The most basic needs are the physiological, or survival, needs (food, clothing, and sex). Next is the need for safety or security (such as protection from physical harm). Third, people need to interact with other humans, to have a sense of belonging; these Maslow called "social needs." The fourth level is the need for esteem (to be considered by oneself and by others as a worthwhile human being). Finally, there is the need for self-actualization (to develop to one's full potential).

Maslow studied the needs of people in general. The second principle of his theory is that since one's needs depend on what one already has, only unsatisfied needs can motivate human behavior. For example, a person who has satisfied his or her survival

FIGURE 11-10 A comparison of Maslow's hierarchy of needs and Herzberg's two-factor theory

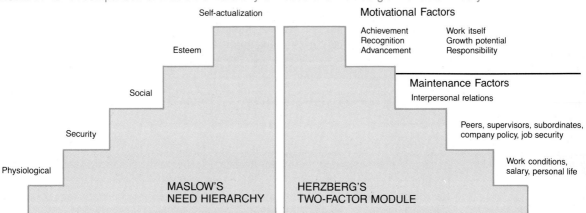

Source: Data for figure on Hierarchy of Needs from *Motivation and Personality,* 3d ed., by Abraham H. Maslow. Revised by Robert Frager et al. Copyright 1954, 1987 by Harper & Row, Publishers, Inc. Copyright © 1970 by Abraham H. Maslow. Reprinted by permission of Harper & Row, Publishers, Inc.

needs will no longer be motivated by these needs and so will move up the hierarchy to satisfy his or her need for feeling safe and secure.

The other side of this theory is that until the basic physiological needs are met, higher needs won't motivate behavior. Maslow explains that "a person who is lacking food, safety, love, and esteem probably would hunger for food more strongly than anything else."[24]

While Maslow's theory does present a broad generalized view of human behavior, it has not been without criticism. This has led to qualifications of the theory over the years. You should be aware of the changed view of Maslow's hierarchy. Among the qualifications are these:

- The theory does not take into account varying needs among cultures and individuals. Such variations are critical in the management of people on the job.
- The satisfaction of one need does not occur independently of other needs. One need does not have to be completely satisfied before another need seeks satisfaction. Moreover, higher-level needs are probably never fully satisfied. The desire for esteem, for example, is a lifelong need and will continue to motivate even after some satisfaction is achieved.

The supervisor should consider Maslow's hierarchy-of-needs theory as a guideline for understanding human behavior in general but should emphasize individual differences in applying them in the workplace.

WHAT CAN THE SUPERVISOR DO?

Use the hierarachy of needs to help you examine the work environment and develop procedures, programs, and conditions that will apply generally to workers. The list shown in Figure 11-11 will serve as a starting point to check your management's status in providing for worker needs. Compare the list to the programs and procedures used in your department. What about the worker who has been efficient and faithful for some time but for whom there has been no suitable spot for promotion? Perhaps that person could become a trainer of other workers, with recognition given to his or her expertise in company publications *along with* a bonus at payday.

Herzberg's Two-Factor Theory

Another explanation of human behavior was proposed by Frederick Herzberg.[25] While Maslow's theory applied motivation to people in general, Herzberg studied the motivation of people in the workplace. Based on a study of engineers and accountants, Herzberg developed a motivational theory of two dimensions: dissatisfiers, which he called "hygiene, or maintenance, factors," and satisfiers, or motivators.

Herzberg found that workers feel dissatisfaction about things *outside of* but related to their jobs, such as relationship with the supervisors, salary, and working conditions.

FIGURE 11-11

WHAT MANAGEMENT CAN DO TO PROVIDE FOR WORKER NEEDS
IN THE MASLOW CATEGORIES

NEED CATEGORY	WHAT MANAGEMENT CAN DO
self-actualization	Provide growth and career opportunities. Provide training and development programs. Encourage creativity. Encourage achievement. Encourage participation in community betterment programs.
esteem	Praise high performance. Publicize individual achievement. Give frequent and prompt feedback for accomplishment. Provide for greater worker responsibility. Promote to higher jobs.
social	Provide for working in groups. Provide for interaction among different levels. Sponsor recreation and company social events. Encourage participation and cooperation in both formal and informal structures.
safety	Provide safe working conditions. Provide a broad benefits program. Provide job security. Provide for fair and equal treatment of all workers.
physiological	Pay fair and equitable wages. Provide comfortable work stations. Provide rest breaks. Provide proper space, light, heat, and air conditioning.

While these are dissatisfiers when they are not present or are not effective, their presence does not satisfy. In other words, the workers *expect* certain basic working conditions; since they are expected as a part of the job, they do not motivate. Herzberg listed 10 of these dissatisfiers and labeled them "hygiene, or maintenance, factors." They are shown on the right in Figure 11-10 on page 339.

In Herzberg's view, certain conditions about the job itself tend to cause satisfaction when they are present and to serve as motivators. Their absence, however, does not prove highly dissatisfying. Note in Figure 11-10 the job-content nature of the six conditions that Herzberg called *motivators*.

As you can see, Figure 11-10 is a comparison of Maslow's hierarchy of needs and Herzberg's two-factor theory. The hygiene features in the Herzberg model generally coincide with Maslow's lower-order needs: physiological, safety, and social. Herzberg's motivators relate closely to Maslow's higher-order needs: esteem and self-actualization. In general, the Herzberg study of worker motivation tends to validate Maslow's hierarchy of needs.

The Herzberg model is very useful to management. A firm that wants to recruit and retain competent workers should examine its workplace, its administrative and supervisory practices, and its salary and benefits plan. But to motivate workers to high productivity, the firm also has to look at the design of its jobs. Job content should provide workers with a feeling of pride of accomplishment and a sense of contribution to the total organization. In addition, the firm should examine its growth and development programs for workers. Employees should have some input into the jobs they perform and should be able to grow and develop on the basis of their potential for and contributions to the firm's growth.

WHAT CAN THE SUPERVISOR DO?

As a supervisor, you can use the Herzberg model in many ways. In the maintenance-factor area, you can:

- communicate departmental policies to workers and administer the policies equitably.
- improve your supervisory abilities.
- monitor working conditions to see that they adequately provide for accomplishing the assigned task.
- maintain workplace safety.
- provide fair, equitable, and objectively determined salary recommendations.
- improve relationships with peers and workers.
- keep workers informed about what is going on, as far as confidentiality will allow.

In the motivational-factor area, you can:

- analyze jobs to see whether they can be enriched or enlarged.
- praise workers for their accomplishments.
- publicize worker achievements via bulletin boards, company publications, and the media.
- let workers know that you feel they are competent and you expect high achievement from them.
- delegate more authority to workers.
- provide training and development programs and encourage (recognize and reward) participation in them.
- assign workers to special projects and recognize results.
- encourage worker participation in problem solving within their work units or within the department.
- assist workers with career planning.
- make objective recommendations for promotions.
- rotate jobs or cross-train workers to provide broader experience.

Vroom's Expectancy Model

A different approach to motivation was presented by Victor H. Vroom. Unlike the Maslow and Herzberg theories, which focus on the inner forces of the individual and the conditions in the workplace as explanations of behavior, Vroom's expectancy theory explains worker motivation as a matter of choices.[26] Vroom asserts that individuals choose to exert work effort or not depending on what the rewards are. Put in the vernacular, this is the "What's-in-it-for-me?" theory.

To simplify the expectancy theory, consider these questions:

● Will my efforts lead to successful performance? This is the *effort-performance expectancy*. It asks, in other words, Do I have the skills and abilities necessary to perform the job well enough to get the reward?

● If I perform the task successfully, will I get the reward? This is called the *performance-reward expectancy*. What evidence is there that the reward will be forthcoming? Does the company live up to its word in giving promised rewards?

● Is the reward worth the effort? This is called *reward attractiveness,* or *valence.*

As an example, let's look at Harold Todd, who works as a counter clerk in a large photo-processing firm. A vacancy is expected in the processing department; it is for a higher-paying, entry-level job in the technical phase of the business. To get the job, Todd must take a processing course.

Knowing that Todd might wonder whether he could do the job even after taking the course, the manager might reassure him by pointing out his success in his present job, his personal interest and experience in photography, and the success of others. Todd might wonder whether he will get the job even if he completes the course successfully. The manager could point to the firm's record of promotions to reassure him. Finally, under the expectancy theory, Todd might wonder if the job is worth the effort involved in taking the course and making the change from his present job. The manager could point out the career opportunities available in the technical phase of the business, opportunities that would open up to him through the change. Interviews might be arranged for Todd with others in the firm who have moved up the ladder through the processing department.

Knowing how the expectancy theory operates to motivate the individual, you can advise the worker through his or her thinking about career or other opportunities within the firm.

Competency Check:

Can you briefly describe the basic concepts of three motivational models?

Other Approaches to Motivation

There are other theories of motivation that you may wish to learn about to improve your supervisory skills. Sources provided in the bibliography at the end of this chapter will be useful for your further study. Also, several motivating devices are presented in the discussion on productivity in Chapter 16. Expanding your knowledge of motivation and human behavior will enhance your ability to provide a proper motivational climate for your workers.

Maintaining a Motivational Climate

Several references have been made in this chapter to the climate of the organization and to the corporate culture. An organization that recognizes its workers as individuals as well as labor resources will have a climate in which workers are motivated to achieve both company and individual goals. As has been pointed out, different situations call for different leadership styles. In addition, while workers are alike in many respects, their individual differences must be taken into consideration when attempting to motivate them. These three generalizations, in addition to an understanding of the theories presented, can serve as general guidelines to creating and maintaining a motivational climate.

The research conducted by one firm into the motivational-climate concept became a landmark study. Over several years, AT&T conducted job studies to identify the training needs of its supervisors. The study, involving 230,000 AT&T supervisors, said this about a motivative environment:

> A motivative environment in the workplace is not necessarily one in which all employees are satisfied and happy. It is a nice "fringe benefit" if they are so, but that is not the purpose for creating and maintaining such an atmosphere. The real purpose is to encourage and induce every member of the work group to contribute his or her *best effort* to the work at all times, and to ensure that environmental conditions foster such behavior.
>
> A motivative atmosphere is not a permissive, easy-going environment; it is rather a *demanding* one in which every member of the work group is expected to do the best work within his or her capability. This is necessary *not only* for the good of the organization— so that the group's goals will be met—but it is actually in the best interests of the individuals involved. For a first-level supervisor to insist and expect each person to do his or her best is a compliment, a mark of respect, to the individual; to ask and accept less than the person's best is demeaning.
>
> If employees can find happiness and fulfillment in the course of applying their best efforts to their own work and contributing their full energies and intelligence to the purposes of the group, then the organization will be highly productive and rewarding to all its members.[27]

In Chapter 2 (Figure 2-6), you read the list of duties that AT&T assigns to its supervisors. Number 6 on that list is "creating a motivative atmosphere." The large number of supervisors employed by AT&T and their importance to the firm led AT&T to establish a structured process for helping its supervisors carry out this responsibility.

The study points out that at AT&T, creating a motivative atmosphere is treated as a total managerial process consisting of 16 discrete steps and is the responsibility of supervisors. The first seven steps in Figure 11-12 identify problems affecting a motivative atmosphere.

Performance standards for evaluating the atmosphere were good attendance and subordinate enthusiasm for the job. Steps 8 through 16 show the process for solving the problems. Standards for this set were few complaints from subordinates, subordinates' willingness to work overtime, and subordinates' meeting output requirements. The method of measurement for the entire process was stated as "measures by the

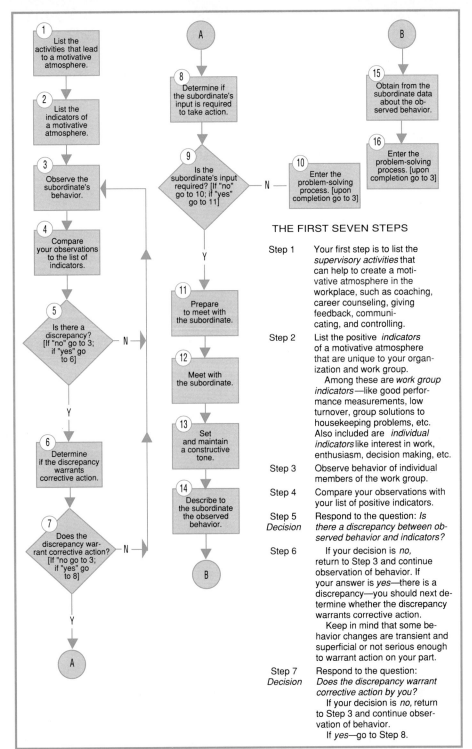

FIGURE 11-12

Creating a
motivative
atmosphere: total
managerial process
(AT&T model)

THE FIRST SEVEN STEPS

Step 1   Your first step is to list the
supervisory activities that
can help to create a motivative atmosphere in the
workplace, such as coaching,
career counseling, giving
feedback, communi-
cating, and controlling.

Step 2   List the positive *indicators*
of a motivative atmosphere
that are unique to your organization and work group.
     Among these are *work group
indicators*—like good performance measurements, low
turnover, group solutions to
housekeeping problems, etc.
Also included are *individual
indicators* like interest in work,
enthusiasm, decision making, etc.

Step 3   Observe behavior of individual
members of the work group.

Step 4   Compare your observations with
your list of positive indicators.

Step 5   Respond to the question: *Is
Decision*   *there a discrepancy between observed behavior and indicators?*

Step 6   If your decision is *no,*
return to Step 3 and continue
observation of behavior. If
your answer is *yes*—there is a
discrepancy—you should next determine whether the discrepancy
warrants corrective action.
     Keep in mind that some be-
havior changes are transient and
superficial or not serious enough
to warrant action on your part.

Step 7   Respond to the question:
Decision   *Does the discrepancy warrant
corrective action by you?*
     If your decision is *no,* return
to Step 3 and continue observation of behavior.
     If *yes*—go to Step 8.

Source: Charles R. McDonald, *Performance-Based Supervisory Development,* HRD Press, Amherst, Mass., 1982, pp. 96–97.

FIGURE 11-13   INDICATORS OF A MOTIVATIVE ATMOSPHERE (AT&T)

WORK GROUP (ENVIRONMENT)	INDIVIDUAL
less hectic pace	asks for more work
fewer "fires" to put out	puts work before breaks
measurements (quantity, quality, absence)	more interested in work
	goes further on own efforts
more promotions	makes own decisions
fewer grievances	tries more on own
higher level of friendly competition	more willing to work overtime
group works out problems among themselves, such as who gets overtime, and so on	generates enthusiasm (talks positively, tries to get others interested or involved)
	keeps supervisor up to date instead of waiting to be asked
	open about problems encountered instead of defensive
	expresses pride in work and confidence in own ability
	self-starter

Source: Charles R. McDonald, *Performance-Based Supervisory Development,* HRD Press, Amherst, Mass., 1982, pp. 99–100.

second-level boss on five areas: reactions of the workforce, attendance, number of grievances, office suggestions, and general attitude."[28]

At the beginning of the AT&T training program, supervisors are assisted in building a model of a motivative atmosphere. In step 1, supervisors learn that a motivative atmosphere is the result of the first-level supervisor's using other managerial processes in an effective way. This managerial knowledge includes knowing that workers are more receptive to new rules and procedures "when the boss takes the time to explain why and considers their feelings."[29]

The study further points out that some indicators of a motivative atmosphere (step 3) are group-related and some are individual-related, as shown in Figure 11-13.

Many companies realize that a motivative atmosphere is important to accomplishing company objectives and take positive steps to create and maintain such an atmosphere in their firms. IBM, Delta Airlines, W. L. Gore and Associates, Johnson and Johnson, and GE are among the firms cited for excellent motivational climates by researchers such as Peters and Waterman[30] and John Naisbitt and Patricia Aburdene.[31]

Competency Check:

Can you cite five demotivators and suggest actions the supervisor can take to eliminate them?

WHAT CAN THE SUPERVISOR DO?

As a supervisor, you need to know both what you can do to create a motivational climate and what you can do to avoid *demotivating* the workers. Lateness, absenteeism, careless work, and a lackadaisical attitude are the earmarks of demotivation. How can you "turn on" demotivated workers? Figure 11-14 shows the signs of eight demotivators and tells you what you can do to turn the situation around.

FIGURE 11-14
SOME DEMOTIVATORS—AND WHAT YOU CAN DO ABOUT THEM

DEMOTIVATOR	SIGNS	WHAT YOU CAN DO
1. Lack of clear objectives: When workers don't know what is expected of them, work tends to slip.	lack of respect for supervisors alibis, beginning with "No one told me" duplication of effort arguments over procedures seemingly pointless questions	Clarify for yourself the standards and expectations of each job. Then make sure you communicate these to your workers.
2. Standards too high: When workers consistently fall short of goals that are too difficult to reach, they become frustrated and disillusioned.	a what's-the-difference attitude disregard for quality standards unwillingness to cooperate cover-up of mistakes	Review your goals. Revise them if necessary by setting smaller goals that are easier to reach within a reasonable time limit.
3. Overly relaxed discipline: When regulations are not enforced, or are enforced haphazardly, the result is often disrespect for both company policies and procedures.	mishandling of equipment too much "horsing around" too many careless errors chronic lateness and absenteeism sloppiness with details	Review the rules. If some are out of date, drop them. Then give fair warning that the remaining rules will be enforced fairly and consistently.
4. Too much pressure from the top: Workers tend to become intimidated when they feel that someone is constantly "riding" them.	complaints about work loads requests for transfer unusual restlessness on the job flare-up among employees irritation with new assignments	Don't relax your standards, but try to become a less "omnipresent" supervisor. Delegate tasks whenever possible, and encourage employees to express themselves to you.
5. Inadequate management contact: When workers have too little access to the boss, they begin to get the feeling that no one higher up on the ladder really cares about them.	Few workers come to see you. Your instructions seem to be deliberately misunderstood. People are sarcastic or derisive about their work. Rumors and gossip flourish. Subordinates avoid you altogether.	Show a greater concern for the problems and interests of employees both on and off the job. Go to them; find out how they are doing, and let them know you really care.
6. Overly heavy criticism: Criticism, even when constructive, can erode the will to produce if not sufficiently balanced with praise.	Workers operate by the "rule book." lack of openness about problems much irritability and tenseness	Look for opportunities to pat workers on the back when they do well, and create opportunities to do so. Balance criticism with constructive suggestions and offers to help.
7. Inadequate working conditions and equipment: Workers may resent what they consider to be handicaps imposed on them by a firm's indifference to their working conditions.	frequent generalized complaints observations that "workers in other departments have it better" unforeseen foul-ups and delays careless use of equipment frequent calls for repairs	Take a complete inventory of equipment and working conditions. If changes are necessary, and you have to fight for them up the line, be sure to let your people know that you are fighting for them.
8. Abandoning leadership: Workers want and need effective leadership. Problems occur when supervisors don't provide it.	emergence of informal leaders in the department disputes about rights or privileges formation of cliques failure to respect authority deliberately "forgetting" instructions strong resistance to change	Reinstate your leadership role— not by just *saying* it but by actually *doing* it.

Source: Office Supervisor's Bulletin, Apr. 15, 1981, issue no. 606, pp. 4–5.

In this chapter, you have studied some of the theories of leadership and motivation. In the remaining chapters of this section, you will learn how you can use these theories to improve supervision of your workers.

COMPETENCY REVIEW

1. Discuss two dimensions of leadership.
2. Contrast the terms *leader* and *manager*.
3. Briefly describe six leadership theories.
4. Cite three forces the supervisor should consider in choosing a leadership style.
5. Describe the basic concepts of three motivational models.
6. Tell what is meant by a "motivational climate."
7. Cite five demotivators, and suggest actions the supervisor can take to eliminate them.

APPLICATIONS

1. The incidents in the beginning of this chapter were deliberately not discussed further in order to give you an opportunity to analyze them in terms of leadership styles. Reread the five incidents, and answer the following:
   a. Which leadership theory is exemplified by the Standing incident?
   b. Classify, on the managerial grid, the leadership positions of Polik, Matson, and Ballou.
   c. Where would you place Smith on the Tannenbaum and Schmidt continuum? Is the position you identified typical of Smith's leadership style? Why?
   d. Where would you place Ballou on the Tannenbaum and Schmidt continuum? Explain.
   e. Classify the supervisors in terms of their X or Y assumptions.
   f. Rank the five supervisors in decreasing order on the basis of whom you'd like to work for. Explain your placement of each.
2. Using the Fiedler model (Figures 11-4 and 11-5) as a guide, complete columns F and G below. In column F, show whether task-oriented, relationship-oriented, or a combination leadership style would be most effective, according to Fiedler.

   In column G, briefly state the probable reasons for the effectiveness of the leadership style you have chosen. Situation 1 has been completed as a sample.

A	B	*Column* C LEADER- MEMBER RELATIONS	D TASK STRUCTURE	E POSITION POWER	F MOST EFFECTIVE LEADERSHIP	G REASON(S) FOR EFFECTIVENESS
SITUATION	EXAMPLE					
1	first-line supervisor at Ford Motor Co.	good	high	strong	task-oriented	Employees respect task expertise, recognize power, and permit supervisor to lead.
2	chairperson of college department	good	high	weak		
3	sales manager at Procter & Gamble	good	low	strong		
4	committee chairperson	good	low	weak		
5	middle-level manager at IBM	poor	high	strong		
6	supervisor in General Mills	poor	high	weak		
7	operating-room nurse director	poor	low	strong		
8	detective in charge of other detectives working on a case	poor	low	weak		

Source: Adapted from James H. Donnelly, Jr., James L. Gibson, and John M. Ivancevich, *Fundamentals of Management,* 6th ed., Business Publications, Inc., Plano, Tex., 1987, p. 392.

3. Using Maslow's hierarchy of needs, give an example of an action the supervisor can take to motivate workers at each level. Try to cite an example not shown in the text in completing the form on page 350.

NEED	MOTIVATING ACTION
self-actualization	_____
esteem	_____
social	_____
security & safety	_____
physiological	_____

4. The following study has been widely used to compare the perceptions held by managers and by employees themselves on what employees want. Complete the activity as directed below.

WHAT EMPLOYEES SAY THEY WANT

ITEM	MY RANKING	CLASS RANKING	SUPERVISOR'S ACTUAL RANKING	EMPLOYEE'S ACTUAL RANKING
1. good working conditions				
2. feeling in on things				
3. tactful discipline				
4. full appreciation for work done				
5. management loyalty to workers				
6. good wages				
7. promotion and growth within company				
8. sympathetic understanding of personal problems				
9. job security				
10. interesting work				

Source: Adapted from Samuel C. Certo and Lee A. Graf, *Experiences in Modern Management, A Workbook of Student Activities,* 2d ed., William C. Brown Publishers, Dubuque, Iowa, 1983, p. 230.

What do people want from their jobs? While this question can't be answered in the same way for all situations, this experience will help you clarify the factors that generally motivate employee performance. It is also designed to provide you with an opportunity to explore why perceptions of these factors vary from situation to situation. Complete the following exercises:

a. Put yourself in the employee's shoes, and figure out what he or she wants from the job. Then rank the 10 items in the table below in terms of importance to employees. In the column headed My Ranking, place a 1 after the item you think employees want most, and so on. Remember, it is not what you want but, rather, what you think employees will say they want.

b. After your ranking in part a, your instructor will help you determine the class ranking and will show you the results from the actual survey of what supervisors think employees will say (for column 3) and what the employees actually said (column 4). Identify any striking similarities or differences and, through discussion with your classmates, try to develop a reasonable explanation for these differences or similarities.

c. After discussing the rationale behind the rankings in part b, discuss in small groups the implications of the data for managers. What should managers do to create a situation in which employees feel motivated?

CASES

Case I:
"Mean-as-a-Snake" Matson

Matson in the beginning of this chapter has been a supervisor of spot welders at Colrain's Ship Repair for 14 years. The company is a small one that specializes in subcontracting parts of ship-repair jobs from big shipyards. Matson has performed all the jobs in the firm in the past and has seemed a "natural" for each one; this was the deciding factor in his promotion to supervisor. He is a brawny, tough, hard-nosed supervisor, who brags that he "never asks a worker to do anything he can't do himself."

He has no patience with slow or sloppy work and will chew out anyone guilty of it in colorful language—usually in front of everybody. "Let them all know at once," he says, "that only good work gets by my inspection." He intimidates new workers. Those with less fortitude don't stay long. But those who do stay learn to respect Matson. They have even gone to bat for him a couple of times in his battles with top management. As one worker said, "He's mean as a snake, but he always rattles before he bites. He's got all the skills, and he sticks up for his workers. When you do your job right, you can count on him for anything."

1. Why, in general terms, do you think workers are willing to work for Matson?
2. Evaluate the situation on the basis of Maslow's needs hierarchy. What worker needs seem to be the motivators here?
3. Based on Tannenbaum and Schmidt, what type of leader is Matson?

4. In view of this additional information on Matson, would you change the classification you gave Matson in application 1? Why, or why not?

Case II: Sam's Natural Style Won't Cut It Anymore

Sam Allen's voice on the telephone sounded strained. ''I can't believe it,'' he said. ''Only a few months ago, I felt confident as a manager; I loved my job. Today, I dread coming to work and doubt my own ability. I think it might be best just to throw in the towel.''

Allen has been working for the same company for more than 15 years. Less than a year before he called me, he had been promoted from production manager at one of the company's plants to plant manager in another. I'd been a consultant to Allen's company for a number of years, and I respected his competence; he was a good choice for plant manager.

When I first met Allen, he was in his first management job: production supervisor. He gave me a tour of his shop and was obviously very proud of it all: the high-tech assembly line he had installed and supervised from start-up, the outstanding productivity figures of his group, and, above all, his people.

Often when managers tour their plants, the workers spread the word down the line to shape up. Not so with Allen. His employees continued working but often paused to make friendly comments to their boss. They were genuinely glad to see him. If Allen stopped to bring to my attention some detail of the production process, he always included a line worker in the demonstration by asking one of them to explain it to me. He asked questions of everyone, and, most important, he praised their work, their ideas, and their contributions to the company. It was a team effort that seemed easy and natural.

The plant has now grown to over 600 employees, and, although most other plants in the corporation are union shops, this plant isn't one of them. The plant supervisors still make major plant decisions through ''town meetings,'' at which managers encourage employee opinions and seek consensus.

When Allen was promoted to a new job as manager of another plant 3 years ago, however, he seemed to face a new labor grievance nearly every day; and relations with his supervisors were awful.

His predecessor, Ed Dolan, had been a tough manager who knew what he wanted and was willing to go ''toe-to-toe'' with the union. The plant never had a strike while Dolan was plant manager, and he retired with a reputation of having been a ''tough cookie,'' feared as much by the supervisors under him as by his employees.

Allen's leadership style seemed a perfect replacement for Ed. But when Allen took over with his same natural, communicative style, trouble began immediately. For example, Allen talked with one of his supervisors about the dangerous clutter in the work area. The supervisor claimed the problem was a lack of people, so Allen arranged to have an employee moved over to the supervisor's department. A few weeks later, the situation hadn't changed. This time, the supervisor said the mess was caused by insufficient equipment.

Allen had story after story like this one. He couldn't trust his supervisors to level with him. Grievances with workers were mushrooming, and Allen was frustrated and bewildered.

Source: Adapted from Marge Yanker, ''Flexible Leadership Styles: One Supervisor's Story,'' *Supervisory Management,* January 1986, pp. 2–6.

1. What do you think is the reason for the problems Allen is having in his new job?
2. What leadership theory or theories seem an appropriate analytical tool in this case? Explain.
3. If you were Allen, what would you do?

REFERENCES

1. David R. Hampton, *Management,* 3d ed., McGraw-Hill Book Company, New York, 1986, pp. 318–319.
2. J. R. P. French and B. Raven, ''The Bases of Social Power,'' in D. Cartwright (ed.), *Studies in Social Power,* The University of Michigan Press, Ann Arbor, 1959, pp. 150–161.
3. Clifford G. Baird, Baird and Associates, Wheaton, Ill., as quoted in ''Are You a Manager or Leader?'' *The Virginian Pilot and Ledger Star,* Norfolk, Oct. 5, 1987, p. 30.
4. See, for example, Edwin E. Ghiselli, ''Managerial Talent,'' *American Psychology,* October 1963, pp. 631–641; J. D. Barrow, ''The Variables of Leadership: A Review and Conceptual Framework,'' *Academy of Management Review,* April 1977, p. 232; and R. M. Stogdill, ''Historical Trends in Leadership Theory and Research,'' *Journal of Contemporary Business,* autumn 1974, p. 5.
5. Edwin E. Ghiselli, *Explorations in Management Talent,* Goodyear Publishing Co., Santa Monica, Calif., 1971.
6. C. A. Schriesheim, J. M. Tolliver, and O. C. Behling, ''Leadership Theory: Some Implications for Managers,'' *Business Topics,* summer 1978, p. 35, in Leslie W. Rue and Lloyd L. Byars, *Management: Theory and Applications,* 4th ed., Irwin Publishing Co., Homewood, Ill., 1986, p. 385.
7. Douglas McGregor, *The Human Side of Enterprise,* McGraw-Hill Book Company, New York, 1960, pp. 16–48.
8. Daniel A. Wren and Dan Voich Jr., *Management Process, Structure, and Behavior,* 3d ed., John Wiley & Sons, Inc., New York, 1984, pp. 399–400.
9. John J. Morse and Jay W. Lorsch, ''Beyond Theory Y,'' *Harvard Business Review,* May–June 1970, pp. 61–68.
10. Arthur G. Bedeian, *Management,* The Dryden Press, Inc., Chicago, 1986, pp. 468–470.
11. Robert R. Blake and Jane S. Mouton, *The New Managerial Grid,* Gulf Publishing Company, Houston, 1978.
12. Robert Tannenbaum and Warren H. Schmidt, ''How to Choose a Leadership Pattern,'' *Harvard Business Review,* May–June 1973, pp. 162–180.
13. Fred E. Fiedler, *A Theory of Leadership Effectiveness,* McGraw-Hill Book Company, New York, 1967.
14. Fred Fiedler and Martin M. Chemers, *Leadership and Effective Management,* Scott, Foresman and Company, Glenview, Ill., 1974, p. 87.

15. Paul Hersey and Kenneth Blanchard, *Management of Organizational Behavior,* 4th ed., Prentice-Hall, Inc., Englewood Cliffs, N.J., 1982.

16. Paul Hersey, *The Situational Leader,* Warner Books, New York, 1984.

17. Ibid., p. 46.

18. Ibid., p. 70.

19. Tannenbaum and Schmidt, op. cit., p. 173.

20. Ibid., p. 175.

21. Terrence E. Deal and Allen A. Kennedy, *Corporate Cultures,* Addison-Wesley Publishing Company, Inc., Reading, Mass., 1982, p. 5.

22. Ibid.

23. A. H. Maslow, *Motivation and Personality,* Harper & Row, Publishers, Incorporated, New York, 1954.

24. Ibid., p. 82.

25. Frederick Herzberg, Bernard Mausner, and Barbara Block Synderman, *The Motivation to Work,* 2d ed., John Wiley and Sons, Inc., New York, 1959.

26. Victor H. Vroom, *Work and Maintenance,* John Wiley & Sons, Inc., New York, 1964.

27. Charles R. McDonald, *Performance-Based Supervisory Development—Adapted From a Major AT&T Study,* Human Resources Development Press, Amherst, Mass., 1982, p. 94.

28. Ibid., p. 98.

29. Ibid., p. 99.

30. Thomas J. Peters and Robert H. Waterman, Jr., *In Search of Excellence,* Harper & Row, Publishers, New York, 1982.

31. John Naisbitt and Patricia Aburdene, *Reinventing the Corporation,* Warner Books, Inc., New York, 1985.

SUGGESTED READINGS

Bass, Bernard M.: "Leadership: Good, Better, Best," *Organizational Dynamics,* winter 1985, pp. 26–40.

Bellman, Geoffrey M.: "The Quest for Staff Leadership," *Training and Development Journal,* January 1986, pp. 36–44.

Certo, Samuel C.: *Principles of Modern Management, Functions and Systems,* 3d ed., Wm C. Brown Company Publishers, Dubuque, Iowa, 1985.

Harbaugh, Norman R., John J. Sullivan, and Joseph J. Walker: "How Does Your Management Style Measure Up?" *Business,* January–March 1983, pp. 51–54.

Margerison, Charles, and Andrew Kakabadse: *How American Chief Executives Succeed—Implications for Developing High-Potential Employees,* American Management Association, New York, 1984.

Schermerhorn, John R., Jr.: *Management for Productivity,* 2d ed., John Wiley & Sons, Inc., New York, 1984.

Snyder, Neil H.: "Leadership: The Essential Quality for Transforming United States Businesses," *SAM Advanced Management Journal,* pp. 15–18.

Teas, R. Kenneth: "Supervisory Behavior, Role Stress, and the Job Satisfaction of Industrial Salespeople," *Journal of Marketing Research,* February 1983, pp. 84–91.

Vroom, Victor H.: "Reflections on Leadership and Decision-making," *Journal of General Management,* spring 1984, pp. 18–36.

12
COMMUNICATING EFFECTIVELY

12

COMMUNICATING EFFECTIVELY

COMPETENCIES

Studying this chapter will enable you to:

1. Define *communication.*

2. Describe the basic communication components.

3. Identify major sources where employees may obtain current information and relate those to the preferred sources.

4. Define *grapevine.*

5. Identify methods of communicating information upward.

6. Explain horizontal communication and Fayol's bridge.

7. Cite ways to communicate information downward.

8. Describe the supervisor's role in a quality circle.

9. Describe ways a supervisor can contribute to a meeting as a participant.

10. Describe activities a supervisor should engage in before, during, and after a meeting.

11. Cite guidelines for effective verbal communication.

12. Describe the functions of action-cued communication.

13. Explain forms of action-cued communication.

14. Cite the Cs of good writing, and give an example of each.

15. Identify techniques for writing effective messages.

CHAPTER OUTLINE

A nne Satchell shook her head. "Why don't they understand the new procedure? It's so much easier than the old way because four steps have been eliminated." Satchell's assistant, Patrick Jones, said, "Well, they don't seem to know why they should use the new procedure, and I'm not sure they understand exactly how to do it. Would it help if I drafted a memo for your signature explaining in detail how to use the new procedure, emphasizing that four steps have been eliminated? I could also ask them if they think they need additional training." Satchell thanked Jones for the suggestion and told him to draft the memo.

Several days later, Jones put the draft on Satchell's desk with a note that asked for her comments or revisions. In a marginal note, Satchell wrote: "This is not what we talked about. Please rewrite." When Jones read the marginal note, he thought, "What we have here is a failure to communicate."

THE COMMUNICATION PROCESS

Communication happens when information is exchanged, and the message is *understood*. The following incident actually occurred—as explained by one of the authors:

"My secretary, Melody, was to mail 100 certificates of completion to participants in a training course. The $8\frac{1}{2} \times 11$ certificates were very attractive, printed by the sponsoring agency and signed by the superintendent, the supervisor, and the instructor. Melody was not at her desk when I left the office, so I wrote a note that read, 'Fold these as little as possible.' Melody did! She folded the certificates to fit into small, personal-sized envelopes."

Did communication take place here? No! There was no mutual understanding (and the certificates had to be redone).

Communication Components

Communication is attempted when one person (the *sender*) wants to convey something (a *message*) to another person (the *receiver*) and the second person acknowledges that the message has been received (*feedback*). As illustrated in Figure 12-1, these are four basic components of the communication process.

The sender initiates the communication because there is something to convey to someone through language that may be oral, written, or action-cued. The message is encoded and then transmitted through a medium (words, numbers, illustrations, or

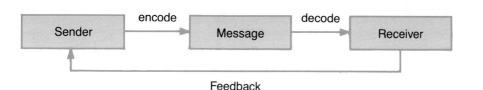

FIGURE 12-1

The components of
communication

actions) that puts the sender's thoughts into a form that can be transmitted. The receiver interprets (*decodes*) the message based on her or his background and experiences and responds to the message through feedback. Feedback lets the sender know whether or not the message was understood. The feedback that Melody gave when she folded the certificates and inserted them in small envelopes was action feedback that gave a clear signal that the message was not understood and that communication had not taken place. Feedback may also be in oral or written form.

Sources of Information

Employees want to know what's going on in their company. Most employees believe that they are entitled to information because they have a vested interest in the company. Where do employees get their information? Where do they *want* to get their information? The answers to these two questions are shown in Figure 12-2 on page 360. These are the responses from a survey of 10,000 employees conducted by Towers, Perrin, Forster, and Crosby, management consultants. The list on the left makes it clear that employees would like to rely on management for their information, but the list on the right shows that only about 60 percent of the employees consider their supervisor to be "a major source of information."

It is interesting to note that both "immediate supervisor" and "small group meetings" as a major source of information showed a small but steady gain between 1980 and 1984. Perhaps the increase in "small group meetings" as a major information source was due to greater emphasis on employee participation in the workplace and on the greater involvement of supervisors in organizational communication.

The survey also asked employees about communication as it related specifically to supervisors and to the organization as a whole. As shown in Figure 12-3 on page 361, supervisors got higher marks as communicators of organizational information in 1984 than they got in 1980. The organization, however, showed a clear decline (Figure 12-4 on page 361) in their ratings by employees on how they were keeping workers informed on matters they believe they need to know to do their jobs or would like to know because it increases their job satisfaction and sense of working as a team.

Employee publications are a preferred major source of information (see Figure 12-2). But what do employees think of the publications? Although many companies have made efforts to improve their publications, the survey respondents did not seem to think their efforts had been successful. A lower percentage of employees found their publications "easy to read," "believable," "up-to-date," or objective ("presents both sides of the story") in 1984 than in 1980 (see Figure 12-5 on page 362).

*Competency
Check:*

Can you describe
the four basic
components of
communication?

*Competency
Check:*

Can you identify
five of the major
sources of current
information and
relate these sources
to the preferred
ones?

FIGURE 12-2 Employee sources of information

Preferred sources

Survey employees were asked to list their "major preferred sources" for job-related information
The numbers change little from year to year; the significance of the list, rather, is in the size of the numbers and the ranking of the sources.

1984 Rank	Source	Major preferred source for		
		'80	'82	'84
1	Immediate supervisor	90.3	91.2	92.3
2	Small group meetings	58.6	60.5	63.0
3	Top executives	50.0	50.2	55.5
4	Annual business report to employees	44.3	40.6	45.8
5	Employee handbook/other booklets	48.4	45.6	41.2
6	Orientation program	45.9	42.6	41.1
7	Regular local employee publication	44.2	42.7	40.4
8	Regular general employee publication	44.7	40.7	38.5
9	Bulletin board(s)	41.4	38.8	37.1
10	Upward communication programs	33.8	34.3	33.8
11	Mass meetings	28.9	26.8	30.3
12	Audio-visual programs	27.7	24.4	23.2
13	Union	21.8	30.8	20.4
14	Grapevine	10.7	9.3	10.5
15	Mass media	11.4	9.7	8.8

Current sources

Survey employees were asked to list their "major current sources" of organizational information
In this list, the numbers do change from year to year. The list shows the immediate supervisor and small group meetings increasingly becoming sources of information.

1984 Rank	Source	Major source for		
		'80	'82	'84
1	Immediate supervisor	55.1	56.9	59.7
2	Grapevine	39.8	38.4	40.4
3	Small group meetings	28.1	30.3	33.1
4	Bulletin board(s)	31.5	28.9	30.1
5	Employee handbook/other booklets	32.0	30.9	26.6
6	Regular general employee publication	27.9	24.8	21.2
7	Regular local employee publication	20.2	21.4	19.2
8	Annual business report to employees	24.6	21.6	16.8
9	Mass meetings	15.9	13.8	16.6
10	Top executives	11.7	11.7	13.3
11	Orientation program	12.5	10.9	12.9
12	Union	13.2	20.7	12.3
13	Mass media	9.7	9.6	10.5
14	Audio-visual programs	10.2	8.0	9.3
15	Upward communication programs	9.0	8.3	9.1

Source: Karen Rosenburg, survey by Towers, Perrin, Forster, and Crosby, in *Human Resources Management—Ideas and Trends in Personnel,* issue 97, Aug. 12, 1985, p. 123. Reproduced with permission from *Human Resources Management— Ideas and Trends,* published and copyrighted by Commerce Clearing House, Inc., 4025 W. Peterson Ave., Chicago, IL 60646.

FIGURE 12-3

SUPERVISORY COMMUNICATION EFFECTIVENESS

MY SUPERVISOR	1980	1982	1984
keeps me well informed.	63.9%	64.9%	67.5%
is kept well informed by higher management.	62.4	63.3	63.5
discusses my job performance once a year.	65.1	70.1	76.1
lets me know when I do a good job.	56.9	59.2	61.8

Numbers are the percentage of the survey sample of 10,000 employees agreeing with each statement.
Source: Karen Rosenburg, survey by Towers, Perrin, Forster, and Crosby, in *Human Resources Management—Ideas and Trends in Personnel,* issue 97, Aug. 12, 1985, p. 122. Reproduced with permission from *Human Resources Management—Ideas and Trends,* published and copyrighted by Commerce Clearing House, Inc., 4025 W. Peterson Ave., Chicago, IL 60646.

FIGURE 12-4

ORGANIZATION COMMUNICATION EFFECTIVENESS

DOWNWARD COMMUNICATION	1980	1982	1984
This organization tries to keep employees well informed.	74.1%	70.9%	68.5%
I've been given the information I need to do my job.	65.6	65.3	65.9
Compared to others, this organization has good communication.	61.4	59.2	57.0
Communication here is candid and accurate.	54.4	51.1	48.9
Official communication doesn't tell the whole story.	64.6	67.8	68.2

Numbers are the percentage of the survey sample of 10,000 employees agreeing with each statement.
Source: Karen Rosenburg, survey by Towers, Perrin, Forster, and Crosby, in *Human Resources Management—Ideas and Trends in Personnel,* issue 97, Aug. 12, 1985, p. 123. Reproduced with permission from *Human Resources Management—Ideas and Trends,* published and copyrighted by Commerce Clearing House, Inc., 4025 W. Peterson Ave., Chicago, IL 60646.

FIGURE 12-5

EMPLOYEE PERCEPTIONS OF COMPANY PUBLICATIONS

| | % responding "always" or "usually" | | |
CRITERION	1980	1982	1984
easy to read	90.9%	85.2%	87.2%
believable	88.9	83.5	84.5
regularly received	87.4	83.2	79.3
thoroughly read by me	76.5	69.5	71.9
interesting	78.9	72.7	71.0
up-to-date	75.5	71.5	68.0
attractive	71.8	68.0	63.7
good source of company news	67.7	60.4	55.8
presents both sides of story	50.2	45.1	42.8
read by my family	27.5	20.9	18.7
helps me in my work	18.2	15.4	14.8

Source: Karen Rosenburg, survey by Towers, Perrin, Forster, and Crosby, in *Human Resources Management—Ideas and Trends in Personnel,* issue 97, Aug. 12, 1985, p. 122. Reproduced with permission from *Human Resources Management—Ideas and Trends,* published and copyrighted by Commerce Clearing House, Inc., 4025 W. Peterson Ave., Chicago, IL 60646.

WHAT CAN THE SUPERVISOR DO?

The supervisor is making progress as a communicator of job-related information. Perhaps even more important, a growing percentage of employees (92.3 percent in 1984) acknowledge the supervisor as their *preferred* source of information (see Figure 12-2). To capitalize on the confidence placed in them, supervisors must know what information employees want. Figure 12-6 provides this information. It should be emphasized that the group polled for this survey was asked, "What subjects are you interested in receiving *further* information on?" The fact that an item falls at the bottom of this list, therefore, does not mean that respondents are not interested in receiving this information; it simply means that they feel they are already receiving adequate information on this subject. "Organizational plans for the future," on the other hand, is apparently a subject that is not communicated fully by many organizations, so employees want to know more about this item.

Overcoming Communication Barriers

Jones in the beginning of this chapter said, "What we have here is a failure to communicate." Communication is often blocked because there are barriers that are

FIGURE 12-6

WHAT EMPLOYEES WANT TO KNOW MORE ABOUT

RANK SUBJECT	1980	1982	1984
1. organizational plans for the future	77.4%	78.4%	79.8%
2. job advancement opportunities	75.2	72.9	72.5
3. job-related "how-to" information	70.8	69.8	68.0
4. productivity improvement	62.2	63.6	63.0
5. personnel policies and practices	67.6	66.4	62.8
6. how we're doing vs. the competition	60.6	60.2	62.7
7. how my job fits into the organization	63.0	62.9	62.1
8. how external events affect my job	58.2	57.8	52.9
9. how profits are used	48.7	44.5	48.6
10. financial results	41.8	39.0	44.1
11. advertising and promotional plans	39.3	40.4	43.4
12. operations outside of my department or division	43.8	41.3	43.3
13. organizational stand on current issues	50.1	44.1	42.7
14. personnel changes and promotions	43.1	41.7	41.1
15. organizational community involvement	45.4	42.4	39.3
16. human interest stories about other employees	27.8	24.8	21.6
17. personal news (birthdays, anniversaries, and so on)	19.5	18.4	16.0

Source: Karen Rosenburg, survey by Towers, Perrin, Forster, and Crosby, in *Human Resources Management—Ideas and Trends in Personnel,* issue 97, Aug. 12, 1985, p. 121. Reproduced with permission from *Human Resources Management—Ideas and Trends,* published and copyrighted by Commerce Clearing House, Inc., 4025 W. Peterson Ave., Chicago, IL 60646.

difficult to penetrate. Some of the more common communication barriers include (1) differing frames of reference, (2) technical language and jargon, (3) information overload, and (4) conflicting signals.

Differing Frames of Reference

Supervisors are in daily contact with people who have varied experiences, education, and backgrounds, which means that they also have differing frames of reference. The expression, "I know where you're coming from" has, of course, no relationship to geography. The expression refers to understanding how another individual feels about something based on his or her frame of reference. Sometimes it is difficult to understand someone whose background is entirely different from yours. For example, a supervisor with 10 years' experience on the job, an associate's degree from a technical school, and a middle-class, suburban background might have difficulty communicating with a dropout from an urban high school. Their experiences, education, and backgrounds are very different, and people use their pasts as their frame of reference.

B.C.

Source: By permission of Johnny Hart and Creators Syndicate, Inc.

Technical Language and Jargon

During World War II, Franklin D. Roosevelt asked an aide to write a memo on the subject of the blacking out of federal buildings. The aide submitted the following memo for President Roosevelt's signature:

> Such preparations shall be made as will completely obscure all federal buildings occupied by the federal government during an air raid for any period of time from visibility by reason of internal or external illumination. Such obscuration may be obtained by blackout construction or by termination of illumination. This will, of course, require that in building areas in which production must continue during the blackout, construction must be provided so that internal illumination will continue. Other areas may be obscured by terminating the illumination.

President Roosevelt revised the memo to read:

> In buildings where you have to keep working, put something across the windows. In buildings where you can afford to let the work stop for awhile, turn out the lights.

Some people use technical language and jargon to try to impress others. The saying "express, don't impress" is a good one. The goal of communication is to deliver your message in a way that the receiver understands. You rarely achieve that goal when you use technical language with people who are not in your field or when you use jargon.

Information Overload

Almost all employees today, whatever their level, get too much information and have too little time to evaluate it. This barrier to effective communication becomes greater as the tide of information increases.

This information overload problem is partly a result of our reluctance to voluntarily decrease the amount of information we receive. We hesitate to say, "Take me off the distribution list. I rarely use this report; and if I need the information, I know where it is available." Perhaps this is because we do not want to admit there is some information we neither need nor use, or perhaps it is because the overflow of information (overwhelming as it may be) makes us feel important.

One organization decided to see whether its managers really used all the reports they were sent and whether they would even notice if the reports were discontinued. First, notices were attached to the tops of all the reports. The notices asked (1) if the managers used the information in the report, (2) if they wished to continue to receive the report, and (3) if the report could be distributed less frequently and still provide the necessary information in a timely manner. Those who returned the notices responded (1) yes (2) yes (3) no.

A follow-up was conducted several months later. This time, the notice was placed about three-quarters through the report. The notice read: "If you wish to continue receiving this report, please return this notice to the data processing center within 10 days." What do you think the response was this time?

Conflicting Signals

When senders convey one message in words and then, through actions, convey a different message, they are guilty of sending conflicting signals. For example, your supervisor may say, "We have an open-door policy here, and I encourage you to drop by at any time to talk to me." Then, when you come by to discuss a problem, not only is the door shut, but the secretary says, "She's busy." When you finally do get in the door, the supervisor shuffles papers, answers the phone several times, and is generally inattentive. Conflicting signals have been given. Supervisors should be aware that conflicting signals cause employee confusion and uncertainty. Which message is to be believed? Care should be taken to send the same messages each time, whatever the form used.

Making the Grapevine Work for You

Every company has an informal communication channel called a *grapevine*. The grapevine is particularly active in firms where the formal communication channels are inactive or ineffective. Employees want to know what's happening in the workplace, and if they aren't given the information through the usual formal channels, the grapevine takes over. The grapevine is typified by "Did you hear about the RIF?" "Diane told me that the new supervisor is going to make a lot of changes." "Sam told Marie that Jim is getting comp time for the extra hour we worked last Friday." Or "Let me tell you about the latest. . . . " As the grapevine spreads information, distortion occurs, but 70 to 90 percent of the details communicated through the grapevine are correct.[1] People tend to think the grapevine is less accurate than it really is because its errors are more dramatic and, consequently, more memorable than are its day-to-day routine accurate reports. Moreover, the inaccurate parts are often more important.[2]

*Competency
Check:*

Can you define
grapevine?

The grapevine is powerful and swift. But employees don't want to get their information through the grapevine. Note that in Figure 12-2, the grapevine is way down on the list of employees' preferred sources of information, while it is far up on the list of current sources of information. So until employees are given organizational information directly through formal communication channels, supervisors must learn to make the grapevine work *for* them and the employees.

WHAT CAN THE SUPERVISOR DO?

Supervisors should feed the grapevine. Since grapevines flourish in information voids, it's best to keep them well-fed. This is especially true during troubled times, when the fears and anxieties of employees often result in false and unproductive grapevine information. To avoid such perils and pitfalls, it is best to do the following:

Keep employees informed about key issues by using the formal channels. The formal channels are staff meetings, posted notices, and announcements in company newsletters and fliers.

Keep employees informed informally—on a one-to-one basis—through the grapevine. To do this, pass information to the key people on the grapevine, sometimes called *liaison communicators.* These are the employees who receive information and pass it on to other staff members.[3]

COMMUNICATING WITH INDIVIDUALS

Supervisors communicate both formally and informally with their superiors, their peers, and their subordinates. This represents upward, horizontal, diagonal, and downward communication.

FIGURE 12-7　UPWARD COMMUNICATION EFFECTIVENESS

UPWARD COMMUNICATION	1980	1982	1984
Communication here is a 2-way street.	55.2%	53.4%	52.3%
Management here acts on employees' ideas.	51.0	49.7	48.4

Numbers are the percentage of the survey sample of 10,000 employees agreeing with each statement.
Source:　Karen Rosenburg, survey by Towers, Perrin, Forster, and Crosby, in *Human Resources Management—Ideas and Trends in Personnel,* issue 97, Aug. 12, 1985, p. 124. Reproduced with permission from *Human Resources Management—Ideas and Trends,* published and copyrighted by Commerce Clearing House, Inc., 4025 W. Peterson Ave., Chicago, IL 60646.

Superiors

Upward communication—communication from subordinate to superior—is declining, according to Towers, Perrin, Forster, and Crosby (see Figure 12-7). While the decline is not great (3 percent in 4 years), the significance is in the trend. A decrease occurred in both 1982 and 1984. Perhaps with the trend toward more participative management, upward communication will receive more emphasis.

Upward communication can also be diagonal. For example, look at the following situation:

Under normal conditions, if Jones in production needs to discuss a problem with Malone in quality control, she would go up the chain of command through McGrath to James and then down the chain of command from Jason to Malone. Using the diagonal communication channel, however, Jones would go directly to Malone. Called "bypassing the chain of command," this practice is not generally encouraged. But if the practice is approved, it saves time and because the communication is direct, there is less chance of distorting the message. Some managers do not like subordinates to use diagonal channels because the managers may not always be informed of the communication and their perception is that their control is diminished.

The purpose of upward communication is to pass information from subordinates to managers. This information may be communicated in a number of ways, including:[4]

- Reports: This is the most frequently used method of upward communication. Reports may be oral or written, formal or informal, long or short.
- Grievance procedures: This form of upward communication allows employees a formal channel of appeal beyond the authority of their immediate supervisors.
- Complaint or suggestion boxes: Boxes for depositing complaints and suggestions are effective when both employee and manager view them as legitimate sources of information.
- Questionnaires and surveys: Information about employee attitudes, morale, views of the organization, and relationships between managers and subordinates may be obtained through questionnaires and surveys.
- Open-door policy: The availability of superiors to subordinates through an open-door policy reflects the degree of managerial commitment to open communication among all levels of employees.
- Grapevine: Although the grapevine is usually a means of downward and horizontal communication, it can work in an upward direction as well. Sometimes the

grapevine information originates at a lower level in the organization and is communicated upward.

● Liaison communicators: Subordinates may supply information to managers, either voluntarily or by request. Sometimes coworkers resent this method of upward communication and consider the source an "informer."

● Special meetings: Employees may call special meetings to discuss items of mutual interest with managers. If these meetings allow for a mutual exchange of information, they may be an effective means of upward communication.

● Quality circles: Quality circles (QCs) are described in Chapters 5 and 16. As management styles have become more participative, quality circles have become a more legitimate way to communicate with upper levels of management through worker presentations.

Competency Check:

Can you identify six methods of communicating information to superiors?

The effectiveness of upward communication is determined by the attitudes of managers toward participative management and the confidence that is placed in the employees. When participation is encouraged, more upward communication results.

Peers

Horizontal communication—communication between peers—presents unique opportunities and challenges. It allows employees to bypass the formal structure and address problems at the level at which they appear. In 1916, Henri Fayol, an early management authority whose contributions to the classical era are discussed in Chapter 1, identified this form of communication and illustrated it with a chart that became known as "Fayol's bridge" (see Figure 12-8).

Horizontal communication is fast. It works in much the same way as diagonal communication. To solve a problem that involves A and B in Figure 12-8, it is not necessary to go through the formal layers of the organization—upward through the chart at the left and then downward through the chart at the right. The directness of this form of communication also helps to reduce the information loss and distortion that often occur when information travels through many different people.

Competency Check:

Can you explain horizontal communication and Fayol's bridge?

One of the greatest dangers of horizontal communication is that it may become a substitute for both upward and downward communication. When this happens, two major channels of communication are bypassed, and information that should be shared through upward and downward communication is not available to these channels.

Subordinates

Most of the information flow within an organization is downward. Managers at different levels within the company communicate with the people they manage. (Refer to Figures 12-3 and 12-4.) Information may be communicated from managers to subordinates in many different forms, including:[5]

FIGURE 12-8

Fayol's bridge

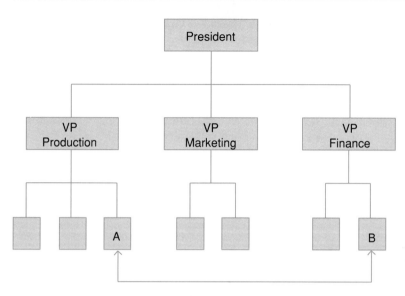

Source: Betty R. Ricks and Kay F. Gow, *Business Communication: Systems and Applications,* John Wiley & Sons, Inc., New York, 1987, p. 11.

● Directives: Company policies and procedures are communicated to employees through directives. Directives may be sent only to employees who are affected by them or may be widely distributed for information purposes.

● Bulletin boards and posters: These communication devices are most effective when placed where employees typically congregate. To be effective, they must also contain topics of interest to employees, be attractive, and contain up-to-date information.

● Company publications: Well-written articles placed in company publications are another method of making information available to workers. As shown in Figure 12-5, however, workers do not always consider these publications the best source of company news.

● Letters and pay inserts: Most employees pay attention to what is put in a pay envelope; inserts may therefore be an effective way to communicate with subordinates.

● Employee handbooks: When workers are hired, they may be given employee handbooks. Employees should be encouraged to read these handbooks because they usually contain information regarding employee responsibilities and benefits.

● Memos: One of the most frequently used forms of business communication, especially among departments, is memos. Memos are an efficient way to communicate in-house information.

● Information racks: Like bulletin boards, information racks should be placed in areas where employees congregate—next to a water fountain, near a drink machine, or close to a snack bar. Information racks should also be kept current and neat and should contain information of interest to employees.

Competency Check:

Can you identify six ways to communicate information from manager to subordinate?

- Loudspeakers: The effectiveness of a loudspeaker as a method of communication depends largely on how often it is used and for what purpose. If the loudspeaker often interrupts work with unimportant messages, it simply becomes a part of the background noise and even the object of ridicule.
- Grapevine: The grapevine is one of the fastest communication methods in any organization, but the information may be distorted as it is passed from one individual to the next. As with any oral method of communication, information sent through the grapevine is susceptible to individual interpretation.

The effectiveness of downward communication is determined largely by the willingness of managers to share information with subordinates. Sharing information builds trust and emphasizes teamwork between managers and subordinates.

WHAT CAN THE SUPERVISOR DO?

Supervisors are looked upon as a major source of information. They provide information to superiors, to peers, and to subordinates. There are many ways to communicate with each group, and supervisors should learn to use all the tools and techniques effectively. All companies do not have all the communication tools and techniques available, nor are all the formal communication channels available used. Supervisors, however, should take advantage of any opportunity to keep their superiors informed about developments in the department, to communicate with their peers when such communication will expedite the work, and to keep their subordinates informed.

COMMUNICATING WITH GROUPS

Supervisors interact not only with individuals—superiors, peers, and subordinates—but also with groups. Although a group is simply a collection of individuals, communicating with a group requires skills different from those used when communicating with individuals on a one-to-one basis.

Two major components exist in all group settings—content and process. *Content* is the task with which the group is charged; *process* is what happens between, among, and to group members as they go about the activities necessary to accomplish the task. Process looks at the interactions of the members of a group—*group dynamics*.

Working with Committees

Supervisors are frequently asked to work with committees, either as committee members, chairpersons, or facilitators. As a member of a committee, it is important that the supervisor be on time for meetings, be prepared, and be an active participant.

To prepare for a meeting, the supervisor should review the committee's charge, note some ideas for reaching the goal, note questions or items that need clarification, and conduct any research necessary to make a contribution to the work of the committee. For example, if a task force has been formed to deal with the problem of employee turnover, the supervisor would want to bring information to the meeting about the turnover in his or her department, any trends that might have been observed, any actions that may have been taken to reduce employee turnover, and specific results that can be attributed to those actions.

With the increase in employee involvement and participation in issues related to the workplace, a supervisor may be asked to chair a committee within the department or to serve as a facilitator for a quality circle.

The supervisor's role in a QC may be as the QC chairperson or as the facilitator. Some companies prefer to have the supervisor act as a resource person and facilitator and have a member of the work group chair the QC. Still others believe the supervisor should act as the chairperson of the QC. As a resource person and facilitator, the supervisor is an observer, stepping in only when it is necessary to keep the group on track or at the request of the chairperson. The role of chairperson for a QC is somewhat different from the role of the traditional chairperson. Even when serving as the chairperson, the supervisor is a part of the QC and has the same vote—one—and the same influence as each of the other members of the group.

One of the techniques used in QCs to encourage each member to participate is to go around the circle asking each person to respond orally to the issue being discussed. Even if a group member has nothing to offer, an oral response such as ''I have no suggestion at this time'' is still required. The chairperson continues to poll each member until there is no additional input.

Competency Check:

Can you discuss each of the roles a supervisor may play when working with a quality circle? Which role do you think is more appropriate? Why?

Participating in Meetings

When supervisors participate in meetings, they should observe the common courtesies of arriving on time, projecting interest, being attentive, and not leaving before the meeting is adjourned.

In addition, the supervisor will contribute more and gain more from the meeting if he or she practices good listening skills. One often-cited study found that adults in various occupations spend 45 percent of their communicating time listening. Listening is not the same as hearing. *Hearing* is the act of perceiving sound(s). (She's hard-of-hearing.) *Listening* is the act of attaching meaning to the sound(s). (He never listens!) Listening skills can be improved if you:[6]

- listen for key words and concepts.
- weigh important points and supporting facts.
- take selective notes.
- form opinions only after hearing all the information to be presented.
- increase your vocabulary to increase your understanding.
- avoid mental debates with the speaker.
- are attentive.
- avoid preconceptions or prejudgments.

Of course, good listening skills are an essential part of the supervisor's daily tools. Effective listening to workers should be an ongoing technique as supervisors build strong relationships with their workers.

When making comments to the group, the supervisor should speak so that other participants can hear. Speaking too softly, trailing off at the ends of words or sentences, or not speaking clearly diminishes your contribution. You may have a great idea, but if no one can understand what you say, the great idea may be rejected or, at best, met with little enthusiasm.

There is seldom universal agreement on anything. So if you disagree with a suggestion, discuss the merits of the idea without attacking the person who made the suggestion. One positive way to disagree with another group member's suggestion is to suggest an alternative.

Competency Check:

Can you describe how the supervisor can contribute as a participant to the success of a meeting?

Conducting Meetings

As the chairperson of a meeting, your responsibilities will vary according to the size, composition, location, and purpose of the meeting. You may be responsible for securing the meeting room, notifying the participants, arranging the seating, controlling the physical environment, and generally overseeing the meeting arrangements as well as for conducting the meeting and for any postmeeting activities.

Before the Meeting

If you are responsible for all the premeeting arrangements, delegate as many of the routine arrangements as possible. You should, however, come to the meeting early and check the room before other participants arrive to be sure all arrangements are complete. A premeeting checklist is provided in Figure 12-9.

As chairperson, you should prepare and distribute an agenda to all participants. The order of the agenda should reflect the importance of the items to be discussed, with the most important ones first. Everyone is more creative; more alert; more prepared to make careful, considered decisions; and more willing to participate in the entire process early in the meeting than they will be later (especially if the meeting is long or runs overtime).

Agendas speed meetings along and keep them on track. They also force the person who called the meeting to specify clearly the items to be covered. Agendas also make participants aware of the items for discussion and give them time to prepare for the meeting by completing assignments and gathering and reading background information prior to the meeting. Agendas minimize the ''If I had known we were going to discuss . . . '' phenomenon. Distribute agendas far enough in advance of the meeting for some preplanning to be done. Agendas are also a tool for handling digressions tactfully. ''That's a good idea, Charlie, but we should defer that discussion either to the end of the meeting, if time permits, or to another time so that we can complete today's agenda.''[7]

FIGURE 12-9 Example of a premeeting checklist

PREMEETING CHECKLIST

Participants
_____ Number invited
_____ Number accepted
_____ Agenda distributed

Facilities
_____ Room reserved
_____ Number of chairs required
_____ Add/remove chairs
_____ Temperature
_____ Lighting
_____ Seating arrangement
_____ Lectern required
_____ Microphone required

Audio-Visual Equipment/Aids
_____ Overhead projector
_____ Slide carousel projector
_____ Film projector
_____ Screen
_____ Tape recorder/player
_____ Video tape player

Refreshments
_____ Coffee
_____ Tea

Refreshments (cont.)
_____ Danish, doughnuts
_____ Cream, sugar, artificial
       sweetener
_____ Spoons, napkins
_____ Cold drinks
_____ Other

Amenities
_____ Notepaper
_____ Pens
_____ Pencils
_____ Ashtrays
_____ Name cards

Miscellaneous Requirements
_____ Video tape recorder
_____ Flip chart
_____ Transparency pens
_____ Chalk/eraser
_____ Extension cord
_____ Handouts _____#
_____ Other (list)
       _____
       _____
       _____
       _____

Did you reserve the meeting room? Do you have enough chairs? Too many? Too few chairs will not contribute to achieving the goals of the meeting because someone is going to be uncomfortable standing. Too many chairs project a message, too. Perhaps many of the people who were supposed to attend didn't show up. A few people scattered throughout a large room gives a feeling of noncohesiveness, not desired in a meeting.

The temperature must be comfortable for most participants. The lighting should be adequate for reading and writing. The seating arrangement should be appropriate for the number of people and for the meeting purpose. If the meeting was called to provide information, make sure everyone can see and hear the speaker. If the purpose of the meeting is to provide an arena for discussion, place chairs so that interaction is possible. It's difficult to have a lively discussion if you are talking to the back of someone's head! Make the environment one that invites group members to participate.

FIGURE 12-10

What to do at the
meeting

AT THE MEETING

The following actions taken during the meeting will help you have a more productive meeting.

_____ Distributed an agenda before the meeting
_____ Be prepared by having reread the agenda and by being informed about the items to be discussed
_____ Have additional background information reproduced (if appropriate) or be prepared to give the information orally (if necessary)
_____ Start on time
_____ Give a short, warm welcome
_____ Introduce new or unknown members (if group size allows)
_____ State purpose of meeting
_____ State amount of time meeting should take
_____ Stop on time
_____ End on a positive note
_____ Be in charge
_____ Know your participants

During the Meeting

As the meeting leader, there are actions you can take to make the meeting more productive. These actions are summarized in Figure 12-10. Several of the actions listed in Figure 12-10 are discussed below.

The chairperson should begin the meeting at the time scheduled, whether everyone is present or not. If you develop a reputation for starting on time, participants will soon realize that you respect the value of their time (and your own) and they will be encouraged to arrive at future meetings on time. State the purpose and time frame of the meeting. End on time. Keep the meeting moving along; if members want to ramble or digress, courteously but firmly return the discussion to the issue. Allow all members to participate in the discussion, but keep the meeting orderly; do not allow it to become noisy or disorganized. Take charge!

After the Meeting

Most postmeeting activities are writing activities and are the responsibility of the chairperson. One of the most important postmeeting activities is to prepare a follow-up summary. Minutes are sometimes recorded, but since minutes include only actions taken, a summary is extremely helpful to all participants. Summaries serve these four important functions:

1. Everyone receives identical written confirmation of the proceedings. We have selective memories, and our recollections of events often differ.
2. Written confirmation of task assignments eliminates any confusion about responsibilities.

3. Summaries provide a clear statement of decisions reached and votes taken.
4. Summaries provide a record for both participants and absentees.

Supervisors should make an effort to obtain feedback from participants regarding the effectiveness of the meeting. Feedback on meeting productivity can be obtained from several sources and in several ways. You may obtain verbal feedback, but this kind of feedback is often distorted because you may hear only the positive comments directly and have to rely on indirect sources for the negative comments. You may conduct a formal meeting evaluation, using an evaluation form that addresses the way the meeting was conducted, the value of the meeting, the physical facilities, and the overall achievement of the meeting goals.

Every meeting is a miniature management cycle. You *plan* the meeting, you *organize* the tasks, you *lead* the group, and you *control* through feedback from the evaluation process.

Competency Check:

Can you describe the activities a supervisor should engage in before, during, and after a meeting?

WHAT CAN THE SUPERVISOR DO?

Meetings often lack mutually understood goals. Some goals aren't even stated; they are merely implied. Supervisors should analyze their meeting goals. Meetings may have several goals, some in conflict with others. All the goals listed below may be legitimate at one point or another in one meeting or another. As a supervisor, can you identify the goals of the meetings you call? Of the meetings you attend?

_____ to block, retard, delay, or confuse action
_____ to fill up time and avoid pressing issues back at the job
_____ to fill a meeting quota
_____ to keep the group divided
_____ to diffuse decision responsibility so that decision failure will be shared
_____ to meet the social needs of the group
_____ to use the meeting arena to impress the boss
_____ to share significant information openly
_____ to set goals, priorities, and plans
_____ to learn some new skill or approach
_____ to coordinate activities
_____ to clarify issues and reach understanding between individuals and with other groups
_____ to identify a problem, assign action to a person, and set a time target
_____ to solve a problem and assign implementation responsibilities
_____ to hear announcements from the boss
_____ to provide mutual assistance
_____ other (specifiy) _____

Source: Richard J. Dunsing, *You and I Have Simply Got to Stop Meeting Like This,* AMACOM, 1978, p. 61.

VERBAL AND ACTION-CUED COMMUNICATION

Communication may be verbal, written, or action-cued. In this section, we will look at *verbal communication* (what we say) and *action-cued communication* (what we communicate by our actions). One of the problems with verbal communication is that no written record exists and each individual's recollection is dependent upon his or her memory of the event.

Verbal Communication

To make verbal communication more effective, the following guidelines should be observed.[8] These guidelines are appropriate whether you are speaking to one individual, to several individuals, or to a group.

- *Know what you want to say.* Whether you are speaking to one person or to a large group, you should have a definite idea of what you want to convey and how you are going to say it. You may want to rehearse mentally how you are going to approach a subject, particularly if it is a sensitive one or one that is likely to cause a confrontation.
- *Consider your listener's point of view.* Your listener may have a viewpoint entirely different from yours, so you should be open to the possibility of another opinion. And it is important to listen to the opinions of others and to be open to another view.
- *Move from the simple to the complex.* If you want to convey more than routine information, plan the order of the items to be discussed. Any background information required for understanding should precede the presentation of new ideas or topics for discussion. Moving from the simple to the complex allows ideas to be developed. Begin with a basic concept, and then expand the information.
- *Select words carefully.* When communicating orally, you do not have the luxury of reviewing and rephrasing your words as you do when communicating in writing. Therefore, before you speak, know your listeners' backgrounds, and select your words carefully so as to send your message clearly without offending your listeners. Try to be sensitive to the way your words may be interpreted.
- *Enunciate clearly.* Speak clearly and naturally in a tone that will be understood. Failure to pronounce words clearly and correctly or mumbling may cause your listeners to lose interest or to feel that you are so unsure of what you are saying that it probably has no value.
- *Use the active voice.* The active voice is more easily understood because it is more direct. Using the active voice will help you speak more concisely, too, because it puts the action right up front. For example, ''Tom called me'' is more direct than ''I was called by Tom.''
- *Be courteous and natural.* No one likes to listen to people who are artificial, pompous, or rude. A natural and forthright manner is the most effective way to

communicate. Your listener will appreciate courtesy in communication, just as you do.

● *Repeat if necessary.* One way to be sure that your message was both received and understood is to briefly summarize the points made. You may also ask the listener to confirm the message by repeating it.

● *Establish eye contact, and be aware of body language.* Establishing eye contact with your receiver encourages communication. Eye contact keeps your mind from wandering and has the additional benefit of making the listener feel more important because of your evident attention.

Competency Check:

Can you cite seven guidelines for effective verbal communication?

Action-Cued Communication

Everyone engages in communication that is neither verbal nor written; it is communication through action. Sometimes it is difficult to understand action-cued communication because it is subject to interpretation by the receiver.

Functions

Nonverbal, or action-cued, communication serves to reaffirm or emphasize, to contradict, to substitute, to complement, and to control.[9] Action-cued communication may be used in conjunction with verbal communication or it may be used by itself.

Gestures and facial expressions may serve to restate or emphasize a particular point. Sometimes a nod of the head emphasizes verbal agreement; a smile may reaffirm "How good to see you"; the manner of dress worn may reaffirm the importance placed on a particular event.

Sometimes nonverbal behavior may contradict verbal communication. You may say, "Yes, I have time to meet with you" and then continue to work on something else instead of listening. The verbal message "I have time" is contradicted by your actions, which clearly say "I'm too busy for you right now."

Nonverbal behavior may substitute for a verbal message. For instance, if you ask someone how the weather is and the response is a flip of the hand, you understand that to mean "so-so."

Complementary nonverbal behavior is often used in speaking. These nonverbal cues serve to reinforce a verbal message. A supervisor may hold up a defective part as she explains how to spot a particular defect.

Nonverbal cues may also be used to control the behavior of others. Silence controls by refocusing attention. A lifted finger may call for quiet.

Action-cued communication is an important part of the communication process. An important point for supervisors to recognize is that their actions speak as loudly as their words, regardless of whether the words are communicated orally or in writing.

Competency Check:

Can you describe five functions of action-cued communication?

Types

How can communication be achieved without words—either written or verbal? What specific action-cued behaviors can be used to communicate a message? The seven types of nonverbal communication are: (1) silence, (2) body language, (3) gestures, (4) facial expressions, (5) touch, (6) space and distance, and (7) personal appearance.[10]

Silence is a very powerful communication tool that can have both positive and negative meaning. Through your silence, you can communicate displeasure, lack of interest, or failure to understand. Silence may be used for emphasis, as when a speaker pauses, or silence may indicate that you are listening carefully, attentively.

A popular subject in recent years, body language as nonverbal communication takes two forms: (1) unconscious movements and (2) consciously controlled or altered movements. When bored, you may yawn or shift positions frequently. When nervous, you may fidget or bite your nails. These movements are usually made unconsciously. Conscious movements may communicate, too. You may cross your arms in a "show-me" attitude, look at your watch, or gaze around the room.

A gesture is a deliberate body movement intended to convey a message. A thumbs-up gesture shows that things are under control; a wave of the hand may indicate "you go first"; standing when introduced to people who are older or in higher-ranking positions shows respect.

Facial expressions are important in action-cued communication because faces express a great range of emotions. The entire face is expressive, especially the eyes. Awareness of how a smile, laugh, frown, or scowl may be interpreted is important; you do not want to send the wrong message through your facial expression.

The first nonverbal communication we have in life is touch. Communication by touch should take into consideration both cultural patterns and individual preferences. Some people prefer a handshake to a pat on the back or a verbal greeting to an arm around the shoulder. You must be aware of cultural differences and individual preferences in using touch as a communication tool.

Distance is a communication tool which, like touch, expresses degrees of intimacy and of cultural and individual acceptance. Better communication is possible at closer ranges because the verbal message is clearer and the nonverbal messages more readily observed. The space you place between yourself and others also communicates a message. If you sit behind a large desk and place your subordinate in a chair in front of the desk, you have communicated that you want the conversation to be formal and that you are in charge. Seating yourself and your subordinate closer together and side by side says that the conversation is to be informal and on an equal level.

Personal appearance and dress communicate a message because there are accepted and expected grooming and dress standards. Those who disregard the accepted standards send the message that they do not choose to conform to company standards and group norms.

Competency Check:

Can you describe six types of action-cued communication?

WHAT CAN THE SUPERVISOR DO?

The supervisor must be aware that communication takes several forms and that conflicting messages can be communicated. Written, verbal, and action-cued communication are all important as supervisors strive to communicate clearly to the employees they supervise.

WRITTEN COMMUNICATION

Many people believe that written communication is more difficult than face-to-face verbal communication because it provides no immediate feedback to the sender, no opportunity to explain unclear messages or answer questions immediately, no way to reinforce the message with nonverbal cues, and no advantage of seeing the reaction of the receiver.

Jones in the beginning of the chapter said, "What we have here is a failure to communicate." Satchell responded to Jones's draft by noting, "This is not what we talked about." Satchell violated at least three of the five Cs of good writing.

Principles of Effective Written Communications

The principles of effective written communications are the five Cs of good writing: (1) clarity, (2) conciseness, (3) completeness, (4) correctness, and (5) courtesy.

Clarity

Clarity means that the message is easy for the reader to understand. The following example shows an unclear message and how that message could be rewritten for clarity:

Unclear: As much as I hate to lose her, I can't recommend her too highly for promotion.

Clear: I recommend her highly for promotion; I hate to lose her as an employee.

Conciseness

Concise messages contain enough words to make the meaning clear without sacrificing courtesy. The following example shows a wordy message and the same message written more concisely:

Wordy: In the event that we find ourselves in disagreement on this issue, it may be necessary that we seriously consider the advisability of continuing to do business with your company.

Concise: If we disagree on this issue, we will consider discontinuing our business relationship.

Completeness

Complete messages provide the reader with enough information to enable him or her to take appropriate action without having to ask additional questions. The following example of incomplete and complete messages illustrates the point:

Incomplete: Can we meet on Wednesday at 8 in the conference room?

Complete: Can we meet on Wednesday, January 22, at 8:00 A.M. in the conference room in Chandler Hall?

Correctness

Correct messages have the facts straight, are free of typographical errors and misspellings, and are grammatically correct. The following example of incorrect and correct messages illustrates the point:

Incorrect: The stationary you delivered on Monday, November 21, is exactly what we wanted.

Correct: The stationery you delivered on Monday, November 22, is exactly what we wanted.

Courtesy

A courteous message conveys the information in a way that creates and maintains goodwill. You should be as courteous and respectful in a letter as you would be in a face-to-face conversation. The following example shows a discourteous message rewritten as a courteous message:

Discourteous: It is obvious that you have made little attempt to meet your obligations. It is also obvious that you do not care about your credit standing with our company.

Courteous: You undoubtedly have a good reason for being unable to meet your financial obligation to our company. If you wish to arrange a payment schedule, please phone me at (524) 771-5555. If not, may we expect your check for $97.80 by June 1?

*Competency
Check:*

Can you cite the
five Cs of good
writing and give an
example of each?

When Satchell responded to Jones's memo, her message was unclear, incomplete, and discourteous. It was concise; whether or not it was correct is not known. Satchell did not tell Jones what was wrong with his memo or what she wanted included that was not in the memo, nor was she very courteous in her rejection note. It is doubtful that she would have used the same language in a face-to-face conversation.

Techniques for Communicating in Writing

When sending messages in written form, you must be careful to use the five Cs of good writing. But that is not enough! There are other techniques that will help the reader understand the message. These techniques include:[11]

● *Write for the reader*. Use vocabulary appropriate for the reader, neither over-estimating nor underestimating your reader's ability to understand.

● *Keep sentences short*. Long, run-on sentences lose the reader's interest quickly. If most of your sentences are longer than 15 to 20 words, consider breaking them up into shorter sentences. Remember that a sentence is a group of words conveying a *single* thought.

● *Use paragraph breaks*. Paragraph breaks divide the message into readable units, dividing the text into main and supporting ideas. Paragraph breaks also improve the appearance of a message by leaving white space.

● *Use short, simple words*. Look at the difference between the memo written by Roosevelt's aide and the revised memo. Long words are rarely necessary and should never be used in an attempt to impress—they rarely do.

● *Avoid jargon*. *Jargon* is pompous, trite, and abstract language. The key here is to ask yourself, ''Is this the way I would express myself if I were speaking to this person rather than writing to her?''

● *Avoid trite words and phrases*. Some expressions are used because they have been around a long time. When these words and phrases become outdated, they should be discarded for more crisp, clean, contemporary language. For example, ''as per your request'' should be replaced with ''at your request,'' ''at the present time'' with ''now'' and ''notwithstanding the fact that'' with ''although.'' One check for trite words and phrases is, Do your phrases often begin and end with little words such as *by, in, as, it, is, of, to,* or *with,* or with words ending in *-ing?* If so, you may want to evaluate your use of these words to see if they are lead-ins to outdated words and phrases.

● *Use action words*. Action words move your message along briskly. For example, ''It is our belief that this change will be of interest to you'' is read more easily if action words such as ''We believe this change will interest you'' are used.

● *Avoid redundancies*. *Redundancies* are repetitions. For example, ''surrounded on all sides,'' ''new beginner,'' ''refer back,'' ''and etc.,'' and ''consensus of opinion'' all contain redundancies.

● *Use a natural style*. Business letters do not have to be formal, stilted, or long. They can be warm, natural, and brief. Write in the style that is natural for you and in a tone that considers the reader.

● *Use personal pronouns*. When we talk to others, we use *I, we,* and *you*. How-ever, this is often not the case in business writing. The informality associated with personal pronouns makes communication more natural. Instead of saying, ''It is the opinion of our company,'' say ''We believe''; instead of ''The association with your company has been a pleasant one,'' say, ''We have enjoyed the association with you and your company.''

● *Use correct punctuation*. Punctuation can make a difference in what the message actually says. For example:

Mrs. Jones, said the secretary, was late.

Mrs. Jones said the secretary was late.

● *Proofread carefully*. Sometimes an error in preparing a letter can be very costly to the company; sometimes an error creates such an impression of incompetence that the customer loses faith in the company; sometimes an error is just a nuisance. As one person remarked, however, ''As long as the document is in your hands, a mistake is a 'typo,' when it is in someone else's hands, it is a *gross error!*'' The person who initiates the message has the responsibility for checking its accuracy.

Competency Check:

Can you cite at least 10 techniques for writing effective messages?

In a recent study by the American Assembly of Collegiate Schools of Business, communication skills were identified as one of the most important skills required of first-line and middle managers.[12] Supervisors, therefore, must develop their oral and written communication skills as they strive to improve the performance of their subordinates as well as their own performance.

COMPETENCY REVIEW

1. Define *communication*.
2. Describe the four basic communication components.
3. Identify five major sources of employee information and relate them to employees' *preferred* sources.
4. Define *grapevine*.
5. Identify six methods of communicating information upward.
6. Explain horizontal communication and Fayol's bridge.
7. Cite six ways to communicate information downward.
8. Describe the supervisor's role in a quality circle.
9. Describe five ways a supervisor can contribute to a meeting as a participant.
10. Describe activities a supervisor should engage in before, during, and after a meeting.
11. Cite seven guidelines for effective verbal communication.
12. Describe four functions of action-cued communication.
13. Explain six types of action-cued communication.
14. Cite the five Cs of good writing, and give an example of each.
15. Identify at least 10 techniques for writing effective messages.

APPLICATIONS

1. Consider the way you think, act, and feel during a given meeting. For each item, circle the number that best expresses the way you participate in the meeting. Then use a second mark to indicate where you'd like your score to be.

Interacting with the Leader

1	2	3	4	5
Very little; try to get along and follow his or her lead			Engage with him or her actively; ask questions and give support	

Influencing Meeting Direction

1	2	3	4	5
Accept what happens			Call for goal clarity, question what's going on, ask for new method	

Getting Involved in "Games"

1	2	3	4	5
Easily hooked by others, start games when anxious or bored			Relatively game free	

Sharing Thoughts

1	2	3	4	5
Hold back, filter, wait for others to say things to me			Fit my thoughts into events; state my position	

Taking Risks

1	2	3	4	5
Play it safe, never push limits, accept customs			Try wild ideas, new approaches; engage power figures in debate	

Using Positive Strokes

1	2	3	4	5
Withhold strokes			Offer freely to a range of people for different reasons	

Being Assertive

1	2	3	4	5
Frequently quiet, inactive, a watcher			Never out of the action, frequent inputs	

Handling Ideas Contrary to Mine

1	2	3	4	5
Reject, counterattack; feel put down and withdraw			Hear the intent, try to use when appropriate, stay open	

Revealing Feelings

1	2	3	4	5
Hide them, fake them, filter them			Share openly without punishing others	

Exercising Leadership as a Participant

1	2	3	4	5
Avoid, let leader lead			Fill the gap when needed, assist	

Listening While Others Talk

. 1	2	3	4	5

| Drift, doodle, rehearse, stare in space | | | Follow each speaker, ask for repeats when point missed | |

Source: Richard J. Dunsing, *You and I Have Simply Got to Stop Meeting Like This*, AMACOM, 1978, pp. 92–93.

2. This form will help you evaluate a working meeting (as opposed to an informational meeting). Select any meeting to evaluate. Circle the number on the scale that best expresses your view of the typical level of that behavior or characteristic. You may want to survey the entire group, or the leader, or a few participants.

To establish your own meeting model, you can place another symbol—a check mark, perhaps—at the number on each item as you believe it should be to best fulfill the meeting needs of your group.

MEETING CHARACTERISTICS AND BEHAVIORS

Goals

0	1	2	3	4	5

| None set; irrelevant or trivial items only | | | | Well-defined, clear, sharpened by the group | |

Roles of Participants

0	1	2	3	4	5

| Not known what to contribute, extent of involvement | | | | Meeting output known, limits known | |

Value of Meeting in Reaching Goals

0	1	2	3	4	5

| Goals best achieved outside a meeting | | | | This meeting and this group best for purpose | |

Priorities Set

0	1	2	3	4	5

| None set; all have equal weight | | | | Clear delineation of relative importance | |

Sense of Time

0	1	2	3	4	5

| Much time wasted on trivia | | | | Best time-fit between group focus and issue needs | |

Straight Talk

0	1	2	3	4	5

| Much fuzzy talk, undefined motives | | | | Issues set up; positions and wants clearly stated | |

Closure of Topics

0	1	2	3	4	5

| Topics end, but decisions and action left unstated | | | All debate ends with a conclusion, decision, or assignment | | |

Leadership Assumed

0	1	2	3	4	5

| Left in the air, with goals and roles not in focus | | | Assumed by leader or led as needed | | |

Participant Commitment

0	1	2	3	4	5

| Each marks time, stays aloof, protects self-interest only | | | Each supports group effort, accepts decision | | |

Participant Utilization

0	1	2	3	4	5

| Some dominate continually; quiet ones never tapped | | | Each shares skill and insight as appropriate | | |

Procedures and Rules

0	1	2	3	4	5

| Many applied to excess, with high need to control behavior | | | A few used to set boundaries, keep on track | | |

A Setting for Human Habitation

0	1	2	3	4	5

| Uncomfortable, "cold" environment; distracting, dull setting | | | Basic air, heat, comfort needs met; seating arrangement facilitates contact | | |

Source: Richard J. Dunsing, *You and I Have Simply Got to Stop Meeting Like This*, AMACOM, 1978, pp. 64–65.

3. What messages do you receive when you see people using the following action-cued communication?

    a. leaning forward

    b. crossing their arms

    c. sighing

    d. pushing their chairs back

    e. rolling their eyes upward

    f. yawning

    g. arriving late

    h. coming unprepared

    i. whistling

    j. putting their hands on their hips

    k. raising their eyebrows

    l. looking at their watches

    m. slinging their legs across the chair arm

CASES

Case I: Guess What's Happening in Marketing!

Samantha Long has been supervisor of the marketing department of Mann and Simpson Classic Autos for 11 years. "Sam," as her customers call her, consistently receives high ratings from both her manager and the customers who call to inquire about their cars. Recently, however, there have been rumors that Long has been having difficulty with Mike Langdon, the person in charge of the sales force. The rumors have reached Paul Chung, vice president for sales and Long's boss.

Chung decides to address the problem before things get really out of hand. He asks Long to see him on Monday at 9 A.M. in his office. Long is puzzled by Chung's rather curt request but decides not to read anything into it.

Monday morning, promptly at 9 A.M. Long goes to Chung's office. Chung is talking to someone on the telephone and will not be available for about 15 minutes, according to his secretary. Long sits down and "cools her heels" for more than 30 minutes. Finally, Chung buzzes his secretary and asks him to send Long in. When she enters the office, before even saying good morning, Chung says, "What's this I hear about you and Langdon having a fight?" Long is really taken aback because, while she and Langdon had a difference of opinion about his going to the production supervisor without talking to her first, she certainly did not consider their encounter a fight. Chung continues, "Langdon says it is much more efficient for him to go directly to the production supervisor than to have to go through you to me, to the vice president for production, and then to the production supervisor. That makes sense to me, too. So why are you making such a big deal about this?"

1. If you were Sam Long, how would you respond?
2. What communication direction was Langdon taking? Is that an appropriate action?
3. What communication errors did Chung commit?
4. How else might the situation have been handled?
5. What role did the grapevine play in this situation?

Case II: What I Meant Was . . .

Satchell in the beginning of the chapter wrote a brief marginal note on Jones's memo telling him to rewrite the memo. Obviously, Satchell disagreed with what Jones had written.

1. How might Satchell have handled the situation so that Jones would understand what she meant?
2. What type of communication would you have used in this instance? Why?

REFERENCES

1. Donald B. Simmons, ''How Does Your Grapevine Grow?'' *Management World.* February 1986, p. 18.

2. Keith Davis, Arizona State University, in ibid.

3. Ibid., p. 18.

4. Betty R. Ricks and Kay F. Gow, *Business Communication: Systems and Applications,* John Wiley & Sons, Inc., New York, 1987, pp. 9-10.

5. Ibid., pp. 7-8.

6. Ibid., p. 292 ff.

7. Ibid., p. 230.

8. Ibid., p. 225 ff.

9. Ibid., pp. 236-237.

10. Ibid., p. 232.

11. Ibid., p. 30.

12. Lyman W. Porter and Lawrence E. McKibbon, *Management and Development: Drift or Thrust into the 21st Century,* McGraw-Hill Book Company, New York, 1988, p. 112.

SUGGESTED READINGS

Ackley, R. Jon: ''Thirteen Ways to a Propitious Meeting,'' *Today's Office,* November 1982.

Auger, B. Y.: ''How to Run Better Business Meetings,'' *Supervisory Management,* August 1980.

Denton, D. Keith: ''A Manager's Toughest Job: One-on-One Communication,'' *Supervisory Management,* May 1985.

Fuller, Rex M.: ''How to Make Communication Work,'' *Pace Magazine, Piedmont Airlines Inflight Magazine,* September–October.

''How to Make Your Next Meeting Meaningful,'' *Personnel Communique,* February 1984.

Jay, Anthony: ''How to Run a Meeting,'' *Harvard Business Review,* March–April 1976.

Porco, Carmen: ''Developing a Proactive Communication Style in Employees,'' *Supervisory Management,* April 1985.

Tombari, Henry A.: ''Making Your Meetings Count,'' *Supervisory Management,* July 1979.

Wakefield, D. Gay: ''Gender and Power Communication in Middle- and Top-Level Administration,'' presented to the seventeenth annual convention of the southeast region of the American Business Communication Association, Apr. 5, 1984.

13

MANAGING THE PSYCHOLOGICAL ENVIRONMENT

COMPETENCIES

Studying this chapter will enable you to:

1. Identify sources of organizational stress and cite several stressors within each source.

2. Describe the measures of stress.

3. Describe actions that organizations, supervisors, and individuals can take to reduce employees' job-related stress.

4. Cite the reasons for burnout and describe the stages of burnout.

5. Identify ways in which to handle mental and emotional health problems.

6. Identify methods of recognizing employee needs.

7. Describe methods supervisors can use to offer assistance to employees.

8. Describe the individual consequences of an unmanaged psychological environment.

9. Describe the organizational consequences of a mismanaged psychological environment.

CHAPTER OUTLINE

The "invisible" work hazards are less visible than safety and health hazards, but no less dangerous to employees.

James C. Quick and Jonathan D. Quick[1]

Maxine DuBois and Brian Riley, on their coffee breaks in the company cafeteria, were commiserating with each other about the problems they are each experiencing with some of the workers they supervise.

DUBOIS I wish I knew what's wrong with Sharon. She used to be one of our most dependable workers, always reported to work on time, followed the rules—I could count on her. And what was really nice was that she was always so cheerful and cooperative. But recently all of that seems to have changed. Sharon is often late, extends her breaks, is surly, and sometimes is even rude to her fellow workers and to me.

RILEY I know what you mean. Although Sam is not surly or rude, he just doesn't seem to have the stamina or enthusiasm for the job that he used to have. Sam was almost a workaholic. He came to work early and was always so interested in his work. Now he just does his job.

DUBOIS I've heard about how stress can affect an employee's performance, but frankly, I don't know what I can do. In fact, I don't even know that Sharon is under any particular stress. Look at me: I'm a nice person to work for. How could Sharon possibly think her job is stressful? And if stress *is* Sharon's problem, what can I do to help?

RILEY Everybody says I'm a great guy, too. Sure I have my moments, but I don't believe I caused Sam's changed attitude toward his job. I read an article in the new training and development journal last night about employee burnout. It made me wonder if burnout is Sam's problem. And if it is, what can I do to restore the "old Sam"?

THE SUPERVISOR'S ROLE IN MANAGING THE PSYCHOLOGICAL ENVIRONMENT

The conversation between DuBois and Riley may be a common one because supervisors are encountering more and more troubled employees. Employees are having various types of mental and emotional problems, and they are bringing these problems and their effects into the workplace. Among these problems are substance abuse, stress, burnout, and a variety of other mental and emotional problems. The problem of substance abuse was covered in Chapter 7. The primary role of the supervisor here is simply to recognize the symptoms and make assistance available to the workers they supervise.

Stress

Stress is not an event or a circumstance; it is a response to it. The actual event or circumstance that demands a response and produces stress is the *stressor*. *Stress* is a patterned, unconscious response to a stressor.[2]

Contrary to a somewhat popular belief, stress is not associated solely with unpleasant events such as losing your job, receiving an unsatisfactory performance appraisal, or losing a loved one. Stress is also present when good things happen. When you get a promotion, meet the "perfect" mate, move to a new location after landing a new job, or even as an anticipated holiday approaches, various levels of stress will be present.

Not all stress is "bad." Some level of stress does, in fact, stimulate performance, as shown in Figure 13-1. Note that when there is little stress, performance is low; but when stress is present in appropriate amounts, performance increases. High stress levels, however, are counterproductive, and performance decreases. Therefore, both too little and too much stress are harmful in terms of employee performance.

Some occupations are more vulnerable to stress than others. The National Institute of Safety and Health (NIOSH) studied 23,300 workers in 130 different job categories and ranked the jobs according to their degree of stress. Figure 13-2 on page 393 lists the 12 jobs found to have the most stress, 28 additional jobs considered to be high-stress occupations, and 12 low-stress jobs.

Sources of Organizational Stress

The four major sources of organizational stress are (1) task demands, (2) role demands, (3) physical demands, and (4) interpersonal demands.[3]

Task demands are demands concerned with specific work activities that must be accomplished. Organizational stressors that result from task demands include:

occupational category (high-stress vs. low-stress jobs)

managerial jobs (when time and decision-making activities are restricted and managers are given little latitude in their activities)

career progress (major job changes or lack of career progress)

routine jobs (lack of variety, underutilization of skills)

boundary-spanning activities (working with other departments both within the organization and between organizations)

FIGURE 13-1 Stress and performance

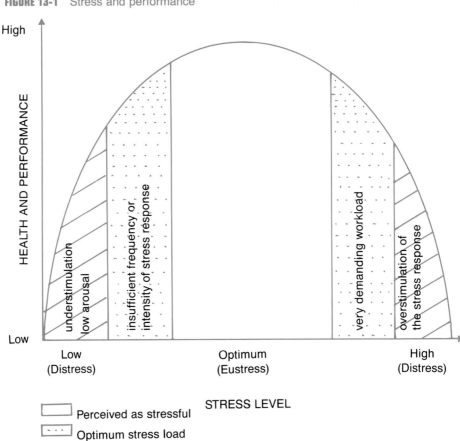

Source: James C. Quick and Jonathan D. Quick, *Organizational Stress and Preventive Management,* McGraw-Hill Book Company, New York, 1984, p. 154.

negative performance-appraisal feedback (negative feedback that must be given and received; see Chapter 9)

work overload (too much work assigned; too little time)

job insecurity (especially in economic downturns)

Role demands are demands related to the behavior others expect of us as we fulfill our organizational roles. Organizational stressors resulting from role demands include:

role conflict (when a worker's perception of his or her role is in conflict with the expectations of others)

role ambiguity (when the worker has inadequate, unclear, or confusing information about what behaviors are expected)

FIGURE 13-2

HIGH-STRESS, LOW STRESS OCCUPATIONS

WHERE THE PRESSURE BUILDS UP
From a ranking of 130 occupations by the federal government's National Institute for Occupational Safety and Health

12 Jobs with Most Stress	*Other High-Stress Jobs* (in alphabetical order)	*12 Low-Stress Jobs* (in order of increasing stress)
1. laborer	1. bank teller	1. clothing sewer
2. secretary	2. clergyman	2. checker, examiner
3. inspector	3. computer programmer	3. stock handler
4. clinical lab technician	4. dental assistant	4. craft worker
5. office manager	5. electrician	5. maid
6. foreperson	6. firefighter	6. farm laborer
7. manager/administrator	7. guard/watchman	7. heavy-equipment opera-tor
8. waitress/waiter	8. hairdresser	8. freight handler
9. machine operator	9. health aide	9. child-care worker
10. farm owner	10. health technician	10. package wrapper
11. miner	11. machinist	11. college professor
12. painter	12. meat cutter	12. personnel worker
	13. mechanic	
	14. musician	
	15. nurses' aide	
	16. plumber	
	17. police officer	
	18. practical nurse	
	19. public-relations person	
	20. railroad switchman	
	21. registered nurse	
	22. sales manager	
	23. sales representative	
	24. social worker	
	25. structural-metal worker	
	26. teachers' aide	
	27. telephone operator	
	28. warehouse worker	

Note: Based on death rates and admittance rates to hospitals and mental-health facilities in Tennessee.

Source: "How to Deal with Stress on the Job," *U.S. News and World Report,* Mar. 13, 1978, p. 80. Copyright, 1978, U.S. News & World Report.

Physical demands are demands that emanate from the physical environment in which we work (see Chapter 7). Organizational stressors related to physical demands include:

temperature extremes (too hot or too cold)

illumination and other rays (not adapted to the needs of the particular job)

sound waves and vibrations (excessive noise and vibration)

office design (settings that do not serve the basic office functions; see Chapters 7 and 16)

Interpersonal demands are demands concerned with the normal course of social, personal, and working relationships found in the organization. Organizational stressors resulting from interpersonal demands include:

status incongruence (actual status and personal expectations do not agree)

social density (too much or too little closeness)

abrasive personalities

leadership styles of supervisors

group pressures

Competency Check:

Can you identify the four sources of organizational stress and cite several stressors within each source?

Strategies for dealing with each of these organizational stressors will be discussed in another section of this chapter.

According to Ken Pelletier in *Healthy People in Unhealthy Places,* certain sources of stress are more common to managers, while other sources are more common to secretaries, computer terminal operators, and blue-collar workers. Figure 13-3 lists the sources of stress for each of these categories.

In some cases, managers and white- and blue-collar workers share the same stressors. There are different stress sources at different levels of the organization for different people.

Measures of Stress

How can supervisors determine that stress is present in the workplace? As DuBois observed in the opening case, sometimes employees exhibit observable behavioral changes for no apparent reason. The changes in behaviors may be the result of stress — worker reaction to stressors on the job.

An increase in tardiness or absenteeism, a rise in the number of grievances filed, an increase in the rate and severity of work-related accidents, a rise in interdepartmental transfers, an increase in employee turnover, or a change in the performance of specific profit centers may be an indication of abnormal levels of stress. In 1984 alone, stress was responsible for 132 million lost workdays.[4] Of course, behavioral

FIGURE 13-3

CAUSES OF STRESS FOR MANAGERS AND FOR
WHITE- AND BLUE-COLLAR WORKERS

MANAGERS	WHITE- AND BLUE-COLLAR WORKERS
work overload and excessive time demands and rush deadlines	work stagnation and helplessness
erratic work schedules and take-home work	erratic work schedules and frequently changing shifts
ambiguity regarding work tasks, territory, and role	rigidity regarding work tasks
constant change, daily variability	monotony; deadening, routinized stability
role conflict (with immediate superior)	too little contact or conflict
job instability and fear of unemployment	job instability and fear of unemployment
responsibility, especially for people	little responsibility or influence
negative competition (cutthroat, one-upmanship, zero-sum game, and hidden aggression)	no competition or stimulation
type of vigilance required in work assignments and team building toward goals	type of vigilance required in inherently stressful work (police, fire fighters, pilots)
ongoing contact with stress carriers (workaholics, passive-aggressive subordinates, anxious and indecisive individuals)	social isolation and lack of support
sexual harassment	sexual harassment
accelerated recognition for achievement (Peter principle)	inadequate recognition for achievement
detrimental environmental conditions of lighting, ventilation, noise, and personal privacy	detrimental environmental conditions of lighting, ventilation, noise, and personal privacy

Source: Kenneth Pelletier, *Healthy People in Unhealthy Places,* Delacorte Press/Seymour Lawrence, New York, 1984, pp. 44–45.

changes may indicate problems other than employee stress. However, the presence of any of these behavioral changes should trigger an investigation into the possible causes.

There are also some objective measures that may be used to identify the existence of stressors. Questionnaires or diagnostic surveys such as the one shown in Figure 13-4 on page 396 may be administered. This survey not only measures the presence of stress but also isolates specific individual stressors by categories. Each item in the

FIGURE 13-4

STRESS DIAGNOSTIC SURVEY©

The following questionnaire is designed to provide you with an indication of the extent to which various individual level stressors are sources of stress to you. For each item you should indicate the frequency with which the condition described is a source of stress. Next to each item write the appropriate number (1–7) which best describes how frequently the condition is a source of stress.

Write *1* if the condition described is *never* a source of stress.
Write 2 if it is *rarely* a source of stress.
Write 3 if it is *occasionally* a source of stress.
Write 4 if it is *sometimes* a source of stress.
Write 5 if it is *often* a source of stress.
Write 6 if it is *usually* a source of stress.
Write 7 if it is *always* a source of stress.

ANSWER

1. My job duties and work objectives are unclear to me. _____
2. I work on unnecessary tasks or projects. _____
3. I have to take work home in the evenings or on weekends to stay caught up. _____
4. The demands for work quality made upon me are unreasonable. _____
5. I lack the proper opportunities to advance in this organization. _____
6. I am held accountable for the development of other employees. _____
7. I am unclear about whom I report to and/or who reports to me. _____
8. I get caught in the middle between my supervisors and my subordinates. _____
9. I spend too much time in unimportant meetings that take me away from my work. _____
10. My assigned tasks are sometimes too difficult and/or complex. _____
11. If I want to get promoted, I have to look for a job with another organization. _____
12. I am responsible for counseling with my subordinates and/or helping them solve their problems. _____
13. I lack the authority to carry out my job responsibilities. _____
14. The formal chain of command is not adhered to. _____
15. I am responsible for an almost unmanageable number of projects or assignments at the same time. _____
16. Tasks seem to be getting more and more complex. _____
17. I am hurting my career progress by staying with this organization. _____
18. I take action or make decisions that affect the safety or well-being of others. _____
19. I do not fully understand what is expected of me. _____
20. I do things on the job that are accepted by one person and not by others. _____
21. I simply have more work to do than can be done in an ordinary day. _____
22. The organization expects more of me than my skills and/or abilities provide. _____
23. I have few opportunities to grow and learn new knowledge and skills in my job. _____
24. My responsibilities in this organization are more for *people* than for *things*. _____
25. I do not understand the part my job plays in meeting overall organizational objectives. _____
26. I receive conflicting requests from two or more people. _____
27. I feel that I just don't have time to take an occasional break. _____
28. I have insufficient training and/or experience to discharge my duties properly. _____
29. I feel that I am at a standstill in my career. _____
30. I have responsibility for the future (careers) of others. _____

SCORING

Each item is associated with a specific individual level stressor. The item numbers and the appropriate categories are listed below. Add your responses for each item within each category to arrive at a total category score.

YOUR SCORE

Role Ambiguity: 1, 7, 13, 19, 25   ____ + ____ + ____ + ____ + ____ = _____
Role Conflict: 2, 8, 14, 20, 26   ____ + ____ + ____ + ____ + ____ = _____
Role Overload—Quantitative: 3, 9, 15, 21, 27   ____ + ____ + ____ + ____ + ____ = _____
Role Overload—Qualitative: 4, 10, 16, 22, 28   ____ + ____ + ____ + ____ + ____ = _____
Career Development: 5, 11, 17, 23, 29   ____ + ____ + ____ + ____ + ____ = _____
Responsibility for People: 6, 12, 18, 24, 30   ____ + ____ + ____ + ____ + ____ = _____

The significance of the total score in each of the stressor categories will, of course, vary from individual to individual. In general, however, the following guidelines may be used to provide a perspective for each score:

Total scores of less than 10 are indicators of low stress levels.

Total scores between 10 and 24 are indicative of moderate stress levels.

Total scores of 25 and greater are indicative of high stress levels.

Source: J. M. Ivancevich and M. T. Matteson, *Stress and Work: A Managerial Perspective,* Scott Foresman and Company, Glenview, Ill., 1980, p. 522.

30-item survey is associated with a specific stressor. The stressors identified are called *role ambiguity, role conflict, role overload (quantitative), role overload (qualitative), career development,* and *responsibility for people.*

Work performance may be affected by stressful events occurring primarily outside of the workplace. A life events scale (LES) used for studying the long-term effects of stress is shown in Figure 13-5 on page 398. The use of the LES as a measure of organizational stress levels is limited because only 7 of the 43 items in the scale are work-related, but it may be used to assess the general level of stress among a group of individuals and to predict the possibility that illness will result from the present stress levels. It should be noted that different people respond to stress in different ways, and the possibility of an individual's becoming ill as a result of stress levels will vary according to the coping skills each possesses. The LES does not, however, provide specific diagnostic information to guide organizations or individuals in their efforts to provide assistance.

A "stress card," a card that turns various colors according to the level of stress being experienced by the holder may be a fad, but many people are purchasing these credit card–sized measures of stress levels. Like the "mood rings" of the 1970s, these cards are chemically sensitive to body heat. The user places a thumb on an area of the card, which changes color to reflect stress level. The card turns black, red, green, or blue, depending on the user's body heat. Black indicates the highest level of stress and blue the greatest level of calm. Some of the card manufacturers have placed tips for controlling stress on the backs of the cards.

Competency Check:

Can you describe three measures of stress?

Strategies for Dealing with Stress

Stress can be dealt with on the organizational level, the supervisory level, or the individual level. We will examine each of these, with special emphasis on the organizational level. If the organization assumes a proactive leadership role, supervisors will be better able to exercise their skills to reduce stress within their own departments.

The organizational level.   You will recall that the sources of organizational stress are task demands, role demands, physical demands, and interpersonal demands. Organizations have a responsibility to respond to these demands on workers in an effort to reduce these stressors. Figure 13-6 on page 399 suggests some strategies for dealing with task and physical demands.

While strategies for dealing with task demands and physical demands primarily focus on reshaping the formal organization, strategies for dealing with role and interpersonal demands focus on both the formal and informal organization. Some of these strategies are shown in Figure 13-7 on page 400.

The supervisory level.   Supervisors have a responsibility and an obligation to implement company policy. Beyond that, however, there are some actions that supervisors can take to reduce stress within their departments. DuBois in the beginning of the

FIGURE 13-5 An example of a life events scale

THE LIFE CHANGE SCALE

Score Yourself on the Life Change Scale
What events have happened to you in the past 12 months?

Event Rank	Event Value	Happened (√)	Your Score	Life Event
1	100			Death of spouse
2	73			Divorce
3	65			Marital separation
4	63			Jail term
5	63			Death of close family member
6	53			Personal injury or illness
7	50			Marriage
8	47			Fired from job
9	45			Marital reconciliation
10	45			Retirement
11	44			Change in health of family member
12	40			Pregnancy
13	39			Sex difficulties
14	39			Gain of new family member
15	39			Business readjustment
16	38			Change in financial state
17	37			Death of a close friend
18	36			Change to different line of work
19	35			Change in number of arguments with spouse
20	31			Mortgage over $50,000
21	30			Foreclosure of mortgage or loan
22	29			Change in responsibilities at work
23	29			Son or daughter leaving home
24	29			Trouble with in-laws
25	28			Outstanding personal achievement
26	26			Wife begins or stops work
27	26			Begin or end school
28	25			Change in living conditions
29	24			Revision of personal habits
30	23			Trouble with boss
31	20			Change in work hours or conditions
32	20			Change in residence
33	20			Change in schools
34	19			Change in recreation
35	19			Change in church activities
36	18			Change in social activities
37	17			Mortgage or loan less than $50,000
38	16			Change in sleeping habits
39	15			Change in number of family get togethers
40	15			Change in eating habits
41	13			Vacation
42	12			Christmas
43	11			Minor violations of the law

This scale shows the relative weight that can be attributed to stress-producing situations. For example, the death of a spouse is a great deal more stress-producing than a change in sleeping habits. After you have added up your score, take a close look at it. If your score is high, you are under a lot of stress. Try to think of ways you could decrease your score. Circle those checked events over which you have some control. Consider the importance to you of exercising control over these events.

Source: Thomas H. Holmes and Monoru Masuda, "Psychosomatic Syndrome," *Psychology Today,* April 1972, p. 106.

FIGURE 13-6   Strategies for dealing with task and physical demands

TASK DEMANDS

Task Redesign

Redesigning jobs to improve the person-job fit and to increase the job incumbent's motivation level is one method of reducing stress caused by task demands. This redesign is accomplished by restructuring one or more of the core job dimensions (see Chapter 5).

Participative Management

Increasing worker participation gives employees greater amounts of discretion and autonomy by decentralizing decision making and increasing participation in the decision-making processes, thus reducing stress caused by lack of personal control over how a task is performed (see Chapter 16).

Flexible Work Schedules

Giving increased discretion over work time enhances individual worker control and discretion in the work environment, leading to reduced stress.

PHYSICAL DEMANDS

Design of Physical Settings

Properly designed physical work environments reduce stress levels and facilitate task accomplishment. Some possible alterations in the physical setting include

Structural changes

Points of entry and exit	Floor angles and elevations
Ceiling height and angle	Wall placement and height
Furniture, fixtures, and placements	Opening for vistas and lighting

Acoustical changes

Wall coverings, finishing, and insulation	Cushions and draperies
Ceiling coverings and finishing	Floor coverings and finishing
	Plants and natural additions

Lighting changes

Natural openings	Placement of artificial lights
Intensity of lighting	Color of interior furnishings

Source: Based on James C. Quick and Jonathan D. Quick, *Organizational Stress and Preventive Management,* McGraw-Hill Book Company, New York, 1984, p. 163. "Task Redesign": From R. W. Griffin, *Task Redesign: An Integrative Approach,* Scott-Foresman and Company, Glenview, Ill., 1982. "Participative Management": From R. Likert, *New Patterns of Management,* McGraw-Hill Book Company, New York, 1961. "Flexible Work Schedules": From S. Ronan, *Flexible Working Hours: An Innovation in the Quality of Work Life,* McGraw-Hill Book Company, New York, 1981.

chapter was concerned about Sharon's behavior and wondered if it was caused by stress on the job. Further, she wonders what, if anything, she could do to relieve stress within her department. DuBois might consider the following supervisory actions:

● Set well-defined objectives. Supervisors should be sure that their workers are fully aware of what is expected of them and what their responsibilities are. Su-

FIGURE 13-7 Strategies for dealing with role and interpersonal demands

ROLE DEMANDS

Role Analysis

Clarify individual work roles to reduce stress. A "role profile" may be developed based on the expectations of superiors, peers, subordinates, and other key people with whom the individual works. When the conflicts between these different expectations are resolved, the employee understands his or her role, and that role is in agreement with his or her role perception, stress is reduced.

Goal Setting

Identify individual's major areas of responsibility and specify performance goals in each area. Clarification of performance expectations and agreement between the individual and immediate supervisor reduces role stress and increases motivation.

INTERPERSONAL DEMANDS

Social Support

Giving emotional, informational, appraisal, and instrumental support needed by individual employees provides a buffer for the impact of stress.

Team Building

Confronting, working through, and resolving natural interpersonal conflicts that evolve within any work group provides a basis for effective team building.

Source: Based on James C. Quick and Jonathan D. Quick, *Organizational Stress and Preventive Management,* McGraw-Hill Book Company, New York, 1984, p. 188. "Role Analysis" and "Team Building": From W. L. French and C. H. Bell, Jr., *Organizational Development: Behavioral Science Interventions for Organizational Improvement,* 2d ed., Prentice-Hall, Englewood Cliffs, N.J., 1978. "Social Support": From J. S. House, *Work Stress and Social Support,* Addison-Wesley, Reading, Mass., 1981.

pervisors should also communicate clearly what kinds of work and work behaviors are rewarded.

● Have more clarity and consistency in policies. Supervisors should communicate to their employees what the policies mean and should be consistent and equitable in their application.

● Develop workers' individual talents as much as possible. Supervisors should help their employees feel important about what they do.

● When possible, even with production lines or routine clerical work, allow employees to make choices that will give them some control over their work environment.

● Define interoffice and interdepartmental relations so that workers are not confused about their roles within and outside of their departments.

● Establish a climate in which employees can meet their objectives without unnecessary conflict, distraction, and interruption.

● Give direct and immediate response to workers' concerns.

● Help employees sort out priorities and work within their comfort zones. Too light or too heavy a work load causes stress.

● Encourage use of company-sponsored exercise facilities. It is commonly accepted today that maintaining an appropriate level of exercise will help a worker to work off frustrations and thereby reduce stress.

The individual level.   Individuals must assume some responsibility for their own stress levels and for engaging in activities that will help reduce stress. Individuals might consider the following actions:

● Deal with the cause of the stress; ignoring the problem will not make it go away.
● Use time-management techniques to help avoid the stress caused by missing a deadline or having to redo work because of inaccuracies.
● Realize your limits, and plan around them; don't take on more than you can handle and still do a professional job. Learn to say no.
● Learn flexibility, and accept imperfection both in yourself and from those with whom you work.
● Talk out your troubles with someone you trust.
● Develop a positive attitude. There is some evidence that positive emotions help fight disease, while negative emotions produce or intensify illness.
● Learn to distance yourself. If you find yourself in a heated disagreement, stop and ask, ''Is this something worth fighting for?'' Act accordingly.
● Streamline your work procedures. Break big jobs down into small components that can be handled more easily.
● Don't fight the inevitable. Stand up for what you believe in, but recognize that there are some things that cannot be changed and must be accepted.

An example of an individual stress-management plan is shown in Figure 13-8 on page 402. Of course each individual will react to the different factors in different ways; therefore each stress management plan must be tailored to the individual.

Competency Check:

Can you describe several actions that organizations, supervisors, and individuals can take to reduce employees' job-related stress?

WHAT CAN THE SUPERVISOR DO?

The supervisor can have a major impact on stress reduction in the workplace. In addition to the supervisory actions discussed above, there are other ways supervisors can personally affect stress levels within their departments. When the company offers stress-management programs, be the first to sign up, and encourage others to join you. Perhaps the most important action a supervisor can take is to get his or her own stress under control. A supervisor's stress level is easily picked up by employees and serves to reenforce and elevate employee stress.

We have said that certain levels of stress are healthy and promote greater productivity. The supervisor should recognize the appropriate stress level for the job (there's one stress level for rotating tires and another for playing professional tennis, for example). Among the skills needed by a supervisor is the ability to key the stress level to the demands of the job, retain worker interest, and keep productivity levels high.

One other action can be taken—the supervisor should keep his or her stress-mobile tuned up and in good running condition!

FIGURE 13-8 An example of an individual stress-management plan

STRESS MANAGEMENT PLAN

Name: *Jon Dickinson*   Date: *11-20-88*

Personal Perceptions of Stress   (1) *Practice constructive self-talk*

(2) *Learn to recognize the inevitable*

(3) _____

Personal Work Environment   (1) *Learn to say No! (nicely)*

(2) *Each day make a do list and daily plan*

(3) _____

Lifestyle Choices

   Leisure time use: (1) *Take an out-of-town 3-day weekend every 2 months*

   Other: (2) *Don't forget vacations*

Relaxation Method(s)   (1) *Practice progressive relaxation each evening*

(2) *Use momentary relaxation at work*

(3) _____

Physical Outlets   (1) *Jog 30 minutes every other day*

(2) *Tennis or golf each weekend*

(3) _____

Emotional Outlets   (1) *Take time to talk out work frustration with spouse*

(2) *Practice controlled expression of anger at supervisors*

(3) _____

Professional Help   (1) *None now*

(2) _____

Source: Joseph W. Kertesz, "Stress Management Plan," unpublished worksheet, Duke-Watts Family Medicine Center, Durham, N.C., 1982, in James C. Quick and Jonathan D. Quick, *Organizational Stress and Preventive Management,* McGraw-Hill Book Company, New York, 1984, p. 269.

Stressmobile

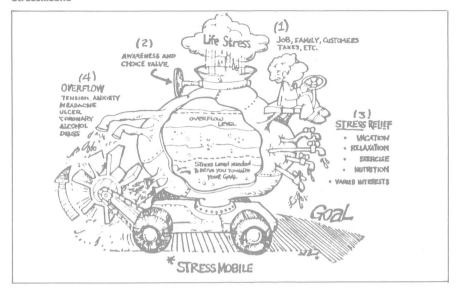

Source: Courtesy Marriott Corporation.

Burnout

Riley in the beginning of the chapter expressed concern that one of the workers in his department might be suffering from burnout. *Burnout* is a condition that results from unrelieved stress or too much of the same routine. As Jeffrey R. Davidson, author and consultant, says, "The labeling of the phenomenon of 'burnout' is a fairly recent happening. But the thing itself, being caught up in the day to day, losing sight of your mission or goal, and failing to pace yourself so your effectiveness falters all have been with us for a long time."[5]

Burnout tends to occur in individuals and professions characterized by a high degree of personal investment in work and high performance expectations. Workaholics may become victims of burnout. *Workaholic* is not a pejorative term; it describes a person who becomes totally immersed in work. It may be difficult to distinguish the workaholic from an employee who is merely a hard worker. Both the workaholic and the hard worker may benefit the organization in the sense that they both produce a great amount of work. However workaholics are, potentially, problem employees because they use work to avoid other problems in their lives. Eventually, these unresolved problems affect their productivity.

Burnout is like the common cold—no one is immune to it. Top executives, middle managers, supervisors, and operational personnel are all susceptible to "catching" burnout. And burnout may be contagious because one employee who is severely burned out can affect the morale of others. The problem of burnout is being recognized in many different industries. For example, Ken Jackson of Continental Telecom in

FIGURE 13-9

SYMPTOMS OF THE BURNOUT SYNDROME

1. early stages
    a. work performance
        - decline in efficiency
        - dampened initiative
        - diminished interest in work
        - progressively lessened ability to maintain work performance in times of stress
    b. physical condition
        - exhaustion, fatigue, run-down physical condition
        - headaches
        - gastrointestinal disturbances
        - weight loss
        - sleeplessness
        - shortness of breath
    c. behavior
        - changing or dampened moods
        - quickness to anger and increasing irritability
        - diminished frustration tolerance
        - suspiciousness
        - feelings of helplessness
        - increased levels of risk taking
2. later stages
    a. attempts at self-medication (tranquilizers, alcohol)
    b. increased rigidity (thinking becomes closed, attitudes become inflexible negativistic, or cynical)
    c. questioning of abilities of self, co-workers, and organization
    d. increase in time spent working with dramatic decline in productivity

Source: Adapted from Leonard Moss, *Management Stress,* copyright © 1981, by permission of Addison-Wesley Publishing Company, Inc., Reading, Mass. All rights reserved. Reprinted in James C. Quick and Jonathan D. Quick, *Organizational Stress and Preventive Management,* McGraw-Hill Book Company, New York, 1984.

Atlanta says, "The technology is changing, there are more demands, and the competitive nature of business means people are putting in longer hours." Another company acknowledging burnout is Food Lion, Inc., of Salisbury, N.C. Blake Bolick says, "All of us feel we have done more than one person can do. When people have been unable to deal with this, it has led to burnout."[6]

Burnout is characterized by chronic fatigue, low energy, irritability, and a negative attitude toward the job. Some symptoms appear in the early stages of burnout; others, in the later stages. Figure 13-9 lists the early symptoms of burnout as they affect work performance, physical condition, and behavior.

Burnout appears to manifest itself in these three stages:[7]

"Here's something for you. They're offering a free seminar on worker burnout!"

1. *Confusion*: In stage 1, burnout victims may have a vague feeling that something isn't going well, feel undefined anxiety, have many days they describe as ''dull'' or ''boring.'' They may complain of minor physical problems—headaches, mild insomnia, or fatigue. Managers will notice that the employee complains more about the job or co-workers, is dissatisfied with scheduling, requires more time to complete jobs, and, while not blatantly rude to customers, may not be friendly either. Many times, the behavior problem is written off as ''just a bad day.''

2. *Frustration*: In stage 2, confusion often turns to frustration and anger. The employee may complain about more specific physical ailments, but headaches and backaches become less severe while occasional fatigue becomes chronic. Employees may begin using or increase their use of alcohol or drugs, have more trouble with their co-workers, and experience feelings of isolation and power-lessness to change things. Open expression of a negative attitude toward the public and resentful and cynical comments about the job and life in general are common. Managers should be alert for increased absenteeism and tardiness, incomplete or inadequate work, signs of drug or alcohol abuse, a deteriorating personality characterized by loss of humor and constant sarcasm, complaints from other employees about the employee's uncooperativeness or decreasing productivity, carelessness, and possible dishonesty. This stage, like the first stage, is gradual. Watch for *trends* in an employee's behavior rather than iso-lated episodes. The behavior can no longer be written off as just a bad day.

Competency
Check:

Can you cite
reasons for burnout
and describe the
stages of burnout?

3. *Despair*: In stage 3, the employee suffers from extreme feelings of inadequacy. Sometimes the hostility has changed to apathy. The stage 3 burnout victim may lower the morale of all employees. He or she often appears indifferent but is actually on a ''short fuse,'' suffers serious personal problems outside the job, and adopts an ''I-don't-care'' attitude about the job and life in general.

Are you susceptible to burnout? Test your own burnout susceptibility by taking the test shown in Figure 13-10.

WHAT CAN THE SUPERVISOR DO?

Goodrich and Sherwood Company has developed a short, eight-question test that may be helpful in identifying someone with workaholic tendencies.[8] Supervisors should observe their employees to see whether the following characteristics are exhibited:

1. Does the employee appear to drive himself or herself to outlast or outperform fellow workers?
2. Does the employee show shifting work patterns so that he or she is working longer hours? Does he or she come in earlier or leave later?
3. Does the employee appear to have few outside interests or to spend less time on those interests than he or she used to?
4. Does the employee continually work on weekends?
5. Do others describe the person as ''overdemanding'' or ''unreasonable''?
6. If a manager, supervisor, or project leader, does the person call meetings on weekends?
7. Does the employee repeatedly indicate that he or she does more than his or her share or is continually sacrificing?
8. Has the person put on excessive weight, and does he or she find work-related reasons for failing to exercise or not having a better diet?

Keep in mind, however, that most employees, at one time or another, have periods of heavy work load. These periods should not be confused with the long-term excessive work patterns that characterize the true workaholic.

Other Mental and Emotional Health Problems

Employees may suffer from a variety of mental and emotional problems other than those resulting from stress and burnout. Some may be afraid, some may worry too much, some may have problems outside the workplace, and some may suffer from

FIGURE 13-10

BURNOUT SUSCEPTIBILITY TEST

Answer the questions using this scale and total the points. Strongly Agree = 3; Mildly Agree = 2; Mildly Disagree = 1; Strongly Disagree = 0.

Physical   **Score**

1. I usually feel fatigued and worn-out _____
2. I seldom get a full night's sleep _____
3. If awakened, it's difficult to fall asleep again _____
4. I exercise less than twice a week _____
5. I ride elevators and escalators rather than climb stairs _____
6. Most people would consider me a worrier _____
7. I don't have a burnout prevention plan _____
8. I seldom eat raw fruits or vegetables _____
9. I often eat sugar and refined foods _____
10. I am overweight _____
11. I add salt to my food without tasting it _____
12. I drink more than four cups of coffee/tea a day _____
13. I drink more than four soft drinks a day _____
14. I eat until I feel stuffed _____
15. I smoke more than ten cigarettes a day _____

Intellectual

16. I seldom introduce an innovation into my work _____
17. I seldom read a journal/book in my profession _____
18. I do not have a plan for intellectual relaxation _____
19. I seldom read anything besides the newspaper _____
20. I don't have a hobby _____
21. I don't express my feeling in any medium—art, music, dance, writing, etc. _____
22. I don't enjoy solving complex problems _____
23. I don't know who represents me in Congress _____
24. I don't keep abreast of current events _____
25. I seldom attend a workshop or professional meeting in my field _____
26. Two opposite opinions cannot both be correct _____
27. I don't know what parts of my job cause me stress _____
28. I can only think of one or two ways to combat stress at work _____
29. I think daydreaming is a waste of time _____
30. Problems at work have only one "best" answer _____

Emotional

31. I am certain of my beliefs _____
32. I am unhappy much of the time _____
33. I seldom compliment others _____
34. I do not approve of anger _____
35. I strike back if my feelings are hurt _____
36. I don't see much that is funny _____
37. I have sexual problems _____
38. I seldom cry and do not believe it is proper _____

39. I am overworked because I can't say no _____
40. I often find fault with myself _____
41. I have no colleagues at work with whom I share important feelings _____
42. I have no one to turn to if I have a personal problem _____
43. I have few interests outside my job _____
44. I am embarrassed by compliments _____
45. I often find fault with others _____

Social

46. I don't have any close friends _____
47. I seldom meet anyone I would like to know better _____
48. My relationships with family members are less than satisfactory _____
49. It is better not to become involved if I see a crime being committed _____
50. I am not liked by most people _____
51. I seldom go out with my family _____
52. I think drinking and driving is acceptable _____
53. I don't know my neighbors and don't care to _____
54. I make no efforts to conserve energy _____
55. I seldom have social relations with my coworkers _____
56. I seldom participate in community affairs _____
57. There are no causes or concerns to which I would contribute money or time _____
58. I think voting is a waste of time _____
59. I am uncomfortable in most social interactions _____
60. I am generally dissatisfied with my interactions with others _____

Spiritual

61. The future does not look promising to me _____
62. I don't think my work is important _____
63. I dislike being alone _____
64. I feel little obligation for the lives of others _____
65. I doubt that I can be a success _____
66. I often take sleeping pills or tranquilizers _____
67. I have more than two alcoholic drinks a day _____
68. I drink when I am depressed or nervous _____
69. I drink at lunch _____
70. I seldom like to do anything unless it is planned _____
71. I don't see much that is positive about life _____
72. I don't do my job especially well _____
73. I refuse to waste my time helping others _____
74. It is impossible to change the system _____
75. I no longer enjoy my work _____

                         Total _____

Source: I. David Welch, Donald C. Medeiros, and George A. Tate, *Beyond Burnout,* Prentice-Hall, Inc., Englewood Cliffs, N.J., 1982, pp. 273–275.

illnesses such as depression. Furthermore, any one of these mental and emotional problems may result in a physical problem.

Causes of Mental and Emotional Health Problems

The NIOSH study quoted previously (Figure 13-2) noted that machine-paced workers tend to have a high incidence of health breakdowns and emotional disorders. Those who work on rotating shifts report more ulcers, other digestive disorders, and sleeping and eating problems. It has been theorized that these workers are more susceptible to these disorders because they work in an environment where they have little or no control.[9]

Worry and fear are prime causes of mental and emotional health problems. Worry creates tensions that affect a worker's efficiency, mental well-being, and even physical well-being. Fear, worry, and anxiety are enemies of the mind.

What are people afraid of? What do they worry about? In a study of fears and anxieties experienced by American businesspeople by psychologists at the Illinois Institute of Psychology, researchers found that businesspeople were subject to 10 major fears.[10] Note that few of the fears and anxieties listed below are directly related to jobs or job performance.

1. *Financial*: 80 percent worried that they were going to lose money or not make enough money.
2. *Job security*: 74 percent worried about losing their jobs as a result of shake-ups, a falloff in business, interoffice politics, or competition from younger employees.
3. *Health*: 69 percent worried about real or imaginary ailments.
4. *Personal appearance*: 59 percent were fearful that their dress and manner were handicapping their chances of success.
5. *Politics*: Apprehensions and anxieties in this area, which affected 56 percent of the businesspeople polled, centered around government trends such as taxation.
6. *Marital difficulties*: 44 percent worried about incompatibility.
7. *Lack of self-confidence*: 40 percent feared they didn't have enough ''on the ball.''
8. *Religious and philosophical convictions*: 37 percent worried about what to believe.
9. *Sexual morality*: 34 percent were subject to worries and conflicts arising from temptations or actual transgressions.
10. *Trouble with relatives*: Anxieties in this area, which affected 33 percent, ranged from problems with a mother-in-law to problems with a husband's brother or problems with grandchildren.

Strategies for Dealing with Mental and Emotional Health Problems

Mental and emotional health problems are ''mind'' problems. To ease these problems, the worker must put his or her mind at ease and in a state over which he or she can exercise some control. Dealing with major mental and emotional problems is beyond the scope of this book. Anyone suffering from severe mental or emotional problems

FIGURE 13-11

WORRY CHART

things that never happen	40%
things that can't be changed by all of the worry in the world	35
things that turn out better than expected	15
petty, useless worries	8
legitimate worries	2
Total:	100%

The point: It's 50:1 against the worry being a real cause for concern.

Source: Secretaries Only, Executives Only, February 1980.

should seek professional help. However everyone worries, has fears, and suffers from anxieties from time to time. There are some techniques for dealing with this worrisome trio. First, it should be recognized that only a small portion of worries and fears ever come to fruition. Figure 13-11 shows that only 2 percent of our worries are legitimate.

Identify the things that are worrying you. Is it your work? Is it your boss? Your health? Write out the list, pinpointing each item. If the worry is your boss, what specifically worries you? Sometimes the fears are vague, with no basis in fact, or simply not as catastrophic as you imagined. After you have made your laundry list of worries, confront your worries by asking, ''What is the worst thing that can happen to me if this were to come true?'' Envision the worst possible consequences, and then think about how you would handle the situation. It all comes back to the mind again. This is why one person reacts to a failure by having a nervous breakdown, falling apart, and giving up, while another person learns from the mistake, decides how to fix it, and then goes about doing it. This person turns a failure into a success by managing the fears and anxieties—this person survives.

Competency Check:

Can you identify three ways to handle your own mental and emotional health problems?

RECOGNIZING EMPLOYEE NEEDS

DuBois and Riley in the beginning of the chapter used one of the methods of recognizing employee needs—observation. In addition to their own observations, supervisors may become aware of employee needs through surveys and diagnostic tests administered by the HR/P department, through a direct appeal from an individual employee, or through feedback from co-workers within the department.

Observation

As you go about your daily supervisory activities, you may notice symptoms of employee stress, burnout, or mental and emotional problems. Recall that DuBois said Sharon was reporting to work late, didn't follow the rules, and was surly and rude. DuBois had gained this information from her own observations.

As you read in Chapter 10, management-by-walking-around is a great way to get to know your workers better. Observing employees as they go about their jobs will give you an opportunity to observe their behavior without being intrusive. If workers are used to seeing you walk around, they are more apt to continue doing their jobs in their usual way when you are present. If, however, you enter their space only when there is a problem or when you are getting ready to complete the scheduled performance appraisals, the workers will not go about their tasks in their normal way. They will be more intent on impressing you than on doing their jobs.

Surveys and Diagnostic Tests

It is unlikely that you, as a supervisor, will decide to administer, on your own, any questionnaires or surveys relating to worker behavior or attitudes. This is usually the responsibility of the HR/P department. You may be asked, however, to administer a survey or a diagnostic test to the employees in your department as part of a companywide effort to gather information. If you are, your responsibility is to introduce the instrument to the employees, explain its purpose, gain their cooperation, and follow the instructions given to you by the HR/P department.

For an organization to gain any benefit from a survey or diagnostic test, the participants must take the activity seriously. As their supervisor, you must set an example by doing your part in a professional manner. ''Look, guys, the front office sent this questionnaire for you to fill out in your spare time. I know it's just another piece of busywork, but let's humor them. When you've finished, drop the thing on my desk.'' This is no way to introduce a questionnaire. Instead, be sure that everyone understands its purpose, understands that it will ultimately benefit both the organization and the workers, and understands that their input will be considered seriously. Convey the message that you are counting on them to respond openly and honestly to the questions. For the best response, a specific time (company time) should be set aside to complete the survey in a place that is relatively comfortable and quiet.

Direct Appeal

Sometimes an employee will make a direct appeal for help. This will happen only if workers feel free to talk to you and know, by your previous actions, that you are available to them and interested in their well-being. Employees must also be confident that anything they tell you will be kept in the strictest confidence and that you will never break that confidence without their permission.

Feedback from Co-Workers

Just as the employee who comes to you with a problem must believe that you are trustworthy and can keep a confidence, so must the co-worker who approaches you on behalf of a friend. The co-worker may feel, on the one hand, that his friend needs help. On the other hand, he may feel that he is "telling tales" and might be getting his friend in trouble if he approaches the supervisor. Assure the co-worker that you have a mutual interest in helping a valued employee, and encourage him to give you any information he feels comfortable sharing with you. You may not get the full story, but you will probably get enough of it so that you can make a judgment about how to proceed in your effort to help the employee.

Competency Check:

Can you cite three ways to identify employee needs?

WHAT CAN THE SUPERVISOR DO?

First of all, be an observant supervisor. Be aware of what is happening in the workplace, particularly of any changes in worker behavior. Develop a reputation for being a caring supervisor by displaying an interest in the well-being of all the workers you supervise.

Practice an open-door policy, and make workers aware that you are available when they need to see you. This does not mean that if you are in the middle of an important task with an immediate deadline, you have to drop everything to see a worker at the very moment he or she asks to see you. Unless the worker has a true emergency, you can explain that you are in the midst of an important project with a deadline that can't be changed but you will be free by, say, 2 P.M. and will clear your calendar so the two of you can spend whatever time is necessary to talk out the problem. To make workers feel at ease in coming to you and not like they are taking up your valuable time, you must learn to balance your own needs with those of the workers to the benefit of both.

PROVIDING ASSISTANCE

Supervisors can provide assistance to employees by counseling them or by referring them to counseling, to company-sponsored employee assistance programs (EAPs) or to outside sources of assistance. (See Chapter 7 for a discussion of EAPs as they relate to physical health programs.) When Riley and DuBois in the beginning of the chapter were discussing Sharon and Sam, each asked, in one way or another, "What can I do to help?"

Counseling

In trained hands, counseling is a powerful tool for helping employees deal with problems they encounter at work and problems outside the workplace that affect their ability to perform effectively on the job. Some say that counseling is an art. Fortunately, it is an art that can be learned. Many companies, realizing the importance of making counseling available to their employees, are providing counseling on two levels:

1. They are enrolling supervisors in counseling classes so that they will be able to counsel workers directly.
2. They are making counseling services available to the workers through professional counselors.

Supervisors should be trained before they attempt to counsel employees. Too often, well-meaning but untrained people do more harm than good when they try to counsel others. Irreparable harm can be done if a supervisor gives advice that is (1) uncalled-for, (2) inappropriate to the situation, or (3) of a clinical nature. Even good advice can be given in the wrong way.

A supervisor trained in counseling is the best person to counsel workers within his or her department. Employees know their supervisor, are comfortable talking with him or her, and realize that their supervisor is interested in their mental and emotional well-being.

Employee Assistance Programs (EAPs)

Employee assistance programs (EAPs) are company-sponsored programs directed toward improving the quality of work life of their employees. EAPs can assist employees in a variety of ways: by improving their physical fitness (as described in Chapter 7), by combating substance abuse, by controlling stress, by teaching them to deal with financial problems, and in a host of other ways. For example, Xerox's employee assistance program (XEAP) provides assistance to company employees and their families in areas such as marital counseling, substance abuse, and financial counseling.

Other companies have invested significant amounts of money to begin their EAPs. Kimberley-Clark's health management program began in 1977 with the stated goal of significantly reducing absenteeism, health-care costs, and cardiovascular risk factors within 10 years. Kimberly-Clark's program includes a physical fitness program; health education programs and activities including nutrition counseling, smoking control, exercises for low-back pain, and diet management; and a series under the heading of Self-Instruction Classes. Its employee assistance program has already helped 561 employees and family members at its corporate offices. Kimberly-Clark thought that with projected reductions in absenteeism and use of medical services, its EAP would break even in about 1987.[11]

Johnson and Johnson has instituted a "Live for Life" program. In an effort to evaluate the cost-effectiveness of the program, J&J is collecting data to determine:

- employee biometric changes (changes in blood lipids, blood pressure, body fat, weight, and maximum oxygen uptake).
- employee behavioral changes (changes in smoking, alcohol use, physical activity, nutrition, heart behavior patterns, job performance, and human relations).

● employee attitudinal changes (changes in general well-being, job satisfaction, company perception, and health attitudes).

A systematic cost-benefit study is possible because Johnson & Johnson is a self-insured company. Any substantial decrease in illness-care claims attributable to a health maintenance program will be of importance to both the employees and the company. Other measures to be analyzed are absenteeism, turnover rates, accident rates, and a host of employee and management attitudes toward themselves, their work, and one another.[12] Johnson & Johnson has already released significant, though preliminary, evaluation data. The results of a 1-year study showed increases in general well-being, improved morale and job satisfaction, and fewer sick days.

Supervisors should encourage employees to take advantage of company-sponsored employee assistance programs to help them become more physically, mentally, and emotionally healthy individuals. If the company studies cited above are any indication, healthy employees are more productive workers. As a supervisor, you should also take advantage of the programs offered.

Outside Groups or Agencies

Sometimes employees need assistance beyond that which is available in the workplace. Perhaps the problems are beyond the capability or expertise of the supervisor or even the company's professional counselor, if such a counselor is even available. Employee assistance programs may not be available when or where the worker needs them. In these situations, the supervisor should know about outside sources of assistance and should direct employees to them.

There are numerous governmental agencies and private groups that offer their services and assistance at no cost or for a nominal fee. Supervisors should try to maintain a list of local agencies or groups to which employees may be referred. In addition, many organizations offer booklets and pamphlets that offer assistance or provide information. For example, the Center for Medical Consumers and Health Care Information in New York offers publications as well as a free phone-in library called "Tel-Med." The Office of Health Information and Health Promotion and the National Health Information Clearinghouse, both in Washington, D.C., provide consumers with information. Supervisors should be aware of the many services offered by these outside agencies or groups and refer workers to them when appropriate.

Competency Check:

Can you describe three ways in which supervisors can provide assistance to employees with problems?

PRODUCTIVITY AND THE PSYCHOLOGICAL ENVIRONMENT

Individuals and organizations both suffer, although differently, in a poorly managed psychological environment. Although the individual consequences and the organizational consequences are different, the bottom line is the same—productivity losses occur. Refer to Chapter 16 for a discussion of the economic costs of low productivity and the relationship of quality of work life to worker and organizational productivity.

Individual Consequences

Competency Check:

Can you describe the three major categories of the individual consequences of an unmanaged psychological environment?

The individual consequences of an unmanaged psychological environment fall into three major categories: (1) behavioral consequences, (2) psychological consequences, and (3) medical consequences, as shown in Figure 13-12. It is obvious from a reading of this list that an unmanaged psychological environment will lead to a loss in worker productivity. Instead of being an asset to the company, workers become a liability unless the problem is addressed and strategies for dealing with it are implemented.

Organizational Consequences

Organizations, too, suffer the consequences of a poor psychological environment. The direct and indirect costs of a mismanaged psychological environment are listed in Figure 13-13. But let's put some dollar costs in the picture. Annually, for example, as a result of cardiovascular disease:

- 52 million workdays are lost.
- $700 million is spent to recruit and train replacements.
- From $500,000 to $1,000,000 is spent for a key-executive death.
- From $25,000 to $50,000 is spent for each nonfatal heart attack.

As a result of back pain, which affects 75 million Americans and is often due to lack of exercise and to stress:

- $1 billion in production costs is lost.
- $250 million is spent for workmen's compensation.

Competency Check:

Can you describe the consequences to the organization of a mismanaged psychological environment?

Headaches alone result in the loss of 124 million workdays. And individuals spend a total of $1.2 billion a year on headache remedies when simple muscle tension–release procedures would have been effective in most cases.[13]

Given these obviously costly consequences to both individuals and organizations, every effort should be made to provide a healthy psychological work environment. Employees benefit. Organizations benefit.

COMPETENCY REVIEW

1. Identify four sources of organizational stress, and cite several stressors within each source.
2. Describe three measures of stress.

FIGURE 13-12

INDIVIDUAL CONSEQUENCES OF AN UNMANAGED
PSYCHOLOGICAL ENVIRONMENT

BEHAVIORAL CONSEQUENCES	PSYCHOLOGICAL CONSEQUENCES	MEDICAL CONSEQUENCES
smoking	family problems	heart disease and stroke
alcohol abuse	sleep disturbances	backache and arthritis
drug abuse	sexual dysfunction	ulcers
accidents	depression	headaches
violence	psychogenic disability	cancer
appetite disorders	burnout	diabetes
		cirrhosis
		lung disease
		skin disease

Source: James C. Quick and Jonathan D. Quick, *Organizational Stress and Preventative Management,* McGraw-Hill Book Company, New York, 1984, p. 301.

FIGURE 13-13

ORGANIZATIONAL CONSEQUENCES OF A MISMANAGED
PSYCHOLOGICAL ENVIRONMENT

DIRECT COSTS	INDIRECT COSTS
participation and membership	loss of vitality
absenteeism	low morale
tardiness	low motivation
strikes and work stoppages	dissatisfaction
turnover	communication breakdown
performance on the job	decline in frequency of contact
quality of productivity	distortion of messages
quantity of productivity	faculty decision making
grievances	
accidents	communication breakdown
unscheduled machine downtime and repair	impaired judgment
material and supply over utilization	quality of work relations
inventory shrinkages	
compensation awards	distrust
	disrespect
court-awarded	opportunity costs
workman's compensation	

Source: James C. Quick and Jonathan D. Quick, *Organizational Stress and Preventive Management,* McGraw-Hill Book Company, New York, 1984, p. 301.

3. Describe several actions that organizations, supervisors, and individuals can take to reduce employees' job-related stress.
4. Cite the reasons for burnout, and describe its stages.
5. Identify three ways to handle mental and emotional health problems.
6. Identify three methods of recognizing employee needs.
7. Describe three methods supervisors can use to offer assistance to employees.
8. Describe the individual consequences of an unmanaged psychological environment.
9. Describe the organizational consequences of a psychological environment that is mismanaged.

APPLICATIONS

1. Identify a current or past situation in your life or on your job that you believe to be stressful.
   a. Describe the situation.
   b. What was involved?
   c. Who was involved?
   d. How did you feel?
   e. What did you do or what are you doing about it?
   f. If it is a past event, would you handle the situation differently today? How? Why?

2. Does your workday include being overloaded with paperwork, scrambling to meet deadlines, rushing late to meetings, playing telephone tag, and even being reprimanded by your supervisor? Are you ever irritated with another employee but must not show your irritation? Do you ever attend a boring meeting in which you must appear to be alert? These kinds of problems can affect your health and well-being more than major crises, such as loss of your job. Job-related issues can cause worry which in turn can cause stress.

   Stress is a condition that results in a strain on one's mental, emotional, or physical being. Your ability to react logically is affected. Of course, some stress can be desirable by stimulating you to perform. But excessive stress can cause physical and emotional problems and can result in less than effective performance.

   What can you do about stress, particularly job stress? In this decision-making activity, you will complete three tests to determine whether you are experiencing stress and how you are coping with stress and will discuss the results with class members. The first two tests, developed by Dr. Perry London and Dr. Charles Spielberger, focus on personality traits and job stress, respectively. The first test, the Temper Test, measures anger as a personality trait. The second test, Job Stress Index, measures the level of stress in a job. The third test identifies methods that you use for coping with stress. You can avoid stress by seeking tasks that you are capable of performing, that you enjoy doing, and that others appreciate.
   a. Complete the Temper Test. Statements that people have used to describe themselves are given below. Read each statement and then circle the appropriate number to indicate how you generally feel. There are no right or wrong answers. Do not spend too much time on any one statement, but give the answer

that seems to describe how you generally feel. When completed, score your responses.

TEMPER TEST: ARE YOU STRESS-PRONE?

	ALMOST NEVER	SOMETIMES	OFTEN	ALMOST ALWAYS
1. I am quick-tempered.	1	2	3	4
2. I feel annoyed when I am not given recognition for doing good work.	1	2	3	4
3. I have a fiery temper.	1	2	3	4
4. I feel infuriated when I do a good job and get a poor evaluation.	1	2	3	4
5. I am a hotheaded person.	1	2	3	4
6. It makes me furious when I am criticized in front of others.	1	2	3	4
7. I get angry when I'm slowed down by the mistakes of others.	1	2	3	4
8. I fly off the handle.	1	2	3	4
9. When I get mad, I say nasty things.	1	2	3	4
10. When I get frustrated, I feel like hitting someone.	1	2	3	4
Total Points				

Source: Perry London and Charles Speilberger, "Job Stress, Hassles and Medical Risk," *American Health,* March–April 1983, pp. 58–63.

Add up the circled points (1–4) for each item to get your total score, somewhere between 10 and 40.

A man who scores 17, or a woman who scores 18, is just about average.

If you score below 13, you are well down in the safe zones, perhaps unresponsive to situations that provoke others. But a score above 20 means you may be a hothead—scoring higher than three-quarters of those tested.

b. Complete the Job Stress Index. This survey lists 10 job-related events that have been identified as stressful by employees working in different settings. Please read each item and circle the number that indicates the approximate number of times during the past month that you have been upset or bothered by each event. When completed, score your responses.

JOB STRESS INDEX: ARE YOU HASSLED?

	Number of Occurrences During the Past Month			
1. I have been bothered by fellow workers not doing their job.	0	1	2	3+
2. I've had inadequate support from my supervisor.	0	1	2	3+
3. I've had problems getting along with co-workers.	0	1	2	3+
4. I've had trouble getting along with my supervisor.	0	1	2	3+
5. I've felt pressed to make critical on-the-spot decisions.	0	1	2	3+
6. I've been bothered by the fact that there aren't enough people to handle the job.	0	1	2	3+
7. I've felt a lack of participation in policy decisions.	0	1	2	3+
8. I've been concerned about my inadequate salary.	0	1	2	3+
9. I've been troubled by a lack of recognition for good work.	0	1	2	3+
10. I've been frustrated by excessive paperwork.	0	1	2	3+

Total Points _____

Source: Perry London and Charles Speilberger, "Job Stress, Hassles and Medical Risk," *American Health,* March–April 1983, pp. 58–63.

To determine how your stress compares with other workers, add the points that you circled for each item (0–3). Your score will be between 0 and 30. Persons who score between 5 and 7 are about average in how often they experience job-related stress. If you score higher than 9, you may have cause for concern. At 4 or lower, you have a relatively nonstressful job.

If your score on the Temper Test is 20 or higher, and if your score on the Job Stress Index is higher than 9, a dangerous situation exists. Double-digit job stress indicates problems, especially if your personality runs high in irritability and temper. If your personality makes you anger-prone, you must avoid jobs that are high in petty aggravations.

c. How do you cope with stress? Here are some methods for coping with stress. Which methods do you use? Complete the checklist, Coping with Stress. When completed, score your responses.

COPING WITH STRESS

Y N **1.** When you are angry or upset, do you work off your stress by participating in physical activities, such as walking, running, swimming, playing tennis, working in the garden, and the like?

Y N **2.** Do you share your worries with someone whom you trust and respect, such as a friend, teacher, minister, or counselor?

Y N **3.** When problems become severe, do you seek a professional listener, such as a guidance counselor or a psychologist?

Y N **4.** Do you accept problems that you cannot change or accept them until you can change them?

Y N **5.** Do you get enough sleep and rest that increases your ability to deal with stress and that makes you less irritable?

Y N **6.** Do you balance your work with recreation?

Y N **7.** Do you concentrate more on others than on yourself, particularly when situations are stressful?

Y N **8.** Do you work on the most urgent tasks first rather than trying to tackle all of your tasks at the same time?

Y N **9.** Do you try to work with others rather than fighting or insisting that you are always right?

Y N **10.** When you are feeling depressed or sorry for yourself, do you seek the company of others?

Source: Eleanor Hollis Tedesco and Robert B. Mitchell, *Office Systems Decision Manual, Administrative Office Management, The Electronic Office,* John Wiley and Sons, Inc., New York, pp. 27–28, 1984.

Your answer to each question should be yes. Examine each question that you answered with a no. Can you use this suggestion to help you cope with stress?

d. After you have completed Temper Test: Are You Stress-Prone?, Job Stress Index: Are You Hassled?, and Coping with Stress, meet with four or five class members. Discuss how to cope with stress and how to avoid stress in your roles as student and as employee. Prepare a list of suggestions for coping with stress, suggestions that you and your group members can easily implement.

CASES

Case I: Where Did I Go Wrong?

DuBois continued to think about Sharon and to worry about her changed behavior. Because Sharon had once been such a productive member of the department, DuBois was anxious to see whether she could help her return to her former level of performance. "Maybe Sharon is suffering from stress and doesn't realize it," DuBois mused. "And maybe others are experiencing stress, too, but haven't reached Sharon's state yet and so their work hasn't been affected. I think I'll give a stress self-test to the whole department. That way I won't be singling Sharon out, and she won't think I'm picking on her."

The next day, DuBois told the workers she would like them to stay for a few minutes after work. She explained that she had a stress test for them to take that should only take about 10 minutes. "It's a self-scoring test," DuBois explained. "No one will see it but you, so you can be really truthful in your responses. The scoring is provided on the test. When you finish grading your own test, take it home with you and decide if you have a high stress level. If you do, come see me and we'll talk about it." (The test Dubois used is shown below.)

Be sure to answer every question, even if it does not seem to apply to you.

1 = almost always true of me   5 = never true of me

1. I eat at least one hot, balanced meal a day.   1 2 3 4 5
2. I get 7 to 8 hours of sleep at least four nights a week.   1 2 3 4 5
3. I give and receive affection regularly.   1 2 3 4 5
4. I have at least one relative within 50 miles on whom I can rely.   1 2 3 4 5
5. I exercise to the point of perspiration at least twice a week.   1 2 3 4 5
6. I limit myself to less than half a pack of cigarettes a day.   1 2 3 4 5
7. I take fewer than five alcoholic drinks a week.   1 2 3 4 5
8. I am the appropriate weight for my height.   1 2 3 4 5
9. I have an income adequate to meet my basic expenses.   1 2 3 4 5
10. I get strength from my religious beliefs.   1 2 3 4 5
11. I regularly attend club or social activities.   1 2 3 4 5
12. I have a network of friends and acquaintances.   1 2 3 4 5
13. I have one or more friends to confide in about personal matters.   1 2 3 4 5
14. I am in good health (including eyesight, hearing, teeth).   1 2 3 4 5
15. I am able to speak openly about my feelings when angry or worried.   1 2 3 4 5
16. I have regular conversations with the people I live with about domestic problems; for example, chores and money.   1 2 3 4 5
17. I do something for fun at least once a month.   1 2 3 4 5
18. I am able to organize my time effectively.   1 2 3 4 5
19. I drink fewer than three cups of coffee (or other caffeine-rich drinks) a day.   1 2 3 4 5
20. I take some quiet time for myself during the day.   1 2 3 4 5

To get your score, add up the figures and subtract 20. A score below 10 indicates excellent resistance to stress. A score over 30 indicates some vulnerability to stress. You are seriously vulnerable if your score is over 50.

You can make yourself less vulnerable by reviewing the items on which you scored 3 or higher and trying to modify them. Notice that nearly all of them describe situations and behaviors over which you have a great deal of control. Concentrate first on those that are easiest to change (for example, eating a hot, balanced meal daily and having fun at least once a week) before tackling those that seem more difficult.

Source: Lyle H. Miller and Alma Dell Smith, Boston University Medical Center.

By the end of the week, not one person had been in to see DuBois, not even Sharon. ''Where did I go wrong?'' DuBois asked herself.

1. Did DuBois ''go wrong''? Why, or why not?
2. Identify the mistakes DuBois made in her effort to help Sharon.
3. How could DuBois have approached Sharon in her effort to try to help her?

Case II: Take This Job and . . .

It is 5:30 P.M. on Friday. Everyone has gone home except David Levine. He rather enjoys the quiet in the warehouse, with the conveyors and forklifts standing silent. But today, Levine's mind is not on the peaceful environment; his attention is on a plan he has been thinking about for a long time—a plan to make ''his'' warehouse more efficient.

When Levine came to work as a stock clerk at Foxfire Industries, the company was a small, family-owned operation. Today, 10 years later, Foxfire is a public corporation and one of the largest manufacturers of airplane parts on the West Coast (the fifth largest in the country). Levine is supervisor of the warehouse, responsible for shipping and receiving.

Recently, David has heard, through the grapevine, that many of the 125 workers in the warehouse are disgruntled. Their work is routine and highly structured. The company has moved away from its family orientation to a strict policy of centralized authority at the top without clearly defining the roles of the employees below the middle strata.

Levine has noticed that there is little camaraderie among the workers. They don't seem to offer each other any support when things go wrong—and things seem to be going wrong a lot recently. The workers are curt with each other; they don't lend a hand when one person has an overload.

Levine squints to read his notes. ''This lighting is really bad; no wonder there are mistakes in routing—you can't read the labels. Maybe Jake was right when he complained about the noise, too.'' David puts his papers aside, picks up the newspaper, and slowly walks to the door.

1. What do you see as Levine's problem?
2. Referring to Figures 13-6 and 13-7, outline a plan for Levine's consideration.

REFERENCES

1. James C. Quick and Jonathan D. Quick, *Organizational Stress and Preventive Management,* McGraw-Hill Book Company, New York, 1984.

2. Ibid.

3. Ibid., p. 155.

4. S. R. Premeaux, R. Wayne Mondy, and Arthur Sharplin, "Stress and the First-Line Supervisor," *Supervisory Management,* July 1985, p. 37.

5. Jeffrey R. Davidson, in Michael J. Major, "Beating Burnout and Promoting Productivity." *Modern Office Technology,* June 1986, p. 66.

6. Michael J. Major, "Beating Burnout and Promoting Productivity," *Modern Office Technology,* June 1986, p. 63.

7. Jack Jones and Dennis Joy, paper written for London House, Inc., Park Ridge, Ill., in *Modern Office Technology,* June 1986, p. 66.

8. "Are You a Workaholic? Consultant Offers Test," Goodrich and Sherman Company, consultants, press release, Sept. 17, 1986.

9. National Institute of Safety and Health (NIOSH), in Adele Greenfield, "Take Pounds of Pressure Off: Reduce Corporate Stress," *Pace Magazine, Piedmont Airlines Inflight Magazine,* March/April 1984, p. 49.

10. Study of fears and anxieties of American businessmen conducted by psychologists at Illinois Institute of Psychology, in John E. Gibson, *How to Size Up People,* Carillon Books, 1977, p.

11. Kenneth Pelletier, *Healthy People in Unhealthy Places,* Delacorte Press/Seymour Lawrence, New York, 1984, p. 144.

12. Ibid., p. 147.

13. Greenfield, op. cit., p. 52.

SUGGESTED READINGS

Anderson, Rebecca Cogwell: "Promote Employee Health with On-Site Programs," *Office Systems '87,* July 1987.

Fitzgerald, Ernest A.: "The Blessings of Being Tense," *Pace Magazine, Piedmont Airlines Inflight Magazine,* June 1985.

McLean, Alan A.: *Work Stress,* Addison-Wesley Publishing Company, Inc., Reading, Mass.

14

TURNING PROBLEM EMPLOYEES INTO PRODUCTIVE WORKERS

14

TURNING PROBLEM EMPLOYEES INTO PRODUCTIVE WORKERS

COMPETENCIES

Studying this chapter will enable you to:

1. Recognize behavioral or attitudinal indicators that point to a potential problem employee.

2. Describe strategies for preventing undesirable behavior.

3. Describe methods for correcting undesirable behavior.

4. Describe a positive time and setting for a counseling session.

5. Cite pitfalls to avoid in counseling and suggest alternative actions.

6. Discuss special types of problems and suggest actions a supervisor might take to correct these problems.

7. Describe how immediate dismissal procedures differ from dismissal following progressive discipline.

8. Cite primary actions a supervisor should take to avoid legal problems as a result of employee termination.

CHAPTER OUTLINE

"**Y**ou've got to fire her," Jackie Hampton said as she stormed around the office. "She can't get along with anybody, and she doesn't do her share of the work. She's always making excuses for poor work, and today was the last straw. Do you know what she's done? She's been hiding her mistakes so no one knows the level of rejects she's been producing. And do you know how I found out?"

"No, Jackie, but sit down, have a cup of coffee, and let's discuss the problem. First, who's '*she*'? This is obviously an ongoing problem, so why don't we start from the beginning," said Mike South, Hampton's supervisor. Hampton has been acting foreman for the paint department of this toy manufacturer ever since Barbara Beasley began her maternity leave 2 months ago.

" 'She' is Suzanne Smith. She's been a real problem for a long time. Barbara was having trouble with her long before she went on leave. I'll sure be glad when Barbara comes back and the headaches are hers again."

"That's something we need to talk about, Jackie, because I just received a letter of resignation from Barbara."

RECOGNIZING PROBLEM EMPLOYEES

It is a rare supervisor who does not have a problem employee, and Hampton is no exception. She is experiencing the frustration associated with supervising employees whose work is less than satisfactory. Typically, unsatisfactory employees exhibit behavioral or attitudinal responses that are different from those shown by productive and motivated workers.

Behavioral and Attitudinal Indicators

Like the proverbial chicken and egg, it is hard to tell which comes first, the behavior or the attitude. Does the behavior cause a change in attitude, or does the change in attitude cause changed behavior? Because of the difficulty in answering this question, and the "blurring" that sometimes occurs when trying to differentiate actions associated with behavioral and attitudinal problems, the problems will be described here without attempting to differentiate between them.

Problem employees reported by managers include those with high lost-time rates, those who do not notify the supervisor when they must be late or absent, those who are continually late or chronically absent, and those who use drugs or alcohol. Other problem employees reported include those with above-average accident rates or safety violations and those with substandard quality and quantity of work. Managers also complain about insubordinate workers, those with "bad attitudes," gripers, gossipers, and those who, in other ways, damage group morale.[2]

"My own experience in dealing with thousands of managers in corporate-sponsored programs [on problem employees] suggests that about 90 percent of managers must deal with at least one problem employee at some time during the year," says Clayton V. Sherman.[3] A generally accepted estimate of the number of problem employees in the work force at any one time is approximately 10 percent, as shown in Figure 14-1. Of this 10 percent, approximately one-half are hard-core problem employees who will be very difficult to turn into productive workers. To avoid creating your *own* stress and subsequent behavioral, attitudinal, and motivational problems, you should recognize the fact that you may not be able to save everyone. Give it your best shot, and then expend your energy on employees who will benefit from your efforts. As one manager put it, "If Jesus Christ had Judas, and Washington had Benedict Arnold, I think you're entitled to at least one of these people."[4]

Competency Check:

Can you identify five behavioral or attitudinal indicators that should alert a supervisor to a potential problem employee?

"Mike and Monica are problem employees. I, on the other hand, am a challenge!"

Problem Employee or Problem Management?

Before labeling an employee a *problem,* consider the possibility that the root cause may be poor or ineffective management. One study found that about half of the employees labeled *problems* by their managers were victims of poor management.[5] These employees had not been adequately trained, had not been provided with counseling when they needed it, and had not received written warnings, as provided for by company policy. Also, some managers have neither the patience nor the ability to develop employees or to change their behavior.

FIGURE 14-1

Distribution of
problem employees

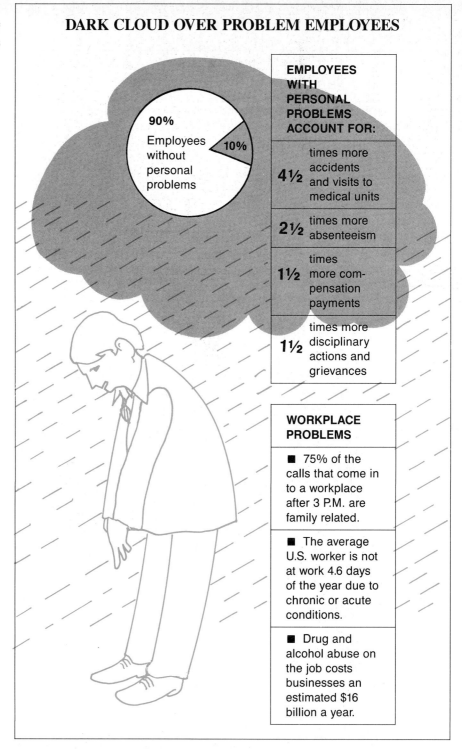

DARK CLOUD OVER PROBLEM EMPLOYEES

90%
Employees without personal problems

10%

EMPLOYEES WITH PERSONAL PROBLEMS ACCOUNT FOR:

4½	times more accidents and visits to medical units
2½	times more absenteeism
1½	times more com-pensation payments
1½	times more disciplinary actions and grievances

WORKPLACE PROBLEMS

■ 75% of the calls that come in to a workplace after 3 P.M. are family related.

■ The average U.S. worker is not at work 4.6 days of the year due to chronic or acute conditions.

■ Drug and alcohol abuse on the job costs businesses an estimated $16 billion a year.

Source: Article by Gordon Borrell, graphics by Judy Jordan-Valloria, *The Virginian Pilot and The Ledger Star,* Norfolk, February 9, 1986, p. E-1.

Some managers think they have a problem employee when, in reality, the employee simply has a different operating style. The outcome of this employee's efforts (productivity) may be acceptable; it is simply the process that is disturbing to the supervisor. Some examples of process concerns include the following:[6]

Physical appearance. Some supervisors prefer a particular type of dress and are disdainful of employees who lack what they consider to be "style consciousness." They should recognize that not all jobs require a clean-shaven face or a suit and tie. Even in jobs that do not require certain dress standards, employees who refuse to conform to the supervisor's perceived requirements are usually deemed *problems*.

Work hours. Some employees are more productive when they work outside the traditional work time. Biological clocks, family responsibilities, and personal preferences all affect an employee's productivity. If flexible work hours can be used to reduce tardiness or absenteeism, some problem employees can be turned around. See the discussion of flextime in Chapters 3 and 5.

Extra hours and weekends. Some supervisors find that they must work overtime and on weekends to catch up. If this is a regular pattern, perhaps the supervisor needs to evaluate the work habits that cause the overtime. In any event, these supervisors may equate extra work with high productivity and expect their subordinates to put in the same overtime. If they don't, these supervisors may perceive the employees as being insufficiently committed to their jobs—or "problem employees."

Participation in activities after work hours. Christmas parties, the July Fourth picnic, and "thank-God-it's-Friday" celebrations all contribute to group cohesiveness and morale. However, employees who choose not to participate should not be penalized or considered "problem employees" just because they are less social than others.

Differences in values, attitudes, and lifestyles. Supervisors may find themselves objecting to the lifestyles, attitudes, or values of the employees they supervise. Some supervisors have difficulty separating what employees do on the job—their productivity—from the opinions they express.

Demographic differences. While we like to think that we are free of bias, prejudice still exists. And where demographic differences occur (differences in age, sex, race, or ethnic origin), some supervisors may believe that it is associated in some way with the employee's ability to do the job.

WHAT CAN THE SUPERVISOR DO?

Supervisors need to be able to separate the *process* of work from the *outcome* of work. Can you do that? React to each of the statements given in Figure 14-2 on page 430 by writing a *P* in the blank if you think it is a process concern or an *O* if you think it is an outcome concern. You will find the answers to this questionnaire at the end of the chapter.

FIGURE 14-2 Process and outcome concerns

In the blank next to each statement, write a *P* if you think it's a process concern and an *O* if you think it's an outcome concern. After you finish, compare your answers to ours.

_____ 1. The employee has written a quarterly report that you feel is too long and disorganized. It needs to be rewritten.

_____ 2. You suspect that the employee has been dating another worker in your office. You're bothered by this, and you've been seriously considering confronting her with your suspicions.

_____ 3. The company vacation policy reads that "All employees shall take their vacations in segments of no less than five days." One of your people has objected strongly to this policy, and he's putting a lot of pressure on you to let him take his vacation days one at a time for a string of Mondays throughout the summer months.

_____ 4. You happen to overhear your receptionist speak rudely over the phone to someone who is obviously a customer. You are wondering whether you should speak to her about it.

_____ 5. The employee has made an arrangement with you to put his hours in on a flexible basis, some days working as few as three hours and others working as many as twelve or fourteen. You're beginning to find his schedule frustrating because you and several of your people are having difficulty reaching him when you need to have the answers to important questions.

_____ 6. The employee is an exceptional salesperson, but you know that she has a strong aversion to paperwork. She's failed to turn in three of the last five weekly progress reports, and you're beginning to get some pressure from your boss to get them in.

_____ 7. You strongly believe that neatness is an important part of high productivity. One of your account executives, who's been a consistently high producer, has an office that looks like it's been stirred with a stick. You're always teasing him about this, but he doesn't seem to take the hint. You're about ready to seriously suggest to him that he neaten the place up so he can be even more productive.

_____ 8. You have a younger person on your staff who frequently disagrees with positions you take. Her tendency to do this is especially strong at staff meetings. You're not bothered so much by what she says as you are by the tone in which she says it. You're about ready to speak to her about it.

_____ 9. Several months ago you instituted a policy in your office that calls for your employees to fill out forms indicating how they spent their time on an hourly basis for each week. One of your younger employees has said that he strongly objects to these forms and thinks they're a waste of his time. He's filled out the forms conscientiously for the first month, but now he refuses to do it. You're confused about how you should deal with his refusal.

_____ 10. One of the managers who works for you frequently conducts group working sessions with her staff. You have serious doubts about this approach to management and are seriously thinking of speaking to her about cutting down on the number of these work sessions.

Look on pages 460 and 461 and compare your answers to ours.

Source: Clayton V. Sherman, *From Losers to Winners: How to Manage Problem Employees . . . and What to Do If You Can't,* AMACOM, New York, 1987, p. 12.

PREVENTING UNDESIRABLE BEHAVIOR

The old adage has it that "An ounce of prevention is worth a pound of cure." Clearly, preventing problems is preferable to correcting them. Smith, the problem employee cited in the chapter opening, is beyond prevention, but perhaps she is not beyond correction. If Smith is to become a productive employee, corrective action rather than preventive measures must be taken.

Establish, Maintain, and Communicate Standards and Discipline Policies

One of the ways to prevent undesirable behavior is to be sure that each employee knows what is expected in terms of job performance (standards) and that workers are made aware of all company policies that directly or indirectly affect them.

What are some of the measures that might have been taken to prevent the behavior that Smith exhibits? Let's briefly review the actions that Hampton has identified as problems.

"She can't get along with anybody . . . "

" . . . she doesn't do her share of the work."

"She's always making excuses for poor work . . . "

"She's been hiding her mistakes so no one knows the level of rejects she's been producing."

Establish, Maintain, and Communicate Standards

Could any of Smith's undesirable behavior be a result of a lack of information about job expectations? Have standards of job performance for the paint department been set, and have those standards been communicated to all employees?

Hampton indicated that the trouble with Smith is not recent, that Beasley was having problems with Smith before she began her maternity leave: " . . . she doesn't do her share of the work." Perhaps no one told Smith what her share is; that is, Smith may not be aware of what is considered an acceptable output for her job. If she *was* told of the standards earlier, Hampton should have a counseling session with Smith to discuss the standards and her performance. Ignorance of job expectations can create problems just like the ones Smith is demonstrating by her behavior. Setting and maintaining standards is one of the topics in Chapter 15.

Establish, Maintain, and Communicate Discipline Policies

An effective discipline policy helps both managers and employees avoid substandard work practices.[7] A well-written and executed discipline policy lets employees know what is expected of them and what the consequences of their violating the policies will be.

Rodney P. Beary has suggested that you evaluate the effectiveness of your discipline policies and procedures by administering the questionnaire in Figure 14-3.[8] If you are less than satisfied with the results of the questionnaire, a review of your disciplinary program may be in order. The first step is to be sure that you have a clear policy on discipline. The policy should include the behavior that employees are expected to observe as a condition of continuing employment. The rules should cover all the usual practices that the firm considers important in the conduct of the job. There should be a general statement, too, that allows action to be taken for any negative behavior not specifically covered in the policy. Not every situation can be covered by a policy; the supervisor needs the discretion to take action when any inappropriate behavior is observed, whether that behavior is specifically defined in the company policy or not.

Management has a reasonable right to expect employees to be on time, to attend regularly, to give a fair day's work, to be physically and mentally able to perform the work assigned, to respond positively to direction, to learn the total job as well as any new jobs, to adjust to changes, to get along with fellow employees, and to know and observe the rules and procedures of the organization.[9] Of course this list is not inclusive. Other employee responsibilities are discussed in Chapter 17.

In addition, the supervisor must recognize that some policy violations are more serious than others—stealing is more serious than lateness, for example. This means that policies should specify whether violations are major or minor and that the con-

FIGURE 14-3   Identifying problem employees

1.	Substandard employees on the payroll?
2.	Excessive number of "nuisance" complaints?
3.	Backing off from discipline taken?
4.	Consistent enforcement of standards?
5.	Open publication of rules and regulations?
6.	Written documentation of specific critical incidents?
7.	Use of a progressive discipline procedure?
8.	Clearly established work standards?
9.	Complaints from employees about other employees?
10.	Poor bottom line results?

Source: Excerpted from Rodney P. Beary, "Discipline Policy—A Neglected Personnel Tool," *Administrative Management,* November 1985, p. 21. Copyright 1985 by Dalton Communications, Inc., New York.

sequences of violations will vary according to the seriousness of the offense. Serious offenses may include possession or use of illegal or intoxicating substances on company property, possession of an unauthorized weapon, theft, fighting, sabotage, gross negligence, and repeated insubordination. Less serious offenses—such as failure to follow directions, leaving the job without permission, minor safety-rule infractions, horseplay, gambling, absenteeism or tardiness, or failure to maintain work standards— may be handled by a progressive discipline approach (discussed later in this chapter). A sample policy on absenteeism and tardiness is shown in Figure 14-4 on page 434.

Merely having a discipline policy does not prevent negative employee behavior. The policy must be disseminated and clearly communicated to all employees by whatever means are available to the supervisors—via orientation meetings, bulletin boards, staff meetings, and so forth.

Clear standards, strictly maintained and communicated to employees, with specific policies for dealing with nonproductive or disruptive workers, discourage substandard work and increase morale and overall productivity.

Provide Ongoing Training

Hampton said Smith is "always making excuses for poor work," has "been hiding her mistakes so no one knows the level of rejects she's been producing," and "doesn't do her share of the work." Perhaps Smith really is a poor performer and the possibility of turning her into a superstar is slim. But let's not give up on her yet! Could it be possible that Smith does not know how to do her job and that is the reason she makes excuses for her work, doesn't do her share, and doesn't want to admit to the number of rejects she has? If this is the case, giving instruction on how to do the job would be appropriate. At this point, however, this constitutes corrective action.

Preventive action would include providing her with the necessary instruction, using one or more of the techniques described in Chapter 10, at the time she was employed. Sometimes, people are hired who do not have all the requisite skills or who have the aptitude for the job but do not yet possess the ability to do the job efficiently. Training is designed to overcome these deficiencies. When too little or inadequate training is provided, work performance is usually substandard. It is important to differentiate between employees who *can't* do and those who *won't* do. The "can't-do" worker benefits from training; the "won't-do" worker doesn't.

Create Awareness of Avenues of Personal Problem Solving

At some time in their employment lives, all employees have personal problems. Some are serious, some are less so, but all are important to the employees. If the firm does not provide a way for its employees to try to solve their problems, the problems will spill over into the workplace as workers seek their own solutions, often in ways unacceptable to the firm. For example, if a company does not offer any way for

FIGURE 14-4 Sample absenteeism and tardiness policy

Subject: Absenteeism and Tardiness

Purpose: To identify the proper procedures for reporting absences and ensure consistent and equitable treatment of absences, late arrivals, and early departures throughout the organization.

Guidelines:

1. All employees are expected to report to work as scheduled and to work their scheduled hours and required overtime. Employees will be charged with an absence occurrence when they fail to report for their scheduled work hours. Employees will be considered tardy and charged with a partial absence occurrence when they report to work more than 6 minutes past their scheduled starting time. Similarly, workers who leave early or extend authorized breaks past their official limits may be charged with a partial absence occurrence.

2. Absences for which employees will be charged with an occurrence include failures to report for such reasons as personal business, an illness or accident not involving hospitalization, or an emergency other than those, such as weather-related closings, officially recognized by the employer. Absences of several days duration will be treated as one occurrence. Absences that will not result in an occurrence charge include those involving jury or military duty, work-related injuries or illnesses, hospital confinement, and the use of authorized bereavement leave. The employer has the right to require workers to submit a doctor's note or undergo a physical examination to verify a claim of illness or injury.

3. Employees must notify their supervisor in advance when possible—and in no case later than 30 minutes after their starting time—of their inability to report for work as scheduled. If a supervisor cannot be reached, workers should inform the personnel office as soon as possible that they will not be able to show up for work. In providing this notification, employees should give a reason for their absence and an estimate of when they will return to work. Supervisors will maintain written records of employees' absences and tardiness, which will include the reasons given by employees for missing work.

4. Employees who are absent for three consecutive working days without notifying the employer are subject to termination as voluntary quits.

5. Once employees have accumulated a total of six occurrences in a 12-month period, their supervisor will discuss with them the reasons for their absences and the organization's need for regular attendance by all workers. The accumulation of two more occurrences within the 12-month period will result in an oral warning. The ninth occurrence will elicit a written warning; the 10th, a 3-day suspension; and the 11th, a 10-day suspension. Employees who are charged with 12 occurrences within a 12-month period will be subject to discharge. Supervisors will provide counseling at each step of this progressive procedure and will refer employees to outside sources of counseling and assistance for help in dealing with medical, physical, or personal difficulties related to their attendance problems.

6. Employees who have perfect attendance for a 1-month period (four consecutive workweeks) are entitled to have one occurrence expunged from their records. Workers who have perfect attendance for a 6-month period will be eligible for a $50 attendance bonus, while a 12-month perfect attendance record will earn employees an additional $100 bonus.

7. In dealing with attendance problems—especially those involving an illness or physical or mental incapacity to report for work—the employer will consider all the facts and circumstances of a particular case, including the employee's overall attendance and performance records, reasons for missing work, and prospects for future improvement and maintenance of an acceptable attendance record. The employer reserves the right to make exceptions to the disciplinary procedures outlined above in the interest of fairness.

8. This policy is effective immediately.

Source: The Bureau of National Affairs, Inc., 40:3, 1986.

employees to take care of personal business that cannot be conducted outside work hours, employees may call in sick rather than lose a day's pay. Stress management training, wellness programs, employee assistance programs, day-care centers, and other types of organizational support systems provide avenues for workers to solve their personal problems before the problems become workplace problems. Many of these support systems are described in Chapters 7 and 13.

Provide and Encourage Feedback

Feedback from supervisor to employee and from employee to supervisor opens lines of communication that may be conducive to identifying potential problems and preventing their occurrence. If workers feel free to ask their supervisor for assistance when they need it, or for tips for doing their work more efficiently, many problems may be prevented.

A supervisor who provides feedback to employees about their job performance also helps prevent problems. When employees are informed early on that their behavior or job performance is unacceptable and are given help in correcting the problem, troublesome situations may be avoided.

Maintain Equitable and Consistent Supervisory Actions

"She can't get along with anybody" is another of Hampton's characterizations of Smith. Smith may say that "Jackie doesn't treat me the same way she treats everybody else. She just doesn't like me, and I can't do anything that pleases her."

One of the outcomes of equitable and consistent supervisory actions is that workers perceive that their supervisors are being fair and that any action taken, whether positive or negative, will be the same, regardless of who the worker is. Employees tend to be less dissatisfied and to exhibit less undesirable behavior in an atmosphere of fair and consistent supervisory treatment. Refer to Chapter 11 for a detailed discussion of motivation theories.

Competency Check:

Can you describe four strategies for preventing undesirable employee behavior?

CORRECTING UNDESIRABLE BEHAVIOR

While it is desirable to prevent unwanted behavior, it is not always possible to do so. Sometimes it is necessary to correct undesirable behavior through disciplinary measures. The purpose of employee discipline is to correct undesirable behavior. This assumes that the employee is well-intentioned and willing to change when shown the correct course of action.

Progressive Discipline

Many firms have adopted a policy of *progressive discipline,* a policy that imposes increasingly severe penalties as violations are repeated. The steps in a progressive discipline policy may range from three to five levels of severity, with correspondingly severe penalties. A typical five-step system would follow these steps:

1. *Verbal reprimand.* On the first occasion of substandard work or violation of a work rule, the employee is given a verbal warning. Nothing is put in writing in the employee's record, but he or she is told that the offense should not be repeated.
2. *Written reprimand.* On the second occasion of substandard work or violation of a work rule, the employee is notified in writing, with a copy put into the employee's work record.
3. *Second written reprimand.* On the third violation, the employee is issued a second written reprimand, which is also placed into the employee's work record.
4. *Suspension.* On the occasion of the fourth work violation, the employee is placed on suspension, usually for a period of from 1 to 3 days.
5. *Discharge.* The fifth repeated violation brings immediate discharge.

Organizations which elect the three-step progressive discipline policy shorten the chain of events by giving a verbal warning, followed by one written reprimand, and finally suspension or discharge.[10]

Figure 14-5 on pages 438–439 shows the usual disciplinary action by a hospital using progressive discipline. Note that the disciplinary action depends on both the type of offense and whether it was the first, second, or third offense.

"Hot Stove" Rule

Douglas MacGregor, who is credited with the theory X, theory Y perceptions of employee behavior (refer to Chapter 11), is also credited with the "hot stove" analogy to disciplinary action. The analogy equates touching a red-hot stove with experiencing disciplinary action. When one touches a hot stove, the reaction is immediate, there was warning, and the result is both consistent and impersonal. Similarly, disciplinary action should be immediate, with warning, consistent, and impersonal (directed toward the act and not against the person).

Immediate

When an employee violates a work rule, whether related to job performance or behavior, the result of that violation should be immediate—just as the result of touching a hot stove is immediate. If the violation calls for immediate dismissal (assuming all facts are known and all disciplinary procedures have been followed), then the employee should be dismissed immediately and required to leave the premises, escorted if necessary. If the violation calls for a verbal warning, then that should be given as immediately after the act as possible, and given privately. In some cases, all facts are not known, and the appropriate action may be temporary suspension. Later, when the investigation is complete, if the recommendation is that disciplinary action was not warranted, then the employee should be returned to the job with back pay and all privileges restored.

With Warning

Does a red-hot stove give a warning, "If you touch me, you're going to be burned"? Of course. Employees should be aware that if they violate company policy, standards, or rules, they will be disciplined. Warning can be provided through posted rules, supervisory information, policy handbooks, orientation, and other types of communication.

What about a policy that has been in existence and clearly communicated to employees at the time of employment but has never been enforced? For example, there may be a policy requiring workers in a particular construction area to wear safety shoes but the supervisors have given tacit approval to not wearing safety shoes by ignoring those who chose not to wear them. Let's assume that a new manager is employed and this manager believes strongly that safety precautions are important. She communicates to the supervisors that from now on, all safety rules will be strictly enforced. The supervisors have an obligation to warn their employees that while the safety-shoe rule has been on the books but heretofore not strictly enforced, from this day on, noncompliance will bring about disciplinary action.

Consistent

When a hot stove is touched, one is burned—the stove is consistent no matter who touches it or when it is touched. Discipline should be administered with the same consistency. Consistency in discipline means that all violations will receive the prescribed disciplinary action. Consistency does not necessarily mean, however, that everyone will receive the exact same measure of discipline. Individual circumstances must be considered before discipline is administered. For example, one employee has a record of arriving late to work and has been previously warned about tardiness and its consequences. Another employee who could always be depended on to be at work on time—even early—has been late twice this week due to a family emergency. The penalty should be different for the two workers, based on the previous work record. This inconsistency in a rule of consistency can also be related to the hot stove. Someone who touches a hot stove repeatedly will receive a more serious burn than will the person who touches the stove only once.

Impersonal

A hot stove isn't selective about whom it burns. The stove doesn't care if you are the one who shined it last week or if you are the one who burned the peas on its surface. The hot stove punishes *the act of touching*.

FIGURE 14-5

USUAL DISCIPLINARY ACTION

OFFENSE	Disciplinary Action		
	FIRST	SECOND	THIRD
repeated tardiness, absenteeism, and abuse of lost-time privileges	VW or WR	WR or D	D
discourteous treatment of patients, visitors, or other personnel	VW, WR, or D	WR or D	D
insubordination (refusal to follow instructions or accept job assignments from a supervisor or properly designated hospital authority)	VW, WR, or D	WR or D	D
late call (failure to call in on time when unable to report for duty as scheduled)	VW	WR	D
incompetent performance of duties or neglect of duty	VW, WR, or D	WR or D	D
evidence of possession of liquor or drug-substance abuse	WR or D	D	
theft, regardless of value	WR or D	D	
conduct endangering the life, safety, or health of others			
deliberate or willful	WR or D	D	
careless or negligent	VW, WR, or D	WR or D	D
possession of unauthorized weapons on hospital premises	WR or D	D	
failure to respect the confidential nature of hospital records and information about patients	WR or D	D	
altering, removing, damaging, destroying, or improperly using hospital property			
negligent	VW, WR, or D	WR or D	D
deliberate	WR or D	D	
malicious gossip about any employee, patient, physician, or hospital representative	VW	WR	D
dishonesty, including falsification or omission of any information pertaining to personal or business records, employment applications, and information on physical and mental condition	WR or D	D	

FIGURE 14-5

(Continued)

| | Disciplinary Action | | |
OFFENSE	FIRST	SECOND	THIRD
accepting monetary tips	VW or WR	D	
violation of parking policies (after three citations)	WR	Final WR	D
solicitation: Employees are not permitted to solicit for donations or to sell any item to others (authorized functions would not apply).	VW or WR	WR or D	D
false recording of hours worked; falsification of or tampering with time cards	WR or D	D	
leaving the premises or unauthorized absence from the work unit during a scheduled working day without permission of supervisor	WR	D	
immoral or unprofessional conduct	WR or D	D	
inability to work with others	VW	WR	D
persistently uncooperative behavior	VW	WR	D
failure to maintain a professional appearance	VW	WR	D
sleeping on duty	WR	D	
gambling on duty	WR	D	
personal phone calls	VW	WR	D
refusal to work overtime in an emergency situation without sufficient cause	VW or WR	WR or D	D
sexual harassment	WR or D	D	

The above list of offenses is not intended to be all-inclusive.

Source: Clayton V. Sherman, *Losers to Winners: How to Manage Problem Employees . . . and What to Do If You Can't,* AMACOM, New York, 1987, pp. 118–119.

Key: VW = Verbal warning
        WR = Written reprimand or probation
          D = Discharge

Discipline should also be impersonal, based on the current violation and applied against the *act*. It should not depend on the supervisor's personal feelings about the employee. It should also be applied without resentment toward the employee who has been disciplined. Impersonal discipline means that the *behavior* is undesirable, not the person. If Hampton approaches Smith by saying, ''You are irresponsible. You cannot be depended on to do your share of the work,'' then she is attacking Smith rather than Smith's behavior. A better, less personal way to approach her is to say, ''The work standard calls for each worker on the paint line to complete 25 toys per hour, or a total of 200 toys per workday. The last count at your station showed only 15 toys per hour, or 120 toys per workday. Is there a problem that I can help you with?'' This approach focuses on the behavior, not on the person, and also offers assistance.

Disciplinary action can be overturned if not properly conducted. When any of the following conditions existed, previous court and arbitration rulings have overturned the disciplinary penalty:[11]

Insufficient evidence.   When there were no witnesses, no production records, and no lost-time records, the supervisory action was overturned.

Inadequate warning.   When there was no policy, the policy was not publicized, and the employee received no warning that there was a violation of a rule prior to the penalty being imposed, courts ruled that the warnings were either nonexistent or inadequate.

Too severe punishment.   When the penalty did not fit the offense, the disciplinary action involved a first offense, and the worker had an otherwise good work record, courts did not respond favorably to the organization administering the penalty. When the organization did not have a progressive discipline policy (that is, it went directly to suspension or discharge without due process), courts exhibited an unwillingness to support the firm's actions.

Actions based on prejudice.   Prejudice rears its ugly head in many guises. Prejudice and bias are not limited to issues such as sex, age, race, religion, and national origin. They may also include unwarranted preferences for educational or experience levels, physical appearance, or attitudes and values. Any act of discrimination places the supervisor's recommendations for discipline in jeopardy.

No clear-cut violation of policy.   If a policy did not specifically prohibit the action for which the employee was penalized, it is difficult to persuade the courts to uphold the disciplinary action.

Inadequate documentation.   A supervisor who hopes to uphold a penalty imposed for substandard work performance or for poor attitudes affecting the employee's performance or the performance of other members of the group must have *documentation* (written evidence) to show that the discipline was justified. Unable to produce documentation, the supervisor may find that the case is considered suspect.

Nonpunitive Discipline

Nonpunitive discipline is discipline without punishment. This more contemporary approach encourages a disciplined work force by recognizing that workers themselves must be the real source of discipline and by reinforcing self-discipline.[12]

The traditional disciplinary system assumes that all violations must be punished and that the supervisor must be sure that the punishment fits the crime. Proponents of nonpunitive discipline feel that the traditional system forces the supervisor to play the "heavy" and wear a black hat. According to the traditional approach, supervisors are supposed to monitor workers, note the black marks in their records, and ultimately build a case for dismissal, if that is appropriate.

Like progressive discipline, nonpunitive discipline follows a series of steps. The difference is in the approach. These steps are as follows:[13]

- *Oral reminder*. An oral reminder is given to the employee in a private meeting between the supervisor and the employee. The purpose of the meeting is to gain the employee's agreement to solve the problem. Instead of warning the employee of the consequences if the offense is repeated, the employee is reminded that he or she has a personal responsibility to meet reasonable standards of performance and conduct. Documentation of the meeting is made in a working file only.
- *Written reminder*. If the problem continues, the supervisor and employee meet again. The supervisor reviews the good business reasons for the desirable behavior, discusses, without threats, the employee's failure to abide by the original agreement, and, through counseling, again gains the employee's agreement to solve the problem. Together, the supervisor and employee create an action plan, which is then summarized in a memo to the employee with a copy placed in the employee's personnel file. Note the difference between "warnings" of future consequences and "reminders" that restate the need for the rule and the individual's responsibility to abide by the rule. Figure 14-6 summarizes the differences between warnings and reminders.

FIGURE 14-6 WARNINGS VS. REMINDERS

	WARNINGS	REMINDERS
timing	before the conversation	after the conversation
focus	next step	individual responsibility
purpose	threaten further negative consequences	remind employee of performance standard
time perspective	past	future
responsibility for action	supervisor	employee
supervisor's role	judge	coach

Source: David N. Campbell, R. L. Fleming, and Richard C. Grote, "Discipline Without Punishment—At Last," *Harvard Business Review*, July–August 1985, p. 169.

● *Further action.* If the above steps are ineffective in correcting the behavior, the employee may be placed on a 1-day paid decision-making leave. The company pays the employee for this day, with the understanding that she or he will return on the following day either to make a total commitment to the job and to change the undesirable behavior or to quit and find another job that will be more in keeping with his or her philosophy. The employee does not begin work immediately on returning to the work site. First, there is a meeting with the supervisor to announce the decision. If the decision is to stay, the supervisor and employee set specific goals and develop an action plan and a timetable. The employee clearly understands that if a change is not made and the requirements of the action plan not met, the result will be termination.

*Competency
Check:*

Can you describe
three methods of
correcting
undesirable
behavior?

According to its proponents (John Huberman, David Campbell, R. L. Fleming, Richard Grote, and others), nonpunitive discipline, properly implemented, is successful in terms of retaining potentially good employees and reducing turnover, disciplinary incidents, grievances, and sick leave. These benefits are shown in Figure 14-7, along with the company experiencing the benefits.

WHAT CAN THE SUPERVISOR DO?

When employees exhibit performance or behavioral problems, using a uniform method of recording the incident is helpful. Figures 14-8 and 14-9 on pages 444 and 445 show two forms used to differentiate performance violations from behavioral misconduct. A uniform format allows the same type of information to be recorded regardless of who the person is.

COUNSELING EMPLOYEES WITH SPECIAL PROBLEMS

Employees with special problems require counseling. The counseling may be provided by the supervisor, if she or he is trained in counseling, or it may be provided by counseling professionals. As noted in Chapter 13, before supervisors attempt to counsel employees for any reason, they should be knowledgeable in counseling methods. Too much damage can be done when untrained persons try to counsel troubled employees.

Counseling Techniques

Assuming that the supervisor understands counseling methods, the techniques described here will make the counseling sessions more effective.

Plan your timing, setting, and opening. Meet with the employee as soon as possible following the infraction. The best time to meet is early in the shift and early in the workweek. If you wait until just before the worker's shift is over, you will both be

FIGURE 14-7   Benefits of nonpunitive systems

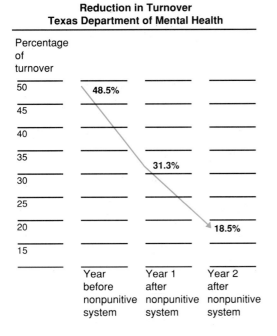

Reduction in Turnover
Texas Department of Mental Health

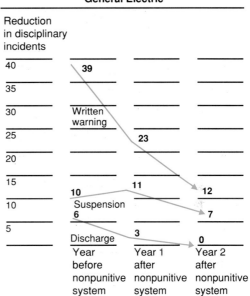

Reduction in Disciplinary Incidents
General Electric

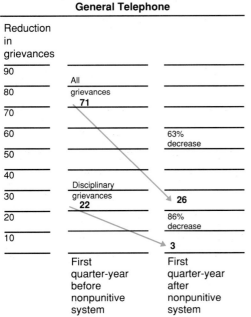

Reduction in Grievances
General Telephone

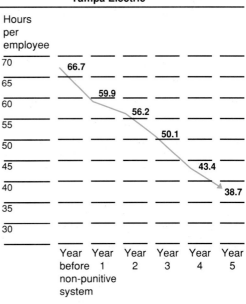

Reduction in Sick Leave Usage
Tampa Electric

Source: David N. Campbell, R. L. Fleming, and Richard C. Grote, "Discipline Without Punishment—At Last," *Harvard Business Review,* July–August 1985, p. 178.

FIGURE 14-8   Corrective action form: Behavior-standard violations

Employee's
Name _____   Department _____   Date _____

Violations of behavior standards are corrected through a progressive disciplinary procedure.

( )   1.   Excessive absenteeism.
( )   2.   Excessive tardiness.
( )   3.   Job duties performed below standard.
( )   4.   Abusive physical behavior.
( )   5.   Sleeping on the job.
( )   6.   Disregarding personal hygiene or standards of dress and appearance.
( )   7.   Unauthorized personal visits or telephone calls.
( )   8.   Discourteous or inappropriate interpersonal relations.
( )   9.   Parking in unauthorized parking zone/failure to display parking sticker.
( )   10.   Failure to follow safety practices.
( )   11.   Other behavior problems.

DISCIPLINARY STEP	First Discussion ( )	Second Discussion ( )	Probation ( )	Suspension ( )	Discharge ( )
DATE	___/___/___	___/___/___	___/___/___	___/___/___	___/___/___
TIME					
ACTION TO BE TAKEN					
EMPLOYEE'S COMMENTS					

The employee's signature indicates that this matter was discussed with him/her and does not necessarily mean that the employee agrees with what is stated.

Employee's Signature _____   Date _____
Supervisor's Signature _____   Date _____

For probation, suspension, and discharge actions:
Reviewed by:
Personnel Director   _____   Date _____
Department Director   _____   Date _____
Vice President   _____   Date _____

Source: Clayton V. Sherman, *From Losers to Winners: How to Manage Problem Employees . . . and What to Do If You Can't,* AMACOM, New York, 1987, p. 108.

FIGURE 14-9   Corrective action form: Work-rule violations

Employee's
Name _____ Department _____ Date _____

Violations of work rules are regarded as major infractions subject to immediate termination of employment.

( )   1.   Mistreatment of patient.
( )   2.   Theft, reasonable basis for suspicion of theft, or attempted theft.
( )   3.   Willful destruction of property.
( )   4.   Assault with intent to do bodily injury.
( )   5.   Insubordination: refusal to perform assigned work.
( )   6.   Willful breach of confidentiality.
( )   7.   Sexual harassment.
( )   8.   Use of alcohol or drugs on hospital premises or reporting to work under the influence to the extent that job performance is in any way impaired or to the extent that others are aware of their use.
( )   9.   Willful falsification of personnel, time and attendance, or other hospital records.
( ) 10.   Solicitation or distribution.
( ) 11.   Possession of firearms or other dangerous weapons on hospital premises.
( ) 12.   Violation of major safety rules.
( ) 13.   Any absence without notification to supervisor prior to shift start.

DISCIPLINARY   Suspension   Discharge
ACTION   ( )   ( )

Date _____ Time _____

INVESTIGATION   _____
RESULTS   _____
                  _____

EMPLOYEE'S   _____
COMMENTS   _____
                  _____

The employee's signature indicates that this matter was discussed with him/her and does not necessarily mean that the employee agrees with what is stated.

Employee's Signature   _____ Date _____
Supervisor's Signature   _____ Date _____
Reviewed by Personnel Director   _____ Date _____
Department Director's Signature _____ Date _____
Vice President's Signature   _____ Date _____
For additional space, use the reverse of this form.

Source: Clayton V. Sherman, *From Losers to Winners: How to Manage Problem Employees . . . and What to Do If You Can't,* AMACOM, New York, 1987, p. 109.

tired and tempers may be short. You also might not have enough time to complete the discussion, and an already disgruntled employee will become more so because the shift is over and he or she cannot go home. An early meeting also allows you to note whether there is a change in behavior or performance during the shift—in other words, to see if your counseling had any effect. Late sessions mean that the worker leaves soon after the meeting and the effect may be minimized by the next day. The same rationale is true for sessions on Friday. If the discussion is held on Monday, Tuesday, or Wednesday, you will have an opportunity on Thursday and Friday to observe any change in behavior or work performance.[14]

The setting must be private. If your office is glass-enclosed and therefore visible to other workers, go to a conference room or to another office. Privacy is a must. Make arrangements for uninterrupted time, and unless the plant is on fire, allow no one to interrupt your privacy.

Review the employee's work record. However, deal with the current problem, not with the past. Prepare your opening comments. Be serious. This is not the time to begin the meeting with a joke to put the employee at ease. Be professional in attitude and in appearance.

Some pitfalls to avoid in counseling sessions include the following:[15]

Competency Check:

Can you describe a positive time and setting for a counseling session?

● Avoid historical absolutes, such as "You're never on time" or "You're always arguing with me." These absolute statements put the receiver on the defensive. Instead, focus on the present situation and how to correct it.

● Avoid public scenes in which you openly discipline an employee in front of others. Publicly humiliating others accomplishes nothing in terms of improving performance. Instead, give correction in private; praise in public.

● Avoid emotional reactions. Nothing is accomplished by emotional outbursts other than the triggering of an emotional response. Instead, stay in control of your own emotions, even if you have to take a deep breath and count to 10.

● Avoid rejecting the person. Putting employees down and attacking their self-esteem only makes a bad situation worse. Instead, focus on specific behaviors and ways to correct those undesirable behaviors.

● Avoid "garbage dumping." "Not only did you make five mistakes on the report you completed, but last week you made two mistakes on the financial statement. And last month, you neglected to send that memo on the new policy to two of the supervisors." This is *garbage dumping*—piling criticism on top of criticism when one does not relate to the other. Instead, deal with one issue at a time.

● Avoid "shrinkspeak." "You're a perfectionist because you could never get approval from your father unless everything was just right. You're still insecure and trying to get approval the same way." Unless you are a psychiatrist, psychologist, or trained therapist, this is out of your area of expertise. Instead, focus on describing the unacceptable behavior and attempting to correct the deficiencies.

● Avoid closing your mind. "Don't confuse me with facts; I've made up my mind." Instead, take the time to listen and talk out the dimensions of the problem. You could be wrong!

● Avoid indirect communication. Don't give critical communication through the grapevine or through a second person. Instead, give the message yourself, no matter how unpleasant you anticipate its being.

● Avoid doing all the talking. Instead, let the worker have an opportunity to talk about his or her frustrations.

The culmination of the counseling session should be a plan of action developed jointly by the supervisor and the employee, with a date for follow-up set.

Competency Check

Can you cite pitfalls to avoid and suggest an alternative action?

Special Types of Problems

Every day, a supervisor in some company faces the results of employee absenteeism, tardiness, substance abuse, insubordination, and various other performance and behavioral problems. Dealing with these problems is one of the supervisor's job responsibilities.

Absenteeism and Tardiness

Employee abuse of sick leave results in an estimated loss of $10 to $20 billion a year to American industry. Controlling the abuse requires a continuous effort.

Usually, a supervisor tries to remedy the absenteeism problem by counseling. Some absentees respond to counseling; others do not. Counseling will probably benefit employees whose:[16]

● pressures off the job are so strong that they affect the employees' commitment to work.
● work appears to them to be disagreeable and dissatisfying.
● working relationships with others are unpleasant and distasteful.
● absence or tardiness is not based on an underlying serious problem and who could benefit from a straightforward "word to the wise."

On the other hand, counseling will probably *not* work with employees for whom:

● the pay level or the job itself holds no strong attraction.
● off-hour activities have a greater appeal than do on-the-job activities.
● the whole purpose of being absent is to inconvenience, punish, or disrupt the organization.

For this latter group, discharge may be the only appropriate course of action.

A suggested 12-point absenteeism checklist for supervisors is shown in Figure 14-10 on page 448.

Substance Abuse

Abuse of both legal and illegal substances is an ongoing problem for many companies. Typical employee behavior changes related to a drinking problem are shown in Figure 14-11 on page 449. Many of these problems were addressed in both Chapter 7, where substance abuse was related to problems in the physical environment, and Chapter 13, where substance abuse was related to problems in the psychological environment.

FIGURE 14-10 12-point absenteeism checklist

☐ Insist on prompt notification *always* when someone in your department must be absent unexpectedly.

☐ Insist on prior discussions about necessary absences for personal reasons, rather than explanations *after* the stay-away. In any event, call for *real* explanations rather than imaginative stories and "phony" excuses.

☐ What is the "Blue Monday" situation in your department? Keep a running record of absences on Monday or the day after each holiday, compared with absences on the best-attendance day (which will probably be payday!). The difference is a good indicator of "phony" absenteeism.

☐ Avoid crises due to unexpected absences by having standard operating procedures and standard backstop procedures: who is to be kept informed of what details, who is to pinch hit for whom.

☐ Be sure to give prompt notification to other departments that may be affected by delays caused by unexpected absences in your bailiwick.

☐ Maintain good departmental and individual absence records. Make periodic checks to see who are the "Absence-proners."

☐ Have heart-to-heart discussions with the ones who cause most of your absentee problems. See if there are personal problems on which counsel by you or someone in the Personnel or Medical Department can help.

☐ Is a group meeting in your department called for? Collect some facts and figures on actual costs of absenteeism to the department and to the company, including *related costs* as well as direct costs, to drive home the seriousness of the problem.

☐ Check your departmental record with that of other departments. Is yours out of line? Where does the basic fault lie? *Turn the mirror on yourself!*

☐ Know your employees. Without prying, show an interest in their personal lives. Encourage after-hour discussion of problems that affect attendance and productivity.

☐ Wear "mental safety goggles" periodically: Look for safety hazards in equipment and operations, and for poor housekeeping that can cause accidents.

☐ Insist that every employee report to you *any* injury, no matter how minor it may seem. It's your responsibility to see that every injured employee gets proper first-aid and/or medical treatment. This applies even to minor injuries, to prevent infection and possibly serious after-effects.

Typically, substance abusers have a greater incidence of absences and partial absences (leaving early or coming in late), with these absences spread out through the week. A summary of approaches for supervisors to take with alcoholics, from a

FIGURE 14-11 Typical employee behavior changes related to a drinking problem

EMPLOYEE BEHAVIOR PATTERN	EMPLOYEE'S RESPONSE TO CRISES	OBSERVABLE SIGNS
Early Stage • drinking to relieve tension • increase in tolerance • memory lapses • lying about drinking	90% Supervisor's Evaluation Actual Job Deterioration Criticism from Boss Family Problems	Absenteeism tardiness (at lunchtime) absent from post General Behavior complaints from fellow workers overreacts to real or imagined criticism complains of not feeling well makes untrue statements Performance on Job misses deadlines errors due to inattention or poor judgment lowered job efficiency
Middle Stage • sneaking drinks • feeling guilty • tremors • loss of interest	75% Loss of Job Advancement Financial Problems, e.g., Wage Garnishment Warning from Boss	Absenteeism frequent days off for vague ailments or implausible reasons General Behavior — Marked Changes statements are undependable begins avoiding associates exaggerates work accomplishments hospitalized more than should be expected repeated minor injuries on and off job Performance generally deteriorating spasmodic work pace lapses of attention — cannot concentrate
Late Middle Stage • unable to discuss problems • efforts for control fail • neglect of food • drinking alone	50% Typical Crisis In Trouble with Law Punitive Disciplinary Action Serious Family Problems, Separation Serious Financial Problems Job Performance	Absenteeism frequent time off (maybe for several days) does not return from lunch General Behavior grandiose, aggressive and/or belligerent domestic problems interfere with work seems to lose ethical values financial problems (garnishments) more frequent hospitalization will not discuss problems problems with the law Performance far below what is expected
Approaching Terminal Stage • now thinks "my job interferes with my drinking"	25% Final Warning from Boss Termination Hospitalization Years of Alcohol Addiction	Absenteeism prolonged unpredictable absences General Behavior drinking on job completely undependable repeated hospitalization physical deterioration visible serious financial problems serious family problems — divorce Performance uneven generally incompetent

7   11   14

Source: Reproduced with permission from *Human Resources Management—Ideas and Trends,* published and copyrighted by Commerce Clearing House, Inc., 4025 W. Peterson Ave., Chicago, Ill. 60646.

booklet published by the U.S. Department of Health, is shown in Figure 14-12 on page 450.[17] While specifically targeted toward alcoholics, many of the techniques are appropriate for those who use illegal substances.

FIGURE 14-12 Guidelines for dealing with alcoholics

1. The supervisor need not act apologetic about confronting the employee and bringing up the issue of alcoholism.

2. If a deterioration in work performance, behavior, or attendance has been noted, the employee should be asked for an explanation. He should be specifically questioned about the possibility of a drinking problem.

3. The supervisor should refrain from moralizing or implying that the employee has no right to drink (off the job, that is).

4. The supervisor should also refrain from asking the employee to drink less or make other changes in his or her consumption of alcohol.

5. Sometimes the employee will offer an excuse (or even several excuses) for the increased drinking (marital difficulties or sizable and pressing expenses, for instance). Since these are basically side issues, not directly job-related problems, the manager should not be distracted into attempting to help the employee cope with them. The manager must keep the focus on the primary concern: how the employee's drinking affects his job performance.

6. The problem employee may claim to be under a physician's care for alcoholism or to be attending counseling sessions; he may further claim that the problem is therefore under control. The employee may even go so far as to state that his consumption of alcohol was found by a health-care professional to be well within the limits of normal social drinking. Even granting the truth of these assertions, the supervisor shouldn't be deterred from actively pursuing the issue. Any health-care professional who became aware of the employee's deteriorated job performance would quite probably reconsider the seriousness of the problem and reassess whether the drinking was in fact under control.

7. The supervisor should not lose sight of the fact that the alcoholic employee is suffering from a disease and that, as with any other disease, the emphasis should be on treatment and rehabilitation, not on fault finding and moralizing.

8. At this point, suspension or discharge should be firmly raised by the supervisor as very real possibilities should the employee fail to control his work performance. The employee should also be told that he bears the responsibility for seeking professional help in managing the problem. The manager should approach the situation in a businesslike manner—making it clear that his actions are prompted strictly by a desire to help upgrade the employee's present unsatisfactory job performance.

9. The supervisor should make sure the company is doing everything it can to provide assistance to the problem drinker. The employee in question should definitely be referred to the employee assistance program or to health services, if these or similar functions exist with the organization. The supervisor should also ask the employee what help he needs and see whether it can be provided by the company or, if not, whether the company can refer the employee to an outside source of assistance.

Insubordination

Insubordination can take one of two forms: (1) An employee may willfully refuse or refrain from carrying out a direct order or instruction given by a supervisor and (2) an employee may direct threats, abusive language, or physical violence at the supervisor.

Before accusing a worker of insubordination based on a refusal to carry out a direct order, the supervisor should mentally reconstruct the conversation to recall if a direct order was given. ''Anne, I think this layout would be more attractive if the colors were more distinct'' is not a direct order; it is a suggestion, an opinion. If Anne fails to change the colors on the layout, her supervisor may be upset; but Anne did not refuse to carry out a direct order.

Even when a direct order is refused, it is wise to try to determine the reason for the refusal before charging insubordination. Was the refusal based on an inability to comply? Was the box too heavy to lift, for example? Was the refusal based on religious convictions? Were you asking someone to work on a religious holiday? Was the refusal based on the employee's perception that the order was irrationally conceived?[18]

Schedule a face-to-face conversation, *not a confrontation,* with the employee whom you believe has been insubordinate. Ask for an explanation. Explain the consequences of insubordination in your firm.

Insubordination that takes the form of physical violence toward the supervisor is not so easily handled. The policy of many firms is that physical violence or a threat of physical violence in the presence of others is grounds for immediate dismissal. No counseling is required or expected when the supervisor's personal safety is threatened.

Competency Check:

Can you discuss several special types of problems and suggest actions a supervisor might take to correct these problems?

THE LAST RESORT

There comes a time when, having exhausted all the means available and having expended as much time as is economically sound, you may have to discharge a worker. This is sometimes referred to as ''terminate,'' ''fire,'' ''let go,'' ''permanent layoff,'' ''dismiss,'' or even ''derecruit.'' Whatever the act is called, it is an unpleasant event for both participants—the person being discharged and the person who does the discharging.

Termination of Problem Employees

Hampton in the beginning of the chapter said, ''You've got to fire her''—speaking to South about Smith. But before South makes the decision to discharge Smith, he must review her work history and all the efforts that have been made to date to turn this problem employee into a productive one. After the review, if he decides to discharge Smith, the process must be carefully planned and executed to protect the supervisor and the organization's image and legal position and to allow the employee to leave without loss of self-respect and dignity.

Immediate Dismissal

As explained earlier in this chapter, it is sometimes necessary, because of the seriousness of the offense, to discharge an employee immediately. When this is the case, the discharge should be clean and swift. As a procedural matter, keys or other security devices should be collected by the supervisor prior to the employee's leaving the premises. Personal passwords and codes used by the employee should be deleted from the access list. General passwords and codes should be changed immediately. As with any dismissal, careful documentation should be made and the files made available to the personnel department.

Dismissal Following Progressive Discipline

Dismissal, even when conducted in a professional manner, is unpleasant. Most employees who are discharged feel rejected, shocked, and often bitter toward the company. And these feelings are projected toward the company representative who has the responsibility for dismissing the employee. Because this is an emotion-charged situation, the supervisor should remain objective and avoid emotionalism in order to defuse the situation as much as possible.

The meeting in which the employee is told of his or her termination should be planned with the help of the HR/P department. The staff of the HR/P department can make available information that should be a part of the discharge meeting. For example, a written benefits package should be prepared for the discharged employee, including any outplacement services or counseling that is available. The supervisor should also review the company policies and procedures for termination to be sure that he or she is operating within the boundaries prescribed by the company.

The meeting should take place in a private location when the supervisor has ample time to devote exclusive attention to the employee who is about to be discharged. It should *not* take place 10 minutes before quitting time with an "I'm sorry, Joe, but this is it. We've tried everything with you, so there's nothing else we can do. You can pick up your paycheck and not come back." Instead, the supervisor, prior to the meeting, should have reviewed all the documentation and be prepared to tell the employee exactly why the discharge is necessary, giving specific documented examples of substandard performance or unacceptable behavior.

Competency Check:

Can you describe how immediate-dismissal procedures differ from dismissal following progressive discipline?

Once you have planned thoroughly what you are going to say and how you are going to say it, you are ready to face the employee. The discharge meeting typically lasts about 30 minutes, with the termination being given first. It is cruel to subject an employee who is about to be discharged to idle chitchat about the weather or the health of the economy. Get to the issue at hand. Without being defensive or emotional, convey the fact that this employee has not been performing up to the standard expected, review the progressive discipline procedures, and then give the termination message. The remainder of the time should be spent providing the employee with information about the benefits package and other services available through the company and explaining what the employee should do next. Most of the time, the discharged employee is unaware of what follows a discharge. For example, you should tell the employee how the final paycheck will be handled (mailed or picked up), remind the employee to collect personal belongings, and explain how references will be handled. This meeting is not a discussion; it is an announcement of a decision and the format for carrying out the decision.

Legally Responsible Termination

As explained in Chapter 17, employees are legally protected from arbitrary dismissal based on a number of factors. This present chapter examines termination of employment as it relates specifically to problem employees; that is, dismissal for cause. Throughout this chapter, the actions that supervisors should take in regard to problem employees have been described. Many of these actions also keep the supervisor from making illegal discharge decisions or from implementing the discharge in a way that might later be deemed illegal. Following company policies and procedures regarding employee discipline, being fair and consistent in dealing with employees, and providing feedback are examples of these actions.

Perhaps two of the most important precautionary measures a supervisor can take to protect the company from charges of illegal termination are (1) to carefully and regularly document any action taken and (2) to be sure that there is no discrimination involved in any termination decision.

Document, document, document! Documentation means keeping records of every time you speak to a problem employee about deficiencies in work performance and any subsequent actions you take to help improve the individual's performance. These records may take various forms, including the following:[19]

- A memo to file stating that you spoke to the employee about a certain matter on a certain date. Note the specific actions or efforts you agreed to take and those the employee agreed to make. A memo to file can also be written when someone makes a major complaint to you about the employee's performance.
- A copy of any performance agreement you and the employee work out and a memo to file on whether or not the agreement was followed through satisfactorily.
- Any memos written in conjunction with the progressive discipline procedures.

Whatever form of documentation you use, it is important that you keep a copy of the communication in the employee's personnel file. Except for a memo to file, the employee should receive a copy of all correspondence directed to his or her attention. In addition, all appropriate people should receive copies of the documentation. For later support, your supervisor and the HR/P department should be aware of the situations leading to an employee's termination.

Be sure there is no discrimination involved in the termination action. Carefully review the procedure. Did you have any bias against the employee's age, sex, race, color, religion, or national origin? Did the fact that the employee was pregnant have anything to do with your decision? You have to be able to answer no to all these questions. Be aware of any actions that might later be called *discriminatory*. For example, it is unwise to say to an employee, "Joan, now that your children are in

Competency
Check:

Can you cite the
two primary actions
a supervisor can
take to avoid legal
problems as a result
of employee
termination?

high school, wouldn't you feel better if you were at home with them? You know how the high school drug scene is'' or ''Jack, you're getting along in years, and the pressures of this job are increasing every day. Think of how great it would be to be fishing instead of what you're having to put up with in this job.'' Any comments along these lines are open to an interpretation of discriminatory termination of employment.

WHAT CAN THE SUPERVISOR DO?

Was the employee discharged for just cause? Before making the decision of last resort, ask yourself these questions:[20]

Was the employee aware of the work rule and the possible consequences of violating it?

Was the work rule reasonable; that is, was it related to the safe and efficient operation of the business?

Was an investigation conducted to determine whether the employee actually violated the rule?

Was the investigation fair and objective?

Did the investigation show that the employee was at fault?

Were the rules, orders, and penalties applied evenhandedly and without discrimination?

Was the penalty imposed in this instance related to the seriousness of the violation and the employee's past work record with the company?

A ''no'' answer to any of these questions means that there is no just cause for discharge.

COMPETENCY REVIEW

1. Identify five behavioral or attitudinal indicators that should alert a supervisor to a potential problem employee.
2. Describe four strategies for preventing undesirable behavior.
3. Describe three methods for correcting undesirable behavior.
4. Describe a positive time and setting for a counseling session.
5. Cite eight pitfalls to avoid in counseling, and suggest alternative actions.
6. Discuss several special types of problems, and suggest actions a supervisor might take to correct these problems.
7. Describe how immediate-dismissal procedures differ from dismissal following progressive discipline.

8. Cite two primary actions a supervisor can take to avoid legal problems resulting from an employee's termination.

APPLICATIONS

1. How can you identify a problem employee? What specific behavioral or attitudinal indicators should you look for? Respond to the questions below by placing a check mark in the blank beside the question to which you might respond yes. If your response is no, leave the question blank.

_____   **a.**   Do you receive complaints from customers about the worker's attitude toward customers?

_____   **b.**   Do co-workers complain to you about the employee's rudeness, about trying to dump work on them, and so on?

_____   **c.**   Does your boss tell you about mistakes in the employee's work?

_____   **d.**   Do your peers complain to you about how the worker has treated them or their workers?

_____   **e.**   If you don't check the employee's work, will it often go out with major mistakes?

_____   **f.**   When you give the worker an assignment, does it rarely come back done the way you wanted it?

_____   **g.**   Do you often have to reschedule the work of your other employees at the last minute because the worker fails to show up?

_____   **h.**   Do you frequently spend time doing work that you should be able to delegate?

_____   **i.**   As soon as a task is finished, does the worker wait until you assign another one?

_____   **j.**   Does the employee rarely complete assignments on time?

_____   **k.**   After you give the worker an assignment, is it frequently returned with a number of reasons why it can't be done?

_____   **l.**   Do you receive reports that the employee has been complaining about you to other people?

_____   **m.**   Are you always at least a little concerned that the worker will say something to embarrass you in front of other people?

_____   **n.**   Do you find it difficult to get your own work done because of the time you spend on the employee's problems and mistakes?

_____   **o.**   When you decide to give an important assignment to someone, do you rarely pick this employee?

_____   **p.**   Do you assign work that the employee should be able to do to other employees because you know they'll do it better and faster?

_____   **q.**   When you point out mistakes the worker has made, does he or she almost always have an excuse or put the blame on someone else?

_____   **r.**   Do you occasionally learn that the employee has lied to you or at least stretched the truth?

Source: Peter Wylie and Mardy Grothe, _Problem Employees_, Pittman Learning Inc., Belmont, Calif., 1981, p. 9.

If you respond yes to any one or more of the questions given, you may have a problem employee, especially if the question addresses something that is particularly important to you or to your department. What if you answered "yes, but . . ." to the questions? This could mean that you may have problem employees but it is difficult for you to accept and admit that these problem employees exist. Admit it, and get to work helping them fix their problems!

2. How effectively do you deal with mistakes made in your department? How well do you learn from them? If a mistake is made, do you regard it as a disaster and disgrace, or as an opportunity to develop and grow? The following checklist quiz will help you evaluate your handling of mistakes and, hopefully, call to your attention techniques that will enable you to convert goofs into learning experiences that will lead to ultimate improvement and gain.

	Yes	No
When a mistake is committed, do you always try to deal with it as quickly as you can?	_____	_____
Do you first assess its importance and significance so that you can view it in proper perspective?	_____	_____
Do you make it a point to investigate every error made in your department to get to the root and cause of it?	_____	_____
In tracking down error causes, do you take care to investigate thoroughly without jumping to conclusions?	_____	_____
Do you take explanations and alibis with a grain of salt, getting all sides of the story before arriving at a judgment?	_____	_____
When a subordinate makes a mistake, do you make every effort to treat it objectively, unemotionally, and impersonally?	_____	_____
Are you careful not to show resentment against individuals who commit errors?	_____	_____
After an error is make, do you take positive steps to prevent its recurrence?	_____	_____
Do you openly and honestly own up to errors you yourself make?	_____	_____
Are your people open and honest about their errors, knowing they won't be persecuted or maligned as a result?	_____	_____
Do you try hard to keep criticism constructive, designed to correct and improve, not to belittle and lay blame?	_____	_____
Do you keep a record of past mistakes and remedies as a history and guide to future corrective measures?	_____	_____

Do you conduct periodic error analysis to pinpoint chronic mistake-makers and determine that the right people are assigned to the right job?   _____ _____

Do you call people to account for their errors on a private and personal basis, without embarrassing them before others?   _____ _____

In trying to initiate controls to prevent error recurrence, do you consult your people, including the one who committed the error, for ideas about the best steps to take?   _____ _____

Total number of *Yes* answers   _____

Score 5 points for each *Yes* answer. If your total is 70 or higher, you're to be congratulated—you handle mistakes like a pro.

Source: Dartnell Corporation, 4660 Ravenswood Avenue, Chicago, Ill. 60640.

CASES

Case I: Give Me My Reprimand with Pay!

The company you work for has been using a three-step progressive discipline approach. The newly hired director of HR/P is "appalled" at what he considers this old-fashioned approach to discipline and has scheduled a meeting with all supervisors to discuss the nonpunitive discipline process that was used by the company he formerly worked for. He has distributed the following article for your review:

Punishing Workers with a Day Off

When Tampa Electric Co. first told Dean Broome about "positive discipline," he sneered at the idea of dealing with problem employees by giving them a paid day off. "It sounded like a reward for bad behavior, like a gimmick from some consultant," confesses Broome, manager of a Tampa Electric power station. Then Broome confronted a lazy mechanic. "We gave him a day off to decide if he wanted his job, and we sure got his attention. He turned around on his own."

Did the "gimmick" really transform Broome's lackadaisical employee into a workhorse? Is so-called positive discipline a legitimate management tool? Or is it, as some labor leaders claim, a veiled attempt by management to quietly slip unwanted workers out the door? A lot of managers are trying to find out. So far, some 200 companies are experimenting with the technique peddled for the last eight years by two personnel managers-turned-consultants in Dallas.

Dressed up.   Companies such as AT&T, General Electric, New York Air, and Union Carbide are trying this approach. Concerned that traditional methods have failed, they contend that positive discipline may improve employee morale and lower turnover.

Advocates of positive discipline say that typically the problems of white-collar workers are ignored until it's too late, while blue-collar workers are simply punished. Positive discipline, they say, generates more "humanistic" tête-à-têtes between managers and employees and reminds managers to tell subordinates when they do a good job.

On its face, positive discipline sounds a lot like traditional discipline dressed up in euphemisms. It works like this: Employees who come in late, do a sloppy job, or mistreat a colleague first get an oral "reminder" rather than a "reprimand." Next comes a written reminder, then the paid day off—called a "decision-making leave day." That sounds a lot better than a suspension.

But this is still serious business. After a pensive day on the beach, naughty employees must agree in writing—or orally, at some union shops—that they will be on their best behavior for the next year. The paid day off is a one-shot chance at reform. If the employee doesn't shape up, it's curtains. The process is documented, so employees often have little legal recourse.

In the eight years since Tampa Electric began using positive discipline, Broome claims, more employees have improved their job performance than have left the company. "Before, we punished employees and treated them worse and worse and expected them to act better," he says. "I don't ever recall suspending someone who came back ready to change."

Positive discipline is far from new. A Canadian industrial psychologist, John Huberman, began promoting the idea more than two decades ago. He didn't find a receptive audience until the mid-1970s, when positive discipline attracted the attention of Richard C. Grote, then a director of training and development at Frito-Lay Inc. Grote was searching for a better management technique after a disgruntled worker wrote a vulgar message on a corn chip and it was discovered by a consumer. When Grote employed positive discipline, morale improved, and terminations at his 210-employee plant fell from 58 to 19 per year. In 1978, Grote and partner Eric L. Harvey opened Dallas-based Performance Systems and began selling the idea. The pair charges $50 per employee, and it takes a year to teach corporations to use the technique.

Managers at a General Electric Co. refrigerator plant in Decatur, Ala., decided to test it in 1979, when they realized that "the existing disciplinary system was cold, harsh, and punitive, and it didn't work," says Bob Burnaska, a personnel consultant at GE headquarters in Fairfield, Conn. Since then, GE has implemented the system at 10 of its 200 plants. At Martin Marietta Corp.'s uranium-enrichment plant in Paducah, Ky., personnel director Bill Thompson says the system has eliminated the need for firing in at least one case.

'Slapped early.'   Bruce Withers, a 24-year-old construction worker for the highway department in Pinellas County, Fla., was given a paid day off last year to think about his absenteeism. "It got me to change my attitude," he says. "I was embarrassed in front of everyone when they told me I had the day off. I didn't want that to happen again." Since the day off, Withers has gotten two promotions and a 50% raise. It doesn't always work, of course. One "positively disciplined" worker who was ultimately dismissed complains that the prescribed process simply gave his boss the guidelines and documentation he needed to give him the boot.

So it may come as no surprise that labor unions dislike this management style. "It's better to get slapped early than to be lulled by a boss who acts like you should trust him," says Victor Crowley, an official of the Communications Workers of America, which represents the hourly workers at Southwestern Bell Corp., a user of the method. "Under positive discipline, employees who are unjustly pushed out of a company won't fight back. How can you get mad when you're paid for a day off?"

But Southwestern Bell takes a more positive view of positive discipline. Says James Graham, Southwestern Bell's labor-relations manager: "It simply removes the adversarial relationship between the workers and management." When it comes to management techniques, it seems, one man's gimmick is another man's panacea.

Source: Laurie Brown, "Punishing Workers with a Day Off." Reprinted from June 16, 1986 issue of *Business Week* by special permission, copyright © 1986 by McGraw-Hill, Inc.

1. Make a list of questions you want to ask at the meeting.
2. Would you support the change? What is your basis for accepting or rejecting the nonpunitive-discipline process?
3. List the pros and cons of both the traditional approach to discipline and the nonpunitive approach.
4. Remember theory X and theory Y? Do you think traditional-discipline approaches and nonpunitive discipline relate to these theories?

Case II: But I've Been Sick

Patricia Mangan was described by management at the metalworking plant as a "fine individual with good work habits when present on the job." She was, unfortunately, not on the job more than she was on the job.

Of the 210 working days in the 10 months preceding her discharge, Mangan was able to work only 43 days. The balance of that period was devoted to surgery and convalescence during excused absences and leaves of absence. There was no question that her ailments were genuine; what troubled her supervisor was that Mangan was usually unfit to perform her work even when she was present, and her doctor did not anticipate that her condition would improve to the point where she would be able to do her job any time in the near future. She was therefore discharged.

Mangan challenged her discharge with a grievance, charging that the discharge was not for just cause. Management countered that it had no choice but to discharge her because her absences seriously disrupted production and no change for the better could be expected. The case was taken to arbitration.

The union argued that every one of the grievant's absences had been for a valid health reason and had been excused by management. It conceded that the year preceding the discharge had been a particularly severe one because it had included surgery—first on a hand and then on a dislocated shoulder. A statement from Mangan's doctor confirmed the nature of her medical problems.

Management did not dispute the genuineness of the ailments and emphasized that the discharge had not been for disciplinary reasons. Instead it presented, as exhibits, the following record of the woman's employment with the company:

She failed to reveal, on her job application 4 years earlier, a mishap prior to that time that caused a recurrent shoulder-separation problem. She was hired; 7 months later, she quit on the advice of her doctor. Two months later, she reapplied, again failing to note her preemployment injury, and was rehired. For better than a year thereafter, her attendance was satisfactory; then, toward the end of the following year, there was a sharp increase in her absences, on an erratic basis.

Early in the year that preceded her discharge, she requested and was granted a leave of absence for surgery, indicating, at the time, that she expected to return after 6 weeks. But she did not return for 3 months beyond that anticipated date, asking for and getting two extensions of the leave. One week following her return, she again sought and was granted a leave, which lasted an additional 2 months. Then, for the first 6 weeks after the next return to work, she had some irregular daily absences. One month later, she asked for another leave, at which time she was terminated.[21]

1. Was the discharge for good cause?
2. If you were the arbitrator, how would you rule?

Figure 14-2: Answers and Discussion

O   **1.** *Disorganized quarterly report that needs to be rewritten*
This is an outcome concern because it is clearly related to the *quality* of the employee's work.

P   **2.** *Employee dating another worker*
This is a judgment call. We see it as a process concern. Even though office dating has the *potential* for having a negative impact on an employee's work, you don't have any evidence of that here.

P   **3.** *Employee objects to company vacation policy*
Another judgment call. Depending upon work schedules and priorities, we think people ought to be able to take their vacation when *they* want to, not when the personnel department thinks they should.

O   **4.** *Receptionist is rude on the phone*
Rude behavior to customers is not a matter of individual style; it's dumb.

O   **5.** *Employee on flex time schedule is unavailable when needed*
Flexible time schedules are one thing; not being able to reach employees when you really need to is quite another.

O   **6.** *Salesperson delinquent in turning in reports*
Even though we think that progress reports are frequently ignored by the people who ask for them, the fact that they're not being turned in regularly, in this case, is having a negative impact on your work. Something has to give. Either your boss has to change the policy or the salesperson has to get the reports in on time.

P   **7.** *Account executive with messy office*
We happen to think that people with neat offices often *are* better organized and more efficient than those with messy offices. But we think it's the employee's *productivity* that should govern your suggestions regarding the neatness of his office, *not* the office itself.

  O   **8.** *Younger staff person disagrees in objectionable tone at staff meetings*
We think that managers not only should tolerate disagreement from their employees, but should encourage it. The problem here is not one of disagreement. It's the disrespectful way in which the disagreement is expressed. *That* you can't tolerate.

  P   **9.** *Younger employee refuses to fill out time sheet*
Another judgment call. We think that time sheets are a *big* waste of time. In this case the employee has given you some empirical evidence that supports our position. He's got better things to do with his time. This does not apply to organizations whose accounting divisions bill customers according to the number of in-house hours spent on a project. A publishing house or an advertising agency, for example, needs time sheets to accurately assess the service costs that have accrued on a job in addition to the production and manufacturing costs.

  P   **10.** *Manager frequently holds group work sessions*
Here the focus is on the way she manages, rather than the results she's getting. If the results aren't so hot, then it's time to take a look at how she's getting those results.

REFERENCES

1. George Odione, *Strategic Management of Human Resources,* Jossey-Bass, Inc., San Francisco, 1984.

2. Clayton V. Sherman, *From Losers to Winners: How to Manage Problem Employees . . . and What to Do If You Can't,* AMACOM, New York, 1987, p. 11.

3. Ibid., p. 13.

4. Ibid.

5. Ibid., p. 14.

6. Peter Wylie and Mardy Grothe, *Problem Employees,* Pittman Learning, Inc., Belmont, Calif., 1981, p. 10.

7. Rodney P. Beary, ''Discipline Policy—A Neglected Personnel Tool,'' *Administrative Management,* November 1985, p. 21.

8. Ibid.

9. Ibid.

10. Sherman, op. cit., p. 105.

11. Ibid., p. 106.

12. David N. Campbell, R. L. Fleming, and Richard C. Grote, ''Discipline Without Punishment—At Last,'' *Harvard Business Review,* July–August 1985, p. 162.

13. Ibid., p. 168.

14. Sherman, op. cit., p. 130.

15. Bruce A. Baldwin, ''Critical Communication: Giving Negative Feedback with Positive Results,'' *PACE Magazine, Piedmont Airlines Inflight Magazine,* November–December 1982, p. 12.

16. Sherman, op. cit., p. 93.

17. U.S. Department of Health, *The Supervisor's Guide on Alcohol Abuse,* in Sherman, op. cit., pp. 94–95.

18. R. Bruce McAfee, and Arno F. Knapper, *Employee Relations Management,* Old Dominion University, Norfolk, Va., 1983.

19. Wylie and Grothe, op. cit., pp. 203–204.

20. Mark A. Hutcheson, "Dismissal Lawsuits: Keeping Firing Decisions Out of Court," *Today's Office,* May 1986, p. 14.

21. "Discipline and Grievances," National Foreman's Institute, Waterford, Conn., 1979.

SUGGESTED READINGS

Blishak, Sylvia: "Anger in the Workplace and How You Can Diffuse It," *Office Systems '87,* March 1987.

"Company Responses to Drug Abuse from AMA's Nationwide Survey," *The Medical-Economic Digest,* April 15, 1987.

Davidson, Jeffrey P.: "When You Have to Face the Problem Employee," *Office Systems '85,* June 1985.

"Drug Addiction in the Workplace," *Supervisory Sense,* vol. 6, no. 12, June 1986.

George, Claude S.: "How to Supervise Effectively," *Datapro,* 1978.

Greenhalgh, Leonard: "Managing Conflict," *Sloan Management Review,* Summer 1986.

"Gripes, Complainers, and Bad Attitudes," *Supervisory Sense,* vol. 4, no. 1, July 1983.

"Inner View," *Personnel Communique,* October–November 1985.

Jernigan, Dale: "5 Ways to Deal with a Problem Employee," *Office Systems '87,* August 1987.

Leap, Terry L., and Michael D. Crino: "How to Deal with Bizarre Employee Behavior," *Harvard Business Review,* May–June 1986.

Ludeman, Kate: "Nine Steps to Resolving Employee Complaints," *Office Administration and Automation,* June 1983.

MacKenna, Neil S: "How to Deal with the Corporate Misfit," *Supervisory Management,* July 1985.

Morin, William J.: "A Professional Approach to Employee Firings," *Office Administration and Automation,* August 1983.

Pulich, Maria Ann: "What to Do with Incompetent Employees," *Supervisory Management,* vol. 31, no. 3, March 1986.

Ward, Richard H., and Nancy A. Hirsch: "Reducing Employee Absenteeism: A Program That Works," *Personnel,* June 1985.

"What to Do About Drugs in the Workplace," *Office Systems '86,* June 1986.

"What to Do About Plateaued Employees," *Supervisory Sense,* vol. 6, no. 7, April 1986.

SECTION VI

THE SUPERVISOR AND THE CONTROLLING FUNCTION

SECTION VI

THE SUPERVISOR AND THE CONTROLLING FUNCTION

15

THE SUPERVISOR'S ROLE IN CONTROLLING

COMPETENCIES

Studying this chapter will enable you to:

1. Define *control*.

2. Cite characteristics of effective standards.

3. Describe the steps in the control process.

4. Define and give examples of types of control.

5. Identify areas in which the supervisor is responsible for control.

6. Compare fixed, flexible, and zero-based budgets.

7. Describe scheduling techniques.

8. Describe the difference between 100 percent inspection and sampling, and explain sampling techniques.

9. Describe types of time controls.

10. Distinguish between economic order quantity and "just in time," explaining the purposes of each.

11. Describe uses of the computer as a control tool.

12. Describe General Electric's front-line control concept.

CHAPTER OUTLINE

Suzie Quarters and Jerry Bezuka are standing by the coffee machine during their morning break. Bezuka has noticed that Quarters has been preoccupied for several days. As he hands her a cup of coffee, he says, "Suzie, do you want cream in your coffee? Suzie . . . ?" "Oh, sorry, Jerry, I guess my mind wandered for a moment. What did you say?" Bezuka shakes his head and decides to meet the situation head-on.

BEZUKA: Suzie, what's the matter? You haven't been your usual outgoing self for several days. Anything you want to talk about?

QUARTERS: Yes, maybe you can help. Remember yesterday when Tom Marco told all of us supervisors that we will have to develop a control system for our departments? I know he said we would have a 2-day workshop on how to establish controls and identify areas for control, but, frankly, that word *control* scares me. What do you think will happen? Will this change our jobs?

BEZUKA: Well, Mr. Marco did say we had to change the budgeting process and move to a zero-based budget. The whole idea seems so big, but the possibility of getting a handle on how to use our resources to produce a better product is kind of exciting—not to mention a challenge!

THE CONTROL PROCESS

Controlling is the function of comparing actual performance with planned performance and taking action when appropriate. There are four steps in the control process: (1) setting standards, (2) observing and measuring performance, (3) comparing performance with standards, and (4) taking whatever corrective action is necessary.

One of the major responsibilities of supervisors is controlling. Controlling, or riding herd on operations, is the raison d'être of first-line management. However, as Quarters pointed out, the word *control* is scary, and a lot of people resent the idea that they are being controlled. They see control as a negative force (using authority to exercise command over their entire work life) rather than as a positive force (using certain activities to produce a quality product or service in the quantity planned for).

A study of the controlling activities of supervisors by the authors revealed that supervisors believe they spend more time on measuring productivity than on any other controlling activity. The total responses are shown in Figure 15-1, including the percentage of responses by level of choice—first, second, third, fourth, and fifth. Note that supervisors reported spending a large percentage of their time controlling a varied range of activities.

Competency Check:

Can you define *control*?

FIGURE 15-1

CONTROLLING ACTIVITIES OF SUPERVISORS

ACTIVITY	FIRST	SECOND	THIRD	FOURTH	FIFTH
measuring productivity	14.7%	29.4%	8.8%	2.9%	8.8%
evaluating departmental objectives	14.7	14.7	11.8	8.8	5.9
quality control of output	14.7	14.7	2.9	8.8	8.8
reporting control results to management	11.8	8.8	11.8	14.7	2.9
comparing planned with actual budget expenses	8.8	5.9	14.7	11.8	5.9
salary administration	8.8	—	5.9	11.8	8.8
appraising performance	5.9	11.8	14.7	14.7	14.7
follow-up of training program	5.9	2.9	2.9	8.8	11.8
evaluating standards	2.9	5.9	11.8	5.9	11.8
measuring plant & equipment efficiency	—	—	8.8	—	2.9
other (expense reduction, controlling stock)	8.8	5.9	5.9	11.8	17.6

Source: Anne Scott Daughtrey and Betty Roper Ricks, supervisory management survey, 1985.

Setting Standards

Chapter 2 described how setting standards of performance is a part of the planning process. Standards provide the link between planning and controlling, as shown in Figure 15-2 on page 470. Knowing what is expected provides the basis for the control function.

Setting standards provides a yardstick against which to measure the firm's movement toward its goals. To serve as effective yardsticks, standards themselves must be effective, and to be effective, they must possess certain characteristics.

Standards Must Be Realistic

For example, let's suppose that Quarters's and Bezuka's firm set a standard of a 5 percent increase in productivity in the next quarter. Is that expectation realistic? Is adequate leadership on board to motivate workers to that level of productivity? Is the skill level of the workers adequate to the task? Are enough workers available? Is the equipment technologically capable of the increased production? Is inventory available? Are there areas where cost cutting might contribute to the accomplishment of the goal?

FIGURE 15-2 Linking planning and controlling

These and other questions must be addressed by management in Quarters's and Bezuka's firm. If the answer to most of the questions is no, the standard is probably not realistic.

Standards Must Be Stated Clearly

A *standard,* by definition, is a "stated level of acceptable performance." The standard should be as precise as possible. Quantitative standards lend themselves to precise statements (200 units per hour per machine with a 5 percent scrap rate, for example). Behavioral standards, such as "No profanity may be used in dealing with customers," are more difficult to quantify. But Figure 15-3 shows that some behavioral standards *can* be quantified. Fuzzy statements provide no yardstick for measuring and are therefore a waste of time. "Good attendance is required" is a fuzzy statement. What is "good attendance"? It is open to a variety of interpretations by different supervisors, and this may lead to different treatment of workers. Stated tolerances, showing allowable deviations from a standard, will make standards clearer and more measurable.

Standards Must Be Communicated

Workers need to know what is expected of them. Quarters in the beginning of this chapter had no idea what was expected of her. Knowing on what basis their performance will be appraised increases workers' confidence by removing their uncer-

FIGURE 15-3

QUALITATIVE AND QUANTITATIVE STANDARDS

STANDARD	TOLERANCE
3.1" shaft diameter	± 0.05"
perfect attendance	two absences per month
8 A.M. starting time	5 minutes late
1-minute waiting time	15 seconds more
clear polished surface	two visible defects
130 over 80 blood pressure	± 20 points

Source: R. Wayne Mondy, Jerry M. DeHarp, and Arthur D. Sharplin. *Supervision,* Random House, Inc., New York, 1983, p. 104.

tainties. Confident workers perform better than do those who are frustrated by wondering how they are doing or how they will be judged.

Standards should be communicated to the appropriate people through the appropriate channels. For example, if attendance standards are imposed on all workers alike, the standard should be printed in the company handbook or communicated orally during orientation sessions. Standards for sales, however, need be communicated only to the people involved in that function. Communication of standards for specific functions may be done through line management, as it was in Quarters's case; that is, from headquarters to division manager, to supervisors, and, finally, to workers.

Communicating standards is a part of the supervisor's responsibility. Telling workers what is expected of them sets up the controlling process. In participative management, workers might actually be involved in setting the standards.

Competency Check:

Can you cite three characteristics of effective standards?

Observing and Monitoring Performance

Observing and monitoring performance is not limited to the performance of employees. Supervisors must observe and monitor equipment, materials, processes, costs, and the quality and quantity of the output. This is the information-gathering phase of the control process. This is the activity through which supervisors gain the information needed to compare performance with standards. The tools and techniques used to generate the information are explained in a later section of this chapter.

Comparing Results to Plan

Comparing the actual performance to the planned performance is the third step in the control process. Comparison is the step in which deviations from the standard are identified.

Taking Corrective Action

A comparison of actual performance to planned performance may reveal deviations that bring into question the standard itself in addition to—or rather than—actual performance. The supervisor is responsible for monitoring performance and noting deviations from the standard. Taking corrective action to revise the standard may or may not be within the supervisor's purview. Let's look at an example.

In a tool and die factory, a standard for a new stamping machine is to stamp out 100,000 tool parts per week, with a tolerance of plus or minus 5 percent. The parts move from the stamper to the assemblers. During the first week, the supervisor observes that some assemblers are idle. The process is traced to the stamping machine, which is found to be producing only 15,000 parts per day—or 75,000 per week. Acceptable performance would be between 95,000 and 105,000 (100,000 plus or minus 5 percent). The supervisor tries to determine whether the cause is:

● the training or performance of the operator—in which case the corrective action would be to retrain or motivate the operator.

● the process—in which case the supervisor would review the work flow and the process and redesign to improve it (in some cases involving sophisticated technology, a specialist such as an engineer might be needed).

● the machine—in which case the supervisor would check the installation to the extent that he or she is expected to be knowledgeable about such things (it might require a specialist in engineering or maintenance).

● the standard—in which case the supervisor might have total, partial, or limited responsibility for taking corrective action.

*Competency
Check:*

Can you describe
the four steps in the
control process?

If the worker's performance is causing the deviation, the supervisor might have total responsibility for bringing the worker up to the expected standard. In some cases, training might be handled by the HR/P department; if so, the supervisor's responsibility might be simply to refer the worker for retraining and to work cooperatively with the HR/P staff until the worker's performance is up to par. In cases where the technology is beyond the supervisor's skills, his or her responsibility might be limited to reporting the deviation to the division heads. If the standard for the machine is found to be unrealistic, the appropriate level of management should take the matter up with the vendor. Whatever the cause of deviation from expectations in operations, the supervisor plays a critical role in early detection and either takes corrective action or refers it to someone who can.

PHASES OF CONTROL

There are three major opportunities for exercising control: (1) before the product is manufactured or the service provided, (2) during the time the product is manufactured or the service is rendered, or (3) after the product is manufactured or the service is provided. These types of controls are referred to as *precontrols, concurrent controls,* and *postcontrols.*

Precontrols

Precontrols (short for ''preliminary controls'') are the controls that are in place before the product is manufactured or the service is performed. These controls are preventive in nature; that is, their purpose is to prevent problems that may occur rather than to correct problems. Precontrols are directed at the resources coming into the organization (*input*)—resources such as people, material, and money (see Figure 15-4).

One way to prevent problems with human resources would be to have an effective selection process that carefully screens potential employees in order to select those who have the skills necessary to perform the jobs. Ensuring that the materials pur-

Resources

FIGURE 15-4
Precontrol

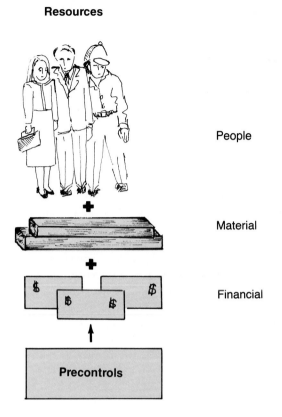

People

Material

Financial

chased are of the correct quality for the job and that they are available in the quantity required is the way to prevent problems occurring because of inadequate materials. Precontrols that can prevent money problems include ensuring that enough money is available to pay for the items ordered or that the dollars spent do not exceed the amount budgeted.

Concurrent Controls

Concurrent controls are controls exercised during the manufacture of the product or when the service is provided. These controls are primarily implemented through observation of the activity. The purpose of concurrent controls is to spot errors when they occur and to correct them at that point. Concurrent controls are directed at the activity or transformation process, as shown in Figure 15-5 on page 474. As the word implies, *transformation* is the process by which inputs are used to produce a product or to provide a service (*output*).

Identifying problems as they occur allows the supervisor to take immediate cor-

FIGURE 15-5 Precontrols and concurrent controls

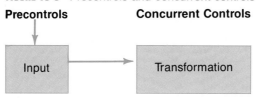

rective action. For example, if a floor supervisor notices that a salesperson is experiencing problems with the computerized register, the floor supervisor (using concurrent controls) would discuss the problem with the salesperson, demonstrate correct use of the register, and have the salesperson show, through operation of the register, that the problem is resolved. Or if a foreman sees that a worker is not wearing the required safety equipment, he or she would bring this violation to the worker's attention immediately and correct it at that time.

Postcontrols

Postcontrols are controls exercised after the product is manufactured or the service provided. These controls are directed at the results of the process (*output*) and are primarily implemented through feedback. The process from precontrols to postcontrols is shown in Figure 15-6.

When a supervisor receives a report from quality control on the number of rejects for a given period, the supervisor is exercising postcontrol. When a service supervisor receives reports from the service representatives each week on the number of service calls made, the supervisor is exercising postcontrol. When a supervisor compares expenses with the budget, the supervisor is also using postcontrol. Information received after the product is manufactured or the service is rendered provides the basis for postcontrols. Did we meet or exceed our goals? Were customer complaints down? Were we within budget? These questions are answered through postcontrols. Of course, when deviations are found during the postcontrol process, the supervisor must then make plans (or implement plans already in existence) to correct the problems. A recap of the major points about precontrol, concurrent control, and postcontrol is shown in Figure 15-7. The three types of controls—precontrol, concurrent control, and postcontrol—provide three opportunities to identify problems and correct them.

Competency Check:

Can you define and give examples of the three types of control?

FIGURE 15-6 Control process using precontrols, concurrent controls, and postcontrols

FIGURE 15-7

SUMMARY OF DIFFERENCES IN THE 3 TYPES OF CONTROL

	PRECONTROL	CONCURRENT CONTROL	POSTCONTROL
directed at	resources	activity	results
process	input	transformation	output
when	before	during	after
how	preventive measures	observation	feedback
purpose	preventing problems	observing problems	identify deviations

WHAT CAN THE SUPERVISOR DO?

The supervisor can make sure that all three types of control are in place and that each control is exercised regularly and consistently. Remember that the purpose of the three controls is to give you three opportunities to check on the quality and quantity of the goods and services you produce. Precontrol allows the supervisor to check the resources that go into producing the goods or providing the service. When this control is not properly exercised, there is little check on the quality and quantity of the resources used. Concurrent control is primarily a supervisory responsibility, for this control is exercised through observation of day-to-day operations. Supervisors must be aware of deviations from standards and be prepared to take immediate corrective action. Postcontrol is the final check on goods and services. This is the supervisor's last opportunity to put the stamp of approval on the department's output. Supervisors must take advantage of each of these opportunities to detect deviations from the standard and to take the necessary corrective action.

WHAT TO CONTROL

Supervisors have responsibility for exercising control over all the activities in their departments. For our purposes, however, we will categorize these control responsibilities as time, behavior, materials and equipment, processes, cost, and quality and quantity of output.

Time

Exercising control over time is a critical element in keeping the work schedules on track. When employees don't report to work on time, if they leave before the end of the workday, or if they take breaks or lunch periods that exceed those granted, then time control is not being exercised effectively.

Behavior

Behavior refers to the way in which employees conduct themselves in the performance of their jobs. Exercising control over behavior means, first, providing employees with standards against which their actions can be compared. These standards may be qualitatively or quantitatively expressed. For example, "working cooperatively with others" may be defined as "helping co-workers complete their jobs if they require such aid." This is a qualitative standard. Qualitative standards are more subjective than are quantitative standards, but, if they are based on observation and critical-incident reports (recall this from Chapter 9), qualitative behavioral standards can be effective.

Materials and Equipment

Using materials wisely and equipment efficiently is vital if a firm expects to make a profit. Supervisors are the people most closely involved in day-to-day operations and, therefore, the ones who will see materials wasted or equipment improperly used. Their responsibility, then, is to ensure that controls are in place to prevent waste and improper use of equipment, to be aware of any of these undesirable actions, and to take whatever corrective action may be necessary (training, retraining, and so on).

Processes

Sometimes the process used to convert inputs into outputs (transformation) is flawed. Perhaps the flow of work is inefficient. Work is not moving through the organization in a smooth flow; it is bottlenecked and slowed at one or more stations. Or perhaps the distribution of work is skewed, with the result that one person has too much work while another has too little. When this occurs, the supervisor needs to examine the situation and look for a more efficient method (process).

Cost

Cost refers to the amount of money expended to produce a good or a service. Costs are usually stipulated in the expense budget for the department. When precontrols are not in place, too many dollars may be spent for materials, for example. The materials may be of a higher quality than that required for the job or the quantity ordered may be greater or less than needed (leaving unused materials or having to slow down production when materials are not available). Observation of waste as a cost is also a supervisor's responsibility. Finally, comparing the costs for the period with the budget for that period provides the information needed for postcontrol of cost. In the case of costs, however, taking corrective action for the period past is impossible. The expenditure has already been made.

Quality and Quantity

Perhaps the supervisor's greatest concern is meeting the standards of quality and quantity of goods produced or services provided. Certainly if there are too many defective goods produced or too many services rendered that require repeat calls, then the unit, department, and, ultimately, the company will not be a profitable operation. Quality has become a focus of many U.S. companies as they compete with other countries for consumer dollars. The slogan used by Ford Motor Company, for example, is "Quality is job one." Other companies, both large and small, are emphasizing quality as they promote their product or their service.

Quantity is the other side of the coin. Quality without quantity does not make for profits; nor does quantity without quality. The supervisor is responsible for maintaining a balance between the two by ensuring that one is not sacrificed for the other. In an effort to increase production and turn out greater numbers of widgets, workers cannot ignore the importance of maintaining a quality product. On the other hand, if workers are trying so hard to produce a 100 percent defect-free product that it is taking them twice as long to produce the number required by the standard, then quantity is being sacrificed for quality. It's quite a balancing act for supervisors; but it's their job.

Competency Check:

Can you name at least five things a supervisor is responsible for controlling?

CONTROL TOOLS AND TECHNIQUES

Quarters in the beginning of the chapter expressed concern over how the change to a formal control system would affect her job. And Bezuka mentioned that Marco (the plant manager) was insisting that supervisors use zero-based budgeting. Bezuka also said, "The whole idea seems so big." Quarters and Bezuka will be relieved to know that in the workshop the company is providing, certain tools and techniques will be explained to help them as they implement the new formal control system.

Budgets

A *budget* is a statement that specifies anticipated amounts of revenues and expenses for a given period. Some supervisors may submit only an *expense budget,* which specifies only the costs the supervisor expects to incur as the product or service is produced. This is because some departments are not profit-generating in themselves but only a part of the process that ultimately produces the product or the service that generates the revenue. For example, on an assembly line, the department responsible for wiring refrigerators is not a profit center; the sales department of the plant is a profit center. *Profit centers* are the departments or units that actually bring in revenue to the company.

Budgets link the planning and control processes. As a planning tool, the budget identifies anticipated revenues and expenses. As a control tool, it is used to compare

FIGURE 15-8

BUDGET FOR OPTICAL DEPARTMENT (JANUARY—MARCH 198_)

	BUDGET	ACTUAL	OVER	UNDER
EXPECTED REVENUE				
glasses	$93,750	$98,674	$4,925	
services	350	200		$150
miscellaneous	200	250	50	
EXPECTED EXPENSES				
frames	$56,000	$60,000	$4,000	
lenses	3,000	3,400	400	
miscellaneous materials	3,000	2,500		$500
labor	13,500	13,500		
machine maintenance	500	200		300

the planned revenues and expenses with the actual revenues and expenses. An example of a budget used as a control tool is shown in Figure 15-8.

The budget shown in Figure 15-8 is a *fixed budget;* that is, a budget that does not change with the number of units produced or the amount of services rendered. A *flexible budget* is one that allows for fixed expenses for costs that remain constant even as production or service levels change (property taxes, basic overhead expenses, and depreciation) and for different levels of expenditures based on the level of production. Costs that vary according to level of production or service include direct labor, materials, and some general and administrative expenses.

Regardless of the type of budget used—fixed or flexible—supervisors should be realistic as they project their expenses and revenues. At the end of the budget period, supervisors should examine the budget deviations, both over and under budget projections. Let's look at Figure 15-8 again. Note that revenue from the sales of glasses was greater than anticipated, by $4925; expenses for frames and lenses were also greater than anticipated, by $4400. The supervisor should try to determine why there were deviations. Perhaps the cost of frames and lenses increased during the 3-month period. Maybe the opticians were careless and broke frames or dropped lenses, requiring reorders and thereby increasing expenses. Or perhaps the supervisor was on target for the expenses as they related to the projected revenues but, as revenues increased, so did expenses. Did expenses increase proportionately to revenues?

The *zero-based budgeting* concept was developed by Texas Instruments Incorporated and used by President Carter's administration in his Office of Management and Budget. Unlike traditional budgets, which allow departments to build their current budget based on previous years' budgets and which include an inflation adjustment, a zero-based budget starts from scratch, or from zero. It requires each program to be justified each year.[1] Every program, whether new or ongoing, is put to the same test. No supervisor can take the continuation of a program for granted simply because

"We've always had it." For example, assume that Bezuka's and Quarters's company has a program that pays employees for courses taken at the local community college. Each year at budget time, this program starts with a clean slate and is proposed along with all other programs. These proposals are placed in priority order, and if the reimbursement program does not compete successfully with all other programs, it may be modified or dropped.

Competency Check:

Can you describe fixed, flexible, and zero-based budgets?

Scheduling Techniques

A *schedule* is a plan that specifies time periods for completing specific activities. A number of techniques may be used to schedule activities, but we will limit our discussion to Gantt charts, critical path method (CPM), and program evaluation and review technique (PERT).

Gantt charts were described in Chapter 3 as they related to planning. They may also be used as control tools when a comparison is made of scheduled output and actual output. Figure 15-9 on page 480 shows such a use of the Gantt chart as it relates to task completion. The Gantt chart in Chapter 3 focused on scheduling human resources, while the Gantt chart in Figure 15-9 focuses on activities. Note that in Figure 15-9, the design phase took longer than planned, but scheduling, ordering, and materials delivery were accomplished in less time than planned. Note also that a period of time planned for was not available. Assembling, inspecting, and shipping have not begun.

Critical path method (CPM) and program evaluation and review technique (PERT) are time-scheduling techniques for projects that require a sequence of activities; some activities can be performed concurrently, while others have precedence requirements. CPM and PERT charts show a network of time requirements and relationships for all activities necessary to complete a project. The activities are the tasks that must be performed and are represented by arrows. Activities are the time-consuming elements in the network chart. The circles in the chart represent events—decision points or the accomplishment of some activity. Events do not consume time or resources. Figure 15-10 on page 481 shows a critical path method network. The term *critical path* denotes the sequence of activities that require the longest period of time to complete. The path is critical because a delay in it means a delay in the project itself. Delays in other paths are not necessarily critical because there is some additional time built in to the paths taking less time than the critical one. Let's look at Figure 15-10 first and then determine the critical path for this activity.[2]

The figure shows, in network form, the work activities necessary to construct an electric power plant. Note that it is necessary to complete some activities before others. For example, the plant design, as shown in activities 1-2, must be completed before any other activity can take place. However, site, vendor, and personnel selection can take place concurrently. The installation of the generator shown in activities 5-7 cannot begin until the site preparation has been completed (activities 3-5) and the generator has been manufactured (activities 4-5). There are really four paths through the network from first event to last (events 1-8). The site preparation (activities 3-5) and the generator manufacture (activities 4-5) are on different paths, but since they converge

FIGURE 15-9 Gantt chart

Activity		Sept.				Oct.		
	14	21	28	5	12	19	26	
schedule								
design								
order								
materials delivery								
machine components								
assemble								
inspect								
ship								

⌐ planned start of activity   ⊠ time not available
                                  (due to maintenance,
                                  material shortages, etc.)   ☆ review date

⌐ planned end of activity   ▭ completed work

Source: John R. Schermerhorn, *Management for Productivity,* John Wiley & Sons, Inc., New York, 1984, p. 529.

at event 5, either activity could delay the generator installation.[3] Note that the estimated time to complete an activity is shown on the line between events.

Now let's look at Figure 15-11 and determine the critical path, or the path estimated to take the longest time to complete. If you add the time required to complete the paths, path 2 becomes the critical path.

The major difference between CPM and PERT is in the way estimated time is calculated. CPM uses one estimate of the time required to complete an activity. PERT uses three estimated times to arrive at a time requirement. PERT time is calculated by determining expected time from (1) *optimistic time* (the time required if everything goes as planned), (2) *pessimistic time* (the time required if Murphy's law is at work—what can go wrong will go wrong); and (3) *most-likely time* (the time required when some activities go as planned and others do not). The formula for calculating expected time is:

FIGURE 15-10 Network diagram

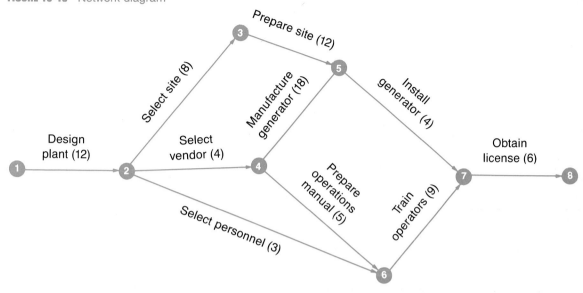

Source: David R. Hampton, *Management for Productivity*, McGraw-Hill Book Company, New York, 1986, p. 702.

$$\frac{OT + 4(MLT) + PT}{6}$$

Therefore, if optimistic time for activity 1 is 9 weeks, pessimistic time is 15 weeks, and most-likely time is 12 weeks, expected time would be calculated as follows:

$$9 + 4(12) + 15 = \frac{72}{6}, \text{ or } 12 \text{ weeks}$$

FIGURE 15-11

DETERMINING THE CRITICAL PATH

PATH	TIMES
1. 1−2−3−5−7−8	12+8+12+4+6
2. 1−2−4−5−7−8	12+4+18+4+6
3. 1−2−4−6−7−8	12+4+5+9+6
4. 1−2−6−7−8	12+3+9+6

Source: David R. Hampton, *Management for Productivity*, McGraw-Hill Book Company, New York, 1986, p. 682.

Competency
Check:

Can you describe
three scheduling
techniques?

Use of PERT in scheduling the activities of the Polaris missile is said to have reduced the time required to produce Polaris by more than 2 years.

Computers are used to generate CPM and PERT charts and to update information in a timely manner, making network scheduling techniques more available to other than top-level managers.

WHAT CAN THE SUPERVISOR DO?

Although supervisors may not be called upon to generate a CPM or PERT chart, they may be held responsible for providing some of the input. It may therefore be important for them to know the basics of network scheduling so they can provide the information required to schedule their departments as a part of a network (CPM, PERT) schedule.

Quality Controls

To maintain high-quality output, goods or services must be evaluated in terms of how they meet quality standards. Products may be evaluated by 100 percent inspection or by sampling.

100 Percent Inspection

Inspecting every product or evaluating every service may not be feasible. Suppose you checked every flashbulb to be sure it worked or tasted every cookie to be sure it was done. What would you have left to sell? But 100 percent inspection is appropriate for some products and services. Custom-made suits and handmade furniture are examples of products for which 100 percent inspection is not only feasible but recommended.

Sampling

Sampling is used when 100 percent inspection is not a feasible or cost-efficient method for determining quality. Sampling may be conducted *randomly* (choosing an item to be inspected on a random basis) or *statistically* (choosing an item to be inspected on a mathematical basis; for example, every tenth item). Sampling assumes that if 95 percent of the items tested are acceptable, then 95 percent of the total output is acceptable.

Competency
Check:

Can you describe
the difference
between 100
percent inspection
and sampling, and
can you explain two
sampling
techniques?

A sample may be judged on either an *acceptability standard* (sampling by attributes) or on a *variability standard* (sampling by variables). If sampling is done by attributes, the product or service sampled is determined to be either acceptable or unacceptable; there is no maybe. For example, a light bulb either lights or it doesn't; a microwave oven is either repaired and working properly or it is still not working. The acceptability standard is often referred to as ''go/no go.''

Sampling by variables allows for some leeway from the standard. A watch may gain or lose up to a given number of seconds per day; a tire tread may be within plus or minus 1/16 of an inch; eyeglass lenses may be plus or minus 0.012 diopters. As long as the sample is within the tolerances, it is considered to be within the quality standard.

Time Controls

Most large and many small firms have some means of recording employee work attendance, including, in some organizations, detailed accounts of times of arrival, breaks, and times of departure. Factories have always been leaders in timekeeping, using a time clock in most cases for keeping track of worker time. Since the early days of time clocks, other options have become available for keeping employees' time records. Kinnie and Arthurs have identified three options they label "old tech," "no tech," and "new tech."[4] Old tech retains the traditional electromechanical time recorder; no tech has discarded automatic time recording and replaced it with supervisory recording or an employee honor system; and new tech uses a computer to record time and to provide a range of other information beyond simple timekeeping.

Old tech uses time clocks in which workers take their time cards and place them in a time recorder, which prints the time on the card. Breaks may be recorded in the same manner, as is "clocking off" at the end of the workday. The hours of work are calculated by the payroll department, and wages are paid according to the hours recorded on the time card.

No tech records time manually through (1) supervisory recording, which may use *exception reporting* only (the supervisor records only those times when an employee is absent or late, leaves early, or takes extended breaks), (2) through employees signing in, or (3) through an employee honor system, in which employees record only the exceptions.

New tech uses a computer to record attendance and to provide organizationwide data collection, automatic analysis, selective access control, and automatic wage computation. The more sophisticated new-tech devices can provide a supervisor with information about an entire department, an individual employee, or even a particular work station. This information can then be made available via a computer screen or hard copy to both the supervisor and others in the firm who need this information for various planning and decision-making purposes.

Figure 15-12 on page 484 shows the three methods of recording employee time and the benefits and costs of each. The choice of method is dependent on the needs of the organization and of the individual departments.

Competency Check:

Can you describe three types of time control?

Materials Control

Supervisors have the primary responsibility for ensuring that materials are available in the quantity and of the quality required and that these materials are on hand when needed. Materials not needed for the job must be stored somewhere; workers must be

FIGURE 15-12

BENEFITS AND COSTS OF ALTERNATIVE TIME-RECORDING METHODS

	BENEFITS	COSTS
1. time clock	low cost of purchase, installation, and maintenance	administration costs
	permanent record for payroll and discipline	possible abuses
time clocks clock cards	acceptable and established	feelings of inequity
2. manual	very low costs of purchase, installation, and maintenance	possible abuses
	harmonization of timekeeping arrangements	time-consuming for supervisors
log books time sheets honor cards	reinforces supervisor's authority	inconsistent treatment of employees?
3. computerized	simplified payroll and lower administration costs	cost of purchase, installation and maintenance
cards or badges	improved management information	will it work?
micro, mini or mainframe computers	fewer errors and abuses	is it acceptable?

Source: Nick Kinnie and Alan Arthurs, "Clock, Clock, Who's There?" *Personnel Management,* August 1986, p. 45.

assigned to account for and distribute materials as needed. On the other hand, if materials are not available when needed, workers are idle—an expensive delay. One technique used to ensure that materials are ordered in the least expensive quantity is economic order quantity (EOQ). EOQ takes into consideration (1) the cost of maintaining materials and (2) the cost of ordering materials. The formula for determining economic order quantity is the square root of (two times actual demand for inventory use times ordering cost) divided by carrying cost.

$$\text{EOQ} = \sqrt{\frac{2DO}{C}}$$

where

$$D = \text{actual demand for inventory use}$$
$$O = \text{ordering cost of inventory}$$
$$C = \text{carrying cost of inventory}$$

Figure 15-13 shows an inventory driven by economic order quantity. Let's suppose that the demand for a particular part for your department is 200 per year, the cost of each order is $60, and the carrying cost is $10 per unit annually. The EOQ is determined by calculating the square root of 2 times 200 times $60 divided by $10. This shows that the supervisor should order 50 units of this particular part to minimize inventory cost. When materials are ordered more frequently, ordering costs go up and carrying costs go down. Conversely, when orders are placed less frequently, ordering costs go down and carrying costs go up. Therefore, supervisors should try to balance the costs by using economic order quantity to arrive at the most economical amount of inventory to keep on hand.

The second problem, mentioned earlier, is that of having excess materials or not enough materials. A technique developed in Japan and now used by many firms in this country is called "just in time" (JIT). Don't confuse this with the JIT (job instruction training) described in Chapter 10. The "JIT idea is simple: Produce and deliver goods in time to be sold, subassemblies just in time to be assembled into finished goods, fabricated parts just in time to go into subassemblies, and purchased materials just in time to be transformed into fabricated parts."[5]

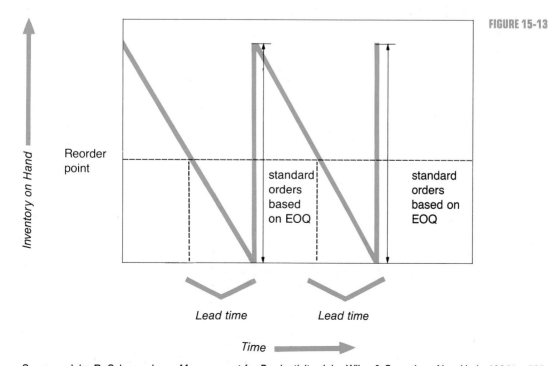

FIGURE 15-13

Inventory on Hand

Reorder point

standard orders based on EOQ

standard orders based on EOQ

Lead time   Lead time

Time

Source: John R. Schermerhorn, *Management for Productivity*, John Wiley & Sons, Inc., New York, 1984, p. 532.

The following describes how one Ford Motor Company assembly plant uses "just in time."[6]

On a typical day, at least 25 rail cars and 30 tractor trailers laden with parts pull into the Ford Motor Company's light-truck assembly plant. "A couple of years ago, we could have survived four days, maybe five, without this daily replenishment," said Percy Eason, the plant's material manager. "These days," said Eason, "Ford's assembly line here would be starved for parts within 24 hours if deliveries did not arrive daily."

"You can't keep a large inventory when it's costing you 20 cents on the dollar—the combined cost of insurance, interest, and other expenses of maintaining inventory. Kanban, a technique for controlling inventory, requires that parts be supplied "just in time." Eason was quoted as saying "having a leaner inventory of parts has uncovered assembly-line snags that had been masked by a comfortable cushion of spares." However well Kanban works for the Japanese, American automakers have to allow some flexibility. The companies that supply Japan's automakers with parts tend to be concentrated around the assembly plants and are able to deliver their products in a matter of hours. Because suppliers in the United States are dispersed throughout the country, the flow of parts are more susceptible to interruptions. Therefore, American automakers are often forced to maintain reserves that would be unnecessary in Japan.

Eason also commented that the concern with inventory levels has focused attention on several less visible matters, including the accuracy and timeliness of inventory records. Ford has installed video display terminals in the plant that allow supervisors to refer more quickly to inventory information in the computer.

Competency Check:

Can you distinguish between EOQ and JIT and explain the purpose of each?

Both EOQ and JIT are techniques supervisors can use to better manage the material resources for which they are responsible.

Computer Controls

Computers are used as control tools to provide information about the progress being made toward accomplishing the objectives of the organization, the department, and the individual. Computers may be used for counting, reporting, and updating to help supervisors make comparisons between what was planned and what was achieved for a given period.

Counting

Computers may be used to count work and compare the results against a standard. For example, in a word prcessing center, standards may be established for (1) the number of pages, lines, or documents to be produced during a standard workday, (2) turnaround time, and (3) errors. As work is received in the word processing center, it is logged in on a computer. When the work is completed, it is logged out. From this information, a weekly employee performance report such as the one shown in Figure 15-14 can be generated.

FIGURE 15-14

WEEKLY EMPLOYEE PERFORMANCE REPORT

EMPLOYEE PERFORMANCE SUMMARY BRUCE PAYNE & ASSOCIATES, INC.

EXHIBIT 1a

DEPARTMENT/BRANCH NO. SECTION SYSTEMS & DATA PROCESSING NO. UNIT NO. WORD PROCESSING

FOR WEEK ENDING 10/5

EMPLOYEE NUMBER		NAME	PERFORMANCE %		Standard Allowed Hours	CHARGEABLE HOURS							NONCHARGEABLE HOURS			Total Straight Hours	Overtime Hours Incl.
			13 Week	Cur. Wk.		MEASURABLE		Delay	Errors	Paid Not Worked	Service and Admin.	Total Available	Loaned	Approved Activity	Absence Vacation Holiday		
						Measured	Unmeas.										
9231	S	M. Holms		147	1.5	1.0	—	—	—	—	37.5	38.5		1.3		39.8	1.0
3653		J. Sammons		80	14.6	18.2	7.0	.3	—	—	12.0	37.5		1.3		38.8	
6275		D. Boger		74	17.8	27.1	8.8	—	—	—	1.3	37.2		1.6		38.8	
4628		D. Smith		72	29.5	40.7	1.9	—	—	—	—	42.6		1.3		43.9	5.1
3241		S. Engle		68	22.2	32.6	4.2	—	—	—	—	36.8		2.0		38.8	
1352		D. Kellogg		64	10.8	16.9	8.4	—	—	—	0.4	25.7		1.3	11.8	38.8	
4158		C. Richardson		63	21.6	34.3	2.8	—	—	—	0.4	37.5		1.3		38.8	
8573		V. Grennel		48	15.9	32.8	4.1	—	—	—	0.6	37.5		1.3		38.8	
1478		L. Alton		42	15.9	37.9	3.7	—	—	—	1.0	42.6		1.3		43.9	5.1
8756		M. Music		—	—	—	—	—	—	—	—	—		—	38.8	38.8	
		TOTALS			149.7	241.5	40.9	.3			53.2	335.9		12.7	50.6	399.2	11.2

Adjusted Total SAH 175.0

COVERED BY STANDARDS GOAL 90 ACTUAL 86

AVERAGE STAFF PERFORMANCE GOAL 100 ACTUAL 62

STAFF EFFECTIVENESS GOAL 89 ACTUAL 52

Source: Walter Kleinshrod, Leonard Kruka, and Hilda Turner, *Word Processing Operations, Applications, and Administration,* The Bobbs-Merril Company, Inc., Indianapolis, 1980, p. 179.

Reporting

The information stored in the computer may be used to generate a variety of reports in a variety of formats, depending on the needs of the supervisor. If an analysis of individual work is required, a report similar to Figure 15-14 can be requested.

At a General Electric facility, six weekly printouts derived from job forms provide information on the number of jobs handled for various word originators. One report summarizes a week's output by one operator, with totals provided for dictation, long-hand manuscript, and cut-and-paste methods of input.[7]

Different reports for different management levels can be generated. For example, Figure 15-15 on pages 490–491 shows a higher-level management report for 8 weeks. It tabulates the average performance, coverage, and effectiveness of the center and shows how many workers were used compared to how many should have been used to produce the indicated volume of work.

Competency Check:

Can you describe three uses of the computer as a control tool?

Updating

Use of the computer makes updating files relatively easy and allows supervisors to make changes in a timely manner. Reports can then be generated based on the most up-to-date information available.

WHAT CAN THE SUPERVISOR DO?

A checklist can be developed to help decide the measures best suited for evaluating performance. From such a list, the supervisor can select appropriate measures needed to supervise effectively. These measures can then be used to design a customized measurement system. A portion of such a chart for a word processing supervisor is shown in Figure 15-16 on page 492.

Front-Line Control

Front-line control, a process developed at General Electric, focuses on the people costs resulting from pressure to complete work and meet schedules. Front-line control makes it easier for supervisors to formulate daily objectives for their units and to develop a plan to meet them, communicate expectations to workers, check performance frequently against the plan, take corrective action before it's too late, and report interferences promptly.[8]

The seven basic principles of this approach are:

1. Each work element must have a time standard or target that is current and reasonable. The standard should reflect expected output from a qualified employee working at a normal pace without interruption.

2. Specific performance expectations for every job must be communicated to every worker. Accepting these targets, even tacitly, amounts to a contract between the supervisor and worker. It is therefore important that the employees understand what is expected, have an opportunity to agree or disagree, and know how performance will be measured.

3. The unit must be staffed at the level needed to meet current output requirements. Staffing at historical performance levels can only perpetuate inefficiencies. If you staff your unit to meet the peak loads, your unit will be operating inefficiently in the slack periods.

4. Every supervisor, at the beginning of every shift, must have a production plan that he or she can reasonably expect to meet. The plan must reflect scheduling priorities based on today's "hot" lists and reflect today's resource availability— the materials, tools, and people to do the job. For long-cycle and white-collar operations, the planning period may be a week rather than a shift; but the planning principle still stands.

5. At frequent intervals during the scheduled period (every hour or two in the shop, perhaps daily in the office), progress must be evaluated against the plan. This means monitoring output either from every worker or just from key checkpoints. If the plan is not being met, corrections can be made before the end of the shift.

6. Problems must be identified, addressed, and resolved. Document and classify lost time or variances from the plan and see that a formal problem-solving procedure is in place.

7. Every supervisor, every day, should be able to specify what his or her productivity is. This daily indicator reflects performance today. If you are asked, "How did you do yesterday?" instead of answering, "I met schedule," you should be able to say, for example, "I met schedule, and I achieved 90 percent labor utilization." Let's look at GE's plan for implementing front-line control.[9]

Planning

The first thing you must do, planning, entails deciding what time values are appropriate for each work activity in your unit. If you have good time standards, or if you can apply percentage factors to your time standards to bring them up to date, you should use them. But if your time standards are nonexistent or hopelessly outdated, you should develop an estimate for each product family at each work station. Your target should not be based on what you have been getting from the work station but on what you should get if operating without interruption. To formulate your target, you should consider what constitutes a normal machine cycle with allowances for setups and material handling and what represents a good hour's production.

Next, you should develop a target table for each work station and include on your tables the common tasks that make up 80 percent of your operations. Incidental tasks or product varieties can often be grouped with the common tasks, or you can add them to your tables as the need occurs. But if you have a large variety of operations or products, you should select a limited number of key volume indicators—those operations or output measurements that are representative of the whole unit's output.

FIGURE 15-15

MANAGEMENT REPORT

	COST CONTROL PROGRESS				BRUCE PAYNE & ASSOCIATES, INC.			EXHIBIT II
DEPARTMENT/BRANCH NO.				SECTION NO. SYSTEMS & DATA PROCESSING	UNIT NO. WORD PROCESSING		FOR WEEK ENDING 10/5	
	PERCENTAGES				EFFECTIVE NUMBER OF STAFF		VARIANCE FROM GOAL	
FOR WEEK ENDING	Covered by Standards	Average Staff Performance	Effectiveness	Adjusted Total Standard Allowed Hours	Actual	Required	Current Week	Cumulative to Date
goal	90	100	89					
8/24	77	52	51	178	9.0	4.6	$406	$ 406
8/31	97	65	60	210	9.0	5.4	306	712
9/7	73	57	56	153	9.0	5.0	284	996
9/14	86	61	56	185	8.7	5.0	328	1324
9/21	71	65	56	175	8.3	4.7	320	1644
9/28	80	44	38	126	8.5	3.3	524	2168
10/5	86	62	52	175	8.7	4.5	380	2548
10/12	87	72	60	214	9.2	6.2	312	2860

FIGURE 15-15 (continued)

HOURS PAID PER STANDARD ALLOWED HOUR

FOR WEEK ENDING	CHARGEABLE						NONCHARGEABLE			TOTAL
	Substandard Performance	Delay	Errors	Paid Not Worked	Service and Admin.	Total Per SAH	Approved Activity	Absence Vacation Holiday	Overtime Premium	
goal	1.00	0.02	0.02	—	0.09	1.13	—			1.13
8/24	1.94	0.02	—	—	—	1.96	—			1.96
8/31	1.55	0.11	—	0.03	—	1.66	—			1.66
9/7	1.76	0.01	—	—	0.01	1.81	0.03	0.46		2.30
9/14	1.63	0.02	—	—	0.13	1.78	0.02	0.04		1.84
9/21	1.54	0.01	—	—	0.24	1.79	0.01	0.35		2.15
9/28	2.20	0.02	—	—	0.36	2.64	0.02	0.12		2.78
10/5	1.61	—	—	—	0.31	1.92	0.07	0.29	.03	2.31
10/12	1.39	—	—	—	0.27	1.66	0.03	0.26	.07	2.02

AVERAGE HOURLY EARNINGS $2.75

Source: Walter Kleinschrod, Leonard Kruk, and Hilda Turner, *Word Processing Operations, Applications, and Administration*, The Bobbs-Merrill Company, Inc., Indianapolis, 1980, p. 189.

FIGURE 15-16

Measures that could be developed in a Word Processing performance measurement and control (PMC) system:		For your center the measure at the left is (check one):				
Description of measure	What the measure indicates or how used: *Ref:*	**5**	**4**	**3**	**2**	**1**
		Degree of importance 5 high-1 low				
1 Productivity (A) Productivity of total center, e.g., work units/keyboard hours	1 (A) Indicates performance rate or efficiency for overall center — I (A)					
(B) Productivity of each secretary	1 (B) Same as I (A), calculated for each secretary — I (B)					
2 Turnaround (A) A single turnaround average for all documents processed by the center	2 (A) Indicates overall level of service as it relates to speed of getting documents back to users — II (A)					
(B) Turnaround average by secretary for all documents processed by that secretary	2 (B) Same as II (A), calculated for each secretary — II (B)					
(C) Turnaround average by user department for user department's documents	2 (C) Same as II (A), except indicates service provided to each user department — II (C)					
(D) Turnaround averages for original, revision, and rush work. Total of three averages for average center	2 (D) Indicates level of service provided by center on three classes of work. Recognizes differences in priority of the three classes — II(D)					
(E) Turnaround averages by secretary for original, revision, and rush work. Three averages for each secretary	2 (E) Same as II (D), calculated for individual secretaries — II (E)					
(F) Turnaround averages by user department for original, revision, and rush work. Three averages per department	2 (F) Same as II (D), except indicates service provided to each user department — II (F)					
3 Work Volume (A) Total volume of work processed by the center, e.g., pages, documents, or other units of work	3 (A) Indicates quality of work produced or through-put of center — how much was done — III (A)					
(B) Total volume of work processed by each secretary	3 (B) Same as III (A), calculated for each secretary — III (B)					
(C) Total volume of work processed for each user department	3 (C) Same as III (A), except indicates work done for each user department — III (C)					
7 Quality (A) Volume of secretary-made errors. Total for center	7 (A) Indicates level of quality for work leaving center — VII (A)					
(B) Volume of secretary-made errors. Total for each secretary	7 (B) Same as VII (A), calculated for individual secretaries — VII (B)					
8 Other						
Suggested frequency for preparing above measures	(A) Prepare these measures on a regular basis, e.g., weekly. (B) Prepare on an irregular basis. (C) Do not include these measures in PMC system.	**A**	**B**	**C**		

Source: Walter Kleinschrod, Leonard Kruk, and Hilda Turner, *Word Processing Operations, Applications, and Administration,* The Bobbs-Merrill Company, Inc., Indianapolis, 1980, p. 198.

The Daily Schedule Control

The best format to use for your tables is the schedule control sheet.

For short cycle operations you should use Figure 15-17. Under "work assignment" you can express your "target" in units per hour. Under "follow-up" you can document "actual" performance against "plan" at regular intervals throughout the shift. And under "report" you can generate the productivity percent per worker by dividing the "actual" quantity produced for the day by the "planned" quantity. Finally, you can generate the productivity percent for all the workers on the shift combined by dividing the total "actual" quantities by the total "planned" quantities.

For long cycle operations you should use Figure 15-18 on page 494. Under "work assignment" you can express your "target" in hours per unit. Under "follow-up" you can document target "hours earned" against actual "hours worked" at regular intervals throughout the shift. And under "report" you can generate the productivity percent for each couple of workers by dividing the "hours earned" by the "hours worked." Finally, you can generate the productivity percent for all the workers on the shift by dividing the total "hours earned" by the total "hours worked."

On the back of the worksheets is a variance summary (see Figure 15-19 on page 495), codifying the causes of lost time to highlight repetitive problems, explaining each problem, and listing immediate and future corrective actions.

Now let's look at how you could utilize the worksheets when you make each work assignment.

FIGURE 15-17

Sample performance measurement and control system

SCHEDULE CONTROL SHORT CYCLE OPERATIONS

Supervisor _____   Area _____   Date _____

Work Assignment					Follow-up								Report		
					PERIOD 1		PERIOD 2		PERIOD 3		PERIOD 4				%
Name	Station	Job	Quantity	Target	Plan	Actual	Plan	Actual	Plan	Actual	Plan	Actual	Planned	Actual	Productivity
											Totals				

Source: Harlan R. Jessup, "Front Line Control," *Supervisory Management,* October 1986, p. 14.

Recording Assignments

Before shift startup, you should fill out the first part of the schedule control. It might read like Figure 15-20 or 15-21 on page 496. Then you should make sure you communicate the specific assignments and your expectations to your workers. For Jones and Smith, you may do this by posting the target tables at the presses. For Black and White, you might say to them, ''I want you to wire Unit 2 completely. Let me know how it goes during the day today because it should be ready for test by the end of the shift tomorrow.''

Follow-Up

Next, you should follow up on the worker's performance.

In the press room, for example, if after checking performance every hour you find that by noon Smith has produced the expected 200 parts, you should note 200 planned and 200 actual in the Period 4 ''follow-up'' column on the schedule control sheet (Figure 15-17) and comment to Smith, ''Looks good!''

On the other hand, if you find that Jones has produced only 300 parts against the 400 planned, you should record the results in the Period 4 ''follow-up'' column (Figure 15-17) and ask him why. If it was a materials, equipment, or operator problem, you should record the lost time (one hour) and its cause on the variance report.

On the assembly floor, if everything goes according to plan, Black and White should be 25 percent through their wiring job at noon. If you find that they both lost an hour trying to find the engineer in order to get the latest revision of the wiring diagram, you should record six hours earned against eight hours worked in the Period 2 columns of the ''follow-up'' section (Figure 15-18). Then you should talk to Black and White to find out what caused the problem and to determine how to correct it. Did they act appropriately,

FIGURE 15-18

Schedule control—
short-cycle
operations

SCHEDULE CONTROL LONG CYCLE OPERATIONS												
Supervisor _____ Area _____ Date _____												
Work Assignment				**Follow-up**							**Report**	
				PERIOD 1		PERIOD 2		PERIOD 3		PERIOD 4		Hours Worked	Hours Earned	% Productivity
Job	Names	Operation	Target	Hours Worked	Hours Earned	Hours Worked	Hours Earned	Hours Worked	Hours Earned	Hours Worked	Hours Earned			
											Totals			

Source: Harlan R. Jessup, "Front Line Control," *Supervisory Management,* October 1986, p. 16.

or did they just put in a call and then sit and wait? Can they recover the time, or should you take other action? On the variance report, you should record the problem and document actions taken and future action needed.

At the end of the shift, you should enter the final data for each worker or pair of workers and talk to the operators about the day's performance. Then you should summarize the results for all of them combined and calculate the shift's productivity performance against plan. To cite two other examples: If you have a total of 20 operators, their performance might be recorded as 140 hours earned against 160 hours worked for a productivity factor of 88 percent. And if you have an assembly line with a total of ten operators, their performance might be recorded as 800 units produced against 1,000 units planned for a productivity factor of 80 percent.

Reporting

Once you have completed all the forms, you should discuss your unit's performance with your manager, making sure he or she understands what you are doing and what real problems need his or her attention. You can never win by concealing the real situation

FIGURE 15-19

Schedule control— long-cycle operations

VARIANCE SUMMARY					
Supervisor _____		Area _____		Date _____	
Work Station	Codes	Hours Lost	Problems	Corrective Action	Action Complete (Y/N)

Variance Codes:
A–Materials Quality
B–Materials Availability
C–Tooling and Equipment
D–Design and Planning
E–Operator
F–Other

Source: Harlan R. Jessup, "Front Line Control," *Supervisory Management,* October 1986, p. 16.

FIGURE 15-20

PRESS ROOM SCHEDULE CONTROL

NAME	STATION	JOB	QUANTITY	TARGET
J. Jones	press #1	part A	400	100/hr
S. Smith	press #2	part B	200	50/hr

Source: Harlan R. Jessup, "Front Line Control," *Supervisory Management,* October 1986, p. 18.

until the last day of the shipping period. But if you reveal a current problem, you will gain some understanding.

You should also track performance trends for yourself. Your day-to-day calculations won't mean much without a trend comparison, especially if you haven't had good measurements in the past. Tracking trends will help you to understand and communicate real performance gains. It will also help to reveal some of the chronic problems that look insignificant today but that will lead to significant lost opportunity if they persist.

The Bottom Line

As you can see thus far, front line control can be a powerful tool to improve the performance of your unit. But to really improve productivity you must go one step further and increase the workload or reduce the workforce.

If more work is coming, you need to figure out how to do it without a proportionate increase in headcount. But if work levels are staying the same, you must reduce overtime, take advantage of attrition, and perhaps ask your boss to help transfer employees out of your unit.

Your new control procedure, your improved communication, and your problem-solving routines should give you confidence that you can do it. You might set yourself a goal of 10 percent or 15 percent more output per employee and take the necessary steps, painful as they may be, to achieve this goal in the next three months. If you succeed, you can congratulate yourself for a job well done.

Competency Check:

Can you describe GE's front-line control concept?

FIGURE 15-21

ASSEMBLY HOUR SCHEDULE CONTROL

JOB	NAMES	OPERATION	TARGET
unit 1 assm.	B. Brown G. Green	pipe complete	16 man-hours
unit 2 assm.	W. White B. Black	wire complete	32 man-hours

Source: Harlan R. Jessup, "Front Line Control," *Supervisory Management,* October 1986, p. 18.

WHAT CAN THE SUPERVISOR DO?

As the cartoon says, "The Fairy Godmother Is Not Coming" to take care of all of your problems. Therefore, if you want your plan to work, you have to take control of your resources and, perhaps by using General Electric's front-line control approach, be a supervisor actively involved in the daily control activities that help to ensure that your unit or department does, indeed, meet its goals.

THE FAIRY GODMOTHER
IS NOT COMING!

COMPETENCY REVIEW

1. Define *control*.
2. Cite three characteristics of effective standards.
3. Describe the four steps in the control process.
4. Define and give examples of the three types of control.
5. Identify at least five areas in which the supervisor is responsible for control.
6. Compare fixed, flexible, and zero-based budgets.
7. Describe three scheduling techniques.
8. Describe the difference between 100 percent inspection and sampling, and explain two sampling techniques.
9. Describe three types of time controls.
10. Distinguish between EOQ and JIT, explaining the purposes of each.
11. Describe three uses of the computer as a control tool.
12. Describe GE's front-line control concept.

APPLICATIONS

1. Answer the following true or false questions to test your knowledge of cost control:

   _____ **a.** A supervisor does not have to involve his or her employees in a cost-control program.

   _____ **b.** A good cost-control program can eliminate a future need for a cost-cutting effort.

   _____ **c.** It is important to question the value of every procedure in your department.

   _____ **d.** Employees are always eager to contribute ideas on how to cut costs.

   _____ **e.** Automated equipment is always the most cost-effective method.

   _____ **f.** A cost-justification study is useful when purchasing new equipment.

   _____ **g.** Overtime is one of the most common reasons that departments go over their budgets.

   _____ **h.** Once a cost-control program is in place, it requires very little follow-through.

   _____ **i.** Small businesses cannot be expected to keep a budget.

   _____ **j.** Cost control in useful only if initiated by top management.

Source: "Keeping Costs Under Control," *Supervisory Sense*, vol. 7, no. 5, November 1986, p. 12.

2. **a.** Name six situations in which 100 percent inspection is appropriate (other than the examples given in the chapter). Explain why you selected these situations.
   b. Name six situations in which "go/no go" sampling is appropriate (other than the examples given in the chapter). Explain why you selected these situations.

    c. Name six situations in which variable sampling is appropriate (other than the examples given in the chapter). Explain why you selected these situations.

3. Construct a CPM or PERT network diagram for getting up in the morning and getting to class. Mark the critical path in a different color.

4. Given the following information, determine the economic order quantity for this particular situation: Jimmy Monroe, supervisor of the printing department, must determine the most cost-efficient inventory of paper. The department uses 1000 reams of paper per month at a cost of $2.40 per ream. The carrying cost per ream is 15 cents per month.

CASES

Case I: Clerks Get
Whistle While They Work

BOISE, Idaho (AP)—It has been called insulting, degrading and disruptive. But the man in charge says it's the best way he knows to weed out those who aren't working.

In a program begun Monday, whistles are blown seven times each day in an Idaho Department of Health and Welfare office. Each time, 30 clerical workers are ordered to fill out forms describing what jobs they were performing at the moment.

Theo M. Murdock, the new chief of the welfare division, is conducting a "random moment time study" of efficiency in his department. But the secretaries and some other administrators aren't pleased with the arrangement.

The study's purpose is to eliminate three secretarial positions and meet Gov. John Evan's recommendation that Health and Welfare reduce its budget $110,000.

"It's insulting to my intelligence the way they go about these things," fumed Lois Morland, a secretary for eight administrators.

"It's degrading and for no purpose," said Alma Keto, another secretary. "It's disruptive. . . . They could save themselves money by not doing it."

Complained co-worker Angie Stelling, a secretary for 11 office employees in the welfare division: "Yesterday morning there wasn't a single whistle. They all blew in the afternoon and everybody was sitting on pins and needles afraid to take a break or go to the bathroom."

Murdock, however, said he doesn't expect even the most dedicated secretary not to take a coffee break once in a while.

"That's part of a working day," he said. "If none of those showed up, I would be concerned."

The biggest bone of contention seems to be the whistle blower.

"They're paying him a good salary to lay off three of our people," said Mrs. Morland.

"It's the most economical way to evaluate the activities of different individuals in a group. It's also 99.9 percent accurate," said Robert Jensen, Murdock's administrative assistant and head of the project.

The secretaries have gained the support of some supervisors and the division's lower-level administrators.

1. Evaluate this form of work measurement.
2. What actions could have been taken to make this work measurement more effective?
3. Do you think these employees would be honest in reporting their activities? Why, or why not?
4. Would you accurately report your activities if you were one of the employees in this office? Explain your answer.

Case II: And the Bells Tolled!

Chief Inspector Ben Halley boarded bus 41 and dropped a token in the fare box. It gave the usual satisfying "ting" as it passed through the mechanism. He sat in the first seat to the right of the driver and watched.

Halley is responsible for checking fare thefts for City Suburban Transit. He likes his job, which involves traveling extensively to subsidiary companies and making sure that drivers are not taking cash fares instead of reporting them. None of the drivers know who he is, and at times his job is much like a detective's.

The company has fare boxes that register the fares with a small meter and a "ting." The meter is deliberately designed so that inspectors like Halley can unobtrusively observe it from the front seat. At the moment, this meter showed 27 fares collected.

The bus stopped, and six people boarded. One gave a transfer, the others dropped tokens and coins into the box. There were five "tings" as they did so, but the man with the transfer blocked Halley's view of the fare box. When he moved away, the register showed only 30 fares collected.

Halley was on the scent now. He carefully noted the next stops, mentally keeping track of the fares collected by counting the "tings." At the end of the run, he had counted 226 fares, but the meter showed only 122. He recalled that Jake Jackson, the supervisor, had complained about the low earning power of this run, considering its traffic potential.

Halley got up to leave the bus as five people boarded. He deliberately situated himself so that he could watch the driver. There was a slight bulge in the driver's jacket pocket. The driver took four fares in his hand and held his hand over the box. Four "tings" registered, but the meter moved only once. Halley's trained ear caught several "tings" coming from the driver's pocket. It was the old familiar game in the transit business—the bell machine in the pocket. This one was quite small and pretty good. Halley smiled as he got off the bus to phone in his preliminary report to the main office and prepare the written report that would be the basis for action against the driver.[10]

1. Identify 2 to 4 precontrols that might be used to prevent this type of behavior.
2. Identify 2 to 4 concurrent controls that might be used to prevent this type of behavior.

3. Identify 2 to 4 postcontrols that might be used to prevent this type of behavior.
4. What action would you take against the bus driver?

REFERENCES

1. David R. Hampton, *Management for Productivity,* McGraw-Hill Book Company, New York, 1986, p. 702.

2. Ibid., p. 681.

3. Ibid.

4. Nick Kinnie and Alan Arthurs, "Clock, Clock, Who's There?" *Personnel Management,* August 1986, p. 40.

5. Richard J. Schonberger, *Japanese Manufacturing Techniques: Nine Lessons in Simplicity,* The Free Press, New York 1982, p. 16.

6. Tom Shean, "Ford Is Geared Up to Achieve Leaner Inventories," *The Virginian Pilot and The Ledger Star,* Nov. 21, 1982.

7. Walter Kleinschrod, Leonard Kruk, and Hilda Turner, *Word Processing Operations, Applications, and Administration,* The Bobbs-Merrill Company, Inc., Indianapolis, p. 181.

8. Harlan R. Jessup, "Front Line Control," *Supervisory Management,* October 1986, pp. 12–13.

9. Ibid., p. 15.

10. Richard N. Farmer, Barry M. Richman, and William G. Ryan, *Incidents in Applying Management Theory,* Wadsworth Publishing Company, Inc., Belmont, Calif., 1966.

SUGGESTED READINGS

Berry, Waldron: "The Human Side of Control," *Supervisory Management.* June 1985, pp. 34ff.

Beyer, Janice M., and Harrison M. Trice: "A Field Study of the Use and Perceived Effects of Discipline in Controlling Work Performance," *Academy of Management Journal,* December 1984, pp. 743–764.

Carlson, Richard G.: "The Organizational Control System," *Journal of Property Management,* May–June 1987, pp. 7ff.

Duncan, W. Jack, Robert A. Scott, and James L. Beeland: "Interorganizational Relations and Perceived Patterns of Control by Lower Participants," *Akron Business and Economic Review,* Spring 1984, pp. 34ff.

Gibb, Peter: "Appraisal Goals and Controls," *Personnel Journal,* August 1985, pp. 89ff.

Green, Stephen G., Gail T. Fairhurst, and B. Kay Snavely: "Chains of Poor Performance and Supervisory Control," *Organizational Behavior and Human Decision Sciences,* July 1986, pp. 7ff.

16

PRODUCTIVITY AND THE QUALITY OF WORK LIFE

COMPETENCIES

Studying this chapter will enable you to:

1. Define *productivity*.

2. Cite the economic costs of low productivity.

3. Identify areas of productivity improvement.

4. Explain the relationship between quality of work life and productivity improvement.

5. Show how the supervisor might use the characteristics of standards in the productivity improvement process.

6. Describe the major approaches to productivity improvement and state an advantage and a disadvantage of each.

7. Tell why supervisors have resisted participative management.

CHAPTER OUTLINE

I. LOOK AT PRODUCTIVITY

    A. What Is Productivity?

    B. Productivity Problems in American Business

        1. Economic Costs of Low Productivity

        2. Variations Make Measuring Productivity Difficult

        3. Some Causes of Low Productivity

    C. Identifying Areas for Productivity Improvement

        1. Product

        2. Process

        3. People

II. QUALITY OF WORK LIFE AND PRODUCTIVITY

    A. What Is QWL?

    B. Relationship of QWL to Productivity Improvement

    C. Legal Aspects of QWL

        1. Equal Employment Opportunity

        2. Occupational Safety and Health

        3. Output Quality

    D. Ergonomics and Productivity

III. STANDARDS AND PRODUCTIVITY

    A. The Planning, Organizing, and Controlling Follow-Through

    B. Using Characteristics of Standards to Analyze Deviations

IV. APPROACHES TO IMPROVING PRODUCTIVITY

    A. Quality Circles

    B. Job Rotation

    C. Job Design and Redesign

    D. Positive Reinforcement

    E. Other Approaches

V. WHY SUPERVISORS RESIST QWL PROGRAMS

    A. Classification of Resisters

    B. Training Is the Key to Employee Involvement

J im Connard, a supervisor at World Techtonics, Ltd., left the meeting with the division manager's words ringing in his ears. "Headquarters expects a 5 percent productivity increase in this quarter or some heads will roll. You're the supers—get that 5 percent or it won't be my head that gets chopped."

"Here we go again," thought Connard, "passing the buck to the supers. They expect us to work miracles. Well this time, no way!"

A LOOK AT PRODUCTIVITY

Does Connard have a legitimate complaint? What is the supervisor's responsibility in increasing productivity? What role does productivity play in the controlling function? And what effect does productivity have on the firm and its employees? This chapter will address these questions and other productivity concerns, beginning with an explanation of the productivity concept.

What Is Productivity?

Note that Connard's boss did not offer to add any workers to help Connard achieve the 5 percent increase. He may have done so had headquarters asked for an increase in production, but the increase demanded was an increase in *productivity,* meaning an improvement in output from the same—or less—input. It meant a more efficient use of resources—working smarter rather than harder. For our purposes, *productivity* may be defined as the ratio of output to input, or:

$$\frac{\text{output}}{\text{input}} = \text{productivity}$$

For example, you might measure the energy efficiency of your car by dividing the miles traveled (output) by the gasoline used (input). The result would be a productivity rate expressed as miles per gallon.

Input refers to the resources used by a business or an agency—resources such as employees, materials, equipment, time, or capital—to carry out its mission. *Output* can refer to many things: to the products or services produced, to the workers trained within a certain period of time, to the increase in capital value, or to the number of customers served. Typically, when a business uses the term *productivity,* it is referring to the quantity of goods or services produced per worker per hour. A word processing operator producing 1400 lines of copy in an 8-hour day, for example, would have a productivity rate of 175 lines per hour ($1400 \div 8 = 175$). A manufacturing firm producing 3000 units (output) using 125 hours of labor (input) would have a productivity ratio of 24 (24 units per hour). If the 3000 units required $1500 in labor costs, the productivity ratio would be 2 (2 units per dollar). The supervisor might use these and other measures of productivity to compare month-to-month or year-to-year performance.

Measuring productivity is a part of the manager's controlling function—a feedback to indicate whether things are going according to plan, as you read in Chapter 15. Ideally, productivity should be a concern of every member of the organization. Historically, however, productivity has been a major responsibility of first-line management.

Competency Check:

Can you define *productivity?*

Productivity Problems in American Business

For most of the twentieth century, the American worker was among the most productive in the world. Whatever American consumers wanted—food, cars, houses, washing machines, or tennis rackets—American workers produced it in a quantity, quality, and at a price to satisfy them. In doing so, these workers helped their employers to prosper, the economy to grow, and Americans to develop a standard of living that is among the highest in the world.

In the 1960s and 1970s, however, American productivity growth began to decline. By 1977, while America still had the highest productivity rate in the world, Japan, France, and Germany had passed the United States in productivity gains. Since that time, American productivity has made no substantial gains. Annual productivity increases have become smaller and smaller, and, a few times, we have experienced actual decreases. Department of Labor statistics showed a negligible 0.5 percent gain in U.S. productivity in 1985 compared to a gain of 1.8 percent the previous year, as shown in Figure 16-1. The figure also shows that there were small increases in nonfarm

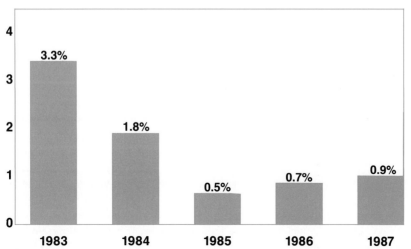

FIGURE 16-1

Productivity gains—nonfarm business

Source: Department of Labor for 1983–1986 data; *The Wall Street Journal,* March 4, 1988, for 1987 data.

productivity growth in 1986 and 1987. Economists debate over whether this reverses the declining trend. The recent gains are too slight to be predictive at this point. This declining or sluggish growth has caused some serious problems in the economy. We shall look at some of these problems next.

Economic Costs of Low Productivity

The price of a product or service is largely determined by the cost of producing it, including a reasonable profit for the owner. In the case of Connard, the firm may have experienced an increase in the cost of production materials. Without any offsetting action, that would have increased the cost of each item produced. When the same level of input is used to produce less output, the difference is inflated prices; that is, low productivity creates inflation.

Connard's management might look at several ways to meet the competition; not all of them are good ones, as indicated in the cartoon. Suppose that Connard's top management decided that to meet the competition, it would be unwise to increase the

B.C.

Source: By permission of Johnny Hart and Creators Syndicate, Inc.

price of the product to offset the increased cost of materials. They also decided that the profit margin was too narrow to be cut. To put it in the vernacular, Connard's management found itself between a rock and a hard place. If productivity remained at its present level, the profit squeeze may have forced Connard's company out of business. Other businesses may also fail. Those affected would include the firms that supply materials to Connard's company and those from whom the now-unemployed workers buy their goods and services. The rippling effect may be localized to one community or it may spread throughout a region or the nation, depending on the size and scope of the failed business. For example, the failure of a multinational auto manufacturer employing thousands of people in many locations would have a greater economic impact than would the failure of a corner grocery store employing only a half dozen workers.

Among the economic costs of low productivity are higher prices, rising unemployment, decreased income from taxes to the government to pay for goods and

Competency Check:

Can you cite the economic costs of low productivity?

services, increased taxes to pay for the social costs of unemployment, a lower standard of living for all those affected, and increased competition from foreign firms.

Variations Make Measuring Productivity Difficult

A study of productivity reveals many variations. It differs among countries, among segments of the economy, and among types of business activity. When productivity is higher in a foreign country with whom we trade, such as Japan, Americans tend to buy more imported products from that country because they are cheaper.

Productivity also varies among parts of the economy. Farming is usually more productive than manufacturing. That is largely due to the fact that for decades, farming, with government help, has concentrated on improving output per acre through the application of research, science, and technology. U.S. farming is among the most efficient in the world in terms of yield per acre. The goods-producing sector is also usually more productive than the service-producing sector.

Finally, productivity varies among business activities. Businesses carry out different kinds of activities—production, sales, finance, research and development, and management, to name a few. Most of the activities can be categorized into production/operations and information-based functions.

Most efforts at measuring productivity during this century have been directed toward production/operations workers. It was fairly easy to count cars coming off the production line in a day or bushels of corn grown on an acre of land in a season. It was more difficult to measure the productivity of the accountant who recorded the financial transactions or of the manager who made the decisions about meeting company objectives. These variations made measuring productivity difficult and the data on productivity levels sometimes confusing.

Some Causes of Low Productivity

In the past decade, serious analysts as well as some hindsight seers have cited many reasons for lower productivity in the United States. The finger of blame has been pointed in many directions: at management for not including workers in decision making nor sharing with them the rewards of productivity gains; at the government for adding to business costs through ever-increasing environmental/consumer protection programs and reporting demands; at the modern worker for being lazy, demanding, and unmotivated; at society for not meeting the needs of the unskilled, uneducated workers who can't fit into a labor market changing from a factory system to a service/information technology-based workplace; and at many others. Like most simple answers to complex problems, each accusation may have a degree of plausibility; but none, considered singly, provides an adequate explanation. A more comprehensive set of reasons has been provided by Arthur G. Bedeian:[2]

- a decline in the rate of investment in capital plant and equipment necessary to increase output
- heavy investment in antipollution devices and safety programs that do not contribute to output

- a younger, less experienced work force than in past years
- reduced expenditures on research and development
- more employees working in service occupations, which are inherently less productive
- labor unions' demands for higher wages and job security without commensurate increases in output
- economic recessions, where output is reduced without proportional work-force reductions
- a lessening of the work ethic, where employees simply don't want to work as hard as they used to

A supervisor reading this list of causes might ask, "But what can I do about capital investment, governmental regulations, or a sluggish economy?" Such concern would be understandable. A supervisor has little or no control over many of the reasons cited. Changing the direction of overall productivity calls for the rallying of forces both internal and external to the firm. Internally, productivity improvement must be the concern of every member of the firm. As members of the management team, supervisors play a vital role because they are the bridge between management and operations—the people who produce the goods and services. As a supervisor, you should be able to identify areas in which productivity might be improved.

Competency
Check:

Can you cite causes
of low productivity?

Identifying Areas for
Productivity Improvement

As Connard returned to his desk with the boss's mandate ringing in his ears, his thoughts turned to past experiences with the firm's finance managers. "Those number crunchers will probably beat me back to the shop floor, calculators in hand, ready to begin their cost-cutting routine." Connard's thinking, even though negative, is right on target. Cost cutting heads the list of most managers who are looking for productivity increases. But cost cutting is not the only way to improve productivity. Major areas that Connard might examine can be grouped into three categories: (1) product, (2) process, and (3) people, as shown in Figure 16-2. These three Ps of productivity and some questions about each that Connard might consider are:

Product

Look at the final product. Can it be made at less cost without sacrificing desired quality?

Materials.   Can they be purchased at lower cost? Can lower-cost materials be substituted? Will a different mix of materials achieve better results?

Equipment and facilities.   Are the equipment and facilities used in producing the product adequate to the task? Is the equipment of proper design and output capability? Is it performing up to expectations? Is maintenance minimal?

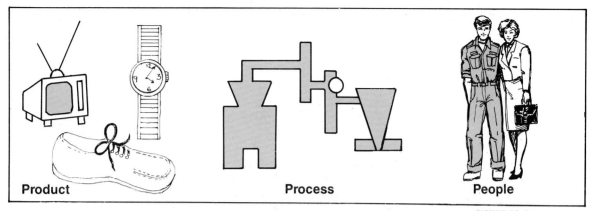

Product   **Process**   **People**

FIGURE 16-2

The 3 Ps of
productivity

Process

Can the work flow be redesigned for greater efficiency? Can process steps be simplified, combined, mechanized, or eliminated? Can scrappage be reduced?

People

Are there too many workers? Too few? Are workers' skills commensurate with the tasks assigned to them? Is training or retraining needed? Are workers performing up to standards? Are absence, tardiness, or morale problems affecting productivity? Are the workers motivated?

Competency Check:

Can you identify the areas of productivity improvement?

Of course, there are other areas which may be related to productivity, particularly in view of the variations noted above. Exploring the three Ps of productivity, however, will undoubtedly disclose productivity improvement possibilities.

WHAT CAN THE SUPERVISOR DO?

1. Develop a climate of productivity improvement awareness among employees and, after top management's approval, reward workers whose suggestions are implemented.
2. Even with an ongoing improvement program, supervisors may be called upon to go another mile on occasion, as Connard was. In such cases, begin a systematic examination of the three Ps. Daily observation may dictate the order in which the search should proceed. For example, if there has been concern about workers crisscrossing and backtracking as they complete an assembly task, you might begin with a study of the work flow (process) or the work-station layout. Look also at absences, tardiness, extended break time, idleness, and early leaving to see that work hours are adhered to (people). Examine the downtime

record of equipment—frequently broken machines play havoc with productivity (product/equipment).

3. Get workers involved in the improvement process. They do the job. Who should know more about it? Moreover, their participation will probably increase their motivation, which in and of itself may lead to increased productivity. As many studies have shown, workers' participation in solving the firm's problems increases the quality of their work life and, thus, their motivation to be better producers.

QUALITY OF WORK LIFE
AND PRODUCTIVITY

There is a consensus that focusing on the human aspects of the workplace is the key to increased productivity. A recent device to improve productivity through better management is the quality of work life (QWL) movement. A look at that movement shows that a positive correlation between QWL and productivity has been experienced by many firms.

What Is QWL?

Because QWL has been shown to affect production, the supervisor should know what QWL is and how it can be applied to the workplace.

Since the beginning of the QWL movement in the early 1970s, many definitions have emerged. This diversity led the American Center for the Quality of Working Life to develop this definition in 1977.

> Quality of work life improvements are defined as any activity which takes place at every level of an organization which seeks greater organizational effectiveness through the enhancement of human dignity and growth . . . a process through which the stakeholders in the organization—management, union(s) and employees—learn how to work together better . . . to determine for themselves what actions, changes and improvements are desirable and workable in order to achieve the twin and simultaneous goals of an improved quality of life at work for all members of the organization and greater effectiveness for both the company and the union(s).[3]

The core of a QWL program is an effort by management to encourage its employees to participate in key decisions that affect their day-to-day work patterns. In addition, QWL encompasses all efforts to stimulate workers by making their jobs and their work environment more interesting. To be successful, a QWL program must have the total commitment of top management which, in turn, must engender the support and participation of every member of the organization. A comprehensive 1982 study of people and productivity found that lack of management commitment and union problems were encountered in efforts to implement employee involvement in a tenth of the companies reporting. Nevertheless, 82 percent of the managers, in assessing the future of QWL, responded that participative management was a promising new approach and not a fad.[4]

Relationship of QWL to Productivity Improvement

The QWL concept assumes that there is a positive relationship between worker involvement and higher productivity. This assumption is supported by many theorists in the field of motivation. Maslow and Herzberg, whom you read about in Chapter 11, are among these theorists. Maslow's hierarchy of needs model and Herzberg's motivation model suggest that people are motivated to higher-level behavior (translated as ''better performance in the workplace'') when they have some control over the conduct of their jobs and are made to feel that they have a direct stake in the accomplishment of company goals.

Peter Drucker showed the importance of management's solicited input from employees this way: ''The greatest boost to productivity would be for management people to learn to ask, 'What do we do in this organization that helps you do the job you're being paid for, and what do we do that hampers you?'''[5] Certainly it makes sense to ask those who work regularly on a production line how the process might be improved. Who knows better? The payoff for the company is not only higher productivity and greater profit but a more satisfied worker who, when properly recognized and rewarded for his or her effort, will strive toward even greater efficiency.

Competency Check:

Can you explain the relationship between quality of work life and productivity improvement?

Legal Aspects of QWL

The degree to which QWL is developed in a company is a managerial option, but certain aspects are controlled by law. The manager must, therefore, address at least the legally mandated environmental components.

The QWL concept embodies philosophical, psychological, and physiological components of the corporate culture. While interpretations of QWL may differ widely among firms, managers must be aware of laws governing certain basic rights of workers. (You will study more about worker rights in Chapter 17.) Of course, there is no law that says a firm must reward a worker for a suggestion that improves productivity; the firm can choose to do that or not. But as you read in Chapter 7, a firm *must* adhere to OSHA standards for maintaining a safe workplace. For example, a firm would be culpable for allowing employees to work with exposed electric wires on a damp factory floor. As a supervisor, you might recommend a reward for a worker's suggestion, but in the case of the exposed electric wire, you would immediately report the situation and insist that the dangerous electric system be corrected. You might want to review Chapter 7, where the physical environment is treated in greater depth. For our discussion of QWL, the legal guidelines presented below are pertinent.

Equal Employment Opportunity

As you read in Chapter 8 on staffing, Equal Employment Opportunity (EEO) laws require equal treatment of workers in all personnel decisions, including recruiting, selecting, training, promoting, and terminating. The degree to which management promotes participative decision making is a managerial option, but nondiscriminatory personnel practices are legally mandated.

Occupational Safety and Health

The Occupational Safety and Health Agency administers certain laws pertaining to the safety and health of employees in the workplace. As noted in Chapter 7, management is required to maintain at least a minimally safe and nonhealth-threatening environment. The firm must meet OSHA standards for work factors such as building, equipment, operating procedures, and quality of air and water.

Output Quality

The fact that there are legal parameters for producing pharmaceuticals or selling airplane tickets may seem somewhat removed from QWL, which pertains to workers. The pertinence may be indirect, but the legal guidelines for producing and marketing certain products and services give to management in these industries a foundation for building an attitude of quality awareness among employees. When workers know that the Food and Drug Administration requires that a food-processing firm such as Birdseye operate under cleanliness standards, management will have a basis for creating and maintaining quality awareness among the workers.

Other agencies, such as the Department of Health and Human Services and the Federal Aviation Administration, also have an impact on the legal environment of business. Whether the relationship to QWL is direct or indirect, management has a responsibility to operate within legal bounds, including all aspects of the environment.

Ergonomics and Productivity

The work-environment relationship has undergone intensive examination in recent years. As you learned in Chapter 7, *ergonomics* is a science that tries to design the work, the workplace, and the tools to fit the worker, and not vice versa. A firm might be producing a safe product in a safe environment and still, if the work environment is neither physically comfortable nor aesthetically pleasing, it might have trouble motivating its workers to higher productivity.

The aim of ergonomics is to increase productivity while, at the same time, making life more comfortable for the worker. Your responsibility in managing the physical environment has already been addressed. Here we look at the relationship of the physical environment to productivity.

In Chapter 7, you learned that G. Gordon Long, referring to effective planning of the office environment, cited four factors to be considered which are related to productivity: (1) utilities, (2) lighting, (3) acoustics, and (4) furnishings.[6] They involve technological, psychological, and aesthetic considerations.

According to Long, ergonomics can show the way to efficiency and productivity. Supervisors need to be aware of ergonomics, not to the degree of becoming ergonomics engineers, but out of concern for the worker and what it will do to improve the quality of the worker's life, with the resultant potential of increased productivity.

WHAT CAN THE SUPERVISOR DO?

1. Train yourself and your workers to be alert to factors in the environment which may contribute to stress, strain, or dissatisfaction and thus lower productivity. Correcting these factors may be as simple as moving a desk to reduce glare or regulating the thermostat for better comfort. Some situations may be more complex and require the involvement of other managers, engineers, or external consultants. A temperature problem in a building where the atmosphere is centrally controlled might require the services of the maintenance staff or an engineer. The supervisor might need to propose that lighting in the computer room be redesigned to reduce eyestrain.
2. Read publications that deal with environmental management, ergonomics, and productivity improvement. This will sharpen your understanding of the relationships among these factors and the possible implications for your firm. Suggestions made from a knowledgeable base have a better chance of being accepted and implemented.

STANDARDS AND PRODUCTIVITY

Chapter 3 pointed out that setting standards of performance is a part of the planning process. Knowing what is expected of resources—whether human, capital, or natural—provides the basis for the controlling function.

The Planning, Organizing, and Controlling Follow-Through

When standards are established in the planning process and the work is organized and assigned to conform to these standards, controlling can be considered follow-through in the manager's ongoing responsibilities.

As you learned in Chapter 15, standards are control devices. They serve as the criteria against which actual performance is measured. Standards must be established for all resources. These standards are usually expressed in terms of quantity, quality, value, time limitations, and behavior. Management might set standards, for example, for the level of sales, return on investment, British thermal unit output from a heating plant, printer lines per minute, customer satisfaction (measured by number of complaints), employee absence reduction, or productivity. Standards provide a yardstick against which to measure the firm's movement toward its goals. A major part of the supervisor's job is to follow through to see that the standards are met.

Using the Characteristics of Standards to Analyze Deviations

Since standards are the basis for control, your daily observation will usually preclude a crisis in deviation from expected performance. The following characteristics of standards provide guidelines for analysis of deviations which occur from either a crisis or from gradual erosion:

Competency Check:

Can you show how the supervisor can use the characteristics of standards in the productivity improvement process?

● *Are they realistic?* What is the history of accomplishment since the standards were set? Production data will help you spot the points of departure and identify the contributing factors. Compare standards to industry, to competing firms, to other departments, and among the workers doing the same tasks. Check equipment. Is it performing as expected? Is training or retraining needed?

● *Are they stated clearly?* Read them. Are they specific? Ask several workers for their interpretations of the standards. Are there differences in understanding? Try a team approach to restating ambiguous standards.

● *Are they communicated clearly?* What medium was used for communication? Is there a more effective medium? Has the follow-up to orientation and initial training been adequate? Ask for feedback from workers who use the standards.

APPROACHES TO IMPROVING PRODUCTIVITY

In the history of American business, an old axiom has prevailed: To increase profits, sell more, cut costs, or both. That axiom is still true, at least for the short term. However, current thinking modifies the axiom to focus more on increasing productivity through concern for the most important resource of all—the workers. As pointed out in Chapter 11, a growing body of research findings sustantiates the belief that workers are motivated to higher performance if they perceive that their employers value them as human beings, encourage their participation in decision making, and share the company's success with them through some type of gain-sharing system. These concepts are embodied in the QWL programs presented earlier in this chapter.

Many approaches have been used in recent years to improve productivity. An interesting study by Lou Harris for an insurance firm asked employees and business executives how they thought productivity could be improved at their place of work. A comparison of their attitudes is shown in Figure 16-3. The top choice for both

FIGURE 16-3

COMPARISON OF EMPLOYEES' AND BUSINESS EXECUTIVES'
ATTITUDES TOWARD IMPROVING PRODUCTIVITY

Question: *To what extent could overall productivity at your place of work be improved by (read each item)—a great deal, somewhat, only a little, or not at all? (Percentages represent those who say "a great deal.")*

	EMPLOYEES	BUSINESS EXECUTIVES
employees getting financial rewards for productivity gains	43%	55%
more and better information from management about decisions that affect employees	42	40
employees being treated with more respect by their supervisors	42	37
better relations between management and labor	39	52
more favorable attitudes toward (your) employer	38	50
employees having more say in decisions that affect them	37	16
employees having a greater chance for recognition and promotion	37	40
employees having more job security	36	11
employees getting bonuses that rise or fall depending on the company's profits	36	34
having better fringe benefits	35	5
use of better equipment and tools	29	67
employees having less pressure on the job	26	3
employees having safer working conditions	20	8
having more pleasant physical surroundings at work	19	8
employees having more convenient working hours	17	3

Source: Daniel Dickinson, *It's Their Business, Too,* American Management Association, New York, 1985, p. 26.

groups was financial rewards for productivity gains. The employees' answers that tied for second place are more interesting. They were "more and better information from management" and "being treated with more respect by . . . supervisors." Information and respect, which can't be pocketed, scored higher than did job security, bonuses, better tools, fringe benefits, or safer working conditions.[7] Does that remind you of the Herzberg model from Chapter 11? It should. Also, if you note the difference between the responses on employee participation in decision making by employees (37 percent) and executives (16 percent), you should recall the discussion of traditional and participative management in Chapters 1 and 2. Would you say that most of these executives have a traditional management orientation?

Many methods are being used in the search for higher productivity. Some firms, for example, have established QWL programs for the entire firm; others have used single techniques designed to motivate the worker. Some of these methods are more closely related to the supervisor's function than others. Gain sharing, for example, may be largely a communicating/reporting function for the supervisors, who are expected to let top management know of workers whose efforts meet the criteria of the company's gain-sharing programs. Of the widely used methods which might involve the supervisor, four are presented below.

Quality Circles

During the past 15 years, American industry, faced with sluggish productivity and other problems, has discovered and implemented quality circles (QCs)

Often a part of a QWL program, *quality circles* are small groups of workers who meet regularly but voluntarily, usually with their supervisor, to identify and solve work-related problems. QCs have come to epitomize the QWL movement, but the terms are not synonymous. After over 25 years of use, notably in Japan, QCs by the mid-1980s had proliferated in America to a point where a national association of QC leaders had been formed. A 1982 study disclosed that QCs were operating in one out of three companies with from 500 to 5000 employees, in two out of three with over 5000 employees, and in three out of four manufacturing companies with 10,000 or more employees. The study also identified the QC as the fastest-growing human resource activity in companies with 500 or more employees. Moreover, these companies ranked QCs among the 10 activities with the highest percentage of "very successful" ratings for productivity improvement.[8]

QCs meet on a regular basis, typically once a week. Composed of from 7 to 12 members of a work group, generally with their supervisor as leader, the QC attempts to identify and, in a brainstorming mode, find solutions to work-related problems. A supervisor at a Ford plant who started a QC by calling a meeting of all employees said, "The more we talked, the more we understood each other. That's a big step forward." In another Ford location, hourly employees were trained in problem-solving skills and then used their talents to solve a nagging machine-operation problem.[9] Many firms have used QCs successfully. Among them are Lockheed, credited with setting up the first American QC; Westinghouse; General Motors; Harley Davidson; and Honeywell. Military and public agencies have also used QCs.[10]

Viewed from both Maslow's and Herzberg's theories of motivation, the QC meets the personal needs of the individual and gets the worker involved in meeting company goals.

To be successful in improving productivity, QCs must have the commitment of top management and the support of all management. The supervisor is the key link. If a supervisor goes to a meeting with an attitude of indifference, boredom, or even disdain, the QC workers will follow suit and the effort will fail. On the other hand, the supervisor who approaches the QC as a cooperative team effort by labor and management to meet common goals will find the QC an effective way to motivate workers.

The supervisor's role as QC leader is not as an authority figure. It is as a discussion leader, a facilitator of group participation, who helps the group formulate and refine solutions to problems. The supervisor's attitude, therefore, is extremely important. In leading a group, a supervisor must be able to analyze and adapt to the situation since groups differ in their abilities and behavior just as do individuals. A review of leadership models in Chapter 11 and of group behavior in Chapter 12 is appropriate in preparing to work with QCs.

How can the supervisor start a QC? If the technique is not already being used in the firm, the supervisor can recommend, through channels, that QCs be studied as a way to improve productivity. First, however, the supervisor must learn as much as possible about QCs and how the technique has benefited other firms. Presenting a knowledge-based rationale along with the recommendation will help to influence top management to pursue the suggestion.

Connard in the beginning of this chapter might well consider taking a QC approach to achieving the 5 percent productivity increase mandated by his top management. The workers themselves are often in the best position to see where improvements can be made. Connard should understand that a QC cannot be created overnight, but simply asking the workers for their suggestions for meeting the goal could establish the climate for a more formalized implementation of QCs as an ongoing productivity program.

Job Rotation

Simple boredom can result in lowered productivity. In an attempt to prevent or alleviate boredom on the job, some firms use job rotation. Under a system of *job rotation,* workers are transferred from one job to another on a systematic basis. Station assignments may be for different lengths of time—1 week, 6 weeks, or even 6 months. It is probably used more commonly for crosstraining of the skills of various jobs in firms where there is high worker movement, turnover, or absence.

Job rotation is also used as a management training device. For example, a bank management trainee might be moved through a series of assignments—including transit, credit, and marketing—serving with a manager-mentor for a period of from 1 to 6 months, depending on the length of the training program.

Automated production-line jobs can very quickly become monotonous. Rotating a worker through a series of related jobs will help to relieve that monotony—for a while. It will also give the worker a greater understanding of the entire process and of the co-workers who perform various parts of a task. A production worker might rotate through jobs such as monitoring the automated production process, quality control of output, and inventory control.

The greatest advantage of job rotation, other than the temporary relief from monotony it provides, is that it helps the company carry out the production process when one worker is absent. Job rotation is not the most widely used technique. Only 18 percent of all firms surveyed in one study used job rotation, ranking it seventeenth out of the 23 techniques they reported using.[11] There are some obvious reasons. First, job rotation provides only temporary relief from boredom, at best. Workers soon become familiar with all the jobs in a rotation work group, each with its own kind of monotony. Second, additional training is involved, and this adds to labor costs. Third, there is an adjustment period, usually with lowered productivity each time a worker moves to a new station. Fourth, job rotation really does not involve the workers in decision making concerning their or the company's goals.

Job Design and Redesign

The organizing function includes identifying the tasks to be done and grouping those tasks into jobs to be assigned to workers. In Chapter 5 you learned that a job may be described in terms of its depth, scope, and core dimensions. The more restrictive any of these elements is, the more routine the job. For example, if a worker in a microchip assembly line is assigned the task of tracing one circuit on the chip on a terminal schematic before passing it to the next worker, the job is extremely limited in all these elements. Such a job could very quickly lead to boredom, eyestrain, and fatigue. As suggested in the cartoon, boring jobs do nothing for productivity.

Source: Reprinted with special permission of King Features Syndicate, Inc.

To improve productivity, the job might be redesigned. One method is called *job enlargement;* that is, increasing the tasks included in the job. The microchip assembly-line worker might have the tasks of examining all circuits, testing the chip, and recording the number of chips accepted or rejected at that station added to the job. A WP operator might have his or her job enlarged from simply entering data to proofing and collating the documents produced. Job enlargement increases one of the core dimensions—variety—but it does little to increase the scope or the other core dimensions of the job. It does not increase the worker's freedom to make decisions regarding the method of doing the job. One study involving a sample of approximately 49,000 U.S. corporations with 100 or more employees, representing 41 million workers, showed that only 22 percent of the respondents used job enlargement, while 46 percent used job design/redesign in their productivity improvement programs.[12] While job enlargement offers some relief in a highly specialized job, other techniques have been more successful.

Job enrichment has been used to increase the scope and core dimensions of a job. *Job enrichment* involves giving the worker more autonomy, more responsibility, and more control over the job. It also upgrades the core dimensions by increasing the variety of operations, providing task identity by giving the worker a feeling for the completion of the job. It upgrades the significance of the job for the worker, for co-workers, and for others in and out of the firm. It increases autonomy, allowing the worker to set both personal and company goals. Finally, it provides feedback by involving the worker in each step of the production of the item.

It is easier to enrich some jobs than others. Assigning more autonomy to a manager might be relatively easy because decision making is a basic responsibility of management. It might be more difficult to assign autonomy to specialized workers in an assembly line because they usually work on assigned, routine tasks. Automated assembly lines tend to narrow the scope even more. But the workers in routine jobs may need enrichment more than anyone. As noted in Chapter 5, General Motors recently announced that it will use, in its planned Saturn auto plant, a team approach in which unionized workers and management will design jobs together. This cooperative approach is somewhat revolutionary and raises legal questions, but GM believes that its workers will be more productive in jobs they help design.

There is some evidence that the improved productivity that results from the team approach to job enrichment cannot be sustained over a long period. General Foods successfully enriched the jobs in a new pet food plant in 1971 by establishing work teams and upgrading the core dimensions of jobs. The plan worked well for several years but had begun to weaken by the late 1970s. Non Linear Systems, a manufacturer of digital electrical measurement instruments, experimented with job enrichment by using teams of 3 to 12 employees in place of a straight assembly line. Minimal supervision was provided, and the teams were allowed to decide on methods and on the pace of production. They were also expected to resolve their own conflicts and handle their own discipline. At first, both productivity and morale improved. But the lack of structure within the groups slowed decision making and eventually led to worker dissatisfaction. After 4 years, the experiment was ended.[13]

In using any job redesign approach, the supervisor should take into consideration all elements of the job: the work itself, the worker, and the work context, including co-workers, supervision, and the rewards system. The fact that job design and redesign was reported to be "very successful" (26 percent) or "somewhat successful" (48 percent) in a comprehensive productivity survey of American corporations shows that this approach has potential as a way of improving productivity.[14]

Positive Reinforcement

In Chapter 9, you learned that appraising and rewarding employees is a critical part of the staffing function. Reinforcement theory, rooted in the works of Pavlov, Thorndike, and Skinner, is based on the assumption that behavior which brings a pleasing outcome is likely to be repeated and that behavior which has an unpleasant outcome is not likely to be repeated. Our concern here is with the use of positive reinforcement as an approach to improving productivity. *Positive reinforcement* refers to the use of rewards—such as praise, bonuses, or recognition—to encourage the repetition of a desired behavior. Suppose that you, as a manager, require that expense reports be submitted on time and that Sue Nguyen consistently fulfills this requirement. You want her to continue this "good" behavior. Using positive reinforcement, you could thank Nguyen and praise her timely reporting, post an "exemplary employee" profile of Nguyen on the company bulletin board, or recommend her for a bonus. Any of these actions might motivate Nguyen to keep up the good work and might also motivate others to get their reports in on time in order to share in the rewards.

A bank president described his firm's use of positive reinforcement this way:

> The reinforcement we now use focuses on the positive or reward forms controlling behavior. Positive control has paid off for our employees and the bank. Our bank rewards performance through increased merit salary increments, bonuses, days off, and educational benefits. In most cases, the employees have become advocates of our positive reward program. I have heard person after person express the wish that the program had been introduced years ago. We are more than pleased with the program and plan to continue using it with all employees.[15]

There has been some criticism of positive reinforcement. Some believe it is a form of payoff or bribery and is used to modify the behavior of workers to fit management's conception of "a good worker." They question the use of extrinsic rewards such as pay to modify behavior in order to fit someone else's model. It should be remembered, though, that a pat on the back for good performance, or a "Good job, Harry" comment to a worker from a manager can go a long way toward improving the psychological climate of the organization. In such a climate, productivity improvement can be achieved much more easily than it can in a negative work environment.

Other Approaches

The approaches to productivity improvement discussed above are by no means the only ones available. In a recent study of 171 manufacturing and nonmanufacturing companies, cost reduction, employee participation, and productivity incentives were ranked as the three methods most often used to improve productivity. Figure 16-4 shows the top nine methods reported by the companies. Gain sharing, salarying blue-collar workers, appraisal and feedback, training and development, and personalized work hours have also been used successfully.

Competency Check:

Can you discuss the major approaches to productivity improvement and state an advantage and a disadvantage of each?

The worker who has a piece of the action will surely be more willing to see that the company succeeds. Gain sharing, in particular, is increasing in importance as a means of making workers feel a part of the firm and thus motivating them to produce more.

Training is fundamental to the achievement of productivity gains. A supervisor is certainly in a position to observe workers in action and to see where training or retraining is needed to improve performance. Developmental programs are also a way of motivating workers to move up in the corporate family.

The creative supervisor is alert to the methods that have been used successfully by

FIGURE 16-4

COMPANY PROGRAMS TO IMPROVE PRODUCTIVITY

TYPE OF PROGRAM	AVERAGE RANKING*
cost reduction	2.3
employee participation	3.1
productivity incentives	3.3
goal setting with productivity focus	3.5
increased automation	3.8
quality improvement	3.9
increased employee training	4.7
better labor-management relations	4.9
increased research and development	5.3

*The rankings were based on a scale where 1 represents the most used programs.
Source: Y. K. Shetty, "Managerial Strategies for Improving Productivity," *Industrial Management*, November–December 1984, p. 24.

other firms as well as to the new techniques that are reported in business literature from time to time.

WHY SUPERVISORS RESIST QWL PROGRAMS

"The people in the middle are the ones who will make it go or not go," according to a consulting services director.[16] Yet it is the people in the middle who have been hardest to convert to participative management. In a study of 139 firms using some form of participative management, 72 percent of the responding supervisors felt that an employee involvement program was good for the company and 60 percent felt it was good for employees. But only 31 percent felt that they themselves benefited from the program.[17] What is the reason for the negative attitude of supervisors?

The major reason is concern for job security. When a QC or work team is established to identify and solve work-related problems, supervisors often feel it will erode their authority. After all, keeping the wheels turning daily has traditionally been the essence of the supervisor's job. If problem solving is to be assigned to workers, where will that leave the supervisor?

Overt reaction to QWL takes different forms. Some supervisors simply withhold their support without visibly disregarding management policy. In one plant, supervisory resistance took the form of a hands-off policy as newly formed semiautonomous work teams tried to solve problems. When questions arose that the teams could not handle, the supervisors said the job was not theirs but the teams'. In this case, the supervisors were trying to regain their authority by undermining the team approach.

Other reasons often cited for supervisors' resistance to employee involvement programs include (1) the new definition of the supervisors' jobs, (2) the additional work created, and (3) the fear of change. A participative management program begun in

1984 at Corning Glass Works met with some supervisory resistance. But it was accepted when a work team of five machinists, assigned a die-manufacturing problem, came up with a solution within 5 hours, costing less than $200. Under the firm's traditional management, a department head, supervisors, and an engineer would have huddled to find a solution and then presented it as an edict.[18] Worker motivation would have been very low at best, and some type of resistance would have been encountered.

Classification of Resisters

Competency Check:

Can you tell why supervisors have resisted participative management?

Janice A. Klein suggests that supervisory resisters can be classified into five types: (1) theory X proponents, (2) status seekers, (3) skeptics, (4) equality seekers, and (5) deal makers. Figure 16-5 shows why each type resists and gives clues to the behavior of the resisters.

In any of these resister attitudes, the supervisor should recognize that he or she is in a no-win situation. If top management is clearly dedicated to changing the organizational culture to one of a more participative nature, supervisors must adapt or lose their jobs. A review of McGregor's theory X-Y in Chapter 11 may be needed here as a checkpoint on your assumptions about people at work.

Training Is the Key to Employee Involvement

Training of supervisors has been seen as the key to implementing successful employee involvement programs to improve productivity and the quality of work life. Florida Light and Power Company began a program and found that middle managers were confused about their new roles. The company tailored special training sessions to help them adjust to the new program.[19] Training is a powerful tool. It can help you change your attitude from one of skepticism and insecurity to one of willing participation. There are also other steps you can take to prepare yourself for participative management.

WHAT CAN THE SUPERVISOR DO?

As a supervisor, you should learn as much as you can about participative management in all its forms. Develop a peer network so that you and other supervisors can share in a study and discussion program. Begin by referring to Figure 2-6, which lists nine duties of first-line supervisors in a plant with semiautonomous work teams. Then read from other sources, such as those in References and Suggested Readings at the end of this chapter.

Moreover, be aware that management today sees employee involvement as a way to motivate workers to higher productivity. And higher productivity is the name of the game in today's workplace. That thrust is not going to go away in the

FIGURE 16-5

SUPERVISORS AS RESISTERS

TYPE	WHY THEY RESIST	CLUES TO BEHAVIOR
1. proponents of theory x	The concept goes against their belief system.	Comments such as "Employees are children, not adults" and "Employees will just take advantage of the program to get out of work."
2. status seekers	They fear losing prestige.	Unwillingness to let go of behavior associated with control. Fear of losing leadership role. Comments such as "Foremen can't be equal members of a team; they will always be the leader."
3. skeptics	They doubt the sincerity and the support of upper management.	Comments such as "This program is no different from past ones. It will fade away in a few months"; "The problem is the next level up"; and "They don't really practice what they preach."
4. equality seekers	They feel that they are being bypassed and left out of the program.	Comments such as "Why do we have to change before the employees do?" Nonsupport and "hands off" as problems arise.
5. deal makers	The program interferes with one-on-one relationships with workers.	Comments such as "We've been stripped of our power" and "We have no control over the process."

Source: Janice A. Klein, "Why Supervisors Resist Employee Involvement," *Harvard Business Review,* September–October 1984, p. 90.

near future. Becoming knowledgeable about participative management, leadership styles, human motivation, and communication skills will help reduce your fear of the unknown and thus make you more amenable to change.

If you are a student preparing to enter supervisory management, you can benefit from the suggestions above for the practicing supervisor. You are on the right track by taking this course.

COMPETENCY REVIEW

1. Define *productivity*.
2. Cite several economic costs of low productivity.
3. Identify three areas of productivity improvement.
4. Explain the relationship between quality of work life and productivity.
5. Show how the supervisor might use the characteristics of standards in the productivity improvement process.
6. Describe the major approaches to productivity improvement, and state an advantage and a disadvantage of each.
7. Tell why supervisors have resisted participative management.

APPLICATIONS

1. National Manufacturing Corporation was finally overwhelmed by falling productivity, competition from imports, and union demands. When it closed its doors, its 50,000 employees joined the ranks of the nation's unemployed. Trace the economic costs of National's closing to the city where it operated. How might the state and the national economy be affected?

2. For each department listed below, name an input and an output that would provide an appropriate production measure for a manufacturing firm. The first is filled in as an example.

DEPARTMENT	INPUT	OUTPUT
a. accounting	computers	fiscal reports
b. delivery		
c. building maintenance		
d. sales		
e. safety		
f. training & development		

3. Tracy Carter, a production supervisor at Ace Plastics, makes monthly comparisons of her group's productivity. The production and labor input for June and July are as follows:

   June: production, 2800 units; labor input, 300 hours
   July: production, 3000 units; labor input, 330 hours

   a. Find the productivity rate for each month.
   b. What conclusions might Carter draw from the results?

c. At the June rate of efficiency, how many hours should have been adequate to produce the 3000 units in July?

d. What do you suggest that Carter do now?

CASES

Case I: Popping the Quota

World Techtonics, Ltd. (WTL), in the beginning of the chapter is a large manufacturer of consumer electronics products, including items such as solid-state radios, boom boxes, hand computers, disc and cassette players, and pagers. Competition from imports from Japan and Taiwan have been intensifying in recent years, and WTL has barely been holding its market share. Top management is determined to increase productivity to maintain its lead for its biggest seller, the Jogger's Mate belt radio and ear domes. Connard supervises the assembly work groups. For some time, his workers have been hard-pressed to meet the 3000 units per week for his group. The division manager has turned down his two requests for overtime. Connard has been concentrating on cutting lost time; he checks closely on tardiness, overstaying break time, and early leaving. The workers grumble at the change from a relaxed atmosphere to a sweatshop. Their resentment is beginning to show in their attitude toward Connard and their co-workers, as well as in their performance. Productivity has fallen behind the daily quota several times in the past quarter.

At the quarterly division manager's meeting, the supervisors were told that the company expects a 5 percent productivity increase in the approaching quarter. "Jeez! That's 150 more units—my gang can't meet the quota now!" Connard muttered to another supervisor. As Connard left the meeting, he thought, "Here we go again—passing the buck to the supers. They expect us to work miracles. Well this time, no way!"

1. How might Connard use the three Ps of productivity to achieve the 5 percent increase?
2. What do you feel are the causes of Jim's resistance?
3. How might quality circles be used at WTL? What does Connard need to do to prepare himself for the QC technique?

Case II: Move It!

Lem Johnson supervises a work group of eight persons at Wikson Furniture's retail warehouse, where furniture is displayed in showrooms and sold from adjoining warehouse storage. The furniture is delivered to the warehouse by container trucks and off-loaded at the incoming pier. It is uncrated, coded, moved into sections of the warehouse by type of item, and stored in 15-foot shelving until it is sold.

When a sale is made, an order is sent to the section supervisors' desks in the warehouse. Each supervisor assigns an order to a member of his or her work group, who drives a cartlift to the appropriate section, loads the item, and delivers it to the customer pickup station.

After a customer selects and pays for the purchase, he or she is asked to wait in a lounge until a number is called indicating that the item is ready for pickup. Customers often complain about the long wait to pick up purchases. There have been several unpleasant scenes at the pickup desk; the warehouse manager has been called to the desk several times recently to calm an irate customer and salvage the sale.

The warehouse manager has told Johnson to shape up and get his group to deliver the furniture faster. Johnson, who wants to move up in the company, is enrolled in a community college course in supervision and management. He has recently been studying productivity improvement and has decided to try the three Ps of productivity as an approach to his group's duties.

1. What is Johnson's "product" at Wikson?
2. What questions might Johnson ask about each of the three Ps that would lead to greater efficiency in delivering the furniture?
3. If you were Johnson, which of the questions would you try to answer first?

REFERENCES

1. Quoted in New York Stock Exchange, Inc., *People and Productivity—A Challenge to Corporate America,* Office of Economic Research, New York, 1982, p. i.

2. Arthur G. Bedeian, *Management,* The Dryden Press, Inc., Chicago, 1986, p. 218.

3. Lee M. Ozley and Judith S. Ball, "Quality of Work Life: Initiating Successful Efforts in Labor-Management Organizations," *Personnel Administrator,* May 1982, p. 27, copyright, 1982, The American Society for Personnel Administration, Alexandria, Va.

4. New York Stock Exchange, Inc., op. cit., p. 27.

5. Marilee S. Niehoff and M. Jay Romans, "Needs Assessment as Step One Toward Enhancing Productivity," *Personnel Administrator,* March 1982, p. 35.

6. G. Gordon Long, "Ergonomics Can Show the Way to Efficiency and Productivity," *Office Systems,* December 1985, pp. 65–68.

7. Daniel Dickinson, *It's Their Business, Too,* American Management Association, New York, 1985, pp. 25–27.

8. New York Stock Exchange, Inc., op. cit., p. 26.

9. "Employee Involvement—What's It All About?" UAW-Ford National Joint Committee on Employee Involvement, Dearborn, Mich., 1980, p. 2.

10. John Bank and Bernhard Wilpert, "What's So Special About Quality Circles?" *Journal of General Management,* Autumn 1983, p. 24.

11. New York Stock Exchange, Inc., op. cit., p. 44.

12. Ibid., pp. 44, 47.

13. James N. Donnelly, Jr., James L. Gibson, and John M. Ivancevich, *Fundamentals of Management,* Business Publications, Inc., Plano, Tex., 1984, pp. 333–334.

14. New York Stock Exchange, Inc., op. cit., p. 47.

15. John M. Ivancevich, James H. Donnelly, Jr., and James L. Gibson, *Managing for Performance,* rev. ed., Business Publications Inc., Plano, Tex., 1983, p. 364.

16. "Middle Managers and Supervisors Resist Moves to More Participatory Management," *Wall Street Journal,* Sept. 16, 1985, p. 27.

17. Janice A. Klein, ''Why Supervisors Resist Employee Involvement,'' *Harvard Business Review,* September–October 1984, p. 88.

18. ''Middle Managers and Supervisors Resist Moves to More Participatory Management,'' loc. cit.

19. Ibid.

SUGGESTED READINGS

Asselin, Gerald A., and Walter D. St. John: ''Promote Productivity: User-Friendly Management,'' *Personnel Journal,* December 1986, pp. 40–47.

Campion, Michael, and Paul W. Thayer: ''Job Design: Approaches, Outcomes, and Trade-Offs,'' *Organizational Dynamics,* Winter 1987, pp. 66–79.

Dale, Barrie G.: ''Quality Circles in the UK,'' *Journal of General Management,* Spring 1984, pp. 71–87.

Gmelch, Walter H., and Val D. Miskin: ''The Lost Art of High Productivity,'' *Personnel,* April 1986, pp. 34–38.

Horton, Forest Woody, Jr.: ''Redefining Productivity for the Information Age,'' *Information Management,* January 1983, pp. 26–27.

''How A&P Fattens Profits by Sharing Them,'' *Business Week,* Dec. 22, 1986, p. 44.

Marek, William, and Gene W. Dalton: ''Managing the Mundane,'' *Personnel Administrator,* October 1986, pp. 59–64.

McTague, Michael: ''Productivity Is Shaped by Forces Beneath Corporate Culture,'' *Personnel Journal,* March 1986, pp. 20–23.

Midas, Michael T., Jr., and William B. Werther, Jr.: ''Productivity: The Missing Link in Corporate Strategy,'' *Management Review,* March 1985, pp. 44–47.

Rowland, Daniel C.: ''Incentive Pay: Productivity's Own Reward,'' *Personnel Journal,* March 1987, pp. 48–57.

Saleh, S. D., and Siva Pal: ''Robotic Technology and Its Impact on Work Design and the Quality of Work Life,'' *Industrial Management,* May–June 1985, pp. 1–15.

Sherman, H. David: ''Improving the Productivity of Service Businesses, *Sloan Management Review,* Spring 1984, pp. 11–23.

Skinner, Wickham: ''The Productivity Paradox,'' *Management Review,* September 1986, pp. 41–45.

Smeltzer, Larry R., and Ben L. Kedia: ''Training Needs of Quality Circles,'' *Personnel,* August 1987, pp. 51–55.

Thiers, Richard J.: ''Bradford-White: A Study in Employee Relations and Productivity,'' *Personnel,* March 1987, pp. 74–77.

17

EMPLOYEE RIGHTS AND RESPONSIBILITIES

COMPETENCIES

Studying this chapter will enable you to:

1. Describe methods of communicating rights and responsibilities to employees.

2. Explain the supervisor's role in communicating employee rights and responsibilities.

3. Identify and describe the following employee rights:

- **a.** legal rights
- **b.** company-granted rights
- **c.** general rights

4. Identify and describe the following employee responsibilities:

- **a.** legal responsibilities
- **b.** moral and ethical responsibilities

5. Describe actions the supervisor might take when provided with any situation involving employee rights and responsibilities.

CHAPTER OUTLINE

" **Y**ou can't do that—I know my rights!"
"That's not my responsibility."
"I have a right to my opinion."
"My rights are spelled out in the employee's manual, so forget it."
"That's not in my job description; I don't have to do it."

These comments are not unusual in the workplace. Patricia Mayes, supervisor of employee relations for Management Associates, Inc., hears this every day. So does Jason Fremont, Management Associates' supervisor of word processing services. Both Mayes and Fremont have noticed that employees are quick to express what they consider to be their rights as workers but rarely discuss their responsibilities to their employer, Management Associates.

"It seems," said Mayes, "that rights are a one-way proposition. What workers fail to understand is that MAI has rights, too! Jason, what can we do to impress on the workers in our departments that we recognize their rights and they have to recognize that they have responsibilities, too?"

As first-line managers, Mayes and Fremont must themselves understand Management Associates' employee rights and responsibilities. Then they must clearly communicate these rights and responsibilities so that workers will understand and accept them as a part of their employment conditions.

COMMUNICATING EMPLOYEE RIGHTS AND RESPONSIBILITIES

Management has a responsibility to communicate to employees their rights as individual employees and their responsibilities as individuals to the organization. Employee rights and responsibilities may be communicated during the orientation process, via company handbooks or manuals, by written notice, during scheduled meetings, or through a combination of these communication channels. Whatever the vehicle, it is important that employees be made aware of their obligations to the company as well as their rights.

The Orientation Process

When workers are employed, they usually go through an orientation process to both their jobs and to the company. The orientation may be a structured formal program or informal sessions with immediate supervisors of the new employees.

Formal orientation programs are discussed in Chapter 10. Informal orientation is often provided by the new employee's immediate supervisor. The informal sessions may be in addition to, in lieu of, or as a follow-up to the formal program. Regardless of its purpose, the supervisor should plan as carefully for the informal orientation sessions as for a formal program.

WHAT CAN THE SUPERVISOR DO?

The planning checklist shown below provides some guidelines for supervisors as they plan their orientation session.

_____ **1.** Block out time in your schedule.
_____ **2.** Choose a good location for the session.
_____ **3.** Plan an agenda, and put it in writing.
_____ **4.** Provide an orientation that is consistent with each new employee or group of employees.
_____ **5.** Evaluate the content regularly and update as required.
_____ **6.** Allow time for questions and discussion.
_____ **7.** Provide ancillary materials (manuals, handbooks, fringe benefit information, and so on).
_____ **8.** Arrange for group or individual follow-up session, as required.

Company Handbooks

Company-issued employee handbooks usually contain information about employee benefits; some specific rights (such as grievance and appeal rights); and company policies, procedures, and rules. Organizations should be very careful that handbooks neither imply employee rights nor suggest an implied contract. (There is a discussion of implied contracts later in this chapter.) Handbooks are informational tools only and should be viewed as such by both the employee and the employer. It should be made clear to employees that the handbook is not an employment contract.

Written Notice

When changes are made in company policies, procedures and rules that will affect employees, the company has a responsibility to communicate these changes to the employees in writing. It is helpful to make it easy for employees to add the new or updated versions to their employee handbooks. The changes should be dated, the new pages should be numbered, and the old policy, procedure, or rule that is affected should be identified. Further, supervisors who distribute the new or updated information should encourage employees to make the change in their handbooks at the time the information is issued.

*Competency
Check:*

Can you describe
four methods of
communicating
responsibilities to
employees?

Scheduled Meetings

In conjunction with written notices of new or updated policies, procedures, and rules, supervisors may call meetings to distribute the information. The meeting provides employees with an opportunity to ask questions regarding the changes.

EMPLOYEE RIGHTS

Employees' rights can be legally granted or granted by the company. There are also some general rights that accrue from employment. In the beginning of this chapter, Fremont and Mayes were discussing the issue of employee rights and recounting some of the comments that employees often make regarding what they consider to be their rights. It is important for Fremont and Mayes to be knowledgeable about what is an employee right and what is not so that they can deal with situations as they arise.

Legal Rights

Just as each citizen is protected by certain inalienable rights, so is each employee. Employees have legal rights to a safe work environment and a nondiscriminatory and harassment-free workplace. They also have last-resort termination rights, privacy rights, and the right to participate in union activities. Though the focus was different, many employee rights were discussed in previous chapters. For example, Chapters 7, 8, and 14 examined some aspects of employee rights.

Safe Work Environment

Each employee is entitled to a safe work environment. The Williams-Steiger Occupational Safety and Health Act of 1970 legitimized what employers had long accepted as a moral contract with their employees. In addition to the specific safety requirements, the "general-duty" clause in the law protects employees from unsafe and unhealthy conditions in areas in which no standards have yet been adopted. Therefore, the absence of standards does not negate the necessity of providing workers with a safe and healthy work environment.

What can employees do if they believe their employer is violating a job safety or health standard? Each employee has the right to request from the Department of Labor (DOL) an inspection of any perceived safety or health problem. The request must identify specific violations rather than general ones. A copy of the request must be sent to the employer. While the request to the DOL must be signed by the complainant, no signature is required on the copy that goes to the employer.

Do employees have the legal right to refuse to work or perform an assigned task if the work itself or the work environment is perceived by them to be unsafe? The following are legal conditions for refusing to work when safety is the issue:[1]

1. Normal procedures to resolve the problem(s) resulting in unsafe work conditions have not been successful.
2. The employee(s) notified the appropriate management officials and tried to have the condition(s) corrected, but the unsafe condition(s) remains.
3. The workers' fears are supported by objective physical evidence, and workers show a good-faith belief that the conditions are, indeed, unsafe.

Nondiscriminatory Workplace

Every employee is entitled to a workplace that is free from discrimination. As a supervisor, your responsibility is to see that discrimination does not occur in any of the employment processes for which you are responsible (selection, promotion, termination, demotion, or transfer). If you observe discrimination in other areas of the company, it is your responsibility to protect the organization by reporting the discriminatory practices to the appropriate person. Even the *perception* of discrimination must be avoided. The issue of nondiscriminatory staffing is discussed in Chapter 8.

Workers who believe that they are victims of employment discrimination may appeal internally if the organization has a grievance and appeal procedure. Grievance and appeal procedures are discussed later in this chapter. The grievant may also file a complaint with the local or regional office of the Equal Employment Opportunity Commission (EEOC). If the EEOC believes that a prima facie case exists, an investigator will be assigned to the case. First-line managers should be aware of the process and, if charges are brought, be prepared to present documentation that would clearly show nondiscriminatory intent and action.

Harassment-Free Workplace

Employees also have a right to a workplace that is free from harassment. Harassment can take many forms—from verbal abuse (insults, suggestive comments, and demands) to subtle forms of pressure for sexual activity to physical aggressiveness that may go as far as attempted rape.

Verbal harassment may also be a form of discrimination. Ethnic, racial, or sex-related jokes, slurs, or derogatory remarks are extensions of discrimination; and employees have a right to expect their supervisors to stop this form of harassment. If verbal harassment affects a worker's ability to perform job responsibilities, and the worker perceives the verbal abuse as discriminatory in intent, the worker may go the grievance and appeal or EEOC route for relief and compensation.

Unwanted and unreciprocated sexual advances, requests for sexual favors, and certain other verbal or physical conduct is considered sexual harassment in the following cases:[2]

● Submission to the conduct is either explicitly or implicitly a condition of the individual's employment ("Before I decide whether to offer you this position, why don't we discuss it further over a drink—at my place?").

● Submission to or rejection of such conduct by an individual is used as the basis for employment decisions affecting the individual ("I could probably change my decision about your promotion, but you need to be a little nicer to me").

● Such conduct has the purpose or effect of unreasonably interfering with an individual's work performance or creating an intimidating, hostile, or offensive work environment ("Every time I walk by Sally's office, she gets up and gives me a good morning hug or pat. I hate it, and it's beginning to affect my work.").

Two major issues are important to first-line managers:

1. The employer is liable for sexual harassment even if the employer had no knowledge that the harassment was taking place.
2. Sexual advances toward an employee are considered unlawful harassment even if the employee suffered no loss of job benefits, not even a threat of loss.

The first issue means that the supervisor is liable for sexual-harassment charges if he or she knows *or should have known* that the unwanted sexual advances were taking place. This language means that supervisors must be aware of what is happening in their areas of responsibility and put an immediate stop to improper activity or actions that even *hint* of impropriety. Sexual harassment may take place male to female, female to male, or between members of the same sex.

The second issue is not as clear-cut. In *Vinson v. Taylor,* a savings and loan branch manager allegedly made demands on a female employee. The trial judge dismissed the case because the employee admitted she had suffered no loss or threat of loss of job opportunity. However, the U.S. Court of Appeals ruled that the employee could claim unlawful harassment. That decision has been appealed, and the company has asked the justices to rule on the two issues described above.

WHAT CAN THE SUPERVISOR DO?

The Virginia Department of Personnel and Training has issued a question-and-answer guide to help employees and supervisors recognize and avoid some terms that may be considered improper. A description of these guidelines is contained in the following newspaper article:

RICHMOND—Calling a male colleague a "stud" is out if you are a state employee.

Also taboo are such sexually charged words and expressions as "the fair sex," "I'll have my girl check that," "lady lawyer," "authoress" and "usherette," says the Virginia Department of Personnel and Training.

Do not use "boy" when referring to males or "the girls" or "the ladies" when referring to females. And a wife is not "the little woman," "the better half" or the "ball and chain," the department says.

The terms are examples of ones that "connote a patronizing or condescending tone and should be avoided," the department said in a state policy banning sexual harassment that went into effect last week.

Sexual harassment can encompass such things as sex-oriented verbal kidding, pinching, winking, brushing against another person's body and demands or subtle pressure for sexual favors that carry promises of preferential treatment, the department said.

But what about jokes told in "good clean fun?" asked the department's guidebook.

"Women and men should be treated with the same respect, dignity and seriousness," was the department's answer. "Neither should be trivialized or stereotyped either in jest or in illustration. Sexual innuendoes, jokes and puns should be avoided."

When a female finds herself in a non-traditional job and is subjected to catcalls and whistles or is faced with defending her right to hold the job, is she a victim of sexual harassment?

"Yes. Jokes, whistles, teasing, catcalls are all forms of sexual harassment, especially when such conduct interferes with job performance," the guidelines say. "When the rejection of unwelcome advances jeopardizes employment or creates a threatening or fearful work environment, this constitutes sexual harassment."

There is nothing illegal about romances or relationships between subordinates and superiors, but the guide advised against fishing off the company pier.[3]

Last-Resort Termination Rights

Employees have certain rights connected with employment-termination practices. An employee's discharge may be declared invalid if any of the following conditions exist:[4]

The employee was discharged for a reason specifically prohibited by federal or state standards. For example, termination in direct violation of Title VII of the Civil Rights Act of 1964, the National Labor Relations Act, or the Occupational Safety and Health Act is specifically prohibited by law.

The employee was discharged for complying with a statutory duty. Courts have refused to uphold an employee's discharge for performing jury duty, for example; for refusing to commit perjury as requested by the employer; for objecting to violating the law; or for complaining to public authorities about illegal activities of employers.

The discharged employee had an implied contract under the terms of employment. Some courts have ruled that personnel manuals containing statements such as "You can be dismissed only for sufficient cause" or "Termination is based on unsatisfactory performance" are implied commitments. On June 5, 1985, the Wisconsin Supreme Court ruled that an employee handbook is an offer by management of a set of employment terms and conditions. If a Wisconsin employee accepts management's offer, then a contract has been formed.

The American Society for Personnel Administrators has suggested that to avoid the perception of an implied contract, employers use the following disclaimer:

> I understand that this employment application and any other company documents are not contracts of employment, and that any individual who is hired may voluntarily leave employment upon proper notice, and may be terminated by the employer at any time for any reason. I understand that any oral or written statements to the contrary are hereby expressly disavowed and should not be relied upon by any prospective or existing employee.

Other companies, such as Sears Roebuck and Company, have chosen to insert a disclaimer in their applications and other employment documents, including the employee handbook. Sears' disclaimer, which has been upheld by several courts, reads as follows:

> I agree to conform to the rules and regulations of Sears, Roebuck and Co., and my employment and compensation can be terminated, with or without cause, and with or without notice, at any time at the option of either the company or myself. I understand that no store manager or representative of Sears, Roebuck and Co., other than the President or Vice-President of the company, has no [sic] authority to enter into any agreement for employment for a specific period of time, or to make any agreement contrary to the foregoing.[5]

Disclaimers, when used, should be inserted in the personnel or employee manual and on the employment application. Any employer using a disclaimer, however, should make sure that its rules and regulations and other policy statements do not conflict with the disclaimer. Some companies are using the statement "No employee has any contract with this company except for documents titled Employment Contract."

Oral statements made during an employment interview, or even during a performance appraisal interview, may constitute an implied contract. In one case, a person being hired was told that "she could stay and grow with the company." When she was let go several months later, she sued for breach of contract—and won. The same result can occur if a supervisor, during a performance appraisal interview, tells an employee, "Don't worry, Sally. As long as you do good work, you'll always have a job here."

Any comment that suggests that passing a probationary period leads to job security should be avoided. Even "Don't worry, Ms. Daily, no one ever gets fired around here" can be held as a valid promise of guaranteed employment.

The discharged employee has been deprived of due process rights guaranteed under the Fourteenth Amendment. Arguments have been made that dismissal from employment can be regarded as the taking of liberty or the taking of property. "Due process" therefore gives a discharged employee the right to certain procedural steps, including a hearing and the right to know the reason for dismissal.

The employee's discharge was motivated by bad faith or malice or based on retaliation which violates public policy. The primary determinant of public policy protection is the court's judgment as to what type of conduct violates public policy and the determination that an employee's discharge was wrong and actionable.[5]

WHAT CAN THE SUPERVISOR DO?

The supervisor can take the following steps to protect the organization against charges of "unjust discharge."[6]

1. Be sure that employees are forewarned regarding possible disciplinary consequences of their actions.
2. Examine the company's requirements of the employee to see that the requirements are reasonable in relation to the orderly and efficient operation of the company's business and of the employee's ability.
3. Before discharging an employee, make a reasonable effort to discover whether the employee's performance was, indeed, unacceptable. Do not rely on hearsay, opinions, or rumors. The employee should also have a chance to respond to any charges.
4. Conduct the investigation in a fair and objective way, keeping an open mind.
5. Treat each employee the same way as others have been treated, given the same or similar conditions.
6. Document unsatisfactory performance, and maintain any records needed to substantiate a termination decision.
7. Consider the time span between the unacceptable performance and the termination.

Privacy Rights

Privacy is a person's right to keep personal information from those who have no need to know. This right to privacy covers many areas of employment, including employment references, private information disclosed to other employees, medical screening, on-premises security systems, personnel files, and employee searches.[7]

Employment references.   The best rule to follow when responding to a request for a reference for a former employee is the "bare-bones" rule—supply only the most basic employment information to a potential employer. Basic information includes a confirmation of prior employment, dates of employment, and the specific position held. One exception to this rule should be noted: An employer is ethically bound to pass on negative information about the moral character of a former employee. For example, suppose you discharged an employee in your child care center for improper conduct toward his or her charges and failed to inform the prospective employer about the reason for the discharge. Later, if a child is molested by your former employee, your company could be liable for failing to pass on information that the prospective employer had a right to know.

Private information disclosed to other employees.   Unless other employees need to know private employee information to do their jobs, this information should not be disclosed. For example, it is usually not necessary for all employees in a department to know the reason for an individual employee's discharge or transfer.

Medical screening.   Screening employees for drug and alcohol problems may be permissible if it is coupled with a program for rehabilitation. If the screening is used simply to identify employees for possible discharge, however, it may be subject to challenge. Employers must be able to present documentation of incompetence *on the job* caused by drug or alcohol use *off the job* if the results of the medical screening are to be used for discharge or disciplinary action.[8]

On-premises security systems.   Generally, on-premises security systems that are known to employees, announced by managers, and offer no surprises to employees do not violate employees' privacy.[9] However, care should be taken to design formal policies and to train supervisors in the application of the security system so that they do not violate the company policy and leave the company open to a charge that it both invaded an employee's privacy and ignored its own rules in doing so.[10]

For example, Carmie Watkins Carr was employed by a company that sold Yellow Pages advertising. Employees of the firm knew that the company occasionally monitored their calls to make sure proper sales procedures were being followed—a reasonable procedure for a company that conducts most of its business by telephone. But in violation of company policy, supervisors listened to a call she received during lunch one day inviting her to interview for another job.

Carr's consequent lawsuit, charging a violation of the federal wiretapping laws, was eventually settled out of court. However, the eleventh U.S. Circuit Court of Appeals ruled that employers could monitor only calls that were clearly related to company business. Further, supervisors were obliged to hang up, the court said, as soon as they realized a call was personal.[11]

Personnel files.   Information that might be considered ''private'' by the employee and is irrelevant to the employee's job or performance should be purged from the personnel records. First-line managers often retain information in their files that might be considered ''personal.'' Again, if the information is not pertinent to the worker's performance on the job, remove and destroy it.

IBM has established the following employee privacy guidelines:[12]

- Management can collect and keep in its personnel files only those facts about employees that are required by law or that are necessary to manage operations.
- Performance evaluations more than 3 years old must be removed from employees' personnel files.
- Employees are entitled to know how filed information about them is being used.
- Employees are entitled to see most of the information in their files. Management may withhold some information, such as a confidential discussion of an opportunity for a promotion that was never given.

Employee searches.   Constitutional protection against unreasonable searches, as provided by the Fourth Amendment, has focused on searches and seizures by *government officials*. It would appear that private employers can conduct searches without fear of any *constitutional* violations. This does not, however, mean that an employer can search ''at will.'' If a company plans to invade an employee's privacy by search, the employer must be protected from litigation. A search procedure should be carefully planned, and guidelines for implementation should be provided to all managers. A case involving employee searches follows.[13]

> *General Motors Corp. v. Piskor* is a primary example of the disturbing recent case law developments in the area of state tort law and employee searches. *Piskor* is particularly troublesome in that it involves a situation which most personnel executives would consider quite ordinary. In *Piskor,* the employer's security guards detained an employee attempting to exit its plant at the end of his shift. The employee had been seen wandering through areas away from his normal work station where radios and tape players were assembled. Serious inventory shortages had been recently reported in this area, and Piskor's pockets, according to the foreman, were "bulging." Piskor shouted and created a disturbance when the guards sought to question him, and when apprehending him, after he refused to cooperate and attempted to flee, the guards found nothing. Piskor sued for assault, false imprisonment and slander charges, and was ultimately awarded approximately $27,000 in damages.

The manner in which a search is conducted is also important. In the case of *Bennett v. Norban,* the Pennsylvania Supreme Court found that an individual whose sensibilities are offended because of the manner in which a search is conducted can sue. The plaintiff, who was searched in front of a number of onlookers, was told to take her coat off so that the pockets of her dress could be searched. When nothing was found, her purse was examined. Nothing was found in her purse either. Given the manner in which the search was conducted, the court found that the events suggested to the crowd that the plaintiff was a thief. This constituted slander and invasion of privacy.[14]

The cases that have been litigated to date seem to indicate that the primary factor examined by the courts is whether there was any regulation or policy placing employees on notice that routine searches would be conducted. Employers who are considering adopting any search policy should make sure that adequate advance notice is given to its employees. If possible, advance consent for the search should also be obtained. This is the safest insurance against any claim an employee may make regarding invasion of privacy through search.[15]

WHAT CAN THE SUPERVISOR DO?

The supervisor should take steps to ensure that these guidelines are followed in any search procedure:[16]

1. The search-and-seizure policy should be based on legitimate employer interests. The prevention of theft, drinking, or the use or possession of drugs on company property are legitimate employer interests.
2. The policy should include all types of searches, including searches of the person, lockers, and personal possessions.

3. The policy should advise employees that lockers are company property, issued for the convenience of employees; that the company has a master key to all lockers; and that lockers will be routinely searched.
4. The search procedure should be applicable to all employees.
5. A statement should be included in the policy that a request to undergo search does not imply an accusation.
6. The search policy should be communicated to all employees prior to its implementation. Post the policy in locations where employees congregate; include the policy in all supervisory manuals and employee handbooks; have employees sign a consent statement at the time of initial employment; and, where applicable, include the policy in collective bargaining agreements.
7. Security personnel and others responsible for searches should be given instructions regarding the search procedure. An employee should not be touched in the search process. If this is not possible, touching should be limited to personal effects and pockets. The search should be conducted in a dignified and reasonable manner and away from other employees.

Union-Participation Rights

Competency Check:

Can you describe employees' legal rights?

Employees have a right to participate in organizing and maintaining membership in a union. This right is guaranteed by the National Labor Relations Act (Wagner Act), which gives the right to nonunion as well as union employees.

The right is based on two premises: (1) the activity must be of common interest to a group of employees and (2) the concerns must involve wages, hours, or other conditions of work protected under the act. Many cases from nonunion groups are now being processed by the National Labor Relations Board.[17]

WHAT CAN THE SUPERVISOR DO?

The supervisor can be aware of actions that are permissible under the law and actions that should be avoided. These are shown in Figure 17-1.

Company-Granted Rights

In addition to legal rights, employees are often granted rights by their company. These rights may include grievance and appeal procedures and equitable compensation.

Grievance-and-Appeal Procedures

To avoid the dollar and morale costs of court action, companies may establish formal channels for resolving grievances. Procedures for appealing management decisions may also be a part of the process.

FIGURE 17-1

DO'S AND DON'TS ABOUT UNIONS

YOU MAY:	YOU MAY NOT:
● tell employees about current wages and benefits and how they compare to other firms.	● promise employees pay increases or promotions if they vote against the union.
● tell employees you will use all legal means to oppose unionization.	● threaten employees with termination or discriminate when disciplining employees.
● tell employees the disadvantages of having a union (especially cost of dues, assessments, and requirements of membership).	● threaten to close down or move the company if a union is voted in.
● show employees articles about unions and negative experiences others have had elsewhere.	● spy on or have someone spy on union meetings.
● explain the unionization process to your employees accurately.	● make a speech to employees or groups at work within 24 hours of the election (before that, it is allowed).
● forbid distribution of union literature during work hours in work areas.	● ask employees how they plan to vote or if they have signed authorization cards.
● enforce disciplinary policies and rules in a consistent and fair manner.	● urge employees to persuade others to vote against the union (such a vote must be initiated solely by the employee).

Source: Robert L. Mathis and John H. Jackson, *Personnel,* 4th ed., West Publishing Company, St. Paul, Minn., 1985, p. 576.

Companies may elect to resolve grievances in one or a combination of the following ways:[18]

● Assign the personnel director the responsibility for resolving employee complaints.

● Create specific procedures for discrimination grievances, using staff members who are adept at counseling.

● Appoint an internal mediator to hear employee complaints and to intervene between grievant and supervisor.

● Authorize employees to select an internal representative to participate in grievance discussions.

● Establish an open-door policy under which any employee has the right to talk directly with a designated top manager.

● Establish a review board made up of employees on various levels throughout the company. Their decisions can be either advisory or binding.

● Provide for an outside mediator or arbitrator to make final decisions in the grievance process.

Although grievance and appeal procedures may differ depending on whether the company is unionized, the first step in any grievance procedure is to determine whether the grievance is legitimate. Some grievances may not be legitimate. If company policy or the union contract states that a grievance must be related to work hours, conditions, or pay, a grievance related to personal relations with another employee is not legitimate.

There are typical steps that follow in the grievance procedure for employees working under a union contract. The grievance does not have to proceed through all steps to be settled; it may be settled at any point along the procedure. The steps in a union grievance process are shown in Figure 17-2.

One survey revealed that 62 percent of nonunion companies had formal grievance mechanisms in place for the employees. Of the 38 percent who lacked formal procedures, nearly one-third had informal open-door policies. The remaining companies had no set policies but provided an open door to the immediate supervisor only, to the immediate supervisor and a personnel representative, or, in some cases, to higher levels of management.

The breakdown of the types of formal grievance mechanisms in 32 nonunion companies is shown in Figure 17-3. The open-door policy in all these cases included levels of management above the immediate supervisor. The procedure usually began with the immediate supervisor and progressed through the ranks if the problem could not be resolved. Figure 17-4 shows the levels of management involved in a formal open-door policy in 23 companies. Note that many of the companies named more than one level of management.

FIGURE 17-2

Steps in a union grievance process

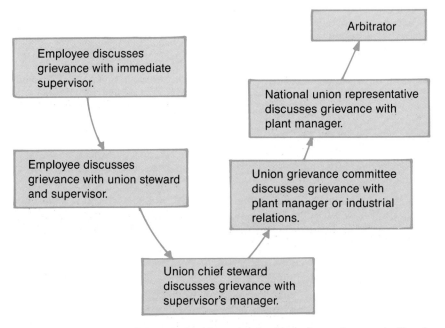

Source: Adapted from Robert L. Mathis and John H. Jackson, *Personnel,* 4th ed., West Publishing Company, St. Paul, Minn., 1985, p. 596.

FIGURE 17-3

TYPES OF FORMAL GRIEVANCE MECHANISMS
IN NONUNION COMPANIES

	NUMBER OF RESPONDENTS
exclusive open door	5
exclusive step procedure without arbitration	5
exclusive step procedure with arbitration	1
open-door and step procedure without arbitration	8
open-door and anonymous line	4
open-door, step procedure without arbitration, and anonymous line	3
open-door and step procedure with arbitration	1
open-door, step procedure with or without arbitration and anonymous line	1
open-door, step procedure with arbitration, and jury	1
step procedure with arbitration, jury, and hearing	1
step procedure without arbitration, jury, and hearing	1
have not decided	1

Source: Maryellen Bo Bosco, "Concensus on Nonunion Grievance Procedures," *Personnel,* January 1985, p. 61.

One of the basic differences in the procedures used in unionized and nonunionized companies is that nonunion workers normally have to file their complaints without assistance while union workers are assisted by union representatives. The other basic difference is that the final decision on grievances lodged by nonunion workers is made by the chief executive officer or the personnel director of the company, while the final decision on a grievance lodged by a union employee is made by an arbitrator.

FIGURE 17-4

LEVELS OF MANAGEMENT INVOLVED IN A FORMAL
OPEN-DOOR POLICY (n = 23)

immediate supervisor	23
human resources manager	22
division manager	20
plant or office manager	17
vice-president	17
president	13

Source: Maryellen Bo Bosco, "Concensus on Nonunion Grievance Procedures," *Personnel,* January 1985, p. 62.

WHAT CAN THE SUPERVISOR DO?

The following checklist provides some guidelines for action by the supervisor. The first seven items are preventive actions; the remainder are actions to be taken after the complaint has been filed.

1. Be aware of what is happening in your area of responsibility. Try to see problems before they become formal grievances.
2. Keep an open channel of communication. Encourage employees to discuss their problems with you.
3. Really listen when employees come to talk with you. Express your interest in their work-related problems.
4. Be consistent in your decisions.
5. Give clear answers in language that employees will understand. Do not try to "snow" employees.
6. Document your actions.
7. Avoid quick and irrational decisions made in the heat of a discussion.
8. Define the problem stated in the grievance. Determine if the stated complaint is the real problem or if it is only a symptom of the problem.
9. Determine if the complaint is grievable.
10. Investigate the grievance objectively and fully to determine if the problem can be settled quickly. Try to settle the complaint at the supervisory level. Get all the facts available to you at the time.
11. Act promptly on the complaint.

Equitable Compensation

Most employees believe they have a right to fair and equitable compensation for the work they perform. Compensation includes both wages and fringe benefits. Companies base their salary scales and fringe benefits on a number of factors, including their ability to pay, the salaries paid by other companies in the industry for similar jobs, economic conditions, union contractual obligations, and their willingness to pay. Reward systems also reflect the organization's philosophy and culture. Some companies want to set the compensation pace; others simply want to be in line with what competing companies are paying, and still others want to pay as little as possible.

Competency Check:

Can you describe employees' company-granted rights?

Pay equity means rewarding employees fairly in relation to what other employees are given for the work they perform. Every employee wants to be treated fairly when wage decisions are made. Employees believe that equitable pay is a right.

General Rights

In addition to legal and company-granted rights, employees have certain general rights. As workers become more and more involved with the company's business through participative management, and as they become more and more desirous of participating in their own work management, a change in their values and their perceptions of their legitimate rights occurs. Supervisors must be aware of this change in the workplace.

Employees now believe they have a right to:[19]

- understand their roles within the organization.
- know the degree of authority they are granted to perform their jobs successfully.
- participate in goal setting when it relates to their own performance.
- trust, respect, and confidence from their managers.
- use their creative skills in the performance of their jobs.
- receive a regular and consistent flow of information, particularly as that information relates to their jobs and performance.
- timely and honest feedback through an effective performance appraisal system that examines both their strengths and their weaknesses and provides for an action plan and follow-up.
- participate in training and development programs that help them overcome their weaknesses and prepare them for advancement.
- become vital and valued members of the company family.

Competency Check:

Can you describe employees' general rights?

EMPLOYEE RESPONSIBILITIES

There are two sides to every coin, and employee responsibilities are the flip side of the employee rights coin. Employee responsibilities become organizational rights. At the beginning of this chapter, you read some of the comments that Mayes and Fremont frequently overhear. You will recall that Mayes and Fremont noticed that although employees are quick to express what they consider to be their rights as workers, they rarely discuss their responsibilities to Management Associates, Inc. And as representatives of MAI, Fremont and Mayes also have rights.

Legal Responsibilities

The legal responsibilities of workers fall into two categories: (1) the responsibility to perform the work for which hired and (2) the responsibility to follow organizational policies, procedures, and rules.

Perform Work for Which Hired

When workers are employed, there is an agreement between the parties that the employees will perform the work contracted for and that the employer will pay for that work. The job description spells out the job parameters. To minimize the problem of ''It's not in my job description'' excuses, there should be a final statement in the job description reading, ''and any other duties as requested by the supervisor.'' Employees have the responsibility not only to perform the work for which they are hired but to perform it properly. The employee should live up to that unspoken agreement made at the time of employment and to the presumption of a "good employee."

Follow Organizational Policies, Procedures, and Rules

Competency Check:

Can you describe employees' legal responsibilities?

Employees are responsible for following company policies, procedures, and rules. The company has a right to expect voluntary compliance from its employees. And when employees do *not* behave according to the established policies, procedures, and rules, the company has a right to enforce compliance by administering discipline. It is important for employees to play by the rules and support the organizations that employ them.

Moral and Ethical Responsibilities

In addition to the responsibility to perform the jobs for which they were hired, there are certain moral and ethical actions for which employees are held responsible. These actions include the general responsibility for contributing to the organization's image, promoting the organization, and other, more specific, responsibilities.

Contributing to the Organization's Image

Employees are major contributors to the image of any company. They *are* the company, and their actions reflect, either positively or negatively, on how others view the firm. For example, when you telephone a company and the person who answers is courteous, eager to assist, and projects a pleasant personality, your immediate impression of that company is positive. Conversely, if you deal with a salesperson who is abrupt, discourteous, and chomps on gum while impatiently waiting for you to make a selection, your impression of the entire company is negative. Your image of the organization is built on your view of its employees.

Promoting the Organization

Because employees *are* the company, they serve as representatives—ambassadors, if you will. Whenever there is an opportunity, employees should speak positively about their company, letting others know about the good things that are happening there. If an employee has a gripe about the company, that complaint should be presented to the appropriate person within the organization, not to persons outside. Loyalty to the company is an ethical responsibility of employees.

Specific Responsibilities

There are a number of specific moral and ethical actions for which an employee should be held responsible. Employees should:[20]

- come to work every day, unless ill or a real emergency has occurred.
- follow a code of ethics in their behavior.
- be sober and drug-free on company time, on company property, or while conducting company business.
- comply with instructions issued by supervisors.
- complete assigned work and accept responsibility for determining any additional needs.
- be safety-conscious so as not to endanger themselves or others.
- take care of company materials and property.
- be honest in their dealings with the company and with others.
- be competent and efficient in the performance of their jobs.
- avoid abusive, threatening, coercive, indecent, and discourteous language when talking to supervisors, peers, subordinates, or customers.
- keep accurate records and avoid any hint of intentional falsification of time reports or other company records.
- maintain appropriate conduct while on duty or on company property.
- avoid instigating or participating in physical or verbal disturbances.
- come to work on time and give a full day's work.
- not abuse break time or, in other ways, be a "time thief."
- cooperate with fellow employees.

Competency Check:

Can you describe employees' moral and ethical responsibilities?

WHAT CAN THE SUPERVISOR DO?

As a supervisor, you must be aware of the legal, moral, and ethical responsibilities of your workers and be sure that each employee understands these responsibilities. Further, each employee should know specifically what your expectations are, how you will communicate whether these expectations are being met, and the consequences of not meeting these expectations. Employees need to have confidence that you, as their supervisor, are aware of both their rights and their responsibilities and that you respect both.

COMPETENCY REVIEW

1. Describe three methods of communicating rights and responsibilities to employees.
2. Explain the supervisor's role in communicating employee rights and responsibilities.
3. Identify and describe these three types of employee rights:
   a. legal rights
   b. company-granted rights
   c. general rights
4. Identify and describe these two types of employee responsibilities:
   a. legal responsibilities
   b. moral and ethical responsibilities

APPLICATIONS

1. Which of the following supervisor's comments are inappropriate, and why?
   a. I don't want to hear your gripes about the rail being loose.
   b. I know Joe shouldn't be making those comments about Jean's ''bod,'' but it's not hurting anyone.
   c. Sue called Jane a ''black slob,'' and I had to chuckle because Jane *is* kind of sloppy.
   d. I had to fire Jose today because he blew the whistle on us to OSHA.
   e. Meg, your work is always outstanding. At this rate, you'll soon be ready for my job.
   f. Why should I give you 15 reasons? You're just fired, and that's that!
   g. Keep *all* employee records in your desk. We might need some of that personal stuff one day.
   h. You better not let a union in because if you do, we'll just close down. We will never be a unionized company.
   i. Don't tell *me* your troubles. What do you think I am, a chaplain?
   j. I'm surprised by the reasons Joe was fired. It's all in his personnel file.
2. Which of the following employee comments are inappropriate, and why?
   a. I want to know exactly what I am supposed to do in this job.
   b. I don't care if it is company policy; it doesn't make sense, and I'm not going to do it.
   c. (answering the phone) Yea, what can I do for you?
   d. If I'm late, I'm late. I'll catch up on my work.
   e. Yes, I have a beer at lunch, but lunch is *my* time.
   f. When I finish my work, I read a magazine. I'm not going to do anyone else's work.
   g. If Sue would stay away from my work station, I wouldn't make those remarks to her.
   h. I'm not responsible for anyone's safety but my own.
   i. I never start a fight, but if someone else starts one, I'm always ready to duke it out.
3. If you were a supervisor for Management Associates, Inc., how would you respond to the following:
   a. a formal complaint about sexual harassment
   b. a grievance that is filed by an employee whom you have reason to personally dislike
   c. an informal conversation with Robert Stevens, who laughingly tells you that Janice Ohrbach thinks he is sexy and usually pats him on the head as she passes his desk.
   d. an employee who says that she heard that Richard Burns was fired because he was drinking on the job
4. As a supervisor, which of the methods of communicating employee rights and responsibilities would you prefer to use? Why?

CASES

Case I: Here Is My Two-Weeks' Notice

Fremont in the beginning of this chapter is not sure how to handle several problems within his department. Fremont is new in his position, and he is trying very hard to solve employee problems at the supervisory level before they escalate. Just this morning, Cathy Sims, one of WP services' most efficient operators, told Fremont that she was resigning and gave him two weeks' notice.

FREMONT   Cathy, is there a work-related problem, or have you been offered another job that you feel it is in your best interests to accept?

SIMS   No, I don't have another job.

FREMONT   Then why are you resigning? You're one of our best operators.

SIMS   I appreciate the compliment. . . .

FREMONT   It's not a compliment; it's a statement of fact. You always get merit raises in addition to the regular salary increases.

SIMS   Well, I haven't wanted to complain, but since you asked . . . I often do the work assigned to several of the other operators. They take extended coffee breaks, often come in late and leave early. They call in sick on Fridays and Mondays, or both; and I hear them laugh about their paid long weekends. One time I asked if they didn't feel guilty for cheating the company; but they only laughed and said, "As long as we don't get caught, what's the big deal?"

1. What problem(s) does Fremont have in his department?
2. In retrospect, if you had been Fremont, what action would you have taken that he did not take?
3. What action would you recommend that Jason take now
   a. about Cathy?
   b. about the other employees?

Case II: I Promise You . . .

It didn't take long for Nicholas Chuffey, a personnel interviewer for the Serdlebank Company, to make up his mind about Harry Lumbard.

"We're ready to hire you," Chuffey informed him. "When can you start?"

Lumbard looked pleased and responded: "Immediately. However, the minimum salary I require is $20,000 a year." The response jolted the interviewer. "Well, the position starts at $19,000,'' he said, ''but I wouldn't let that worry you. I'll see to it that you're raised to $20,000 in a few months.''

The promise overcame the applicant's hesitations, and he accepted the job. However, no raise came through for Lumbard. Higher-ups at the Serdlebank Company repeatedly vetoed Chuffey's requests for the additional money for the new employee. Lumbard became so furious at the company's stand that he resigned his position and sued the Serdlebank Company for damages for breach of contract. In court, Lumbard recited the following:

● ''My bottom-line figure for accepting the job with Serdlebank was $20,000. I took less initially only because Serdlebank's interviewer made a commitment to have my salary raised.''
● ''That commitment was violated.''

A Serdlebank functionary countered with the following:

● ''Whatever promises Chuffey may have made were not binding on our company. He has no power to set pay scales.''
● ''If Lumbard chose to believe Chuffey, he did so at his own risk.''[20]

1. How binding are an interviewer's pay promises to a job applicant?
2. Did the ex-employee win in court?

REFERENCES

1. John J. Hoover, ''Workers Have New Rights to Health and Safety,'' *Readings in Personnel and Human Resource Management,* 2d ed., Randall S. Schuler and Stuart A. Youngblood (eds.), West Publishing Company, St. Paul, Minn., 1984, pp. 396 ff.

2. Stuart A. Youngblood and Gary L. Tidwell, ''Termination at Will: Some Changes in the Workplace,'' ibid., pp. 409 ff.

3. Virginia Department of Personnel and Training, Richmond.

4. Youngblood and Tidwell op. cit., p. 406.

5. Thomas H. Williams, ''Fire at Will,'' *Personnel Journal,* June 1985, p. 76.

6. George E. Stevens, ''Firing Without Fear,'' reprinted from *Management World,* March 1984.

7. John C. O'Meara, ''The Emerging Law of Employees' Rights to Privacy,'' *Personnel Administrator,* June 1985, p. 159.

8. Ibid., p. 160.

9. Loc. cit.

10. Jim Schachter, ''Courts Are Arena for Battle over Privacy in the Workplace,'' *Virginian Pilot and Ledger Star,* Dec. 20, 1987.

11. Loc. cit.

12. Interview with Frank Cary, ''IBM's Guidelines to Employee Privacy,'' *Harvard Business Review,* September–October 1976, pp. 82–90, in *Foundations of Personnel and Human*

Resource Management, rev. ed., Ivancevich, Glueck, Business Publications, Inc., Plano, Tex., 1983, p. 576.

13. Robert J. Nobile, ''Employee Searches in the Workplace,'' *Personnel Administrator,* vol. 30, no. 5, May 1985, p. 89.

14. Ibid., p. 94.

15. Ibid., p. 91.

16. Ibid., pp. 96–97.

17. Stevens, op. cit.

18. Robert Coulson, ''Termination Can Be Trouble if Dismissal Is Unfair,'' *Office Systems '85,* December 1985, p. 32.

19. Lee Ginsburg, Neil Miller, and Robert Brien, ''A New Charter of Rights,'' *Management World,* January 1983, p. 15.

20. *White Collar Management,* Business Research Publications, Inc., 1983, sample newsletter.

SUGGESTED READINGS

Condon, Thomas J., and Richard H. Wolff: ''Procedures That Safeguard Your Right to Fire,'' *Harvard Business Review,* November–December 1985.

Donovan, Timothy G.: ''Businesses Facing Truth About Lie-Detector Tests,'' *Office Systems '86,* June 1986.

Elliott, Ralph D., and James R. Hoffman: ''The Impact of Right-to-Work Laws on Employer Unfair Labor Practice Charges,'' *Journal of Labor Research,* vol. 5, no. 2, Spring 1984.

Hershizer, Brian, and Harry Graham: ''Justice Without Juries,'' reprinted from *Management World,* March 1984.

Leonard, Maria: ''Challenges to the Termination at Will Doctrine,'' *Personnel Administrator,* February 1983.

''Letting Workers Help Handle Worker Gripes,'' *Business Week,* Sept. 15, 1986.

Manley, Marisa: ''Charges and Discharges,'' *INC.,* March 1988.

McAfee, R. Bruce, and Betty R. Ricks: ''Communicating Employee Responsibilities and Rights: The Influence of Role Modeling,'' in Chimezie A. B. Osigweh (ed.), *Communicating Employee Responsibilities and Rights: A Modern Management Mandate,* Greenwood Press, Westport, Conn., 1987.

18

FACILITATING CHANGE

COMPETENCIES

Studying this chapter will enable you to:

1. Discuss the nature of organizational change.

2. Identify the internal targets for change.

3. Discuss several external forces for change.

4. Compare reactionary and planned change.

5. Explain why recognizing the need for change is an inherent part of the supervisor's controlling function.

6. Identify in order and describe the steps in the change process.

7. Define the term *change agent* and show how it relates to the supervisor.

8. Illustrate ways through which supervisors can develop in workers a receptive attitude toward change.

9. Give several examples of how supervisors can minimize resistance to change.

10. Explain the supervisor's role in the changing phase.

11. Explain what is meant by "stabilizing at a higher level of effectiveness."

CHAPTER OUTLINE

I. THE NATURE OF ORGANIZATIONAL CHANGE

    A. Internal Forces Create Targets for Change

    B. External Forces Provide Ongoing Challenges and Opportunities

        1. Consumers

        2. Suppliers

        3. Technology

        4. Social Trends

        5. Politics

        6. Economics

        7. Labor

        8. Disasters

II. MAKING PLANNED CHANGE

    A. Recognizing the Need for Change

    B. Identifying the Internal Targets

    C. The Change Process

        1. Unfreezing

        2. Changing

        3. Refreezing

III. THE SUPERVISOR'S ROLE IN MANAGING CHANGE

    A. The Supervisor as Change Agent

    B. Preparing Workers for Change

        1. Making Workers Receptive to Change

        2. Minimizing Resistance to Change

    C. Making the Change

    D. Stabilizing After Change

"I give up!" George Comiski spat out the words to his co-workers as he sat down for his morning coffee break. "Wasn't that session this morning the pits? Another change! Before we really get the hang of one routine around here, in pops some management pencil pusher with another. Doesn't anybody up there know what they're doing? I say, let them come down here and do our jobs for a while to find out what's going on. Or let us set the routine—we could do a better job of it. This time they've overdone it—new machines, new routine, and teams, yet! Who's going to call the shots? You? Me? Hell, we all know this all-for-one and one-for-all routine won't work around here—and it sure won't get the quality boost they're after."

Comiski was griping about changes announced by headquarters of his firm, Apogee Power Equipment Company, Inc. (APEC), to its mower divisions. The changes meant that Comiski's division, which manufactured and assembled gasoline mowers and which, 18 months ago, completed installation of a partially automated assembly-line method, would change to a team method of operations. Comiski, a 10-year assembly-plant worker with a high productivity rating, was fearful that the new process would deemphasize individual performance, which he was good at, and reward group performance, which he knew would involve some inefficient and lazy workers. He was unhappy about the prospect and vowed to himself to fight the change.

Comiski is not alone in his reaction to change. The fears and frustrations of workers and managers alike are reflected in media headlines every day: Downsizing. Layoffs. Acquisitions. Plant closings. Lawsuits. Labor-management disputes. Bankruptcy. Re-organization. Government regulations and deregulations. The list goes on.

As suggested in the opening quote, excellent firms consider constant improvement and constant change essential to their survival. Even those that are less than excellent are affected by change, whether they welcome it or not.

This chapter will focus on organizational change. First, we will examine the nature of that change.

THE NATURE OF ORGANIZATIONAL CHANGE

Change is a natural phenomenon. One has only to look at the weather, the seasons, the human life cycle, or a flower. All represent natural change. Other changes occur through environmental forces. Depletion of a resource, for example, will force the company using that resource to change to another. Some changes occur through human interaction. People get new jobs, move, join clubs, marry, create families, and interact in many ways that change their lives and the lives of others. Changes also occur through human and environmental interaction. A recent example is the change in the way we manage resources such as water and air in order to correct the pollution that we caused in the past. Change comes from so many sources that every person and organization is touched by it.

It has been said that change is inevitable. While this is largely true, some organizations adapt to change more successfully than do others. To some, as suggested in the cartoon, change is to be tolerated only as long as it does not alter the status quo.

Source: Reprinted with special permission of King Features Syndicate, Inc.

Firms seeking a competitive edge in today's global markets are treating organizational change not only as inevitable but as necessary to survival. The popularity of recent best-sellers such as *Theory Z—How American Business Can Meet the Japanese Challenge,*[2] *Reinventing the Corporation,*[3] and *Thriving on Chaos*[4] reflect the urgency with which executives in recent years have not only accepted change but have searched out and made changes in order to make their organizations more productive. They need not look far. The nature of organizational change suggests that we have two places to look: inside and outside the organization. Forces in both environments constantly create the need for organizational change. A good place to start is inside the firm.

Internal Forces Create Targets for Change

Organizations are dynamic entities. Even in firms that seem to be operating smoothly, there are forces at work that will upset the equilibrium. The success of a firm engenders growth. Growth causes change. More sales mean more production demands which, in turn, call for more people, more equipment, and perhaps new processes. Adding people creates new relationships through reassignment or reorganization. New equipment or processes trigger the need for new training programs. Amended or new policies and procedures may be required.

Internal change often stems from management's recognition that there is a gap between what should be and what is. This gap may be perceived as a problem to be corrected or as a possibility for improvement. As a supervisor, you might view low productivity as a problem that changed training methods might solve. You might also view increased rejects on the assembly line as an opportunity to get workers involved in problem solving by having them participate in finding ways to improve product quality. Comiski's remarks in the beginning of the chapter suggest that his firm plans to reorganize its workers into teams as a way to improve product quality. While Comiski and his firm are not in agreement at this stage as to method, Comiski's comments suggest that he would be receptive to participating in improving the work process.

Internal forces for change permeate the entire organization. They may be subtle forces that if not recognized and acted on, will cause a gradual erosion of effectiveness in the organization. For example, errors in communication that are ignored over time can evolve into a pattern of faulty communication that becomes accepted as the firm's norm. Product blemishes allowed to slip through quality control over time may put faulty products on the market and damage a firm's reputation for quality products and seriously affect its bottom line. Outdated job design or job descriptions may result in inefficiency, low morale, supervisory problems, or even lawsuits. Obsolescent equipment may strain the maintenance budget, decrease productivity, or cause morale problems. Whether internal changes are subtle or overtly planned, effective managers stay alert to all elements of the organization to see what and where changes are needed.

John R. Schermerhorn, Jr., cites seven internal targets for organizational change. These targets, shown in Figure 18-1, involve all the elements of the organization.[5] Here are some questions to consider when determining where changes should be made:

- *Purposes and objectives:* What is the mission of the organization? Is the mission current? Is it properly translated into objectives? Are the objectives well-communicated?
- *Culture:* Are the basic principles of operation clarified and communicated? Are the basic values of the firm shared by all its members?
- *Strategy:* Do the strategies fit the mission? Are they meeting the objectives?
- *Tasks:* Are the jobs well-designed? Are the workers motivated by their jobs? Are standards being met?
- *Technology:* Are the equipment and facilities adequate? Is more cost-effective equipment available? Are the processes and the work flow efficient?
- *People:* Is the human resources management system effective? Are the workers

FIGURE 18-1

Internal targets for change

○ Purposes and objectives	○ Technology
○ Culture	○ People
○ Strategy	○ Structure
○ Tasks	

Source: Adapted from John R. Schermerhorn, Jr., *Management for Productivity,* 2d ed., John Wiley & Sons, New York, 1984, p. 516.

motivated? Are training and career development programs utilized? Are worker attitudes positive?

● *Structure:* Is the organizational structure effective? Are roles clarified? Is co-ordination among the various units effective? Does authority distribution need modifying in order to provide for worker participation?

The targets are interrelated, of course; and a change in one may necessitate a change in another, which may necessitate a change in still another, and so on, in a rippling effect involving many targets throughout the organization.

While the nature of organizational change involves internal forces and targets, many changes stem from forces outside the organization, forces over which the supervisor has no control.

Competency Check

Can you identify the internal targets for change?

External Forces Provide Ongoing Challenges and Opportunities

Business exists in an ever-changing environment. External events become forces that present a constant challenge to organizational effectiveness. Figure 18-2 on page 558 illustrates the virtual bombardment of organizational effectiveness by external and internal forces. The major external forces are consumers, suppliers, technology, social trends, politics, economics, labor, and disasters.

Consumers

Consumers make the ultimate decisions about which products and services will succeed in the marketplace. If consumers don't buy—for whatever reason—the producer must change to another product or go out of business. You don't see many horse-drawn carriages being manufactured in the United States. Who would buy them?

When Coca-Cola tried to sell its new-formula cola, consumers said no. The company had to bring back the "classic" Coca-Cola. Consider the internal targets affected by this consumer decision. Coca-Cola had to decide not only what to do with the new formula but also how to reclaim the customers lost in the changeover. A strategy to reduce the demoralizing effect on the culture of the firm was also needed. The equipment and processes needed to produce and market two formulas instead of one brought about technological changes. Certainly there had to be people changes. Those assigned to the production of the new cola had to be reassigned. How would you like to have been the person whose idea it was to change the formula in the first place?

As you can see, consumer actions can force changes in many internal targets.

Suppliers

Suppliers have a high impact on an organization. Suppose your suppliers go out of business, eliminate or reduce their supply of product, change the quality of the product, increase the price, reduce their services, relocate, experience a strike, or change their relationship with your firm in some other way. Any of these changes could be a direct "hit" on one or more of the internal targets and thus have an impact on organizational effectiveness unless compensatory changes are made.

FIGURE 18-2   External forces and internal targets can erode organizational effectiveness

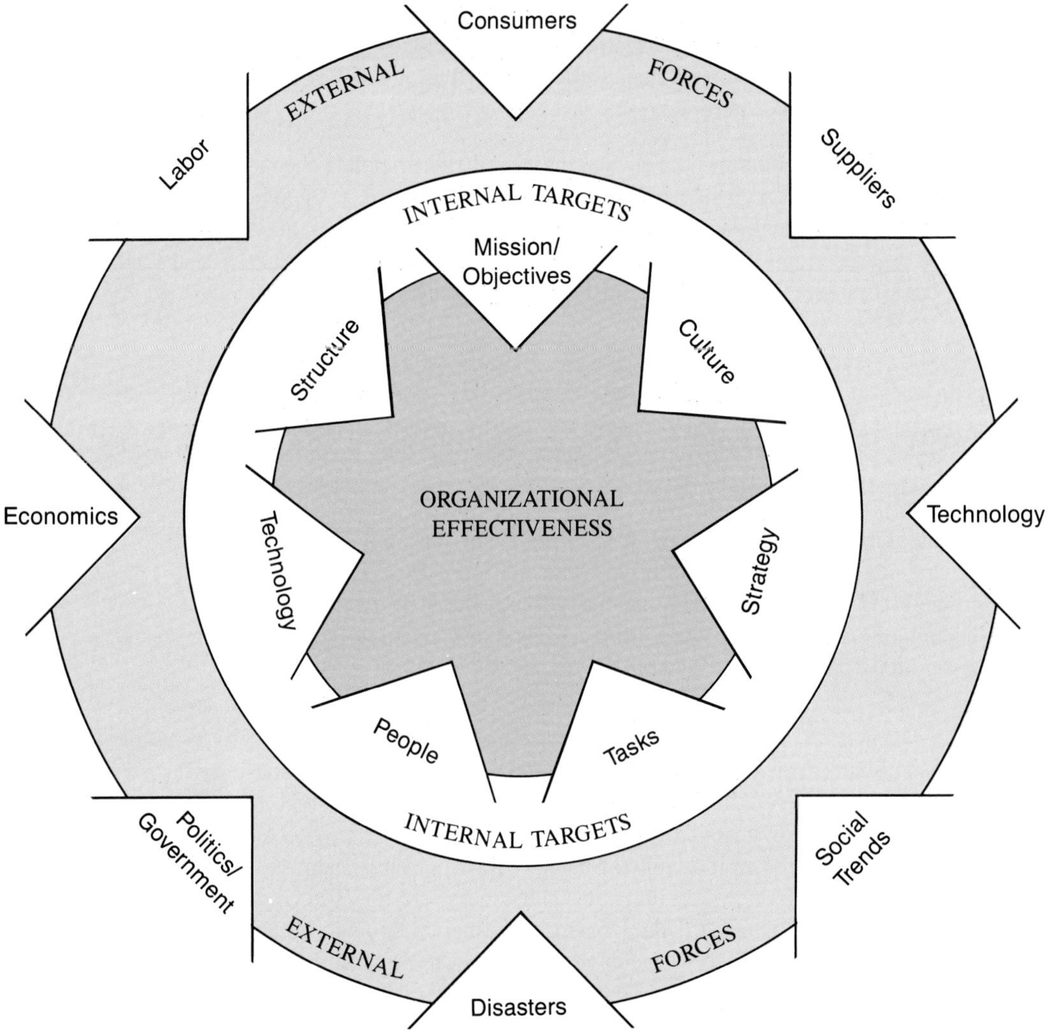

Technology

Technology is constantly changing. Think of the computer industry, for example. New products that are better, faster, cheaper, and often smaller are being introduced so frequently that keeping up to date seems an impossible task. Efforts to do so result in changes in internal technology that can affect all internal targets, with significant repercussions for people and tasks.

Social Trends

Social trends often have subtle origins, develop slowly, and then suddenly mushroom into mandates for change. Efforts by consumer activists and others to improve auto safety began several decades ago. Changes came slowly, mostly through legislation. The catalytic converter and seat belts are examples of these changes. Laws requiring the use of seat belts are still emerging from state legislatures.

Another example of a change brought about by social trends is smoking. Beginning with a mandate for a health-hazard warning on cigarette packages and developing over several years, the trend toward reduced smoking is resulting in social action that has caused many changes in the organizations affected. Among these organizations are those in the tobacco industry, transportation, enforcement agencies, and the restaurant industry.

Demographic trends also have an impact on the organization. Migration to the south and southwest caused changes in the strategies of many industries located in the northeast and the midwest. The trend toward an older population may have an impact on the purposes, objectives, strategies, and other internal targets of many organizations. MacDonald's, aware of the changing demographics, and finding it difficult to hire enough young workers, has begun hiring older workers in their fast-food business.

Politics

Politics can also cause organizational change. Elected officials are influenced by their constituencies. Special-interest groups spend great sums of money apprising politicians of the merits of their particular causes. This process, together with other political activities, results in actions being taken that may necessitate organizational changes. Examples are decisions on routes for highway construction, zoning, public-use contract negotiations, and budgetary allocations.

Economics

Economics is a frequent force for organizational change. The availability and cost of money can cause sudden and dramatic changes in the daily operations and the long-term investments of firms. For example, the 1987 stock market crash sent organizations in a variety of industries back to the drawing board to restructure after investment losses and their rippling effects—from a decrease in customers for products and services to reduced book value of their corporations. Drastic personnel reductions were made in the securities industry, for example, which suffered lost business from lowered investor confidence.

Economics plays a large role in the daily operation of a business and in its planning for the future. The state of the economy, the level of inflation or deflation, consumer confidence, and other economic factors affect the cost of financing, which, in turn, often necessitates changes in internal targets.

Labor

Labor encompasses the entire human resources management function. Changes may be needed in the way an organization forecasts, recruits, selects, orients, trains, appraises performance, or terminates its employees. Labor-intensive organizations such as retail firms have a greater sensitivity to change than do organizations that are technology-based. But all work requires human resources, and all managers need to address change in this area on an ongoing basis.

Workers themselves have changed in recent years. For one thing, they are more knowledgeable about their rights and are more vocal in exercising them. While most are better-educated than were their predecessors, there remains a large segment of undereducated and unskilled workers. In addition, many newly created jobs require a higher level of skill than did former entry-level jobs. All of these factors affect the labor supply to which employers must accommodate. Training often requires programs for divergent skill levels, and more training within the industry is becoming mandatory.

Labor legislation also necessitates change. New antidiscrimination, workplace-safety, handicap-accommodation, compensation, and benefits laws have necessitated changes in recent years. Labor legislation involving unions has long been an external force for change. Unionized firms face changes periodically as they negotiate new labor contracts.

Disasters

Competency Check:

Can you discuss several external forces for change?

An organization may also have to undergo sudden and pervasive change as a result of a disaster. Earthquakes, fires, and floods have disrupted, even decimated, many firms. Other disasters that have forced many changes include explosions, chemical or nuclear accidents, and crime. A plan for crisis management may lessen the effects of the changes that emanate from such disasters.

Organizational effectiveness is continually threatened by these external forces. To remain effective, organizations must manage change as an integral part of the system. Peters says, ''There are no excellent companies . . . '' only those that believe in '' . . . constant improvement and constant change.''[6]

Competency Check:

Can you discuss the nature of organizational change?

You have learned that change, by nature, is ongoing and stems from both internal and external sources. You have also seen that change may, at times, be a reaction by management to external forces. The challenge is to keep reactionary change to a minimum by anticipating the operating forces for change and modifying the organization through advance planning and orderly change. The next section will address the change process.

MAKING PLANNED CHANGES

Some reactionary change is inevitable. For example, when several deaths were attributed to Tylenol that had been poisoned, its manufacturer, Johnson and Johnson, had to make many changes quickly. Some of these changes, such as pulling the product from retail shelves, were immediate. Others, such as investigating the cause, analyzing the returned Tylenol, and communicating with the public to calm fears, followed soon after. Still other changes, such as redesigning the product and packaging, while still reactionary, could be planned. Fortunately, crisis-induced changes represent a small percentage of all the changes that are made by organizations.

The majority of changes are planned, with varying degrees of effectiveness in the planning. According to Comiski's comments in the beginning of the chapter, APEC did not plan for its changes very effectively. But it did take the first step when it recognized that change was necessary. That is a critical step, which we shall look at next.

Recognizing the Need for Change

Alert managers keep a sharp watch on their organizations' movement toward the accomplishment of objectives. As you learned in Chapter 15, many glitches can happen between expected and actual outcomes. These glitches may be a symptom of a problem and may suggest a need to modify one or more internal targets. Figure 18-3 lists symptoms that may signal a need for change.

Symptoms are sometimes mistaken for the actual problem. You might view a symptom as the visible part of an iceberg. Usually the real danger is hidden beneath

FIGURE 18-3

Symptoms that may signal a need for change

1. Morale is low. Employees are uncooperative, cliquish, and unfriendly to new hires and show no loyalty to the firm.
2. There is a high turnover of personnel.
3. Customer complaints about service have increased.
4. There is an increase in goods returned because of defects.
5. Waste material in production and operation has increased.
6. Equipment maintenance costs have skyrocketed.
7. Workers complain of equipment inefficiency and downtime.
8. Overtime costs have increased.
9. Accident claims have increased.
10. Absenteeism and tardiness have increased.
11. Worker grievances have increased.
12. A sexual-harrassment suit has been filed against the company.
13. Productivity has steadily declined.
14. Transfer of company resources to new acquisition slows down production of older units, demoralizing morale of managers and workers in older units.
15. Little interest is shown in training and development programs.
16. Housekeeping has become lax.
17. Job descriptions rarely portray the job being performed.
18. Workers complain that tasks are inequitably distributed.
19. Breaking of policies and rules is commonplace.
20. Supervisors often complain that management does not back them up in their decisions.

the surface. For example, if your workers complain about equipment inefficiency and downtime, do you assume your problem is workers who like to grumble? Not if you're an effective supervisor. Instead, you view the complaints as a symptom of a deeper problem that needs investigation. You look into the age of the equipment; its volume of use; the ability of its operators; the process, frequency, and effectiveness of repairs; its environment, especially if it is electronic equipment; and, yes, the morale of the workers who might, indeed, be grumblers.

The symptom is a cue that change is needed. This will lead you to the internal targets to determine what should be changed.

Identifying the Internal Targets

As you learned in the first section of this chapter, seven major elements of the organization are targets for change. In making planned changes, these targets should be examined carefully to see which ones will be affected in the planned change. As already noted, a change rarely affects only one area. Instead, the rippling effect may cause changes in the whole organization. All affected targets should be identified so that planning can be complete.

In 1986, AT&T decided that a change in strategy was needed to make the company more competitive. One of several planned changes was to restructure its research and development (R & D) function. Where the firm had before and since divestiture used the *"baby Bells" for R & D,* it decided to break away from the family of Bell firms and buy components from other firms. Such a strategy would have been unthinkable in the old AT&T culture. Now managers found themselves in a different culture— they were being encouraged to think freely about using suppliers other than Bell as well as non-Bell markets for AT&T products. This new concept has been accompanied by a complete restructuring of the organization, a refinement of its mission, and a revised set of objectives. Changes permeate the organization, affecting every internal target. Through careful planning and execution of the changes, AT&T's management, by 1988, had already headed the once-great company back on the road to profitability. Planned changes have been carried out in every aspect of the business, and more are expected in the 1990s.[7]

All the events at AT&T involved people changes. Layoffs, terminations, reassignments, and transfers affected thousands of workers. When identifying internal targets for change, managers should be aware that any change will affect people. Because of the behavioral changes involved in any organizational modification, the change process focuses on people, as we shall see next.

The Change Process

Change is complicated. If it involved only moving equipment or installing computers, there would be little difficulty. But as noted above, change involves people. People are creatures of habit, and change upsets habits. Therefore, even when people intellectually accept the reasons for a change, they tend to resist it. How can firms maintain effectiveness through change under these conditions?

FIGURE 18-4 The change process

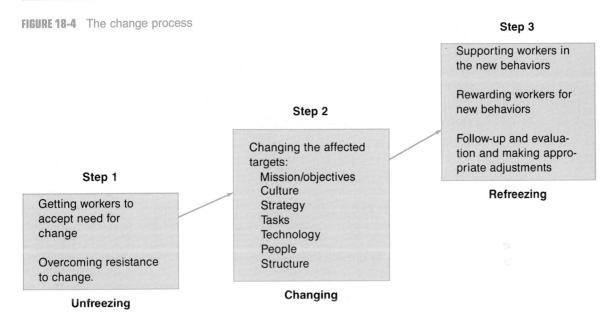

Source: Adapted from Kurt Lewin, "Frontiers in Group Dynamics: Concept, Method, and Reality of Social Sciences: Social Equilibria and Social Change," *Human Relations,* June 1947, pp. 5–14.

Kurt Lewin says that change should be viewed as a people-oriented, three-step process: (1) unfreezing, (2) changing, and (3) refreezing.[8] A graphic view of the change process is shown in Figure 18-4. A brief discussion of the three steps, based on Lewin's classic thesis, follows.

Unfreezing

The first step in making a change is making workers aware of the need for it and making them receptive to it. They must be made aware that their present behavior is ineffective, and they must be persuaded that the new behavior will make them more effective. This thawing-out process is a difficult one because people are usually comfortable in their present behavior and resist changing.

To encourage the unfreezing, managers must recognize the nature of resistance to change. Resistance stems from the workers' feelings of comfort and security in the status quo and their fears of the unknown in the new situation. Workers may fear many things, including their ability to handle the new situation, the changes it will make in their social or work relationships, or the change it may make in their economic status. While it may not be possible to completely eliminate these fears, they can be minimized. Ways to do this will be discussed later in this chapter.

Changing

According to Lewin's thesis, workers, once unfrozen, begin to try out the new behavior. This tends to catch on so that one worker follows another in changing. This is especially evident when one worker has some expertise in the new behavior. As you learned in Chapter 11, expertise can carry the power to influence others. Workers will identify with the expert, who then serves as a role model.

Getting workers to exercise the new behavior over a period of time helps them *internalize* the behavior; that is, make it a part of their normal behavior. As time passes, the new behavior becomes routine, replacing the old behavior.

Refreezing

Lewin's third step in making a change occurs when the worker has accepted the new behavior experimented with during the second step. At this point, the workers' attitudes should have changed to a point where they support the new behavior as a normal part of their lives.

During this third stage, management should try to maintain the momentum set in motion during the changing stage. Supporting the workers in their new behavioral modes is important in the refreezing process. Encouraging workers who may falter during this stage by providing both emotional support and needed resources will speed refreezing. Rewarding workers who successfully make the change and assimilate it into their work routine is imperative. Workers who were persuaded to change through promised benefits will quickly be turned off if they see no rewards forthcoming. The quality of the refreezing stage will depend greatly on management's reinforcement of the desired outcomes.

Follow-up and evaluation are also essential during the refreezing stage. They not only provide information on the success of the behavioral change but also provide cost-to-benefit data that will allow management to quantify the value of the change to the firm. Follow-up and evaluation also give management an opportunity to make appropriate adjustments in the new system, if needed. A word of caution regarding adjustments: Too many modifications during this stage may undo progress made in the first two stages. Adjustments themselves constitute change. While some adjustment is to be expected, too many adjustments can create chaos, causing workers to lose confidence in the managers, their planning ability, and the change itself as a means of improvement. Do you think that some of Comiski's negative reaction stems from too frequent change at APEC?

In the next section, you will examine your role in the change process.

Competency Check:

Can you identify in order and describe the steps in the change process?

THE SUPERVISOR'S ROLE IN MANAGING CHANGE

While major organizational changes are usually initiated at the top level of management, you will be directly involved at the departmental level. Supervisors should be a part of the planning for any change that involves operations. You will, in fact, be expected to handle the changes that occur on a routine basis. You will also be expected to be innovative in initiating changes that will improve your workers' performance. Making adjustments, as you recall from Chapter 15, is a part of your controlling function.

For larger changes that emanate from top management, you may be expected to serve as the change agent for your department.

The Supervisor as Change Agent

A *change agent* is a person who has responsibility for altering or modifying the behavior of persons in an organization and of the organization itself. In other words, the change agent is the one who makes change happen.

For more pervasive change programs, such as organizational development (OD), a change agent may be a manager appointed to the role or an outside specialist engaged by the firm to direct the change program.

OD, a specialized management approach to change, is a process focused on changing the behavior of people throughout the firm and thus changing the firm and its culture. You will be called on, as will all managers, to assist with OD when this approach is used. More often, however, you will serve as a change agent to effect group, departmental, or divisional changes on a somewhat smaller scale. This means that as a change agent, you will have two responsibilities: (1) identifying departmental needs and initiating appropriate changes and (2) managing the change process when the change is initiated by your superiors.

Much of the first responsibility will be handled through your controlling activities (see Chapter 15). Monitoring the internal and external environment for improvement opportunities will also help. This responsibility should keep before you the question, "How can we do this job more effectively?"

As a change agent executing planned change, you need to understand and be able to lead workers through the change process steps of unfreezing, changing, and refreezing.

One way to make your job easier is to prepare your workers for both accepting change and making changes.

Competency Check:

Can you define the term *change agent* and show how it relates to the supervisor?

WHAT CAN THE SUPERVISOR DO?

Understanding the change process is essential if you are going to be an effective change agent. Sometimes you will need to abandon the textbook approach and summon all your creative resources to help you manage change. Figure 18-5 on page 566 lists 14 steps to creative change. It encapsulates strategies for change ranging from inspiration to implementation. It also advises that success as a change agent can help you move up the corporate ladder.

Preparing Workers for Change

Comiski in the beginning of the chapter clearly was not prepared for the changes announced by APEC management. His attitude illustrates the two areas that are the supervisor's major concern in preparing workers for change.

1. helping workers develop an attitude of receptivity to change as a means of improvement
2. minimizing resistance to change

FIGURE 18-5 14 steps to creative change

With a great idea in your pocket and seriousness written all over you, follow these 14 strategies to guide an idea from inspiration to implementation.

1. Always stay within your personal resources of time, skills, and courage. We only have so much of the three to offer. If you extend yourself beyond that, you will feel and create stress, experience burnout and hostility, and become negative about both your proposed change and the process of organizational change.

2. If your change takes a lot of extra money, reconsider it. No matter how useful, needed, and potentially successful your new idea is, if large amounts of extra money are called for, you are taking on a battle that is unrelated to the issue of change and the strengths of your idea. What is always needed is more intelligent reallocation of existing resources.

3. When you decide on a change, do it well. Be skillful in what you do. Brilliant ideas are shot down by sloppy performance, and they should be.

4. "If it ain't worth doing, it ain't worth doing well." Bad ideas should be shot down, too, even if the leaders of the change are skillful operators. Think through your desired change and make certain it is needed in the organization.

5. Take leadership. Be authoritative, not authoritarian. You are going to have to do it, and the change will be better because of that. Those involved must also feel a sense of creative ownership about the process and the outcome. They need leadership.

6. Plan and arrange success—don't wait for it to happen or be discovered. You have to make it happen and deliver it. You must structure and sculpt it.

7. Ignorance of what you are doing is not a sin. You must, again, take the lead in promoting your change within your organization. Analyze, evaluate, and don't ever repeat your mistakes. Talk calmly, clearly, and confidently of your successes.

8. Take care of the administrative needs of the organization. It's not that painful, and if your proposed change is worth doing, it is probably more efficient than what exists. It may even be more accountable and flexible.

   If you overlook or do a sloppy job of administrative chores, you won't even make it to the primaries. If you prove that you can meet those needs in a more efficient, accountable, and flexible manner than has been done in the past, you are far along in getting executives and top managers to meet your needs and take you seriously. It is a good tradeoff.

9. Don't try to do too much too fast. You will have time to keep chipping away. Decide what is most important and what you can do best, and do it well.

10. Know your audience. Speak its vocabulary, not your own jargon. It's strategically vital. You must meet people where they are to build a constituency.

11. Know the tradeoffs necessary for your change to materialize. Of course, something will have to be modified or given up. Somebody will cling to that and see you as a threat. You are.

    Your boss may ask, "How do we know what you are proposing is better than what we have?" Your answer should be, "Of course we don't, but is what we are doing working so well?" Don't hesitate with that answer. Many of us with good ideas have been intimidated because we can't produce data to "prove" the merits of our proposals. Produce data to document the present flaws; then once your idea is in operation, produce data to document your successes. And continue generating the data for as long as you wish to sustain your change.

12. Most people in your organization feel they personally cannot effect change. They probably can't. Teach them how you can do it together. That's the role of leadership.

13. Use the successes from your work in organizational change to promote your own career. Very few at the top of the organizational ladder were discovered for their well-kept secrets. They arranged for their successes and were proud to talk about them. Gaining career recognition is *your* responsibility, and it takes planning.

14. Memorize the following magic formula for organizational change (but be cautious about trusting magic formulas): Build a constituency; don't go outside others' experience; learn the territory; have a clear agenda for change; dazzle them with data; and be serious.

Source: Jerry Conrath, "Solving Problems Creatively," *Management World,* January 1985, p. 19.

Making Workers Receptive to Change

In helping workers become amenable to change, supervisors should first be enthusiastically entrepreneurial in seeking out ways to improve the entire department. Enthusiasm is usually contagious. Workers are more likely to submit innovative suggestions if they know that the suggestions are welcome; will be explored and, if feasible, implemented; and, if successfully implemented, will be rewarded. Treating suggestions and resultant changes over time under such a policy will help to develop the workers' trust in the supervisor and the organization. In a climate of trust, change is always easier to implement.

Getting started in developing a receptive attitude to innovation and change may be difficult. Talking with and listening to the workers will help the supervisor identify those with innovative potential. Comiski probably would have been a willing contributor to APEC's change plan if he had been asked.

You might ask workers if they have suggestions for improvement in a specific area, such as waste reduction or work flow. Having them submit their proposals and having a work group try it out may motivate others to submit suggestions. Continued encouragement may lead to the attitude you are seeking: receptivity to change as a means of improvement.

If your firm is attempting to develop an innovative attitude throughout the firm, it may wish to find out what level of innovative thinking currently exists. This information may be gathered through a questionnaire such as the one in Figure 18-6 on page 568. If the criteria are valid and reliable, and if the questionnaire is administered and the results evaluated by trained personnel, it can help develop a climate in which your workers are not only receptive to change but actively search for ways in which to improve the process through change.

Competency Check:

Can you illustrate ways through which the supervisor can develop in workers a receptive attitude toward change?

Minimizing Resistance to Change

The second area of concern to the supervisor in preparing workers for change is minimizing resistance to it. If your workers have developed a receptive attitude to change, there will be much less resistance. That will make your job easier. But human nature being what it is, some resistance will surface when change is introduced. Understanding why people resist change is the first step toward minimizing that resistance.

As you read in the discussion of unfreezing, people resist change for many reasons. The resistance is sometimes overt and sometimes covert. Comiski freely expressed his displeasure to his buddies over coffee but kept his fears and his planned resistance to himself. Can you identify Comiski's reasons for resisting APEC's changes among those listed in Figure 18-7 on page 569?

If you cited fear of having his salary reduced as one reason for his resistance, you are right. APEC rewards individual performance, and Comiski is a good performer. He knows that some of his co-workers are not good performers, and he does not know how rewards will be handled after the change. He fears that with the change to group performance, his high productivity will be averaged with the low productivity of others in his group and thus lower his pay. He fears the unknown.

FIGURE 18-6 How interested employees are in work innovation

INTEREST IN WORK INNOVATION INDEX

The first characteristic of people at work which we wished to assess is interest in work innovation. From an organizational point of view, much benefit can come from a search by employees at all levels for better ways to do things. For individuals, a continuing interest in innovation may represent an alertness which permits them to use well their minds and their abilities. For employees, interest in innovation may be also an indicator of general interest and involvement in their job.

Questionnaire Items

The following items appear to be the best indicators of interest in innovation (numbers in parentheses preceding each response category indicate the score assigned to each response):

1. In your kind of work, if a person tries to change his or her usual way of doing things, how does it generally turn out?
   - (1) _____ Usually turns out worse; the tried and true methods work best in my work.
   - (3) _____ Usually doesn't make much difference.
   - (5) _____ Usually turns out better; our methods need improvement.

2. Some people prefer doing a job in pretty much the same way because this way they can count on always doing a good job. Others like to go out of their way in order to think up new ways of doing things. How is it with you on your job?
   - (1) _____ I always prefer doing things pretty much in the same way.
   - (2) _____ I mostly prefer doing things pretty much in the same way.
   - (4) _____ I mostly prefer doing things in new and different ways.
   - (5) _____ I always prefer doing things in new and different ways.

3. How often do you try out, on your own, a better or faster way of doing something on the job?
   - (5) _____ Once a week or more often.
   - (4) _____ Two or three times a month.
   - (3) _____ About once a month.
   - (2) _____ Every few months.
   - (1) _____ Rarely or never.

4. How often do you get chances to try out your own ideas on your job, either before or after checking with your supervisor?
   - (5) _____ Several times a week or more.
   - (4) _____ About once a week.
   - (3) _____ Several times a month.
   - (2) _____ About once a month.
   - (1) _____ Less than once a month.

5. In my kind of job, it's usually better to let your supervisor worry about new or better ways of doing things.
   - (1) _____ Strongly agree.
   - (2) _____ Mostly agree.
   - (4) _____ Mostly disagree.
   - (5) _____ Strongly disagree.

6. How many times in the past year have you suggested to your supervisor a different or better way of doing something on the job?
   - (1) _____ Never had occasion to do this during the past year.
   - (2) _____ Once or twice.
   - (3) _____ About three times.
   - (4) _____ About five times.
   - (5) _____ Six to ten times.
   - (6) _____ More than ten times had occasion to do this during the past year.

Source: Samuel C. Certo, *Principles of Modern Management,* 3d ed., Wm. C. Brown Company Publishers, Dubuque, Iowa, 1986, p. 262.

FIGURE 18-7 Fears cause resistance to change

People resist change often because they are comfortable in their present way of doing things. They fear that their lives will be upset and that their future will be uncertain in the changed environment. Below are some of the fears that cause workers to resist change.

Fear

- of the unknown
- of losing their job
- of having their salary reduced
- of losing status, rank, or power
- of their inability to perform the new job
- of new responsibilities

- of required training
- of changes in social/work relationships
- of a required relocation
- of challenges to their values, attitudes, or beliefs
- of change itself

If you were Comiski's supervisor, what would you do to dispel his fears? Figure 18-8 on page 570 presents four worker-oriented approaches that can be used to deal with resistance to change. The first of these, education and communication, is one appropriate method to use with Comiski. All APEC workers need to be shown how they will be affected by the change. A one-on-one conference with Comiski should be used to explain that one benefit of the change will be an increase in productivity, and, as a high producer, his pay could increase. Any new compensation system should be thoroughly explained to all workers. If decreases will, in fact, be involved, the facilitation and support approach should be used.

One of the most effective methods of dealing with resistance to change is the participation-and-involvement approach. This participative approach results in longer-term acceptance of and internalization by the workers.[9] Helping to plan and execute the change not only helps dispel workers' fears but also motivates them by increasing their self-esteem. As you learned in Chapter 11, worker participation in decisions about their work life is one of the best motivators. Here is an example of worker enthusiasm about participation in a team mode at Goodyear Tire and Rubber.

At the morning shift change in Goodyear Tire and Rubber's radial-tire plant in Lawton, Okla., workers crowd into supervisor Bill Jackson's office to check yesterday's production figures against those of the other three shifts. Average tire-production time is down to 10 minutes, half that of most other plants in the world. Up the line in the spotless 1.5-million-square-foot plant, tire builders on Ron Wood's team go over personal ''business plans'' to meet or exceed factory standards, such as 1 percent absenteeism and 1 percent product waste. On the floor, an automatic tire-trimming machine and tread-gluing machine invented by employees do what five employees per shift used to do. ''There is so much talent in this plant, it is unreal,'' says Jackson. ''You think of all the years it wasn't used.''

Harnessing worker power—encouraging pride even in such little things as waxed floors and commitment to big goals such as turning out a high-quality, low-cost product—is one of the keys to Goodyear's success in the global tire market.[10]

FIGURE 18-8

WORKER-ORIENTED METHODS OF DEALING WITH RESISTANCE TO CHANGE

APPROACH	EXAMPLES	COMMONLY USED IN SITUATIONS	ADVANTAGES	DRAWBACKS
1. education and communication	Use one-on-one discussions, group presentations, written communications to educate people prior to change ahd help them see benefits of change.	where there is a lack of information or inaccurate information and analysis	Once persuaded, people will often help with the implementation of the change.	can be very time-consuming if lots of people are involved.
2. participation and involvement	Allow workers to help design and implement change; ask for ideas and advice; form task forces, committees, teams to work on the change.	where the initiators do not have all the information they need to design the change, and where others have considerable power to resist	People who participate will be committed to implementing change, and any relevant information they have will be integrated into the change plan.	can be very time-consuming if participants design an inappropriate change
3. facilitation and support	Provide social and emotional support for hardships of change; actively listen to problems and complaints; provide training in new ways; help overcome performance pressures.	where people are resisting because of adjustment problems	No other approach works as well with adjustment problems.	can be time-consuming, expensive, and still fail
4. negotiation and agreement	Offer incentives to actual or potential resistors; work out trade-offs to provide special benefits in exchange that change will not be blocked.	where someone or some group will clearly lose out in a change, and where that group has considerable power to resist	Sometimes it is a relatively easy way to avoid major resistance.	can be too expensive in many cases if it alerts others to negotiate for compliance

Source: Adapted from John P. Kotter and Leonard A. Schlesinger, "Choosing Strategies for Change," *Harvard Business Review,* March-April 1979, p. 111, and John R. Schermerhorn, Jr., *Management for Productivity,* 2d ed., John Wiley & Sons, Inc., New York, 1986, pp. 519–521.

In addition to participation by workers, such as that experienced at Goodyear, communication is important in managing change.

Minimizing resistance to change can occur only through effective communication. Workers don't like surprises. Too often in recent years, large groups of workers have been handed pink slips on a Friday morning, to take effect that afternoon. No matter how compelling the reason for the change, workers need a chance to prepare for the economic and emotional trauma that may accompany it. Knowledge of these events has caused workers to lose trust in their firms. This has made them suspicious of change and has increased their fear of losing their security. Clear, honest, and timely information should precede any organizational change. This applies to companywide change as well as to the routine departmental changes that you, as supervisor, will manage. When your workers trust you and the information you disseminate, they are less resistant to change.

A caveat for the unfreezing stage is that the supervisor follow company policy in the change process as in all other functions. Sometimes you may not be made aware of major changes, such as downsizing or plant closings. Or if apprised by management, you may be sworn to secrecy. Such conditions put supervisors who have tried to create a climate of trust in an awkward position with the workers. The only recourse is to try to persuade management to communicate openly with workers. Failing that, providing emotional support for the affected workers may be all you can do.

Competency Check:

Can you give several examples of how supervisors can minimize resistance to change?

A second caveat is that supervisors keep in close touch with workers who are slow to unfreeze. These workers will need additional support throughout the change. If the worker maintains an attitude of resistance, refusing to conform to the change, sooner or later the supervisor will have to make the hard decision to terminate the worker. Continuing the supportive role in the change step that follows will, hopefully, help the supervisor avoid this unpleasant possibility.

Making the Change

According to Lewin, many change agents enter the change step before the situation is adequately unfrozen.[11] When change occurs before workers feel that it is necessary and will be beneficial, there is an increased risk that resistance will resurface and that the change will fail.

If the workers have been properly prepared during the unfreezing stage, the actual change can be fairly easy. For example, before the installation of a new check-acceptance system in a supermarket, the checkers should complete a training program that includes hands-on experience at the register. The old system required that the manager be called to the register to approve and initial each check. The new system includes the following steps:

- Verify that the printed information on the check is accurate and current.
- If the customer has a store check-cashing ID, record the number on the left front corner of the check or ask for two IDs—a driver's license and a credit card (do not accept gasoline cards).

- Stamp the back of the check with the store stamp.
- Record the IDs on store-stamp form on check.
- Insert the check into the check slot in the cash register and key in customer's SS number.
- Press the enter key to automatically endorse the check for deposit.
- Thank the customer for shopping FreshFoods.

During the change to the new system, the checkers should be given much support. For example, the supervisor should recognize that production will be slower at the beginning, while checkers are learning the new system. Exercise patience while they are developing their skill in using the new procedure. Encourage them to ring for you to come to the checkout counter when questions arise that they aren't yet prepared to handle. At the end of their shifts, ask whether they encountered any problems. Ask for their suggestions as to how to handle them. For example, Mark Bodinsky, a checker, might suggest that the new process steps be posted on the cash register, where he can refer to them until he commits them to memory. If you agree that this "crutch" would be helpful, have the steps duplicated and posted on the registers of Bodinsky and any other checker who needs help. And do so before Bodinsky's next shift.

Competency Check:

Can you explain the supervisor's role in the changing phase?

Note: In the change phase, your role is largely supportive. Recognize that mistakes will be made and that some workers will revert to the old system simply out of habit. Let them know that you are there to help them make the change. The greater their trust in you, the faster will be their internalization of the change and their move into the refreezing stage.

Stabilizing After Change

Lewin's refreezing stage is an attempt to restore equilibrium to the environment at a higher level of effectiveness. Properly implemented, refreezing helps to phase out the feeling of chaos that some people experience during change. Your efforts should be concentrated on maintaining the momentum that the change engendered and supporting the workers making the change.

Stabilizing at a higher level of effectiveness requires evaluation and feedback. Lines of communication must be kept open so that workers will continue to feel comfortable in giving negative as well as positive feedback.

Suppose, for example, that Bodinsky, the checker, comes to you with a comment that customers in line are complaining about the new requirement that two IDs be presented for check cashing. If you respond with, "Mark, are you back again with another problem? What am I going to do with you? No other checker has complained," you're going to turn Bodinsky off and thereby lose some valuable feedback.

Instead you might say, "I'm sorry to hear that, Mark. Do you have any suggestions for improving the situation?" Bodinsky might surprise you with, "Yes, why don't we tell the customers that they can reduce the inconvenience by getting a store check-cashing card approved and put on file? We could explain that they can then show just the store card instead of getting out two IDs in a busy checkout line. We could give them the form to fill out and return, or we could even provide a small desk in the store where they could do it right then.''

Bodinsky's good idea might both speed his refreezing at the new level of effectiveness and also help retain valuable customers for the store.

Another method of refreezing is to reinforce desired outcomes by offering rewards. Offering increased pay or benefits for greater productivity is one way to reward workers for adjusting to the change. Giving them a share in increased profits or cost reductions is another. A cost-benefit analysis of the change will provide data that might be used in a companywide reward policy. If, for example, Bodinsky's firm experienced a 10 percent reduction in bad-check costs, a portion of this amount might be shared with those involved in suggesting, planning, and implementing the change. Bodinsky's suggestion for reducing customer complaints might be rewarded with a bonus or, at least, recognition, such as a feature in the firm's newsletter to its employees.

If conditions are not stabilized after change, some workers might revert to doing things the old way or the entire change might even be abandoned, resulting in significant costs to the firm.

Competency Check:

Can you explain what is meant by ''stabilizing at a higher level of effectiveness''?

COMPETENCY REVIEW

1. Discuss the nature of organizational change.
2. Identify seven internal targets for change.
3. Discuss eight external forces for change.
4. Compare reactionary and planned change.
5. Explain why recognizing the need for change is an inherent part of the supervisor's controlling function.
6. Identify in order and describe the steps in the change process.
7. Define the term *change agent,* and show how it relates to the supervisor.
8. Illustrate ways in which supervisors can make workers receptive to change.
9. Give four examples of how supervisors can minimize resistance to change.
10. Explain the supervisor's role in the changing phase.
11. What is meant by ''stabilizing at a higher level of effectiveness''?

APPLICATIONS

1. Recently a new procedure was implemented for assembling a unit in your department. Everyone but Carmen Ross is using it. She is still assembling the unit in the old way. You've talked with her about this several times and have demonstrated the new steps to her. Still she hasn't come around. What do you do? List several actions which you might take to handle the situation with Carmen Ross.
2. Many events in your lifetime have caused changes in the world of work.
   a. List 10 changes that have occurred in the environment in the last 20 years.
   b. Classify the changes on your list according to the eight external environmental forces in Figure 18-2 on page 558.
   c. Show how the changes have caused organizational change.

3. Supervisors are often on the firing line when it comes to coping with resistance to change. They may be told by their superiors that a change is to be made and that they must squelch any resistance in their departments. Even when the supervisor is initiating the change, he or she may have to cope with a resister who prefers to do things ''like we've always done them.'' This chapter has given you some guidelines to managing change. But what about your own attitude toward change? The questionnaire below will help you analyze your own feelings about change and meeting resistance to it. Respond to the questions by checking under the Yes or No column to reflect your feelings about change.

	Yes	No
Do I personally resist change in my life or in my work?	____	____
Do I resent being told by superiors that a better way is needed for a process in my department?	____	____
Do I offer suggestions for changes up the line as well as down the line to workers?	____	____
Have I ever personally tried to sell an idea for change to my superior?	____	____
When making changes in my department, do I plan the entire change and then announce it to the workers?	____	____
Do I invite suggestions for improvement from workers on a regular basis?	____	____
Do I ever assign problems to committees or teams to find solutions?	____	____
Do I insist that rules and procedures be followed without exception and without question?	____	____
If I see a worker using a nonstandard procedure to perform a task, do I observe, ask for an explanation, and evaluate the variation according to its effectiveness?	____	____
Do I provide clear and valid information about a change in departmental procedure?	____	____
Do I encourage workers to be innovative in improving tasks?	____	____
Do I demonstrate the benefits of a planned change to workers?	____	____
Do I try to time changes so that they will occur on Fridays or before a holiday to provide workers a cooling-off period?	____	____
Do I enlist key workers to help in planning changes?	____	____
Do I provide meet-and-confer time to plan, implement, and evaluate changes?	____	____
Do I recognize workers' insecurity by clarifying intentions, methods, and expected results of change to relieve their fears?	____	____

Do my workers freely come to me to offer suggestions for change? _____ _____

Do I usually hear about worker complaints or fears from the grapevine when changes are made? _____ _____

CASES

Case I: The Changes Begin Monday . . .

Reread the incident in the beginning of the chapter about the changes at APEC. Then consider the following:

A new CEO came on board at APEC 6 months before the changes announced at the mower plant. According to the grapevine, the board of directors thought some change was necessary at the top to get the company moving again after a profit slide that lasted over 3 years. The new CEO had a mandate to make whatever changes he thought necessary to turn things around and recapture the market share recently lost to foreign competitors.

Several changes have been made in recent years, but they have not significantly reduced customer complaints about the quality and safety of Apogee mowers. These complaints, and an impending lawsuit against the firm for an injury supposedly caused by a broken lawn-mower housing, led the new CEO to select product design and quality control as his first attack on the company's problems. He moved fast, setting up the project at headquarters.

Research into design, process, quality control, and management methods were completed at headquarters by management with the aid of an outside consultant. The resultant design and process changes were proudly announced by top management to the affected divisions. Changes were to be effective on Monday, 4 days away. As reflected in Comiski's comments, the workers' reactions were less than enthusiastic.

1. Was APEC's change reactionary or planned? Explain.
2. Based on your study of change in this chapter, do you consider any of APEC's actions to be ''right'' at this point? If so, name the action, and give your reason.
3. List the actions of APEC that might be considered ineffective.
4. If you were Comiski's supervisor, how would you handle him and the situation now?

Case II: Tracy's Bright-Idea Light Burns Overtime

As supervisor of one of six groups of assembly-line workers at GenCo Manufacturing Company, Jim Peterson tries to encourage his workers to be innovative in improving their jobs. The assembly line is designed, installed, and maintained by the engineering department. Peterson's group is part of the production department.

One of the workers, Tracy Cummins, is one of the brightest workers on the line. She has just come to Peterson's office to tell him that she has a great idea concerning the new jigs that engineering is installing on the line.

"Why don't you buck my idea over to Sam in engineering? I'll bet that crew will grab it as if it were their idea in the first place! And you know, if they install it, I won't even care if they do steal my idea!"

She is exuberant—certain that her idea is a good one. The conversation is overheard by Mike Rogers, a 12-year employee who has resisted every change made during that time. Rogers' and Cummins' paths cross as they return to the line.

"You pushing another of your crackpot ideas, Tracy?" he asks sarcastically.

"Oh, crawl back in your shell, Mike. You're just afraid something will kick you out of your rut and make you work for a change. No pun intended—I know how you hate the word."

Peterson overhears the exchange and agrees somewhat with both parties. The trouble is, Peterson thinks that Cummins does seem to have a "great idea" about everything. Some have, indeed, been good and have been implemented. But many have been impractical, and some have been really far out.

There must be, Peterson thinks, a way to handle the situation. But what . . . ?

1. What suggestion for handling the situation can you offer to Peterson?
2. What should Peterson do about Rogers?

REFERENCES

1. Tom Peters, *Thriving on Chaos,* Alfred A. Knopf, Inc., New York, 1987, p. 4.

2. William Ouchi, *Theory Z, How American Business Can Meet the Japanese Challenge,* Addison-Wesley Publishing Company, Reading, Mass., 1981.

3. John Naisbitt and Patricia Burdine, *Reinventing the Corporation,* Warner Books, New York, 1985.

4. Tom Peters, op cit., pp. 1–4.

5. John R. Schermerhorn, Jr., *Management for Productivity,* 2d ed., John Wiley & Sons, Inc., New York, 1984, p. 516.

6. Tom Peters, op. cit., pp. 1, 4.

7. "AT&T: The Making of a Comeback," *Business Week,* Jan. 18, 1988, pp. 56–62.

8. Kurt Lewin, "Frontiers in Group Dynamics: Concept, Method, and Reality of Social Sciences: Social Equilibria and Social Change," *Human Relations,* June 1947, pp. 5–14.

9. John R. Schermerhorn, Jr., James G. Hunt, and Richard N. Osborn, *Managing Organizational Behavior,* 2d ed., John Wiley & Sons, Inc., New York, 1985, p. 637.

10. "Unleashing Workers," *U.S. News & World Report,* Aug. 24, 1987, p. 44.

11. Lewin, loc cit.

SUGGESTED READINGS

Ackerman, Linda S.: "Don't Fight Change, Guide It Instead," *Office Administration and Automation,* July 1984, pp. 26–29, 65.

Certo, Samuel C.: *Principles of Modern Management,* 3d ed., Wm C. Brown Company Publishers, Dubuque, Iowa, 1986.

Hallett, Jeffrey J.: "Worklife Visions," *Personnel Administrator,* May 1987, pp. 57–65.

Kanter, Rosabeth Moss: *The Change Masters,* Simon and Schuster, New York, 1983.

Kanter, Rosabeth Moss: "Managing the Human Side of Change," *Management Review,* April 1985, pp. 52–56.

London, Manual, and John Paul MacDuffie: "Technological Innovations: Case Examples and Guidelines," *Personnel,* September 1987, pp. 26–38. Focuses on barriers to technological change and presents three cases in the telecommunications industry illustrating three methods of change. See also Lori Henry, "Reorganization at McCormick and Dodge: Getting Everybody in on the Act," in this issue, pp. 48–52.

Moores, Tommy: "Making Changes—Smoothly," *Management World,* June 1986, pp. 26–28.

Morgan, Brian S., and William A. Schiemann: "Employee Attitudes: Then and Now," *Personnel Journal,* October 1986, pp. 100–106.

Mosley, Donald C., Leon C. Megginson, and Paul H. Pietri: *Supervisory Management,* South-Western Publishing Company, Incorporated, Cincinnati, 1985.

Schoonover, Stephen C., and Murray M. Dalziel: "Developing Leadership for Change," *Management Review,* July 1986, pp. 55–60. This is a special issue on "Managing the Future."

Shea, Gordon F.: *Building Trust in the Workplace,* American Management Association, New York, 1984.

West, Michael, and Nigel Nicholson: "Coping with the Job That No One Did Before," *Personnel Management,* July 1986.

Wright, Wayne L.: "Escape from Mediocrity," *Personnel Administration,* September 1987, pp. 109–118.

Tichy, Noel M., and Mary Anne Devanna: "The Transformational Leader," *Training and Development Journal,* July 1986, pp. 27–30.

Index